Internationale Politik und Sicherheit

herausgegeben von der
Stiftung Wissenschaft und Politik, Ebenhausen
Redaktion: Dr. Albrecht Zunker

Band 48

Hannes Adomeit

Imperial Overstretch: Germany in Soviet Policy from Stalin to Gorbachev

An Analysis Based on New Archival Evidence, Memoirs, and Interviews

Nomos Verlagsgesellschaft
Baden-Baden

Die Deutsche Bibliothek – CIP-Einheitsaufnahme

Adomeit, Hannes:
Imperial Overstretch: Germany in Soviet Policy from Stalin to Gorbachev : An Analysis Based on New Archival Evidence, Memoirs, and Interviews / Hannes Adomeit. – 1. Aufl. – Baden-Baden : Nomos Verl.-Ges., 1998
(Internationale Politik und Sicherheit ; Bd. 48)
ISBN 3-7890-5133-0

1. Auflage 1998

Contents

PREFACE

This book has been long in the making. Its constituent parts were scattered over twenty-five years of my specialization in Soviet, Russian, and German affairs in the form of articles, research papers, recorded interviews, and conference protocols. The many fragments have now been integrated into one single entity. Despite its quest for objectivity, the book is likely to reveal personal commitment. If so, this would in part be due to my checkered background and a reflection of recent European history. I was born in 1942 in Memel, then a German city in East Prussia, incorporated into the Soviet Union in the Second World War under the name of Klaipeda and now the main sea port of independent Lithuania. I developed a personal interest in Soviet and post-Soviet affairs, and divided Germany and Europe, also because my parents had been forced to leave their homeland in East Prussia and because the extended family was separated during the war, some members ending up in North-Rhine Westphalia and Bavaria in West Germany, others in Mecklenburg-Vorpommern in East Germany. Personal involvement with the subject matter was further shaped by my experience as a student at the Freie Universität Berlin and the direct exposure to the artificiality of the division of the city and the arrogance and petty chicaneries of East German border guards on the access routes. Interest and involvement were enhanced in my many years of work at the Stiftung Wissenschaft und Politik (SWP) in Ebenhausen that gave me the opportunity to establish lasting contacts with other research institutes in Germany and abroad, academic specialists and policy makers in Moscow, and officials at the Auswärtige Amt and the Chancellor's Office in Bonn.

It is to these colleagues and officials that I would like to offer my sincere thanks. All three German ambassadors to Moscow during the Gorbachev era, Jörg Kastl, Andreas Meyer-Landrut, and Klaus Blech very much contributed to my understanding of the course of events by providing me with their perspectives on official negotiations and more informal talks with Soviet party and government officials. The book also profited from conversations with other Western officials who participated, conceptually or at the operational level, in managing the relations between the Soviet Union and the West on the German problem. These officials include Rudolf Adam, Bob Blackwill, Sir Roderic Braithwaite, Ulrich Brandenburg, Frank Elbe, Wolfgang Ischinger, Klaus Neubert, Horst Teltschik, Malcolm Toon, Jack Matlock, Dennis Ross, Gebhardt Weiß, Phil Zelikow, and Robert Zoellick. Especially important were the interviews and conversations with former Soviet and East German officials, including Vladimir Bykov, Anatoli Chernyaev, Gennadi Gerasimov, Andrei Grachev, Sergei Grigoriev, Egon Krenz, Hans Misselwitz, Yuli Kvitsinsky, Igor Maksimychev, Viktor Rykin, Georgi Shakhnazarov, Thilo Steinbach, Sergei Tarasenko, and Vadim Zagladin.

The specialists on international affairs at the various research institutes in Moscow who were most helpful over the years in clarifying the context and the course of events are Volodya Benevolensky, Viacheslav Dashichev, Andrei Kortunov, Viktor Kremenyuk, Sergei Karaganov, and Vitali Zhurkin. At the Stiftung Wissenschaft und Politik, valuable insights were provided by its director, Michael Stürmer, and current or previous colleagues Falk Bomsdorf, Peer Lange, Friedemann Müller, Uwe Nerlich, Christoph Royen, Reinhardt Rummel, Klaus Schröder, Gebhard Schweigler, Klaus Segbers, Peter Stratmann, and Bernhard von Plate. The researchers at the Bundesinstitut für ostwissenschaftliche und internationale Studien in Cologne who were most helpful and influential in shaping my views on the topic were its director, Heinrich Vogel, and Fred Oldenburg, Gerhard Wettig, and Heinz Timmermann. Much of the writing for this book was done while I was teaching at the Fletcher School of Law and Diplomacy at Tufts University. Thanks at that school are due in particular to Dean Jack Galvin and Alan Henrikson. I also would like to convey my very personal gratitude to Tim Colton and Lis Bernstein, director and associate director respectively at the Kathryn W. and Shelby Cullom Davis Center for Russian Studies at Harvard University, for their encouragement and support. Two projects were most valuable in advancing my understanding. One is the Cold War International History Project at the Woodrow Wilson International Center for Scholars, with Jim Hershberg as its director, the other the Harvard Project on Cold War Studies, directed by Mark Kramer. Many of the results of the projects' conferences and papers have been integrated here. I am most grateful for the insights provided by both colleagues and officials and hope that the ideas and information they provided are accurately represented in this book. I also very much appreciated the research assistance which Mark Vail rendered so efficiently and cheerfully, no matter how seemingly unsurmountable the task.

Many thanks, finally, are due to the Fritz Thyssen Stiftung in Cologne. The book would not have been possible without the generous grant which the foundation provided.

Transliteration of Russian Terms

The transliteration of Russian terms follows the style used by United States Library of Congress. To enhance readability and avoid pedantry, however, some modifications have been made. The soft sign, indicated by an apostrophe in standard style, has been deleted in political household words. In such words, the italics have also been dispensed with. Hence, the stylistically correct *glasnost'* and *oblast'* according to the Library of Congress system have been rendered here simply as glasnost and oblast. The scientific transliteration was also abandoned in many proper nouns and names.

For instance, the text features Yuri Andropov, Alexander Yakovlev, Alexei Arbatov, Vladimir Petrovsky, Lavrenti Beria, and Boris Yeltsin rather than Iurii Andropov, Aleksandr Iakovlev, Aleksei Arbatov, Vladimir Petrovskii, Lavrentii Beriia, and Boris El'tsin. Accordingly, the book refers to Yekaterinburg and Yaroslavl instead of Ekaterinburg and Iaroslavl'. Perhaps at the risk of offending Ukrainian sentiments, Kiev has not been altered to Kiyev, Kiyiv, or Kyyiv. Moscow, too, at least its spelling, has remained unaltered.

INTRODUCTION

Why was Germany divided after the Second World War? Why was the division of Germany maintained for almost half a century? Why did the Soviet Union accept German unification? And why did it consent to unified Germany as a full member in the Atlantic alliance? These questions form the subject of this book. Its main focus is the *Soviet* role in these fateful events of the second half of the twentieth century. It is therefore concerned with party and government leaders in Moscow, their political ambitions, the ideological stereotypes they shared, the institutional pressures they faced, and the systemic constraints with which they had to contend.

The context into which the examination is placed is that of the rise, decline, and fall of empires. The underlying assumption is that it is appropriate to consider the Soviet Union an imperial entity consisting of three concentric rings. The first and innermost ring is that of the USSR itself with its fifteen constituent republics. The second consists of what in the era of the Cold War was called "Eastern Europe," that is, the non-Soviet countries of the Warsaw Pact. The third and outermost ring comprises Moscow's dependencies and its friends and allies outside the Central Eurasian landmass, including at one time or another Cuba, North Vietnam, Laos, North Korea, Iraq, Syria, Libya, Egypt, Ethiopia, South Yemen, Angola, and Mozambique.

This examination deals with Eastern Europe as the ring of empire most closely linked to the center and considered by successive Soviet leaderships as the most important staging area of their influence in Europe. This necessitates scrutiny, above all, of the Soviet-East German relationship and developments in East Germany as the most exposed and most important entity of the Soviet strategic *glacis* in Europe. Since West German "revisionism" was regarded in Moscow as the main challenge to the post-war order and West Berlin as a painful "thorn in the flesh" of the East German body politic, the Soviet Union's relations with the Federal Republic and Soviet reactions to West Germany's Ostpolitik form another major focus of this book.

No claim will be advanced here that the division of Germany was part of a blueprint drawn up by Stalin for the construction of an empire in Eastern Europe. Soviet planning and consistency in the execution of a deliberate design were much more in evidence, for instance, in the treatment of Poland. Nevertheless, the integration of the part of Germany occupied by the Red Army in the misnamed "socialist community" followed an imperial logic and was reinforced by Soviet ideology. To that extent, it is erroneous to contend, as many Russians still do, that since there was no design in Moscow, the *West* was obviously responsible for the division.

The inexorable imperial and ideological logic also explains the tenacity with which the Soviet Union clung to its possessions for such a long time. However, it will be argued here, the attempt to incoporate the eastern part of Germany, including part of the former capital of the German *Reich,* in the empire was worse than many a crime committed in the Stalin era.. It was a serious political blunder. It was a major and, in Europe, the *central* part of what in the title of this book has been called imperial overstretch: the expansion of Soviet control to areas that initially contributed to the reconstruction of the Soviet Union but then became a serious economic liability. Politically and militarily, Moscow's attempt to hold on to the eastern part of Germany locked the Soviet Union even more firmly into competition and confrontation with the West than the ideology, under which its leadership operated, seemed to require. Furthermore, without East Germany, the Soviet empire in Eastern Europe would have looked quite different. It would have been more self-contained and hence relatively more manageable for Khrushchev, Brezhnev, Andropov, and Chernenko. As a result, early in the history of the Soviet empire the attempt at incorporating the German chunk produced major symptoms of pathology. Such symptoms became clearly visible in the Berlin blockade of 1948-49 and the workers' uprising in East Germany in 1953. They remained suppressed for some time but flared up again in the protracted crisis of 1958-61 that led to the building of the Berlin wall. In the 1970s and 1980s, it appeared to many Soviet and Western observers that normalization of the difficult imperial condition had set in. But this proved to be a major misperception, as the rapidly unfolding events in 1989-90 and the collapse of empire were to prove.

The story to be told here is full of paradoxes. One of them is the incongruity of Soviet perceptions of East Germany. In the period of normalization, the GDR came to be seen in Moscow as a successful example in the construction of socialism. Gorbachev, as will be shown in detail, very much admired the East German economic and technological achievements and for quite some time was prone to accept at face value Honecker's progress reports about the GDR's progress in microelectronics, computer technology, industrial engineering, and biotechnology. He even went as far as to concede expressly Honecker's argument that Soviet perestroika was essentially a delayed response to the challenges of the revolution in science and technology of the second half of the twentieth century which the GDR had already met. In principle at least there could also be little doubt that the political regime established by Ulbricht and maintained by Honecker rested on Marxist-Leninist foundations, and excessively so, as Gorbachev was to complain privately to his reformist colleagues in Moscow. However, in stark contrast to such perceptions of the GDR's economic resilience and political conservatism, Soviet leaders from Khrushchev to Gorbachev and their German experts repeatedly expressed the concern and even alarm, both in private conversation among themselves and in talks with the East German leaders, that East Germany was becoming ever more dependent financially and economically on West Germany, making political concessions, and permitting an erosion of its system structure. Such contradictions of perception that found their reflection in contradictory policies were never meaningfully addressed let alone resolved until the collapse of the GDR and the Soviet empire rendered any such possible efforts obsolete.

Gorbachev's eventual acceptance of German unification and his consent to unified Germany's membership in NATO as an integral part of this collapse receive major attention here. The drama and enormity of these two decisions can hardly be overestimated. They meant liquidation of four decades of time-honored Soviet ideological and strategic precepts; abandoning what seemed to be one of the most reliable allies of the Soviet Union; relinquishing a crucial military component in the "correlation of forces"; dispensing with what apparently was an indispensable factor in the Soviet economy; signing the death warrant of the Warsaw Pact and CMEA; and giving birth to a new Europe. Furthermore, the two decisions were taken against the background of other paradoxes of Soviet empire and the German problem. In the 1970s and 1980s, the Soviet Union had amassed tremendous military power. Its nuclear arsenal appeared to have made its imperial position unassailable for all time. The nuclear age, it seemed, had not only made Clausewitz obsolete but also all traditional theories on the rise and fall of empires, including the idea that "No empire is permanent."[1] Part of the explanation of why the Soviet Union divested itself of its empire, it will be argued, lies in the discrepancy between economic stagnation and global expansion and between an apparently thriving military-industrial complex and a corroding socio-economic base – a gap correctly recognized by Sovietologists as the "paradox of super-power."[2]

One of the crucial factors in the rise and fall of empires is the political will of the political establishment in the metropole to maintain the empire. Churchill is on record of having said that he had not become prime minister in order to preside over the dissolution of the British empire. What about Gorbachev? Had *he*, according to his self-perception, become party leader in order to give history a push and preside over the dissolution of the Soviet empire? Specifically with respect to the Soviet Union's East German imperial legacy, what were his perceptions of the problem when he took office in March 1985? Did he subscribe to the notion that in an era of nationalism and the nation state the division of Germany was unnatural and artificial, and that the division of Germany had to be ended in favor of the construction of his Common European House? There is no evidence for such an initiative, to introduce another paradox. Gorbachev's acceptance of German unification and his consent to unified Germany's membership in NATO, it will be shown, like the division of Germany under Stalin, was not part of overall foresight and planning but occurred within a new framework – the New Thinking – that left little room for alternative options.

---

1 Michael W. Doyle, *Empires* (Ithaca, NY: Cornell University Press, 1986), p. 137.
2 See, for instance, Seweryn Bialer, *The Soviet Paradox: External Expansion, Internal Decline* (New York: Alfred A. Knopf, 1986).

This interpretation of history allocates a role to both objective and subjective factors in the rise, decline, and demise of the Soviet empire. As for the latter set of factors, a particularly interesting and important feature is the increasing alienation, animosity, and antipathy between Gorbachev and Honecker in the period from 1985 until 1989. Outwardly, everything looked normal in that relationship, with all the embraces, the kisses, the awarding of medals, the cordial receptions, and attendance of congresses.[3] But beneath the surface in the relationship between Gorbachev and Honecker, there was smoldering suspicion, resentment, and scheming, much of it fueled by Gorbachev's realization that the East German leader was risking serious instability by stubbornly refusing to go with the times and, conversely, by Honecker's conviction that the Soviet leader was pursuing disastrous policies that undercut the legitimacy of his rule in the GDR and the fabric of the "socialist community." In that context, yet another paradox is to be noted. Given the dominant position of the Soviet Union in the bloc and that of the Soviet party leader in inter-party relations, one would have expected Gorbachev to exert severe pressure on Honecker to change his policies. However, the record of private conversations between the two leaders reveals that such pressure was not exerted. Matters were left to drift and problems to accumulate until the end of the East German regime and the Soviet empire.

Such observations underline the important role of the party leader in communist systems, no matter whether it is one of omission or commission. But even in communist systems, foreign policy cannot not be formulated and carried out by one person single-handedly. What is needed for both policy making and the implementation of decisions are appropriate domestic structures, institutions, and organizations. This fact of international life raises questions at another level of analysis: Which of the established Soviet institutions played a significant role in breaking new ground on the German problem? Obvious contenders for such a role are several party institutions, such as the Politburo, the Central Committee's International Department (ID) and the CC's Department for Liaison with the Communist and Workers' Parties; government agencies, such as the foreign ministry, the KGB, and the armed forces; and the Defense Council, an institution whose membership consisted of top foreign and security policy personnel from both the party and the state.

These institutions can be regarded as having had a vested interest in adhering to imperial policies and opposing change on the German problem. This raises the question as to how Gorbachev was able to overcome bureaucratic inertia and latent opposition to his policy changes. Several hypotheses for answering this question suggest themselves.

3 Soviet foreign minister Shevardnadze used such formulations to characterize the relations among party leaders in the Soviet bloc in general; see Eduard Ambrosievich Shevardnadze, *Moi vybor. V zashchitu demokratii i svobody*, 2nd ed. (Moscow: Novosti, 1991), p. 199. They certainly apply to the relations between the Soviet and the East German party leader.

One is the seriousness of the internal crisis. It could be argued that the deterioration of economic and social conditions, the spreading of ethnic violence and secessionism, and of obstructionism and opposition in the party were so severe that international affairs were simply a side-show. A second hypothesis, prevalent among analysts who are fond of easy and straightforward solutions to intricate problems, is the notion that the disastrous economic state of affairs in the Soviet Union persuaded Moscow to cut a deal with rich West Germany: the consent to unification was given in exchange for huge financial and economic benefit. A third hypothesis is the idea that the severe internal crisis interacted with an equally severe crisis of empire and that Gorbachev's consent to German unification was a rational response to overcommitment and overextension of empire.

But what approaches should be used in order to answer such questions? To what extent is it still appropriate to utilize tools developed by the now extinct field of Soviet studies? Sovietology, contrary to now popular criticism, underwent significant transformations before the collapse of the Soviet Union. In the 1940s and 1950s, the most widely accepted framework of analysis was that of totalitarianism, which posited complete state control of politics, society, and the economy; one-man and one-party dictatorship; terror as a functional element of the system; and the impossibility of reform: the system would either endure or collapse. In revised versions of the model, the "totalitarian" was replaced by "authoritarian." There was also a realization that one-man dictatorship after Stalin's death had been replaced by collective leadership and terror by less bloody forms of repression. In essence, however, the proponents of the revised model still assumed that the main features of the system had remained unchanged.

The behavioral revolution in communist studies of the 1960s and 1970s took issue with this framework of reference and focused on diversity and differentiation behind the façade of monolithism. Various "bureaucratic politics" and "interest group" models were applied to the study of Soviet-type systems. But whereas such studies did advance our understanding of unplanned processes in communist systems, they also created some serious impediments. This applies in particular to the notion that Marxist-Leninist regimes bore many of the pluralist features characteristic of Western political systems. It was probably this perceptual lens that produced the erroneous assumption that communist systems were amenable to major structural reform. In retrospect, it appears that the revised "totalitarian" or "authoritarian" school was right after all in the sense that despite all the attempts at reform the communist parties and the Soviet-type system in the Soviet Union and Eastern Europe proved unreformable. Thus, what is evidently needed and will be applied here is a combination of traditional Kremlinological and more modern behavioral approaches to decision making.

The design constructed here to tackle the theoretical and empirical problems as outlined is as follows: Chapter 1 establishes conceptual foundations by looking at such theories on the rise, decline, and fall of empires as may be useful for analysis. The theories examined will be called metrocentric, pericentric, international systemic, transnational, and integrative. Although several of the approaches shed some light on the Soviet problem, one of the most useful designs applied here can be found in Paul Kennedy's book, *The Rise and Fall of the Great Powers*. This includes in particular the author's argument that economic potential is required to underpin military power, and military power is usually needed to acquire and protect wealth. If, however, too large a proportion of the state's resources is diverted from the creation of wealth and allocated instead to military purposes, then this will lead to a weakening of national power, to overcommitment and overextension. As the subsequent chapters of the present book will show, this became an important political problem once the Soviet Union had entered a period of economic decline.

Chapter 2 features a discussion of Soviet perceptions and policies on the German problem from the division of Germany under Stalin through Khrushchev's tenure in office to Brezhnev's "era of stagnation." The analytical thread that will help the reader through the maze of Soviet policies on Germany in this period from the 1940s to the late 1970s will be called the Ideological and Imperial paradigm. Its constituent elements can be said to have been competitive and confrontational, with ideological, geopolitical, and military-strategic factors playing a dominant role and providing the rationale and conceptual basis for the Soviet policy of imperial control – notably in Central and Eastern Europe – and global expansion.. Power and ideology in this paradigm are regarded as having reinforced each other.

Chapter 3 demonstrates how this framework of analysis and policy underwent a serious crisis in the last years of the Brezhnev era and during the Andropov and Chernenko "interregnum" from the late 1970s to the mid-1980s. One of the major research questions in this period concerns the role of military and economic power in the management of the Soviet empire. The thread of Ariadne running through the analytical labyrinth indicates that an increasing number of policy-makers and academic analysts in Moscow had begun to doubt the political utility of Soviet military power, to express concern about the country's ability to keep up with the United States in the military-technological competition, and to appreciate the importance of economic and technological factors as a source of global influence. A politically significant part of the Soviet political establishment also began to recognize the stark fact of imperial decay and the necessity of comprehensive reform if damaging trends were to be arrested and reversed. Such realization, however, remained politically irrelevant until the very end of the interregnum. Practical policies continued to be mired in bureaucratic inertia. They took a particularly vicious form in the severe pressure that was exerted on West Germany to desist from consenting to the stationing of intermediate-range nuclear missiles on its territory and on East Germany to cease making political concessions to Bonn for allegedly short-term and short-sighted economic and financial benefit and to submit to bloc discipline.

Chapter 4 portrays the Gorbachev leadership's recognition of the comprehensive crisis in domestic and international affairs and the lessons it derived from that crisis. Since the role of statesmen in history and the role of the party leader in communist systems are important issues to consider, the chapter contains a political profile of Gorbachev. Under his leadership, a new paradigm was constructed, tentatively and hesitatingly at first, but then in a more determined, consistent, and comprehensive fashion. The new philosophical and practical approach – the New Thinking – put the emphasis on internal political, economic, and social development and international cooperation. In domestic affairs, the new paradigm provided for policies of democratization, federalism, and market-oriented reform. In foreign policy, it emphasized devolution of empire; eradication of regional military preponderance; abandonment of military-strategic parity; membership in international economic institutions, such as the GATT, IMF, and the G-7; and cooperation within the framework of the United Nations.

The chapter then deals in detail with Gorbachev's perceptions and policies on Germany in the period from his assumption of power in March 1985 until his visit to West Germany in June 1989. The new Soviet leader, it will be argued, had no intention to liquidate the empire but wanted to reform it and make it more cost effective. East Germany was meant to help in this endeavor. Since he considered that country as advanced in the production of high technology, he even thought that it could make an appreciable contribution to the modernization of the Soviet economy and to undercutting President Reagan's Strategic Defense Initiative (SDI). The impact of Western policies on both the demise of the Soviet empire and the changes in Gorbachev's policies will also be examined in this chapter. Evidence will be presented concerning the question as to whether the decline of empire was accelerated by the Reagan administration's policy of forcing the pace of the military-technological competition and deepening the "fault lines of the Soviet empire," or whether such attempts were essentially counterproductive, delaying the fundamental changes that were bound to come anyway, given the deep internal contradictions of the Soviet empire.

Chapter 5 examines the institutional and domestic political setting of the imperial collapse. In particular, it dwells on two internal Soviet paradoxes. The first concerns the role of the German experts, or *germanisty*, in policy-making on the German problem. On the basis of observations derived from Western systems of government to the effect that the regional experts' detailed knowledge of and empathy with developments in their area of specialization often predisposes them to become advocates of the viewpoints and even interests of "their" countries, one would have assumed that the Soviet experts on Germany were instrumental in developing, advocating, and helping to implement fundamental policy changes. Such assumptions do not apply in the Soviet case. Almost at every stage in the rapid evolution of events, the German experts in both party and government institutions remained wedded to traditional views and policies and engaged in procrastination and delay. The second paradox relates to the role of the power institutions in the Soviet system. The comparative history of the rise and fall of empires knows of many examples when the mainstays of the system actively resisted imperial devolution and decline and deposed those at the top who either looked with equanimity at that process or even promoted it. A revolt of Soviet "young Turks," however, failed to occur in the Soviet Union, and the old guard staged an ineffective coup only in August 1991, when the external empire had already disappeared. The two paradoxes can be linked to each other: If the *germanisty* in the party and the foreign ministry had a vested interest in the continuation of the conceptual and practical approaches they had developed over several decades of policy, why did they not conspire with officials and officers in the defense ministry, the armed forces, the military-industrial complex, and the KGB – institutions opposed to German unification and unified Germany's membership in NATO – to bring down the whole edifice of the New Thinking and the devolution of empire? Part of the answer provided in this chapter is the shift in decision-making authority to a small circle of leaders and their advisers and personal assistants; an extraordinary improvement in the academic institutes' access to and involvement in policy-making; effective cooperation of these institutes with the top echelon of the foreign ministry; and the traditional organizational culture of the armed forces that mitigated against their taking an active role in politics.

Chapter 6 covers the period from the fall of 1989 until the fall of 1990. The argument will be developed here that the parameters of the New Thinking did *not* extend to relinquishing Soviet control over the GDR and that Gorbachev continued to cling to the idea that it would be possible to have the cake and eat it, too: to retain East Germany in a Soviet sphere of influence *and* to improve economic cooperation with West Germany. This notion, furthermore, would still have been in accordance with his idea of preserving the empire and making imperial rule more humane and cost-effective. This period also reveals one of the major dynamics leading to the collapse of empire: unintended consequences of conceptual change, the occurrence of unplanned and unforeseen events, and loss of control. The force of events, as will be demonstrated, began to reveal its decisive impact with the dismantling of the iron curtain by Hungary in May 1990. It continued with the exodus of East Germans in the summer. And it culminated in the unintended and, from Moscow's perspective, unauthorized opening of the Berlin wall on 9 November. But Soviet loss of control over events in the GDR also combined with Gorbachev's *loss of will* to maintain the Soviet imperial position in Central and Eastern Europe – an important fact that is evidenced most of all by his refusal in principle to use force in order to arrest the fundamental processes of change taking place there.

The chapter differentiates between Gorbachev's *acceptance* of the reality of German unification in January 1990 and his *consent* to unified Germany's membership in NATO, which occurred officially at the Soviet-West German talks in Moscow and Arkhyz in July 1990. The driving forces behind both the passive acceptance and the more active consent were basically the same as in the previous phase. *Faits accomplis* were incessantly being created and ratified by the Soviet leadership. As Gorbachev was to acknowledge at a meeting with East German prime minister Hans Modrow in Moscow on 30 January 1990, time was exerting an impact on the process and lending dynamism to it.

Acceptance of German unification was facilitated by changes in Soviet perceptions concerning the importance of the GDR as an economic asset and, as Gorbachev still was to say at the Malta summit in December 1989, its function as a "strategic ally" of the Soviet Union. By that time, however, the Soviet leadership had already come to realize that both the internal political stability and the economic and technological advances of the GDR had been exaggerated; that, relatively, a unified Germany and the other Western industrialized countries had more to offer to the Soviet Union than the GDR and the Council on Mutual Economic Assistance (CMEA); that a unified Germany would be willing and able to make a significant contribution to the modernization of the Soviet economy; and that for all of these reasons leaving the GDR to its fate could be reinterpreted as a logical and consistent application of the new paradigm.

Similar observations are warranted regarding the decision on unified Germany's membership in NATO. The thought of the inevitability of taking this domestically highly sensitive step ripened in the minds of a top circle of policy-makers in the period from the end of January to May 1990. The institutions that would ordinarily have been involved in preparing such a momentous decision were simply confronted with the outcome of largely confidential deliberations. Analysis of decision-making, based on the background provided in the preceding chapter on the institutional setting reveals that these institutions, notably the party apparatus, including the Central Committee's International Department, but also the defense ministry and the general staff, the KGB, and the foreign ministry bureaucracy, were deliberately shunted aside. The same tactics of exclusion governed the top decision makers' treatment of the *germanisty*, the German experts, who almost across the board either opposed or attempted to put the brakes on German unification and, even more vehemently, on unified Germany's membership in NATO.

The consent to unified Germany's membership in NATO, the argument continues in that chapter, had not only domestic but also international dimensions. The small circle of decision-makers around Gorbachev ultimately realized that, as his foreign policy adviser put it, the West had the better arguments.[4] Another lay in the absence of viable alternative options: the Soviet Union was internationally isolated on the issue of German neutrality and on Gorbachev's idea of dual membership of unified Germany

4 Interview with Chernyaev.

in both military alliances. There was simply no support for it in Western and Eastern Europe, let alone from across the Atlantic. There was also concern among the top decision-makers in Moscow that a non-aligned Germany might one day seek access to nuclear weapons in order to safeguard its security. A contributory factor to the consent was their illusion that the Warsaw Pact could be reformed and would continue to play a role in European security. The chapter concludes with an examination of the role of economic factors in the Soviet consent to unified Germany's membership in NATO.

Sources of Evidence

The validity of answers to the questions set forth in the introduction depends of course on the availability and effective utilization of different sets of sources. This author adopted the following procedure for the establishment of evidence. On the most basic and conventional level, he used treaties and agreements on Soviet foreign policy commitments and statistical data on Soviet military and economic power and potential, the strategic and conventional military balance, and demographic and social developments in order to reconstruct objective trends and the substantive context in which decisions were made.

In addition, four types of sources were consulted: (1) the *public record*, consisting of published diplomatic correspondence, government statements, memoranda and notes, documentary materials of CPSU congresses and Central Committee meetings and speeches, and articles and interviews by government officials and party leaders; (2) the *archives* of the East German communist party – the *Zentrale Parteiarchiv des Instituts für Geschichte der Arbeiterbewegung* (Institute for the History of the Workers' Movement, Central Party Archives), now under the administration of the German federal government; (3) *interviews* conducted by this author with past Soviet government and party officials and their Western counterparts; and (4) the *memoirs* of these officials.

In order to get a reliable picture, the author checked and cross-checked all four types of sources. Thus, the circumstances of particular Politburo sessions and bilateral Soviet-East German and multilateral Warsaw Pact or CMEA meetings, as reflected in the published materials and unpublished documents, were verified in interviews with the government and party officials privy to concomitant information. Inconsistencies or contradictions in the memoir literature were taken up with the interview partners. Especially valuable were the perspectives received in interviews with the personal assistants on foreign policy to Gorbachev, Soviet foreign minister Eduard Shevardnadze, (West) German chancellor Helmut Kohl, and East German prime minister Lothar de Maizière.

Paraphrasing Mark Twain, one might be inclined to think that there are lies, damned lies, and archives. This adage does not, however, apply to the SED archives. The "red Prussians," like their predecessors, faithfully practiced *Deutsche Ordnung und Gründlichkeit*, decreeing that their activities be neatly recorded for posterity. Presumably not in their worst nightmares did the Soviet and East German leaders suspect that the record of their private conversations, secret Warsaw Pact meetings, and talks behind closed doors of that organization's ordinary conferences would some day be accessible to Western scholars. Their erroneous notion about the confidentiality of the talks is one of the reasons why this author assumes that there was no deliberate attempt at falsification of the record. Another reason is the importance of the Soviet connection for the survival of the regime. The members of the SED Politburo wanted to have reports, as complete and accurate as possible, on every nuance and shading of what the Soviet comrades thought, said, and did. Given this circumstance, it is difficult to imagine scribes putting gloss, negative or positive, on the Soviet position in secret, confidential, or open meetings.[5] For further information on sources the reader may want to refer to the Bibliographical and Biographical Note.

5 Interview with Krenz.

PART ONE: THE SOVIET EMPIRE

Chapter 1: Theoretical and Conceptual Considerations

1. Conceptual Approaches

The term "empire" is used with deliberation in this book. Obviously, this word has no independent existence. It can encompass only the meaning which social convention allocates to it. Unlike definitions of imperialism, nationalism, or ideology, however, the notion of empire is less controversial and the mental associations produced by it more uniform.[1] The word is derived from the Latin *imperium* which can be rendered as "command," "authority," or "power." *Imperium Romanum* thus denoted the supreme power in Rome and the realm which it commanded. Modern theorists have variously defined empire as "any successful attempt to conquer and subjugate peoples with the intention of ruling them for an indefinite period;"[2] as relationships of "control imposed by some political societies over the effective sovereignty of other political societies;"[3] and as a state entity in "which one ethnic group dominates others."[4] Empire, according to these definitions, embodies elements of political inequality, military domination, and economic exploitation. These features distinguish empires from federations, confederations, and alliances and explain the more pejorative and emotionally charged "imperialism" – a term that originated in nineteenth century France to denote the grandiose foreign policy designs of Napoleon III and that was used in Britain by supporters and opponents of Prime Minister Disraeli to describe his policies of global expansion.[5] Imperialism here will be understood to mean a process or policy of establishing or maintaining an empire.[6]

There is a curious anomaly, however, when it comes to the consideration of the American and the Russian experience. Imperialism, at the end of the nineteenth century, was considered primarily an activity of the European maritime powers, the British, French, Germans, Spanish, Portuguese, and Dutch, and less so of the United States or Russia. Perhaps surprisingly, *their* cross-continental expansion was not labeled

1 The discussion of empire and imperialism draws on Ariel Cohen, "The End of Empire: Russian Imperial Development and Decline," Ph.D. thesis, The Fletcher School of Law and Diplomacy, Tufts University, December 1993, pp. 12-106. This author (H.A.) was thesis supervisor. The thesis was revised and published as *Russian Imperialism: Development and Crisis* (Westport, Conn.: Praeger, 1996). A useful conceptual apparatus and rich empirical data can also be found in Karen Dawisha and Bruce Parrott, eds., *The End of Empire? The Transformation of the USSR in Comparative Perspective*, Series "The International Politics of Eurasia," Vol. 9 (Armonk, NY: M.E. Sharpe, 1997).

2 John Starchey, *The End of Empire* (London: Victor Gollanz, 1959), p. 319.

3 Michael W. Doyle, *Empires* (Ithaca, N.Y.: Cornell University Press, 1986), p. 19.

4 Maxime Rodinson, as quoted in Jan P. Nederveen Pieterse, *Empire and Emancipation* (New York: Praeger, 1989), p. 245.

5 Benjamin J. Cohen, *The Question of Imperialism* (New York: Basic Books, 1973), p. 10.

6 This is the definition used by Doyle, *Empires*, pp. 44-45.

imperialism but "nation building."[7] The internal structure of the state rather than external expansion was the conceptual lens through which the American "manifest destiny" and Russian "gathering of lands" (*sobiranie zemlei*) were viewed.[8] In the American case, this lens would seem to be appropriate since the massive influx of white settlers did not lead to a system of imperial control but rather to the destruction of the social structure and culture of the Indians and the formation of an entirely new nation state. But the failure to call Russian cross-continental expansion by its proper name is less comprehensible. Certainly, Czarist foreign minister Prince Alexander Gorchakov, one of the architects of Russian imperial expansion, left no doubt as to the nature of the exercise. In a circular letter in 1864, he explicitly told his European colleagues that he did not think that the Russian imperial quest was in any way different from the *mission civilisatrice* of other European powers. "The position of Russia in Central Asia [and by implication in other areas subjugated by the Czars] is that of all civilized states which are brought in contact with half-savage nomad populations possessing no fixed social organization." In such cases, he explained, "the more civilized state is forced in the interest of the security of its frontier to exercise a certain ascendancy over its turbulent and undesirable neighbors."[9]

In some respects, however, Russia's expansion in the west, south, and east did deviate from previous imperialist patterns. Traditionally, the metropolis was economically, technologically, and culturally the most advanced part of the empire and was able, for this very reason, to spread its influence and maintain control. Yet although military force loomed large in other states' empire-building, Russia's expansion was almost exclusively based on force rather than commercial or cultural preeminence. This certainly applied to her subjugation of more advanced peoples and states, such as Poland, Finland, the Baltic nations, the Crimean Khanate, Khiva, and Bukhara. As Count Witte, prime minister under Czar Nikolai II, pertinently remarked, "Who created the Russian empire, transforming the semi-Asiatic Muscovite Czardom into the most influential, most dominant, grandest European power? Only the power of the army's bayonet. The world bowed not to our culture, not to our bureaucratized church, not to our wealth and prosperity. It bowed to our might."[10]

The failure to regard Russia as an empire extended into the Soviet era, despite the fact that the Bolsheviks, after having espoused the Wilsonian principles of self-determination, set out to restore the Russian empire. By the end of the civil war, the territorial domain

---

7 Cohen, *The Question of Imperialism*, p. 10.

8 Andreas Kappeler points out that the scholarly literature distinguishes between a "classic overseas colonialism" and an "internal" form; see his "The Multiethnic Empire," in James Cracraft, ed., *Major Problems in the History of Imperial Russia* (Lexington, Mass.: D.C. Heath, 1994), p. 401.

9 Quoted in James Cracraft, ed., *Major Problems in the History of Imperial Russia* (Lexington, Mass.: D.C. Heath, 1994), pp. 410-11.

10 I am indebted to Robert Legvold for this quotation but have been unable to verify its source.

of the USSR largely coincided with the Russia of the Romanovs. Russians were the dominating ethnic component in the realm. As Lenin correctly observed, one only needed to "scratch a communist to find a Great Russian chauvinist," someone who would advance traditional geopolitical arguments in favor of acquiring warm ports on the Indian Ocean, "liberating" Constantinople, stirring up revolution in China and India, or who just wanted to ensure a steady supply of Uzbek cotton for the Red Army soldiers, Azeri oil to fuel the tank engines, or Yakut diamonds to pay for the Comintern's revolutionary activities.[11]

Several factors may explain the failure conceptually to consider post-World War I Soviet Russia as an empire. First, the vigorous campaign waged by the Bolsheviks to undermine the British empire in the Middle East and India deceptively made the new Soviet state appear as *anti*-colonial and *anti*-imperialist. Second, the new Leninist connotation of imperialism as the "highest stage of capitalism" applied only to states with a specific systemic structure and by definition not to the Soviet Union. Left-wing political forces in the West and revisionist theorists adopted and disseminated this point of view. Third, European nineteenth-century and early twentieth-century imperialism was based on nationalism and a strong state; Soviet ideology, in contrast, rested on internationalist principles, aimed at the establishment of a universal classless society, and foresaw the withering away of nationalism together with the state. Finally, the sordid business of suppression of national self-assertion and independence, from the Baltic to the Caucasus, and from the Arctic to the Hindukush and the Amur, was not accompanied by much publicity, let alone by television crews. The Soviet armed *reconquista* proceeded largely concealed from world public opinion.

The conceptual muddle was left undisturbed after World War II – despite the Soviet Union's incorporation of the Baltic states; territorial expansion in Europe and Asia; establishment of a sphere of influence in Eastern Europe; and transformation of the country from a regional to a world power. The USSR was largely seen as a case *sui generis* to which it was inappropriate to attach the imperial label. The closest approximation of Soviet realities to Western images of empire occurred during the Cold War when the Soviet Union and Eastern Europe were collectively called the "Soviet bloc" and the Eastern European countries referred to as "satellites." But these terms became politically incorrect during the detente period of the 1970s, when Western political leaders attempted to construct a working relationship with the Soviet Union and Western scholars persuaded themselves that they were discovering tendencies of diversity, autonomy, pluralism, and emancipation in the "former" bloc.

Obviously, such terms as "empire" and "satellites" were regarded as anathema by Soviet political leaders and propagandists. Even in retrospect, former Soviet officials have been reluctant to accept such labels. Gorbachev, both when he occupied the highest

11 Cohen, "The End of Empire," pp. 492-93.

office in the Soviet Union and after the collapse of the country, refrained from using the two terms. He also resented the characterization of the relationship between the Soviet Union and its Eastern European dependencies as "colonial." For instance, when Czechoslovak President Vaclav Havel visited Moscow in February 1990 and told Gorbachev that his people would "comprehend that finally the chapter of the traditional, as it were, colonial relations has been closed," his host resented the epithet: "Once again I had to object and ask the president not to ascribe to us a colonial [design] in our relations with Czechoslovakia."[12] Even in retrospect, his terminology on Soviet relations with Eastern Europe has remained euphemistic and apologetic.[13]

Georgi Shakhnazarov, his advisor on Eastern European affairs, has adopted a similarly equivocal and euphemistic stance on the issue. *He,* at least, acknowledged that one could "consider the people's democracies an organic part or the periphery of a Soviet empire." He also admitted that it was true that "the social and state structures of all the countries belonging to the socialist system were initially, soon after the Second World War, brought under a common roof, that of one and the same Soviet system;" that the Soviet Union "held its allies on an economic leash and, often to its own detriment, supplied them with a considerable amount of oil, ore, metals, and at times even grain;" and that the Eastern European countries were pulled into military-political bloc, that their armies were equipped with Soviet weapons, and that in the event of war they had to act together with the armed forces of the Soviet Union under the orders of our High Command." But, then, he incongruously states that the term empire "explains litttle." He sees no difference between the position of the United States in the Western Hemisphere and that of the Soviet Union in Eastern Europe. Furthermore, he rejects the notion that Moscow had been able to behave in the socialist community as it saw fit: "Nothing of the sort! ... Within the general principles of relations in the socialist system, there existed specific confines, within which governments could act independently."[14]

Vadim Medvedev, the former CPSU Central Committee secretary and head of the Department for Liaison with the Communist and Workers' Parties, in his reflections on the collapse of the Soviet empire, eschews the sensitive word but aptly considers the Soviet Union and the countries of Eastern Europe as a single entity, with the latter having formed the "outer ring of the Soviet bloc."[15] His former Politburo colleague and Gorbachev confidant Alexander Yakovlev has been less inclined to mince words. To him the "socialist community" represented a "strange empire," and one where, although every leader

---

12 The exchange took place over the content of a joint Soviet-Czechoslovak declaration; see Mikhail Gorbachev, *Zhizn' i reformy* (Moscow: Novosti, 1995), Vol. 2, pp. 360-61.

13 For details see *infra*, pp. 272-73.

14 Georgi K. Shakhnazarov, *Tsena svobody. Reformatsiia Gorbacheva glazami ego pomoshchnika* (Moscow: Rossika, Zevs, 1993), pp. 96-97.

15 Vadim A. Medvedev, *Raspad. Kak on nazreval v "mirovoi sisteme sotsializma"* (Moscow: Mezhdunarodnye otnosheniia, 1994), p. 3.

played his own game and no one derived any special gains from cooperation with the Soviet Union, "no one could have even dreamt about the servility of the vassals."[16] Along the same lines, Vitali Zhurkin, the director of the Institute on Europe, deplored in a discussion at the Central Committee's Commission on International Policy in June 1990 the "amazing (*udivitel'nyi*) empire that we created" in Eastern Europe – a zone of economic inefficiencies and one where "resentment and even hatred toward the Soviet Union could grow."[17]

If, then, it is analytically useful to treat the Soviet Union as an empire subject to pressures and processes similar to those that affected empires in the past, what are some of the major conceptual approaches that may help us understand both the general and the specific features of the Soviet experience? Four major theoretical approaches can be distinguished. They can be called the metrocentric, the pericentric, the international systemic, and the transnational orientation.

2. Metrocentric Approaches

The first orientation can essentially be subdivided into three schools – (1) the radical liberal school, with John A. Hobson as the main proponent; (2) the Marxist school, which includes Rosa Luxemburg, Rudolf Hilferding, and Lenin as the founding theorists, and "neo-Marxist" authors, such as Paul Baran, Henry Brailsford, Michael Barratt Brown, Victor Kiernan, Harold Laski, John Starchey, and Paul Sweezy; and (3) a political and sociological approach, with Austrian political economist Joseph Schumpeter as the founding father, which emphasizes expansionist inclinations of anti-democratic, militarist elites.[18]

Hobson was the first to treat imperialism as a disposition of metropolitan society to extend its rule. He was also the first to connect imperialism and capitalism, disregarding all available evidence that there existed empires based on slave and feudal social organization, and there was at least a theoretical possibility that there would be empires under a different form of societal formation than capitalism. Taking Britain as a point of departure, Hobson portrayed imperialism as the result of forces emanating from the metropole. Special interests, led by financiers, encouraged an expansionist foreign policy designed to promote the needs of capitalist investors for investment outlets. These interests succeeded in manipulating the metropolitan politics of parliamentary Britain

---

16 Alexander N. Yakovlev, *Gor'kaia chasha: Bol'shevism i reformatsiia v Rossii* (Yaroslavl: Verkhnye-volzhskoe knizhnoe izdatel'stvo, 1994), p. 191.

17 "Peremeny v Tsentral'noi i Vostochnoi Evorope. S zasedaniia Komissii TsK KPSS po voprosam mezhdunarodnoi politiki 15 iiunia 1990 g.," *Izvestiia Tsk KPSS*, No. 10 (October 1990), pp. 107-8. Apparently for reasons of what then was still considered to be politically correct, the editors of the journal chose to put Zhurkin's "empire" in quotation marks.

18 For a critique of neo-Marxist theories of imperialism see Hannes Adomeit, "Neo-Marxist Theories of Imperialism: Clarification or Confusion of a Concept in International Relations," *Co-existence*, Vol. 12, No. 2 (October 1975), pp. 126-48.

through their influence over the press and educational institutions, which provided them with imperialistic propaganda.[19]

Lenin's "territorial division of the world" broadened Hobson's concept of formal territorial annexation to include the exercise of controlling influence by economic means – one of the modes of so-called "informal imperialism." For Lenin, imperialism was not only the product of high finance. It was capitalism in its final, monopolistic stage driven to search for overseas profits, raw materials, and markets.[20] Thus, the connection between capitalism and imperialism was both consistent and central for "mature" capitalist states. "The necessity for exporting capital," he argued, "arises from the fact that in a few countries capitalism has become 'over-ripe' and ... capital cannot find 'profitable' investment."[21] Imperialism, therefore, was not amenable to reform. It is for this very reason that Lenin attacked the "revisionist renegade" Karl Kautsky for arguing that "the urge of present-day states to expand ... can best be promoted, not by the violent means of imperialism, but by peaceful democracy."[22]

Schumpeter rejected the Marxist approach. "It is not true," he countered, "that the capitalist system as such must collapse because of immanent necessity, that it necessarily makes its continued existence impossible by its own growth and development."[23] To him, capitalism and imperialism were not only unrelated but antithetical to each other. He defined imperialism as the objectless disposition of a state to unlimited forcible expansion. This phenomenon originated in atavistic, militaristic institutions, such as the "war machine" of ancient Egypt, and similarly aggressive political systems with a dominant social and economic position enjoyed by undemocratic elites and the armed forces. Modern capitalism's only link to these aggressive forces of imperialism lay in the deformation imposed by the war machines of the absolutist monarchies of seventeenth and eighteenth century Europe. Their monopoly position in the economy was benefitted by the use of military force abroad. Force, in the perception of the elites, could "serve to break down foreign customs barriers;" they "can use cheap native labor without its ceasing to be cheap; they can market their products, even in the colonies, at monopoly prices; they can, finally, invest capital that would only depress the profit rate at home."[24]

The Dutch scholar Jan P. Nederveen Pieterse also rejects the Marxist idea of economic determinism underlying imperialism. To him war and the "bloodstained fetish

---

19 Doyle, *Empires*, p. 20; summary by Cohen, "The End of Empire," p. 15.

20 This was authoritatively stated by V. I. Lenin in his *Imperialism: The Highest Stage of Capitalism* (New York: International Publishers, 1939, new. ed.: 1969).

21 Ibid., p. 63.

22 Karl Kautsky, *Nationalstaat, imperialistischer Staat und Staatenbund* (Nürnberg, 1915), pp. 70 and 72, as quoted by Lenin, *Imperialism*, p. 112.

23 Joseph A. Schumpeter, *Imperialism and Social Classes*, transl. Heinz Norden, ed. and with an introduction by Paul M. Sweezy (New York: Augustus M. Kelley, 1951), p. 108.

24 Ibid., pp. 109.

of empire" are not simply expressions of economic dynamics but "primarily political phenomena, a manifestation of political will. Economic theories of imperialism, while elucidating many pertinent dynamics, at the same time conceal a more important logic in the course of affairs." They failed "to address the question of power, which lies with the 'will to power,' especially the will to power of strata who feel insecure in their status. By failing to see power clearly in the past, this perspective clouds the future."[25]

Consideration of the rise and fall of the Soviet empire makes it necessary to focus not only on developments in the imperial center, the inner ring of empire, but also in the outer rings. Historians and political scientists have provided some conceptual and comparative approaches which are applicable here.

3. Pericentric Approaches

Following the summary of Cohen, as a reaction to the prevailing views of the metrocentrists, British historian John Gallagher, along with a number of students and colleagues, such as Ronald Robinson and Anil Seal, developed a theory of imperialism primarily concerned with events in the imperial periphery.[26] This approach is conceptually useful in its assertion that empires typically collapse as a result of decay at the center, severe difficulties of control at the periphery, or a combination of both. Prior to the writings of the pericentrists, empire had been analyzed as if rulers had no subjects and as if Europe's pursuit of profit and power had taken place in a world in which external forces did not exist.[27] The pericentrists, in contrast, proceeded from the assumption that "global power, carried by a ruling nation, cannot in the long run be supported solely by the people of that nation ... In its relations with other peoples such a power must satisfy them and give them an interest in the continuance and stability of the whole."[28] They regarded expansion as a set of "unequal bargains" between metropolitan agents, sometimes with little support from the center, and their indigenous allies and opponents, who were concerned with defending or improving their positions inside their own societies.[29] Such concerns obviously provided the center with levers of influence in accordance with the time-honored Roman imperial principle of *divide et impera*.

A distinction can thus be drawn between formal and informal empire. The former applies to peoples and nations that are integrated fully into the political and legal system

25 Nederveen Pieterse, *Empire and Emancipation*, p. 216.

26 J. A. Gallagher and R. E. Robinson, "The Imperialism of Free Trade," *Economic History Review*, 2nd Ser., Vol. 4 (1953), pp. 1-15; summary by Cohen, "The End of Empire," pp. 75-76.

27 Anil Seal, Preface to John A Gallagher, *The Decline, Revival and Fall of the British Empire* (London: Cambridge University Press, 1973), p. viii; quoted by Cohen, "The End of Empire," p. 75.

28 G. Modelski, quoted in Geoffrey Parker, *The Geopolitics of Domination* (London and New York: Routledge, 1988), p. 6.

29 Cohen, "The End of Empire," p. 76.

of the imperial state, typically with career opportunities for them in the central administration, with only the lower levels of the imperial bureaucracy manned by "natives" of the periphery. The latter pertains to those dependent and penetrated societies which retain varying degrees of autonomy and where "the governance of extensive districts of the colony is entrusted to members of the native elite under the supervision of imperial governors."[30] In accordance with this classification, the first ring or inner core of Soviet empire can be understood to be the *formal* empire, while the second and third rings – Eastern Europe first and foremost, but also the dependent states, proxies, and allies outside the Warsaw Pact scattered around the globe from Angola to Mongolia, and from Cuba to Vietnam, can be regarded as forming the *informal* empire.

It can be argued that the more geographically expansive the imperial realm, the more important the levers of informal and indirect control wielded by the center. One of the major reasons for this lies in the fact that, with the help of cooperative local elites, the direct use of military force can be avoided. Another potential benefit of informal control is the limitation of risk through proxies. In the Soviet empire, East Germany played such a role vis-à-vis the Western allies in and on the access routes to Berlin; Cuba in Central America, Angola, Mozambique, and Ethiopia; and Vietnam in Southeast Asia. "Sub-imperialisms" are able to develop on the basis of indirect rule. This can be another bonus of informal empire but also potentially a threat since the power of the subordinate entity might turn into a challenge to central influence and control.

Some of the most important factors in the demise of empires are nationalism and tendencies of emancipation. Marxists have been notorious for underestimating this important force of history, assuming that "objective" class forces rather than "subjective" factors such as nationalism propelled world events. Indeed, it was the quest for national emancipation that seriously shook the colonial system of the European powers after World War I and II, and finally, in the late 1950s and the 1960s, destroyed it. Willem Wertheim is thus correct in arguing that emancipation is "a decisive force in both revolution and evolution, and has to be incorporated from the outset as a basic element, instead of being viewed as a force alien to social reality."[31] Nederveen Pieterse specifies this general observation by stating that the determining forces in the development and decline of empire are not Dialectical Materialism and Historical Materialism à la Marx, Engels, and Lenin, but the dialectics of "domination and liberation" and of "empire and emancipation."[32] He also discovered an important dialectic relationship between nationalism and imperialism.

---

30 Doyle, *Empires*, p. 38.

31 Willem F. Wertheim, *Evolution and Revolution: The Rising Waves of Emancipation* (Harmondsworth: Penguin, 1974), p. 86, as quoted by Nederveen Pieterse, *Empire and Emancipation*, p. 83.

32 Nederveen Pieterse, *Empire and Emancipation*, pp. xiv-xv, 353-81.

> Imperialism creates nations: It naturally highlights the international domain and interstate conflict, and compels resistance to take on a similar form, the form of the nation-state, to act as its counterpart in the arena it has created. If empire building in its earlier stages is actually nation building, empire in its later stages is still building nations: in the process of emacipation from empire by means of defensive assimilation.[33]

The Soviet leaders from Lenin to Gorbachev were conscious to varying degree of the significance of nationalism. But they regarded it as one of the "remnants of the past" (*perezhitki proshlogo*) that would, with their assistance, be relegated to the "rubbish bin of history." To that extent, the Bolshevik leaders hardly differed from Prince Gorchakov and his conviction that the blessings of progressive ideas and a more advanced social system had to be brought to "backward" societies. As shrewd political leaders, however, both Lenin and Stalin knew that the remnants of the past were forces to be taken seriously and could be exploited for the consolidation of power. Thus, within days of assuming power, the Bolshevik government issued a Declaration of Rights of the national minorities. Without qualification, it affirmed that every nation had the right to self-determination up to and including secession. The mistaken belief of many of the nationalities that their fate would be better placed with the Reds than the Whites in the civil war following the Bolshevik revolution, helped decide the outcome of the war. Yet the slogan of "self-determination" not only failed to persuade the nationalities to become more than temporary allies against the Whites and to support the Bolshevik regime unconditionally but gave them the legitimate excuse to go their own way. Wilsonian principles of self-determination, therefore, gave way to "proletarian self-determination." On its basis, the leaders in Petrograd dispatched pro-Bolshevik armies to topple the newly formed nationalist regimes. Although the attempt to restore Russian control over Finland and the Baltic states failed, it was successful in Ukraine, Belorussia, Armenia, Azerbaijan, Georgia, and in Central Asia.[34] As a consequence, the nationalist movements of the regions of Eurasia incorporated into the Soviet Union were suppressed, but their aspirations were only subdued rather than eradicated.

Nationalism and the forces of national emancipation also played a significant role after World War II, in the establishment of the Soviet empire in Eastern Europe. Two major problems affected Soviet control. One was the unwillingness of the Eastern European nations to reconcile themselves with their dependent status and their resulting desire to emancipate themselves from Soviet rule. The other is the geographical extension of the problem noted above in the context of the Czarist empire: the subjugation of nations politically and economically more advanced than the metropole. The consequences became visible, from the Soviet perspective, in the relatively benign phenomenon of

---

33 Ibid., p. 359.

34 See Richard Pipes, *Russia under the Bolshevik Regime* (New York: Random House, 1995), the chapter entitled "The Red Empire," esp. pp. 149, 151.

"national communism" in Eastern Europe. But it also manifested itself in the more dangerous popular revolts in East Germany in 1953, Hungary in 1956, Czechoslovakia in 1968, and the unrest in Poland in 1956, 1970, 1976, and 1980-81.

Such events serve to clarify that what was at issue in Soviet-East European relations was not a matter of "involuntary imperialism" or "autocolonization" – at least not on the societal level. As Karen Dawisha has argued, the nondemocratically elected elites in Eastern Europe adopted a pro-Soviet stance in order to receive Soviet security assistance that would keep them in power. They continued to do so and sought to maintain their autocolonial status even as the impulse for empire was receding under Gorbachev.[35] However, in larger perspective, neither was the establishment of the Soviet empire in Eastern Europe involuntary nor did society there ask to be subjugated. The relationship between the center and the periphery in this case essentially followed an all-too familiar imperial story. The regimes put in place by the outside power proved to be exceedingly unpopular. This forced the metropole recurrently to embark on rescue operations.

The consequences of the extension of Soviet control to Eastern Europe were not always properly recognized. George Kennan, American diplomat, scholar, and author of the influential "Mr. X" article published in *Foreign Affairs* in July 1947. In retrospect, he admitted that "a serious deficiency of the article was the failure to mention the satellite area of Eastern Europe – the failure to discuss Soviet power ... *in terms of* its involvement in this area."[36] The attentive reader had every reason to believe that he "was talking only about Russia proper" and that the weaknesses of the Soviet system to which he was drawing attention "were ones that had their existence only within the national boundaries of the Soviet state." He would have been able to resent a far stronger argument about the tenuous nature of Soviet rule, he continued, if he had added the "embarrassments of imperialism which the Soviet leaders have now taken upon themselves with their conquest of Eastern Europe" and the "unlikelihood that Moscow would be permanently successful in holding that great area in subjection."[37]

During the Cold War, mental and political maps included East Germany as part of "Eastern Europe" – despite the fact that Berlin is located further west than Prague and that no part of Germany was ever considered part of that area at any time in European history. East Germany and the unresolved problem of a separate East German identity turned out to be one of the reasons why Kennan was right in that Moscow would be unsuccessful in holding on to Eastern Europe. Indeed, from the very beginning of the post-war era, the division of Germany and thereby the potential resurgence of German

---

35 Karen Dawisha, "Constructing and Deconstructing Empire," in Dawisha and Parrott, *End of Empire?*, p. 344.

36 George F. Kennan, *Memoirs: 1925-1950* (Boston: Little, Brown & Co., 1967), p. 357 (italics in the original).

37 Ibid.

nationalism were central to Moscow's problem of managing the new bipolar security order and the Soviet empire in Europe.

Concerning this issue, Stalin was not blinded by ideology but demonstrated political realism. He furthermore exhibited a great degree of skepticism, even cynicism, about the prospect of communist revolution without the direct support of Soviet power. This was amply demonstrated when he told visiting Yugoslav communist Milovan Djilas that in Germany "you cannot have a revolution because you have to step on the lawn;"[38] when he commented dryly on a pre-1941 Soviet war film, which showed rebellious elements of the German proletariat disrupting the rear, that "the German proletariat did not rebel;"[39] and when he told Polish leader Mikolajczyk that communism fitted Germany "as the saddle a cow."[40] He appears to have recognized German nationalism as a strong force that had to be taken into consideration in any post-war European security structure.[41]

The realization of the "costs of empire" associated with the processes of national emancipation in Eastern Europe and the unresolved "German problem" surfaced periodically in the deliberations of Soviet leaders. Several times, latent crises turned acute. However, after the building of the Berlin wall in 1961, awareness of the problem in Moscow was to wane and was to preoccupy the Soviet leadership in a major way only under Gorbachev.

4. International Systemic and Structural Approaches

Yet another explanation of imperialism focuses on the international system. One such approach, as developed originally by Morton Kaplan, is based on the assumption that basic structural features of the system, and the distribution of power within it, determine the behavior of states and create strong pressures for states to act in certain ways in order to safeguard vital interests. Furthermore, the system would allow the analyst to detect and predict patterns of behavior.[42] However, as critics have pointed out, Kaplan weakened his argument by asserting that changes of the system occurred as a result of *processes within states*. The fundamental dynamics of international politics, they have charged, thus remained unclear: Does the international system shape the behavior of states or does the internal make-up of the states determine the structure of the

---

38 Milovan Djilas, *Conversations with Stalin*, transl. Michael B. Petrovich (New York: Harcourt Brace & World, 1962), p. 79.

39 Ibid., p. 103.

40 Charles Bohlen in a seminar session, Columbia University, 19 March 1970.

41 For evidence see Hannes Adomeit, *Soviet Risk Taking and Crisis Behavior: A Theoretical and Empirical Analysis* (London: Allen & Unwin, 1982), esp. pp. 129-31.

42 Basic for this approach is Morton A. Kaplan, *System and Process and International Politics* (New York: John Wiley, 1957), pp. xvii-xviii; see also Kaplan, "Systems Theory and Political Science," *Social Research*, Vol. 35, No. 1 (Spring 1968), pp. 30-47.

international system? Since Kaplan had made both assertions, "the logic of his analysis, and hence its capacity for forecasting, was questionable."[43]

In an attempt to rescue structural theory, Kenneth Waltz has drawn a sharp distinction between what he calls "systems level" and "unit level" phenomena, stressing the tight limits set on state action by the international system.[44] Such limits certainly existed in many areas of the political and military competition between the superpowers. They also explain the tenacity with which the Soviet Union clung to its imperial possessions. However, there was no particular reason why two superpowers should have been locked in intense struggle had it not been for a specific conception of struggle shared by both of them. As for the United States with its pluralist and democratic structure, it can hardly be said that it was *inherently* prone to define itself as part of an uncompromising, "antagonist" world. It was only through the definition imposed by the Soviet Union, that of international relations as an "historically inevitable" struggle between two "opposed socio-economic systems, capitalism and socialism," that the United States perceived the conflict in antagonist terms. But any major alteration of such a definition in Moscow would cause both the functioning and the basic structure of the bipolar system to change. This was shown conclusively in the second half of the 1980s, when the introduction of perestroika, glasnost, and the New Thinking fundamentally altered international politics. A separation of the international system and the state actors, therefore, is not very helpful.

Jack Snyder, in his *Myths of Empire*, is conscious of the inextricable links between (1) the international system, (2) perceptions, and (3) the domestic politics of states.[45] In an attempt to come to grips with the origins and processes of imperialism in comparative perspective, he tests various hypotheses about these interrelationships in five states: Germany, Japan, Britain, the Soviet Union, and the United States. In the process, he distinguishes three theories which, in his opinion, can serve to explain imperial expansion and overexpansion of great powers.

Concerning the first – international systemic – dimension, Snyder tests in particular the theories of the Realist school, according to which expansion is a rational response to international anarchy and the best means of achieving security. Realism, as he explains, imputes to imperial statesmen and strategists the idea that conquest increases power by adding human and material resources that can be used in the competition with other great powers. Conversely, these actors have thought that losses at the empire's periphery could lead to collapse of power in the imperial core. Furthermore, they have maintained that

43 John Lewis Gaddis, "International Relations Theory and the End of the Cold War," *International Security*, Vol. 17, No. 3 (Winter 1992/93), p. 31.

44 Kenneth W. Waltz, *Theory of International Politics* (New York: Random House, 1979), pp. 97-98, as summarized by Gaddis, "International Relations Theory," p. 31.

45 Jack Snyder, *Myths of Empire: Domestic Politics and International Ambition* (Ithaca, N.Y.: Cornell University Press, 1991).

"the best defense is a good offense." In this view, cumulative gains in the imperial periphery can be reaped through assertiveness and aggressive action, the establishment of a strategic *glacis* and the creation of buffers, denying the adversary territory and manpower, and allowing a cheap defense of empire, whereas defending closer to home would be more costly. Expansion and aggression occur whenever a state's power in the international system is expected to decline. Preventive action then seems required in order to forestall such a development. Finally, as he writes, political leaders in the Realist perspective have acted in accordance with the idea that threats make other states compliant. This belief often implied a contradictory image of the opponent as posing an immense security threat but at the same time as being too weak or irresolute to counter remedial measures adopted by the adversary.[46]

Snyder calls the idea of expansion as a rational response to international anarchy and allegedly the best means of achieving security the "central myth" of empire but also the "major force propelling every case of overexpansion by the industrialized great powers."[47] He sees the tendency toward overexpansion as correlated with each state's position in the international system. Germany and Japan, in this view, were the least buffered from the dangers of international anarchy due to their size, geographical location, and resource endowments. They, consequently, had the most to gain by attempting to expand to a position of economic and military self-sufficiency. Furthermore, changes in a state's international power position over time correlated with its inclination to overexpand, as shown by German and Japanese policies in the 1930s. As for the post-war period and the Soviet Union, he concludes, the period of Moscow's most militant expansion "coincided with the time of fluid global power relations in Europe; the rise of revolutionary movements in Asia; and significant fluctuations in the nuclear balance." This "created an environment that spurred domino fears and worries [in Moscow] about windows of vulnerability."[48]

His second explanation of expansion and imperial overstretch is cognitive. It addresses the problem of whether imperial myths are predicated upon genuine belief or are mere instruments of policy. Since information for rational decision-making is incomplete, political actors store what they have learned in simplified, structured form. These actors often tend to see current and future events as a rerun of formative experiences in their political career, and "when a whole generation undergoes the same formative experiences, such as the lessons of Munich, the strategic policy of the whole state is likely to be affected for many years."[49] Yet on the basis of his case studies, Snyder casts doubt on the value of cognitive explanations for imperialist policies. He

46 Ibid., pp. 1-18.

47 Ibid., p. 1.

48 Ibid., pp. 306-307. The same was true for the United States in this period, he argues.

49 Ibid., pp. 27-28.

holds that "beliefs and 'lessons' correlate more strongly with personal and institutional interests than with formative experience."[50]

As for the third – the domestic political – explanation, he sees imperialist expansion as based on parochial interests and emanating from political coalitions, typically including important segments of the military, the military-industrial complex, economic groups seeking to profit from autarky and arms production, and government bureaucracies that stand to gain from aggressive external policies. The theory of domestic coalition politics, he writes, passed both cross sectional and time series tests. In what can be considered a common sense conclusion not necessarily requiring rigorous testing he concludes: "Cartelized political systems like Germany and Japan were the most recklessly overexpansionist; democratic systems and systems ruled by unitary oligarchies were less so."[51]

Snyder's "scientific" inquiry has both strengths and weaknesses. On the international systemic dimension, useful for analysis here is his observation that "the strategy of gaining security through expansion is rarely effective because the ideas underlying it contradict two of the most powerful regularities in international politics: the balance of power and the rising costs of expansion."[52] Indeed, in balance-of-power systems, individual states tended to form coalitions in order to counteract power imbalances created by revisionist states. As will be demonstrated *infra,* similar dynamics applied to the post-World War II bipolar system where both coalitions aimed at military preponderance. However, one of the weaknesses of Snyder's examination is the fact that he draws no clear-cut distinction between expansion and overexpansion; the terms are used interchangeably. But surely there is a major difference. Imperial expansion, where benefits outweigh costs, will frequently command widespread domestic support and pose relatively mild analytical and political problems. Imperial overexpansion, where costs exceed benefits, is more difficult to explain. It raises the question as to when, in the opinion of the analyst and political leaders, the advantages of empire turn into liabilities – a difficult question to answer and one that Snyder fails to address.

Another weakness in the international systemic dimension of analysis is Snyder's assertion that imperial expansion is likely to occur whenever a state's power is perceived to decline. International politics typically offer windows of both vulnerability and opportunity. This was no less true for the international system and Soviet foreign policy in the 1940s. The more militant line was not only the result of Moscow's security concerns and fears about falling dominos but also because *opportunities* existed for weakening the American position in Europe, undermining the Western colonial system in Asia, exploiting the communist victory in China, and reaping diplomatic capital from the

---

50 Ibid., p. 30.
51 Ibid., p. 308.
52 Ibid., p. 6.

first explosion of a nuclear device. Similarly, the findings about a power responding with assertiveness and aggression to perceived shifts in the "correlation of forces" in favor of the adversary are at odds with the course of events in the mid-1980s. In that period, the international power position of the Soviet Union had indeed declined, but the Soviet leadership under Gorbachev responded by pursuing *conciliatory* policies and embarking on a *reduction* rather than an expansion of imperial commitments.

Equally unsatisfactory are some of the author's findings in the second dimension of analysis: the cognitive explanations and their relevance in international politics. In fact, the book harbors a major unresolved contradiction. On the one hand, it denigrates the importance of beliefs and ideas as "ex post facto justifications for policy and elements of a strategic ideology" and "rationalizations."[53] On the other hand, it sees various "myths" of empire, that is, erroneous ideas, beliefs, and images as lying at the root of every case of overexpansion by the great powers. Its author concludes that beliefs correlate more strongly with personal and institutional interests than with formative experience. However, to posit congruence between images and interests is denying the possibility that political leaders may free themselves from established beliefs, images, and lessons, and even from dependency on interests, and provide a detached, even though incomplete, "cognitive" analysis of new challenges and new problems. The evolution of the New Thinking, as will be demonstrated, is an example of just such a conceptual revision.

Domestic coalition politics is the third and most important explanatory variable in the author's research design. Unfortunately, the findings under this heading are so complex and contradictory as to be almost meaningless. Focussing on the Gorbachev era, he discerns a dissolution of the "more cartelized" domestic structure of the Soviet Union in the period between 1953 and 1985 and the emergence of a "more unitary" and "more democratic" system that produced more "moderate" outcomes.[54] But was the Soviet Union under Gorbachev really more "unitary" than under Brezhnev? Assuming that it was, the author generalizes that "[i]f strong cartels face a situation of weakly institutionalized democracy and truncated debate, ... then increasing mass participation will exacerbate the cartel's inclination towards overexpansion."[55] However, although the conditions of weak democracy and increasing mass participation did apply in the Gorbachev era, the policies of overexpansion were ended rather than continued, let alone reenforced.

Almost as an afterthought, and briefly mentioned in the discussion of domestic politics, he makes a final point: "simple logrolling does not explain most of these [five] cases without resort to ideology. In some cases ideology was so integral to the political process that it played a central role in determining what the individual 'interest groups'

53 Ibid., pp. 306, 308.
54 Ibid., p. 311.
55 Ibid., p. 310.

wanted."[56] This finding raises an interesting as well as fundamental question. Earlier, cognition was declared only marginally significant. But who is to say with precision what part of ideology is genuine and cognitive, what part constitutes formalized perception and dogma, and what part is instrumental? This is a complex but crucial problem for the analysis of each and every major Soviet foreign policy decision that cannot simply be swept under the analytical rug. Ultimately, the reader is left wondering what really is more important for imperial expansion and overstretch: interests or ideology?

Imperial expansion and overstretch are also at issue in studies by Charles Kupchan and Paul Kennedy. In *The Vulnerability of Empire*, Kupchan asks why imperial powers often engage in self-defeating behavior.[57] Such behavior, in his view, occurs in response to perceived external threats and is characterized either by overly competitive behavior, which tends to lead to "overextension," or by overly cooperative behavior, which results in "strategic exposure."[58] He focuses on selected historical periods in which the United States, Germany, France, and Great Britain engaged, in response to shifts in the international distribution of power, in behavior that tended to erode their strategic position. Metropolitan vulnerability, he writes, not only results from shifts in the global distribution of power but also from previous elite efforts to enlist public support for imperial policies, support which later constrains the elites from readjusting when the international political landscape changes. Like Snyder's approach, Kupchan's study is of limited utility for the study of the Soviet empire. Elite perceptions of vulnerability are only one part of the explanation of Soviet overextension under Brezhnev and cooperative behavior under Gorbachev. To arrive at a fuller more accurate understanding of both imperial expansion and contraction in the Soviet case, many more factors need to be taken into consideration.

Kennedy's *The Rise and Fall of the Great Powers* is more relevant to the issues discussed in this book.[59] He argues that the relative strengths of the leading nations in world affairs never remain constant, principally because of the uneven rate of growth among different societies and technological and organizational breakthroughs which bring greater advantage to one society than to others. Once their productive capacity is enhanced, they find it easier to sustain the burdens of paying for large-scale armies and fleets. It may sound crudely mercantilistic, he continues, but wealth is usually needed to underpin military power, and military power is usually needed to acquire and protect wealth. If, however, too large a proportion of the state's resources is diverted from the

---

56 Ibid., p. 314.

57 Charles A. Kupchan, *The Vulnerability of Empire* (Ithaca, N.Y.: Cornell University Press, 1994).

58 Ibid., p. 14.

59 Paul M. Kennedy, *The Rise and Fall of the Great Powers: Economic Change and Military Conflict from 1500 to 2000* (New York: Random House, 1987). Except for some deletions and some minor changes, the summary in this paragraph has been rendered *verbatim*.

creation of wealth and allocated instead to military purposes, then that is likely to lead to a weakening of national power over the longer term. In the same way, if a state overextends itself strategically – by, say, the conquest of extensive territories or the waging of costly wars – it runs the risk that the potential benefits from external expansion may be outweighed by the expense of this endeavor. He considers this a dilemma which becomes acute if the nation concerned has entered a period of relative economic decline.[60]

Kennedy's analysis of the great powers' resource allocation dilemma – how much to allocate to "guns" or to "butter," to "profit" or to "power" – could have been discussed above under metrocentric approaches. However, it also fits into the present framework since the author is interested in the consequences of the state's resource allocation policies for its international power position and policies. He applies this interest to the bipolar system of the post-war era and the competition between the superpowers until the mid-1980s and concludes that the process of a "nation overextending itself, geographically and strategically" and "leaving less for 'productive investment'" with its "economic output slowing down ... and dire implications for its long-term capacity to maintain both its citizens' consumption demands and its international position" was already "happening in the case of the USSR, the United States, and Britain."[61] In retrospect, as with many a good book, there is some doubt as to whether its conclusions and predictions correctly reflected current realities; certainly, it failed accurately to predict future events. Leaving aside again the issue of American economic and military power and the United States' role in world affairs, the book correctly reconstructed what Sovietologists in their analyses of the Soviet Union then diagnosed as dilemmas of internal decline and external expansion, and a widening gap between a deteriorating economic base and rising military capabilities, referring to this phenomenon as a "paradox of superpower" and describing the Soviet Union as an "incomplete superpower," "a military giant and economic dwarf" and "giant on clay feet."[62] West German Chancellor Helmut Schmidt even referred to the Soviet Union as an "Upper Volta with nuclear weapons."[63] Yet, Kennedy thought that this "does *not* mean that the

---

60 Ibid., pp. xv-xvi.

61 Ibid., p. 539.

62 Some of the best examples is Seweryn Bialer, *The Soviet Paradox: External Expansion, Internal Decline* (New York: Alfred A. Knopf, 1986) and Paul Dibb, *The Incomplete Superpower* (Urbana, Ill.: University of Illinois Press, 1988); see also Hannes Adomeit, "Soviet Foreign Policy: The Internal Mechanism of External Expansion," in Hannes Adomeit and Robert Boardman, eds., *Foreign Policy Making in Communist Countries: A Comparative Approach* (Farnborough: Saxon House, 1979), pp. 15-48. Pointing to the widening gap between economic and military power in the period from the late 1970s until the mid-1980s was "almost becoming a *cliché* among Western Sovietologists," according to Arnold Horelick, "External Implications of Soviet Internal Development," in Uwe Nerlich and James A. Thomson, eds., *The Soviet Problem in American-German Relations* (New York: Crane, Russak, 1985), pp. 123-51.

63 In several semi-official speeches and privately.

USSR is close to collapse" and considered it "highly unlikely that even an energetic regime in Moscow would either abandon 'scientific socialism' in order to boost the economy or drastically cut the burdens of defense expenditures and thereby affect the military core of the Soviet state." The implications of this for the West were unpalatable since there was "nothing in the character or tradition of the Russian state to suggest that it could ever accept imperial decline gracefully."

> Indeed, historically *none* of the overextended, multinational empires – the Ottoman, the Spanish, the Napoleonic, the British – ever retreated to their own ethnic base until they had been defeated in a Great Power war, or (as with Britain after 1945) were so weakened that an imperial withdrawal was politically unavoidable.[64]

None of these predictions turned out to be accurate. The Soviet leadership, already in office when the book was written, did embark on an attempt at fundamentally realigning the relationship between economic and military power. It drastically reduced its imperial commitments. It aimed at significant cuts in defense expenditures. It accepted imperial decline more or less gracefully, certainly without producing cataclysmic international conflict. And the country over which the leadership presided finally collapsed. All this makes the task of analyzing the Gorbachev era even more challenging.

5. Transnational Approaches

Doyle is among the few theorists of empire who appreciate the fact that transnational forces in the past influenced both imperialist policies and the form which empires assumed. Settlers, missionaries, merchants, and public officials, as he points out, were such forces.

> Settlers destroyed native society altogether and welcomed formal imperial rule provided it gave them a substantial voice in colonial policy. Commerce tended to create local oligarchies, which could then become the collaborating classes on which indirect rule depended. The military, which preferred direct rule, destroyed armed tribal opposition and with it many of the leaders who might have collaborated in indirect rule.[65]

But he and other theorists have inadequately focussed on the reverse process: the influence which peripheries have exerted on the metropole, often through the same transnational forces that helped shape the dependencies.[66] Theories of international relations, rather than of the rise and fall of empires, provide the scholar with some guidance in understanding the impact of these forces in general and in the imperial context.

---

64 Kennedy, *The Rise and Fall of the Great Powers*, pp. 513-14.

65 Doyle, *Empires*, p. 179.

66 Doyle, *Empires*, p. 38, notes this fact only in passing.

Karl Deutsch, for instance, in his seminal *Nationalism and Social Communication*, analyzed social, economic, and technological processes largely beyond the control of the nation-states and the influence which these processes exert on world development.[67] Far from being prisoners of the nation-state, in his view, citizenries can effect positive change through "social communication," or transnational, popularly centered activities towards a more peaceful and constructive international order. Accordingly, in the late 1970s, in a statement directly applicable to the Soviet-American competition, he thought that the best hope for change in relations among countries that seemingly remain locked in conflict may lie in a "combined strategy of both internal and external change."[68]

Several British and American scholars have placed this approach into the general paradigm of global transnational influences and looked at it through the lens of international political economy (IPE). In Britain, these scholars include Robin Brown, Robert O'Brien, and Julian Saurin. IPE is regarded by O'Brien as "a methodology that identifies the interaction of economic and political domains as the central phenomenon in international relations."[69]

While he does not focus on any particular context, he notes that transnational influences are more properly examined under the broader aegis of IPE than treated either as a case of simple technology transfer or an issue of international security studies. He, as well as Brown, regards both of the latter as subordinate to the increasing internationalization of politics and economics, in the wake of which the influence of the state will be reduced.[70] Finally, in this group of scholars, Julian Saurin contends that the state "has been taken as a model" in traditional international relations theory and "become the constitutive unit of the international system." He regrets that "[t]he ontological primacy ascribed to the assumed state has effectively foreclosed alternative accounts of global social change and order that derive from the actual historical experiences of people across the world."[71] These scholars, while focusing on theory rather than the empirical dimension of East-West relations, do reflect the growing importance of IPE in the study of international relations. Their theoretical constructs,

---

67 Karl Deutsch, *Nationalism and Social Communication* (Cambridge, Mass.: MIT Press, 1953).

68 Karl Deutsch, *The Analysis of International Relations*, 2nd ed. (Englewood Cliffs, N.J.: Prentice-Hall, 1978), p. 196.

69 Robert O'Brien, "International Political Economy and International Relations: Apprentice or Teacher?," in John Macmillan and Andrew Linklater, eds., *Boundaries in Question: New Directions in International Relations* (London: Pinter, 1995), p. 90; similarly Richard Higgot, "International Political Economy," in A. J. R. Groom and Margot Light, eds., *Contemporary International Relations* (London: Pinter, 1994), pp. 156-69.

70 Ibid.; Robin Brown, "Globalization and the End of the National Project," in John Macmillan and Andrew Linklater, eds., *Boundaries in Question: New Directions in International Relations* (London: Pinter, 1995), p. 55.

71 Julian Saurin, "The End of International Relations? The State and International Theory in the Age of Globalization," in John Macmillan and Andrew Linklater, eds., *Boundaries in Question: New Directions in International Relations* (London: Pinter, 1995), p. 244.

furthermore, are applicable to a variety of specific historical or political contexts, including the disintegration of the Soviet empire.

While British theorists have traditionally focused primarily on the interaction between national political and economic systems, American contributions to the field of International Political Economy have been informed by a larger, international, and institutional approach. Led by Robert Keohane and Joseph Nye, these scholars have devoted their energies to understanding the extent to which the largely institutionalized post-1945 international regime (anchored by such institutions as the IMF, the United Nations, and the World Bank) has altered or limited the authority of states and their ability to make policy. Grouped under the headings of Transnational Theory and Neoliberal Institutionalism, these theorists have posited that the role of international institutions and other non-state actors, while largely beneficial, has limited the power of states in ways that have yet to be fully understood. Charles Kegley and Eugene Wittkopf have argued that transnational forces can be grouped into four major categories: trade and capital flows, military alliances, technological forces, and political influences.[72] Nye and Keohane have informed their study with the idea of "regime change," which tries to explain how the evolution of the international institutional landscape has altered the place of states in the international system. They have observed that international institutions act as "transmission belts" through which the behavior of one state affects that of another.[73] They also point out that "interests are constructed, not given," and that they "derive not only from considerations of geopolitical position but also from both material interest and conceptions of principle as interpreted through varying domestic political structures."[74]

The Neoliberal and Institutionalist perspectives have a bearing on the hotly debated question about the role of external pressure in the collapse of the Soviet empire. To look first at the probably still dominant, alternative Realist interpretation, in a mirror image of Marxist-Leninist concepts, the Soviet system was regarded as being driven by an inherent proclivity to conduct expansionist policies. If it were denied the option of external expansion, the system would either collapse or have to concentrate on internal development. These two outcomes of a strategy of "containment" were first suggested by Kennan in 1947. The United States, in his view, had it in its power "to increase enormously the strains under which Soviet policy must operate [not only] to force upon the Kremlin a far greater degree of moderation and circumspection [but also] ... to

---

72 Charles W. Kegley, Jr. and Eugene R. Wittkopf, *World Politics: Trend and Transformation*, 3rd ed. (New York: St. Martin's Press, 1989), p. 24.

73 Joseph S. Nye, Jr. and Robert O. Keohane, "Transnational Relations and World Politics," *International Organization*, Vol. 25 (Summer 1971), pp. 325-49.

74 Robert O. Keohane and Joseph S. Nye, "Introduction: The End of the Cold War in Europe," in *After the Cold War: International Institutions and State Strategies in Europe, 1989-1991*, eds. Robert O. Keohane, Joseph S. Nye, and Stanley Hoffman (Cambridge, Mass.: Harvard University Press, 1993), p. 4.

promote tendencies which must eventually find their outlet in either the *break-up* or the gradual *mellowing* of Soviet power."[75]

But several scholars and policy makers, looking at the world through Realist lenses, went beyond the idea of containment to *isolation* of the Soviet Union in order to achieve either of the two outcomes posited by Kennan. A restrictive technology policy and the curtailment of trade and credit relations were considered to be the appropriate means for this purpose.[76] In the late 1970s and early 1980s, corresponding policies culminated in the deliberate acceleration of the Soviet-American military-technological competition and efforts at raising the "costs of Soviet empire," exploiting its "fault lines" and making sure, to paraphrase Reagan, that it would go down with a whimper rather than a bang.

Neoliberal and Institutionalist perspectives may have conceded the point of the inherent proclivity of the Soviet system towards expansion but, for the most part, they ruled out the idea of collapse. Its adherents stressed instead the evolutionary and reformist potential of the system. A policy of deliberate isolation of the Soviet Union was regarded as too dangerous, since it would increase the risk of military conflict, and also as counterproductive, since it would delay adjustment processes.[77] Some of its adherents thought that the structural deficiencies of the Soviet system made it unnecessary to increase pressures from the outside, and that governmental and transnational interaction, including trade and credit relations, rather than strengthening the system, would *sharpen* the contradictions and induce reform. Such diagnoses, in the late 1960s and early 1970s, gave rise to a mushrooming literature on "convergence" of the capitalist and socialist systems. Marxist theorists in the United States, "Eurocommunists" in Western Europe and some communist party officials in Eastern Europe shared these visions and propounded the ideas of "reform socialism" and a "third road" between the two systems.

In the West, such notions also provided a conceptual underpinning for the policies of detente, "bridge building," "constructive engagement," Ostpolitik and *Wandel durch Annäherung*, or change through rapprochement. Western technology, trade and credits, and businessmen and bankers, were not the only transnational forces that were being regarded as having an impact on the Soviet empire. Other, equally important forces were held to include Western European social democracy; the Eurocommunist parties, notably

75 George F. Kennan, "The Sources of Soviet Conduct," in id., *American Diplomacy, 1900-1950*, Mentor Books (New York: The New American Library, 1951), p. 105 (italics mine). The quote is from his "Mr. X" article, referred to above.

76 Some of the more prominent Sovietologists that can be regarded as belonging to this school are Zbigniew Brzezinski, Richard Pipes, Abraham S. Becker, Charles Wolf, Andrew Marshall and Michel Tatu. See especially Richard Pipes, *Survival is Not Enough: Soviet Realities and America's Future* (New York: Simon and Schuster, 1984), p. 266.

77 Sovietologists belonging to this group can be said to include Alexander Dallin, Raymond L. Garthoff, Jerry F. Hough, George F. Kennan and Marshall D. Shulman. Among German scholars, one of the best corresponding *exposés* is Christoph Royen, *Die sowjetische Koexistenzpolitik im Wandel: Voraussetzungen, Ziele, Dilemmata*, Series Internationale Politik und Sicherheit, Vol. 2 (Baden-Baden: Nomos, 1987).

those of Italy, France, and Spain; the trade unions; cultural and church groups; and the "peace movement." In the East, they were thought to exist in the form of reform communist parties or reformist factions in orthodox parties. Such forces were interpreted as having been effective in their impact on the Soviet system and empire primarily throughout the second half of the 1970s and in the 1980s. In that period, the Conference on Security and Cooperation in Europe (CSCE) was regarded as having provided a particularly useful umbrella under which they could deploy and operate.

One of the most contentious issues analytically is the question as to what hastened the demise of the Soviet imperial system: the strategies associated with Realist isolation of and pressure on the Soviet Union, or the Neoliberal and Institutionalist approaches of containment, cooperation, and constructive engagement? It will be shown here that both approaches played a role. The external pressures, applied primarily by the United States, initially served their purpose well in concentrating the Soviet (Gorbachev's) mind on internal development. Once this had happened, the mainly Western European policy of constructive engagement first facilitated and then reenforced policy shifts in the Soviet Union. Completing the circle of interaction, after Gorbachev's desire to play by the Western rules of interdependence and integration, rather than by adhere to the traditional Leninist principles of antagonism, had become credible, the Realist stick was increasingly put aside (this happened already under Reagan) and replaced by Neoliberal and Institutionalist carrots.

6. An Integrative Approach

What are the conclusions of this discussion of various theories on the rise and fall of empires? Which of these theories, or parts thereof, can meaningfully be employed in the subsequent inquiry into the collapse of the Soviet empire? One conclusion is that *none* of theories are able to give a satisfactory explanation of the phenomenon of imperialism; *all* of them can contribute something to our understanding. International relations, of which the imperialist phenomenon is an integral part, are exceedingly complex. They include ideological, political, military, economic, technological, social, and psychological dimensions, all of which in one way or another impinge on the behavior of political leaders, elites, and nations. The selection of one single dimension can, therefore, at best illuminate one segment of international relations but never the whole picture.

A similar reasoning can be applied to what in the international relations literature has been referred to as the "level-of-analysis" problem.[78] Three levels can be distinguished, that of the individual leader or statesman; the nation state with different groups, elites

78 J. David Singer, "The Level-of-Analysis Problem in International Relations," *World Politics*, Vol. 14, No. 1 (October 1961), pp. 77-92; see also id., *Models, Methods, and Progress in World Politics* (Boulder, Colo.: Westview, 1990) and Kenneth Waltz, *Man, the State, and War: A Theoretical Analysis* (New York: Columbia University Press, 1959).

and institutions involved in foreign policy decision-making; and the international system. As with the various disciplines, each of the analytical levels and "cuts" can shed light on a given problem of international relations and foreign policy; none is able to explain the "essence" of decisions and events.[79] Thus, while it is useful for heuristic purposes to separate different dimensions and levels, the analyst should try to reconstruct their complex *interaction* and to provide the reader with a hierarchy or *rank ordering* of their importance.

To apply these considerations to the study of imperial development and decline, empires first and foremost need military power in order to expand and maintain control. But they can hardly survive for long by the mere exercise of raw power. Some semblance of legitimacy is called for; they therefore need an ideological underpinning. They also require a viable political organization and an efficient economic base in order to sustain effective armed forces. Finally, they must pay attention to social costs in order not to lose the modicum of consent of the governed necessary for imperial policies. None of these factors should be neglected.

An integrative approach is also appropriate when considering the relevance of the four major approaches discussed in this chapter. Obviously, just as foreign policy, imperial construction and decline begin at home. The *metrocentric* view, therefore, is basic to an understanding of the problem of imperialism. But this is not saying very much. It leaves open the whole plethora of problems touched upon, including the question as to the role of individual leaders in the rise and fall of empires and whether the underlying dynamics of the process are power acquisition and aggrandizement, economic determinism, or ideological zeal. The state of affairs at the center, in turn, cannot be looked at in isolation from what is happening in the imperial possessions and dependencies. A *pericentric* perspective, therefore, has to supplement the metrocentric view. Conditions there decide on the cost effectiveness of imperial rule. This pertains in particular to such questions as to whether the subjects of imperial possessions and dependencies are compliant or prone to resist; whether local elites can be coopted or have to be tightly controlled; and whether the periphery contributes to the power and wealth of the metropole or constitutes a constant drain on its resources. Depending on the answer to these questions, the periphery can present a formidable challenge to the imperial control. The same is true for the *international system*. Historically, both the "balance of power" and the "bipolar" system have acted as constraints on imperial expansion; the dynamics of both also contributed to imperial decline. Typically, competing powers will attempt to affect the power position of the opposing empire's core not only by denying it new territory and resources outside its domains but also by fomenting resistance, revolt and revolution in the periphery. Finally, it is not only the impact of the policies conducted by

79 Graham Allison, *Essence of Decision: Explaining the Cuban Missile Crisis* (Boston, Mass.: Little, Brown, 1971).

states in the international system that affects the metropole and the periphery of empires, but also *transnational forces*. Such forces made themselves felt in previous centuries. However, the introduction of modern communications technology, including the telephone, telefax, radio, television, and satellites, vastly enhanced their importance and made insulation of the empire from external influences even more difficult than before. The Soviet empire, as it turned out, could not evade this fact of twentieth-century life.

There are, of course, pitfalls in adopting an integrative approach. "Scientific" inquiry in practice often consists of isolating a few selected "variables" in order to verify or falsify clearly stated hypotheses. A research design that pays attention to the complex interaction of a variety of factors at various levels of analysis will, therefore, surely expose the analyst to the charge of "overexplanation" of the problems to be explained, that is, the reasons and rationales for the division of Germany, the long duration of the division, the Soviet acceptance of German unification, and the consent to German unification under NATO auspices in the context of the rise and fall of the Soviet empire. If so, he has been accused of worse things and will take consolation in the thought that it is better to overexplain than to underexplain. Given the insights gained from archives, memoirs, and interviews, it would be a disservice to the reader to deprive him of rich data simply because they do not fit into a narrowly defined analytical framework.

Having stated the research problem, outlined some of the theories applicable and the approach to be taken here, it is now appropriate to begin the next chapter, which consists in a reconsideration of Soviet perceptions of and policies toward the German problem from the division of Germany under Stalin through the hardening of the division under Khrushchev and until the last years of the Brezhnev era. The analytical thread that will help the reader find his way through the empirical maze will be the Ideological and Imperial paradigm.

PART TWO: EXPANSION

Chapter 2: The Imperial and Ideological Paradigm

1. Parameters of the Paradigm

At the Twenty-eighth and last CPSU Congress, in July 1990, Foreign Minister Shevardnadze asked the assembled party officials: "We have grown accustomed to certain German realities. We have seen in them a guarantee of our security. But let us think about this: Can there be a reliable guarantee [of security] based on the artificial and unnatural division of a great nation? And how long can it last"?[1] Why, in the more than forty years of the division of Germany, had no one before him dared stand up and ask such a pertinent question?

The disadvantages of the division should always have been obvious to the more perceptive among Soviet leaders: a perennial state of confrontation with the West, interrupted intermittently by periods of detente. The problem, therefore, arises as to what may have led Stalin to opt or, as the case may be, settle for a divided rather than an undivided Germany. Was it *not* patently obvious from the very beginning that the division of Germany could not last? If so, will the historical record now confirm Gorbachev's "belief" that Stalin was ready, "until the very end, to pay a price for a neutral Germany"?[2] Similarly, how credible is Politburo member Aleksandr Yakovlev's assertion, made at the same congress, that "We always advanced the question of Germany's unification," notably at "the end of 1945 or the beginning of 1946, and then repeatedly during the 1950s"?[3] Is it true, as a Russian expert on Europe has stated, that the Soviet leadership, in the period from the end of the war until the mid-1950s, "more or less consistently supported German unification"; that a "peaceful, democratic, and neutral Germany" was a "genuine" goal of Soviet diplomacy; and that this conclusion is supported by "geopolitical logic – perhaps the only kind that Stalin mastered"?[4]

To answer these questions, it is useful to put Soviet policies on the German problem under Stalin, Khrushchev, and Brezhnev into an appropriate framework of analysis. Such a framework can be called the Ideological and Imperial paradigm, the essence of which will be held to consist of a close interrelationship between power and ideology in domestic politics and between imperial and revolutionary purposes in

---

1 "Otchety chlenov i kandidatov v chleni Politbiuro, sekretarei TsK KPSS," *Pravda*, 5 July 1990.
2 Michail Gorbatschow, *Erinnerungen* (Berlin: Siedler, 1995), p. 701.
3 "Otvety na voprosy uchastnikov s"ezda," *Pravda*, 11 July 1990.
4 Sergei A. Karaganov, "Implications of German Unification for the Former Soviet Union," in Paul B. Stares, ed., *The New Germany in the New Europe* (Washington: The Brookings Institution, 1992), p. 332. The author is deputy director of the Institute on Europe at the Russian Academy of Sciences.

foreign policy.[5] The confluence of these two dimensions is, of course, the norm rather than the exception. Empires cannot be built without power. Imperial control, in turn, is difficult to maintain without universal appeal and purpose. In the period from the ancient Egyptian theocracies to Europe in the age of absolutism and the "divine right of kings," power was legitimized primarily by religious belief and dogma. After the Enlightenment, this form of legitimation was replaced by more rational constructs, of which Marxism-Leninism is one example. For the present purposes, to explain the ideological part of the dual paradigm, it is appropriate to clarify what is meant by ideology, to relate Marxism-Leninism to that clarification, and to describe its impact on Soviet foreign policy.

The Ideological Dimension

Ideology can be defined as a comprehensive system of political beliefs that consists of cognitive, normative, and operational components.[6] The cognitive or analytical element provides a theory about the nature of social and political life and provides a set of concepts and categories for interpreting specific situations and events. The normative aspect articulates a set of fundamental values and purposes that are considered the ultimate objectives of political life and provide a legitimation of behavior. The tactical, instrumental, or operational properties refer to principles of conduct and axioms of behavior that guide concrete action toward the attainment of objectives. Its coherence, rigor, and claim to absolute truth distinguish ideology from looser categories of belief systems, such as liberalism, conservatism, as well as *mentalité* and culture.[7] Ideologies also differ from two other kinds of ideational systems of comparable rigor: unlike philosophies, they include an explicit commitment to the use of force for the attainment of political objectives; and unlike

---

5 This paradigm was first developed in my article, "Russia as a 'Great Power' in World Affairs: Images and Reality," *International Affairs* (London), Vol. 71, No. 1 (January 1995), pp. 35-68. The utility of such a framework was recognized also by Zubok and Pleshakov. In what is one of the best recent reconsiderations of the Stalin and Khrushchev era –like the present book based on new archival evidence and memoirs – the authors proceed from the assumption that Stalin saw no contradiction between strengthening the Soviet Union and empire building, on the one hand, and advancing the cause of world revolution, on the other. They argue that "It was this revolutionary-imperial paradigm that the USSR followed consistently from the early 1920s;" Vladislav Zubok and Constantine Pleshakov, *Inside the Kremlin's Cold War: From Stalin to Khrushchev* (Cambridge, Mass.: Harvard University Press, 1996), p. 13.

6 This enumeration of the components of ideology and the subsequent formulations draw on Nigel Gould-Davies, Introduction to *Ideology and Soviet Foreign Policy*, Ph.D. Dissertation, Harvard University (in progress). The threefold differentiation of ideology is also adopted by Stephen White and Alex Pravda, eds., *Ideology and Soviet Politics* (Houndmills and London: Macmillan, 1989).

7 The difference between ideology and political beliefs was aptly made, and applied to the Soviet Union and the United States respectively, by Zbigniew Brzezinski and Samuel P. Huntington, *Political Power: USA–USSR* (New York: Viking Press, 1964).

religions, they are founded upon claims to knowledge about the nature of social existence rather than on faith in a transcendent reality.[8]

If, then, an ideology can be understood to be a highly structured and absolutist system of political beliefs, a *revolutionary* ideology is one that is incompatible with the existing political order. Its interpretation of history and social life is radically different from that of the other members of a given international order; its objective is not the improvement but the fundamental transformation of this order and its replacement with a new system based on higher principles. For this purpose, it uses methods not normally sanctioned by the established order. Marxism-Leninism was clearly an example of such a revolutionary ideology. It claimed to furnish a "scientific" explanation of political and socio-economic phenomena. It purported simultaneously to provide a philosophical method (dialectical materialism); a teleological interpretation of world history (historical materialism); and principles of political economy with "laws of development" pertaining to capitalist and socialist systems.

This is not the place to repeat at length the arguments of various schools of thought concerning the significance of Marxist-Leninist ideology for Soviet foreign policy. Stated briefly for the present purposes, it is useful to proceed from the premises that there is no necessary contradiction between Marxist-Leninist ideology and the Soviet "national interest"; that national interests are not self-evident but have to be defined by the political process; that such a definition in the Soviet case certainly had strong ideological components; and that ideology was *adapted* to new conditions, not abandoned. Soviet foreign policy, furthermore, was not that of a traditional state, formulated by the foreign ministry, but that of a revisionist power whose policies were determined primarily by the Communist Party, the institutional embodiment of ideology.[9]

Additional working assumptions here are that the analytical properties of ideology, or at least its core elements, provided a filter through which the Soviet leaders interpreted reality and that the "balance of power" also had an ideologically determined equivalent: the "correlation of forces."[10] Concerning the issue of

---

8 Gould-Davies, Introduction to *Ideology and Soviet Foreign Policy*.

9 This is a summary of the main argument this author made in "Ideology in the Soviet View of International Affairs," in Christoph Bertram, ed., *Prospects of Soviet Military Power in the 1980s* (London: Macmillan, 1980), pp. 103-10.

10 The ideological content of the '"correlation of forces" was aptly described by Raymond L. Garthoff, "The Concept of the Balance of Forces in Soviet Policy-Making," *World Politics*, Vol. 4, No. 1 (October 1951), pp. 84-111; for an updating see Hannes Adomeit, "The Political Rationale of Soviet Military Capabilities and Doctrine," in *Strengthening Conventional Deterrence in Europe: Proposals for the 1980s*, Report of the European Security Study (ESECS) (London: Macmillan, 1983), pp. 67-104, and Vernon Aspaturian, "Soviet Global Power and the Correlation of Forces," *Problems of Communism*, Vol. 29, No. 3 (May-June 1980), pp. 1-18. Some of the Soviet portrayals are Georgii Shakhnazarov, "Deistvennye faktory

legitimation versus mobilization, the question as to whether the Soviet leaders genuinely believed in ideological precepts is immaterial, since even false priests, apostates, and cynics, in order to serve and stay in power, are constrained to act in accordance with the official belief system and institutional requirements. The Marxist-Leninist claim to "scientific" – absolute and universal – truth required eradication of actual or potential challenges. Hence, whatever their preferences and convictions, the Soviet leaders from Stalin to Gorbachev had to contend just as much with deviationist phenomena of the "socialist" variety, such as Maoism, the Prague Spring, and Eurocommunism, as with Western liberalism and capitalism. Ideology, therefore, of necessity had not only an *ex post facto* but also an *ex ante*, motivating and mobilizing, function.

As codified in Lenin's *Imperialism, the Highest Stage of Capitalism* and subsequent party documents, the constituent elements of the ideological part of the paradigm can be summarized as follows:

(1) International relations are an extension of domestic class struggle to the international arena.

(2) There is an irreconcilable contradiction between two opposed socioeconomic systems – socialism and capitalism.

(3) Imperialism, the highest stage of capitalism, is inherently militaristic and aggressive.

(4) There is a constant redistribution of power among the capitalist countries and changing coalitions and power centers. The contradictions between these centers – the United States, Western Europe, and Japan in post-war conditions – are irreconcilable; the forces that divide these centers are more basic than those that unite them.

(5) Conflict ("a series of frightful collisions") among the imperialist states, that is, military conflict (war), is as inevitable as war between imperialism and socialism.

(6) In the long run, the correlation of forces will shift in favor of socialism. Conflict will end only with the victory of socialism. This is historically predetermined. The shift will occur because of (a) the sharpening of contradictions in the imperialist system; (b) the superiority of the socialist over the capitalist mode of production; (c) the growing strength of national-liberation movements; and (d) the emergence of new states with a non-capitalist and ultimately socialist orientation.

(7) Since class relations are the determining factor of international affairs, nationalism will wither away. Nationalist phenomena under socialism are merely *perezhitki proshlogo:* the remnants of an outdated socio-economic system.

---

mezhdunarodnykh otnoshenii," *Mezhdunarodnaia zhizn'* (Moscow), No. 1 (1977), pp. 87-96, and Vadim V. Zagladin, "World Balance of Forces and the Development of International Relations," *International Affairs* (Moscow), No. 3 (1985), pp. 65-79.

The conduct of Soviet foreign policy was constrained by a narrow spectrum of interpretation, within which a "correct" and "principled" policy had to be pursued. Furthermore, ideology gave rise to certain axioms or "operational principles" of Soviet foreign policy behavior, which can be defined as follows.

(1) Since individual nations and coalitions of states are divided internally along class lines, Soviet foreign policy has to be conducted on two tiers or tracks: the ideological, or socio-economic, level and the state-to-state level. "Internal contradictions" within and among capitalist countries are an important asset that should be utilized, wherever appropriate, with the help of "peace movements" and the communist parties.

(2) Since "peaceful coexistence" can never be a goal in itself but is only a *tactical* device, and since only countries with the same or similar system structure as that of the Soviet Union can be regarded as trustworthy, cooperation with the West can only be *limited* and *temporary*.

(3) Since the adversary "power centers of imperialism" must be expected to exploit economic weaknesses of the socialist countries and exert pressure, it is necessary, in economic affairs, to pursue *autarkist policies*.

(4) Since the restoration of capitalism in a socialist state ("counter-revolution") is a betrayal of principles and could be the prelude to a general "roll back" of socialism, *counter-revolution must be prevented*. In doing so, however, limits set by the risks of a military conflict with the West have to be observed.

(5) Since ideology ("history") provides legitimacy, the *use of force* presents no moral problem; it is only a *matter of expediency*.

To turn to the "imperial" dimension of the paradigm, a paradox must be noted first. There is very little in Marxist-Leninist ideology that can be construed as providing the basis for the establishment of an imperial system. The essence of this body of thought was the idea that *socio-economic forces* rather than political or military power propel history. State institutions, military establishments included, were supposed to "whither away." Yet, as noted, the Czarist empire was reconstituted under Soviet rule and extended, first regionally, then globally. Military and geopolitical factors in Soviet policy began to take precedence over economic considerations. Despite all the Soviet claims about the greater sophistication of the "correlation of forces" theory as compared with bourgeois Western "balance of power" constructs, Soviet leaders conformed in their foreign policy behavior to the most primitive notions of Realist theory and all of the above-noted "myths of empire."

The Imperial Dimension

The dichotomy between Marxist-Leninist ideology and the Soviet brand of Realism, however, is more apparent than real. Before attempting to demonstrate this, the basic elements of the "imperial" part of the paradigm will be enumerated. These elements, which here have been distilled primarily from what Soviet leaders had to say privately and derived from their conduct in foreign policy rather than from official, publicly accessible sources, include the following:

(1) Power, prestige, status, and influence of any given country in world affairs depend on the size of its population, geographical expanse, endowment with natural resources, volume of industrial and agricultural output, and access to or control over human and material resources abroad. Expansion will add to the country's resources and thereby to its power and prestige.

(2) The single most important factor determining the influence of a great nation in international affairs is military power. Qualitative indicators are important, as is the morale of the armed forces, but so are quantitative indicators, such as the number of divisions, tanks, aircraft, and artillery, and the number of nuclear missiles and warheads. In fact, quantity can make up for deficiencies in quality.

(3) Military threats, whether explicit or implicit, will make opponents compliant. The greater the discrepancy between one's own military capabilities and that of the opponent(s), the more effective the threat. Both the domestic political orientation and the foreign policies of allies and adversaries can be influenced by external pressure.

(4) Close attention, therefore, has to be paid to the "correlation of forces." The Soviet Union, and the coalition of states over which it presides, must be at least as strong as all of the potential enemies combined, and preferably stronger.

(5) Given the anarchic nature of the international system, the lack of common values and the objective condition of conflict between two antagonist socio-economic systems, security cannot be left to the good intentions of the adversary. It must be sought through unilateral efforts.

(6) Political means to achieve security, including the utilization of contradictions within and between inimical countries, should not be neglected. However, these are only supplementary to the military-technical means at one's disposal.

(7) The Western countries' clamor for the universal dissemination of human and civil rights, pluralism, democracy and the "free flow of information" as well as the encouragement of nationalism and the deployment of what their theorists call "transnational" forces have to be considered attempts at subverting Soviet global and regional influence and control. Vigilance and counteraction are required to stave off such attempts.

The enumeration of imperial elements shows that they *supplement* rather than supplant the ideological aspects of the dual paradigm. As early as 1924, Stalin had clarified this when he declared: "Soviet power in Russia is the base, the bulwark, and the refuge of the revolutionary movement of the entire world."[11] In the 1930s, he had reiterated the confluence of ideological and imperial dimensions in Soviet foreign policy by providing a standard definition of a "true internationalist" as someone who "is ready to defend the USSR without reservation, without wavering, unconditionally."[12]

One explanation lies first and foremost in the fact that Marxist ideology has many facets and that Lenin and Stalin, in the course of the "creative development of theory" and adaptation of Marxism to Russian conditions, emphasized certain portions of the theory to the almost complete exclusion of others. This led to the perversion or deformation of some of the main principles of Marxist thought. It pertained above all to the *de facto* emphasis placed by the Soviet leaders on military power as an agent of international change rather than socio-economic development.

A second explanation for the confluence of ideological and imperial dimensions of the paradigm, rather than their contradiction, is connected with the dogma of the "irreconcilable" and "inevitable" conflict between two opposed systems. This notion is essentially the ideological equivalent of the Realist view of international relations as a zero-sum game, in which one side's loss is the other's gain, and victory and defeat are the only possible outcomes.

A third explanation has much to do with the fact that the revolution did not occur in the advanced capitalist countries, such as Germany and England, but in backward Russia. Apart from the basic structural deficiencies of the system itself, this was one of the reasons why the heralded "superiority of the socialist over the capitalist mode of production" could not be achieved, and why the communist system was imposed, maintained, and expanded by force, rather than established and supported by popular will. As time went by and imperial overstretch began to set in, the attractiveness of the Soviet-type system and model of development waned even more. This reenforced the reliance on military means to maintain influence and control.

Having established the Ideological and Imperial paradigm as a basic framework of analysis, it is now appropriate to look in detail at its practical consequences for Soviet policies toward Germany.

2. The Division of Germany: Design or Default?

The main propositions flowing from the paradigm are that (1) there was considerable continuity in Soviet policy on the German problem, the Kremlin leaders from Stalin to Gorbachev adhering to the principle of the existence of two German states and

11 J. V. Stalin, *Sochineniia*, Vol. 6 (Moscow: Politizdat, 1947), p. 265, as quoted by Zubok and Pleshakov, *Inside the Kremlin's Cold War*, p. 13.

12 J. V. Stalin, *Sochineniia*, Vol. 10 (Moscow: Politizdat, 1948), p. 53.

relying on East Germany as a strategic ally in their attempt to build an empire and control Eastern Europe; (2) these and other top ranking party leaders may have realized the high costs and negative consequences of clinging to the *status quo* on the German problem (and that this may have especially been true for Lavrenti Beria, the former secret service chief) but that an overwhelming majority of the collective leadership rejected the idea of abandoning the GDR; and (3) that most of the initiatives on the German problem, including Stalin's "peace note" of March 1952, were primarily political and propagandistic exercises rather than a genuine search to end the division of Germany.

It is also one of the central arguments of this book that the establishment of the Soviet empire in Eastern Europe and the concomitant division of Germany may not have been the inevitable consequence of Stalin's adherence to the paradigm but that it was a logically consistent and *probable* result. An apt description of this nexus between the paradigm and the division of Germany can be found in the observation that

> It was nothing but imperial ideology and policy, the wish to create the most favorable external conditions for socialism and for the USSR, that prompted the start of the race of nuclear and other arms after 1945, just when the crushing defeat of fascism and militarism was, it would seem, offering a realistic opportunity for building a world without wars and a mechanism of international cooperation – the United Nations – had been created for this purpose. But imperialism's nature asserted itself that time again.[13]

Only one word was changed in this statement made by Gorbachev at the Twenty-sixth party congress in February 1986. The "favorable" in the above citation is "unfavorable" in the original, and the imperialism referred to is not that of the Soviet Union but purportedly that of the United States.

As this example of mirror imaging in the interpretation of international politics indicates, there is no shortage of Soviet and Russian attempts, both of a scholarly and political nature, to prove that Stalin did not really want the division of Germany and that, consequently, the Western allies were responsible for the division. The fatal flaw in this argument lies in the fact that the latter does not follow from the former. There is indeed, as will be shown, a fair amount of evidence to suggest that Stalin was aware of, and averse to, the risks that a division of Germany would pose; that he was conscious of the potentially disruptive strength of German nationalism that could never be reconciled with a divided country; and that he would, therefore, have preferred, as he is reported as having stated at a Politburo meeting at the end of May

13 *Pravda*, 26 February 1986.

1945, a "united, peaceloving, and democratic state."[14] However, what was meant by peaceloving and democratic? In Moscow's definition, the Soviet Union, too, was peaceloving and democratic, as was the GDR after its foundation. The question thus needs to be posed as to whether a systemic structure of a single Germany as required by Stalin would have been acceptable to the German population and to the Western allies. If not, the preference for a united Germany from a practical political point of view would have been meaningless. This would have been even more true if each occupation power, sovereign in its area of control, were to proceed unilaterally and impose there its own socio-economic and political system. The central dynamics of the division can be found precisely in this process. Stalin recognized this as early as April 1945 when he told a visiting Yugoslav delegation that "this war is not as in the past; whoever occupies a territory also imposes on it his own social system."[15] The conclusion to be drawn from this is that the division of Germany occurred by *default rather than design*. Nevertheless, to repeat, the default was less than accidental or coincidental. The exigencies of ideology and empire played a large role in the unplanned outcome.

To deal systematically with this proposition, it will first be assumed that Stalin acted neither on the basis of revolutionary zeal nor of an expansionist imperial blueprint but simply attempted to achieve limited Soviet security interests and that, within that context, four main options can be distinguished. On this basis, Soviet interests and behavior will then be more directly related to the pressures and requirements generated by the Ideological and Imperial paradigm.[16]

The starting point of analysis could be the battle of Stalingrad, after which victory over Germany became a distinct possibility. This raised the question for the Soviet leadership as to what the post-war European order should look like, which in turn

---

14 As reported by Vladimir Semenov, who attended the Politburo meeting; Wladimir S. Semjonow, *Von Stalin bis Gorbatschow: Ein halbes Jahrhundert in diplomatischer Mission, 1939-1991* (Berlin: Nikolaische Verlagsbuchhandlung, 1995), p. 201.

15 Milovan Djilas, *Conversations with Stalin*, trans. Michael B. Petrovich (New York: Harcourt Brace & World, 1962), p. 114.

16 The four options are discussed more fully by Adomeit, *Soviet Risk Taking and Crisis Behavior*, pp. 112-161. This author's approach and conclusions coincide with those of Hans-Peter Schwarz, *Vom Reich zur Bundesrepublik: Deutschland im Widerstreit der außenpolitischen Konzeptionen in den Jahren der Besatzungsherrschaft, 1945-1949* (Neuwied und Berlin: Luchterhand, 1966), pp. 201-270. Schwarz's Study is probably the most comprehensive and analytically most satisfactory treatment of Germany in the international context. Although new archival evidence, much of it generated under the auspices of the Woodrow Wilson's International Cold War History Project, has thrown more light on Stalin and his policies in general, there is nevertheless very little that has come to light concerning his thinking and policies on the German problem. This was a problem which was encountered not only by this author (H.A.) but also by Zubok and Pleshakov, *Inside the Kremlin's Cold War*; Vojtech Mastny, *The Cold War and Soviet Insecurity: The Stalin Years* (Oxford: Oxford University Press, 1996); and Norman M. Naimark, *The Russians in Germany: A History of the Soviet Zone of Occupation, 1945-1949* (Cambridge, Mass.: The Belknap Press of Harvard University Press, 1995).

concerned in particular the role of Germany in that order. Twice in the course of a quarter of a century the very existence of the state had been threatened by Germany. Considering Stalin's near paralysis for several weeks after the German attack and the seemingly unstoppable offensives deep into Soviet territory, with German troops reaching the outskirts of Moscow in the winter of 1941, it would have been astonishing had he not seen Germany as the main security issue for years to come.

But how was security *vis-à-vis* Germany to be safeguarded? The answer is, probably by adopting any one of four broad options: (1) a revolutionary transformation of the social and economic system of the whole of Germany under the leadership of a communist party controlled by the Soviet Union; (2) a substantial weakening of the economic and military potential of Germany in conjunction with territorial reductions; (3) division or dismemberment and its long-term enforcement by the four powers; (4) a united, neutral Germany.

Option One: The "Revolutionary Transformation" of Germany

According to classic Marxist theory, prospects for a revolutionary transformation of Germany in the early post-World War II period were bright. The country, as Stalin commented, had "an extremely qualified and numerous working class and technical intelligentsia."[17] In theory, capitalism had reached its highest stage and had become "ripe" for the next stage in the historical transformation process. Fascism, an extreme form of "imperialism" in Marxist terminology, had been discredited. Its collapse had set in motion far-reaching processes of socio-economic change. Conditions for a socialist transformation of Germany could be considered as favorable also because, in one part of Germany, the Soviet Union exerted unchallenged control and could impose its own policies. In the other part, the influx of several millions of refugees from the formerly German regions under Soviet and Polish control, as well as from Czechoslovakia and Hungary, had produced fertile ground for social unrest. In fact, strikes and mass demonstrations against inadequate living conditions and low food rations plagued the Western zones until the spring of 1948. Furthermore, there was a widespread realization among the members of the two parties of the Left, the Social Democrats (SPD) and Communists (KPD), that the disunity of the working class had facilitated the rise of fascism in the 1930s and that it was now necessary to cooperate in the construction of a new Germany.

However, as after World War I, the course of events after World War II took an entirely different direction from what ideology seemed to predict. Such socialist and communist organizations, as well as democratic and antifascist committees, as had sprung up spontaneously after the war, were dissolved in July 1945 by the Soviet

---

17 Stalin as quoted by Djilas, *Conversations with Stalin*, p. 114.

Military Administration (SMA) in Germany. Political activity "from below" was replaced by political manipulation "from above." The communist *apparat* triumphed over what could have been a powerful independent socialist movement.[18] Resented for its attempts to rally socialists around its flag in an organized as opposed to voluntary fashion, burdened by its association with an occupation power whose internal structure had been consistently rejected by German socialists as a model of development and guilty by association for a hasty and damaging reparations policy pursued by that power, the KPD was losing out in the race with the SPD for the political support of the German population. This led to a sudden reversal by the SMA of its initial preference for separate development of the two parties. In April 1946, therefore, it ordered the merger of the two parties, with control firmly placed in the hands of the communists. Autonomous political development was anathema, as shown by the fact that the merger occurred against the will of the majority of the SPD membership. In that single instance, in the three Western sectors of Berlin, where the merger proposal was put to a test it was rejected by a vast majority (82 percent) of the SPD membership.[19] And despite the fact that, organizationally, the SPD had ceased to exist in the Soviet zone and the SMA was heavily favoring the new Socialist Unity Party (SED), the latter party did not manage to win an absolute majority of the votes in the October 1946 elections for the regional parliaments. It fared even worse in the elections held in the same month for the city government in Berlin, where the SED received only 19.8 percent of the vote as against 48.7 percent for the SPD, 22.2 percent for the Christian Democrats, and 9.3 percent for the Liberals.[20]

If this was the fate of the political forces favored by the SMA in the area directly under its control (the Soviet zone), or acting in the shadow of its power (in Berlin), it was clear that the chances for a successful communist revolution, or even the hope of influencing the course of events through a strong communist party, were quite remote in the western parts of Germany. The option of a "revolutionary transformation" of the whole of Germany, therefore, was only theoretical.

Option Two: Emasculation of Germany

A second possibility for safeguarding Soviet security interests and preventing German aggression was the weakening of the economic and military potential of

---

18 Wolfgang Leonhard, *Child of the Revolution*, trans. C. M. Woodhouse (London: Collins, 1957), pp. 325-27.

19 In a ballot on 30 March 1946; see Eberhard Schneider, *Die DDR: Geschichte, Politik, Wirtschaft, Gesellschaft* (Stuttgart: Verlag Bonn Aktuell, 1975), p. 28.

20 To clarify this point, the SPD had only ceased to exist in the *Soviet zone of occupation*, not in Berlin. The two parties, SPD and SED, were therefore pitted against each other in the city elections.

Germany and the reduction of German territory. The pursuit of this option was implied in what Stalin said at the Politburo meeting at the end of May 1945, that it was "unrealistic to think of breaking up Germany into splinters or to destroy its industry and reduce it to an agrarian state. ... The task is not to destroy Germany but to deprive it of the possibility to rise again as an aggressive power in Europe."[21]

One aspect of weakening Germany were territorial reductions. At the Tehran conference in 1943 it was agreed that the northern part of East Prussia should be transferred to the Soviet Union and a strong Poland created with substantial territorial compensation, at Germany's expense, in the north and west. Churchill's warnings at Yalta about not "overstuffing the Polish goose" were thereby completely ignored. Polish sovereignty was extended *de facto* to the *western* Neisse river, Stalin thereby laying the basis for the most probable development in the circumstance: long-term Polish-German hostility and Polish dependence on the Soviet Union.[22] Events seemed to drift precisely in that direction because of the expulsion of more than 10 million Germans from the areas east of the Oder and Neisse rivers, the westward shift of several million Poles, and the consolidation of the Soviet and Polish administration in the new territories.

Another important aspect of weakening Germany were reparations. In internal memoranda, at the Allied Control Council, and in the foreign ministers' meetings, Soviet representatives never tired of pointing to the enormous losses the USSR had incurred during the war. Ivan Maisky, head of a reparations commission, commented on one of its reports that "Our direct material losses surpass the national wealth of England or Germany and constitute one-third of the overall national wealth of the United States." He also thought that five million Germans, if they were to work at Soviet plants for ten years, could contribute about $35-40 billion to the Soviet economy.[23] At the Yalta conference, the United States had agreed on $20 billion (half of which for the USSR) as a "basis for discussion," which Soviet representatives had taken as an agreement in principle. According to the Potsdam Protocol, the Soviet Union was allowed to satisfy its own reparation claims and those of Poland from its own zone of occupation. This it proceeded to do rapaciously even before the war had ended, transferring large amounts of industrial equipment from its zone and removing

---

21 Semjonow, *Von Stalin bis Gorbatschow*, p. 201.

22 Herbert Feis, *Between War and Peace: The Potsdam Conference* (Princeton, N.J.: Princeton University Press, 1960), pp. 221-74. The difference between the western and eastern Neisse, which was at issue at Yalta, was not negligible as it involved the fate of about 2.7 million ethnic Germans and hence the problem of future German revanchism. The significance of the point will be explored below.

23 In comments on a July 1944 report, I. Maisky and G. Arkadiev, "Osnovnie linii reparatsionnoi programmy SSSR," and in a 19 December 1944 letter to Stalin, as quoted by Zubok and Pleshakov, *Inside the Kremlin's Cold War*, p. 31. Zubok and Pleshakov provide additional information on the reparations issue based on new archival evidence.

German (and non-German) assets in Eastern Europe on a large scale.[24] According to the Protocol, the Soviet Union was also to receive 15 percent of such usable and complete industrial capital equipment as was unnecessary for the German peace economy *in exchange* for an equivalent value of food, coal, oil products, and other commodities to be agreed upon (category A) and 10 percent of such industrial capital equipment as was not essential for the German peace economy *without payment or exchange* (category B).[25] Removal of equipment as stipulated under A and B was to occur simultaneously, and the amount to be extracted from the Western zones was to be determined within six months after the Potsdam conference.[26] As General Lucius D. Clay observed in September 1945, concurrently with the extraction of reparations from their own zone, the Russians were "most anxious to get industrial facilities and equipment out of the *Western zone[s]* as quickly as possible."[27]

The Soviet reparation demands were perfectly understandable from a practical economic point of view because of the USSR's desperate need for capital equipment. This point was emphasized by Semenov and other Soviet foreign ministry officials in talks with Rudolf Nadolny, the German ambassador to Moscow from 1933-34. In 1946, one of the officials told the former German ambassador that

> Germany should again become big and strong, and be friends with Soviet Union. It should have the right to self-determination. In principle, the Soviet government accepted the Weimar Constitution as a basis [for the political organization of] Germany but the constitutional question was one for Germany to decide. However, the Soviet government *could not compromise on the [question of] reparations from current production; Russia had to be rebuilt first, and then Germany, but not vice versa.*[28]

It would be erroneous, however, to ascribe simplistic Marxist reasoning to Stalin and to assert that he looked at economic issues without regard to their political implications. The Soviet insistence on the breakup of trusts, syndicates, cartels and monopolies, the dismantling of German industry, demands for reparations, and international control over the Ruhr were all part of an overall objective: the weakening of Germany and, in particular, the emasculation of her military-industrial potential. All this was, in fact, frankly acknowledged by Molotov when he said that

24 Concerning the impact on and the estimated magnitude of the losses incurred by the East German economy because of Soviet occupation policy, see Adomeit, *Soviet Risk Taking and Crisis Behavior*, pp. 127, 233-34.

25 US Department of State, *Foreign Relations of the United States: The Conference of Berlin (Potsdam)*, Vol. II (Washington, DC: Government Printing Office, 1960), pp. 1478-98.

26 Ibid.

27 Letter from Clay to McCloy, 3 September 1945, in Smith, ed., *The Clay Papers*, doc. 30, p. 64 (italics mine).

28 Rudolf Nadolny, *Mein Beitrag* (Wiesbaden: Limes Verlag, 1955), p. 179 (italics mine). This statement was made during one of Nadolny's visits to Berlin-Karlshorst, the Soviet military headquarters.

"The aim of completely disarming Germany militarily and economically should also be served by the reparations plan. The fact that until now no such plan has been drawn up, in spite of the repeated demands of the Soviet Government, ... is a dangerous thing from the point of view of safeguarding the future peace and security of nations."[29]

By 1948, however, the Soviet reparations policy in Germany had come to a dead end, and it appears that the unfolding of the Berlin crisis of 1948-49 was not an unrelated fact.[30] This was so because the blatantly exploitative nature of that policy had not only produced negative political consequences for the "competition between the two opposed socio-economic systems" on German soil but also had begun to affect the economic base of the Soviet zone itself, and to a lasting degree. In 1946, Soviet reparation demands and zonal production had risen sharply. In 1947, when reparation policies had changed (the removal of capital stock had largely been replaced by the extraction of commodities from current production) and reached unprecedented heights, production had still suffered only slightly. But after April 1948, the volume of industrial production in the Soviet zone had reached its peak, dropped sharply and in later years flattened out despite all efforts to reverse this trend. As events were to show, neither the currency reform in the Soviet zone nor newly founded East Germany's Two-Year Plan (1949-50) achieved their stated purpose of substantially increasing production. Stringent limits of growth had resulted from the depletion of raw materials stocks and the small net total of new and replacement investments after subtraction of reparations in the form of capital goods. As the Soviet Union had not been averse to taking food as reparations and continued to remove industrial goods from current production, a wide gap in the standard of living between the Western zones and the Soviet zone could easily be predicted.

In contrast to the developments in the Soviet zone, economic recovery in the Western zones had begun in the latter half of 1947. Industrial production was catching up with that in the Soviet zone relative to the 1936 level, and in June 1948 it surpassed it, only to be given an additional boost by the successful currency reform promulgated in the same month. As Germany was considered the key to the success of European economic reconstruction, the prospects for the successful implementation of the European Recovery Program (Marshall Plan), signed in April 1948, and of the objectives of the Organization for European Economic Cooperation (OECD), formed in the same month, appeared bright indeed.

---

29 At the 10 July 1946, meeting of the Council of Foreign Ministers in Paris; see V. M. Molotov, *Problems of Foreign Policy: Speeches and Statements, April 1945 - November 1948* (Moscow: Foreign Languages Publishing House, 1949), p. 66 (italics mine).

30 The treatment of economic developments in the Soviet zone draws on J. P. Nettl, *The Eastern Zone and Soviet Policy in Germany* (London: Oxford University Press, 1951), pp. 240-41.

Two points about the weakening of Germany still need to be made. One concerns the suspension, in effect the end, of the dismantling of capital equipment in the American zone, and with it reparations deliveries to the Soviet Union (and also to Western claimants), in May 1946. Molotov was to deplore this decision at the Moscow Foreign Ministers' Conference in March 1947, where he noted that, since the Potsdam conference, the Soviet Union had received only the insignificant sum of $7.5 million in reparations deliveries in exchange for commodities (pursuant to category A of the Potsdam Protocol) and $5 million in reparations free of charge (category B).[31] But as the cooperation of the prime ministers of the German *Länder* and other German political and economic leaders was needed for the implementation of the London recommendations for the establishment of a separate West German state, it was simply no longer politically feasible to resume reparations deliveries to the Soviet Union. If reparations from *the whole of Germany* were meant to be an element of safeguarding Soviet security within the overall program of emasculating Germany, matters by 1948 looked bleak.

The same can be said for a second issue still to be considered: the controversy about international control of the Ruhr. In the early four-power discussions such control, as the extraction of reparations, was conceived of only within the framework of the whole of Germany. Thus, from the Western point of view, it appeared objectionable for the USSR to retain complete control over the economy in the Soviet zone *and* demand additional rights in the economy of the Western zones. Clay was in full agreement with predominant American and British (and on this issue also French) views when he stated bluntly that "we should not enter into an agreement for international control [of the Ruhr] until we know that such an agreement will not involve Soviet representation in such control."[32]

Stalin, as early as April 1945, appeared to be pessimistic about the likely effectiveness of political and economic measures to curb the military and industrial potential of Germany. He assumed that defeated Germany would "recover, and very quickly" because of its high level of industrialization and, as quoted above, its "extremely qualified and numerous working class and technical intelligentsia."[33] He drew the conclusion from this that the Germans would be "on their feet again" in twelve to fifteen years.[34] On another occasion, as Djilas reported, Stalin rose from the

31 Yuri Zhukov, reporting Molotov's statements at the conference, *Pravda*, 31 March 1947. The figures may very well have corresponded to the facts.

32 Clay, Eyes Only, for Draper, Top Secret, CC 3129, 7 February 1948, in Smith, ed., *The Clay Papers*, doc. 329, p. 556.

33 Djilas, *Conversations with Stalin*, p. 114.

34 Ibid. The Soviet foreign ministry official quoted above expressed a very similar opinion to Nadolny. He told his German visitor that "the Soviet government was not out to transform Germany into a Soviet satellite (*es zu sowjetisieren*). The Germans at the moment were hungry

table, "hitched up his pants as though he was about to wrestle or to box, and cried out almost in transport, "The war shall be soon over. We shall recover in fifteen or twenty years, and then we'll have another go at it."[35] It is fair to infer from all of this that, in Stalin's mind, doubts about the viability of economic and political measures to control Germany, expectations for the speedy recovery of Germany, and apprehensions about the possibility or even inevitability of another military conflict, were all closely linked.

For all of these reasons a fundamental conflict between economic and political priorities had to be resolved by Stalin. If Germany was to be preserved or reestablished as a single nation state, the time to abandon a politically harmful economic policy had come in the spring and summer of 1948. By that time, the insistent knocks at the door of the three Western zones for the payment of reparations and the demands for international control of the Ruhr had come to sound hollow and anachronistic. A radical change in Soviet economic policy in Germany was required if a united Germany was to respect the security interests of the USSR and economically cooperate with it in good faith.

A similar conclusion had to be drawn if the *division* rather than the emasculation of Germany was to be the main objective of Soviet policy in Germany. If the creation of a West German state were to be answered by the formation of an East German counterpart, the viability of such an entity also necessitated the abandonment of the counterproductive economic policy. What evidence is there that such a course aiming at the division of Germany was deliberately adopted by Stalin and, if so, at what time?

Option Three: Division and Dismemberment

As argued at the beginning of this section, it would be erroneous to say that Soviet policy at the end of World War II had consciously and consistently aimed at the dismemberment or division of Germany. On the contrary, as the end of the war approached Stalin had increasingly rejected this option. His rationale, to the extent that it can be accurately reconstructed, was rooted primarily in applying lessons of the past. Historically, war-time coalitions in Europe had a tendency to disintegrate after the achievement of victory, and inter-allied agreements had proven difficult to enforce as a consequence. As for Germany, the experience of Versailles had amply demonstrated the ineffectiveness of international controls. In fact, international restrictions and tutelage had provided powerful stimuli to revisionist and nationalist

---

and downcast, but gradually they would recover, and then they would turn against Russia." (Nadolny, *Mein Beitrag*, pp. 178-79).

35 Djilas, *Conversations with Stalin*, pp. 114-15.

tendencies, even though the extent of territorial reductions of Germany after World War I had been limited.

It was reasonable, therefore, to assume that the division or dismemberment of Germany after World War II, too, would unleash powerful forces of German nationalism and create new security risks. Stalin's recognition of this danger is reflected in his statement that "The experience of history shows that Hitlers come and go but the German nation, the German state, remains";[36] in the appeals to German nationalism rather than to "progressive forces" by founding, in July 1943, the Nationalkomitee Freies Deutschland (Free German National Committee) and the Bund Deutscher Offiziere (Federation of German Officers) in an attempt to bring about an early political solution to the war;[37] in his refraining from pushing the idea of dismemberment at Tehran, being reluctant about it at Yalta and declaring on Victory Day (9 May 1945) that the USSR "has no intention of either dismembering or destroying Germany."[38]

The Soviet concern about a possible recrudescence of German nationalism and the difficulty of enforcing a division of Germany was evident in what Soviet UN ambassador, Andrei Vyshinsky, stated to British war correspondent Alexander Werth in 1947: "If there isn't a central German government, there will be before long a militarist West German government."[39] In the same year, Foreign Minister Molotov even opposed the idea of a federalization of Germany as "dangerous" because it would "play into the hands of the militarists playing on the German people's longing for 'German unity.'"[40]

The view that Stalin did not intend to divide Germany is supported also by the extent of the transfer of German territory to Poland and the scale of the expulsion of ethnic Germans. If Soviet post-war policy had provided for an East German state under Soviet protection, it would have been much better to establish an East German state of roughly the same geographical extent, population, and economic potential as Poland. For Moscow, this would have meant agreeing on the *eastern* rather than the western Neisse river as the border between the two countries: the area separated by the two rivers would have made an important difference because it would not only have added significantly to East Germany's natural resources and production capacity (the area in question had a diverse industrial base) but also to its population (2.7 million people were living in this area, almost all of them ethnic Germans). The

---

36 J. V. Stalin, *The Great Patriotic War of the Soviet Union*, 5th ed. (Moscow: Foreign Languages Publishing House, 1950), p. 84.

37 See Bodo Scheurig, *Freies Deutschland: Das Nationalkomitee und der Bund Deutscher Offiziere in der Sowjetunion 1943-1945* (Munich: Nymphenburger Verlag, 1960).

38 *Pravda*, 10 May 1945.

39 Werth, *Russia: The Post-War Years*, p. 234.

40 At the Foreign Ministers' Conference in Moscow, March 1947, ibid., p. 236.

problem of the viability of the GDR, which came to haunt the Soviet Union perennially, but most acutely in the June 1953 popular revolt and the Berlin crisis of 1961, could have been alleviated to a considerable extent by adopting such a course of action.[41]

In retrospect, it appears that the stronger the momentum towards the creation of a separate West German government, the more insistent the Soviet demands for the preservation of German unity. At the December 1947 Foreign Ministers' Conference in London, Molotov was reported in *Pravda* as having advocated a "united, independent, and democratic Germany" and the formation of an "all-German Consultative Council," but that this had been rejected by the West and "instead Western Germany was being turned into the breeding ground for another world war."[42]

These arguments were repeated in 1948. The note of the Soviet Government to the three Western powers of early March and the justification provided by Marshal Sokolovsky for the termination of Soviet participation in the Control Council at the end of March took issue with the London conference and charged that the West had deliberately excluded the USSR from decision-making and even consultation on problems concerning Germany as a whole.[43] On 26 March, that is, only a few days after Sokolovsky's dramatic walk-out from the Allied Control Council, Lieutenant General Luk'ianchenko of the Soviet military administration in Germany stated for the historical record that "The division of Germany is already an established fact" and that it was clear to all that "this division was caused by the USA, Britain, and France."[44]

The fact that the USSR increasingly portrayed itself as the champion of German unity and even advocated the holding of a referendum on this question can be

---

41 In recognition of the importance of the border problem for the viability and legitimacy of a future East German state, the United States ambassador in Moscow, Walter Bedell Smith, wrote in August 1948 that if the Western powers "should be forced out of Berlin" and, following the establishment of a Western German government, a communist dominated government were to be established in eastern Germany, the "latter's prestige and power of attraction throughout the country might be vastly increased by return of part of" the area east of the Oder and the western Neisse rivers; telegram to Secretary of State Marshall, Secret, 21 August 1948, US Department of State, *Foreign Relations, 1948,* Vol. IV, p. 910.

42 *Pravda*, 18 December 1947.

43 The Soviet government's note to the three Western powers was published in *Pravda*, 9 March 1948; the Soviet version of the crucial events of 20 March (the walkout of the Soviet representative at the Control Council) according to *Pravda*, 22 March 1948.

44 TASS report from Berlin, ibid., 29 March 1948. The phrase "The division of Germany is now an accomplished fact" was the line of the day carried verbatim by *Neues Deutschland* and *Tägliche Rundschau*, and it was amplified in an article by *Pravda* correspondent Yuri Korol'kov, *Pravda*, 1 April 1948. However, one of the Soviet Union's experts on German problems, Danil Mel'nikov, interpreted the separate *currency reform* of 18 June as completing the division of Germany, ibid., 20 June 1948.

explained by the Soviet desire not to be held responsible in a court of history for the powerful drift towards the division of Germany, a drift which the Soviet Union itself had helped to set in motion. But since the division of Germany contained the threat of territorial revisionism and nationalism, it could still have appeared preferable from the Soviet point of view, even in 1948, to be included in the making of decisions concerning Germany as a whole rather than be excluded and faced with a West German state hostile to the USSR by the very circumstances of its creation. Maintenance of unity may also still have appeared advantageous to the Soviet Union since it did not seem to have given up hope of gaining access to reparations from the Western zones, and from the Ruhr in particular.

A detached consideration of Soviet "national" interests, it would seem, would favor maintaining a unified German state, neutral and noncommunist, based in its internal structure on a system somewhere between socialism and capitalism, with a small army and police force for internal security and self-defense. This is the kind of policy suggested in essence by Stalin in his note to the three Western powers on 10 March 1952, in proposals made by his successors in 1954 and, as applied to Austria, in the State Treaty of 1955. Was this option really ruled out by Stalin or foreclosed by the post-war conditions?

Option Four: Neutralization of Germany

In principle, the option of a unified Germany was not foreclosed. But adopting it would have made it necessary for the Soviet Union to meet certain conditions. It would have required repudiation of the "two camp" theory with all its implications of militant tactics. It also presupposed a willingness to cooperate with the Western powers in the establishment and management of a new European order. More specifically, the prevention of German revisionism might also have required the return of the areas east of the Oder and Neisse rivers – areas which many Germans, with Western allied encouragement, had already begun to consider as only "temporarily under Soviet and Polish administration." Even those Germans who, like Nadolny, were favorably inclined towards the Soviet Union, considered the return of most of these areas an indispensable precondition for an overall Russian-German settlement. This was clearly stated in Nadolny's memorandum of 30 April 1947 to Molotov, in which he expressed his conviction that the

> intended expulsion of nine million Germans from their traditional homeland and the *de facto* separation of the eastern German provinces [from the Reich] *will never be accepted by the German people*. However, the German people are prepared to sacrifice as much territory as would be

> necessary for Polish access to the sea. It is to be hoped that the Russian statesmen will find an appropriate solution.[45]

In the light of what has been said here about the non-viability of a revolutionary transformation of the whole of Germany and the anti-Soviet and, by implication, anti-Russian bias of German nationalism, the option of neutralization, if adopted in the post-war era, would in all likelihood have resulted in a Germany that was orienting itself toward the West. Such a development would probably have been no different than the one that could be observed in Finland and Austria, and indeed also in West Germany. The difference, a crucial one in Stalin's eyes, was one of scale. To prevent a country without a major industrial base and with a population of only about 7 million (Austria) or 5 million (Finland) from becoming a threat to Soviet security was quite a different proposition from one that involved a country with a heavy industrial base and a population of approximately 80 million people.

The maintenance or reestablishment of German unity in the post-war era, if it involved an expression of preferences by the German people, would undoubtedly have led to a substantial defeat for the Soviet-type system in the eastern zone. There is much merit to the argument, therefore, that Stalin, rather than risking such a development, chose what appeared to him a lesser risk, namely, to hold fast to the area occupied by the Red Army, complete a series of pacts "with all the states at its western border, from the Black Sea to the Baltic and, after the conclusion of the Soviet-Finnish treaty, right up to the Arctic ocean," deal a "powerful blow to all instigators of a new world war"[46] and make the resulting sphere of influence safe for the USSR by incorporating the whole of Berlin in it – were it not for the equally valid argument in Stalin's view that the enforcement of the division of Germany was improbable or impossible.

Given these apparently insoluble dilemmas for Soviet security in the post-war era, it would have been entirely understandable if Soviet policy had merely drifted into acceptance of the division of Germany as inevitable, trying to contain emerging dangers by pursuing conciliatory policies. Instead, militant rhetoric was employed almost throughout the early post-war period and, in the 1948-49 Berlin blockade, a strategy of coercion was adopted, utilizing conventional military superiority in the area and Soviet leverage over "progressive forces" as means of forcing Western compliance to ill-defined Soviet demands. Perhaps this strategy cannot be explained entirely in rational terms, as a policy arrived at by the careful weighing of ends and means. Beyond the vague feeling or anxiety that Germany had been a threat to Soviet security in the past and that it was likely to be one in the future, Stalin may never

---

45 Nadolny, *Mein Beitrag*, p. 180 (italics mine).

46 "Sovetskaia politika ravnopraviia natsii," *Bol'shevik*, No. 9 (1948), p. 5.

really have had a clear conception on how to approach, let alone solve, the German problem.

To that extent, one would also be looking in vain for a single "decision" that decided the issue of whether Germany should be divided or remain whole. The division occurred as a consequence of a *process* of interaction which, in turn, was driven in large measure by the pressures and requirements generated by the Ideological and Imperial paradigm. Their impact on the process will be analyzed in the following sections.

3. The Paradigm Applied: East Germany and Eastern Europe

The paradigm provided powerful reasons for integrating East Germany into a Soviet sphere of influence. The primary function of this sphere, as Shevardnadze later deplored, became that of a "buffer zone, ... a chain of 'allied' countries that would protect us from the West and [justify] the deployment of large Soviet troop contingents in those countries."[47] Such a conception also "implied that the Soviet Army had not liberated certain countries of Europe, but seized them as war trophies."[48] It also conforms to the basic attitudes of the architects of Soviet imperial policies in the post-war era: a rigid and doctrinaire outlook on international affairs, amply reflected in private conversation and memoirs.

Stalin, for example, is reported in the summer of 1945 at a meeting in one of his dachas as having pinned to the wall a map showing the prospective post-war frontiers. Stepping back, he pointed to the north and said that he liked what he saw. The same was true for what he found in the northwest: "The Baltic area – Russian from time immemorial!" He then looked to the east: "all of Sakhalin, the Kuriles, Port Arthur, and Dalny are ours. Well done! China, Mongolia, the Chinese Eastern Railway – all under control." Then, stabbing a finger at the southern Caucasus, he exclaimed: "But *here* is where I don't like our frontiers!"[49]

The imperial mind-set of the supreme leader (*vozhd*) was shared by Molotov. He explained the origins of the cold war by saying, paradoxically, that the Western leaders were responsible because "we were on the offensive" and then went on to clarify the history of the creation of the Soviet empire in Eastern Europe: "They were,

---

47 Shevardnadze, *Moi vybor*, pp. 210-11.

48 Ibid., p. 211.

49 As reported by Foreign Minister Viacheslav M. Molotov, *Sto sorok besed s Molotovym. Iz dnevnika F. Chueva* (Moscow: Terra, 1991), p. 14. This book essentially can be regarded as having a memoir quality. It contains the transcripts of 139 conversations (and a neighbor's remarks at Molotov's funeral) between the former Soviet foreign minister and Felix Chuev. For details about the background of the "memoirs" and excerpts from the book see Woodford McClellan, "Molotov Remembers," *Cold War International History Project Bulletin*, No. 1 (Spring 1992), pp. 17-20.

of course, bitter about us, but we had to consolidate our conquests. Create our own, socialist Germany out of a part of [the whole country]. Czechoslovakia, Poland, Hungary, Yugoslavia – they were feeble, we had to restore order everywhere."[50] And what were the limits to such a "restoration"? They were obviously not set by moral considerations and, in principle, unlimited. Thus, when Averell Harriman asked Stalin whether he was pleased with the fact that while earlier the Germans had been at the gates of Moscow, he was now engaged with the Western powers in an effort to divide Berlin, he replied coldly: "Tsar Aleksandr went [all the way] to Paris."[51] The limits of imperial consolidation and expansion, therefore, were set by expediency. This is confirmed by Molotov. "Of course, you have to know when to stop. In this regard I think Stalin observed strict limits."[52]

The structure of the emerging empire conformed to the ideological part of the paradigm and required close approximation of the dependencies to the Soviet system. For tactical reasons, some experimentation and deviation were allowed in East Germany and other parts of Eastern Europe, but only until about 1948.[53] From then on the principle of "proletarian internationalism" was to govern the relations between the Soviet Union and the satellite countries. This carried with it the sub-principle of limited sovereignty and the Soviet Union's self-proclaimed right of armed intervention when the socialist order appeared threatened. Although the latter principle, held to be separate from and superior to "bourgeois" international law, was formally asserted only in the Warsaw Pact intervention in Czechoslovakia (the Brezhnev Doctrine), it existed in practice from the very beginning of the imposition of Soviet control in Eastern Europe.

One of the important issues connected with the ideological part of the paradigm concerns the issue of popular consent. Marxism-Leninism and traditional imperial exigencies again reenforced each other. The will of the people(s) in the peripheral areas is typically of little or no concern to the metropole. The rationale of empire is to enhance the power and glory of the center and to discourage and suppress processes of emancipation at the periphery. In the Soviet case, this rationale was enhanced not only by the universalist pretensions and anti-nationalist content of Marxist-Leninist ideology but also by the Leninist disdain for "spontaneity" and "subjectivism" as opposed to the allegedly objective requirements of history. It is useful in this context to present some evidence from secret reports of the Soviet Military Administration in Germany about the conditions and results of Soviet policies in this strategically

50 [Molotov], *Sto sorok besed*, p. 86.

51 Ibid., p. 103.

52 Ibid.

53 Zbigniew K. Brzezinski, *The Soviet Bloc: Unity and Conflict*, rev. ed. (New York: Praeger, 1961).

important outpost of empire.[54] One of these reports was based on talks between SMA officers and Prime Minister Steinhof of the *Land* Brandenburg concerning "the attitude of the German population to the Soviet occupation powers" and drew on a "number of materials from various districts of the Brandenburg *Land*."[55] Despite the severe constraints on the free flow of information under Stalinism, the report was quite sanguine about popular German attitudes. It cited the Oberbürgermeister (chief mayor) of the city of Forst, Worter (SED), as having stated at a meeting of *Volksvertreter* (people's deputies) to the city assembly that "We can't go on this way. The Russians only give orders, and we have to be quiet, listen and, without any complaint, carry out these orders." These remarks by a communist party member (!) "were met by stormy applause" among the CDU and LDP deputies. Similarly, at a meeting in Greifenberg, the representative of the SED was reportedly insulted by members of the CDU who left the room calling the SED "hirelings of the Kremlin" and shouting: "Down with the Traitors of the Fatherland!"[56]

SMA reports also accurately reflected the popular attitude to Russians and the Soviet Union. Thus, at a meeting of the FDJ (Freie Deutsche Jugend, the communist youth organization) in Wittenberg, the chairman of the CDU is reported to have objected to the idea of holding a bicycle race in support of the all-German referendum on German unity (on the referendum see below). His argument was that the Russians would stop the bike riders along the way and take away their bikes: "they are very keen on these things." Bikes, of course, he went on to say, "are not the only thing the Russians take."[57]

On the basis of such information the Soviet Military Administration lamented the fact that "it is not easy to reeducate the German people in the spirit of friendship and respect for the Soviet Union." In essence, it saw three reasons for this difficulty: (1) the "anti-Soviet propaganda" before the war, which had exerted a powerful influence on popular images; (2) quoting Steinhof, a "disastrous" occupation policy which had

---

54 The reports are to be found in the CPSU archives renamed Russian Center for the Preservation of Contemporary Documents (Tsentr khraneniia sovremennoi dokumentatsii – TsKhSD) in Moscow. This author was able to use see the documents in 1992. However, in the spring of 1993, when returning to continue with the work, the registry (*fondy*) of documents had pencil marks next to military security related documents to the effect that they could "not be checked out to the reading room."

55 "Prem'er ministr zemli Brandenburg d-r Steingof [Steinhof] ob otnoshenii nemetskogo naseleniia k sovetskim okkupatsionnym vlastam," Biuro informatsii SVA, *Biulleten'*, No. 23, 18 June 1948, Top Secret, CPSU Archives, Tsentral'nyi Komitet VKP (b), Otdel vneshnei politiki [hereafter TsK VKP (b), Otdel vneshnei politiki], *fond* 17, *opis* 128, *ed. khr.* 579. It was quite typical in the Stalin period and thereafter that, when subordinates felt that they had to transmit unpleasant information to the center, a direct evaluation and commitment was avoided. Instead, other opinion is cited.

56 Ibid.

57 Ibid.

reenforced the prevalent negative stereotypes; and (3) skillful exploitation of SMA "mistakes and shortcomings" by the opponents of the new order.[58]

Some background information is appropriate with respect to the second of Steinhof's observations. Even before Soviet occupation policy began to take shape, large-scale plundering and rape committed by Red Army soldiers had seriously damaged the chances of Russian-German reconciliation and the successful introduction of a Soviet-type system.[59] When the Soviet army entered East Prussia and crossed the Vistula into Silesia and Pomerania, it was common for Soviet soldiers to rape every female over the age of twelve or thirteen in a village, killing many in the process, to pillage the homes for personal possessions, food, and alcohol, and leave the village in flames. They acted in conformity with Ilya Ehrenburg's calls for retribution, which were widely disseminated in the armed forces: "We shall kill. If you have not killed at least one German a day, you have wasted that day ... If you kill one German, kill another – there is nothing funnier for us than a pile of German corpses."[60] Since Stalin had rejected any criticism of the savage behavior of the Soviet troops in Eastern Europe and the northeastern part of Yugoslavia,[61] it was not surprising that he would respond even more negatively to complaints by East German communists, saying that "I will not allow anyone to drag the reputation of the Red Army in the mud."[62] The rampages and rapes committed by marauding and often drunk soldiers did not stop with the conquest of Berlin and Germany's formal surrender on 9 May. Although many Soviet officers and Stalin had come to realize even before the end of the war that letting the armed forces run berserk eroded army discipline and harmed Soviet interests in Germany, it was not until the troops were confined to strictly guarded posts and camps during the winter of 1946-47 that German women were freed from the persistent threat of rape.[63]

Lasting damage to the chances for Russian-German reconciliation and successful economic reconstruction in the Soviet zone of occupation was done also by the rapacious reparations policy discussed in the previous section. The policy went beyond the dismantling of industrial plants and the shipment of products from current production to the Soviet Union. It also included the deportation of nuclear scientists, missile engineers, and technicians. For instance, in October 1946, in a carefully

---

58 Ibid.

59 The account of the large-scale plundering and rape in which the Soviet soldiers engaged in the areas conquered in 1944-45 follows the careful and detailed study by Naimark, *The Russians in Germany*, pp. 69-140.

60 Ehrenburg as quoted ibid., p. 72.

61 Djilas, *Conversations with Stalin*, pp. 95, 101.

62 The source for this is Wolfgang Leonhard, *Child of the Revolution* (Chicago: H. Regnery, 1958), p. 365, as quoted by Naimark, *The Russians in Germany*, p. 71.

63 Naimark, *The Russians in Germany*, p. 79.

planned operation code-named Osoviakhim, thousands of German scientists and technicians were rounded up and, with their families and possessions, transferred to the Soviet Union in ninety-two trains and, in special cases, in airplanes.[64] Finally, it included the requisition of forced labor. In fact, perhaps nothing can demonstrate more convincingly the practical application of the paradigm than the utilization of such labor for the extraction of uranium.

Ever since the United States had tested nuclear weapons and used them in the war against Japan, Stalin had considered the manufacture of atomic weapons a high-priority project.[65] General Leslie Groves, the chief administrator of the American nuclear weapons program, had thought at the end of the war that it would take the Soviet Union about ten years to produce an atomic bomb. He had estimated that the Czech and Russian supplies of uranium constituted no more than 5 percent of the world's supply and that, as a result, even if the Soviets could produce a bomb, based on their small stores of uranium, they would never be able to keep up with Western bomb production.[66] A Russian informant confirmed Groves's assessment of the Soviet predicament when he told American intelligence that "the biggest drawback to making a Soviet atom bomb is the terrific lack of pure uranium which is available to the Soviet Union." However, the western Erzgebirge region of Saxony, located across the mountains of the Jáchymow mines in Czechoslovakia, contained huge deposits of pitchblende, usable for pure uranium extraction. In the first months of 1947, the entire region was cordoned off by Soviet military units, while the mining districts themselves were placed under the administration of Moscow's State Security Ministry (NKVD) and guarded by troops of the Ministry of the Interior (MVD). Within a relatively short time, the region was turned into one of the richest uranium producing areas in the world and became an almost indispensable asset for the Soviet nuclear weapons project. The was made possible only because tens of thousands of workers were forcibly recruited for work in the mines and thereby exposed to dangerous levels of radiation and frequent accidents. The NKVD administrators were completely unresponsive to complaints voiced even by East German communist party officials. In the secret police's and Stalin's view, the extraction of strategically important resources took precedence over long-term political interests. The viability and legitimacy of the East German communist regime fell victim to Soviet military requirements.

---

64 Ibid., pp. 220-35.

65 See the carefully researched reconstruction of this top political and military priority by David Holloway, *Stalin and the Bomb: The Soviet Union and Atomic Energy, 1939-1956* (New Haven: Yale University Press, 1994).

66 Citations and the subsequent analysis according to Naimark, *The Russians in Germany*, pp. 235-36.

There was no particular need to engage in any skillful exploitation of Soviet "mistakes and shortcomings" – the third point Steinhof had made. The image problem of Russians and the Soviet occupation authorities, as well as that of their East German communist collaborators, was of their own making. The consequences clearly surfaced in reports to Moscow by Colonel Tiul'panov, the chief of the SMA's information department, on the referendum on German unity. The referendum had been decided upon by a Second People's Congress in March 1948 and was held from 23 May to 13 June 1948. The effectiveness of the referendum campaign could be taken as an indicator of the degree of political support for the SED in the spring of 1948 in the Soviet zone of occupation, in Berlin, and to a lesser extent (the referendum was allowed only in the British zone) in the Western zones. On the surface, the "preliminary results" reported by the SMA in the Soviet zone were very encouraging, from the SED's point of view. A total of 11.6 million people of the 12 million eligible voters (96.4 percent) there had signed the petition for German unity.[67] In stark contrast, the results in the British zone showed only single-digit figures.

The outcome of the referendum in the four sectors of Berlin, where the Soviet and Western presence and interests intersected, was especially revealing:

Table 1 – Results of the May-June 1948 Referendum in Berlin

Soviet sector	681 000	79.8%
British sector	54 000	12.2%
American sector	48 000	6.6%
French sector	34 000	10.3%

In his report to Moscow, Tiul'panov presented a fair assessment of the results in Berlin. The referendum had revealed that a "significant part of the population" was negatively disposed towards the Soviet occupation power and the SED. There "appeared to be a lack of influence of the FDJ on broad segments of the youth." When propagating the referendum, communist party workers had been told: "*We are all for unity. You don't need to persuade us. Let the Russians pack up and leave, and we'll have unity immediately.*" Furthermore, the chief of the SMA's information department was skeptical and suspicious of the high percentage of signatures in the Soviet zone of occupation. He candidly described the "negative attitude among

67 SMAG, Information Department, Report by Colonel Tiul'panov [chief of the information department of the SMAG] to Comrade Baranov, CPSU Central Committee, "Predvaritel'nye itogi provedeniia Narodnogo oprosa 'Za edinstvo Germanii,'" Secret, CPSU Archives, Otdel vneshnei politiki, *fond* 17, *opis* 128, *ed. khr.* 568.

certain segments of the population towards the Soviet occupation powers, the SED, and the democratic camp." Such attitudes, he thought, could be observed especially among "the refugees, church organizations, and the religious sects." The Protestant Church, in particular, was regarded by him as still being able to play an important role in shaping popular perceptions. Finally, Tiul'panov pointed to the expulsion of Germans from their homeland in the east – "ethnic cleansing" as one would say today – as posing serious problems for the occupation authorities. He quoted one of the refugees from East Prussia as saying: "We refugees would vote for the unity of Germany if the referendum question were to state that the borders of Germany will be moved to the east."[68]

Despite the candor, even Tiul'panov remained captive to traditional Bolshevik misperceptions or, contrary to better judgment, considered it expedient to use them in his reports to Moscow. He, too, constructed unconvincing rationalizations, advocated unworkable remedies and engaged in what German critics have called *parteichinesisch* (party political jargon or gibberish). True to standard Marxist-Leninist and Stalinist rhetoric, he tried to convince his superiors that, despite all the problems with youth in Berlin, the attitudes of refugees, and the *petite bourgeoisie*, "the referendum was supported by the working class and peasantry."[69] In other reports he even insinuated that not all was lost in the relationship with German social democracy. Adopting a traditional Leninist approach, he detected a "growing rift between the provocative, anti-Soviet course of the leadership of the SPD and the rank and file" of the party. He also spoke reassuringly of a schism between the followers of Kurt Schumacher (one of the SPD leaders firmly committed to a Western orientation), the "*Shumakherovtsy,*" as he called them, and the party base.[70] Irrespective of the glaring deficiencies of the Soviet system, the deep inter-war rift between German social democracy and Russian communism, and the behavior of the Soviet forces after the war, the comforting notion was being conveyed to Moscow that the strategic line on Germany was sound, that what needed to be done was simply to correct "tactical" mistakes, errors and shortcomings; "improve party political work"; and "strengthen organizational activity." "The CC of the SED," reads one of these ritualistic fragments, "must work out a clear ideological platform for

68 Ibid. (italics of the quote above are mine).

69 Ibid.

70 This is in reference to the party congress of the SPD held in Berlin, 8-9 May 1948; see SMAG, Department of Information, Report by Colonel Tiul'panov, chief of the information department, to Comrade Baranov, CPSU Central Committee, 12 May 1948, CPSU Archives, Otdel vneshnei politiki, *fond* 17, *opis* 128, *ed. khr.* 568.

work with the social democrats and take organizational measures that will ensure the mobilization of regional and lower echelons of the SED for this work."[71]

The SMA expressed similarly utopian views on the CDU, its "conservative" party creation in the Soviet zone. Apparently assuming that the "pro-American" and "anti-democratic line" of the adherents of party leader Jakob Kaiser, the *Kaizerovtsy*, had been defeated, the eastern CDU was now considered to be "in a position to act as a wedge that can begin to loosen the front of Christian Democratic parties in West Germany and perhaps, in the future, in other European Christian Democratic Parties as well."[72]

Finally, SMA portrayals of the economic state of affairs were characterized by the same wishful thinking characteristic of its political reports. Again in conformity with the paradigm, emphasis was put on the "correctness" of the main strategic line and the "progress" made in its implementation. Only some "temporary" or "transitory" problems had to be overcome. One report reassured the imperial center that "The achievements in industrial work in 1947 provide the basis for stating that the economy of the Soviet Zone is developing on a correct path; the public sector is preeminent, and the private sector is losing its commanding position."[73] But another report revealed that not everything was well at the periphery. "The supply of the population of the Soviet zone of occupation in several *Länder*," it stated, "even though "not catastrophic," had nevertheless "significantly deteriorated."[74]

These glimpses into the day-to-day problems of the administration of empire and the kind of reporting provided to the center confirm the validity of the present working hypothesis: the division of Germany occurred not by design but by default. The partition was determined by the requirements of a narrowly circumscribed paradigm, and once the division of Germany had become a *fait accompli*, it was maintained by bureaucratic inertia.

---

71 In response to decisions adopted at the party congress of the SPD held in Berlin, 8-9 May 1948; see SMAG, Department of Information, Report Colonel Tiul'panov, chief of the information department, to Comrade Baranov, CPSU Central Committee, 12 May 1948, CPSU Archives, Otdel vneshnei politiki, *fond* 17, *opis* 128, *ed. khr.* 568.

72 SMAG, Department of Information, Report by Colonel Tiul'panov, chief of the information department, to Comrade Baranov, CPSU Central Committee, "Polozhenie v Khristianstvo-Demokraticheskom Soiuze Sovetskoi zony okkupatsii i Berlina," 23 April 1948, Secret, CPSU Archives, Otdel vneshnei politiki, *fond* 17, *opis* 128, *ed. khr.* 568.

73 Report by V. Semenov [political counselor at the SMAG] and G. Arkad'ev [his deputy] to the Ministry of Foreign Affairs, Comrade V.M. Molotov; Secretary of the CPSU Central Committee, M.A. Suslov; and Deputy Minister of Foreign Affairs, A. Ia. Vyshshinskii, Secret, "Kratkii ekonomicheskii obzor po sovetskoi zone okupatsii Germanii," 27 March 1948, CPSU Archives, Otdel vneshnei politiki, *fond 17*, *opis* 128, *ed. khr.* 573.

74 SMAG, Information Bureau, "K voprosu o prodovol'stvennom polozhenii v Sovetskoi zone," *Biulleten'*, No. 32, August 1948, pp. 1-10, CPSU Archives, Otdel vneshnei politiki, *fond* 17, *opis* 128, *ed. khr.* 578.

Since bureaucrats are the agents of inertia, some words are in order about the *personnel* responsible for both policy formulation and implementation. One of the features characteristic for imperial appointments, such as the satraps in Persia or the provincial governors in the Roman empire, is the fact that officials are often sent abroad to distant and undesirable provinces as punishment for mistakes or failures or, if dispatched to more important and desirable places, as a reward for faithful service. Typically, the officials' ability to impose the will of the metropole, rather than their special knowledge of or sensitivity to local conditions, is the primary criterion for their appointment abroad. This also applied to Soviet practices in Eastern Europe. Former SMA political advisor Semenov, for instance, has reported in a matter of fact fashion that Stalin "transferred the operational work [i.e. everyday business] in the SMA to the Chief of the Political Department of the Fifth Shock Army, General Fedor Efimovich Bokov." Why? Stalin had known Bokov "since the beginning of the war, when he was a secretary in the party committee of the General Staff of the Red Army. He had at times reported to Stalin and he [Stalin had] liked him. He always had his hands at the seams of his trousers, no redundant words, let alone demands."[75] What about Bokov's special qualifications for the assignment to Germany? None whatsoever. "His most important shortcoming was surely that he didn't know Germany and that he was also unwilling to immerse himself in its problems."[76]

Another feature of Soviet control consisted in the fact that, as Shevardnadze knew well when he assumed office, that "Top *party officials* were appointed to ambassadorial posts in Eastern Europe, and those appointments were made exclusively by the Politburo." Their subordination to the party leadership in Moscow determined the way decisions were made. "Former party officials appealed to higher party levels in all questions, bypassing the Ministry of Foreign Affairs. And in the countries where they were posted they would often act in a similar way, going directly to the top and ignoring the foreign ministries of the host country."[77]

Centralization of decision making contributed to this closed system of imperial personnel selection and control. Information passed upward in the decision-making hierarchy, with several drafts working their way to the top through formalized resolutions of the Central Committee of the CPSU and the Council of Ministers of the USSR, the most important decisions ultimately being approved by Stalin personally or, after his death, "collectively" in the Politburo. Once a decision was made, the principle of "democratic centralism" provided that there was no further discussion and no "factionalism" in the party organs and state institutions but strict

---

75 According to Semenov, this is how staff officers described him in their memoirs; Semjonow, *Von Stalin bis Gorbatschow*, p. 222.

76 Ibid., p. 224.

77 Shevardnadze, *Moi vybor*, pp. 194-95.

implementation in accordance with the letter and spirit of the decision. As for decision-making on the German problem, Semenov has aptly observed that

> Stalin personally kept German matters in his hands. In accordance with [his] orders, Viacheslav Molotov dealt with them in the Politburo of the CC ... Policy questions and important operational actions would regularly be discussed in meetings with Stalin. From the German side, Wilhelm Pieck, Otto Grotewohl, and Walter Ulbricht would be present. The Soviet participants as a rule were Stalin, Molotov as well as, from the SMA, Vasili Sokolovsky [the head of the Soviet Military Administration in Germany] and I [Semenov]. [Marshal Georgi K.] Zhukov [the supreme commander of the Soviet forces in Germany] settled many questions directly with Stalin [from headquarters in Berlin] and was seldom called to the discussions in Moscow.[78]

After having provided the basic reasons why the division of Germany occurred, examined the conceptual frame of reference and the mind-set of the top decision-makers, and described the ineptitude of the subordinates supporting the establishment of empire, it is now appropriate to focus on some of the most important milestones in the hardening of the division, as well as on those instances that seemed to indicate that the Soviet leadership was perhaps reconsidering the risks, costs, and benefits of its position in Germany.

4. The Impact of the Berlin Blockade and the Korean War

One of the milestones on the road to the division of Germany and a watershed of European history is the Berlin blockade of 1948-49. The main analytical problem which this ill-advised Soviet venture poses is whether it was meant to be a *lever* with which to impede the Western processes for the formation of a separate West German state and prevent the door from being firmly shut on German political and economic unity, or whether Berlin was the *prize* of the endeavor, with the city to be merged with the Soviet zone of occupation in an effort to consolidate the Soviet empire. There is evidence for both interpretations.[79]

Evidence for the lever theory and more specifically for a Soviet attempt to forestall the disruption of German economic unity can be found in the letter by the chief of the SMAG, Marshal V.D. Sokolovsky, to his British counterpart, General Robertson. On 29 June 1948, eleven days after the promulgation of the currency reform in the Western zones, Sokolovsky wrote: "I would like to assure you that your opinion regarding the restrictions of movements of the German population is correct"; they

---

78 Ibid., pp. 230-31.

79 The evidence is drawn from Adomeit, *Soviet Risk Taking and Crisis Behavior*, the chapter on the Berlin crisis of 1948, pp. 67-182. The partial opening of the Soviet party and foreign ministry archives has not yielded anything that would make it necessary to change that portrayal of the origins, course of events, and consequences of the crisis.

are of a "temporary nature and taken *for the protection of the currency* of the Soviet zone."[80] Later Soviet sources, such as the authoritative *Short History of the USSR*, summed up the currency argument as follows:

> On 20 June 1948 [18 June is the correct date] a secretly prepared money reform was suddenly announced in the three Western Zones. The devalued old German marks instantly flooded Eastern Germany, creating a danger to its economy. The Soviet occupation authorities were compelled to take urgent measures. To block off currency profiteers all vehicles and passengers arriving from Western Germany were thoroughly checked.[81]

The currency issue was put into a broader economic context. In late 1947, as the former US Secretary of State, Byrnes, recalls, Molotov had responded to a question about the "real Soviet motives in Europe" that he (Molotov) "was willing to give up practically anything else" in order to get a quadripartite arrangement on the Ruhr.[82] During the Berlin crisis, half a year later, the Soviet government returned to this issue in its note of 14 July to the Western powers, complaining that "such a very important center of German military industry as the Ruhr district has been removed from the control of the four powers."[83] In discussions with the three Western ambassadors, held from 2 to 30 August 1948 in Moscow, Stalin and Molotov also mentioned the Ruhr repeatedly.[84]

Political and economic objectives were inextricably linked. Thus, the communiqué of the Foreign Ministers' Conference of the Soviet Union, Albania, Bulgaria, Czechoslovakia, Yugoslavia, Poland, Romania, and Hungary, held from 23 to 24 June 1948 in Warsaw, touched upon economic issues but went on to deplore the Western allies' policy toward Germany as expressed in the London agreement of 7 June. By their announced plans for the merger of the three Western zones and the projected creation of a separate West German state, the communiqué stated, the United States, Britain, and France had "complete[d] the division and dismemberment of Germany"; they had "encourage[d] German revanchist elements" and "subordinate[d] the economy of Western Germany to the aims of the USA and

80 *Pravda*, 1 July 1948 (italics mine); for the economic interpretation, see also Marshal Sokolovsky's letters to the American military governor in Germany, General Lucius D. Clay, of 20 and 22 June 1948, *Pravda*, 22 and 23 June 1948.

81 Academy of Sciences of the USSR, Institute of History , ed., *A Short History of the USSR, Part II* (Moscow: Progress Publishers, 1965), p. 274. For the economic justification of the blockade, see also V.G. Trukhanovskii, ed., *Istoriia mezhdunarodnykh otnoshenii i vneshnei politiki SSSR, Vol. III: 1945-1963* (Moscow: Izdatel'stvo "Mezhdunarodnye otnosheniia," 1964), p. 221.

82 Walter Millis, ed., *The Forrestal Diaries* (New York: Viking Press, 1951), p. 347.

83 *Pravda*, 16 July 1948.

84 According to Charles E. Bohlen, State Department Counsellor at that time, as quoted in Millis, ed., *The Forrestal Diaries*, p. 347.

Britain"; they had acted in an "anti-democratic spirit"; and, last but not least, they had committed a "gross violation of the Yalta and Potsdam agreements."[85]

Political issues ostensibly designed to maintain German unity were also advanced by Marshal Sokolovsky at the conference of the four military governors near Potsdam on 3 July. He stated tersely that the traffic restrictions would continue until the Western allies "had abandoned [their] plans for a West German government."[86] Similarly, in their discussions with the three Western ambassadors in August, Stalin and Molotov reaffirmed the point made in the Soviet note of 14 July to the effect that the conversations regarding Berlin were of "no useful purpose except within the framework of conversations regarding all of Germany."[87] According to the account by Walter Bedell Smith, the United States ambassador to the Soviet Union and a participant in the Moscow discussions, Stalin made it clear "in no uncertain terms" that the Western powers had "forfeited their right to occupy Berlin" by their introduction of a new currency in Berlin and by their "decision to set up a Western German government at Frankfurt."[88] Smith also thought that "we could have produced an agreement in fifteen minutes at any time by an offer to abandon the London decisions."[89]

However, the interpretation of the Soviet blockade as having been imposed for the purpose of gaining Berlin as a *prize* can be made equally persuasive. The SMA stridently maintained that Greater Berlin "lies in the Soviet zone of occupation" and "economically forms part of it." It added that the "whole mechanism of joint administration" of Berlin and Germany had collapsed and "with it any legitimate basis for the continued presence of the American, British, and French authorities in Berlin." It then arrived at the *ultima ratio* of the argument, declaring that "the Soviet Military Administration is the only legitimate occupation authority [in Berlin]. As a consequence its orders have the force of law for the whole of Berlin."[90] Such statements clearly implied that Berlin was to be incorporated into the Soviet zone of occupation. Alexander Werth, a former British war correspondent, accordingly wrote that, "Having accepted the *fait accompli* of a separate Western Germany, the Russians tried to put an end to the Berlin 'anomaly' with their 1948 blockade of the former Reich capital."[91]

---

85 Statement of the Foreign Ministers of the USSR, Albania, Bulgaria, Czechoslovakia, Yugoslavia, Poland, Romania, and Hungary, *Pravda*, 25 June 1948.

86 Lucius D. Clay, *Decision in Germany* (Garden City, N.Y.: Doubleday, 1950), p. 367.

87 Walter Bedell Smith, *My Three Years in Moscow* (Philadelphia, Pa: Lippincott, 1950), p. 241.

88 Ibid., p. 244.

89 W.B. Smith, *My Three Years in Moscow*, p. 253.

90 *Tägliche Rundschau* (SMAG newspaper), 24 June 1948.

91 Alexander Werth, *Russia, the Post-War Years* (London: Robert Hale, 1971), p. 248.

Faced with the persuasiveness of both interpretations, a Western scholar has argued that, from the Soviet point of view, Berlin was both a lever *and* a prize."[92] This argument approximates this author's conclusions. Stalin simply had not made up his mind as to what would result from the pressure tactics. Western analysts of Soviet foreign policy have typically sought to identify a single objective underlying Soviet foreign policy initiatives and failed to neglect the possibility that the Soviet leaders may have pursued several goals simultaneously, or were simply testing what could be achieved. This *modus operandi* seems to have applied in the Berlin crisis. Advantageous outcomes, from Stalin's viewpoint, could either have been the Western abandonment of the London recommendations for the formation of a separate West German state or a withdrawal of the Western allies from Berlin. Yet both of these objectives were unacceptable to the Western powers. This, together with the ambiguity of the Soviet stance, accounted for the resounding failure of Stalin's risky venture. The constant fluctuation between narrow objectives (incorporation of Berlin in the Soviet zone) and larger goals (maintaining German unity), interspersed with the absurd assertion that the blockade essentially was a figment of Western imagination since there existed only "technical difficulties" on the roads, railways, and canals to and from Berlin, led to confusion among Western diplomats as to what Stalin really wanted and whether compromise on any of the German issues was feasible. What, then, were the immediate consequences of Stalin's initiative and their impact on subsequent Soviet policies on the German problem?

First and foremost, the blockade, far from arresting the momentum toward the foundation of the Federal Republic, actually accelerated it. This was followed by the establishment of a German Democratic Republic: on 30 May 1949, a People's Congress (*Volkskongreß*) adopted a draft constitution and, with Soviet "consent," constituted itself as the GDR's parliament (*Volkskammer*). The constitution was duly adopted on 7 October 1949, and on the same day the parliament authorized SED leader Otto Grotewohl to form a provisional government.[93] These measures, however, did not terminate the imperial nature of the relationship between the USSR and the GDR. The transfer of sovereignty was limited. There was a name change: the Soviet Military Administration in Germany turned into a Soviet Control Commission in Germany. But this change meant very little. As General Chuikov, the head of the SCCG clarified, he saw the Control Commission as continuing the task of implementing the Potsdam Protocol and other Four Power agreements.[94] Furthermore, the East German constitution did not mention the division of Germany.

---

92 Walter Phillips Davison, *The Berlin Blockade: A Study in Cold War Politics* (Princeton, N.J.: Princeton University Press, 1958), p. 144 (italics mine).

93 Renata Fritsch-Bournazel, *Die Sowjetunion und die deutsche Teilung: Die sowjetische Deutschlandpolitik 1945-1979* (Opladen: Westdeutscher Verlag, 1979), pp. 39-41.

94 Chuikov statement of 11 November 1949, *Neue Welt* (East Berlin), No. 19 (1949), pp. 4-5.

According to its preamble, "the German people" had given itself a constitution, and article 1 referred to Germany as "an indivisible democratic republic." Both the limited transfer of sovereignty and the constitutional constructs clearly pointed to Soviet intentions to maintain control in the GDR and simultaneously to extend its influence through the GDR and residual Four Power mechanisms to West German affairs. Consolidation of empire also meant the drawing of new borders. On the occasion of a visit to Poland, SED leader Walter Ulbricht committed the GDR to the "recognition of the Oder-Neisse line as a border of peace."[95] This commitment was honored and formalized in 1950 in the East German-Polish treaty of Görlitz. But the question was as yet undecided as to whether the new state with its limitations on sovereignty, new borders contested by West Germany, and a regime detested by the East German population were constructs that could endure.

The impact of the failed Berlin venture was reenforced by that of the Korean war of 1950-52. Since the division of Korea, like that of Germany, can serve to reenforce the conclusions about the almost compelling nature of the Ideological and Imperial paradigm for policy-making, some detail on the origins of the partition is appropriate. New archival evidence suggests that Stalin's ideas about Korea were in no way more defined than those on Germany.[96] Publicly, both the Soviet and the North Korean communists adhered to the idea of a unified government for Korea – not, however, because Stalin purposefully aimed at the reestablishment of a single country but, as a Soviet foreign ministry background report written by Jakob Malik openly declared, because "*it would be politically inexpedient for the Soviet Union to oppose the creation of a single Korean government.*"[97] The vehicle which permitted Stalin to assert imperial interests in Korea and which caused the division of Korea were the decisions of the Moscow conference of foreign ministers of December 1945 which stipulated a four-power "trusteeship" for Korea with a joint Soviet-American commission to prepare elections for a Korean provisional government. The directives to the Soviet delegation were to insist that only those political groups that accepted the Moscow decisions should be consulted. Since only the communist party in both halves of Korea supported the "trusteeship" idea and the Soviet delegation held firm to its instructions, the commission's work and the chances for a single Korea ended in May 1946. This did nothing to lessen Soviet verbal support for Korean reunification.

---

95 *Neues Deutschland*, 21 November 1948.

96 The argument and evidence presented follow Kathryn Weathersby, "Soviet Aims in Korea and the Origins of the Korean War, 1945-1950," Cold War International History Project, Woodrow Wilson International Center for Scholars, Working Paper No. 8, November 1993.

97 Jakob Malik, On the Question of a Single Government for Korea, 10 December 1945, Russian Foreign Ministry Archives, *fond* 0102, *opis* 1, *delo* 15, *papka* 1, 1.8-10, as quoted by Weathersby, "Soviet Aims in Korea," p. 14. The terms *fond*, *opis*, *delo*, and *papka* are in accordance with the Soviet archival classification system..

As in Germany, narrowly defined military and economic interests governed a process that led to the partition of Korea. Another internal foreign ministry report bluntly asserted that Cheju island and the ports of Pusan and Inchon "must be controlled by the Soviet military command. By insisting on the allocation of the strategic regions in Korea to the USSR, we can exert pressure on the position of the Americans, using their wish to receive for themselves strategic regions in the Pacific Ocean."[98]

There were also strong parallels between Korea and Germany on economic issues. For the foreign ministry, it went without saying that "the Japanese enterprises of military and heavy industry located in North Korea must be considered trophies of the Red Army."[99] But the economic interests went further and were linked again with strategic interests in the form of a mineral called monazite, a black sand that contains small amounts of thorium, a radioactive material that can be used in the production of nuclear weapons. From the very beginning of the occupation, Soviet officials investigated the exploitation of monazite deposits, and samples were brought to the USSR.[100] In full realization of the strategic importance of these materials, the highest-ranking Soviet officer in Korea, General Terenti Shtykov, wrote to Stalin that he considered it "necessary to take measures to increase the export from North Korea to the USSR of concentrates of monazite, tantalum, and niobium and to begin the export of uranium ore. For this purpose I ask your orders to corresponding Soviet organizations about aiding the Korean government in the development of deposits and in the organization of the extraction of concentrate and the mining of the above indicated rare metals."[101]

The parallels between Germany and Korea extend to perceptions of risks and costs, rather than respect for principles of self-determination, as governing the limits of Soviet imperial expansion. The documentary evidence proves that it was the highly nationalistic North Korean communists under Kim Il Sung who were determined to establish control over the whole country by military means; that Stalin initially opposed the idea because he was concerned about American power in the Pacific region and the risks of US intervention; but that, in January 1950, he endorsed the North Korean invasion plans and aided the military push to the south after the

98 Notes on the Question of Former Japanese Colonies and Mandated Territories, Russian Foreign Ministry Archives, *fond* 0431, *opis* 1, *delo* 52, *papka* 8, 1.40-43, as quoted by Weathersby, "Soviet Aims in Korea," p. 10.

99 Report by Suzdalev, senior advisor to the foreign ministry's 2nd Far Eastern Department, December 1945, Russian Foreign Ministry Archives, *fond* 0102, *opis* 1, *delo* 15, *papka* 1, 1.22-29, as quoted by Weathersby, "Soviet Aims in Korea," p. 15.

100 General [Terentii F.] Shtykov to Stalin, 12 March 1949, Russian Foreign Ministry Archives, *fond* 07, *opis* 22a, *delo* 223, *papka* 14, 1.1-2, as quoted by Weathersby, "Soviet Aims in Korea," p. 21.

101 Ibid.

"correlation of forces" had seemingly shifted in favor of the socialist world system (anti-colonial uprisings in Indonesia and Indochina, guerilla wars in Burma, Malaya, and the Philippines, unrest in the British and French territories in North Africa and the Middle East, the abolition of the US nuclear monopoly in August 1949, and the victory of the Chinese communists in October 1949) and after Mao Tse-tung had committed himself to assist Kim Il-sung if, contrary to expectations, the United States were to intervene.[102]

As in the Berlin blockade, Stalin had miscalculated Western reactions in Korea and had to pay a heavy price. The combined effect of both failed ventures was that the United States was now committing itself to a large security role in Europe. Thus, even before the end of the Berlin blockade, the North Atlantic Treaty was signed. Rather than continuing to dismantle its military bases and "bringing the boys home," the United States reintroduced large forces to the European continent: at the outbreak of the Berlin crisis in June 1948, the US army in Europe had consisted of only 90 000 officers and men. By 1953, this number had risen to 427 000 troops, most of whom stationed in Germany. A huge network of bases and supply depots was constructed for the American forces in Germany, Britain, France, and the Mediterranean countries and later extended to the Near and Middle East, South East Asia, and the Pacific. American strategists were, in Moscow's perspective, thinking of "closing the circle of air bases around Russia" and making that circle "smaller and smaller, tighter and tighter, until the Russians are throttled." They were planning "combined air, naval and ground operations from American bases located near the Russian mainland and their use for intensive bombing raids and attacks by guided missiles."[103]

The obvious Soviet concern now was the possibility that West Germany's manpower, and its economic and military potential, would be added to American economic and technological resources, maritime supremacy, conventional forces, and nuclear weapons in Europe, and that the United States would use West Germany as a "springboard for aggression" against the Soviet Union. There was also the concern that a rearmed West Germany would be intent on "taking revenge" and regaining its lost territories in the east and draw the United States into war. The North Atlantic Treaty, therefore, was interpreted in Moscow as a dangerous scheme which "absolutely ignores the possibility of a repetition of German aggression." Since it created "a closed grouping of states" and did not have "as its aim the prevention of a new German aggression," it had to be "regarded as a treaty directed against the

---

102 See the full documentation of the deliberations between Stalin, Mao Tse-tung and Kim Il-sung in "The Cold War in Asia," Woodrow Wilson International Center for Scholars, Washington, D.C., *Cold War International History Project Bulletin,* Nos. 6-7 (Winter 1995/96).

103 Quoted from a formal protest by the Soviet embassy in Washington in reference to a speech by General Kenney, commander of the Strategic Air Command, and an article based on it in *Newsweek;* text as published in Department of State, *Foreign Relations, 1948*, Vol. 4, p. 887.

USSR, one of the chief allies of the United States, Great Britain, and France in the last war."[104] Even though the Soviet Union had succeeded in exploding a nuclear device in August 1949 and tested a hydrogen bomb four years later, it lacked the kind of intercontinental delivery systems to put America at risk. The United States, in essence, remained strategically invulnerable. It enjoyed unchallenged naval supremacy in the Atlantic and the Pacific. It also possessed vastly superior scientific-technological and economic resources. In fact, until the late 1950s it remained the only superpower, both economically and militarily.

In the light of such unfavorable trends in the "correlation of forces" and the existence of various plans for the rearmament of West Germany and her inclusion in a European Defense Community (EDC), initiatives appeared to be called for in Moscow to prevent, or at least delay, such a development. Stalin's note of 10 March 1952 can be interpreted as such an initiative.

5. Stalin's 1952 "Peace Note": Lost Opportunity or Political Maneuver?

The diplomatic note to the United States, Britain, and France dropped the previous Soviet insistence on a disarmed Germany and raised the prospect of both unification and free elections. A German peace conference was to be convened with participation of an all-German government "expressing the will of the German people." Unification was to be in return for neutralization. A unified Germany would not be allowed to enter any coalition or military alliance directed against the Soviet Union. Its territory would be devoid of foreign troops and foreign military bases. The size and weaponry of its armed forces, as well as arms production, would be strictly limited. And it would be prohibited from harboring "organizations hostile to democracy and the cause of maintaining peace."[105]

Controversy has raged for several decades as to the meaning of the note and the subsequent exchanges between the USSR and the Western powers. One interpretation has been that of a genuine offer and "lost opportunity" for the reestablishment of German unity. Soviet propagandists and government officials advocated this point of view, some styling West German chancellor Konrad Adenauer as the chief culprit in the rejection of the Soviet proposal and asserting that he was "not only a political opponent of Russia but even felt irrational hate towards

104 Memorandum issued by the Soviet government on 31 March 1949 in reaction to the impending conclusion of the North Atlantic Treaty; *Pravda*, 1 April 1949.

105 Text of the note as published in *Foreign Relations of the United States, 1952-1954*, Vol. 7, pp. 167-172.

the Russians."[106] West German social democrats have accused the CDU of having squandered German unity because of its preference for Western integration.

Western scholars, too, have argued this case, one of its strongest advocates being Rolf Steininger.[107] But the evidence adduced to support the notion of a genuine Soviet reunification offer in his and other Western studies was derived from Western archival sources. By their very nature, such sources could not help in the reconstruction of the rationale and reasons underlying the "peace note." They also failed to shed light on Soviet decision-making processes. The problem was compounded by the fact that Western historians and political scientists familiar with Western systems and policies conducted much of the research, and not experts on Soviet affairs. It has now become possible to rely on *Soviet* and *East German* archival materials and the scrutiny of such materials by Western specialists on the USSR and the GDR.

The new archival evidence strongly suggests that the diplomatic note and its sequels were a tactical device designed to achieve some or all of the following objectives: to gain a greater degree of influence over West German public opinion; to counteract then current Western initiatives on "free elections" to be held in both parts of Germany under United Nations supervision; to delay or prevent West German defense integration in the framework of the European Defense Community; and to obtain a gradual pullout of Western allied troops from West Germany.[108]

The following direct and circumstantial evidence justifies this conclusion. First, the manipulative and instrumental character of the initiative was clearly stated by its chief architects in the course of its preparation. The "peace note," according to comments sent by then deputy Foreign Minister Gromyko to Stalin, "would have great political meaning for the strengthening of the struggle for peace and against the remilitarization of West Germany and would help the supporters of the unity of Germany and peace to expose the aggressive intentions of the three Western powers

---

106 Semjonow, *Von Stalin bis Gorbatschow*, p. 269. Semenov fails to provide detail on the origins, main protagonists, processes, and the reasoning behind the 1952 "peace note." One suspects that the reason for this is that he would not have been able to make a convincing case for his assertion that the offer was genuine.

107 Rolf Steininger, *Eine vertane Chance: Die Stalin-Note vom 10. März 1952 und die Wiedervereinigung* (Bonn: Dietz, 1985).

108 The most thorough of the new studies is Gerhard Wettig, "Die Deutschland-Note vom 10. März 1952 auf der Basis diplomatischer Akten des russischen Außenministeriums," *Deutschland Archiv*, No. 7 (June 1993), pp. 786-805. Wettig's conclusions essentially are shared by Ruud van Dijk, "The 1952 Stalin Note Debate: Myth or Missed Opportunity?", Cold War International History Project, Woodrow Wilson International Center for Scholars, Working Paper, No. 14, May 1996. See also Willfriede Otto, "Sowjetische Deutschlandnote 1952: Stalin und die DDR. Bisher unveröffentlichte handschriftliche Notizen Wilhelm Piecks," *Beiträge zur Geschichte der Arbeiterbewegung* (March 1991), pp. 374-81. The account by Otto is based on handwritten notes taken by Wilhelm Pieck, the East German president.

connected with the General Treaty [on the transfer of sovereignty to West Germany]."[109]

Second, the manipulative and propagandist quality of the "peace note" is apparent also in the fact that the note was not quietly discussed among Soviet and Western diplomats but published immediately for maximum political impact. The new evidence clarifies that this purpose was uppermost in the minds of Soviet officials who participated in drafting the note. In full realization of the lack of support for the communist party in West Germany (KPD), the party's grave organizational weaknesses, and the "absence of correct and flexible tactics,"[110] an appeal was to be made to the proverbial "masses." Suitable respondents would be found among the many, allegedly disgruntled, rank and file social democrats and in the "oppositional bourgeoisie."[111] The publication of the note, as Soviet and East German leaders incongruously agreed, had "triggered a great movement of the masses" and this had "put the Western powers and the Adenauer government under considerable pressure." They also thought that the "question of elections without a UN Commission" could be transformed into a "mass struggle for toppling the Adenauer government."[112]

A third important aspect of the Soviet initiative that casts doubt on the "lost opportunity" thesis is the fact that the preparation of the note did not occur in secrecy and over the heads of the East German communists but with their full knowledge and active participation. It is difficult to see why the SED should have joined the project if it had harbored suspicions that it was being invited to provide helpful suggestions for its self-liquidation.

Fourth, the new evidence not only fails to provide support for the notion that Stalin had decided to liquidate East Germany but shows that he was determined to strengthen its "socialist foundations." The details of this objective were discussed in meetings between Walter Ulbricht, Wilhelm Pieck, and Otto Grotewohl of the SED leadership and Stalin and other top Soviet officials in Moscow from 31 March until

---

109 A. Gromyko to I. Stalin, 21 January 1952, Archiv vneshnei politiki Rossiiskoi Federatsii (hereafter AVPRF), 07, 25, 100, 13, A-124/ag (supplement), as quoted by Wettig, "Die Deutschland-Note," p. 799. The sequence of numbers and letters follows the Soviet archival classification system in the following order: *fond, opis, delo,* and *papka*. The last letters and numbers refer to the specific document on file.

110 From a report of 15 March 1952 of the head of the diplomatic mission of the USSR in the GDR, G.M. Pushkin, sent to the Soviet foreign ministry: Ekonomicheskii i politicheskii obzor polozheniia Zapadnoi Germanii v 1951 godu, 15 March 1952, AVPRF, 82, 40, 042-Ge/2, 254, E-1248/A-675/3, as quoted by Wettig, "Die Deutschland-Note," pp. 801-2.

111 Ibid.

112 Based on notes taken by GDR president Wilhelm Pieck on the occasion of the talks held with Stalin on 1 and 7 April 1952, Otto, "Sowjetische Deutschland-Note," pp. 382-83. They do not clarify who exactly made these points and gave the appropriate instructions, Ulbricht or Stalin. The difference is largely immaterial since, as argued here, no major divergence in Soviet and East German viewpoints can be detected.

10 April. The discussion included plans for the replacement along Soviet lines of the traditional *Länder* structure of East German by smaller administrative districts (*Bezirke)*; an expansion of the state and collective sector in agriculture; organizational streamlining of the SED as a "party of a new type"; border protection measures between East and West Germany; and the build-up of national armed forces in the GDR.[113]

Fifth, the enhanced efforts to consolidate socialism in the GDR coincided with determined Soviet attempts at tightening bloc discipline. Starting in September 1949 in Hungary with the arrest, trial and later execution by garroting of Laszlo Rajk (a Politburo member and the minister of the interior), purges began to take place throughout Eastern Europe, the most extensive of which occurring in Czechoslovakia, reaching its zenith in November 1951 with the arrest and later trial and execution of Rudolf Slansky, a deputy prime minister and former party secretary.[114] Deconstructing the socialist foundations in the GDR for the sake of a united neutral Germany simply would not have fit the overall pattern of imperial construction.

A sixth rationale concerns Soviet domestic politics. A genuine Soviet reunification offer, as argued, would have meant a significant change in established policies. This, in turn, would have been reflected in a shift in internal power alignments. However, the note was carefully prepared and continuously "improved" in accordance with routine bureaucratic procedures and decision-making processes. The idea of a note was apparently first suggested to Gromyko by Mikhail Gribanov, the head of the MFA's Third European Department. What was needed, he told his superior, was "a real step to a peaceful settlement with Germany ... in order to counteract the erroneous declaration of the three [Western] powers on the termination of the state of war with Germany."[115] For that purpose, he proposed convening a commission of experts that would draft principles for a German peace treaty.[116] He also suggested to Foreign Minister Andrei Vyshinsky in the same month that the GDR should first propose to West Germany a joint initiative urging the four powers to conclude a peace treaty with Germany. After the expected rejection of this *démarche* by Bonn, the East German government should then unilaterally address the four powers. Only

113 Based on notes taken by Pieck (Otto, "Sowjetische Deutschland-Note," pp. 388-89) and documents from the Soviet foreign ministry archives (A. Gromyko to A. Vyshinsksii, 18 April 1952, AVPRF, 07, 27, 162, 42, E-3347/r.). Both references are from Wettig, "Die Deutschland-Note," pp. 802-3.

114 Brzezinski, *The Soviet Bloc*, pp. 93-94.

115 M. Gribanov to A. A. Gromyko, 3 August 1951, AVPRF, 082, 38, 112, 250, A-1475/Zeo, as quoted by Wettig, "Die Deutschland-Note," p. 792.

116 Ibid.

thereafter would Moscow launch corresponding initiatives.[117] The first draft of the principles of a peace treaty was sent by Gribanov to the commission of experts on 8 September 1951. In the subsequent months, Molotov, who at the time dealt with foreign policy matters in the Politburo, and Gromyko were actively involved in modifying and commenting on the draft. On three occasions it was sent to Stalin for final approval.[118] No evidence has come to light to the effect that disagreements existed among the top leaders or the major institutions involved in decision-making either on substance or procedure. There is also no evidence showing that a pro-German faction in the foreign ministry or the Politburo had suddenly become ascendant and been able to embark on a drastic departure from the traditional paradigm.

This leads to a seventh point in the rebuttal of the "genuine offer" thesis. One would expect that major changes on an issue as crucial as that of Germany would not only be reflected in domestic political changes but also be embedded in an overall change of Soviet ideology, domestic politics, and foreign policy. This, however, was not the case. Concerning ideology, while Soviet foreign ministry officials and diplomats were busy drafting, promulgating, and propagandizing the "peace note," party officials immersed themselves in the task of preparing the Nineteenth Party Congress, to be held in October 1952. Their primary business centered on domestic affairs – the new party statutes, the Fifth Five-Year Plan, the necessity for priority development of heavy industry, and the intensification of the struggle against slackness and corruption in the economic bureaucracy. These topics reappeared in a collection of comments published in *Bolshevik*, *Pravda*, and in tens of millions of pamphlet reprints under the title of "Economic Problems of Socialism in the USSR," written in February, April, May, and September 1952.[119] One would search in vain in these pamphlets if one were to look for ideological justification of new policies.

As for international affairs, matters were only slightly different. Stalin's pamphlets confirmed the validity of the "two camp" theory. The only significant departure from orthodoxy was a revision of the Leninist theory of the inevitability of war. Stalin now declared the "contradictions" among the imperialist states to be more acute than those between the imperialist camp and world socialism. The dogma on the inevitability of war between the two opposed socio-economic systems was thereby not discarded but modified: war among the imperialist states was held to be more likely than war

117 M. Gribanov to A. Ia. Vyshinsksii, 15 August 1951, AVPRF, 082, 38, 112, 250, A-1558/Zeo, as quoted by Wettig, "Die Deutschland-Note," p. 793.

118 Wettig, "Die Deutschland-Note," p. 798.

119 The pamphlets were discussed before and after the Nineteenth Congress and then integrated in a textbook on political economy published in many languages, the English version being Joseph V. Stalin, *Economic Problems of Socialism in the USSR* (Moscow: Foreign Languages Publishing House, 1952).

between the two systems. More specifically, in the Stalinist perspective, West Germany, Britain, France, Italy, and Japan, resentful of American "tutelage," "bondage," "domination," and "oppression," would sooner or later try to throw off the American yoke.[120] Obviously, if this diagnosis were correct, Soviet diplomats would have ample opportunities to exploit "contradictions" both within and between these countries. The note, as argued, attempted to use such opportunities.

Put into the larger foreign policy context, the Berlin blockade and the Korean war had resulted in increased international tensions and a build-up of Western military power. In accordance with previous patterns of behavior, Soviet foreign policy subsequently aimed at the mitigation of these adverse trends by some conciliatory gestures and by playing on Western divergences. As Marshall D. Shulman has written in his seminal *Stalin's Foreign Policy Reappraised*,

> By restraint in the use of overt acts of provocation after the Korean attack, and by encouraging the development of neutralism, nationalism, the peace movement, and anticolonial agitation, Soviet foreign policy was intended to achieve such specific purposes as the weakening of the structure of American strategic air bases abroad ... as well as such general purposes as undermining the cohesion and momentum of the Western alliance.[121]

Stalin's "peace note" on Germany corresponded with these purposes.

This conclusion is reenforced by the fact that, in line with such ideological preconceptions on international affairs, neutrality could not be regarded as anything but, to quote Mao Tse-tung, "a hoax."[122] As will be shown in the next section, this view was reaffirmed and directly applied to the German problem by the top Soviet leaders after Stalin's death.

6. Imperial Dilemmas: Beria and the Crisis in the GDR

As with Stalin's "peace note," a substantial amount of evidence from Soviet archives, memoirs, and interviews has emerged to shed new light on Soviet thinking on the German problem in the 1950s. Some of this evidence has surfaced in connection with the so-called "Beria affair," the alleged attempt by the former chief of the secret police to "sell off" East Germany after Stalin's death in March 1953 in the context of the "new course" adopted by Prime Minister Malenkov.[123] Lavrenti Beria at that time

---

120 Ibid., *pp.* 37-41.

121 Marshall D. Shulman, *Stalin's Foreign Policy Reappraised* (New York: Atheneum, 1965), p. 259.

122 "On the People's Democratic Dictatorship," as quoted in H. Wei, *China and Soviet Russia* (Princeton, N.J.: Van Nostrand, 1956), p. 264.

123 Recent new sources include the memoirs of Andrei A. Gromyko, transl. Harold Shukman, *Memories* (London: Hutchinson, 1989); a supplement to Khrushchev's memoirs, N. S. Khrushchev, transl. and ed. Jerrold L. Schecter with Viacheslav V. Luchkov, *Khrushchev Remembers: The Glasnost Tapes* (Boston: Little, Brown, 1990); and N. S. Khrushchev,

had just taken charge of the new Ministry of the Interior (MVD), created by the merger of the interior and state security ministries. The stenographic record of a top secret CPSU Central Committee meeting, held on 2 July 1953 to discuss and approve Beria's arrest and execution, is particularly interesting.[124] It provides fascinating insights into the mind-set of the adherents to the imperial and ideological paradigm. It is, therefore, appropriate to look at some of the nuggets from this gold mine of information.

The CC meeting was preceded on 27 May by an important session of the Council of Ministers (the government) at which, according to Malenkov, the "topic on the floor" had been the "German problem" and the "serious failure of the situation in the GDR."

> We all concluded that as a result of incorrect policies, many mistakes had been made in the GDR. Among the German population there was huge dissatisfaction, which was particularly evident in the fact that the population of East Germany had begun to leave for West Germany. In the most recent period, approximately in the last two years, about 500,000 people have escaped to West Germany.

Analysis of the internal political and economic situation in the GDR, notably the "mass migration" of East Germans to West Germany, had indicated that "*we are facing an internal catastrophe. We were obliged to face the truth and to admit that without the presence of Soviet troops the existing regime in the GDR is not stable.*"[125]

"Aktsii," in V. F. Nekrasov, ed., *Beria: Konets kar'ery* (Moscow: Politizdat, 1991). Molotov's reminiscences, recorded in numerous conversations with the former foreign minister in the last ten years of his life by an obscure poet and ardent Stalinist named Feliks Chuev, *Sto sorok besed s Molotovym*, have already been mentioned. Malenkov's side of the story can be found in several articles written by his son Andrei, as well as in interviews given to him and others by Dmitrii Sukhanov, Malenkov's closest aide in the 1940s and 1950s; Andrei Malenkov, "Protivoborstvo," *Zhurnalist*, No. 2 (February 1991), pp. 60-66, and Dmitrii Varskii, "Skhvatka" (interview with Andrei Malenkov), *Vostochnii ekspress*, No. 16 (1991), pp. 8-9. East German sources include the memoirs of Rudolf Herrnstadt, a former SED Politburo member, chief editor of *Neues Deutschland* and a major proponent of reform in the period after Stalin's death; Nadja Stulz-Herrnstadt, ed., *Das Herrnstadt Dokument: Das Politburo der SED und die Geschichte des 17. Juni 1953* (Reinbek: Rowohlt, 1990). Furthermore, the Soviet instructions to the East German leadership in June 1953 have now been published: "Ein Dokument von grosser historischer Bedeutung vom Mai 1953," *Beiträge zur Geschichte der Arbeiterbewegung*, Vol. 32, No. 5 (1990), pp. 648-654, and "Dokumente zur Auseinandersetzung in der SED 1953," ibid., Vol. 32, No. 5, (1990), pp. 655-672. This review of the literature draws on James Richter, "Reexamining Soviet Policy Towards Germany During the Beria Interregnum, Cold War International History Project, Woodrow Wilson International Center for Scholars, Working Paper No. 3, June 1992.

124 CPSU, CC, Top Secret, Plenum TsK KPSS, Iiul' 1953 goda. Stenograficheskii otchet, "O prestupnykh antipartiinykh i antigosudarstvennykh deistviiakh Beriia," 2-7 July 1953, *Izvestiia TsK KPSS*, No. 1 (1991), pp. 140-214 and No. 2 (1991), pp. 141-208. All citations of this report will refer to the first installment in the January edition unless otherwise noted. Beria was arrested on 26 June 1953 and executed on 23 December.

125 Ibid., pp. 143-44 (italics mine). The mixture of past and present tense is as in the original.

Foreign Minister Molotov provided some detail about the internal catastrophe facing East Germany, saying that, "in the period from January 1951 until April 1953, 450,000 people have left the GDR for West Germany"; that this movement of people had increased "particularly in the first months of this year"; and that "among the escapees there were more than a few workers, including several thousand members" of the SED and the FDJ, the Union of Free German Youth. Conveniently shunning any Soviet responsibility for the mass exodus, Molotov concluded that all this was "clearly an indication of huge deficiencies in the work of our friends in East Germany."[126]

As the record unequivocally shows, there was no complacency among the top Soviet leaders in May and June 1953. This is confirmed, among other sources, by Pavel Sudoplatov, the head of the MVD's Ninth Department, known also as the Buro for Special Tasks. In that capacity he was directly responsible to Beria and privy to the most sensitive information, including on East Germany. According to Sudoplatov, his chief was aware of the severe economic crisis in East Germany and also in Poland, which had caused thousands of people to flee to the West. A divided Germany would force the Soviet Union to supply both countries with cheap raw materials and foodstuffs until collectivization of agriculture and industrialization could mitigate the problem. German unification, on the other hand, would bring substantial economic benefits. He was "obsessed" by the idea that $10 billion could be obtained for the reconstruction of the Soviet Union. "The Kremlin," he told Sudoplatov, thought that the creation of a unified neutral Germany under a coalition government could be a buffer between the Soviet Union and the United States in Western Europe and the best way to strengthen the Moscow's global position. Ulbricht was to be forced to cooperate and consent to East Germany becoming an autonomous province in the new unified Germany.[127] Sudoplatov was told to explore the feasibility of a concomitant initiative and – through secret contacts in West Germany and Austria – to spread the rumor that the USSR was prepared to make a deal on Germany. The urgency of the matter was reinforced by Ulbricht's statements to the effect that it was the SED's goal to establish a dictatorship of the proletariat in the GDR and by East German reports of a split in the top leadership of the SED.[128] The top leadership of the CPSU was split, too. Molotov, in particular, opposed the idea of a unified neutral Germany. He, Beria, and Malenkov formed a commission to

126 Ibid., p. 162.

127 Pavel Sudoplatov, *Razvedka i Kreml'. Zapiski nezhelatel'nogo svidetelia* (Moscow: TOO "Geia," 1996), pp. 414-15. *Provintsiia* is the term used by the author.

128 In May, the East German State Security chief, General Ernst Wollweber, had been called to Moscow and provided this information; ibid., p. 415.

formulate policy guidelines for future Soviet policy in East Germany and to define the conditions for German unification.[129]

On 5 June, Vladimir Semenov, the newly appointed Soviet High Commissioner in Germany told the top East German leadership to slow down the building of socialism in the GDR and work for German unity. East Berlin asked for a delay of two weeks in order to consider the Soviet directives. Semenov rejected this request, commenting that the GDR would (then already?) be an autonomous area in a unified Germany.[130] At the beginning of June, Ulbricht and other top East German leaders were ordered to appear in Moscow. In a meeting with Beria, Malenkov, Khrushchev, Molotov, Semenov, and General Andrei Grechko (the commander of the Soviet forces in Germany), the East Germans were informed of the Soviet decision against an accelerated construction of socialism in the GDR. Ulbricht is reported as having vehemently opposed this directive, as a result of which Beria, Malenkov, and Khrushchev decided to depose him.[131]

The concern of the Soviet leadership was exacerbated by the outbreak of serious popular discontent, starting in East Berlin on 17 June and then rapidly spreading throughout East Germany, in response to an increase in work norms. This, too, was part of Ulbricht's drive for the accelerated construction of socialism in the GDR. How, then, did Beria react? According to Sudoplatov, his chief ordered Grechko and Semenov to use the Soviet armed forces in order to suppress the popular revolt, hoping that as a result of this demonstration of power he would enhance the chances for compromise with the Western countries. The West was to be under no illusion that Soviet Union could be expelled from the GDR by a popular uprising.[132]

In view of the bankruptcy of Soviet and East German policies, why did the leadership in Moscow not cut its losses and liquidate the imperial outpost? And what about Beria? Was he really prepared to face up to the unpalatable East German realities and determined to free the Soviet Union of Stalin's imperial legacy in Germany? The proceedings at the July 1953 Central Committee meeting appear to confirm Sudoplatov's account that he was. At the meeting, Malenkov charged that Beria (presumably at the May 1953 session of the Council of Ministers) had "suggested a course toward [the establishment of] a bourgeois Germany." Similarly, Khrushchev decried that he (Beria) had "proposed turning away from the construction of socialism in the GDR and heading toward concessions to the West"

---

129 Ibid. Until late in his life, Molotov clung to the view – and disapproved – that Beria was prepared to sacrifice the GDR; see Chuev, *Sto sorok besed s Molotovym*, p. 335.

130 Sudoplatov, *Razvedka i Kreml'*, p. 416. The author uses *oblast'* here.

131 This position was formally adopted in a 12 June 1953 CPSU Presidium (Politburo) decision. Although the decision has been referred to in official documents, a copy of it thus far has not been found, according to Sudoplatov; ibid.

132 Ibid., p. 417.

(which, in Khrushchev's view, would "have meant giving away 18 million Germans to the rule of the American imperialists") and that he had said: "'We must found a neutral, democratic Germany.'"[133]

The problem with these accusations is that the Kremlin leaders responsible for Beria's arrest were sure to find or fabricate the most heinous crimes in his past as justification for his execution.[134] In fact, taking a few leaves from Stalin's Great Book of Purges, they unmasked Beria as a "bourgeois degenerate" (Malenkov); as a "person from the bourgeois camp" (Molotov); as a treacherous "bandit" who behaved "not like a communist but like a provocateur" (Khrushchev); as someone who, "without a doubt, was connected with international imperialist intelligence services as a full-scale agent and spy" (Kaganovich); and an "enemy of the Soviet Union" (Molotov). Even if one chooses to discount the more outlandish allegations, the CC proceedings and evidence from East German sources nevertheless indicate that Beria *was* prepared to go farther on the German problem than his erstwhile colleagues. But how far exactly? Trade union chief Lazar M. Kaganovich only spoke of Beria's "*leanings* towards what amounted to liquidating the GDR,"[135] and Molotov revealed that Beria, in his draft resolution before the Presidium of the Council of Ministers on the German question, had

> proposed that we "concede the error of building socialism in the German Democratic Republic under existing conditions." He also suggested that we "turn away from building socialism in the GDR *at the present time*." This proposal was, of course, completely unacceptable. When I objected, Beria answered that, after all, he was only proposing to turn away from socialism in the GDR "at present."[136]

Such portrayals suggest that Beria only advocated a slower pace in the systemic transformation of East Germany but not to abandon the Soviet outpost altogether.

What, then, was the thinking of the majority of Politburo and Central Committee members? How should one "correctly" have addressed the internal crisis in the GDR?

---

133 CPSU, CC Plenum, "O prestupnykh deisviiakh Beriia," p. 157. Khrushchev, like Molotov, continued to adhere to his position. In November 1960, he told Ulbricht in private conversation that Beria *and Malenkov* had "wanted to liquidate the GDR, but we fired one [Malenkov] and shot the other [Beria];" Record of the Meeting between Comrade N. S. Khrushchev and Comrade W. Ulbricht on 30 November 1960, Russian Foreign Ministry Archives, *fond* 0742, opis 6, *por.* 4, *papka* 43, Secret. The transcript of the meeting as published by Hope Harrison, "Ulbricht and the Concrete "Rose:" New Archival Evidence on the Dynamics of Soviet-East German Relations and the Berlin Crisis, 1958-61," Cold War International History Project, Woodrow Wilson International Center for Scholars, Working Paper No. 5, May 1993 [hereafter Harrison, "The Archival Evidence"], Appendix A.

134 In fact, several Western analyses have considered the charges against Beria to have been motivated almost exclusively by the power struggle in the Kremlin; see, for instance, Victor Baras, "Beria's Fall and Ulbricht's Survival," *Soviet Studies*, Vol. 27, No. 3 (July 1975), pp. 381-395.

135 CPSU, CC Plenum, "O prestupnykh deisviiakh Beriia," p. 199 (italics mine).

136 Ibid. p. 163 (italics mine).

And, above all, what was to be done? Perhaps paradoxically, the remedy they suggested for curing the ills at the periphery of empire was not altogether different from what Beria as a minimum appears to have advocated: reducing the pace in the "construction of socialism" in the GDR. Nothing more than that. As Molotov reported to the CC meeting, "[w]e explained this to our German friends, and they agreed completely that, given current international conditions, it is unwise to force the construction of socialism in the GDR."[137]

No detail was provided as to how effective such a course of action could possibly have been. The common operating assumption apparently was that the problems were only temporary and would somehow disappear. Such notions were nurtured by rationalizations. Molotov, for instance, thought:

> When examining the affair, we must consider that the GDR embarked upon an extremely hurried course of industrialization and that the Germans were involved in construction projects that far exceeded their resources. At the same time, East Germany was also required to bear significant expenditures for the occupation and to pay war reparations. Not to mention the reconstruction necessary after the war. Meanwhile, we must not forget that East Germany finds itself in particularly complex circumstances: The occupying powers in Berlin – the USA, England, and France – as well West Germany, have a disorganizing effect on the political and economic situation in the GDR.[138]

Indeed, these problems did contribute to the severe crisis in the GDR. Given the facts as acknowledged by the Soviet leaders, that much harm had been done by a rapacious reparations policy, that the success of economic reconstruction in West Germany was causing ideological and political problems, and that the East German outpost could only be kept as long as Soviet troops were stationed there, the question needs to be restated even more emphatically: why did the Soviet leaders not follow the path imputed to Beria and stop the construction of socialism in East Germany? And why, in particular, did they not draw the conclusion from the June 1953 workers' uprising that their position in the GDR was even more tenuous than they had thought and abandon it?

The proceedings of the July 1953 CC meeting provide several answers to these questions. The first and foremost was impeccably Marxist-Leninist: a "bourgeois," even though ostensibly democratic Germany, could not possibly be neutral. In Molotov's words, Beria was

> verbose in his explanations to the effect that it would be fine for the Soviet Union if Germany united as a single state on bourgeois foundations – as if it were possible for a modern-day bourgeois Germany *not* to be tightly linked with other imperialist nations; and if, under

---

137 Ibid., p. 143; similarly Molotov, ibid., p. 162.

138 Ibid.

> present conditions, it were possible for a bourgeois Germany to exist that would not be at the same time an imperialist, aggressive Germany.[139]

His central point: "As Marxists, it is clear to us that in the given situation, that is, in the imperialist epoch, the idea that bourgeois Germany might become peace-loving or neutral in relation to the USSR is not only an illusion but, in fact, a position foreign to communism."[140] Khrushchev supported this reasoning and asked:

> Could a democratic bourgeois Germany really be neutral? Is this possible? Beria said, "We shall conclude a treaty." But what would a treaty like this cost us? We know the price of treaties. A treaty is strong only if it is backed by guns. If a treaty is not backed up by force, it is worth nothing. We would be laughed at, we would be considered naive.[141]

A second rationale was that of the importance of the GDR in the struggle for influence in Europe. To Molotov it was self-evident that the very existence of the German Democratic Republic was "a serious blow not only against German imperialism but also against the imperialist system throughout Europe." If the GDR followed the "correct political course," it would become a "reliable friend of the Soviet Union" and "a serious obstacle to the success of imperialist plans in Europe."[142]

A third rationale was moral, psychological and emotional. To have followed Beria's course would have meant "renouncing what was won with the blood of our soldiers, the blood of our people, in the tough battle against Hitlerism."[143]

A fourth and final reason was the importance of East German uranium for the Soviet Union's nuclear weapons program. This was acknowledged by Avrami Zavenyagin, the deputy head of the Ministry for Medium Machine Building, one of the military-industrial ministries responsible for the manufacture of nuclear weapons. "Large quantities of uranium are mined in the GDR," he said, "perhaps no less than what is at the disposal of the Americans. This fact was well known to Beria, and he should have mentioned it to the Central Committee so they could have kept it in mind."[144]

Given the instability in East Germany and Western interference, was it not likely that Moscow could be *forced* to abandon its exposed position in Central Europe? The top leadership assembled in secret thought that it would not have to yield under pressure. Molotov observed that "The correlation of international forces has fundamentally changed after the Second World War in favor of the USSR and the states which are friendly towards it." Among the friendly countries, in addition to

---

139 Ibid., p. 162 (italics mine).
140 Ibid., p. 162 (italics mine).
141 Ibid., pp. 157-58.
142 Ibid., p. 162.
143 Ibid., p. 162.
144 Ibid., No. 2 (February 1991), p. 170.

East Germany, he counted China, North Korea, Poland, Czechoslovakia, Romania, Hungary, Bulgaria, Albania, and Mongolia, and thus arrived at a total of 800 million people who were building socialism.[145] Furthermore, nuclear weapons were assumed to discourage Western adventurism. Zavenyagin told his colleagues that the United States' monopoly in nuclear fission weapons had been "liquidated." Having realized this very fact, the "Americans began developing a hydrogen bomb." This weapon was of a "destructive force ten times greater than that of the conventional nuclear bomb" and had not only technical but global political significance. Prevention of a second US monopoly therefore would be a "most important event in world politics." He assured his colleagues that, in the race for the development of this weapon, "we think that we have not fallen behind the Americans."[146]

To summarize, the Soviet leaders were perfectly well aware of the main problems of imperial control in Germany. The GDR lacked legitimacy. There was a tremendous outflow of people. Politically, the regime was unstable. It could be kept in power only by the presence of Soviet forces. Ideologically, the GDR was in a difficult position because of the presence of the Western allies and the flourishing of a Western way of life in West Berlin. Economically, the GDR had fallen behind its Western counterpart because of the Soviet Union's reparations policy, structural deficiencies, and the diversion of trade. Nevertheless, the competition with imperialism required holding on to East Germany, and the more favorable "correlation of forces" made it possible to do so.

Such assessments, however, posed two basic questions as to future trends: (1) could the shift in the "correlation of forces" in favor of socialism be maintained and external threats to the Soviet position in Germany be warded off and (2) was it going to be possible to achieve viability of the GDR and avert an internal collapse? The course of events from the mid-1950s to the beginning of the 1960s was still to give ambiguous answers to these questions.

To extend this overview of Soviet perceptions and policies on the German problem to the mid-1950s, proposals put forward by the collective leadership under Malenkov in 1954 were in all likelihood, like Stalin's note, a tactical device rather than a genuine offer of reunification and timed to prevent or delay the entry of the Federal Republic in NATO, a step that, in accordance with the October 1954 Paris agreements, was scheduled to take place in May 1955. When Khrushchev became the dominant figure in the Soviet leadership in that year he therefore did not find himself faced with similarly difficult choices and complexities as his predecessors: West Germany was firmly being integrated in the Atlantic alliance and the European Economic Community. East Germany became a member of the Warsaw Pact and

145 Ibid., p. 170.
146 Ibid., No. 2 (February 1991), p. 166.

Comecon, and the Soviet leaders were committing themselves firmly to the GDR's survival and viability. But the achievement of these objectives remained elusive. The next major crisis in the periphery was already brewing.

7. Imperial Dilemmas: The Berlin Wall

The driving forces behind the outbreak of yet another crisis of Soviet control in the GDR and the reasons for the construction of the Berlin wall in August 1961 are by now well understood. As in 1952-53, they consisted of East Germany's ever present lack of political legitimacy, economic deficiencies, and the exodus of significant numbers of East Germans to West Germany that suddenly became acute. Soviet archival sources, memoirs, and interviews have served to clarify this.[147] Formally, at the international diplomatic level, the crisis began at the end of October 1958 with the assertion by East German leader Walter Ulbricht that "The Western powers have destroyed the legal basis for their presence in Berlin" and that they "no longer have any legal, moral, or political justification for their continued occupation of West Berlin." He also *de facto* threatened the replacement of Four Power rights with East German sovereignty by claiming that "All of Berlin lies on the territory of the GDR."[148]

The threat against the Western presence and Western access rights was amplified by Khrushchev two weeks later. On 10 November, at a friendship meeting at the Polish embassy in Moscow, he stated that the Western powers had

> violated the Potsdam Agreement repeatedly and with impunity, while we have remained loyal to it as if nothing had changed. We have every reason to set ourselves free from obligations under the Potsdam Agreement, obligations which have outlived themselves and which the Western powers are clinging to, and to pursue a policy with regard to Berlin that would spring from the interests of the Warsaw Treaty.[149]

Khrushchev also argued that "if the Western powers are interested in any questions regarding Berlin" they should "build their relations with the German Democratic Republic."[150] Implied here was the threat of a unilateral Soviet renunciation of the Potsdam Agreement and the establishment of a system that would take into account vaguely defined interests of the socialist countries and include the GDR as a sovereign, internationally recognized state.

---

147 For the most important presentation of such evidence, see Harrison, "New Archival Evidence," and Vladislav Zubok, "The Berlin Crisis, 1958-1962: New Evidence From Soviet Archives," Conference on the Cold War, Moscow, January 1993.

148 Gerhard Keiderling and Percy Stulz, *Berlin 1945-1968: Zur Geschichte der Hauptstadt der DDR und der selbständigen politischen Einheit Westberlin* ([East] Berlin: Dietz Verlag, 1970), p. 461.

149 *Pravda*, 11 November 1958 (italics mine).

150 Ibid.

This threat was spelled out in more detail in the Berlin ultimatum of 28 November 1958 – identical notes sent by the Soviet government to the three Western powers and a similar note addressed to the Federal Republic of Germany.[151] The central point advanced in the note to the three Western powers is the proposal

> to solve the West Berlin question at the present time by the conversion of West Berlin into an independent political unit [*samostoiatel'naia politicheskaia edinitsa*] – a free city, without any state, including both existing German states, interfering in its life. Specifically, it might be possible to agree that the territory of the free city be demilitarized and that no armed forces be maintained there. The free city, West Berlin, could regulate its own economic, administrative, and other affairs.[152]

The proposal could be regarded as limited in scope. However, the political stakes were raised considerably by declarations of the Soviet government to the effect that it regarded the wartime agreements relating to zones of occupation, administration, and control machinery in Germany and Berlin as null and void; that it proposed, for six months only, "not to make any changes in the present procedure for military traffic" of the three powers between West Germany and West Berlin; and that if this grace period were not used to reach an acceptable agreement, "the Soviet Union will then carry out the planned measures through an agreement with the GDR."[153]

Khrushchev's demands raise the analytical problem, as in the Berlin crisis of 1948-49, of whether Berlin in Moscow's perspective was a *lever* with which to achieve more far-reaching objectives or a *prize* in order to stabilize the GDR. In a strict sense, West Berlin was the primary topic of the note. But at the same time, the "free city" proposal touched upon a whole range of broad issues, such as the extent of Four Power rights and responsibilities in Germany and Berlin; relations between West Berlin and Bonn; access to West Berlin for West German and Western allied personnel and goods; recognition of the GDR, *de facto* or *de iure*; the role of East Germany in European politics; the nature of relations between East and West Germany; and, finally, the question of European security and superpower relations. While it was theoretically possible to separate West Berlin from larger issues, in practice it was impossible.

As in the Berlin crisis of 1948-49, therefore, it is appropriate to abandon the idea of a single objective pursued by the Soviet Union in the crisis and to proceed instead from the idea that Khrushchev, during the prolonged campaign for the conclusion of a peace treaty, pursued a range of objectives. The most important of these goals can be listed as follows: to induce the Western powers to yield their position in Berlin – the goal most unlikely to be realized; to enhance the domestic stability and the

---

151 The full text of the notes and Khrushchev's comments are published in *Pravda*, 28 November 1958.

152 Ibid.

153 Ibid.

international status of the GDR; to limit the influence of West Berlin as a showcase of the West and enhance its sense of vulnerability by weakening its ties with West Germany; to win final and irrevocable acceptance of the postwar political and social order in Europe; and to neutralize the threat to this order emanating from West Germany, that is, her declared policy of non-recognition of the GDR (and the borders) and her desire to see Germany united.[154]

The new archival evidence corroborates previous Western interpretations to the effect that Khrushchev was determined to change the *status quo* and use the demand for the conclusion of a peace treaty for this purpose. At a meeting between Khrushchev and Ulbricht in November 1960, the Soviet leader told his East German counterpart that

> When we put forward the question of a peace treaty we also made allowance for the possibility of concluding an interim agreement, that is, an agreement between the four powers on a temporary status for West Berlin for a limited time, during which both Germanies would have to agree on the issues. If they did not agree, then we would be free to conclude a peace treaty with the GDR. This was our concession to Eisenhower so as to save his prestige and not create the impression that we would expel them [the Western powers] from West Berlin. This continues to remain true now. You Germans probably will not agree amongst yourselves and then we will sign a peace treaty with you, and the Western powers will not conclude any peace treaty at all. But this does not worry us.[155]

What in part may have prompted Khrushchev to take the initiative in autumn 1958 was his assumption that the "correlation of forces" had again shifted in favor of the Soviet Union. The favorable trends, from the Soviet perspective, included the launching of the Sputnik earth satellite in October 1957, which conveyed the notion that the Soviet Union was not only a "revolutionary" power ideologically but also a force to be reckoned with technologically. The feat in space also had military implications: it demonstrated that the Soviet Union was able to produce ICBMs. This in turn raised concern in the United States about the possible emergence of a "missile gap" in favor of the USSR. Despite the fact that the Soviet Union never embarked on the production of first-generation ICBMs, the successful launching of the Sputnik and subsequent highly publicized Soviet ICBM flight tests heralded the end of United States invulnerability to long-range Soviet missile attack. Predictably, the psychological repercussions of this new reality and the concern about actual or

---

154 This interpretation of a range of objectives rather than a single goal pursued by Khrushchev in the Berlin crisis is shared by Thomas W. Wolfe, *Soviet Power and Europe: 1945-1970* (Baltimore, Md.: Johns Hopkins University Press, 1970), pp. 89-90.

155 Record of the Meeting between Comrade N.S. Khrushchev and Comrade W. Ulbricht on 30 November 1960, Russian Foreign Ministry Archives, *fond* 0742, *opis* 6, *por* 4, papka 43, Secret. The transcript of the meeting as published by Harrison, "New Archival Evidence," Appendix A.

potential shifts in the balance of power to the West's disadvantage were skillfully exploited by Khrushchev during the Berlin crisis.[156]

Similar considerations apply to the economic competition between the two world systems. The Soviet Union's economic growth rates in the late 1950s, according to official Soviet data, were quite high, with industrial production growing at more than 10 percent, whereas corresponding American growth rates were only little more than 2 percent. This gave Khrushchev the idea that it would be possible "to catch up with and overtake the USA by 1970" – wishful thinking which, much to later Soviet embarrassment and regret, was enshrined as a goal in the 1959 Seven-Year Plan and the 1961 party program. Finally, favorable trends in the "correlation of forces" also seemed to be inherent in the rapidly accelerating processes of decolonization which severely shook the Western "imperialist" system and, in accordance with Marxist-Leninist theory, threatened to produce the final collapse of the opposed socio-economic system.

By 1961, however, perceptions as to the "correlation of forces" had significantly shifted to the disadvantage of the Soviet Union. Soviet ICBM capabilities and claims had turned out to be exaggerated and the "missile gap" was recognized as what it was: a myth. The rift with China, carefully concealed from the outside world in the late 1950s, became public in 1961. The processes of decolonization did not automatically and invariably favor the Soviet Union. More often than not they merely led to the replacement of direct with indirect Western control, and certainly did not produce the collapse of the capitalist world system as predicted by Soviet ideology. Most important for the present inquiry, the balance of power in Central Europe was decidedly shifting against the Soviet Union. Western security cooperation and defense integration was proceeding at a rapid pace, including in particular the creation of the West German *Bundeswehr* and its projected arming with nuclear weapons under a "dual key" system, with the American president ultimately deciding whether such weapons were to be used in war.[157]

The "arming of the *Bundeswehr* with nuclear weapons, which are now legal," and other disadvantageous trends raised concern among Soviet officials in the periphery and at the center.[158] They led to apprehensions, as Soviet ambassador to East Berlin

---

156 This was carefully documented by Arnold L. Horelick and Myron Rush, *Strategic Power and Soviet Foreign Policy* (Chicago: University of Chicago Press, 1966).

157 It is interesting to note that in the communications between Soviet officials in East and West Germany and the center in Moscow essentially no distinction was drawn between equipping the German armed forces with nuclear weapons under the "dual key" system and independent West German access to such weapons.

158 Record of the Meeting with Ulbricht on 5 October 1958 (Pervukhin's diary, entry of 11 October 1958), TsKhSD, *rolik* 8875, *fond* 5, *opis* 49, *delo* 82, p. 7-8, as quoted by Harrison, "New Archival Evidence," p. 13. Smirnov, the Soviet ambassador to Bonn, in conversation with Ulbricht, Pervukhin and Astavin. Both the "arming" and the "legality" did not correspond to the

Mikhail Pervukhin told Ulbricht in September 1958, that "the West is preparing to carry out a series of significant economic and political measures against the GDR."[159] Ambassador to West Germany A. A. Smirnov agreed, warning that "the Western powers are talking openly about activating the struggle against the GDR" and that it was possible that "the West will not stop at limited local provocations on GDR territory."[160]

Negative trends in the socio-economic sphere were equally important. Western European integration, as epitomized by the success of the European Economic Community, posed the danger of a Western Europe outpacing Eastern Europe in economic performance, power, and prosperity. The West German *Wirtschaftswunder* (economic miracle) made a shambles of Ulbricht's idea, borrowed from Khrushchev's precepts of Soviet-American competition, to "catch up with and overtake" West Germany. Instead of narrowing, the economic gap between the two German competitors threatened to *widen* and exacerbate the problems of ideological competition and East German viability and legitimacy. As ambassador Pervukhin deplored in an internal report, "the uncontrolled borders between the socialist and capitalist worlds unwittingly prompt the [East German] population to make a comparison between both parts of the city, which unfortunately does not always turn out in favor of Democratic Berlin."[161]

Three factors interacted to produce a severe socio-economic crisis in the GDR in 1961.[162] The first was a new wave of collectivization in agriculture. In 1949-58, the pace of conversion of private lands into collective farms had been slow. At the end of 1958 as much as two-thirds of the total agricultural area was still in private hands. In 1959, however, the SED leadership decided to make greater efforts in the "socialist construction in the countryside." Severe pressure was exerted on private farmers to join collective farms, with 300,000 private farms changing ownership in that year, and another 300,000 in the first four months of 1960. As a result, private farming in the GDR practically ceased to exist but at the cost of a severe decline in agricultural production.

---

facts, however. The arming had not begun. A *Bundestag* decision to do so had preliminary character and was not a law; if adopted, its realization would have taken at least two years.

159 Record of the Meeting with Comrade W. Ulbricht on 26 September 1958 (Pervukhin's diary, entry of 30 September 1958), TsKhSD, *rolik* 8873, *fond* 5, *opis* 49, *delo* 76, p. 1, as quoted by Harrison, "New Archival Evidence," p. 14.

160 Record of the Meeting with Comrade W. Ulbricht on 5 October 1958 (Pervukhin's diary, entry of 11 October 1958), TsKhSD, *rolik* 8875, *fond* 5, *opis* 49, *delo* 8276, p. 9, as quoted by Harrison, "New Archival Evidence," p. 14.

161 "On Several Issues Regarding the Economic and Political Situation in Berlin," Russian Foreign Ministry Archives, delo 022/GDR, Referentyra p GDR, *opis* 4, *por.* 3, *papka* 27, p. 1, as quoted by Harrison, "New Archival Evidence," p. 26.

162 The description of the factors producing a socio-economic crisis in the GDR in 1961 follows Adomeit, *Soviet Risk Taking and Crisis Behavior*, pp. 232-37.

A second factor of the crisis lay in an ambitious investment program. In consequence of the disproportionally higher wartime destruction as compared to West Germany, greater dismantling of equipment by the occupying power, reparations extracted from current production, utilization of forced labor for the benefit of the USSR, monetary losses and unequal trade, the aging capital base in the GDR was in a dismal state. The Seven-Year Plan of 1959-65 sought to create *new* capacities, and to create them *rapidly*. Investment was to increase by 142 billion marks, which exceeded the GDR's total net material product of 141 billion marks! Despite a consumer-oriented rhetoric, the emphasis was put on investment in heavy industry. The means with which the unrealistic goals were to be achieved, as an 1953, were demands by the SED for greater efforts by the working population, higher work norms, tightened labor discipline and cutbacks in private consumption.

The two factors interacted to produce a third: an increasing shortage of skilled labor, due primarily to the westward migration of East German farmers, workers, technicians, and managers. To put things in perspective, in the period from the end of the Second World War until 1961 a total of 3.8 million people had emigrated to West Germany but only 565,000 had migrated to the east – a net los of 3.25 million inhabitants.[163] In the period 1949-61 the population of the GDR had decreased from more than 19 million to little more than 17 million. In 1953, the year of the June workers' revolt, more than 330,000 had left the GDR – the highest annual figure at any time in the state's existence. After a decline in 1954 and 1955, the numbers rose to about 279,000 in 1956. They then fell again to 144,000 in 1959. But despite the then much lower base of the population, the number of migrants increased in 1960 to nearly 200,000 people. In the last months of 1960 and the first six months of 1961 the *monthly* rate rose dramatically to reach between 20,000 and 30,000 people. A critical point had been reached. Disruption of the whole complex planning and production process became endemic since qualified replacements for farm managers, skilled mechanics and engineers in heavy industry, or foremen in the construction industry could no longer be found.

As in 1953 (and later, in 1989-90), the serious consequences were well understood in Moscow. The question as to the stability of the GDR and its repercussions on the Soviet empire in Eastern Europe again moved to center stage in the discussions among and between Soviet and East German officials. As early as August 1958, Yuri Andropov, the then head of the Central Committee department on relations with the communist and workers' parties, wrote an urgent letter to the CC in which he pointed

---

163 Sources for these data are *Die Flucht aus der Sowjetzone und die Sperrmaßnahmen des kommunistischen Regimes vom 13. August 1961* (Bonn: Bundesministerium für gesamtdeutsche Fragen, 1961); *DDR-Handbuch*, 3rd ed., Cologne 1985, esp. p. 419; and Thomas Ammer, "Stichwort: Flucht aus der DDR," *Deutschland-Archiv*, No. 11 (1989), p. 1207.

to the significant rise in the number of highly qualified East German personnel among the refugees, an increase of 50 percent as compared to the previous year. The East German leadership, he complained, asserted that the qualified cadres were leaving for the higher standard of living in West Germany. However, reports from refugees indicated that their motives were often more political than material. "In view of the fact that the issue of the flight of [skilled workers and] the intelligentsia from the GDR has reached a particularly critical phase," he warned, "it would be expedient to discuss this with Comrade Ulbricht, using his stay in the USSR to explain to him our apprehensions on this issue."[164]

Discussions did ensue. In Western interpretation, it has generally been accepted that it was Ulbricht who attempted to push Khrushchev toward taking action on both the specific issue of stopping the outflow of refugees and the larger problem of a peace treaty, and that Khrushchev resisted these pressures. In private conversation between the two leaders on 30 November 1960 in Moscow, however, the Kremlin leader was apparently still intent on separating the two issues, his preference being the conclusion of a peace treaty, with Ulbricht in the interim taking measures to close the Berlin loophole. At a crucial juncture in the conversation, Khrushchev asked Ulbricht about his views on the conclusion of a peace treaty.

N.S. Khrushchev: When will we sign it, in 1961?

W. Ulbricht: No!

N.S. Khrushchev: Why [not]?

W. Ulbricht: We don't have the heart.

N.S. Khrushchev: Politically or economically?

W. Ulbricht: Just economically. Politically I am in favor.[165]

In a strange reversal of positions, the Soviet leader then attempted to convince his East German counterpart that the peace treaty was a top priority; that the risks of a Western military response were small; and that economic consequences could be contained. A peace treaty should be concluded in 1961, either with the Western powers or a separate treaty between the USSR and the GDR, after the planned summit conference with President Kennedy in June. As for the risks of Western military counteraction in response to the conclusion of a separate treaty, Khrushchev told Ulbricht that "we are almost certain that the Western powers will not start a war." On the economic front, he said, "we would lose little economically from it. ...

164 Letter from Yu. Andropov to the CPSU Central Committee, 28 August 1958, TsKhSD, *rolik* 8875, *fond* 5, *opis* 49, *delo* 82, pp. 1-3, as quoted by Harrison, "New Archival Evidence," p. 17 (italics mine).

165 Record of the Meeting between Comrade N.S. Khrushchev and Comrade W. Ulbricht on 30 November 1960, Russian Foreign Ministry Archives, *fond* 0742, *opis* 6, *por.* 4, *papka* 43, Secret. The transcript of the meeting as published by Harrison, "New Archival Evidence," Appendix A.

The existing situation really would essentially be preserved."[166] In contrast, the major benefit of proceeding as he suggested lay in the political realm.

> [P]olitically, our situation would improve, since it would mean a defeat of the West. If we don't sign a peace treaty in 1961, then when? If we don't sign it in 1961, then our prestige will have been dealt a blow and the position of the West, and West Germany in particular, will be strengthened. We could get away with not signing a peace treaty if an interim agreement on West Berlin were concluded. If there is not an interim agreement, then we will sign a peace treaty with the GDR and let them see their defeat. They will not start a war. Of course, in signing a peace treaty, we will have to put our rockets on military alert. But, luckily, our adversaries still haven't gone crazy; they still think, and their nerves still aren't bad.

The priority which Khrushchev gave to political issues, however, by no means indicated a lack of concern about East Germany's economic crisis, her vulnerability to West German pressure, and the costs of empire. Like Brezhnev and Gorbachev subsequently, he was incensed about what he perceived to be unacceptable East German economic dependency on West Germany and (in contrast to his successors) the apparent necessity for the Soviet Union and other Warsaw Pact countries to stabilize economic conditions in the GDR for strategic reasons. Both "our and your fault," he told Ulbricht, "lies in the fact that we did not sufficiently think through and work out economic measures. We should have thought more precisely about liberating the GDR economy from the FRG. ... *We did not know that the GDR is so vulnerable to West Germany. This is not good; we must correct this.*" He blamed Ulbricht because "*you did not offer resistance [to the West Germans], you did not disentangle yourselves, you got used to thinking that Germany was [still] one.*"[167]

Furthermore, the record elucidates in vivid detail Soviet awareness of the costs of empire. It also reveals an acute dilemma: the aversion to subsidize the GDR but at the same time the perceived necessity of having to do so in the interest of safeguarding the Soviet strategic position in the center of Europe and to improve the competitive position of East Germany *vis-à-vis* West Germany. In typically colorful and contradictory Khrushchevian fashion, he told Ulbricht: "We must create a special group in our Gosplan with [East German Minister of Economic Affairs, Bruno] Leuschner, which *will receive everything needed on his demand. There is no other way.* The GDR must develop and maintain the increase [sic] in the standard of living of its population." But Khrushchev then clarified that the "everything" should not to be taken too literlly. He complained to Ulbricht that "*you ask [us] for 68 tons of gold. This is inconceivable. We can't have a situation where you buy goods and we must pay for them. We don't have much gold, and we must keep it for an emergency.*"

166 Ibid.
167 Ibid. (italics mine).

Earlier in the private conversation he had warned: "[Y]ou will not encroach on our gold. Why give you gold? If you need cocoa, coffee, rubber, then buy it in Ceylon or Indonesia. Build something there. But free us from this and don't thrust your hands into our pockets." Ignoring the exigencies of central planning and the close involvement of the Soviet Union in East German economic affairs, Khrushchev complained: "By old habit, you try to do everything through us. *You should have learned how to walk on your own two feet instead of leaning on us all the time.*"[168]

The new evidence also confirms that other Warsaw Pact member countries were not at all pleased by the prospect of a massive subsidization of East Germany in the interest of maintaining the viability of the Soviet empire. At the summit conference of leaders of the socialist bloc, from 3 to 5 August 1961, Khrushchev praised Ulbricht for his "heroic job" in the construction of socialism in the GDR, notably the completion of collectivization of agriculture ("you cannot build socialism without it") and without referring directly to the Polish and Czechoslovak party leaders Gomulka and Novotny he chided them for "national narrow-mindedness" and excessive "enthusiasm about peaceful construction" to the detriment of the interests of the socialist community as a whole. He then proceeded to ask two questions, which he both answered in the affirmative: (1) Do we need the GDR as the first line of defense? (2) Do we have to maintain the high living standards in the GDR even at the expense of improvements in the Soviet Union and Eastern European countries?[169] For the benefit of the Polish and Czechoslovak comrades he painted the likely consequences of a failure to support the GDR in stark colors. A lowering of living standards of the GDR to the East European level would lead to East Germany being swallowed by West Germany and would create an intolerable strategic situation: "[T]he Bundeswehr would advance to the Polish border ... to the border with Czechoslovakia ... nearer to our Soviet border."[170]

On the surface the November 1960 exchanges appear to indicate that it was Khrushchev who was pushing for political action despite economic constraints, whereas Ulbricht was attempting to put the brakes on Soviet political initiatives because of economic considerations. However, to repeat, it would appear that the East German leader at that point was more concerned about the practical solution of the problem of open borders around Berlin than about the peace treaty. In general, it was Ulbricht who was trying to persuade Khrushchev to take unilateral action and that the Soviet leader wanted to find solutions within a Four Power framework. This

---

168 Ibid. (italics mine).

169 Transcript of summit conference, TsKhSD, *fond* 5, *opis* 49, *delo* 365, 11. 165, 168, 170, as quoted by Zubok, "The Berlin Crisis," p. 31.

170 Ibid.

basic asymmetry was clearly recognized by Pervukhin. In a "top secret" letter to Foreign Minister Gromyko, he wrote:

> Trying to liquidate the remnants of the occupation period as soon as possible, our German friends sometimes demonstrate *impatience* and a somewhat *one-sided approach* to this problem, not always heeding the interests of the entire socialist camp or the international situation at the given moment. Evidence for this, for example, is their effort to stop the free movement between the GDR and West Berlin *as soon as possible by any means*, which in the present conditions would complicate carrying out the struggle for a peace treaty. Recognizing the correctness of our position that the liquidation of the remains of the occupation period is possible only on the basis of a peace treaty, our friends therefore urge a speedy conclusion of a peace treaty with the GDR.[171]

A decision in principle to close the borders was apparently reached at the 3-5 August 1961 meeting of Warsaw Pact leaders in Moscow. The extensive but still incomplete record does not reveal whether a final decision was made at the conference. There is no mention of a wall to be built. No reference exists as to whether the Soviet and East German leaders met separately before, during, or after the conference to discuss details of implementation.[172] Ulbricht was to state later that the meeting had agreed "to carry out the various measures gradually," which could mean that the details were left up to him as long as there would be no serious complications.[173] Whatever the case may be, by the summer of 1961 Khrushchev had become convinced that drastic unilateral action to close the borders had become inevitable if the empire was to be maintained and that the green light had to be given to the East German leadership to act accordingly. The measures adopted had profound consequences.

8. Consolidation of the Soviet Empire and the "Correlation of Forces"

In a letter written one month after the imposition of border controls, Ulbricht was to inform Khrushchev that the measures of 13 August had been a tremendous success. Not only "must [I] say that the adversary undertook fewer countermeasures than expected," but the following aims had been achieved:

> (1) The protection of the GDR against the organization of a civil war and military provocations from West Berlin.

---

171 Letter from Ambassador Pervukhin to Foreign Minister Gromyko, 19 May 1961, Top Secret, Russian Foreign Ministry Archives, *fond*: Referentyra po GDR, *opis* 6, *por*. 34, *inv*. 193/3, Vol. 1, *papka* 46. The letter as published by Harrison, "New Archival Evidence," Appendix D (italics mine).

172 On these issues see Harrison, "New Archival Evidence," pp. 47-51.

173 Letter from Ulbricht and the SED Central Committee Delegation to the CPSU Twenty-second Congress in Moscow to Khrushchev, 30 October 1961, SED Central Archives, NL 182/1206. Text as published by Harrison, "New Archival Evidence," Appendix K.

(2) The cessation of the economic and cultural undermining of the capital of the GDR by the West Berlin swamp.
(3) A change in the political situation will occur. The Bonn government has understood that the policy of revenge and the plan to roll back the GDR ... have been destroyed for all time. This will later have great effects on the tactics of the Western powers regarding Poland and Czechoslovakia.
(4) The authority of the GDR state, which was weakened by its tolerance towards the subversive measures from West Berlin, was strengthened and a revolution in the thinking of the population of the capital and the GDR has occurred.[174]

Soviet analysts agreed. They noted that "the rug was pulled from under the feet of the adventurist elements, who had hoped to kindle a military conflict at the open border between the GDR and West Berlin."[175] In West Germany, they asserted, Adenauer's policies from positions of strength, or *Politik der Stärke*, came to be seen as unworkable. The building of the wall "significantly consolidated the domestic situation in the GDR and contributed to the successful building of socialism in that country."[176] In fact, that process was regarded as being so successful that the GDR came to be considered, in the 1970s and 1980s, as politically the most stable and economically and technologically the most advanced country in the Soviet bloc. From Moscow's perspective, the GDR had clearly turned from a liability into an important asset. It retained its position as a strategic outpost, but one that no longer needed to be subsidized, and was perceived to contribute to making the Soviet empire in Eastern Europe more viable. However, as will be argued in subsequent chapters, two developments marred Moscow's perceptions of fundamental progress achieved in the consolidation of empire, one rather predictable and consistent with the East German success story, the other seemingly contradicting it: (1) the rising self-confidence of the SED leaders, of both Ulbricht and Honecker, made the GDR a much more difficult country to deal with, and (2) despite its apparent success, the GDR was regarded as drifting again into dangerous dependencies on West Germany.

---

174 Letter from Ulbricht to Khrushchev, 15 September 1961, SED Central Archives, Central Committee files, Büro Walter Ulbricht, J IV, 2/202/130. Text as published by Harrison, "New Archival Evidence," Appendix I.

175 A. S. Grossman, "Granitsa mira," *Voprosy istorii*, No. 10 (1969), p. 201; V. G. Trukhanovskii, ed., *Istoriia mezhdunarodnykh otnoshenii i vneshnei politiki SSSR, Vol. 3: 1945-1963 gg.* (Moscow: Mezhdunarodnye otnosheniia, 1964), pp. 211-212; N. N. Inozemtsev, *Mezhdunarodnye otnosheniia posle vtoroi mirovoi voiny, Vol. 3: 1956-1964 gg.* (Moscow: Politizdat, 1962), pp. 523-34.

176 Grossman, "Granitsa mira," p. 201; similarly Georgii M. Akopov, *Zapadnyi Berlin. Problemy i resheniia* (Moscow: Mezhdunarodnye otnosheniia, 1974), pp. 164-255; and Viktor Vysotskii, *Zapadnyi Berlin i ego mesto v sisteme sovremmenykh mezhdunarodnykh otnoshenii* (Moscow: Mysl, 1971), pp. 237-45.

Soviet perceptions of the important progress that was being made in the consolidation of the empire were also closely tied yet again to the correlation of forces. One of the most important lessons which the Soviet leaders had derived from the Berlin crisis was that of the continued importance of military power, both conventional and nuclear, in international affairs. As a result, as other instruments of exerting influence and retaining imperial control were becoming dull, the military knife was being sharpened in Moscow. Strong attempts were being made by successive Soviet leaderships to change the military balance in their favor. In the early post-war period, the Soviet Union had achieved preponderance in conventional weapons. In both East and West, the asymmetries were generally perceived to be so wide that the Soviet Union was considered to be able to overrun Western Europe. To counteract this advantage, the United States, beginning in 1947, began to build a countervailing force in the form of nuclear weapons. But Western Europe was not to escape its predicament as "hostage" as the USSR, too, transformed itself into a formidable nuclear power. This transformation began at the theater nuclear level in the late 1950s and early 1960s. It was extended thereafter to intermediate-range nuclear forces, with the deployment of a large bomber and missile force. After the Cuban missile crisis, the military build-up was to include intercontinental forces, the Soviet Union achieving rough strategic parity with the United States by the end of the 1960s. Finally, in the 1970s, the Soviet Union embarked on a program of developing capabilities for intervention and power projection far beyond its borders.

The improvement of the Soviet position in the "correlation of forces" was duly noted by Khrushchev. As he was to say later: "No longer were we contaminated by Stalin's fear. No longer did we look at the world through his eyes. Now it was our enemies who trembled in *their* boots. Thanks to our missiles, we could deliver a nuclear bomb to a target at any place in the world. No longer was the industrial heartland of the United States invulnerable to our counterattack."[177] Khrushchev continued: "Of course, we tried to derive maximum advantage from the fact that we were the first to launch our rockets into space. We wanted to exert pressure on American militarists – and also to influence the minds of more reasonable politicians."[178]

Pressure based on vague nuclear threats was exerted not only on American "militarists" but also, and perhaps even more so, on *European* policy makers and public opinion. This design to safeguard Soviet security and expand Soviet influence was first used during the Suez crisis in 1956, when Khrushchev issued nuclear threats against Britain and France. It was also applied during the protracted controversy over Berlin between 1958 and 1961, when he threatened that, in the event of war, NATO

---

177 *Khrushchev Remembers*, p. 53.

178 Ibid.

military bases in various European countries would be destroyed by Soviet nuclear strikes (in Italy, "even if they are in orange groves," or in Greece, in "olive groves");[179] that Germany would be "reduced to dust";[180] and that "the very existence of the population of West Germany would be called in question."[181]

Khrushchev, in retrospect, held such threats to have been effective: If a third world war were to be unleashed, he quoted Adenauer as having said numerous times, West Germany would be the first country to perish. "I was pleased to hear this, and Adenauer was absolutely right in what he said," Khrushchev continued. "For him to be making public statements was a great achievement on our part. Not only were we keeping our number one enemy in line, but Adenauer was helping to keep our other enemies in line, too."[182]

In Khrushchev's perspective, significant gains had been made in Berlin and Germany. The West had "swallowed one bitter pill."[183] Provided the United States could be put under more direct pressure and confronted with a more credible threat, and its sense of vulnerability raised to the European level, conditions in Central Europe would perhaps get "more mature," and the West might then be prepared to swallow another bitter pill. Undoubtedly, this was part of the reasoning underlying Khrushchev's attempt to improve Soviet strategic capabilities and deploy intermediate-range nuclear missiles in Cuba.

The lesson which Brezhnev and his colleagues drew from this failed venture was not that military power in the nuclear age was ineffective. In their perspective even *greater efforts* had to be made to catch up with and overtake the United States in the military competition. Military power came to be regarded by them as one of the main tools with which to advance the claim to political equality with the United States and play a stronger role in global politics. In Eastern Europe, as demonstrated by the Warsaw Pact intervention in Czechoslovakia in 1968, military power remained necessary for enforcing discipline. And towards the Western European countries, above all West Germany, it served as an instrument with which to win acceptance of the *status quo* in Eastern Europe, establish a code of conduct in their relations with the "socialist community" (notably "non-interference in internal affairs"), and influence their domestic and foreign policies in directions favorable to the Soviet Union. In conformity with such notions, Soviet analysts later were to write that "In

---

179 *Pravda*, 12 August 1961.

180 Ibid., 8 August 1961.

181 Ibid., 12 August 1961.

182 *Khrushchev Remembers*, p. 569.

183 This is a phrase used by Khrushchev; ibid., p. 509. The same metaphor occurs in reference to the assumptions of Khrushchev and his supporters in the Presidium of the CPSU, in Oleg Penkovsky, *The Penkovsky Papers*, transl. P. Deriabin, with an introduction and commentary by Frank Gibney and a foreword by Edward Crankshaw (London: Collins, 1965), p. 161.

conjunction with the liquidation of the strategic invulnerability of the United States, the belief of the countries of Western Europe in the so-called 'nuclear guarantees' of their trans-oceanic partner was being eroded. Europe began to recognize what a catastrophe a contemporary rocket-nuclear war would be for the continent. From this stems the general interest of the Europeans to avoid a military conflict, to abstain from military-political confrontation, and to develop diverse contacts between Eastern and Western Europe."[184]

To summarize Soviet attitudes and policies on the German problem under Khrushchev and to look ahead to the Brezhnev era, the building of the Berlin wall had alleviated East Germany's perennial manpower and currency drain, enhanced the country's economic viability, induced the population to come to terms with communist rule, and improved the GDR's chances for political legitimacy. To the extent that the Soviet leaders were still concerned about possible Western challenges to its empire in Eastern Europe, they could find reassurance in the fact that the wall, and with it the post-war borders and order in Europe, were reliably guarded by the East German armed forces and border troops, with the Soviet army in the background. There was a new confidence in Moscow that was reflected in Soviet attitudes towards East-West relations. Detente in the late 1960s and early 1970s was authoritatively explained and widely believed in Moscow to be the result of significant "changes in the correlation of world forces," meaning primarily a shift in the military balance in favor of the Soviet Union.[185] As Georgi Arbatov, one of chief theoreticians of East-West detente claimed, if the "imperialist" powers were now becoming partners in efforts to lessen the threat of war and normalize relations with the socialist countries, this was "not because of any change in the class nature of their policy."[186] It was because of the fact that these powers have had "to adapt their internal and foreign policies to objective realities" – the new "correlation of forces" – which, in turn, had "resulted from the activity of the Communist Party, the Soviet state, and the entire Soviet people to strengthen the economic and defense might of the country and to consolidate the unity of Soviet society and the socialist community."[187] The Kremlin leaders' new confidence as well as a new stridency were apparent also in the Soviet Union's relations with West Germany. Bonn's Ostpolitik, like detente, was seen by them as another example of the West's adaptation to the "new realities."

---

184 A. O. Chubar'ian, ed., *Evropa – veka. Problemy mira i bezopasnosti* (Moscow: Mezhdunarodnye otnosheniia, 1985), p. 135.

185 Brezhnev's report to the Twenty-fifth CPSU Congress, *Pravda*, 25 February 1976.

186 Georgi Arbatov, "O Sovetsko-Amerikanskikh otnosheniakh," *Kommunist*, No. 3 (1973), p. 105.

187 Ibid.

9. Soviet Responses to West Germany's Ostpolitik

In fact, the growth of Soviet military power, the consolidation of the GDR, and the waning prospects of German unification did induce West Germany to modify its policies towards the East. Its standard position to the effect that relaxation of tension and "normalization" of relations in Europe could only take place as a result of German unification became untenable. Reunification, as West German policy makers realized, could only occur in the context of detente, not prior to it. Thus, a *modus vivendi* had to be reached first not only with the Soviet Union but also with its dependencies in Eastern Europe, including the GDR.

Some modifications were put into effect in the period from 1966 to 1969 by the Grand Coalition government of Kurt-Georg Kiesinger (CDU) and Willy Brandt (SPD). The modifications included the willingness of the federal government to enter into negotiations with all the European communist states for a "normalization" of relations, including the establishment of diplomatic relations; consent to the establishment of contacts with the GDR at all governmental and non-governmental levels; inclusion of the GDR in an agreement on the renunciation of force; abandonment of claims that Germany continued to exist as a "legal entity in the borders of 1937"; and adoption of the position that the 1938 Munich agreement was concluded by the threat of force and was invalid *ex post facto*.

However, from the vantage point of the Soviet leadership under Brezhnev, Kosygin, and Podgorny, such modifications were both inadequate and potentially dangerous. They did not go far enough in the direction of the recognition of the GDR as a separate state but too far in encouraging the Eastern European governments to normalize political relations and benefit from the West German *Wirtschaftswunder*. The result was a campaign of severe pressure on Bonn and the attempt to isolate West Germany both in her relations towards the East and within the Western alliance. The campaign had several facets.

First, the Soviet leaders construed a "USA-FRG axis" as a major threat to European security and world peace by declaring that "each one of the peculiar partners conspires to use the other for its own goals," the United States using the German problem as a "pretext with which to continue the stationing of troops in Europe and as a lever with which to influence the politics and economics of Western Europe, and the Federal Republic using the United States for the realization of its revanchist plans to change the map of Europe."[188]

Second, French President Charles de Gaulle's NATO initiatives, France's exit from the military organization of the alliance, and the ensuing Franco-Soviet

---

188 Brezhnev at the Twenty-third CPSU Congress, *Materialy III-ogo s"ezda KPSS* (Moscow: Politizdat, 1966), p. 26.

rapprochement were given exemplary character. West Germany was told to follow the French lead.

Third, the Soviet leaders appealed to latent anti-German attitudes in both Eastern and Western Europe, reminding the "peoples of Europe" that there was still a "threat stemming from the aspirations of the West German revenge seekers."[189]

Fourth, the Soviet leaders refused to differentiate between the major political parties in the Federal Republic. Although Brezhnev, at the Karlovy Vary Conference of European Communist and Workers' Parties in April 1967, had endorsed cooperation between communists and social democrats, in practice the SPD was excluded as a possible partner. The ideological justification used was the charge that after the promulgation of its 1958 Godesberg program the party had fallen into the hands of "rightist leaders."[190]

Fifth, Moscow exploited the fact that in the period from 1966 until 1969 the rightist *Nationaldemokratische Partei Deutschlands* (NPD) was able to poll more than 5 percent of the vote in the parliamentary elections in some of the German *Länder* and gain representation in the state legislature. The Soviet leaders asserted not only that neo-Nazism was on the rise but also that the federal German government had "much in common with the political aims of the neo-Nazis of all shadings."[191]

A sixth issue turned against the West German government was Bonn's presumed quest to gain access to nuclear weapons and, related to this, its alleged refusal to sign the nuclear non-proliferation treaty.

A final argument levelled against the West German government and its Ostpolitik was the assertion that, due to its "militarist," "revanchist," and "neo-Nazi" character, the FRG could "not claim the same equal status" as other sovereign states.[192] The Soviet government gave this argument an ominous twist by demanding, in essence, a right of intervention in German affairs. It did so by referring to Articles 53 and 107 of the United Nations Charter which, as *leges speciales* to Article 2 (*lex generalis*), sanction coercive measures against a former enemy state of the anti-Hitler coalition. On this basis, it threatened that "the Soviet Union together with other peace loving states is prepared, in accordance with the obligations emanating from the Potsdam

---

189 Ibid., p. 27.

190 See, for instance, the analysis by V.G. Vasin, *Godesbergskaia programma SDPG. Otkrytoe otrochenie Marksizma* (Moscow: Politizdat 1963).

191 Soviet Government Declaration on the State of Affairs in the Federal Republic of Germany, *Neues aus der UdSSR*, Soviet embassy, Bonn, 1 February 1967.

192 Aide memoire of the Soviet Government to the Government of the German Federal Republic on the Question of Renunciation of Force, 5 July 1968, *Neues Deutschland*, 14 July 1968.

Agreement and other international agreements, to take, if necessary, all the measures which arise from the state of affairs in the Federal Republic of Germany."[193]

What, then, were the results of this propagandistic assault on Bonn? By and large, they were negligible. By 1969 it was evident that the attempt at isolating West Germany within the Western alliance had failed. De Gaulle refused to bend the Franco-Soviet *entente* into an anti-German direction. The Federal Republic adhered to its close ties with the United States while continuing to build on the Franco-German relationship, and it made new successful efforts at deepening Western European integration. At the same time, the electorate was ready for a change of power in Bonn – a fact that had much to do with the internal divisions and the weakness of leadership in the CDU but very little with Soviet policy. As a result, any "scientifically based" approach in Moscow sooner or later would have had to abandon the approach of circumventing and isolating the government in Bonn and of refusing to deal with the main political forces in the country. Conditions in Eastern Europe were also "ripe" for new Soviet perspectives and policies on Germany. Before the Warsaw Pact military intervention in Czechoslovakia in August 1968, "revisionism," reformism, and the rising attractiveness of West German social democratic ideas and West German capital had posed a challenge to imperial control. The intervention, perhaps paradoxically, untied the hands of the Soviet leadership and facilitated a more favorable response to the Ostpolitik of the new coalition government of SPD and FDP, formed in October 1969.

In his inaugural address, Chancellor Willy Brandt, for the first time in the history of official government statements to the Bundestag, spoke of "two states in Germany." The Federal Republic was thus taking another step towards acceptance of the post-war "realities." The new government, almost immediately after coming to power, also proceeded to sign the nuclear non-proliferation treaty. Transformation of Soviet military preponderance into political influence, stabilization of the empire, and the achievement of a *modus vivendi* based on the division of Germany now appeared to be within easy reach of Soviet policy in Europe. To accelerate the process, Brezhnev committed himself to new appraisals of West Germany by declaring that the formation of the coalition government led by the SPD represented a "significant change in the constellation of political forces in the German Federal Republic."[194] Similarly, the communiqué of the Warsaw Pact summit conference of December 1969 noted trends in West Germany "directed at a realistic policy of cooperation and understanding" in Europe and characterized Bonn's signature of the non-proliferation treaty as a "positive element."[195]

---

193 *Neues aus der UdSSR*, Soviet embassy, Bonn, 1 February 1967.

194 At a Soviet-Czechoslovak friendship meeting, *Pravda*, 29 October 1969.

195 *Pravda*, 4 December 1969.

In the course of the 1970s, West Germany fully participated in the process of East-West detente. It joined the Conference on Security and Cooperation in Europe (CSCE), concluded treaties for the normalization of relations with the Soviet Union, Czechoslovakia, and Poland, set its relationship with the GDR on a new footing, facilitated the September 1971 Quadripartite Agreement on Berlin, played an active role in arms control negotiations, such as the Mutual Balanced Forces Reductions (MBFR) talks in Vienna, provided an important impetus to East-West economic cooperation and boasted some of the highest growth rates in trade of the Western industrialized countries with the USSR. It is not surprising, therefore, that West Germany in the 1970s became an *interlocuteur privilégié* of the Soviet Union in the West.

Soviet analysts predicted that the 1970s would be a period of "broad deployment of political forces in all directions" with an in all likelihood favorable outcome because of the fact that "the majority of the West German population maintains the position of recognizing realities and desires peace and good-neighborly relations with all the peoples of Europe."[196] Indeed, in retrospect, one can classify the 1970s as a golden era in Soviet-West German relations. Soviet analysts were generous in their praise. The relations between the socialist countries and the Federal Republic in the 1970s had been an "important factor of stability and good-neighborliness in Europe."[197] They pointed in particular to the signing of the August 1970 Moscow treaty and its provisions on the non-use of force between the USSR and the FRG; the recognition by the FRG of the European borders and the European territorial realities created at the end of the Second World War; and her contribution to the development of detente.[198]

What, then, is the significance of this era in historical perspective? The Soviet Union and West Germany, it would seem, were engaged in a futile effort at normalizing the abnormal. It is true that some of their interests coincided. They both wanted to reduce the risk of military conflict in Central Europe. They saw benefits in the expansion of trade. Yet their goals remained fundamentally different. The Soviet Union had no intention of permitting a spillover of the improvement in political relations to the ideological sphere. Notwithstanding CSCE, Moscow ruled out any "interference in the internal affairs of the socialist countries." As the continuing military build-up and the lack of progress in the MBFR talks demonstrated, it also

---

196 D. E. Mel'nikov, "Vneshniaia politika FRG," in *Federativnaia Respublika Germanii*, published in the series *Ekonomika i politika stran sovremmenogo kapitalizma* (Moscow: Mezhdunarodyne otnosheniia, 1974), p. 463 (italics mine).

197 See, for instance, V. Iu. Kuz'min, *Vazhnyi faktor stabil'nosti i dobrososedstva v Evrope: sotsialisticheskie strany i FRG v 70-e gody* (Moscow: Mezhdunarodnye otnosheniia, 1980).

198 B.M. Khalosha, *Voenno-politicheskie soiuzy imperializma: osnovnye osobennosti i tendentsiia v 70-kh – nachale 80-kh godov* (Moscow: Nauka, 1982), pp. 271-72.

objected to an extension of detente to the military competition. Specifically on the German problem, it continued to insist on the idea of the existence of two separate German states, on the permanence of the post-war European borders, and on West Berlin as a special entity that was not to be governed by the Federal Republic, with ties between the two entities to be kept at a minimum.

West German political leaders and public opinion, in contrast, hoped that the ideological rigidities in the Soviet bloc would soften and that both the military preponderance of the Warsaw Pact and the pace of the arms competition in Europe would be reduced. Regarding the German problem, they expected that the improvement of political relations would create favorable conditions for overcoming the division of Germany and the continent – a fact underlined by the "Letter on German Unity" attached to the 1970 Moscow treaty.[199] They also expected that the viability of West Berlin would be enhanced by an expansion of contacts between the city and West Germany and by its inclusion in the country's trade agreements with the USSR and other members of Comecon.

The existence of a wide chasm between Soviet and West German expectations connected with the "normalization" of relations can now be corroborated on the basis of new evidence. Two weeks prior to the signing of the Moscow treaty, and as part of the preparations for the removal of Ulbricht from the office of party chief, Brezhnev told Erich Honecker in private conversation in Moscow: "We don't have any erroneous ideas about Brandt and West German social democracy. Illusions are out of place." There wasn't a single example of a social democratic party having embarked on a socialist transformation, and such a development would not occur in West Germany either. West Germany, however, aimed at the transformation and liquidation of the GDR. In that respect, there was essentially

> no difference between Brandt and [Bavarian prime minister and CSU chairman Franz Josef] Strauß. Perhaps one can't put it like that now. But it is true. Both are for the capitalist system, both are for the liquidation of the GDR. Brandt is under ... pressure. He has to come to agreements with us. He hopes in this way to realize his goal in relation to the GDR, the social-democratization of the GDR.[200]

The West Germans, Brezhnev continued, "are strong economically. They are trying to gain influence in the GDR, to swallow the GDR, one way or another." The Soviet

---

199 The letter was delivered by the West German embassy in Moscow to the Soviet foreign ministry shortly before the signing of the August 1970 Soviet-West German treaty on the renunciation of force. Moscow officially acknowledged its existence only in April 1972, as the Bundestag was debating ratification of the treaty; see Michael J. Sodaro, *Moscow, Germany, and the West from Khrushchev to Gorbachev*, Studies of the Harriman Institute (Ithaca, N.Y.: Cornell University Press, 1990), p. 185.

200 Record of a Meeting Between L.I. Brezhnev and Erich Honecker on 28 July 1970. The document is from the Central Party Archives of the SED, publ. by Peter Przybylski, *Tatort Politbüro* [Vol. I]: *Die Akte Honecker* (Berlin: Rowohlt, 1991), Doc. 15, p. 287.

Union and the socialist community, however, would safeguard the results of victory in World War II. They would neither permit a development that would weaken their position in the GDR nor permit an *Anschluß* of the GDR. "On the contrary," he predicted, "the trench between the GDR and the FRG will become deeper."[201] This prediction was tied to a normative statement: "*There is, there cannot be, and it should not come to a process of rapprochement between the FRG and the GDR.*"[202]

Brezhnev made equally blunt statements about the Federal Republic's position concerning the "special nature" of intra-German relations. Special relations between the two Germanys were unacceptable. The GDR "*is part of the socialist camp. That will never be different.* What, then, is the point about the talk [in the FRG] that the GDR 'cannot be a foreign country to us'? Is it a state that is independent from West Germany or not?"[203]

Finally, in a meeting between top leaders of the CPSU and the SED, held less than two weeks after the signing of the Moscow treaty, the Soviet party chief tried to assuage "Comrade Walter [Ulbricht's] disquiet concerning West Berlin." He (Brezhnev) had told Brandt that limited compromises on the issue were possible only if two conditions were met. Brandt had to recognize, first, that "West Berlin does not belong to the FRG and will never belong to it" and, second, that a "political presence of the FRG in West Berlin will not be accepted."[204]

Brezhnev's statements reveal an uncompromising Soviet commitment to maintaining the division of Germany. But the viability of the Soviet Union's stance on the German problem continued to depend on the viability of the GDR. In retrospect, this was recognized by, among others, Valentin Falin, one of the chief architects of the Soviet response to Brandt's Ostpolitik. "At the beginning of the 1970s," he wrote, he was optimistic on that score. "I thought that [the GDR] had reserves in order to solve the existing problems and to correct mistakes that had been committed."[205] Brezhnev and other top Soviet leaders were of the same opinion. However, as will be shown in the next section, they were also becoming increasingly concerned about internal developments in the GDR and went as far as drawing the conclusion that Ulbricht was a satrap who was neither able to correct nor even willing to admit "mistakes."

---

201 Ibid., p. 287.

202 Ibid. (italics mine).

203 Ibid. (italics mine).

204 Excerpts from a secret protocol on the meeting between a delegation of the CC of the CPSU and a delegation of the CC of the SED on 21 August 1970 in Moscow. The document is from the Central Party Archives of the SED, published by Peter Przybylski, *Tatort Politbüro* [Vol. I]: *Die Akte Honecker* (Berlin: Rowohlt, 1991), Doc. 16, p. 290.

205 Valentin Falin, *Politische Erinnerungen* (Munich: Droemer Knaur, 1993), p. 64.

10. Soviet Responses to East Germany's Assertiveness

Ulbricht regarded detente as a threat to East Germany's stability. This perception was not lessened by the fact that, after 1969, the SPD had formed a coalition government in Bonn. Whenever the SED had felt confident enough to compete with the West German Social Democrats for the hearts and minds of *all* Germans, and in the process had opened a horror chamber: the long-declared-dead *Geist des Sozialdemokratismus*, the ghost or spirit of social democracy, had risen in the GDR and haunted the communist party faithful.[206] The ghost had appeared in full view in the 1966 SPD-SED correspondence and projected speakers' exchange, and it was glimpsed during the 1970 visit by chancellor Willy Brandt to Erfurt, who was given an enthusiastic welcome, foreshadowing the equally exuberant welcome given to chancellor Kohl in Dresden in December 1989.

As East-West detente began to develop in 1969, therefore, Ulbricht and other orthodox East European communist leaders were apprehensive and suspicious that the Soviet Union would move too fast and too far in its rapprochement with West Germany, thereby forcing them to participate in a process which they thought they could not easily manage.[207] In particular, there was anxiety in East Berlin that Moscow would make deals with the three Western allies and West Germany at the expense of East German interests; abandon the joint Soviet-East German demand for full recognition of the GDR under international law; fail to support the GDR in its claim to codify the status of West Berlin as an "independent political entity"; refuse to endorse the East German quest for exclusive rights in matters concerning transit to Berlin; and continue to exercise rights on matters concerning Berlin and Germany as a whole, thus limiting East Germany sovereignty.

The East German party leader, in consequence, tried to define the Warsaw Pact's rules of engagement with the West and bend them in a more restrictive and ideologically orthodox direction than was thought expedient in Moscow. He insisted that the West, and notably West Germany, meet some or all of the following conditions before any "normalization" of relations could take place: (1) the codification of the territorial *status quo,* with the post-war borders in Europe to be declared immutable (as opposed to inviolable); (2) the freezing of the post-war socio-economic and political *status quo* in Europe; (3) full international legal recognition of the GDR; (4) a change in status of West Berlin to make the city more dependent on East Germany; (5) full West German respect for a separate East German citizenship;

---

206 *Geist* in German has two meanings. It can be translated either as spirit or as ghost. The *Sozialdemokratismus*, or "social democratism," was communist pejorative usage.

207 Concerning the Soviet-East German rift in the late 1960s and early 1970s, see Gerhard Wettig, *Community and Conflict in the Socialist Camp: The Soviet Union, East Germany, and the German Problem, 1965-1972*, trans. Edwina Moreton and Hannes Adomeit (London: C. Hurst, 1975).

(6) abandonment of the Federal German legal position that East Germans had an automatic right to West German citizenship.

As evidence from the SED's archives has confirmed, the differences between the USSR and the GDR over detente and Soviet-West German rapprochement led to a crisis of confidence in Soviet-East German relations that reached its high point in the winter of 1970 and the spring of 1971 and that was (temporarily) resolved by the replacement of Ulbricht and the appointment of Erich Honecker as new party chief. The archives again provide fascinating insights into the thinking of the Soviet leadership regarding the German problem and the quality of relations between the imperial center and the periphery.

Contrary to public appearances and fraternal kisses, the relationship between Brezhnev and Ulbricht was tense. In July 1970, in private conversation with Honecker, the Soviet leader even admitted to traumatic experiences.

> You know, back in 1964 [at his] *dacha* [in Döllnsee], he [Ulbricht] simply move[ed] my delegation (Tikhonov and others) aside, pushe[d] me into a small room, and start[ed] lecturing me about what is wrong with us and exemplary with you [in East Germany]. It was hot. I was perspiring. He didn't care. I only noticed that he wanted to give me instructions as to how we must work and govern, [he didn't] even let me speak. His whole arrogance became apparent there, his disregard for the thinking and the experience of others.[208]

Brezhnev generalized from this unpleasant personal experience and lamented the tendency in East Germany to portray the GDR as "the best model of socialism" and to assert that "Everything that is being done is done better in the GDR, everyone should learn from the GDR, GDR socialism exerts influence on other countries, and it does everything right." This arrogance, he complained, was insulting to other socialist countries, Poland and Czechoslovakia for instance, but also to the Soviet Union. "We are concerned about this, and this has to be changed; the Politburo of the SED [and] you have to change it."[209]

The archival record also clarifies that Brezhnev and his successors found the East German arrogance particularly irksome because of the GDR's dual dependency – economically on West Germany and in security terms on the Soviet Union. Concerning the first issue, as Khrushchev had already noted, the GDR was economically more dependent on West Germany than was politically expedient. By 1970 the country was also in debt to the Soviet Union and other CMEA countries. Several members in the SED Politburo had begun to realize that Ulbricht's economic policies conducted under the heading of the New Economic System were overly

208 Record of a Meeting Between L.I. Brezhnev and Erich Honecker on 28 July 1970. The document is from the Central Party Archives of the SED, published by Przybylski, *Tatort Politbüro* Vol. I, Doc. 15, p. 287. The original mixes past and present tense.

209 Ibid.

ambitious. His policies, designed to catch up with and overtake West Germany in labor productivity, were predicated on an acceleration of scientific-technological progress. But the huge investments in computer technology and other advanced products and processes exceeded East Germany's resources. They failed to enhance the country's technological competitiveness or to benefit its economy. Significant distortions were the result. Consumer goods production declined. Shortages in supply occurred. The construction of housing was being curtailed.[210]

A faction in the Politburo attacked the "high unplanned indebtedness to the CMEA countries ... and to the FRG and West Berlin" and criticized goals such as "a 10 percent increase in labor productivity and production per annum for [the realization of which] the preconditions are in reality lacking."[211] Reports by informants in the SED Politburo and Pyotr Abrasimov, the Soviet ambassador in East Berlin, made Brezhnev aware of the deterioration of economic conditions in the GDR. As a result, he told Honecker in private: "For us the important thing is the strengthening of the positions of the GDR, its further positive economic development, and a corresponding increase in the conditions of life of the population [and] the working class of the GDR. One should concentrate on these tasks."[212] He obviously thought that Honecker would be more willing and better prepared to perform these tasks.

Brezhnev's second major irritation was connected with a paradox of imperial control. The periphery may completely be dependent on the center for protection, but the provincial governor may nevertheless act contrary to the center's preferences and even refuse to carry out instructions. This typically raises the problem of choosing a suitable successor. The center's emissaries then tend to get embroiled in the domestic power struggles at the periphery. A case in point is Moscow's involvement in Ulbricht's resignation from his position as first party secretary and his "retirement" to the more ceremonial role as president (*Vorsitzender des Staatsrats*).

Expressing his irritation with Ulbricht, the Soviet party leader assured would-be successor Honecker: "I tell you quite openly that it will not be possible for him to govern by leaving us out and to take ill-conceived steps against you and other comrades in the Politburo."[213] Clearly with a view to a possible replacement of Ulbricht with Honecker, he reminded the latter of the GDR's complete dependency on the USSR for protection: "*We do have troops [stationed] with you [in the GDR].*

---

210 Przybylski, *Tatort Politbüro*, Vol. I, p. 103.

211 Paul Verner and Willi Stoph at the plenary meeting of the SED Central Committee, 9-10 December 1970, as quoted by Przybylski, *Tatort Politbüro*, Vol. I, p. 105.

212 Record of the Brezhnev-Honecker meeting of 28 July 1970, Przybylski, *Tatort Politbüro*, Vol. I, Doc. 15, p. 284.

213 Ibid., p. 281.

Erich, I tell you frankly, and never forget this: The GDR cannot exist without us, without the S[oviet] U[nion], its power and strength. Without us there is no GDR."[214]

It was not only the center but also Moscow's emissaries in East Berlin who got directly involved in the power struggle. As reported by Yuli Kvitsinsky (then a foreign ministry official at the Soviet embassy in Bonn and an active participant in the quadripartite negotiations on Berlin, with a previous appointment in East Berlin), ambassador Pyotr Abrasimov was in the picture regarding the struggle for power in the highest echelon of the East German leadership. His relations with Honecker and his supporters had become close over time, and he was kept up to date about all steps taken. This was no secret to the other members of the SED Politburo and it conveyed the impression that a possible change of power would take place at least with Moscow's silent approval.[215]

However, some members of the Politburo in Moscow were against Ulbricht's replacement. The then Chairman of the Supreme Soviet, Nikolai Podgorny, is said to have voiced especially strong opposition to such a step. Brezhnev, too, despite all his complaints about Ulbricht, was still hesitant about having him removed from office, stating at a meeting between high ranking officials of the SED and the CPSU in mid-August 1970 that "We have recently received several signals and rumors that, let us say, frictions and quarrels have arisen in your Politburo." However, he saw as yet "no reason for change." Instead, he appealed to the SED to strengthen the "collective" and the "unity of leadership," and he told Ulbricht and his colleagues to work out their differences – who, in turn, promised that they would behave.[216] Dark clouds were thus brewing over Abrasimov's head. Kvitsinsky realized this when Gromyko, who was otherwise cautious on personnel issues, once unexpectedly said in his presence that he had apparently been mistaken about Abrasimov, personally and politically. Instead of carrying out the line of the CPSU Central Committee, the ambassador had participated in completely inappropriate intrigues, for which he would have to answer.[217]

The scales, nevertheless, began to tilt in Honecker's favor. This was caused in part by massive attacks against Ulbricht from inside the SED and finally direct appeals to Brezhnev to get rid of him. In January 1971, the oppositional faction complained in a letter to the Soviet leader that Ulbricht had reneged on all the promises on party unity

---

214 Ibid. (italics mine).

215 Julij A. Kwizinskij [Yuli A. Kvitsinsky], *Vor dem Sturm: Erinnerungen eines Diplomaten* (Berlin: Siedler, 1993), p. 255. Kvitsinsky served from 1959 until 1965 in the Soviet embassy in the GDR and from 1978 until 1981 in the embassy in Bonn.

216 Secret protocol of the meeting between a delegation of the CC of the CPSU and a delegation of the CC of the SED on 21 August 1970 in Moscow. The document is from the Central Party Archives of the SED, published by Przybylski, *Tatort Politbüro,* Vol. I, Doc. 16, pp. 292-93.

217 Kwizinskij, *Vor dem Sturm*, pp. 255-56.

made in August. In domestic politics as well as on the GDR's policies towards the FRG, they said, "Comrade Walter is pursuing a personal line to which is he clinging stubbornly." At 78 years of age, anyone would have difficulty to manage things effectively, but in his case the age problem was compounded by his "difficult personality." He displayed ever more "irrational ideas and subjectivism," and in his conduct towards "the comrades in the Politburo and other comrades he is often rude, insulting, and discusses things from a position of infallibility."[218]

The combined pressure of his colleagues in East Berlin and from Moscow finally persuaded Ulbricht to yield. On 3 May 1971, he asked the plenum of the Central Committee of the SED to relieve him of the duties of first secretary, referring to his old age which had made it impossible for him to continue his work on behalf of the Central Committee, the party, and the people. In accordance with what he knew to be the Soviet preference, he proposed Honecker as his successor.

Soviet dissatisfaction with Ulbricht and his removal from office are symptomatic of another problem of imperial rule: the aversion of the metropole to recognize the existence of basic structural deficiencies of empire and to blame subordinate bureaucrats and local officials for problems in their nominal sphere of responsibility. But the supreme irony of Ulbricht's replacement is that Honecker proved to engage in the same "mistakes" and turned out to be, in the center's perspective, just as irrational, subjectivist, arrogant, assertive, recalcitrant and, in the end, unmanageable as his predecessor.

This was not immediately apparent. The first two to three years after Honecker had assumed office passed without much conflict. As Kvitsinsky has pertinently observed, Honecker made a significant contribution to the Quadripartite Agreement on Berlin concluded on 3 September 1971. He was flexible but vigorous in his negotiations with West Germany. He supported the idea of socialist integration in the CMEA framework.[219] On domestic issues, one month into his rule – at the Eighth congress of the SED in June 1971 – he submitted a far-reaching program of change to improve the material situation of the population. Incomes of GDR citizens grew by four percent annually. Minimum wages and pensions were increased; paid working holidays and maternity leave were extended; an extensive new housing program was initiated, and so was the construction of numerous sports facilities and public

218 Letter by 13 full and candidate members of the SED Politburo to Brezhnev, dated 21 January 1971. The document is from the Central Party Archives of the SED, as published by Przybylski, *Tatort Politbüro,* Vol. I, Doc. 17, pp. 297-303. The wording is very much reminiscent of what Lenin had to say about Stalin in his "testament," a collection of notes and letters written before his death.

219 Kwizinskij, *Vor dem Sturm*, p. 258.

buildings. Industrial plants that had become outdated were to be renovated as soon as possible.[220]

Yet despite the protective shield of the Berlin wall and the apparent success of his socio-economic programs, Honecker remained conscious of East Germany's insecurity, vulnerability, and lack of domestic legitimacy. This realization as well as East Germany's inferior status *vis-à-vis* West Germany and its international isolation initially made Honecker almost pathologically bent on securing unconditional Soviet support. He expressly asked Brezhnev to view the GDR *de facto* as a Union Republic of the USSR and as such to include it in the Soviet Union's economic plans.[221] He was not content merely with a "close partnership USSR-GDR" but had the GDR declare itself, in Article 6 of its 1974 constitution, to be "forever and irrevocably allied" to the Soviet Union and to commit itself, in article 1 of the 1975 treaty of alliance with the Soviet Union, to maintaining "relations of eternal and unbreakable friendship and fraternal mutual assistance." The reference in the previous GDR constitution to "two German states of [one] German nation" had made it unnecessary to emphasize the specific character of the relations between both German states in each and every Soviet-German or intra-German treaty. Now, however, the substitution of this formula with "eternal friendship" with the Soviet Union, as Falin later was to comment, was "stupidity bordering on provocation" because the political logic of this change was that anyone striving for a united, free, and democratic, rather than a Soviet-type Germany allied with the Soveit Union had to oppose the "special" Soviet-East German relationship.[222]

But then, in the eyes of Soviet policy makers in the 1970s and early 1980s, the new political logic was perfectly acceptable. The consolidation of the empire seemed to require eradication of all ideas about German unification now considered politically harmful, no matter whether under capitalist, socialist, or any other auspices. The new rationale was demonstrated by an exchange between Falin and Foreign Minister Gromyko in 1977. Falin had pointed out to his superior that it was unproductive to emphasize the theme of "two German states" and unprincipled to abandon the vision of a united socialist Germany. The criticism was rejected. Gromyko remarked that "*We don't need a united Germany at all, not even a socialist one. The united socialist China is enough for us.*"[223]

The honeymoon in the relationship between the Soviet leaders and Honecker, however, was destined to come to an end. The first of many reasons is connected with a generational change and the background of the new leadership in East Berlin.

---

220 Ibid., on actual and intended changes in the GDR economy.

221 Ibid.

222 Falin, *Politische Erinnerungen*, p. 238.

223 Ibid., p. 239 (italics mine).

To quote Kvitsinsky again because of his well-informed perspective, he had long observed that in the GDR the group of the so-called "KZ people" (*KZler*, derived from *Konzentrationslager*) was pressing for power. These were party functionaries who had spent the Hitler era neither in capitals of unoccupied Europe nor in quiet Comintern offices in Moscow but in the concentration camps and prisons of the Third Reich. Latent tensions had always existed between them and the emigrants. Honecker was a typical representative of the *KZler* who, in contrast to Moscow emigrants such as Ulbricht and Pieck, were less inclined to place allegiance to Moscow above the interests of their own country. That is why, among other reasons, he was more popular than Ulbricht with the younger SED officials of the second rank, who had gradually ascended to leadership positions at the district and regional levels and who were now moving into the central party organs. One of the indications of this change in the make-up of the party leadership lay in the fact that Honecker, after his appointment as party chief, was single-mindedly surrounding himself with former FDJ cadres. From Moscow's vantage point, therefore, there was a distinct possibility that the policies of the GDR would be determined to a greater degree than before by tendencies of national patriotism and claims for a more independent role in intra-bloc and international affairs.[224]

There was another aspect of Honecker's biography that was to cause concern in Moscow. Honecker was born on 25 August 1912 in Neunkirchen in the Saarland, the son of a miner. At the tender age of 10, pressured by his father, he entered the communist youth organization in the Saarland. He did not do well at school, failed to receive a decent apprenticeship position, went to work for a time as a farm laborer in Pomerania, returned to the Saarland to work as a roofer for his uncle, turned professional communist youth organizer, and then rose through the ranks to become a leading member of the KPD district committee in that *Land*.[225] Although, according to Marxist theory, ethnic, regional, or national attributes are secondary to class characteristics, Honecker's background could be interpreted as establishing an-all German predisposition. Such assumptions turned out to be correct. Furthermore, as will be shown in the next chapter, his background was part of his unbending desire to visit West Germany, to return to the places where he had worked as a youth, and to see the grave of his father.[226] From the Soviet perspective, therefore, the combination of a latent tendency to assert GDR interests and an all-German longing for *Heimat* produced a psychological profile whose political repercussions were unpredictable and perhaps difficult to control.

---

224 Kwizinskij, *Vor dem Sturm*, pp. 256-257.

225 See the biographies by Heinz Lippman, *Honecker: Portrait eines Nachfolgers* (Cologne: Wissenschaft und Politik, 1971) and Dieter Borkowski, *Erich Honecker: Statthalter Moskaus oder deutscher Patriot? Eine Biografie* (Munich: C. Bertelsmann, 1987).

226 Interview with Krenz.

Before this eventuality became reality, it turned out that Honecker's economic program was no less ambitious and impossible to realize than that of his predecessor. Kvitsinsky aptly describes the attendant deterioration in economic conditions and the downturn in Soviet-GDR political relations.

> [W]e received information [in the early to mid-1970s] that the GDR consumed much more than it was able to produce. The result of this development was a rapid increase of the state's foreign debt, which under Ulbricht had remained within acceptable limits. But cautious warnings from Moscow had no effect on Honecker. He explained to us that in today's world only fools would not take up loans, that the GDR had significant reserves of gold and foreign currency, and that it had a broad range of possibilities to increase its exports for freely convertible currency.
>
> Soon, however, it turned out that almost the entire export growth of the GDR was used up to service the loans that had already been taken up. Many of the GDR's economists sounded the alarm, but no one in the Central Committee of the SED seemed to value their opinion much. The GDR now needed such goods from the West as the Soviet Union could not deliver. The Soviet admonitions to be frugal also went largely unheeded: After international recognition and the normalization of its relations with the Federal Republic, the GDR with Honecker at the top now wanted to venture out independently onto the stormy sea of international politics. After all, why not? Was the GDR inferior to Poland or Czechoslovakia?[227]

In late 1974, Soviet officials learned that East Berlin had worked out a package of agreements with Bonn to the effect that the GDR should receive several million West German marks for the improvement of the connections between West Berlin and the Federal Republic and for an expansion of contacts between the population of both German states. This concerned, among other things, the construction or rebuilding of roads, the opening of new telephone lines, and the cession of small parts of East German territory to West Berlin. All this, as Kvitsinsky observed,

> made the impression of a very adroit political and commercial deal. The GDR modernized its roads with its own personnel and was paid for it in foreign currency by Bonn. The GDR improved its telephone network and again the Federal Republic was ready to pay for it. And a whole series of similar deals was in preparation: the modernization not only of the road system but also the railway links, the opening of additional checkpoints on the border with the Federal Republic and the expansion of the already existing ones, the facilitation of tourist trips of West Germans into the GDR and of visits to relatives, the authorization of money transfers, and the lifting of restrictions on postal parcels. For many of these projects the GDR received the money from Bonn in advance, so that it was bound to keep its pledges. Ulbricht's thesis of the strict separation (*Abgrenzung*) of both German states was practically buried quietly. The GDR claimed the

227 Kwizinskij, *Vor dem Sturm*, pp. 258-59.

> right to play a ground-breaking role in the normalization of human relations between Eastern and Western Europe.

The budding relationship between the two Germanys was carefully monitored in Moscow and caused concern that would not cease until the collapse of East Germany. To continue with Kvitsinsky's account:

> Andrei Gromyko viewed this turn in the policy of our German friends with great doubts from the very start. Although its internal stability, due to the national division, was substantially less than that of our other allies, the GDR ventured out far in comparison to the Soviet Union and the other countries of the Warsaw Treaty. It was clear that Bonn would only invest in the GDR in order to advance the political goal of the development of German domestic special relations, that is, to achieve the "change through rapprochement" that Brandt and Bahr had already conceived in 1963.
>
> And one more completely new element in the policy of the GDR aroused suspicion in Moscow: The entire package of agreements with the Federal Republic had been negotiated without consultations with Moscow. Basically, we had simply been presented with a *fait accompli.*[228] ...
>
> Gromyko attempted to bring about a top-level dialogue with the GDR on this whole complex of questions. However, when Honecker heard what it was about, he avoided meeting with Brezhnev. In January 1975, he sent a delegation to Moscow that was led by [SED] Politburo member Hermann Axen, who was in charge of international relations.
>
> The talk led to nothing. Gromyko expounded the Soviet doubts quite directly and openly and indicated that the Soviet general staff had a negative opinion of the measures planned by "the friends" in regard to ensuring the security of the GDR. But what was the reply of Axen who had been sent expressly because no one wanted to change anything in the agreements that had already been signed and made public most hurriedly? He raised up his short arms, appeared insulted by the mistrust of the "Soviet friends" toward the policy of the GDR, praised the agreements and their advantages for the GDR, and swore that in regard to the German question there would always be only a policy closely coordinated with the Soviet Union.[229]

The stage for a serious crisis in Soviet-East German relations had irrevocably been set. Its proportions were far to exceed the scale of the conflict that had existed in the Ulbricht era. Several factors compounded its gravity. One was the fact that Honecker attempted to conceal from his colleagues in the Politburo all the reservations and warnings conveyed to him from Moscow, transferring them to his personal files.[230] Another was the fact that the Soviet leadership had informants in the SED Politburo

228 Ibid., pp. 259-60.

229 Ibid., pp. 260-61.

230 Ibid., pp. 262-63. Further examples of such concealment of information will be provided in the next chapter.

who reported that Honecker spoke more and more disparagingly about Brezhnev and the Soviet Union.[231]

In 1976-78, careful analyses of the internal situation of the GDR were prepared in the Soviet foreign ministry with the participation of the KGB and the defense ministry. The studies predicted a rapid development of relations between both German states and a growing dependence of East Germany on West Germany. The authors anticipated that the Protestant Church would become the crystallization point of opposition forces and warned that the structures of the party, the army, and state security which appeared to be so stable were in reality swiftly eroding.[232]

Why, then, did the Soviet leadership under Brezhnev fail to react more forcefully? One of the reasons is connected with internal factors. The "era of stagnation" seriously affected the top levels of decision making – a weakness that was enhanced by Brezhnev's failing health. Even more importantly, what were the Soviet options? Economic pressures would have had negative repercussions on a deteriorating Soviet economy. Such measures, furthermore, were likely to push the GDR even more quickly into the arms of West Germany. Finally, Honecker's closest followers were now in leading positions in the party, government, and state security. There was no oppositional faction on which Moscow could rely. And in contrast to Ulbricht, it was difficult to imagine that Honecker would cooperate in his removal from office. The imperial center was beginning to lose control.

In the period from the late 1970s to the mid-1980s, this predicament of empire coincided with a serious crisis in all dimensions of Soviet power. As will be shown in the next chapter, the failures of Soviet policies on the German problem were both a cause and a symptom of a deepening overall crisis of the Marxist-Leninist and Imperial paradigm.

---

231 Ibid., p. 263.

232 Ibid., pp. 264-65.

PART THREE: CRISIS

Chapter 3: The Comprehensive Crisis of Empire

1. The Crisis of Ideology

The Soviet empire and the Ideological and Imperial paradigm as its analytical frame of reference had rested on three major pillars: Marxist-Leninist ideology, military power, and economic resources. For the imperial edifice to collapse, it would have been sufficient for one of the pillars to fall. In the period from the late 1970s until the mid-1980s, however, all three supports had begun to crumble. What were the reasons for this turn of events? What role, if any, did developments in the two Germanys play in Soviet imperial decline? And what contribution did the German problem make to the fundamental reconsideration of priorities and policies that was to occur under Gorbachev? These are the central questions to be analyzed in this chapter.

As described in the previous chapter, in any political or imperial system, ideology can be said to play a number of important functions. It can fulfill analytical (or cognitive), utopian (or missionary), mobilizing, and legitimizing purposes. By the end of the1970s, Marxist-Leninist ideology failed to fulfill these functions. As Yakovlev told a conference of communist party secretaries in Varna in September 1989, what had gone wrong with ideology was that there had been grave "deformations," including the following:

(1) Overemphasis on what separates socialism from capitalism and a narrow focus on the differences as they existed at the time and in the specific conditions when socialism arose.

(2) Uncritical adherence to decisions, formulations, approaches, and definitions that had been developed in the past and that subsequently came to be idolized, codified, and cast in basalt, leading to a state of affairs where every attempt to revise them was declared to be a deviation from socialism, subversion, or treachery.

(3) The arbitrary "exclusion" from or "admission" to socialism of whole countries and peoples dictated by practical political interests or dogma. As a result, the Marxist truth was lost that every social order is shaped by the conditions and requirements of life and not by dogmatic belief, no matter how attractive it may seem to be.[1]

What was wrong with ideology was also that each of the major cognitive and predictive elements of Marxist-Leninist ideology had turned out to be faulty. Some of

---

1 Speech by Alexander Yakovlev at the conference of communist party secretaries for ideological questions, Varna (Bulgaria), 26-28 September 1989, included for agenda item 8 of SED Politburo meeting of 17 October 1989; SED, Central Archives, Politburo *Arbeitsprotokolle*, J IV 2/2A/3247.

the dogmas had been revised under Khrushchev, notably the idea that military conflict among the imperialist states was as inevitable as war between imperialism and socialism. But other major formalized perceptions and predictions had remained in force. This concerned the notions that the "contradictions" between the "power centers of imperialism" were more basic than the links that unite them; that in the long run the "correlation of forces" would shift in favor of socialism; that conflict would end with the victory of socialism; that the socialist mode of production was superior to that of capitalism; that the "national-liberation movements" would bring about states with anti-imperialist, non-capitalist, and ultimately socialist orientation; that class relations are a determining factor of international affairs; and that nationalism would wither away. The increasing gap between ideology and reality and the decline in the effectiveness of the Soviet system did not lead to a withering away of the state or of nationalism but rather of the attractiveness of the Soviet model of development. The ensuing crisis of ideology affected all areas of international politics. It was evident first and foremost in the highly developed industrialized world, that is, in Western Europe, the United States, and Japan. But it also pervaded Central and Eastern Europe, and the countries of the Third World.

In Western Europe, in the late 1970s, the principles of individualism, pluralism, democracy, and the market economy clashed with the communist ideas of monolithic politics and society and central planning and control in the economy. In order to enhance their chances to win power, the Italian, Spanish, French, and other Western European communist parties increasingly began to distance themselves from the Soviet model and develop a new system of thought or, more appropriately perhaps, a loose set of ideas, called "Eurocommunism". This tendency was vehemently opposed by Soviet ideologists. By the end of the 1980s, in part as a result of Ssoviet measures, but also because of a significant credibility gap between the communist parties and mainstream political and socio-economic forces in the countries concerned, "Eurocommunism" had run its course by the early 1980s. Even the traditionally strong communist parties of Italy and France found themselves faced with a serious decline in their electoral strength. In other Western European countries things remained as unsatisfactory as ever from the Soviet perspective. In West Germany, for instance, the German Communist Party (DKP) continued to receive less than one percent of the vote in Bundestag and Länder parliamentary elections and thus failed to gain representation at both the federal and the state level. It thus had no measurable influence in West German political life.

In Central and Eastern Europe Soviet ideology had never taken root. The communist regimes in the countries of this area suffered from the defects of having come to and being kept in power by the Soviet armed forces. Society in that region was perennially affected by Western viruses and a low-grade infection called "market socialism" and "socialism with a human face." Moscow was able to suppress acute flare-ups of the disease but unable to provide a cure. The last cycle in this political pathology had been the Warsaw Pact's intervention in Czechoslovakia in August 1968. Some "normalization" had taken place in the early 1970s. However, in the second half of the 1970s and the early 1980s, the medicine contained in "basket three" of the Helsinki final act produced a remission. It occurred throughout Eastern Europe, but from the Soviet perspective in an especially serious form in Poland in 1980-81.

To put the Polish dilemmas in perspective, according to the orthodox Soviet definition, "antagonist contradictions" could exist and crises occur only in *capitalist* systems.[2] Andropov had adhered to this dogma. But he had at least admitted: "Yes, we do experience contradictions as well as difficulties." To think that this could be different would be "abandoning safe, even though harsh realities." History had taught that "contradictions that by their nature are non-antagonist can produce serious collisions if they are not taken into consideration."[3] Several theorists went beyond the ideological euphemisms stilll apparent in the more realistic pronouncements of their chief. They called attention to the absurdity of drawing a distinction between contradictions that cannot be solved at all and contradictions that can be solved in theory but not in practice. To them, as Poland had shown, it was nonsense invariably to hold the *perezhitki proshlogo*, or "remnants of the past," responsible for acute problems. It was more appropriate in their view to look at the policies of the communist party which could produce "political crises with all its dangers for socialism."[4]

The ideological failures were equally momentous in the Third World. In the 1950s and 1960s, it had seemed to Soviet ideologists and political leaders that the rapidly accelerating processes of decolonization would set the newly independent ex-colonial countries on a non-capitalist path of development in internal system structure and on an anti-Western course in foreign policy. From Moscow's vantage point, to accelerate the process it had appeared expedient to provide aid to the so-called "national-liberation struggle." But whereas it turned out that Soviet support could occasionally

---

2 The security implications and management problems of the Polish crisis will be dealt with in the next section. In the present section only the ideological dimension of the crisis will be considered.

3 Yuri N. Andropov, "Uchenie Karla Marksa i nekotorye voprosy sotsialisticheskogo stroitel'stva v SSSR," *Kommunist*, No. 3 (February 1983), p. 21.

4 A. P. Butenko, "Protivorechiia razvitiia sotsializma kak obshchestvennogo stroia," *Voprosy filosofii*, No. 10 (1982), p. 27. The author at that time was a member of the USSR Academy of Sciences and Deputy Director of the Institute for the Economy of the World Socialist System. A similar approach was taken by several other authors, including the Vice President of the USSR Academy of Sciences, P. N. Fedoseev, "Dialektik des gesellschaftlichen Lebens," *Probleme des Friedens und des Sozialismus*, No. 9 (September 1981), pp. 1192-1200.

decide the question of power in the short term, the Soviet Union was incapable of contributing meaningfully to long-term socio-economic development in the Third World. More often than not, after a period of cooperation with Warsaw Pact countries in the security field, the new states turned to the West for development aid. Furthermore, Moscow's overestimation of the importance of the Third World in the East-West competition contributed to the overextension, overcommitment, and rising costs of empire of the late 1970s and early 1980s.

To sum up, as Yakovlev correctly told a conference of communist party secretaries for ideological questions, the model of socialist development as exemplified by the Soviet Union before the advent of perestroika had essentially "exhausted" itself.[5] In retrospect, other communist party officials regretted that significant sums of money had been wasted for an endless procession of visiting communist dignitaries, their medical treatment in Moscow, vacations in Sochi, and hunting trips in Siberia despite the fact that these dignitaries often had no more than a nuisance value in their own countries.[6] In fact, the smaller the party, the greater the profession of loyalty to Moscow. Gorbachev noted this in October 1984 in a conversation with Vadim Zagladin: "We have to ask ourselves, why it is that influential and strong parties separate themselves from us, whereas the small and insignificant parties remain orthodox and faithful to Moscow."[7] Such pertinent questions, it would seem, are an illustration of a more general malaise felt by Soviet leaders and part of their realization that the international communist movement had turned from an asset into a liability. Indeed, as Vadim Medvedev observed in retrospect, whereas earlier "real socialism" had exerted a powerful influence on world affairs, "at the end of the 1970s and the beginning of the 1980s, its development stopped, which contrasted sharply with the rapid progress [achieved] in the West and among some newly industrialzing countries."[8]

2. Military Power and Declining Political Influence

The second pillar on which the Soviet empire had rested was military power. In retrospect, it seems that some fairly simple but stubbornly executed ideas underlay Soviet foreign policy from Stalin to Chernenko: military power could be transformed into global political influence; parity in strategic nuclear power could be used to

5 Speech by Alexander Yakovlev at the conference of communist party secretaries for ideological questions, Varna (Bulgaria), 26-28 September 1989, included for agenda item 8 of SED Politburo meeting of 17 October 1989; SED, Central Archives, Politburo, *Arbeitsprotokolle*, J IV 2/2A/3247.

6 Interviews with Zagladin, Rykin, and Grigoriev.

7 As reported by Chernyaev, *Shest' let s Gorbachevym*, p. 19. Chernyaev, like Zagladin, at that time was one of the deputy chiefs of the CC's International Department.

8 Medvedev, *Raspad*, p. 8.

advance claims to political equality in relation to the United States; preponderance in conventional weaponry and forces and superiority in short and medium-range nuclear systems could serve not only to safeguard Soviet positions in Eastern Europe but to change the domestic and foreign policies of the Western European countries in directions favorable to Soviet interests; and the deployment of naval and airborne forces capable of intervention and power-projection far beyond the periphery of the Soviet Union would deter Western intervention in Third World countries and induce them to cooperate with the Soviet Union.[9] In the 1970s, from Soviet perspectives, favorable developments in international relations had seemed to confirm the validity of such notions. In the early 1980s, however, failures occurred more or less simultaneously in Soviet policies towards the United States, Western Europe, Central and Eastern Europe, Japan, China, and the Third World, necessitating a fundamental conceptual ressessment.

The United States. In the early 1980s, it had become apparent to Soviet ideologists and political leaders that the depth of "antagonist contradictions" in the West had been overestimated and that the forces that bound together the three main "power centers of imperialism" had been stronger than those that put them at odds with each other. In practical political terms, it had proved impossible to separate the United States from Western Europe and Japan. There had, of course, been many divisive issues in Western alliance relations: sanctions in response to the Soviet occupation of Afghanistan; sanctions as a punishment for martial law in Poland; the West German gas, credit, and pipeline deal; the stationing of medium-range missiles in Europe; and doubts about the reliability and loyalty of various European allies. However, after autumn 1983, these controversies had receded in importance or disappeared altogether.

In the United States, the strength, composition, and orientation of socio-economic and political forces had also changed, a fact that Soviet experts on American affairs, or *amerikanisty*, were quick to recognize. Their main line of interpretation at the beginning of the first Reagan administration was the notion that the new conservative philosophy and hard-line political approaches in the United States were essentially short-lived and would soon subside. However, as the Republican Party headed for a resounding electoral victory in 1984, they and other international relations experts increasingly came to adhere to the view that what they called the "conservative wave" in the United States was a more lasting and dangerous phenomenon.[10]

---

9 See Hannes Adomeit, "The Political Rationale of Soviet Military Capabilities and Doctrine," in *Strengthening Conventional Deterrence in Europe: Proposals for the 1980s*, Report of the European Security Study (ESECS) (London: Macmillan, 1983), pp. 67-104.

10 Yakovlev, for instance, as late as June 1985, thought that the "conservative wave" in the United States was generated and supported by that part of the bourgeoisie that was intimately connected with the scientific-technological revolution and high-technology military industry. In his view,

As for American defense policies, it may have appeared to Soviet political leaders and analysts that NATO in the mid-1970s was no longer able successfully to compete with the Warsaw Pact in the arms competition, that the Western countries were primarily reacting to Soviet initiatives, and that they were increasingly putting faith in arms control negotiations to redress, from their perspective, a deteriorating military balance. Such perceptions, to the extent that they existed, were rendered invalid by new realities in the East-West arms competition. In the late 1970s, defense outlays in the United States began to rise sharply. New challenges were issued to the Warsaw Pact, one in the form of laser-guided conventional weapons and computerized command and control systems, the other in the shape of Reagan's Strategic Defense Initiative (SDI). The deployment of intermediate-range nuclear weapons and the resulting capability of NATO to strike at Soviet territory from Western Europe as well as the ongoing US strategic modernization programs also put Soviet Union under pressure to respond and to do so in an area in which it could compete less easily and effectively: military high technology.[11]

The in-flight destruction, on the night of 31 August – 1 September 1983, of an unarmed civilian South Korean airliner *en route* from New York to Seoul (KAL 007) over the waters of the Sea of Okhotsk exacerbated Soviet-American relations and deepened the international isolation into which the Soviet Union had maneuvered itself. It also underlined the pitfalls of a mental attitude that relied uncritically on the military and standard operating procedures. According to Dobrynin, the KAL 007 crisis "illuminated the difficult relations and lack of communication between our civilian leaders and the military establishment, the generals being even more isolated from the rest of the world than the politicians." As invectives were exchanged between the United States and the Soviet Union, a "haggard and worried" Andropov told Dobrynin: "Return immediately to Washington and try to do your utmost to dampen this needless conflict bit by bit. Our military made a gross blunder by shooting down the airliner and it probably will take a long time to get out of this mess."[12] Yet at the same time, as the Soviet ambassador recalled, the Kremlin leadership "did not have enough courage to recognize publicly and immediately with deep regret that it [the plane] had been shot down over Soviet territory by a tragic

---

this explained the interest of the Reagan administration in shifting the East-West competition to the military-technological sphere; see the discussion between him and Vadim Zagladin, chaired by Fedor Burlatsky, "Vostok – Zapad. Tsivilizatsionnye otnosheniia: Neobkhodimost'? Real'nost'? Utopia?," *Literaturnaia gazeta*, 26 June 1985.

11 The impact of SDI on Soviet perceptions and policies will be discussed on pp. 149-50 and pp. 226-27.

12 Anatoly Dobrynin, *In Confidence: Moscow's Ambassador to America's Six Cold War Presidents* (New York: Random House, 1995), pp. 536-37.

mistake. ... It was unusual at that time for the Soviet government to accept [that] it had made any kind of error."[13]

Western Europe. Another crucially important failure in the attempt to transform military power into political influence was the Soviet campaign against the stationing of intermediate-range nuclear weapons, the Pershing 2 and cruise missiles, in Western Europe. Chancellor Schmidt had attempted several times to impress upon the Soviet leadership that legitimate Western European security interests would be violated and that West Germany, above all the SPD, would be pushed into a very difficult political situation if the Soviet Union were to deploy a large force of intermediate range nuclear weapons – SS-20 missiles and Backfire bombers. However, until the break-up of the negotiations in 1983, no Western offer for compromise as part of NATO's "dual track" decision was deemed acceptable in Moscow. Nothing therefore slowed the momentum of Soviet deployments. The Soviet Union continued to improve its quantitative and qualitative superiority in INF systems. It attempted at the same time to delay or to prevent altogether the NATO counter-deployments in Western Europe. Its major instrument was a Western "peace movement" that reached impressive strength in 1983.

What, then, were the results of the INF controversy? Militarily, even after the Western counter-deployments, the Soviet Union had gained some advantage. Politically, however, it had experienced an abysmal failure. The SPD-FDP government under Schmidt had fallen apart as a result of intra-party (SPD) controversies over the issue and after the March 1983 parliamentary elections was replaced by a CDU/CSU-FDP coalition government under Kohl. In Western Europe the Soviet leadership now saw itself faced with governments of varying composition, conservative in West Germany and Britain and socialist in France and Italy, yet all of these governments strongly supported the stationing of US missiles in Europe, the improvement of conventional defense in Europe, and the strengthening of Atlantic ties. The opposition parties seemed far removed from winning power and effectively shaping defense policies. Finally, the "peace movement" as an instrument of Soviet state policy in Western Europe severely declined in importance.[14]

Decline of the "Peace Movement." In 1984, ID officials and propagandists were still trying to reassure themselves and the top Soviet leadership that the Western

13 Ibid.

14 Chancellor Kohl, in a speech on 12 November 1991 in Strasbourg, reflected on the significance of the INF controversy. He stated that the Soviet leadership had come "to recognize the futility of its attempts at decoupling European and American security" and "dividing the alliance." He was convinced that this realization had been "an essential precondition for the policy of the New Thinking in the Soviet Union. *President Gorbachev himself confirmed this in conversation with me*;" Press and Information Office of the Federal Government, *Bulletin*, No. 137, pp. 1115-16 (italics mine).

"peace movement" was far from defeated. They cheerfully claimed that a June 1984 opinion survey in West Germany had revealed that 87 percent of the respondents were still "opposed to the stationing of new intermediate-range nuclear missiles" and that they "supported the withdrawal of the [missiles] already deployed."[15] Soviet propagandists were still consoling themselves with the idea that in the past there had been recurrent waves and periodic ebbs and flows of Western anti-war movements. Each and every wave had tended to be larger and more broadly based. The "peace movement," they acknowledged, had lost the INF-campaign. They thought, however, that it was now entering "a new stage of development" and gradually transforming itself into a "permanent political factor" that would be able to exert "effective influence" on government decisions.[16]

Doubts as to the validity of such interpretations were made official only at the Twenty-seventh party congress. Gorbachev promised that the CPSU would "proceed from the realities of the modern world." Such realities included the fact that "It is, of course, not possible to solve the problem of international security with one or two even very intense peace offensives. Only consistent, systematic, and persistent work can bring success."[17] Subsequently, even *Pravda* commentators were prepared to acknowledge what perceptive analysts had known for some time and discussed in private: "In the last few years a tendency could be noted among the anti-war movements, including among the most active and relatively important ones, to put themselves at a distance from the peace organizations of the socialist countries." This tendency threatened to "divide the progressive forces and thus to diminish their strength."[18]

Afghanistan and the Third World. Soviet failures in the competition over the internal systemic structure and foreign policy orientation of the countries of the Third World were equally glaring. In the 1970s, the dispatch of Soviet military advisers and weapons as well as cooperation with proxies such as Cuba and Vietnam, had seemed to have resulted in substantial gains for the Soviet Union at little risk of confrontation with the United States. The early 1980s, however, began to look different. The Reagan administration appeared to be unaffected by the dual shock of Vietnam and Watergate. It was ready to return to a more active containment policy and even a rollback of Soviet gains. Several opportunities for such a policy presented

---

15 G. Kirillov and V. Shenaev, "FRG: Oslablenie pozitsii praviashchei koalitsii," in Oleg N. Bykov, ed., *Mezhdunarodnyi ezhegodnik: Vypusk 1985 goda. Politika i ekonomika* (Moscow: Izdatel'stvo politicheskoi literatury, 1985), pp. 193-194. The book appeared in 1985 but the article was written in 1984.

16 V. Orel, "Antivoennoe dvizhenie: dostizheniia i perspektivy," *Kommunist*, No. 12 (1984), pp. 87-98 (italics mine).

17 *Pravda*, 26 February 1986.

18 Yuri Zhukov, "The Anti-War Movements," *International Affairs* (Moscow), No. 4 (April 1987), p. 23.

themselves. In Angola, for instance, Soviet and Cuban intervention had failed to arrest the civil war and the government's loss of control over wide areas of the country, thereby opening the prospect that the Marxist regime in Luanda could be overthrown. In Ethiopia, joint Soviet-Cuban intervention had been unable to stop the Eritrean secession and the deterioration of socio-economic conditions. North Vietnam's victory in the south and its occupation of Cambodia had led to significant economic and political costs, complicating Sino-Soviet relations and the relationship between the Soviet Union and the prospering non-communist countries of Southeast Asia. Finally and most importantly, in contrast to previous interventions in Eastern Europe, the Soviet intervention in Afghanistan had not produced a quick military solution and political stabilization. It had led instead to a widening guerilla war supported by outside powers. It remained, as Gorbachev deplored at the Twenty-seventh party congress, an "open wound."[19]

Eastern Europe. The war in Afghanistan had coincided and interacted with the rise of Solidarity in Poland. In fact, in 1980-81, the Soviet leadership under Brezhnev faced an acute dilemma in its attempt to restore control. Shevardnadze later remembered that Afghanistan and the Soviet domestic situation interacted with the events in Poland and anxiety about possible negative reactions from the West. "But that was not all. I think Moscow was given pause by serious and, I suppose, correct fears that the Poles would fight back and that full-scale military actions would have to be unleashed."[20] New archival evidence has revealed the existence of such fears. When the issue was discussed at a Politburo meeting in late October 1981, even traditional hard-liners such as Defense Minister Ustinov and KGB chairman Andropov had to concede that "*it would be impossible now for us to send troops to Poland.*" They thought that the Soviet Union "must steadfastly adhere to [its] line not to send in troops."[21] Suslov, the CC secretary in charge of ideology, is reported to have supported this line. "Under no circumstances are we going to use force in Poland," he exclaimed.[22] However, the collective mind of the Politburo was also made up to the effect that, as Foreign Minister Gromyko put it, "*we simply cannot and must not lose Poland.*"[23] The two positions seemed mutually exclusive. The

19 *Pravda*, 26 February 1986.

20 Shevardnadze, *Moi vybor*, pp. 205-6.

21 For the new documentary evidence, see Mark Kramer, "Poland, 1980-81: Soviet Policy During the Polish Crisis," *Cold War International History Project Bulletin* (Woodrow Wilson International Center, Washington, D.C.), No. 5 (Spring 1995), pp. 1, 116-26; p. 121 (italics mine).

22 According to Shevardnadze, at one point in the crisis, "I happened to be in Mikhail A. Suslov's office. Someone phoned him to report about the worsening situation in Poland and to insist, as I understood it, on an 'activation of forces.' Suslov repeated firmly several times, 'There is no way that we are going to use force in Poland'"; *Moi vybor*, pp. 205-6.

23 At a Politburo meeting in October 1980, Kramer, "Poland, 1980-81," p. 118 (italics mine).

Soviet leadership was nevertheless almost miraculously able to avoid military intervention, having persuaded General Jaruzelski to impose martial law. But the basic structural problems of imperial control in Eastern Europe remained. The internal ferment did not end. No stable solution was achieved.[24] As Poland had shown conclusively, the attempt at transforming military preponderance into legitimate and effective political control in Eastern Europe had failed.

To summarize the discussion of military power and its political utility, by 1983-84 the Soviet leaders found themselves in a position of severe international isolation. Unwilling or unable to embark upon a comprehensive rearrangement of relations with the United States, Western Europe, Japan, and China, they adopted an attitude of "insulted giant" and "bear in hibernation."[25] Based on the conviction that in response to the implementation of NATO's dual-track decision they had to live up to their threats of political and military countermeasures, they showed a stone-hard face to the outside world. In typically Brezhnevite fashion, Andropov continued with the further deployment of SS-20 missiles, the stationing of "operational-tactical missiles" in the GDR and Czechoslovakia and the forward positioning of nuclear-armed submarines "in ocean areas" close to the US coast. He broke off the arms control negotiations on strategic and medium-range nuclear weapons and for a time also those on conventional arms. Chernenko, his successor, abandoned the policy of selective detente toward the Western European countries, his propagandists attacking the West German government for allegedly aiding and abetting "revanchist" and "neo-Nazi" tendencies. Trends for cooperation between China and the West in economic and security matters were growing. In the Islamic world the standing of the Soviet Union continued to be affected negatively by the occupation of Afghanistan and Moscow's support for a pro-Soviet and pro-communist system in that country.

All lines of communication were blocked. The Soviet leadership for all practical purposes ceased to be an active participant in international politics and was relegating itself to the role of bystander. However, behind the façade of defiance and stridency, the realization was beginning to gain ground in Moscow that power in international relations does not primarily depend on quantitative indicators such as the number of weapons and troops, reserves of raw materials, size of the population, and the acreage owned or controlled on the Hindukush or the Horn of Africa but on the effectiveness and efficiency of the socio-economic and political system to develop the human potential, or the *chelovecheskii faktor,* as this was called under Andropov. There also began to develop a greater awareness of the importance of political, cultural, economic, and technological instruments in the competition for influence in world affairs.

---

24 Shevardnadze, *Moi vybor*, pp. 205-6.

25 Terms used in lead articles by *The Economist* at the time.

3. Declining Economic Performance and the "Costs of Empire"

The third pillar on which the superpower status of the Soviet Union had rested was that of economic potential. This pillar, too, was being seriously eroded. To take one of the crudest measures of the erosion, that of the gross national product, in 1961 Khrushchev had quoted unnamed economists as estimating that at the end of the Seven-Year Plan (1959-65) "the USSR will surpass the USA in the volume of production and approximately by 1970 in per capita output."[26] The authoritative CPSU program of the same year improved on this prediction. The "approximately" was dropped and replaced by the assertion that the USSR "*will* surpass the USA ... in per capita output" in 1970.[27] That year, however, came and went, and starting from 1975 the official USSR statistical annuals began to show Soviet national income as unchanged at the same proportion of US national income, namely at 67 percent. The slogan of catching up with and overtaking the United States was abandoned. Furthermore, internally, the Institute of World Economy and International Relations (IMEMO) in Moscow made its own calculations and estimated Soviet national income to amount to only *half* of the American volume. It also concluded that the gap was widening rather than narrowing.[28] Unofficial Soviet estimates later put the Soviet-American national income ratio even lower than that.[29]

The Soviet economists' sense of urgency was sharpened by the fact that in the second half of the 1980s labor and capital inputs were doomed to slow more rapidly and natural-resource exploitation costs to rise faster. Extrapolation of trends indicated that the Soviet economy was heading for zero and negative growth. As Table 2 shows, Western (CIA) and official Soviet statistical time series data coincided in this portrayal of trends.[30]

---

26 Khrushchev on 6 January 1991 at a meeting of party organizations, *Pravda*, 25 January 1961.

27 The embarrassing program was adopted at the June 1961 plenary meeting of the Central Committee of the CPSU; see *Pravda* and *Izvestiia*, 30 July 1961 (italics mine).

28 Information received from IMEMO researchers by Philip Hanson of the University of Birmingham. The subsequent analysis of economic developments is based on Phil Hanson's contribution to *The Gorbachev Challenge and European Security*, Report by the European Strategy Group (Baden-Baden: Nomos, 1988), pp. 53-69. Hanson was the principal author of the economic section of the report.

29 A particularly sophisticated reevaluation of the Soviet official data for the 1970s and 1980s and their downward revision has been provided by Gregory Khanin, "Economic Growth in the 1980s," in Michael Ellmann and Vladimir Kontorovich, eds., *The Disintegration of the Soviet Economic System* (London: Routledge, 1992), pp. 73-85.

30 Sources: *Narodnoe khoziaistvo SSSR* (various years); *Pravda*, 24 January 1988; CIA, *Handbook of Economic Statistics* (Washington, 1986); CIA and DIA, *Gorbachev's Modernization Program: A Status Report*, Paper prepared for the Subcommittee on Security Economics of the US Congress Joint Economic Committee, 19 March 1987; ESG Report, *The Gorbachev Challenge*, p. 58.

Table 2 – Decline of Soviet Economic Growth, 1965-1985

	1966-70	1971-75	1976-80	1981-85
A. Soviet official measures				
NMP produced	7.7	5.7	4.2	3.5
NMP utilized	7.1	5.1	3.9	3.2
Gross industrial output	8.5	7.4	4.4	3.6
Gross agricultural output[a]	3.9	2.4	1.7	1.1
Investment[a]	7.4	7.2	5.2	3.2
Capital stock	7.5	7.9	6.8	6.0
Electric power	7.9	7.0	4.5	3.6
Oil, coal, and gas	5.2	5.4	4.2	2.5
B. CIA estimates[b]				
GNP	5.1	3.0	2.3	1.9
Industrial output	6.4	5.5	2.7	1.9
Agricultural output	3.6	-0.6	0.8	2.1
Investment	5.5	4.3	4.3	3.4
Capital stock	7.4	8.0	6.9	6.2
Labor (man hours)	2.0	1.7	1.2	0.7

Notes. All output series and the investment and capital stock figures are in constant prices, that is, they denote "real" changes. The Soviet official series, however, are known to contain an element of hidden inflation and therefore are upwardly biased. Note a: For five-year periods, the growth rates shown are those between the total for the period and the total for the preceding five-year period. Note b: At 1982 ruble factor-cost.

Growth, of course, is only one aspect of economic development. When looking at a country's status, prestige, and influence in international affairs, other factors are equally important. These concern the quality and technological level of its products, its share in world commodity and financial markets, the volume of foreign direct investment, and the size of private and government assistance programs. In all of these categories, the Soviet Union was performing poorly. Innovation was limited to the military sphere, with hardly any spillover to the civilian economy. The design features, reliability, and technological sophistication of its industrial products were notoriously poor. Even with large price rebates, they were hopelessly uncompetitive in comparison with Western products. The structure of the Soviet Union's foreign trade very much resembled that of a developing country: the USSR exported large quantities of raw materials, notably oil and natural gas, and imported machinery. Its share in world trade in the 1970s and early 1980s hovered around 4 percent, was far lower than that of the United States, West Germany, or Japan and was declining. With an economy run by the state, the Soviet Union provided no private investment, which had proven to be an important factor of growth for many of the newly industrializing countries such as Korea, Taiwan, Singapore and, more recently, China.

The Soviet Union's share in economic assistance programs was also small. It lacked the West's private programs, and government aid lagged far behind Western shares. The *commitments* were sometimes impressive but actual disbursements small. In accordance with the imperial and ideological paradigm, strategic considerations typically determined aid. But there were also major problems with the aid provided. Servicing and spare parts were difficult to obtain, and regimes in the Third World that were shifting from the acquisition to the consolidation of power and economic development frequently found that the benefits of cooperation with the West outweighed those that could be obtained from the Soviet Union.

Specialization and the division of labor in Comecon did not help. The organization's system of economic exchanges was like "trading dead cat for dead dog."[31] Comecon's inefficiencies merely reflected those of the Soviet-type system of planning and management. In a normally functioning empire, the dependencies are meant to provide benefits to the center. This was not the case in the Soviet empire. After a period of blatantly exploitative trade and economic relations in the Stalin era, the Soviet Union began to *subsidize* its hold on Eastern Europe. As noted above, East Germany before the building of the wall was an early example of what came to be a more general pattern under Khrushchev and Brezhnev. Subsidization occurred in the form of the delivery of cheap oil and gas; overpayment for industrial products relative to world market prices; and acceptance of industrial products whose quality was inferior to that of commodities exported by Moscow's allies to the West in exchange for hard currency. Whereas such deficiencies were serious enough *per se*, the main concern of the Soviet leaders, in what an astute analyst of Soviet affairs called the "harsh decade" of the mid-1970s to the mid-1980s, was the impact of the deceleration

31 The claim to fame for this apt characterization is unclear but probably belongs to Hungarian economists.

of economic growth and lagging technological innovation on the military-industrial sector and the armed forces.[32]

The "Military-Industrial Complex" and the Challenge of SDI

A number of special features characterized the "military-industrial complex" (MIC) in the Soviet Union.[33] In conjunction, they amounted to a heavy burden on the Soviet economic mule that it was ultimately no longer able to bear. *Excessive secrecy* was one of the many straws that threatened to break the back of the beast. Secrecy was one of the most pervasive phenomena in both Czarist and Soviet Russia. By the late 1960s, it had penetrated the system to such an extent that during the SALT I negotiations members of the Soviet foreign ministry's negotiation team were denied access to information about force levels and other "secrets" by the members of the Soviet military delegation.[34] Even after the termination of this practice in SALT II, the most important aspects of military affairs remained concealed. These concerned the size and composition of the military budget; the strength, organization, and deployment of the Soviet armed forces; the priorities in military research and development; the scope and rates of weapons production; and the volume, composition, and geographical distribution of arms exports and military assistance. Initiatives in foreign policy were being announced after they had been decided. Discussions in the Politburo and Central Committee on international security affairs remained unpublished.

A second feature of the MIC that was damaging to the overall economy was the *priority given to military industry in the allocation of resources*. Military industry received the best in machine tools and instruments. It paid its workers more and gave them better housing and medical facilities than were available in the civilian sector. Supply bottlenecks were fewer since managers, state officials, and party secretaries learned to attend more quickly to requests from the arms industry.

---

32 See Seweryn Bialer, "The Harsh Decade," chapter 4 in his *The Soviet Paradox: External Expansion, Internal Decline*, Vintage Books (New York: Random House, 1986), pp. 57-80.

33 The term was coined by Eisenhower. In 1961, in his farewell address, he warned against a collusion between "big business" and the military, that is, against the possible emergence of a "military-industrial complex" that might "acquire unwarranted and potentially dangerous political power;" as reported in *The New York Times*, 18 January 1961. The Soviet military, of course, denied the existence of a MIC in the USSR. To General V.N. Lobov, first deputy chief of staff of the Soviet armed forces and a first deputy minister of defense, that idea was "absurd;" "Est' li v SSSR voenno-promyshlennyi kompleks?," *Izvestiia*, 16 October 1988. In contrast, some Western analysts quipped: "Whereas the United States *has* a military-industrial complex, the Soviet Union *is* a military-industrial complex."

34 This fact was first revealed by Raymond Garthoff, an American participant in the SALT I negotiations. It was confirmed recently to this author by a Soviet foreign ministry official.

A third special feature was the *one-way flow of technological innovation*. As part of the priority given to the military sector, great emphasis was put on military research and development. According to Roald Sagdeev, the former head of the Institute for Space Research at the USSR Academy of Sciences, at least 70 percent of the personnel employed in scientific tasks worked in the military, and therefore "closed," sector of science.[35] Military industry was almost exclusively the beneficiary of innovation, with spillover occurring only in one direction: from civilian research and development to the military sector.

Fourth, *military industry was largely exempted from planning constraints*. It was able to enjoy the supply advantages of central planning without suffering its demand disadvantages. Production quotas, for instance, were not assigned to pilot plants and experimental factories, and retooling to upgrade weapons in these enterprises was standard practice.

Fifth, relative to the civilian sector, there was more *effective quality control* in military industry. The defense ministry, as the sole buyer of weapons, made sure that it would get what it wanted. This was achieved mainly by quality-control inspectors attached to each plant. These *voennye predstavitely,* or military representatives, were empowered to reject products that did not conform to the stringent design specifications laid down by the ministry. They received their salaries from the ministry, and since they were neither employed nor paid by the plant, the establishment of cozy and corrupt relations between them and the plant management was made difficult.

Finally, the *high levels of military expenditure* contributed to the burdens of empire and the downfall of the Soviet economy. According to Western estimates, Soviet military spending in current prices was said to have increased from about 50 billion rubles in 1970 to approximately 130 billion in 1986.[36] In the period from the mid-1970s to the mid-1980s, military expenditures were estimated to have increased by 10 percent annually in current prices. Since such rates of growth exceeded that of the economy, the proportion of military expenditures in GNP, according to Western estimates, increased from 12-14 percent at the beginning of the 1970s to 15-17 percent at the beginning of the 1980s.[37] Many Western and Soviet observers, including Gorbachev after he had become General Secretary, thought that such estimates were too low. In conversation with Gromyko, for instance, he assumed that military expenditures constituted 16 percent of national income but "if one added to

---

35 *Novoe vremia*, No. 47 (1988), p. 27.

36 The Soviet Economy under a New Leader, Paper Prepared Jointly by the Central Intelligence Agency and the Defense Intelligence Agency for Submission to the Subcommittee on Economic Resources, Competitiveness and Security Economics of the Joint Economic Committee, Congress of the United States, 19 March 1986.

37 Ibid.

that 4 percent for the MVD [Ministry of the Interior] and the KGB, the total amounts to 20 percent, which is the highest [proportion of] military expenditures [of GNP] in the world."[38]

The level of defense expenditure did not constitute much of a problem in the conditions of relatively high economic growth in the 1950s and 1960s. But as the decline in the growth rates of the Soviet economy continued in the 1970s, objective constraints made themselves felt. The priority allocation of resources to the military sector of the economy became a cancerous growth, a malignant tumor that sapped the strength of the whole economic organism and threatened to destroy it. Starting from the second half of the 1970s, growth of Soviet military expenditures in *real terms*, based on 1970 prices, was estimated as having decreased from about 4 to 2 percent per annum; no growth was recorded any longer in military procurement.[39] Such trends, according to Western analysts, were not the result of a deliberate decision by the political leadership but the inexorable consequence of an the overall slowdown of the Soviet economy.[40] Even political leaders ignorant of economic affairs – essentially all of the Soviet leaders from Stalin to Gorbachev – could no longer ignore the fact that the share of military expenditures in the gross national product could not continue to rise indefinitely; that a technologically advanced military sector could not exist in isolation from the economy; that the future effectiveness and modernity of the armed forces was threatened by the economic deficiencies; and that tinkering with the system and yet another round of "administrative streamlining" were no longer enough to remedy the problem. The Soviet military was certainly getting restless about the political leadership's inability to achieve a level of technological sophistication in the military-industrial sphere that would guarantee parity, or parity plus, with the United States.[41] Perhaps conscious of the dissatisfaction inside the main pillar of Soviet global power, Brezhnev addressed the top military leaders in the Kremlin only two weeks before his death. He attempted to reassure them that they would get everything they needed. But he also had to tell them that "*politics can only be effective if it is based on real economic and military power.*"[42]

---

38 As quoted by Shakhnazarov, *Tsena svobody*, p. 49.

39 According to CIA calculations, *USSR: Measures of Economic Growth and Development, 1950-1980*, Studies Prepared for the Use of the Joint Economic Committee, U.S. Congress, Washington, D.C., December 1982, p. 54.

40 See, for instance, Abraham S. Becker, *Sitting on Bayonets: The Soviet Defense Burden and the Slowdown of Soviet Defense Spending*, Rand / UCLA Center for the Study of Soviet International Behavior, The Rand Corporation, Santa Monica, CA, JRS-01, December 1985.

41 Disagreements over economic and military priorities in all likelihood led to the dismissal of chief of staff Nikolai Ogarkov in September 1984; see Jeremy R. Azrael, *The Soviet Civilian Leadership and the Military High Command*, The RAND Corporation, R-3521-AF, June 1987; see also Dale R. Herspring, "Nikolai Ogarkov and the Scientific-Technical Revolution in Soviet Military Affairs," *Comparative Strategy*, Vol. 4, No. 1 (January 1987), pp. 29-59.

42 "Soveshchanie voenachal'nikov v Kremle," *Pravda*, 28 October 1982 (italics mine).

It is into this setting that Reagan's "Star Wars," or Strategic Defense Initiative, has to be placed. As Dobrynin has observed, "Our physicists, headed by Academician Yevgeni Velikhov, were as skeptical as many of their American counterparts, but their views hardly carried much weight. ... *Our leadership was convinced that the great technical potential of the United States had scored again and treated Reagan's statement as a real threat.*"[43] Such perceptions were not only held in the Andropov and Chernenko interregnum but also by Gorbachev. Since the argument is made in this book that the crumbling of the three main pillars of empire and a grave domestic political crisis formed a compelling rationale for Gorbachev's New Thinking, his views on the SDI issue are of considerable importance. There is little direct evidence how he regarded the problem before his accession to power but there is more in his first months in office. The evidence available shows that he recognized science and technology as crucial factors of global political influence and Reagan's Star Wars not simply as one of the many gyrations of the arms competition but as a *fundamental* challenge to the Soviet Union.[44]

Prior to Gorbachev's accession to power, a growing number of party officials and academic specialists became concerned about the social costs of high defense expenditures. Shevardnadze later recalled that he had expressed his concern about the impact of the arms race on both superpowers. In a private conversation at his (Shevardnadze's) home in Moscow, United States Ambassador Thomas J. Watson had told him that in the United States signs of a falling standard of living had appeared and that this could probably be attributed to the high costs of the arms race. In his opinion, the same applied to the Soviet Union. By taking on the chief burden of the arms race both the USA and the USSR were beginning to sacrifice competitiveness relative to other countries. Shevardnadze agreed and cited the examples of the Federal Republic of Germany and Japan: "While we were competing in the production and stockpiling of state-of-the-art weapons, they, freed from this burden, surged ahead of us."[45] He could have added, as he wrote, that in "our economy only the military-industrial complex operated at peak performance, thriving at the country's expense and making it possible for the country to entertain illusions

---

43 Dobrynin, *In Confidence*, p. 528 (italics mine).

44 Evidence will be presented below; see pp. 226-27. Gorbachev, in retrospect, has attempted to *deemphasize* the importance of SDI for changes in the Soviet approach towards the West. For instance, at a conference on "A World Restored: Reflections on Ending the Cold War," organized by West Point Military Academy, 8-9 October 1995, he stated that the Soviet Union had an advanced research program and was ready for cost-effective responses. "SDI was not decisive in our movement to a new relationship. Change in the Soviet Union was the decisive factor;" quoted from notes taken by one of the participants.

45 Shevardnadze, *Moi vybor*, pp. 149-50. No date was provided for the conversation. From the context, it appears that it took place in 1985, after Shevardnadze's appointment to the post of foreign minister.

of its own might and power. But suddenly it dawned on us that real power is something much more than nuclear warheads."[46]

To return to the main line of the argument, the erosion of the three main pillars of empire reflected long-term structural deficiencies of the Soviet empire and the Soviet system. The crisis of empire which this erosion produced was intimately connected with a domestic political crisis in the Soviet Union.

4. The Domestic Political Crisis

"Stability of cadres" had been the proclaimed hallmark of the Brezhnev era. After the cycles of physical liquidation under Stalin and the hectic administrative reshuffling and frequent discoveries of "anti-party groups" in the Khrushchev era, Brezhnev finally met the ruling elite's longing for predictability and security of tenure – at a price. Stability turned into stagnation (*zastoi*). Corruption and nepotism became rampant. The "new class" of party officials became ever more insulated from society.[47] The system of self-generating and self-selecting appointments according to centrally controlled lists (*nomenklatura*) turned party officials into an oligarchy, or a special caste, something akin to an aristocracy, with life peerage that provided power, perks, and privileges.[48] The elite, if this term can be meaningfully applied, had its own clannish ties, special stores, maternity wards, funeral services, health resorts, and hunting lodges. Its children spent time together, received priority access to higher education, and often intermarried. Brezhnev's son, to take an example from the highest level of the hierarchy, became deputy minister for foreign trade, and his son-in-law was promoted to first deputy minister of the interior.[49]

There was at least one area of growth in the period of stagnation: the bureaucracy. In accordance with Parkinson's Law, the number of bureaucrats in the Brezhnev era rose to unprecedentedly high levels. The party apparat expanded by tens of thousands of officials, many of whom incorporated as a result of the creation of agricultural departments in the party's district committees. About half a million officials filled the hierarchical layers of the party bureaucracy, from the central apparatus (Politburo, Secretariat, CC departments) to the regional and local offices in the Union republics, regions, districts, cities, and territories. Growth occurred also in the number of employees (*chinovniki*) in state and economic administrations. Between 1975 and

---

46 Ibid.

47 This phonemenon in the evolution of Soviet-type systems was aptly described by Milovan Djilas, *The New Class* (New York: Praeger, 1968).

48 Terminology used by Mikhail Voslensky, *Nomenklatura*, transl. Eric Mosbacher (London: Bodley Head, 1984), and Georgi Arbatov, *The Soviet System: An Insider's Life in Soviet Politics*, with an introduction by Strobe Talbott (New York: Random House, 1992), p. 227.

49 Ibid.

1980, their ranks swelled by three million and in 1984 surged to a level of 18.6 million officials. They could be found, some of the time at least, at their desks in 36 councils of ministers, more than 1,000 ministries and state committees, 51,700 executive committees of the regional and locals soviets, 44,600 production and scientific-production associations, 21,600 state farms (*sovkhozy)*, transportation, construction, trading, and service enterprises as well as health and educational institutions.[50]

These data excluded the officers and men in the Soviet armed forces, the KGB, border troops, interior ministry, and the police and the officials in the labor unions, youth organization (*Komsomol*), and other "social formations," including the collective farms, or *kolkhozy*. The strength of the five branches of the armed forces – the army, the navy, the air force, the strategic rocket forces, and air defense – added up to a total of about 5 million officers and men.[51] According to Western estimates, the secret police (KGB) had 720,000 agents on its payroll, and this agency and the interior ministry (MVD) had under their command 570,000 officers and men in military formations, including several divisions of border and internal security troops.[52]

The numerical expansion of the administrative apparatus and the external and internal security services was matched by an increase in their political influence. The defense minister and the head of the KGB became full members of the Politburo. Brezhnev appointed himself Marshal of the Soviet Union and emphasized his role as supreme commander of the armed forces. Important questions of internal and external security were discussed and decided in a reactivated defense council (*sovet oborony*), a select body of top party and state officials and high-ranking military officers. Prominence, status, and prestige of the military were demonstratively elevated. On the occasion of official celebrations in Red Square, the top military leaders were prominently placed atop the rostrum at the Lenin mausoleum, at the right-hand side of the General Secretary; as if to demonstrate equality with the party, they took up half of the rostrum.

---

50 Data as compiled by M.U. Klimko, *Voprosy istorii KPSS*, No. 11 (1984), p. 16, as quoted by Gyula Józsa, "The Party Apparatus under Andropov and Chernenko," in Federal Institute for East European and International Studies, ed., *The Soviet Union 1984/85* (Boulder, Colo.: Westview, 1986), pp. 25-27.

51 Data from various issues of the IISS *Military Balance*.

52 Astrid von Borcke, "The Role of the Secret Service," in Federal Institute for East European and International Studies, ed., *The Soviet Union 1984/85* (Boulder, Colo.: Westview, 1986), pp. 49 and 56, and various issues of the *Military Balance* published by the International Institute for Strategic Studies. The figure of 720,000 KGB agents is based on research by Yevgenia Albats, *The State within a State: The KGB and Its Hold on Russia – Past, Present and Future*, trans. Catherine A. Fitzpatrick (New York: Farrar, Straus, Giroux, 1994), p. 23. For detail on these figures see *infra*, chapter 5, the section on the KGB.

The new "internationalist" function of the army, the new role of a blue-water navy in advancing world-wide "state interests," the priority allocated to military industry in the economy, and the privileged position of the military in politics and society could be interpreted as rampant "Bonapartism" or at least as a successful bid by the military for power at the expense of the party. This, however, would be an erroneous interpretation of the essence of civil-military relations under Brezhnev. The undoubted growth in the military's role did not result from a politicization of the armed forces or their deliberate push for power but from a pull exerted by the party.[53]

The same can be said for the enhanced role of the secret police in the 1970s and early 1980s. The KGB was permitted to increase its influence and representation in the Central Committee and the party bureaus of the Union republics. Gaidar Aliev, the head of the KGB in Azerbaijan, and Boris Pugo, his counterpart in Lithuania, were appointed party chiefs in their respective republics. Under Andropov, KGB chief until his transfer to the party apparatus in May 1982, the secret police became more prominent and active. It was instrumental in implementing a whole series of restrictive measures, curbing cultural expression, religious rights and freedoms, and the free flow of information. It helped stifle and silence dissent. It persecuted and suppressed human rights groups like the Helsinki watch committees formed in the wake of the Conference on Security and Cooperation in Europe (CSCE). But all along the KGB engaged in image building. It fostered the idea that it was a modern, efficient, and reliable institution, devoid of internal corruption and dedicated to furthering the interests of the party, the state, and the people, and hence entitled to a privileged role in politics and society.

Bureaucratization and militarization interacted with a crisis of political leadership. One of its many causes lay in the serious health problems which Brezhnev developed after 1975. In the last years of his rule, he was said to have been able to work only for a few hours each day. His death in November 1982 at the age of almost 76 thus came almost as a relief to reform-minded officials in the party and government. In fact, the Politburo's selection of Andropov as his successor was greeted, according to Chernyaev, with an "outburst of ovations" in the November 1982 plenary meeting of

53 The new "internationalist function" of the Soviet armed forces was advocated by [Marshal] Andrei A. Grechko, "Rukovodiashchaia rol' KPSS v stroitel'stve armii sotsialisticheskogo armii," *Voprosy istorii KPSS*, Vol. 5 (1974), pp. 30-47. The case for using the navy as an instrument for the advancement of Soviet "state interests" was vigorously made by Admiral Sergei S. Gorshkov in a series of articles in *Morskoi sbornik*. For a detailed analysis, see Hannes Adomeit, "Militärische Macht als Instrument sowjetischer Außenpolitik: Überholt? Unbrauchbar? Unentbehrlich?," in Hannes Adomeit, Hans-Hermann Höhmann and Günter Wagenlehner, eds., *Die Sowjetunion als Militärmacht* (Stuttgart: Kohlhammer, 1987), pp. 200-235.

the Central Committee.[54] Such outbursts had occurred previously, some of them carefully stage-managed. This time, however, the enthusiasm appeared to be genuine.

The new leader had the reputation of being intelligent, shrewd, skillful, hard-working, and immune to corruption. He was regarded as having a remarkable mind, political talents, and an intellectual bent and as being incorruptible and selfless, which on occasion bordered on asceticism.[55] His record as ambassador to Hungary during the 1956 revolution, CC secretary in charge of relations with the ruling communist parties in the 1960s, and head of the KGB in the period from 1967 to 1982 made him appear better informed than anyone in the top leadership about the shortcomings of the Soviet system and the problems of empire in Eastern Europe. He seemed to combine perfectly the qualities of enlightened intellectual and efficient technocrat. Nothing, however, was to come of the high hopes that had accompanied his appointment. He merely prescribed the time-honored Soviet medicine of a new campaign to cure the social and economic ills that had befallen the country. The campaign was conducted under the heading of "mobilization of reserves" inherent in the system in order to modernize it. The imposition of discipline was meant to help in this effort.

The structural deficiencies of the system had led to a plethora of activities at the margin or outside the legal framework and a thriving "second economy." Many of these activities were advantageous to the consumer since they mitigated the rigidities of central planning and alleviated supply and distribution shortages. Yet rather than legalizing and constructively channeling these forms of private initiative, the new party leader set out to eradicate them. He decreed a relentless struggle against "social parasites," "idlers," "work shirkers," and "violators of work discipline." New regulations went into effect imposing harsher penalties for certain economic offenses such as bribery, speculation, and theft of products or tools from the workplace. The police were roused from their doldrums and forced to conduct dragnet operations in shops, bars, restaurants, movie theaters, and steam baths to check whether the people found there had legitimate business or were skipping work. The dragnet operation was also employed as part of yet another anti-alcoholism campaign. Drunkards were rounded up and punished by pay cuts, demotions, and public denunciations.

It is possible that Andropov considered the expansion of police powers and intrusion into the private sphere to be a preparatory stage for more far-reaching structural changes, perhaps even in a more liberal direction. If so, such changes were never outlined. A mere three months after his inauguration as Secretary General, he was put on a dialysis machine for kidney failure. In April 1983, rumors abounded that he no longer commanded a majority among the top leadership. Politburo and Central

54 Chernyaev, *Shest' let s Gorbachevym*, pp. 12-13.
55 Andropov as characterized by Arbatov, *The System*, p. 256.

Committee meetings were postponed. The party chief was last seen in public on 18 August 1983. Like actors in a *theâtre absurd* and in a repetition of practices adopted in the last years of Brezhnev's life Andropov's subordinates excused the party leader's absence with claims that he was suffering from recurrent colds. Letters and documents were published on his behalf to prove that the main subject of the charade was keeping abreast of the affairs of state and working indefatigably. Yet Andropov was not at hand to announce and justify the "countermeasures" in response to the West German parliament's decision to deploy intermediate-range nuclear missiles, and he failed to appear in public in order to explain the circumstances that had led to the destruction of the civilian Korean airliner on flight KAL 007. These tasks were left to Marshal Nikolai Ogarkov, the Soviet armed forces' chief of staff. Essentially, Soviet decision-making had reverted to the last years of the Brezhnev era. The political and personal agony, perhaps mercifully, came to an end only on 9 February 1984, when Andropov died.

Another succession and leadership crisis erupted. Reform-minded party officials had hoped that this time the Politburo would chose Gorbachev as party leader. This was not to be. As vividly described by Chernyaev, on 14 February the top leadership was ready to announce its choice for Andropov's successor to the assembled members of the Central Committee.

> "Five minutes before the beginning of the session the candidate members of the Politburo and the CC secretaries, as was customary, entered the hall through a side entrance. [Politburo candidate member and CC secretary] Ponomarev, the perennially first among the second, led the procession. The tension had reached its high point. All eyes were focussed on the left door behind the rostrum, that is, the entrance to the presidium. Who will appear first? Exactly at 11 a.m. Chernenko appeared. Behind him followed [Prime Minister] Tikhonov, [Foreign Minister] Gromyko, [Defense Minister] Ustinov, [CC secretary] Gorbachev and the others. There was dead silence in the hall. No one stirred. When Andropov, after Brezhnev's death, had been first to enter the plenary hall, everyone had stood up. The members of the presidium sat down, Gorbachev directly next to Chernenko. It was still uncertain [who had been chosen]. Chernenko rose, bent over steeply towards his notes on the table and in an asthmatic voice mumbled a few words about the deceased.

Tikhonov then announced that the Politburo had completed its deliberations and instructed him to "propose to the plenum to consider the candidacy of comrade Chernenko." The Central Committee was stunned. It responded to the proposal with lukewarm applause and to Tikhonov's *laudatio* of the candidate with embarrassed silence.[56] Predictably, the new leader proved to be as frail as his predecessor, although less imaginative. One is left to wonder why that selection was made and why Gorbachev was not chosen instead. Some understanding of the reasons may

56 Chernyaev, *Shest' let s Gorbachevym*, pp. 11-13.

shed some light on how one should view Gorbachev's position at that time and the policies he pursued subsequently.[57] Four possible reasons can be advanced.

The first is that the gerontocracy did not understand the seriousness of the Soviet predicament and, to the extent that it did recognize problems, thought that they could be managed. In the light of the Politburo's rejection of Chernenko and preference for Andropov in 1982, however, this rationale is unconvincing.

The second possibility is that the Politburo chose a transitional figure with the idea in mind that it would put its trust in a second-in-command (Gorbachev), who would effectively run party and state affairs and take over from him on Chernenko's departure. This explanation is disingenuous. Its attractiveness lies in the fact that, at least up to a point, subsequent events moved in this direction. There is no evidence, however, that this was the Politburo's reasoning at the time.

The third rationale is the idea that the members of the Politburo had been frightened by Andropov's initiatives and feared for their job if they were to select a younger, more dynamic leader. What speaks for such an interpretation is the fact that in his speech of praise to the CC Tikhonov had emphasized the candidate's "benevolent attitude" towards the cadres. And as Gorbachev discovered at the meeting, there were many happy faces around. These belonged to members of the Central Committee who had felt "threatened by dismissal or who had already retired but still belonged to the CC." They were hopeful that "now their time, the tranquil and 'stable' [time], in a word, the 'time of Brezhnev,' would return."[58]

Finally, opting for someone like Gorbachev, with his only fifty-two years of age at the time of Andropov's death, may have been far removed from the collective political mind of the Politburo. In their view, Gorbachev was simply too young to be allowed to skip several steps on the ladder of seniority. Although no spring chicken at the age of seventy-two, Chernenko was "younger" than other leading candidates for the top party post – Tikhonov was seventy-eight, Ustinov seventy-five, and Gromyko seventy-four. Did they remember and feel encouraged by the remark made by Andrei Kirilenko, a then member of the Politburo, who had stated at Brezhnev's birthday celebrations in 1976 that seventy years of age was being thought of in the Soviet Union as "middle age"?[59] Perhaps.

In conformity with the last argument, a private meeting is said to have taken place shortly prior to the Central Committee plenum, with Gromyko, Ustinov, Tikhonov, and Chernenko in attendance. The four appear to have taken the crucial decision on the succession. Tikhonov was overheard in the corridor as saying, "I believe that we

57 This discussion draws on John Miller, *Mikhail Gorbachev and the End of Soviet Power* (New York: St. Martin's Press, 1993), pp. 39-40.

58 Gorbatschow, *Erinnerungen*, p. 242.

59 *Pravda*, 15 October 1976.

did indeed decide correctly. Mikhail [Gorbachev] is still young. One also doesn't know how he would behave in that position [of General Secretary]. Kostya [Chernenko] is exactly the right man."[60]

Whatever the precise reason for his selection, Chernenko as party chief meant continuation of the pervasive ineptitude, incompetence, inertia, and lack of innovation in the Soviet Union. Collectivism in decision-making and continuity of policy would again be emphasized. As previously, some economic experiments and pilot projects would be authorized but comprehensive reform was put on hold. In foreign policy, matters would turn from bad to worse. Given the party chief's infirmities (he was said to suffer from emphysema) and his long periods of absence from the job (for instance, from 15 July to 5 September he made no public appearance), it is safe to assume that Gromyko was effectively in charge. Some Western scholars have made valiant attempts to portray this interval as rife with Soviet endeavors to reestablish detente with the West.[61] More pertinent, it would seem, are contemporary observations to the effect that under Chernenko's nominal leadership the counterproductive attitudes of "bear in hibernation" and "insulted giant" not only continued but turned into an "aggressively isolationist mood."[62] The number of Jews permitted to emigrate shrank to a trickle. Andrei Sakharov, already exiled in Gorki, was denied a visa for medical treatment in the West. The Soviet Union canceled its participation in the 1984 summer Olympic games. The country's direct-dial international telephone circuits, installed for the 1980 Olympics in Moscow, were unplugged and replaced by old-fashioned Soviet operators.[63] New fences topped with barbed wire went up around foreigners' compounds in Moscow and police were instructed to check Russian visitors more stringently. A new article 13 of the criminal code of the Russian Federation made it a crime to pass on to foreigners "information that constitutes a professional secret." Another law imposed a fine of 50 rubles on citizens who invited foreigners to stay at their home without informing the police. There was an increase in psychological intimidation and even physical assault against Western, notably American, journalists, diplomats, and

---

60 Gorbatschow, *Erinnerungen*, p. 241. Gorbachev thus in essence confirms what American journalist David Remnick had heard. "'Kostya [Chernenko] will be easier to control than Misha [Gorbachev],' one of the Politburo members said as he left the room where they had settled the issue." As quoted in his *Lenin's Tomb: The Last Days of the Soviet Empire* (New York: Random House, 1993), p. 63.

61 For instance, Raymond L. Garthoff, *The Great Transition: American-Soviet Relations and the End of the Cold War* (Washington, D.C.: Brookings, 1984), pp. 168-94.

62 This was the observation made by Richard Owen, "Chernenko Walling Out the West," *The Times* (London), 28 June 1984.

63 This appears to have happened in 1982, still under Brezhnev, but the practice continued under Andropov and Chernenko; see Kevin Klose, "The New Soviet Isolationism: A Sorry Retreat," *International Herald Tribune*, 26 May 1984.

tourists.[64] The list of xenophobic measures could be extended and supplemented by examples of a nationalist and military-patriotic revival. At this stage, however, it is necessary to return to the main topic and examine the interaction between the multidimensional crisis of empire and the German problem.

5. The Impact of the Crisis on Soviet-East German Relations

The accelerating decay at the center also affected East Germany as the most exposed part of the Soviet imperial periphery. Perhaps paradoxically, it was not the GDR's actual or perceived socio-economic decline that prompted a crisis in Soviet-East German relations but contradictory Soviet perceptions and policies conducted on their basis. The Kremlin leaders, on the one hand, believed at least part of what they heard from the East German leadership: that the GDR was a political and economic success story. But, on the other hand, and quite in contrast to the idea of the GDR's political consolidation and economic prowess, they were concerned about the country's allegedly increasing dependence on West Germany and drift away from the Warsaw Pact and Comecon. Not least for this very reason did they resent the SED leadership's newly found self-confidence and assertivness. As described in the previous chapter, early in his tenure Honecker had been willing to consent to a package of quadripartite agreements and understandings on Berlin and bilateral agreements with West Germany on intra-German relations. However, in the second half of the 1970s, the new provincial governor had become more self-confident and independent and just as difficult to manage as his predecessor. There was less coordination and consultation between the GDR and the USSR than in the past. The Soviet leadership reacted with admonitions to the SED comrades not to overestimate their role and, in their relations with West Germany, not to let themselves be drawn into further economic dependencies. However, the admonitions fell on deaf ears. And there was very little the USSR could do since it had transferred most of its occupation rights to the GDR and Honecker was firmly in control of the party.[65]

As for the early 1980s, new archival evidence clearly shows how, in Honecker's perception, the GDR's profile had grown after it had received international recognition and UN membership. A lot of room in SED Politburo meetings is taken up by often exuberant reports on the various visits by Honecker and other Politburo members abroad, visits by Western and other dignitaries to the GDR, exchanges between SPD and SED party leaders, and meetings between East and West German government officials. The new evidence also reveals that, while the relationship with

64 Richard Owen, "Chernenko Walling Out the West," *The Times* (London), 28 June 1984.

65 "Mauerbau mit Genehmigung Moskaus: Kwizinskij als Zeuge im Keßler-Prozeß," *Frankfurter Allgemeine Zeitung*, 23 July 1993.

the Soviet Union remained an important part of East German foreign policy, its relative importance for the GDR was declining. East Germany was diversifying its foreign policy, a reversal of roles and policies was taking place and the sources of Soviet-East German conflict changed In the early 1970s, the controversies had concerned questions of foreign policy. At that time, Moscow had felt confident enough to push for East-West detente. In the late 1970s and early 1980s and most acutely in 1983-84, East German foreign policy deviationism was again at issue. This time, however, it was East Berlin that felt brave enough to make closer contact with the class enemy.

Honecker's confidence was reflected in his new attitudes towards German unification, thereby confirming Soviet anxiety about East Germany's possible drift into an all-German direction. Turning future events on their head, Honecker told SED officials in February 1981 that,

> if today certain people in the West make presumptuous speeches and pretend that reunification of the two German states is more important to them than their wallet, then we would like to tell them: be careful! Socialism will one day knock on your door, and when the day comes that the workers of the Federal Republic decide to transform the Federal Republic of Germany into a socialist state, then the question of German reunification poses itself completely anew. There shall be no doubt how we will decide then.[66]

Contrary to such unrealistic notions, as Gromyko had clarified earlier, a united socialist Germany was no longer in the Soviet interest. Although German unification under socialist auspices had no chance ever to be put on the agenda of practical politics, Honecker's all-German pretensions did produce irritation in Moscow (see *infra* in this section). Whenever it came to a confrontation over specific issues deemed important from the Soviet vantage point, the interests of the center still took precedence over those of the fiefdom. However, the degree of influence the Soviet Union could exert on the broad sweep of East German policies was even more limited than in the past. Frequently it yielded on subordinate issues. In 1983, for instance, Honecker demanded the recall of the two-time Soviet ambassador, Pyotr Abrasimov, who had long conducted himself as if the GDR were his personal fiefdom, attending East German Politburo sessions and interfering almost at will. Andropov obliged.[67] Whereas the CPSU, after Andropov's death and Chernenko's appointment to the post of General Secretary in February 1984, was demoralized, internally divided, and internationally isolated, the SED, in contrast, was able to present an almost undivided front. If the weak and ineffective Soviet leadership had

---

66 "Honecker spricht von Vereinigung beider deutscher Staaten," *Frankfurter Allgemeine Zeitung*, 17 February 1981.

67 See Kwizinskij, *Vor dem Sturm*, pp. 263-64; see also his remarks on the conduct of Yefremov, Abrasimov's predecessor.

wanted to undermine or replace Honecker, it would hardly have known on whom to rely in support of such a design.[68]

The enhanced self-assurance of the SED derived not only from its improved image and standing in the West but also from developments in Eastern Europe. In the late 1960s, the GDR had only been a junior partner in the Warsaw Pact's so-called "iron triangle," comprising East Germany, Poland, and Czechoslovakia – a powerful bulwark based on coal, iron, and steel, ideological orthodoxy and foreign policies of retrenchment. The triangle, however, had disintegrated in 1968, when the Czechoslovak communist party succumbed to the disease of "revisionism" from which, essentially, it was never to recover. In the second half of the 1970s, helped by massive borrowing from the West, Poland became the Soviet Union's preferred partner in bridge-building between East and West in Europe. But that country's role, too, collapsed with the disastrous downturn of its economy, the rise of Solidarity and the downfall of the party. East Germany was the only side of the triangle that seemingly remained unaffected by the virus of internal dissent and the ills of economic decline. Outwardly, throughout the 1970s , it maintained domestic political stability and officially it boasted steady economic progress.. Whereas according to government data of the countries concerned the net material product of Poland and Czechoslovakia decreased at the beginning of the 1980s (in Poland, it fell by 12 percent in 1981, and by 5.5 percent in 1982; in Czechoslovakia, by 0.1 percent and 0.3 percent respectively), the East German economy *grew* by 4.8 percent and 2.5 percent. East Germany's reported economic performance in 1983 and 1984 was even better, the growth of the East German national product outpacing that of any other Comecon country.

What, then, were the consequences of the increased self-confidence of the East German leadership for USSR-GDR relations? In the period from the Soviet Union's intervention in Afghanistan in December 1979 to the Bundestag's consent to the stationing of Pershing II and cruise missiles on West German soil in November 1983 they were difficult to recognize for the outside observer. Both Moscow and East Berlin had a shared interest in maintaining reasonably good political and economic relations with the countries of Western Europe. Thus Brezhnev, Andropov, and Honecker had fostered the notion of the divisibility of detente and the possibilities for Europe to remain a tranquil island in the rough seas of superpower competition. They had portrayed the Reagan administration as the driving force behind an increased danger of war in Europe and exempted the Schmidt government from the worst criticism. The purposes of this policy of differentiation at this stage of Soviet policy

68 See James A. McAdams, "The New Logic in Soviet-GDR Relations," *Problems of Communism*, Vol. 37, No. 5 (September-October 1988), pp. 52-53; see also Kwizinskij, *Vor dem Sturm*, pp. 255-266.

were apparently to undercut American economic sanctions, to enhance the influence of the West German "peace movement," and to exacerbate divisions in the Western alliance. Both Moscow and East Berlin warned that the European idyll could abruptly come to an end. They threatened that if Bonn were to implement the December 1979 "dual track" decision of NATO and deploy intermediate-range nuclear systems, intra-German relations would be one of the first major casualties of a new cold war in Europe. They cautioned that the whole carefully woven network of legal, political, and economic relations between West Germany and its neighbors in the East could suddenly unravel. Gromyko, for instance, stated in East Germany in the fall of 1983 that the deployment of U.S. missiles on West German soil would "contradict the spirit and letter" of the treaties normalizing Bonn's relations with Moscow and East Berlin.[69] Similarly, in October 1983, Honecker warned that if the Bundestag were to consent to the stationing of the missiles, a "new ice age" would ensue in relations between East and West Germany.[70]

But it soon became apparent that Moscow and East Berlin had different reasons for opposing the deployment of missiles in Western Europe. The primary objective of the Soviet leadership was to maintain its military preponderance in Europe and to expand its political influence by means of the "peace movement" and protracted arms control negotiations. By contrast, the East German leadership seems to have been motivated by the desire to avoid being drawn into an accelerated arms race between East and West in Europe and having to bear the brunt of a deterioration in East-West political relations.

In the autumn of 1983, shortly before the Bundestag decision, the attitudes and policies of the Soviet Union and East Germany began to diverge openly. *Neues Deutschland* started publishing letters to Honecker from Evangelical Church congregations, urging him to continue the dialogue between the two German states. Mutual trust, the letters said, should flow from the dialogue and form the basis of a "security partnership and, in your words, a coalition of reason."[71] Honecker, in order to emphasize the East German position, stated at a plenary meeting of the SED Central Committee in November 1983, only two days after the beginning of missile deployments in West Germany, that the countermeasures decided upon by the Warsaw Pact did "not elicit any enthusiasm" in the GDR. He also associated himself with the "coalition of reason" slogan and clarified that it was of "great importance to continue the political dialogue with all forces." Charging that the Kohl government had taken upon itself a great responsibility by agreeing to the stationing of missiles, he nevertheless assured the Central Committee: "We are in favor of limiting the

69 *Pravda*, 19 October 1983.

70 In a letter to Chancellor Kohl, *Neues Deutschland*, 10 October 1983.

71 *Neues Deutschland*, 22 October 1983.

damage as much as possible."[72] Thus, new seeds of East German deviation from the Soviet foreign policy line had been sown.

From the Soviet point of view, the problem was difficult to manage since party leaders in several other Eastern European countries continued to be interested in normal relations with the West. Most of them, including East Germany, Hungary, Romania, and to a lesser extent, Bulgaria, were openly asserting their own foreign policy preferences. There was even sweeping ideological justification for the divergence from the Soviet line and the challenge to Soviet authority. Such justification was developed by Matyas Szürös, the head of the international department of the Central Committee of the Hungarian Communist Party, in October 1983.[73] In the era of the Comintern and the Cominform, he argued, the national interests of the member states of the "socialist community" had "unconditionally" been subordinated to international interests. Such subordination, he stated emphatically, should no longer obtain. Differences in experience were completely natural since there was no "single correct model" to imitate. Both historic traditions and contemporary conditions made it possible for "relations between individual socialist and capitalist states to continue to develop despite the fact that the deterioration of East-West relations and the contraction of contacts are the general trend."[74]

In 1983-84, the SED also began to deviate from the CPSU's internal policies, notably on the issue of the relationship between the state and society. In contrast to the Soviet leadership under Andropov and Chernenko and its attitudes towards dissent, the East German government granted a certain degree of autonomy to the Evangelical Church. It also permitted the establishment of some transnational links between the two German societies, including the churches and the "peace movement." On the ideological plane, the SED began to cultivate a new "special relationship" with Western European social democratic parties. In April 1983, for instance, it organized a major conference in East Berlin on the legacy of Karl Marx, at which the SED argued that the cause of preserving international peace had assumed priority over the promotion of social change. Not only were communist parties of all orientations invited to send delegations to the conference, but so too were numerous social democratic parties, including the SPD. Then, in the following year, the SED began a series of direct negotiations with the SPD on common security

---

72 Ibid., 26-27 November 1983.

73 In a lecture delivered on 20-21 October 1983 at a conference on the teaching of history after World War II. The lecture was not published at the time. However, an article by Szürös based on it appeared in the Hungarian journal *Tadarsalmi szemle* (Budapest), No. 1 (January 1984), pp. 13-21.

74 Ibid.

issues, first, on a proposed chemical weapons-free zone and later on a European nuclear-free corridor.[75]

Soviet concern was reinforced not only by the fact that Honecker was toying with the idea of German unification under socialist auspices but also by another phase East Germany was now entering in its perennial search for national identity. It still emphasized its socialist roots but no longer derived its existence exclusively from the "revolutionary" strands of German history. It retained the claim that the GDR was the culmination of the tradition associated with the peasant wars of the early 16th century and its leaders (e.g., Thomas Münzer, Götz von Berlichingen, and Florian Geyer), the bourgeois revolutions of 1830 and 1848, and the proletarian revolution of November 1918. But it now also began to associate itself with the "whole richness of German history." Thus, the SED discovered precursors and parallels to its own world view in the writings of Johann Wolfgang von Goethe and Immanuel Kant and began to reinterpret the historic role of Martin Luther, Frederick the Great, and Otto von Bismarck. To the chagrin of the Soviet comrades, it also began to reevaluate the conspiracy to assassinate Hitler on 20 July 1944.[76]

Thus, on the eve of the twentieth anniversary of the assassination attempt, at a meeting of the (East) German Society of Historians and the Central Institute on History at the Academy of Sciences, SED court historians and ideologues claimed that the resistance group under Colonel Graf Stauffenberg had included "patriotic officers" who deserved "a place of honor in the history of the German anti-Fascist resistance struggle." Their cooperation with other leading personalities from different sections of German society had to be regarded as an incipient "coalition of reason" (!) and their attempt against the life of Hitler on 20 July 1944 as "a courageous act of historic and national significance."[77] Contrary to such reinterpretations, an article in the Soviet army newspaper scathingly attacked the Stauffenberg circle as having consisted of forces close to the German "monopoly bourgeoisie" and having "advocated an alliance with American imperialism and the creation of a united imperialist front against the Soviet Union." In obvious allusion to the East German historiographical departures, it warned that current efforts aimed at elevating such forces to the "rank of national heroes" could not be considered separately from the "activation of revanchist and nationalist tendencies in West Germany."[78]

The most important issue, however, and one that was to provide the first of two main triggering mechanisms for a severe crisis in Soviet-East German relations, was the extension of substantial amounts of West German credit to the GDR. In July

---

75 McAdams, "The New Logic in Soviet-GDR Relations," p. 53.

76 *Neues Deutschland*, 20 July 1984; *Krasnaia zvezda*, 19 July 1984.

77 *Neues Deutschland*, 20 July 1984.

78 *Krasnaia zvezda*, 19 July 1984.

1983, the West German government had guaranteed a credit to East Germany in the amount of DM 1 billion. In June 1984, on a visit in Moscow, Honecker was again warned not to increase GDR dependence on West Germany. Honecker chose to ignore the comradely advice and in late July 1984 another major West German government-guaranteed credit to East Germany in the amount of DM 950 million was agreed upon. Unacceptably from Moscow's perspective, the West German economic and financial benefits were linked to East German political concessions. For instance, when Bonn announced the second credit, it stated that East Berlin had consented to a list of eleven measures for the improvement of intra-German travel and visits and had given firm assurances that it would permit several thousands of its citizens to emigrate to West Germany in the current year.[79] In fact, in the first half of 1984 a larger number of East German citizens – almost 30,000 – visited West Germany than ever before. Given the importance of the issue for the increasing alienation in Soviet-East German relations and the animosity between Honecker and Gorbachev, the problem of debts and dependency will be analyzed later in more detail.

The second triggering device for the severe crisis in Soviet-East German relations in the summer of 1984 was the preparation of an official state visit by Honecker to the Federal Republic of Germany. For the East German party leader such a visit was, in the opinion of former SED Politburo colleagues, an "important, even emotional issue" and the "crowning of his career."[80] To provide some background, in November 1981, Brezhnev had visited West Germany for the third time during his tenure in office and had warmly supported the idea of a meeting between Schmidt and Honecker. On 11-13 December 1981, Chancellor Schmidt and Foreign Minister Genscher paid an official visit to East Germany and held talks with Honecker at Lake Werbellin and in Güstrow. However, the German chancellor and his foreign minister, as indeed international public opinion, were shocked when General Jaruzelski, on the last day of Schmidt's visit in the GDR, declared martial law in Poland. The "internal intervention" in Poland that made it unnecessary for the Soviet Union to intervene could not possibly have been carried out without Brezhnev's endorsement.[81] It was not unlikely, therefore, that the Soviet and, in association with them, the East German stage managers had intentionally attempted to embarrass Schmidt. They could at least have had the decency to delay their action until after Schmidt's return to West Germany. But now, as Polish internal security forces were rounding up Solidarity

79 See the reports on this linkage in *Frankfurter Allgemeine Zeitung* and *Süddeutsche Zeitung*, 26 July 1984.

80 Interview with Krenz; Schabowski, *Das Politbüro*, p. 35.

81 See Sidney I. Ploss, *Moscow and the Polish Crisis: An Interpretation of Soviet Policies and Intentions*, Westview Special Studies on the Soviet Union and Eastern Europe (Boulder, Colo.: Westview, 1986), pp. 135-153.

activists, the intra-German handshakes looked strangely out of place. In fact, not having been given discreet advance warning for a timely cancellation of the visit to East Germany, the chancellor and his foreign minister appeared duped to the West German public. Schmidt nevertheless extended an invitation to Honecker to visit the Federal Republic.

In the circumstances, that is, the continuing East German support for the repression of Solidarity in Poland and the widening controversy over the stationing of intermediate-range missiles in Europe, a visit by Honecker to West Germany at any time in the period from December 1981 to November 1983 seemed completely out of the question. But in 1984, after Honecker's deviation from the harsh Soviet line and the extension of the second West German credit to East Germany, the visit advanced from a dim prospect to specific planning. September was the month agreed upon for the visit . But the Soviet leadership, as will be shown, was adamant that it should not take place. Before examining this hotly debated issue, it is appropriate to sketch the deterioration of Soviet-West German relations that coincided with the crisis in Soviet-East German affairs.

6. The Impact of the Crisis on Soviet-West German Relations

In March 1984, the Soviet leadership under Chernenko's frail guidance responded to the challenge in the bloc with an ideological counteroffensive and at the April plenum of the Central Committee decided to show a stone-hard face to the outside world.[82] Part of the new harsh attitude was the abandonment of selective detente, that is, the policy of relative goodwill and inducements to West Germany and Western Europe, while adhering to an uncompromising attitude toward the United States. The first indications of the new Soviet policy toward West Germany appeared in a communiqué issued at the end of the conference of foreign ministers of the Warsaw Pact countries in Budapest on 20 April 1984, which expressed concern that once again "concepts are being propagated which put into question the borders of the European states and their social order and which are directed against the political and territorial realities in Europe."[83]

Thus, yet another propaganda campaign against Bonn began to take shape. As if in preparation for Foreign Minister Genscher's visit to Moscow at the end of May,

---

82 On the ideological counteroffensive, see the article by Oleg Rakhmanin, deputy head of the Central Committee's Department for Liaison with the Communist and Workers' Parties: O. V. Borisov (pseud.), "Soyuz novogo tipa," *Voprosy istorii KPSS*, No. 4 (1984), pp. 34-39. The Soviet ideological counteroffensive was supported by two members of the Czechoslovak Communist Party; see Michael Stefanak and Ivan Hlivka, "Narodni a internacionalni v politice KSC," *Rude pravo*, 30 March 1984.

83 *Izvestiia*, 21 April 1984.

Soviet politicians and party hacks suddenly found a new growth of "revanchism," "militarism," and "neo-Nazism" in the Federal Republic. Whereas accusations of the West German government had until then been based only on guilt by association, that is, on the idea that Bonn was supporting or at least not resisting the policies of the Reagan administration, it was now held *directly* responsible for the sharp deterioration in East-West relations and for an increased risk of war in Europe. In particular, Soviet propagandists attacked Bonn and the decision by the Western European Union (WEU) to lift the restrictions, imposed on West Germany when it entered NATO in 1955, on the production of long-range conventionally armed aircraft and missiles. They claimed that the WEU decision had to be seen in the context of the current "policy of the militarist circles" in NATO, including in West Germany. This policy had entered a highly dangerous phase, they charged, its manifestations being plans for the deployment of new American missiles in Europe, increased defense cooperation in WEU, and demands of leading Christian Democratic politicians for the creation of a European nuclear force.[84] Although the Soviet campaign against Bonn is on public record, the question arises why it took so long – almost half a year after the Bundestag vote on missile deployment – to get underway. Several reasons may explain the time lag.

First, the Soviet leadership may not have foreseen the likely evolution of West German domestic politics after the November 1983 Bundestag vote and regarded the position of the SPD on international security issues as promising. In fact, a considerable transformation of the SPD had taken place in the period from 1977 to 1983. In 1977 chancellor Schmidt had commented on the need to maintain a balance between NATO and the Warsaw Pact countries in the "gray weapons" area, that is, the realm between the strategic and tactical nuclear levels. He had been one of the principal architects of NATO's dual-track decision in 1979. But there was widespread opposition within the party. It remained to be seen, from Moscow's perspective, whether majority opinion in the party would distance itself further from NATO and move towards neutralism or return to the political center in West German politics.

Second, in the immediate aftermath of the stationing of the missiles, no one could predict with certainty the reaction of the West German "peace movement" and its future influence. The Central Committee's International Department still assumed or at least hoped that major sections of the opposition outside parliament would continue to demonstrate against the stationing of missiles and draw upon the impressive strength of the more than one million people that it had been able to

---

84 Danil Proektor, "Wenn die letzten Limits fallen," *Neue Zeit* (Moscow), No. 19 (May 1984), pp. 18-21; see also V. Nikanarov, "Indul'gentsiia militarizmu: NATO pooshchriaet narashchenie voennoi moshchi FRG," *Krasnaia zvezda*, 18 May 1984.

muster in the fall of 1983. In Moscow it seemed unlikely that the "peace movement" would decline quickly to relative political insignificance in the West German body politic.[85] The probable degree of success or failure of Soviet military pressure and selective detente, therefore, may not have been clear in the arteriosclerotic collective mind of the Soviet leadership.

Third, the Politburo may have hesitated to impose a new line on West Germany because, as noted, the Eastern European countries were quite averse to a deterioration of political and economic relations with Western Europe. Party leaders and propagandists in these countries had no illusion about the great difficulty to make a new "revanchism" and "militarism" campaign against West Germany appear credible. Thus, the Soviet Politburo may initially have wanted to act behind the scenes in order to avoid a damaging public dispute and to force the issue only after the incontrovertible failure of such attempts.

Fourth, the Kremlin may not have realized until the first months of 1984 that vigorous efforts needed to be made to restore the credibility of the Soviet threat posture. Beginning in early 1984, the West German government began to claim triumphantly (but perhaps unwisely) that the Soviet countermeasures at the military level did not really amount to much and that countermeasures at the political level were practically non-existent. Above all, as they pointed out in private as well as in public, intra-German relations and the status of Berlin had remained unaffected. No "new ice age" had occurred. And economic relations had not suffered, neither with the USSR nor with other Comecon countries. Such interpretations of "business as usual" may gradually have increased the pressure on the Soviet leadership to demonstrate that it indeed meant business.

Finally, Chancellor Kohl's political philosophy and the evolution of intra-German affairs had become an irritant in Moscow. In July 1983, when Kohl had visited Moscow, he had forcefully portrayed reunification as a major foreign-policy goal of the West German government. Subsequently, after his return to the Federal Republic, he had insisted that the German problem was still *eine offene Frage* – an unresolved question – and that, as codified in the 1972 Basic Treaty, "special relations" existed between the two German states. In principle, this was nothing new. Officials in the Soviet foreign ministry and the Central Committee's International Department, however, thought they had detected a new stridency on the German problem by what, after all, was no longer a government coalition led by social democrats but by conservatives.[86]

Thus, given the persistence of the traditional paradigm in 1984, the Soviet Union's relations with both East and West Germany were becoming a problem. But the tense

85 Interview with Zagladin.

86 Interview with Rykin.

relations with its recalcitrant and obstructionist *gubernator* in East Berlin were the problem that had to be dealt with immediately. In late July and early August, the Soviet leadership finally lost ist patience. It went public with its criticism and forced the unruly East German satrap to reappear in Moscow to face another round of accusations. This important juncture in center-periphery relations in Europe will be described and analyzed next.

7. Debts, Dependency, and Intra-German Relations

In Haydn's "Surprise" Symphony (No. 94 in G Major), a possibly slumbering audience is rudely awakened in the *andante* of the second movement when, at a second pianissimo, the full orchestra suddenly plays a fortissimo. At this stage in the book, after the *tour de force* on paradigms and parameters, the reader may need a jolt to reinvigorate his interest. If so, nothing could serve that purpose better than two *Pravda* articles that appeared in the summer of 1984. At that time certainly the sensitivity of the subject, the timing of the articles, and their high-level political backing converged to catch the attention of political leaders and slumbering Sovietologists. The articles also tell a fascinating story of empire and ideology.

Perhaps paradoxically for the uninitiated in the defunct art of Kremlinology, the articles were ostensibly not about East Germany but nevertheless infuriated its leadership. Equally paradoxically for the untrained eye, the first article was written by a certain Lev Bezymensky who – in contrast to the pseudonyms often used by the editors of *Pravda* to lay down the party line – actually existed but who was almost unknown beyond a small circle of specialists in both the Soviet Union and the West.[87] Nevertheless, the article was also published in *Neues Deutschland*, the East German party newspaper. The second article did not even have a byline, and the East German party newspaper failed to publish it.[88] However, the issues it dealt with were considered serious enough by both Soviet and East German party leaders to break off their vacations and hurry to a hastily arranged secret meeting in Moscow. According to widespread Western opinion, it was the advent of perestroika and glasnost that caused a deep political rift between the CPSU and the SED and personal animosity between Honecker and Gorbachev. It can be argued, however, that the chasm between them opened earlier, with the publication of the two articles and the ensuing emergency meeting in Moscow.

The background for the Soviet-East German acrimony lies in the extension of two major government-guaranteed credits by West Germany to the GDR. The first, granted in July 1983, amounted to DM 1 billion (*Milliardenkredit*); the second was

87 Lev Bezymensky, "Pod sen'iu amerikanskikh raket," *Pravda*, 27 July 1984.
88 "Na lozhnom puti," ibid., 2 August 1984.

extended in July 1984 and was almost in the same amount – DM 950 million. Since credit to communist countries in one form or another was to become a normal part of East-West interaction and indeed had already played such a part in Soviet-American relations in the period of detente, it is easy to overlook the significance of the dramatic measure. Except for "swing" credits to facilitate intra-German trade, credit to East Germany was unprecedented. Furthermore, the political sensitivity of the arrangements was heightened by the fact that they did not occur in a period of renewed detente but rather in one of unabated East-West tensions over the stationing of intermediate-range nuclear missiles in the Soviet Union and Western Europe. In addition, the credits were arranged by Franz Josef Strauß, who in the past had been the *bête noire* of Soviet and East German propagandists and had been attacked by them as a rabid revanchist harboring nuclear ambitions. For the Soviet Union the main issue was whether East Germany was carelessly embarking upon a slippery path that would lead from economic to political dependency and ultimately erosion of the socialist foundations of East Germany.

Günter Mittag, the chief architect of the New Economic Mechanism under Ulbricht and the leader responsible for economic affairs under Honecker, was to acknowledge in retrospect that there had indeed existed a close linkage between politics and economics. At the beginning of the 1980s, he wrote, the GDR had no longer been in a position "to achieve on its own the necessary qualitatively higher level of labor productivity." CMEA could not be relied upon to provide new impetus either. On the contrary, in his view, this organization "counted on the GDR for the development of new technologies." Thus, the only thing that remained was "closer cooperation and closer rapprochement" with West Germany although we "implicitly had to accept the fact that the Federal Republic always granted assistance under the premise of preparing for future reunification."[89]

Soviet-East German controversies over the issue began in earnest at the beginning of the 1970s.[90] The deteriorating performance of the centralized command economies, including that of the GDR, threatened to erode living standards and political stability. In order to avert that danger, Honecker developed an ambitious *sozial-politisches Programm* that was to provide not only for the continuation of subsidies for cheap food, rent, health care, education, and transportation but also the expansion of housing construction and social benefits, such as old-age pensions, child-care benefits, maternity leave, and a reduced work week. Laudable as the

---

89 Günter Mittag, *Um jeden Preis: Im Spannungsfeld zweier Systeme* (Berlin: Aufbau Verlag, 1991), p. 83.

90 Parts of this section draw upon Patrick Stuart, "Perceptions and Reality in Erich Honecker's Formulation of Economic and Foreign Policy," The Fletcher School of Law and Diplomacy, unpublished seminar paper, written for this author's seminar on "Russia and Germany in the New Europe," fall term 1992.

program may have been, the question was how to finance it. If severe cuts in investment were to be avoided, an increase in borrowing was the answer. When the possible risks of such a strategy were pointed out to Honecker at a Politburo meeting in February 1972, he made it clear that he accepted these risks and that borrowing from the West was meant to be long term, saying that "We do not have the intention to repay the debts of the GDR within two years."[91]

The "oil shock" significantly enhanced the pressures for borrowing. For whereas the Soviet Union managed to postpone the ultimate hour of reckoning by the huge windfall profits it was able to reap, East German economic specialists estimated that the price explosion for oil and raw materials on the world market would "lead to an enormous additional burden for the national economy of the GDR, amounting to an estimated 25-30 billion marks at present." That, precisely, was the sum which Honecker had intended to spend on the core of his *sozial-politische Programm*, the construction of housing.[92]

East Germany's level of indebtedness subsequently began to increase. This did not go unnoticed in Moscow. In the mid-1970s, Prime Minister Kosygin told Mittag that East Germany should refrain from increasing its level of Western indebtedness above DM 6 billion.[93] To put this figure in perspective, according to the head of the GDR Staatsbank, even this limit would have been "3.6 times higher than the total export volume" of the GDR and meant that "the national income consumed [would have been] higher than the national income produced."[94] But Honecker and Mittag ignored all warnings and considerations of economic rationality and went beyond this level. In fact, at that time, GDR indebtedness was already well over the DM 6 billion threshold. In 1979 the total hard currency debt reached about DM 30 billion.[95]

Werner Krolikowski, a Politburo member and CC secretary for economic affairs in 1973-76, later revealed that "at every meeting with Honecker the Soviet party leaders – Brezhnev, Andropov, Chernenko, and Gorbachev – warned of the great danger of indebtedness to the West."[96] At one of these meetings in East Berlin, in October 1979, on the occasion of the thirtieth anniversary of the foundation of the GDR, "Brezhnev pounded his fist on the table and, in front of the assembled [SED] Politburo, accused Honecker of leading the GDR into bankruptcy."[97] The East

91 Przybylski, *Tatort Politbüro*, Vol. II, p. 49.

92 Ibid., p. 54.

93 Przybylski, *Tatort Politbüro*, [Vol. I], p. 325.

94 Przybylski, *Tatort Politbüro*, Vol. II, p. 50. Grete Wittkowski was the head of the GDR state bank. Her figure of 3.6 is calculated on the basis of a projected debt of DM 5.9 billion (rather than DM 6 billion) for the end of 1973.

95 Przybylski, *Tatort Politbüro*, Vol. I, p. 327.

96 Hand-written notes by Krolikowski, dated 16 January 1990, ibid., Doc. 22, p. 327.

97 Ibid.

German party leader pretended to take the criticism seriously and had proposals put before the Politburo to halve the total debt of the GDR in the 1980s. But these proposals were as unrealistic as his previous policies. No serious attempt was made to fulfill the plans, and the level of debt continued to increase.

Honecker and Mittag then began to use an extensive business network under the auspices of Alexander Schalck-Golodkowski, a shrewd and shadowy figure, to raise as much hard currency as possible. The network went under the name of *Kommerzielle Koordinierung* (Coordination of Commerce), referred to by insiders as KoKo, which Schalck also used to amass a private fortune. One of the avenues he pursued was the export of weapons, a scheme that began in earnest in 1982 and earned the GDR about DM 300 million in that year.[98] KoKo expanded commercial exports, too, even if it meant engaging in transactions that would yield only DM 0.10 per commodity unit at a production cost of 1 East German mark. Schalck finally used KoKo to exchange East German for West German marks at commercial banks in West Berlin. Since the banks kept each other informed about the volume of such exchanges, Schalck's operatives synchronized their transactions in order to avoid a precipitous fall in the exchange rate.[99]

The imperial center was apparently well informed about Honecker's economic strategy and, indeed, about internal SED concerns and opposition to the increasing level of indebtedness. One of the informants was Krolikowski, who told the Kremlin in March 1983: "The deliveries in the export plan with the Soviet Union have not yet been specified 100 percent. Products in the amount of 1.3 billion marks are still missing."[100] He commented that this state of affairs "unmasks [the fact] that the most important task [of planning] is the balancing of trade with the NSW [non-socialist world] through [an increase in] exports." Furthermore, according to Krolikowski, it also showed the GDR's intention "*to sell to the Soviet Union such commodities as cannot be sold in the NSW* and in that way to fulfill the plan for exports to the Soviet Union."[101] Such reports in all likelihood confirmed the Soviet leaders' worst suspicions. Indeed, since politics and economics are linked, they could not have been very surprised about a further observation in Krolikowski's report to the effect that "the attitude by E[rich] H[onecker] to the Soviet Union and CMEA is characterized by great cunning." Honecker avoided open criticism of Andropov, but everything he had to say about the new Soviet leader was said with "cool sobriety, without personal

98 Ibid, Vol. II, p. 63.

99 Ibid.

100 Ibid., Vol II, p. 65. Krolikowski by then had already been demoted (in 1976) to the position of deputy prime minister.

101 Ibid. (italics mine).

involvement and dedication," and there wasn't "a word of praise." He was merely "adopting an attitude of watchful waiting to the events in the Soviet Union."[102]

Western estimates of the GDR's debt, too, became more ominous. The *Wall Street Journal*, which had calculated the GDR's debt to the West as being $11.8 billion at the end of 1980, estimated that this amount would rise to $18-20 billion by the end of 1985. The *Neue Zürcher Zeitung* provided a figure of $12 billion in July 1982. The United Nations calculated an even higher figure. However, none of these estimates included East German obligations to West Germany in the amount of approximately DM 3.4 billion at that time, which were not counted as foreign debt.[103] Forty percent of these debts had a payment period of less than one year. This required that half of all hard currency receipts be used for the repayment of principal and interest. But these obligations could only be met by raising new credit. To compound matters, the deterioration in the terms of trade as a result of the huge increase in the world market price for oil and raw materials made it more difficult to acquire hard currency. But new credits were urgently required.

In June 1983, Honecker sent Schalck as his personal emissary to a secret meeting with Franz Josef Strauß. In a personal letter, which Schalck handed to the Bavarian prime minister and head of the CSU, the East German leader revealed economic and financial information that he had withheld even from his own government and party.[104] He effectively bared his soul and confessed to Strauß the GDR's economic predicament. As Strauß later wrote, Honecker told him that he "could ask for CMEA's help, which for all practical purposes meant Moscow's, but Western assistance was a [preferable] alternative, since he intended to cooperate with [the West] more closely on economic matters." The letter culminated in the plea to Strauß to use his good offices in Bonn in order to break the barriers which had thus far stood in the way of the realization of his wishes.[105] Schalck insisted on having the letter returned to him to take back to East Berlin. Secrecy, evidently, was of the highest order. Only Schalck and Mittag knew of Honecker's plans. If the wheeling and dealing with Strauß had been discussed in the Politburo, his associates would probably not have dared move against Honecker but someone would undoubtedly have informed the Soviet leaders, and this would most likely have spelled the end of his plans.[106]

Another important part of the background to the *Pravda* articles was Honecker's unbending determination to visit West Germany. Chancellor Schmidt and Foreign

---

102 Ibid. [Vol. I], Doc. 25, p. 351.

103 Wolfgang Seiffert, "Zur Verschuldung der DDR und ihren Konsequenzen," *Deutschland-Archiv*, Vol. 15 (December 1982), p. 1241.

104 Przybylski, *Tatort Politbüro*, Vol. II, p. 63.

105 Franz Josef Strauß, *Die Erinnerungen* (Berlin: Siedler Verlag, 1989), p. 524.

106 Przybylski, *Tatort Politbüro*, Vol. II, p. 67.

Minister Genscher, as noted above, had paid an official state visit to the GDR in December 1981 and had invited Honecker to visit the Federal Republic. Consultations with the government in Bonn had advanced far enough by the summer of 1984 to make it seem quite realistic that the visit would take place some time in the autumn. Given the divergence of Moscow's and East Berlin's *Westpolitik*, the impending visit assumed supreme symbolic significance. The *Pravda* articles for obvious reasons did not refer to it. But, as will be seen, whether or not the visit should take place was a hotly contested issue in the August 1984 emergency meeting in Moscow.

8. *Pravda* Articles of Faith

To turn to the *Pravda* articles themselves, the diatribes by Bezymensky appeared just two days after the announcement of the second credit. The author attacked Bonn for "using economic levers as well as political contacts" in order to gain concessions by the GDR on matters of sovereignty. He reminded his readers that the Federal Republic had still not responded favorably to any of the four demands that Honecker had put forward in Gera, East Germany, in October 1980. The "Gera demands," as they were later called, had been issued by Honecker during a period of perceived risks of East German infection by the Polish Solidarity bacillus and had deliberately been designed to be unacceptable to Bonn. The demands consisted of (1) West German recognition of and respect for a separate East German citizenship; (2) upgrading of the permanent representations in Bonn and East Berlin to the status of embassies; (3) abolition of the Zentrale Erfassungsstelle (central registration office) in Salzgitter for criminal acts committed by East Germans for possible later prosecution; and (4) delineation and readjustment of the East-West German border at the Elbe river.[107] Bezymensky also reminded his readers of statements made by Honecker prior to the stationing of intermediate-range nuclear missiles in Western Europe to the effect that good-neighborly relations could not flourish "in the shadow of the missiles."[108]

The second, unsigned, article appeared a few days later. It was even more blunt in its attack on Bonn and drew the connection between the new credit and East German concessions more sharply. It warned that the "economic lever has frequently been used in the past for the disruption of the postwar peace order in Europe and above all for the destruction of the stability of the GDR." The lever at present was the "credit agreement between the Deutsche Bank and the foreign trade bank of the GDR." With the help of the credit and its deliberate linkage with demands, such as an increase in

107 For the text of Honecker's speech in Gera, see *Neues Deutschland*, 10 October 1980.
108 This, in fact, is the title of Bezymenksy's article.

the number of West German visitors to East Germany and of the volume of printed material imported by the GDR, Bonn attempted "to gain new channels of political and ideological influence." Finally, according to the editorial, West Germany tried, "under the pretext of 'damage limitation,'" to achieve its "long-standing revanchist plans" in Europe.[109]

Before focussing on the Moscow emergency meeting and providing an analysis of the Soviet-GDR controversies, three brief observations are in order. First, although the articles were ostensibly directed against Bonn, they were pointed to an even greater degree at East Berlin. Simply put, they outlined how Bonn had more or less skillfully laid a trap and East Berlin had stepped into it. From this perspective, the crucial question concerned the reason for the SED's ill-advised behavior. Was it a mixture of stupidity, naïveté, overconfidence, and pan-German illusions? Or was it part of a conscious and deliberate policy to construct a "special relationship" with the other Germany?

A second observation concerns the forum of the attack. Ordinarily, inter-party controversies were carefully shielded from international public scrutiny so as not to detract from the appearance of unity and cohesion of the "socialist community." The Sino-Soviet rift is a perfect example of this. Soviet criticism of China, as is by now well established, was first voiced in the late 1950s behind closed doors. Moscow then moved to indirect attacks (ostensibly against Albania, but Beijing was the actual target) and finally to open polemics. This pattern strongly suggests that public criticism was a procedure that was only adopted as a matter of last resort when all other avenues of redress had been exhausted. In the specific example at issue here, therefore, the Soviet initiative clearly indicates the prior existence of a pattern of conflict and controversy in Soviet-East German relations, not a mere collective quirk of temper or bad mood in Moscow.

These interconnections and inferences can be drawn *inter alia* on the basis of Honecker's remarks at the secret high-level meeting in Moscow, where he told his critics:

> As regards the first article, I was informed about it and I decided to have it published because it shows the position of the GDR in its controversy with the FRG. We did not print the second article because it was directed against some of the positions of the CC of our party. We are of the opinion that open polemics do not conform to the norms in the relations between our parties. We are against polemics [in our relationship] with the CPSU; all questions that arise can be solved among ourselves. I called you [Comrade Chernenko] on Monday [12 August] to make clear that

109 "Na lozhnom puti," *Pravda*, 2 August 1984.

there should be no public attacks since they only harm us and the whole [socialist] community.[110]

The third observation concerns the author of the attack. Bezymensky was known by CC International Department insiders as being a close confidant of Falin.[111] Honecker was perfectly aware of this.[112] Thus, there could not have been much doubt in the mind of anyone familiar with Moscow power politics that the signed article had the backing of the most senior officials in the CC's International Department involved in policy making on the German problem. Similarly, the unsigned article published subsequently merely reenforced the importance of the matter since this form of publication was usually adopted by the chief editors of *Pravda* authoritatively to enunciate party policy. In fact, Konstantin Rusakov, the head of the CC department for relations with the ruling communist parties, explicitly acknowledged in the Moscow meeting with Honecker that the articles "did not pass me by" and that he had "consented" to their publication.[113] But they also appeared to have the high-level support of the foreign ministry. Gromyko had frequently warned the East German comrades not to overestimate their role and in their relations with West Germany not to let themselves be drawn into economic dependence.[114]

A final observation is related to the previous point. The articles unquestionably not only had to have high-level backing in the Politburo but also that body's *approval*. However, when such authorization would have had to be given, Chernenko was on vacation. The second in command in Moscow was Gorbachev, and it is precisely he whom Honecker suspected of having been responsible for clearance of the articles. This suspicion was fully confirmed in the East German party leader's mind at the August 1984 emergency meeting in Moscow. According to what Honecker later told Krenz, Gorbachev both in the car to the Kremlin from the airport and in the Kremlin meeting showed himself well informed about the content of the articles.[115]

---

110 The source for this *exposé* and analysis of the Honecker-Chernenko meeting in Moscow is the verbatim East German protocol (*Niederschrift*) of the discussion; as usual, there is little doubt that the record of the proceedings was kept with customary German bureaucratic accuracy; see SED Politburo, *Arbeitsprotokolle*, J IV 2/2.039/280, transcript of meeting, p. 59 of typed original (italics mine).

111 Interviews with Grigoriev. Later, Falin and Bezymensky appeared as co-authors of an orthodox Soviet version on the origins of the Cold War; see *Pravda*, 29 August 1988.

112 Interviews with Krenz.

113 Transcript of meeting, p. 73 of typed original.

114 "Mauerbau mit Genehmigung Moskaus: Kwizinskij als Zeuge im Keßler-Prozeß," *Frankfurter Allgemeine Zeitung*, 23 July 1993.

115 Interview with Krenz; Gorbachev, at the August 1984 emergency meeting with Honecker in Moscow, refers to having talked to Honecker in the car; see transcript of the meeting, p. 64 of the typed original.

9. The Chernenko-Honecker Emergency Meeting in Moscow

The record of the meeting which took place on 17 August 1984 provides instructive insights into the reality of "fraternal relations" behind the façade of harmony and consensus. It provides a vivid example of what at the meeting euphemistically went under the name of "open" and "frank" exchanges – party jargon for the blunt expression of serious disagreement.[116] It clearly brings into focus the state of relations between the Soviet Union and East Germany, the sharp differences in their interpretation of international affairs, the sources of conflict between the two countries and their leaders, the personalities of the top leaders, and the origins of the personal animosity and alienation between Gorbachev and Honecker.

The character of meetings and their outcome are usually predetermined by the participants. This was no different at the Moscow conference. The participants included on the Soviet side the most senior representatives of empire and ideology: Chernenko, the party chief; Gorbachev, the second in command; Dmitri Ustinov, Politburo member and defense minister; Viktor Chebrikov, Politburo member and head of the KGB; and the aforementioned Rusakov, Central Committee secretary in charge of relations with the ruling communist parties. The MFA was represented only by Georgi Kornienko, one of its first deputy ministers; as the proceedings would show, his presence amounted to little more than token participation: the meeting was evidently intended to be an exercise in "proletarian internationalism" and the reassertion of communist party discipline in the bloc rather than a matter of diplomacy.[117] On the German side the delegation similarly included the most senior and powerful figures of the party and security hierarchy – Honecker as chief of the delegation; Politburo members and party secretaries Kurt Hager, responsible for ideology, and Hermann Axen, the party secretary for international affairs; Erich Mielke, Politburo member and chief of state security; and Günter Sieber, the head of the CC department for international relations.[118]

The tone of the meeting was set by Chernenko's terse welcoming remarks and his disingeneous observation that "the leadership of the GDR [sic] has apparently seen the need to achieve clarity concerning certain important questions in our relations" and that this "coincides with the wish of the Soviet party leadership." It was, of course, obvious to everyone in the room what this "need for clarity" was all about. Honecker was first given the opportunity to outline the East German position. He did

116 The terms were used several times by the participants to characterize the meeting.

117 The reader does not need to be troubled with the enumeration of the other participants mentioned in the verbatim record. They included V.V. Sharapov, a personal assistant to the general secretary; A.I. Martynov, sector head in one of the CC departments; and A.N. Tarasov, another CC official, as translator.

118 Also included in the talks was Bruno Mahlow, Sieber's deputy; he acted as translator.

so without the slightest trace of regret or remorse. On the contrary, in what must have been at least one full hour of presentation, he vigorously defended his point of view and policy.[119] In the process, at least from the perspective of an impartial debating judge, he effectively destroyed the Soviet argument.

Honecker initially made three technical and procedural points to undercut the Soviet position. First, "in the name of the Politburo of the CC of the SED," he extended "cordial greetings to Comrade Chernenko and the other comrades of the Soviet party leadership" and reported: "On Tuesday [13 August], a session of the Politburo of the CC of the SED took place which dealt with several questions arising from some articles in *Pravda.*" In accordance with "instructions of the Politburo" of the SED, he wanted to respond to the questions at issue. He thus conveyed the idea that he had discussed his response to the Soviet attack with his colleagues in the Politburo and that he had their full backing. He had apparently anticipated Soviet criticism to the effect that his policies were "subjectivist," that they perhaps did *not* have the backing of the SED leadership, and that he was deliberately attempting to conceal the extent of the rift between him and the Soviet leadership. Indeed, later in the meeting, Chernenko pointedly asked: "Do the members of the Politburo of the CC of the SED actually proceed from [the assumption] that everything that happens in the relations between the GDR and the FRG, including the preparation of the visit [of Honecker in West Germany] is coordinated in advance with the Soviet Union and that there is mutual agreement about that? If this were the case," he told Honecker, "it would mean that your comrades are not properly informed about our positions."[120]

A second procedural issue raised by the East German party leader was that of the form and venue of the Soviet attack. He flatly denied that there was anything to talk about concerning East Germany's relations with West Germany. "For the SED, [West German] revanchism and the necessity of unmasking it is not at issue. In the struggle against revanchism, the SED has always taken a firm position." At issue in reality were "speculation and efforts made in the West to drive a wedge between our two parties." The SED, Honecker claimed, based its policies on the view that one should not allow public rifts ("not even one millimeter") to occur in the relations between the GDR and the USSR since they only benefitted the class enemy. The CPSU apparently did not act accordingly. He made this perfectly clear later in the acrimonious exchanges when he said that he thought "that there should be no newspaper articles of this kind without prior" consultation and coordination and that such a procedure should be no problem.

---

119 His opening statement amounted to a total of 42 double-spaced pages. To deliver one page of text would probably have taken about one and a half minutes.

120 Transcript of the meeting, p. 52 of the typed original.

> Surely, it should be possible without much difficulty for the chief editor of *Pravda* to call the chief editor of *Neues Deutschland* over the VCh [top secret] line [linking the Warsaw Pact countries] ... to say, "Listen, Günter [Schabowski, chief editor of the East German party newspaper and a candidate member of the Politburo in 1984], we are planning this or that. We should talk about it and coordinate things and we could jointly consider what formulations are the most appropriate.

Such coordination had not occurred, Honecker implied. On a third technical point, although he had already insinuated that on matters of substance everything was perfectly clear and there was really nothing to discuss, he attempted to deflect in advance possible Soviet criticism of complacency by reminding his hosts that he had "somewhat cut short" his vacation (something that any German, East or West, would do only in a true emergency) "to deal with these questions."

On substantive issues, the East German party leader embarked upon a broad *tour d'horizon*. He referred to the summit conferences of the Warsaw Pact countries in Prague (January 1983) and Moscow (June 1983) and the foreign ministers' conference in Budapest (April 1984) and claimed that a common line had been agreed upon. In essence, it consisted of the idea that "the struggle for peace is the most important question of the contemporary era." This struggle and the consistent application of the principles of peaceful coexistence by the Warsaw Pact had not failed to impress the political leaders in the capitalist states. For instance, it had "put the adherents of a confrontational course in the USA government on the defensive." Furthermore, he thought, "one could not overlook a process of differentiation" in these countries. To explain, differentiation was seen by the Soviet leadership of the day as part of a pernicious Western policy directed against the cohesion within and among *socialist* countries. Honecker thus reminded his Soviet critics that the tables could be turned, with the member states of the Warsaw Pact playing on the differences within and among the countries of the Western alliance.

He then dealt with the enhanced role of the GDR in world affairs. The country's international stature was portrayed by Honecker – more implicitly than explicitly – as one of the more important results of the activist, peace-oriented policies of the GDR. Almost in passing he mentioned that the SED had had the opportunity recently to explain its approach to international affairs not only "in talks with the representatives of the communist and workers' parties and the national-liberation movements" but also with the chiefs of government of Canada, Sweden, Greece, Italy, the Federal Republic of Germany, Great Britain, France, Austria, Finland, Spain, the Netherlands, India, Syria, Egypt, Nicaragua, Mexico, and Malta, and also "the presidents of parliament of numerous countries of the world."[121]

121 Ibid., pp. 6-7.

To look ahead briefly at this stage, in the subsequent months of its continued defiance of Moscow, the SED was to emphasize even more strongly the theme of the enhanced international recognition, status, and influence of East Germany. For instance, in an internal report on the visit of British foreign secretary Geoffrey Howe to East Berlin in April 1985, the SED Politburo adopted the by then typical posture of self-congratulation and confidence. It thought that the visit had "clarified" the fact that Britain in its European policies had "to take into account more strongly than before the growing international position of the GDR and its authority as a political and economically stable state." The visit had further "strengthened the international position of the GDR and the international influence of its peace policy."[122] Even more importantly, the SED leadership went beyond the idea of differentiation as a useful concept for the socialist community's approach to the West. It commented favorably on Great Britain's alleged aim of reducing the "evident lag" in her relations with the socialist countries and that she was now "*actively taking part in the [Western] policy of differentiation among the member states of the Warsaw Treaty.*"[123] However, this flatly contradicted the current Soviet line to the effect that, as mentioned, Western policies of differentiation were considered detrimental to Warsaw Pact cooperation and cohesion.

The next move in Honecker's justification of his policies was a bow in the direction of the USSR. It came in the form of an endorsement of the Soviet Union's military strategy and doctrine. He criticized the United States for wanting to "increase its first-strike capability" against the countries of the Warsaw Pact by deploying nuclear missiles in Western Europe, including West Germany. He charged that the United States "*de facto* refuses to accept the principle of military parity and equal security," "strives for military superiority," and is ready to "start a new, extremely dangerous round in the arms competition, connected above all with the militarization of space and the creation of anti-missile and anti-satellite systems." He reminded his Soviet hosts that the United States had used nuclear weapons in Hiroshima and Nagasaki and had not renounced future use of these weapons, despite the fact that the USSR had already done so. Finally in his review of strategic matters, he lashed out against Washington for intensifying war preparations in Asia and in the Pacific and intervening in Central America, the Near and Middle East, and southern Africa. For all of these reasons, he went on, the GDR was determined to contribute to "maintaining the military-strategic balance under any circumstance." After the beginning of the stationing of intermediate-range nuclear missiles in Western Europe it had for that reason "taken the appropriate countermeasures agreed upon with the USSR."

---

122 SED Politburo, *Arbeitsprotokolle*, Politburo meeting of 16 April 1985, J IV 2/2A/2748.

123 Ibid. (italics mine).

On the surface, this seemed to be a mere confirmation of Soviet viewpoints. However, one of Honecker's central points was his insistence on the advantages of a *balanced* approach, consisting of both military countermeasures and a peace offensive. Turning specifically to Germany, he asserted that the "peace movement in the FRG is far from exhausted." It actively continued its struggle and had to be taken seriously by all the political forces in the FRG, also by the government. There was consequently "every reason on our part to encourage this struggle by an offensive, forward-oriented activity." This should include reiterating that the military countermeasures of the Warsaw Pact would be rescinded if the West were to stop and reverse its stationing decision.[124]

Continuing with the diagnosis of political and socio-economic forces in West Germany and the plea for a flexible response, Honecker adopted the traditional Marxist-Leninist view as to the "contradictory nature" of developments in that country. He asserted that Kohl and Genscher conducted policies even more strongly focussed on the United States than those pursued by the previous left-liberal government of Schmidt and Genscher. Nevertheless, it saw itself confronted with the necessity to continue *Ostpolitik* and, in essence, to adhere to the treaties concluded earlier. Furthermore, after the government of SPD and FDP under Chancellor Schmidt had so resolutely advanced NATO's dual-track decision and the stationing of missiles, the social democrats had now changed their tune. They now opposed the stationing of these weapons and supported a number of Warsaw Pact proposals on international security. This change of heart had been the result of (1) the "peace policy of the socialist countries," (2) the "pressure of the peace movement," (3) past "electoral results" in West Germany and (4) "future electoral decisions" in that country. The SED, for that reason, had "used the altered state of affairs as an opportunity significantly to expand its contacts with the SPD at all levels."[125]

East Germany, in Honecker's summary, had to conduct policies towards West Germany that would meet four criteria. The policies had

- "to be understood and supported by the popular masses in our country;"
- "to be understood and increasingly accepted by the greatest possible number of citizens in the FRG;"
- "to [contribute] to mobilizing the forces of peace and opposition in the FRG rather than letting them fall into a state of resignation;"
- "to make it more difficult for the Kohl government to be a good and active ally of the Reagan administration."[126]

124 The beginning of Honecker's review of the importance of the "peace movement," the SPD and the labor unions is on p. 9 of the original transcript and continues on pp. 19-23. For reasons of coherence, the two parts are presented in conjunction by this author.

125 Transcript of the meeting, p. 23 of the typed original.

126 Ibid., p. 33.

After this review of East-West relations and the principles of East German policy vis-à-vis West Germany, Honecker finally dealt with the first of the two most important issues in the Soviet-GDR controversy – his impending visit to West Germany. (The other issue, it will be recalled, was credit and dependency.)

> Concerning the question of my visit to the FRG, we let ourselves be guided by the inevitable task of the mobilization of all forces for peace, against the USA course of confrontation, and against the destruction of the European treaty system. *When the question is being posed when this visit shall take place the answer should be "Now,"* and [it should take place] in conjunction with the thirty-fifth anniversary of the GDR [on 7 October] when we will demonstrate the strength of our socialist GDR.[127]

He needlessly reminded Chernenko and the other CPSU Politburo members that the idea of the visit was nothing new. The invitation had been issued "three years ago by Chancellor Helmut Schmidt. It has been renewed by Chancellor Kohl. A corresponding invitation has also been issued by President [Richard von] Weizsäcker."

The following arguments, in Honecker's view, supported the idea of the visit to take place as soon as possible.[128] First, it would *enhance the standing and prestige of East Germany relative to West Germany*. Honecker explained that he would travel in his capacity as the head of state of the GDR. His counterpart, the federal German president, "has assured me that he will treat me in the same way as Todor Zhivkov [the Bulgarian president] who, as is known, will visit the FRG before me." This, he boasted, would "demonstrate that the socialist German worker and peasant state is a sovereign and independent state that conducts relations with the FRG on the basis of international law."

Second, the visit would *strengthen East Germany's influence in West German politics;* it would affect the orientation of the political parties and the outcome of elections scheduled in several of the West German Länder in autumn 1984. Almost all the political parties in West Germany welcomed the idea of the visit, Honecker told his critics. This applied first and foremost to the Greens and to the "peace movement." But it was true also for other political parties and forces. The FDP supported the visit because it saw it as improving the party's electoral prospects in the upcoming parliamentary elections. As for the SPD, their leaders

> have let us know that they place great value on the visit to take place in the next few weeks. The chairman of the SPD, Willy Brandt, recently again addressed himself directly to me and expressed his hope that he will [be able to] meet with me. He let it be known that he expected me to have

---

127 Ibid., p. 38 (italics mine). As a matter of nuance, the record has Honecker saying that the visit *soll* (shall) rather than *sollte* (should) *stattfinden* (take place). This reenforces his point that there was no doubt that the visit would take place.

128 The numbering and sequence of the arguments are mine.

> dinner with him in Bonn. Similar statements have been made by [SPD leaders Hans-Jochen] Vogel, [Egon] Bahr, [Horst] Ehmke, and others. Vogel told me at the beginning of August that the SPD has a special interest in the visit because it [the party] expects from it a strengthening of its position in view of the upcoming elections. [Johannes] Rau, SPD prime minister of North Rhine Westphalia, and [Oskar] Lafontaine, the SPD chairman of the Saarland, have expressed themselves in the same way. Elections will take place in both of these federal states. If the SPD were to win, the correlation of forces in the Bundesrat would be changed. On the whole, the leadership of the SPD expects assistance from my visit and the propagation of our policy so that it [the SPD] will be able to create in the FRG a new majority against the CDU-CSU.

Even in the conservative party there were circles that supported the visit, Honecker claimed. The CDU, as everyone knew, was "connected with important groups of the West German economy" for whom the continuation of trade relations with the USSR, the GDR, and other socialist countries was an important matter.

Third, Honecker argued, the visit would *improve the international standing and prestige of East Germany*. In this context, he once again reported that in the past months he had met with the heads of government of Sweden, Greece, and Italy. Soon he would travel to Finland, and in late fall he expected the French prime minister and the chancellor of Austria to visit East Germany. The French president, François Mitterrand, had sent him a message. And Egon Krenz, his deputy, was at present on a visit to Greece. His own visit to West Germany, therefore, "would be part of a series" of visits and exchanges and would "underline that the relations of the GDR with the FRG are of the same quality under international law as those with other capitalist countries."

Fourth, the visit would contribute to a *normalization of East-West relations in Europe*. Not too long ago, he reported, Chancellor Kohl had visited Budapest. Zhivkov was getting ready to travel to Bonn. Comrade Chnoupek, the Czechoslovak foreign minister, had visited Bonn and issued an invitation to the German chancellor to visit Prague. Representatives of other socialist countries were planning to have meetings in Bonn. "In this context, my trip to the FRG would be a normal occurrence, whereas if this visit were not to take place this would create the impression of an extraordinary event."

Finally, the visit could serve as an opportunity for *more effective coordination of Soviet-GDR and Warsaw Pact policies toward West Germany*. At the moment, there were no coordinated proposals on the details of the visit, otherwise the East German foreign ministry would already have entered in consultations with its Soviet counterpart. There was still time and the opportunity for the Soviet Union and other Warsaw Pact countries to provide inputs. East Berlin was ready for consultation and coordination with its partners. Honecker completed the explanation and justification of his policies by saying that

> All in all, after consideration of all factors, we have arrived at the conclusion that the visit in the FRG would be right and beneficial for our joint policy of struggle for lessening the danger of war and against the arms policy of the USA and NATO. ... We have, of course, also considered the question of canceling the visit. A cancellation, [however], if it were not explained convincingly to the population of the German Democratic Republic as well as the peace forces of the FRG and the international public, could really satisfy *only the extremists in the FRG and the USA who are intent on preventing the visit.*[129]

Before turning to the rebuttal by the "Soviet comrades," it is necessary to explain that Honecker had studiously avoided raising the very subject that had been central to the *Pravda* attacks: the allegedly successful West German strategy of undermining the political reliability and stability of the GDR by using the "economic lever." The implication of this – no doubt deliberate – omission was apparently that the Soviet argument was so wide of the mark that it was unworthy of serious consideration.

Chernenko's Response: The Empire Strikes Back

The Soviet Politburo had obviously discussed and formulated the line to be taken in response to its unruly German satrap. Chernenko graciously made a few polite references to the "great respect" the Soviet comrades had for the "achievements of the GDR" and even asserted that "we are learning from the experience of the German comrades." He then ungraciously replied to Honecker's statement: "Much of what you, Comrade Honecker, have just told us, is well known to us. But your account confirms the necessity of a timely and open talk."[130]

Almost predictably, he began by adopting the time-honored approach used by Stalin and his successors in order to enforce bloc discipline: the portrayal of a dangerous world that required vigilance. He claimed that the main cause of increased tension in the world lay in US imperialism and the "striving of the USA to unite the Western countries in the struggle against socialism." Europe remained the main arena of the East-West competition. "Here lies the main border between the two systems, here is the most forward line of the controversy between socialism and capitalism, and exactly here can be found the main direction of the attacks by the West against us."

What about West Germany, then? Chernenko called it Reagan's European bailiff, the "main force militarily, economically, and ideologically" carrying out Reagan's policies "on our continent." Continuing, the Soviet party leader did not mince words.

---

129 Ibid., pp. 38-44 (italics mine).

130 Transcript of the meeting, p. 45 of the typed original.

The [speaking with a] forked tongue [in international relations] and the militarist tendency in the policy of the FRG [today] are comparable to Bonn's actions under Adenauer. Bonn and Washington act in full accord with each other. The USA is stationing new missiles in Europe, calling for a crusade against socialism and calling in question the realities of post-war development. Bonn has declared the German problem to be unresolved, has officially demanded [reestablishment of] the borders of 1937 and speaks of special German relations. More vigorous efforts are being made to undermine the socialist order in the GDR. That can be recognized by the naked eye.

The second club used traditionally by Soviet leaders to enforce bloc discipline was the assertion that disobedience threatened common security interests. This, too, was argued by Chernenko. For him, the relations between the GDR and FRG directly affected "the security of the Soviet Union and the socialist community as a whole."[131] The conclusions to be drawn were unambiguous:

The policy of revanchism is a policy of war. I talked about this on 14 June 1984 [when you visited Moscow for talks with us] and I said that we couldn't really understand why the GDR is exercising such restraint towards the revanchist and nationalist policy of the FRG. To respond favorably at present to [the West German desire for a] broadening of relations with the FRG means to provide it with additional channels for ideological influence in the GDR. The state of affairs itself and Bonn's positions dictate the necessity of a line of delimitation. What is required is stubbornly to put to the FRG the principled demand for the strengthening of the sovereignty of the GDR and the unconditional respect of this sovereignty by Bonn. [It is] in this context that one should put the question of your visit in the FRG.

A third club used in the past by Soviet hard-liners and interventionists in the bloc was the charge that the satraps had in previous meetings promised to mend their ways but had subsequently reneged on their promises. This approach was also used by Chernenko and put squarely in the credit-and-erosion-of-socialism context.

You, Comrade Honecker, in our talks in June, did not voice any doubt and said that the GDR completely agreed with the Soviet Union on all international questions. Putting it mildly, the state of affairs after our talks has not improved. Nevertheless, [GDR] declarations have been issued concerning new measures for facilitating contacts and the improvement of possibilities for visits of citizens and children from the FRG. *These measures, from the point of view of internal GDR security, are dubious and constitute unilateral concessions to Bonn.* You receive financial benefits as a result. But these are in reality only illusory advantages. The point here is [the danger of] additional financial dependencies of the GDR on the FRG.[132]

131 Ibid., pp. 48, 50.

132 Ibid., p. 48 (italics mine).

As if the warning had not been clear enough, Chernenko added: "The events in Poland are a grave lesson from which one should draw conclusions."[133]

The Soviet party leader denied that the process of East-West German rapprochement in any way enhanced the status of the GDR relative to West Germany. On the contrary, he asserted, "Whereas the positions of Bonn in the affairs of the GDR and West Berlin have been strengthened, the GDR has not made progress on any of the vital questions." This applied, for instance, to the recognition of a separate East German citizenship, the borders, the change of the status of the GDR representations to embassies, and the recognition of Berlin as an inseparable part of the GDR.

What, then, was Chernenko's response to the alleged opportunities for exploiting differentiation in the West German body politic and influencing the orientation of political parties and public opinion? What about the possible benefits of "damage limitation" after the stationing of the missiles and the presumed advantages of constructing a "coalition of reason" across the systemic divide? His reply was unequivocal: "Yes, in the FRG there are some anti-missile and anti-war sentiments. In the ruling circles there are also some politicians who proceed from sober positions." However, all of that "does not provide any rationale for the slogan of an all-German coalition of reason. This slogan is being used by those who are attempting to camouflage their policy and to deceive the people by phraseology without class content."[134] Honecker, of course, had used the phraseology in question.

Another part of the party leader's rebuttal probably reveals more about the basic conceptual approach adopted by party leaders Brezhnev, Andropov, and Chernenko than does anything else they may have said publicly. The whole matter really came down to this, Chernenko explained. It was necessary "not to convey the impression that the hard line of the Reagan administration is producing results [because conciliatory responses would lead to even stronger and more brazen pressure."[135] Within this frame of reference, Chernenko returned for the third time in his rebuttal to the issue of the impending Honecker visit to West Germany. Incongruously, he mused that this was, "of course, a matter that has to be decided by the SED." However, the Soviet comrades believed "that they [the SED leaders] would collectively and mutually, taking into account the considerations expressed by us, reexamine this question ... *We also would like to tell you that we Soviet communists would react positively if in the circumstances that have arisen you were to cancel the visit.*"[136]

---

133 Ibid.

134 Ibid. p. 51.

135 Ibid.

136 Ibid., p. 53 (italics mine).

Just in case, so that the point of Soviet displeasure would not be lost, Chernenko concluded by thanking Honecker for his invitation to attend the thirty-fifth anniversary celebrations of the foundation of the GDR and informed him that "we have taken the decision to send a representative delegation led by Comrade Gromyko" to East Berlin – a clear *affront* since such a delegation ordinarily would be headed by the party chief or his deputy.

In essence, this completes the effort at extracting nuggets from the gold mine of the Moscow secret meeting. But there are two sets of exchanges that are of special interest here, one between Defense Minister Ustinov and Honecker and the other between the East German leader and Gorbachev.

The Ustinov-Honecker Exchanges

Ustinov's participation in the proceedings confirms the notion of him as a leader of narrow intellectual ability. In his interjections he twice repeated the Chernenko theme on West Germany as the main executor of Reagan's policies in Europe. He then moved on to explain to Honecker the nature of the Bundeswehr as the "main strike force of NATO." Honecker predictably and disdainfully brushed off Ustinov's attempt at lecturing him on a topic he thought he knew more about.

> '*Comrade Honecker:* Comrade Ustinov, we are very well informed about what you are saying. Just recently I decorated two female comrades who worked in NATO staffs. We know very well how things are going. Concerning the FRG and the role of NATO in US policy, I've also made clear our view to Comrade Ceausescu who didn't want to believe it. You can forget about any further remarks on that issue.
>
> *Comrade Ustinov:* It would be good, Comrade Honecker, if you were to remind [Ceausescu] of this during your visit to Romania. There are other facts. The Bundeswehr provides 50 percent of all land forces of NATO and 30 percent of the air forces. I only mention this here in order to make it clear what this is all about. You shouldn't take it the wrong way.
>
> *Comrade Honecker:* I know all this, Comrade Ustinov, and have to deal with it daily. ...
>
> *Comrade Ustinov:* I know that you know this, Comrade Honecker. What we are talking about here is unmasking the FRG – the NATO – line. It's important for that reason to work with the facts such as, for instance, the existence of refugee organizations with 2.5 million members, soldiers' associations with 4 million members, 80 Nazi organizations, associations of reservists, etc.
>
> *Comrade Honecker:* Well, all that is obvious, Comrade Ustinov, and we don't mutually have to convince ourselves [that these things exist. However, ...] as for the questions we are dealing with, I think that we can arrive at the conclusion that *it is up to the SED to decide on the question of the visit in the FRG.*

Comrade Ustinov: We would like to point out that with the greater opportunities for citizens of the FRG to enter the GDR the danger of espionage is rising. We also ask whether, when the gates are opened more widely, the [reliabililty of the] soldiers will not be affected negatively.

Comrade Honecker: First, we haven't opened the gates more widely. Second, *there is no linkage between credit and the easing of travel.* Naturally, we have to continue ideological work on this problem. There are only very few citizens in the GDR who do not have any relatives in the FRG. We have to be aware of this. And concerning the children from the FRG who come to us, they won't be able to push us around. And the pensioners who go from [the GDR] to the other side – they all come back.[137]

The *théâtre absurd* of "I know that you know, comrade" and the reflections on the potentially disruptive behavior of the capitalist kids on the socialist block need no further comment. But to complete this insight into the inner workings of metropole-periphery relations and the further evolution of Soviet policies on the German problem, it is necessary to look at Gorbachev's participation in the proceedings.

The Gorbachev-Honecker Exchanges

Gorbachev's role in the meeting amounted to a reenforcement of the pressure on Honecker to cancel the visit and toe the Soviet line. Yet his performance was typical for him in several respects. It demonstrated his apparent proclivity for compromise and consensus, his notion that persuasion is preferable to coercion, and that one only needed patiently to explain one's own point of view for the adversary eventually to relent and agree to a common position. As "history" – the collapse of empire and the implosion of the Soviet Union – was to underline, serious problems with this philosophy of political life arise when there is a serious clash of interest and the opponent is unwilling to change his mind. This is precisely what happened in the Moscow meeting.

Gorbachev began, in effect, by assuring the unrepentant sinners in the dock that the Soviet comrades were well-meaning. He "would like to state unambiguously that our common opinion proceeds from the view that what is at issue here is not a crisis situation in our relations." ("We are not talking about a crisis situation," he repeated later.) But on certain questions some "clarification" needed to be achieved and this should be, as Honecker himself had stated earlier in the car, the main purpose of the meeting. But even more than that: "Our meeting should lead to reconciliation and bring about trust." Having thus cast himself in the role of a lenient judge, he nevertheless lashed out against the culprits on the *banc d'accusés*, telling them that the rift that had opened up in Soviet-East German relations needed to be repaired and

137 Ibid., pp. 69-72 (italics mine).

harmony had to be reached so as to preclude the adversary from exploiting the differences. He then joined Chernenko and Ustinov in their scathing criticism of East German gullibility and susceptibility to the Western strategy of differentiation, quoting an unlikely source in his support:

> Even the Italian ambassador in Washington, in his talks in the State Department, has – in connection with the [planned] visit by Comrade Honecker in the FRG – drawn the conclusion that new processes are developing in Eastern Europe which needed to be watched carefully and that the [Western] policy of differentiation was producing results. We proceed from the view that this will be taken into consideration [by you].

He also reiterated the Soviet Politburo line on the more acute state of international affairs that had developed "as a result of the policy of the Reagan administration" and West Germany acting as its "main ally." As proof of the enhanced dangers, he referred to President Reagan, who had tested a microphone before giving a speech, jokingly counting down to zero for a hypothetical missile launch against the Soviet Union. Gorbachev took or pretended to take the countdown seriously. "As we say," he told Honecker, "what the sober person keeps in his head, the drunk betrays by his tongue. This is surely revealed by the Reagan 'joke.'" (Honecker agreed or pretended to agree, adding that the East German press had published the TASS statement that had decried the apparent Reagan outrage.) Gorbachev pressed on relentlessly on this theme: "In its draft party platform, the Republican Party states that the course of confrontation and pressure has to be strengthened. The Soviet Union is portrayed there as an unnatural state and as the central danger for the USA."

Turning specifically to the German problem, Gorbachev demonstrated that he had done some homework prior to coming to the meeting. He used the commemoration of the building of the Berlin wall on 13 August, held in West Berlin, to attack the very "people by whom you would be received if you were to visit the FRG." He charged that in their speeches at the commemoration

> President [Richard von Weizsäcker], [Intra-German Affairs Minister Heinrich] Windelen and [Secretary of State in the Foreign Ministry Alois] Mertes have issued declarations to the effect that Berlin is the capital of Germany. They spoke of the German problem as being unsolved. They criticized [Hans] Apel [the leading SPD candidate in the Berlin city council elections] and his statement to which you just referred [that the German problem was no longer open].

He then looked at the problem through the lens of the traditional Politburo paradigm and the alleged necessity of having to punish West Germany for having consented to the stationing of missiles.

> When the missiles were put up and the social democrats consented to the stationing, we stated that if nothing were to happen [to reverse this], a new element would be created, things could not go on as before, and there would be repercussions also on the relations between the two

German states. And what is happening now? The contacts are being broadened, the visit is being prepared and credits are being extended. This does not match up with our declarations.

In light of the changed circumstances, Gorbachev summarized, it was necessary to "think carefully about all this." And as for the *Pravda* articles, he claimed that "each and every one of the arguments [made there] can be supported."[138]

To conclude, once the Soviet leaders had made public their opposition to Honecker's planned visit to West Germany, the trip became a test of wills that a dutiful ally "could not afford to win."[139] On 4 September, East Germany's permanent representative in Bonn announced that the date for the trip was "no longer real," or in plain English, that the trip was canceled.[140] In justification of the cancellation, East German spokesmen cited – in the circumstances probably convenient – remarks by CDU parliamentary leader Alfred Dregger to the effect that West Germany's future did "not depend on Herr Honecker doing us the honor of a visit."[141] Todor Zhivkov was to follow suit and also excused himself.

Summary

The following conclusions and lessons can be drawn from the period stretching from the end of the 1970s until the beginning of the Gorbachev era. First, the controversies between East Berlin and Moscow, like Bonn's differences with Washington, were not about adherence to the alliance *per se* but about the direction of alliance policies. This concerned first and foremost the Warsaw Pact's relationship with the West. But as will also be seen in the next chapter, the differences pertained to global affairs, including relations with China. Nevertheless, the Moscow meeting and the cancellation of the Honecker visit served to demonstrate the as yet limited scope and purpose of the East German deviation from the Soviet line. It was certainly preposterous to assert that an attempt was made by both Germanys to "try reunification on the sly," that a decade later the world would "learn of secret negotiations in these years that took place between Germans who put Fatherland ahead of ideology" and that this attempt "should not be a surprise" because it was "only natural."[142] Even then it was evident that the "natural" political inclination of a party leader like Honecker was to strengthen the political and economic viability and

138 Ibid., pp. 64-66.

139 This was the pertinent observation by *The Economist* ("Russia Rules its Allies"), 15 September 1984.

140 Evaldt Moldt, who announced the East German decision; see *Neues Deutschland*, 5 September 1984. A new date for the visit was not set.

141 As quoted by *Neues Deutschland*, 25-26 August 1984.

142 William Safire, "The Germanys: Trying Reunification on the Sly," *International Herald Tribune*, 14 August 1984.

international standing of his régime. He had made his career in the pursuit of these objectives, not least by taking charge of security during the building of the Berlin wall. The improvement of intra-German relations and a search for more leeway in the GDR's relations with the Soviet Union were quite compatible with these objectives. But as the great number of applications for exit visas to West Germany showed, the legitimacy and viability of the régime remained in doubt. The political system of the GDR still very much depended upon Soviet support and so did its economy under conditions of high prices for energy and the limited competitiveness of East German industrial products on the world market. Whatever the objective consequences of his policy, Honecker had no intention to destroy the Soviet-East German relationship.

Second, despite the fact that the overt controversies in East-West relations of the late 1970s and early 1980s were very much about international security issues, such as the Soviet intervention in Afghanistan, the threat of intervention in Poland, and the stationing of nuclear missiles in Europe, *economic* factors were becoming an increasingly important part of East-West relations. The Soviet leaders could not escape this reality, notwithstanding their vigorous and vicious criticism of West Germany and its alleged strategy of undermining the political and ideological foundations of the GDR. This was proven, for instance, by the fact that 1984, the year of the Soviet punitive countermeasures to the missile deployments, was also the year of a DM 25 billion trade turnover – a new record in the volume of Soviet-German trade.

Third, the Soviet-East German differences neither stemmed from nor did they result in Soviet pressures on the GDR or on other CMEA countries to sever their economic and credit links with West Germany. The June 1984 summit meeting of the East bloc's economic organization supported the maintenance and expansion of such links. It did so with good reason, for if the economic fortunes of the GDR and other members of the bloc had declined or declined further, the Soviet economy, too, would have been damaged. Soviet interests would have been even more negatively affected if economic stringencies in Eastern Europe had led, as in Poland, to political upheaval and the erosion of party control. Soviet criticism of East Berlin, therefore, concerned the *scale* of East German indebtedness and had a primarily *political* rather than economic rationale.

Fourth, it was predictable that there would be a shift in the priorities of East German foreign policy after the cancellation of the planned visit. From late 1983 through most of 1984, the SED had by and large achieved its immediate goal of preventing superpower tensions from rupturing the fabric of contacts between East and West Germany. It had noted with satisfaction the resumption of Soviet-American talks about strategic and intermediate-range nuclear arms and space weapons. As a result, as Hans Modrow, the party secretary of the SED for the Dresden district, stated in December 1984: "The 'separate German track' has come to an end, at least for the time being." Henceforth, "we will be very active in seeking to broaden our contacts with all Western countries, ... not only with West Germany."[143]

Fifth, as so often in the past, the Soviet Union's change of policy towards West Germany after the April 1984 Central Committee plenum was rendered obsolete soon thereafter by a change of tack in its policy towards the United States. The Soviet proposal at the end of June to hold negotiations in Vienna on space weapons was a clear indication that the attempt at influencing American policy indirectly with the help of West Germany had run its course and had been superseded by the primacy of Soviet-American relations. The Gromyko-Reagan meeting in September 1984 confirmed this trend. Bonn was now politically less important to Moscow than Washington – a state of affairs that meshed well with the Soviet campaign of teaching West Germany a lesson.

The final and most important point about this period, however, is the comprehensive nature of the crisis that the Soviet empire was facing. The central features of the crisis, as described here in detail, were the transformation of ideology from an asset to a liability; the inability to transform military power into political influence; the failure effectively to compete with the Western industrialized countries in the scientific-technological revolution; and the inability to provide effective political leadership either for a revitalization or for a fundamental change of the Soviet domestic system. Cutting through all of the fog of innuendos, charges, and countercharges on the German problem, both within the Soviet bloc and between East and West, the central problem for the Soviet leaders from Stalin to Chernenko was their inability to "digest" the part of Germany it had acquired in the Second World War. They remained caught up a dilemma that became acute in the late 1970s and early 1980s. They were incapable of providing legitimacy for their control of Eastern Europe or of making it cost-effective. Yet imprisoned by the parameters of the Ideological and Imperial paradigm, they were as yet unprepared to divest themselves of the imperial burden in the center of Europe. It took a new leader and an entirely new approach to international relations to make possible the solution of the seemingly intractable German problem.

---

143 Hans Modrow, in an interview with US correspondent Henry Tanner, *International Herald Tribune*, 14 December 1984.

PART FOUR: COLLAPSE

Chapter 4: Gorbachev's Old and New Thinking

1. The Paradigm of New Thinking

The "Gorbachev revolution" began with only minor revisions of theory but ended in the complete replacement of the Ideological and Imperial paradigm. The then party leader and his chief advisors have acknowledged the gradual and essentially unplanned progression of change. "It would be a great exaggeration to say that we envisaged from the very beginning the scope and difficulties of perestroika," Gorbachev has explained in retrospect. "Its initial designs, furthermore, did not go beyond the framework of the system, neither ideologically nor politically. For us it was then a matter of improving the existing society, 'forcing the system to work.'"[1] Similarly, Yakovlev remembers that "at the beginning, we had little idea where events would take us."[2] There was only a general "understanding of what needed to be cast aside."[3]

This general understanding, however, is precisely what explains the progressive, and in its ultimate scope unintended dismantling of the Ideological and Imperial paradigm and its replacement by the New Thinking. As in the Left and Right dichotomy of traditional Marxist-Leninist approaches, an inner logic existed that linked a set of policies of either one or the other orientation in domestic and foreign policy.[4] To illustrate this abstraction by an example, Brezhnev's approach to détente was bound to fail because of a dual violation of the logic of interconnectedness. A repressive policy at home contradicted an ostensible policy of opening in foreign policy. In the foreign policy realm, rejection of "interference in the internal affairs of socialist countries," notably in Eastern Europe, a vigorous arms build-up and support for the "national-liberation movement" did not square well with attempts to improve East-West economic exchanges and gain access to Western technology, credits, and know-how. The theoreticians of the new paradigm recognized such deficiencies and realized that the effectiveness of the new approaches depended upon comprehensiveness, consistency, and coherence.

1 M. S. Gorbachev, "Mir na perelome," *Svobodnaia mysl*, No. 16 (November 1992), p. 10.

2 Lecture at Harvard University, 7 November 1991.

3 Alexander N. Yakovlev, *Muki prochteniia bytiia. Perestroika – nadezhdy i real'nosti* (Moscow: Novosti, 1991), p. 330.

4 This logic was best described by Alexander Dallin, "Linkage Patterns: From Brest to Brezhnev," in Seweryn Bialer, ed., *The Domestic Context of Soviet Foreign Policy* (Boulder, Colo: Westview, 1981), pp. 344-47, and earlier in his "Soviet Foreign Policy and Domestic Politics: A Framework of Analysis," *Journal of International Affairs*, No. 2 (1969), pp. 250-65.

What, then, were the main ingredients of Gorbachev's New Thinking? The new paradigm included the following major principles:[5]

(1) The use of military power, geopolitical expansionism, and empire building are outdated forms of international conduct. They impose significant costs and impede socio-economic development.

(2) Status and power in international affairs are determined by qualitative indicators, such as effectiveness of the political system, economic efficiency, and the ability to adapt to rapid scientific-technological progress.

(3) The internal resources of a nation, including a high level of education and technical skill of the population as well as the country's quality and way of life are important factors of international influence.

(4) Interests in world affairs are to be promoted through multilateral approaches and participation in international institutions. This also applies to security, which cannot be safeguarded unilaterally through military-technical means but only cooperatively and by political means.

(5) Although the nation state continues to be an important organizing principle in the international system, nationalism is one of the many forms of unilateralism that needs to be replaced by processes of integration.

(6) The main actors and factors of stability in the international system are the industrialized countries (G-7), which adhere to a common system of values, laws, and norms.

(7) The main factors of instability and threats to world peace are nationalism, ethnic conflict, religious fundamentalism, political extremism, migration, terrorism, environmental catastrophes, weapons proliferation, and armed aggression from the south.

To explain and provide some detail about the evolution of the new paradigm, the first and foremost realization was that of a close interrelationship between domestic and foreign policy and, as time went by, even the priority of domestic over foreign

5 On the origins, content, and evolution of the new paradigm through the eyes of their architects, see M. S. Gorbachev, *Perestroika i novoe myshlenie dlia nashei strany i dlia vsego mira* (Moscow: Politizdat, 1988); Shevardnadze, *Moi vybor*; Yakovlev, *Muki prochteniia bytiia*; and Chernyaev, *Shest' let s Gorbachevym*. For Western analyses of the new paradigm, see Falk Bomsdorf and Hannes Adomeit, "Das 'Neue Denken': Grundzüge und Verwirklichung," in Hannes Adomeit, Hans-Hermann Höhmann, and Günter Wagenlehner, eds., *Die Sowjetunion unter Gorbatschow* (Stuttgart: Kohlhammer, 1990), pp. 261-296; Seweryn Bialer, "New Thinking and Soviet Foreign Policy," *Survival*, Vol. 30, No. 4 (July/August 1988), pp. 291-309; Stephen M. Meyer, "The Sources and Prospects of Gorbachev's New Political Thinking on Security," *International Security*, Vol. 33, No. 2 (Fall 1988), pp. 124-63; and Coit D. Blacker, *Hostage to Revolution: Gorbachev and Soviet Security Policy, 1985-1991* (New York: Council on Foreign Relations, 1993). In the present chapter, only a summary of the New Thinking will be provided. For more detail and the practical application of the theory, see chapter 6, section 2.

policy. Statements made by Gorbachev himself reflect this progression of viewpoints. In an interview with *Time* magazine in September 1985, he remarked that

> somebody [Lenin?] said that *foreign policy is a continuation of domestic policy*. If that is so, then I ask you to ponder one thing: if we in the Soviet Union are setting ourselves such grandiose plans in the domestic sphere [perestroika], then what are the external conditions that we need to be able to fulfill those domestic plans? I leave the answer to that question with you.[6]

In February 1987, at an international peace forum in Moscow, he went one step further when he said that

> our international policy is *determined* more than ever before by our domestic policy, by our interest in concentrating on creative work for the perfection of our country. For that very reason we need a more stable peace, predictability, and a constructive direction of international relations.[7]

There is another aspect of significance to the relationship between domestic and foreign policy in the Gorbachev era . That is the idea of learning by trial and error in both dimensions of policy. Reflecting in his memoirs on the felt necessity at the beginning of his tenure in office to embark upon a fundamental change in foreign policy, he explains that "perestroika in domestic [affairs] and in the foreign policy realm took shape only gradually; success in one area had a positive impact on the other, whereas, correspondingly, failures put a brake on the development in both areas."[8]

A central point to be made at the outset, however, is that the trial-and-error process had its limits. Gorbachev was not much of a conceptual thinker. To the extent that he adhered to abstractions, he remained wedded to the utopian ideas, in politics, of "reform socialism" and "socialism with a human face" and, in economics, the harmonization of the plan with the market. Fundamental reconceptualization, both in domestic and foreign policy, was urged upon him, in part by events and in part by advisers who had a keener intellectual bent and greater analytical potential. Obviously, such sweeping assertions need to be supported by evidence – and will be later.

Reconceptualization of domestic and foreign policy also meant abandoning Marxist-Leninist ideology. The necessity for taking such a momentous decision was

---

6 Gorbachev interview with *Time*, 9 September 1985 (italics mine). The "somebody" Gorbachev referred to may have been Lenin, who is on record as having stated: "There is no more erroneous or harmful idea than the separation of foreign from domestic policy;" V.I. Lenin, *Sochineniia*, 4th (Russian) ed., Vol. 15 (Moscow: Politizdat, 1948), p. 67.

7 *Izvestiia*, 17 February 1987. This was not some inadvertent slip but an example of progression in his thinking. In April, in a dinner speech in London, he reiterated that "Our foreign policy, to a greater degree than ever before, *stems directly from our domestic policy*;"*Pravda*, 1 April 1987.

8 Mikhail Gorbachev, *Zhizn' i reformy*, Vol. 2 (Moscow: Novosti, 1995), p. 7.

understood by hardly anyone in a position of responsibility at the beginning of the Gorbachev era. But it was clearly stated in the midst of change by seven dissident Soviet émigrés living in the West: Vasili Aksyonov, Vladimir Bukovsky, Eduard Kuznetsov, Yuri Lyubimov, Vladimir Maximov, Ernst Neizvestny, and Alexander Zinoviev. "Ideology is that hard core of the Soviet system that does not allow the country to deviate too far for too long," they wrote in March 1987. Unless the central ideological tenets were changed, "long-term Soviet strategy would remain imprisoned by its assumptions." If the Soviet leadership was really serious about radical change, they concluded, it "would have to begin by discarding the ruling ideology."[9]

In the process of discarding Marxist-Leninist ideology, Vadim Medvedev, the CPSU CC secretary responsible for ideological questions, told his colleagues from the Warsaw Pact countries assembled in East Berlin in September 1989 how damaging Marxism-Leninism had been. He admitted that, "When we ideologized foreign policy in an unbalanced fashion, it often harmed the prestige of the Soviet Union as well as socialism as a whole." It did not at all contribute to the normalization of relations "but at times even [achieved] the very opposite."[10] Shevardnadze, in retrospect, confirmed this point. The notion of peaceful coexistence as a form of class conflict had inevitably led to perceptions of the "world as an arena of a perennial struggle between systems, camps, and blocs." It had blurred the difference between ideological competition and psychological warfare and "erected insurmountable barriers on the road towards mutually beneficial cooperation between countries with different socio-economic structures."[11] According to Medvedev, the emphasis on ideology in international affairs had also "furnished a pretext to our opponents to accuse us of expansionist and aggressive designs and of wanting to 'export revolution.'" It had "contributed to the enhancement of 'enemy images.'"[12] A daring statement at the dusk of the Soviet era! The problem with such courage in the Gorbachev era, however, was that the seeming or real abandonment of one ideological tenet after another was accompanied by qualifications and counteracted by euphemisms and ambiguities. Gorbachev's speech at the seventieth anniversary of the Bolshevik revolution provides a glaring example of this. Given its perceived importance in the Soviet ideological context at that time, some analysis of its content is appropriate here.

9 "The Time has Come Now to Reject the System Itself," *International Herald Tribune*, 24 March 1987.

10 Speech by Vadim Medvedev, the CPSU CC secretary responsible for ideological questions at the conference of the ideological secretaries of the socialist countries, on 21 September 1989 in East Berlin; SED Politburo, *Arbeitsprotokolle*, J IV 2/2A/3248.

11 Shevardnadze, *Moi vybor*, pp. 95 and 101.

12 Medvedev speech in East Berlin, 21 September 1989.

Despite its many departures from ideological orthodoxy, the speech brimmed with Stalinist or, if one prefers, neo-Stalinist rationalizations.[13] "Under the conditions at that time [the 1930s]," he asked, "was it possible to choose a course [of action] other than the one adopted by the party?" He unequivocally replied: "No, it was not possible." He saw collectivization, as indeed it was, as a "fundamental alteration of the whole way of life of the main mass of the population in the countryside." But he gave a positive spin to this generalization by saying that it had "created the social basis for the modernization of the agricultural sector." Yes, one should not overlook the "complicated nature of this period." There were such deplorable things as "excesses" (this was a term used by Stalin). "There were also – I say this openly – real crimes because of the abuse of power. Thousands and thousands [sic] of party members and non-party people were subjected to mass repressions."[14] As for foreign policy, he chastised the "ruling circles of the West" for distorting the truth and attempting to show that "the Soviet-German non-aggression pact of 23 August 1939 had provided the starting shot for the attack of the Nazis on Poland and thus for [the beginning of] the Second World War." Nothing was said about the secret protocols. There were no regrets and apologies about the occupation and treatment of the Baltic states. There was no hint about the Soviet deliveries of strategically important commodities, which helped Nazi Germany to build up its war machine.

Whatever the merits of the anniversary speech concerning specific points of Soviet history, its most noteworthy feature was the absence of any moral dimension. Yakovlev later was to express his regret to the meeting of ideological secretaries in Varna that adherents of both socialism and capitalism had "convinced themselves by the trial-and-error method that there are more urgent factors and necessities than the abstractions turned into dogmatic clichés that have nothing to do with morality, and that have led to deafness and blindness towards good and evil."[15] Gorbachev's speech is a sorry example of such blindness. In contrast to the period after the collapse of the Soviet Union, the records of the secret meetings and private conversations from the Gorbachev era that have now become available fail to provide clear-cut statements by the leading adherents of the New Thinking to the effect that Marxism-Leninism was a fundamental aberration that had led Russia into a comprehensive crisis. For them a socialist future remained the utopia to be achieved. As Medvedev told the East Berlin gathering in September 1989, it was an "illusion" of the forces inimical to perestroika

---

13 Text in *Pravda*, 3 November 1987.

14 For more realistic data on the number of party and non-party members who fell victim to mass repressions see *infra*, pp. 368-69.

15 Speech by Alexander Yakovlev at the conference of communist party secretaries for ideological questions, held in Varna (Bulgaria), 26-28 September 89, included for agenda item 8 of SED Politburo meeting of 17 October 1989; Central Party Archives, SED Politburo, *Arbeitsprotokolle*, J IV 2/2A/3247.

to assert that "our society could evolve in the direction of capitalism and abandon the socialist values." Such speculation was "built on sand."[16] Yakovlev adopted a similar stance at the Varna meeting a few days later. No matter how one looked at it, he said, whether "from a political, ideological, or simply a pragmatic point of view," it was "absurd" for both the "conservatives of conviction and the conservatives of privilege" to charge that perestroika was tantamount to the abandonment of the "principles and ideals of socialism."[17]

What explains the retractions and reservations and the continued adherence to utopian goals? First, outright rejection of Marxism-Leninism would have destroyed the very basis on which power and legitimacy of the political leadership rested. Second, in the perceptions of the *perestroichniki,* retreat from utopia would have provided the orthodox elements in the party apparat with the ammunition they needed to mount a political counteroffensive with the aim of ousting the new leadership. Third, many of the supporters of New Thinking, including Gorbachev, remained incapable of ridding themselves of the ideological baggage accumulated in the seventy years of travel that was intended to lead to a bright future. "Why do I sit surrounded all the time by Lenin's works?," Gorbachev asked in July 1986. "I leaf through them, I look for solutions ... Because it is never too late to consult Lenin."[18] Who, then, was this man who embodied such contradictory attitudes but who had such an enormous impact on world history?

2. Gorbachev: A Political Profile

Gorbachev was born in 1931 in the small village of Privolnoe in Stavropol krai (region or territory), a fertile agricultural area in southern Russia.[19] His outlook on life and his career in the communist party, as his own memoirs and testimony from relatives, friends, and acquaintances show, were shaped by the rural character and agricultural base of this region.[20] "Privolnoe" means the expanse of land that was

16 Speech by Vadim Medvedev, the CPSU CC secretary responsible for ideological questions at the conference of the ideological secretaries of the socialist countries on 21-22 September 1989 in East Berlin; Central Party Archives, SED Politburo, *Arbeitsprotokolle*, J IV 2/2A/3248.

17 Yakovlev speech, as quoted above (fn. 15).

18 Speech to members of the Soviet Union of Writers, Kremlin, 19 July 1986; excerpts as published in *Détente*, No. 8 (Winter 1987), pp. 11-12.

19 A *krai* in both past Soviet and current Russian definitions refers to a large administrative entity located in strategically important borderlands (*krai* literally means edge). In functional terms, there is no difference between the administration of a *krai* or an *oblast'* (region or province).

20 This sketch of Gorbachev's political profiles draws heavily on his memoirs, which first appeared more or less simultaneously in both Russian and German; Mikhail Gorbachev, *Zhizn' i reformy*, 2 vols. (Moscow: Novosti, 1995) and Michail Gorbatschow, *Erinnerungen* (Berlin: Siedler Verlag, 1995). The English version appeared several years later and has not been used here. The memoirs are by far the best source for a political profile of Gorbachev. They reflect his political philosophy, his rationalizations, and his analytical strengths and weaknesses. Where there are

steppe when the first peasants came, and it also means freedom.[21] The customs and traditions of the Cossacks – soldiers and peasants who, at the Czars' orders, settled the frontiers of the empire and pushed them south and east – have helped to mould the area. Peasants from Russia and Ukraine fled from serfdom. "Later," as Gorbachev explains, "they were forcibly settled here – a human drama that claimed many victims. My family on the paternal side, the Gorbachevs, settlers from the Voronesh province (*guberniia)* but also my ancestors on the maternal side, the Gopalkos – settlers from the Chernigov province – had arrived here in this way."[22]

His childhood was overshadowed by three major political and socio-economic events: collectivization, the purges, and World War II. His maternal grandfather had been one of the first after the Bolshevik revolution to help establish a cooperative, a voluntary organization of peasants who kept and farmed their own land. His grandmother and mother also worked there. "In 1928," Gorbachev writes tersely, "grandfather entered the CPSU. He participated in the foundation of our *kolkhoz*, named Khleborob (Wheat Farmer) ... and became its chairman ... In the 1930s grandfather took over the leadership of the collective farm Krasnyi Oktiabr (Red October) in a neighboring village, located twenty miles from Privolnoe."[23] Whether because of idealism or a sense of self-preservation, the Gopalkos became active supporters of Stalin's collectivization drive.

The Gorbachevs, in contrast, initially refused to submit to Stalin's plans. "[Paternal] grandfather Andrei," as the grandson remembers, "did not participate in the collectivization [campaign]; he did not enter a collective farm but remained a [private] farmer." He was arrested in 1934, convicted as a "saboteur," and sent to do hard labor "in the form of cutting timber" in the Irkutsk region. He was released after two years, before he had served his full sentence. He returned from camp "with two documents which certified him as an activist of labor, and he immediately joined a

---

discrepancies between the two editions – there are some which are meaningful – they will be pointed out. His own portrayal will be critically evaluated and checked against information provided by persons whom he met during his life and political career. Such information is contained in memoirs as well as in biographies, the best of the latter including Archie Brown, *The Gorbachev Factor* (Oxford: Oxford University Press, 1996); Robert G. Kaiser, *Why Gorbachev Happened: His Triumphs and his Failure* (New York: Simon & Schuster, 1991); Moshe Lewin, *The Gorbachev Phenomenon: A Historical Interpretation*, exp. ed. (Berkeley, Cal.: University of California Press, 1991); Zhores Medvedev, *Gorbachev* (Oxford: Basil Blackwell, 1986); John Miller, *Mikhail Gorbachev and the End of Soviet Power* (New York: St. Martin's Press, 1993); and Gerd Ruge, *Gorbachev: A Biography* (London: Chatto & Windus, 1991).

21 Ruge, *Gorbachev*, p. 13.

22 Gorbachev, *Zhizn'*, Vol. 1, pp. 32-33.

23 Ibid., pp. 37-38.

collective farm. Because he worked assiduously, he soon rose to become head of the pig farm of the *kolkhoz*."[24]

What about the human and material costs of collectivization, the methods used and the moral problems involved? The approach Gorbachev adopts to deal with these issues in his memoirs is essentially the same he had used in his speech on the seventieth anniversary of the 1917 revolution. The portrayal bears a euphemistic and apologetic quality, is devoid of moral opprobrium and follows the typically Gorbachevian "on the one hand ... but on the other hand" pattern. He acknowledges that "In 1933, a famine erupted in the Stavropol region ... The famine was terrible. In Privolnoe, at least one third if not half of the village population died. Whole families perished and long thereafter, essentially until the beginning of the war, [many] cottages stood there abandoned, near collapse, like orphans. Three [of the six] children of grandfather Andrei also perished of hunger."[25] Yet he also thinks that "historians argue until this very day about the origins [of the famine] and whether it was perhaps organized deliberately so as to finally subdue the peasants. Or did adverse weather conditions after all play the most important role in it? I don't know what things looked like in other regions but we [in the Stavropol area] were indeed visited by a terrible drought." Did the famine, then, have natural causes? No, essentially, it didn't. "The calamity did not lie in [the weather] alone. Mass collectivization ... in my view tipped the balance."[26] Was mass collectivization gratuitous mass murder, then, organized by the communist party, a heart-rending tragedy that could and should have been avoided? No, it wasn't. He fails to understand "what "golden age" of the Russian village the current advocates of peasant happiness are talking about. These people either know absolutely nothing, or they knowingly do not tell the truth, or they have lost their memory."[27]

The refusal unambiguously to condemn mass murder is also evident in his treatment of Stalin's purges in the late 1930s. Typically for the period, no one was immune from denunciation, arrest, and execution. This was true also for his grandfather Gopalko. He was arrested in 1937, accused of sabotage, charged with being a member of a "counterrevolutionary, Right-wing Trotskyite organization," and severely tortured in order to extract a confession. The arrest, according to Gorbachev,

---

24 Ibid., p. 42.

25 Ibid.

26 Ibid.

27 Ibid., p. 38. He adds that *he* certainly remembers the vestiges of the "way of life that was characteristic for the Russian village before the revolution and before the foundation of collective farms." This characterization as well as the treatment of the subject on the seventieth anniversary of the October revolution implies that collectivization was not only "objectively necessary" but improved life on the farm. The "in principle" positive assessment of collectivization may provide one of the explanations why Gorbachev, until the very end, refused to contemplate major changes in agriculture in he direction of private farming and the market.

produced "the first [major] upheaval in my life" and "ingrained itself forever in my memory." This was in part due to the fact that "enemies of the people" were shunned by society. "I still remember today that after grandfather's arrest, the neighbors passed by the house in a wide circle as if we had the plague and that our relatives only stopped by secretly at night." Gopalko was fortunate to be released in December 1938 and reinstated in his job as collective farm chairman in 1939. His wife's grandfather, however, was not so fortunate. He was arrested, also in 1937, in the Altai region in southern Siberia and shot.[28]

What is also lacking in Gorbachev's published recollections, despite the traumatic experience of the arrest of his maternal grandfather, is a reflection on Stalin's personal responsibility, the function of the communist party in the Soviet system, and his own willing (guilt by) association with a criminal régime as a judge or prosecutor. It was only after the collapse of the Soviet Union, when he was asked when he had begun to understand the role played by the NKVD and its successor, the KGB, that he said that he had begun to comprehend it long ago, from the time his grandfather was under arrest, but that there was much that had remained obscure to him, adding that even his grandfather had said of his arrest: "I am sure Stalin does not know."[29]

The third major influence on Gorbachev's life was the Second World War. For the purpose of reconstructing Gorbachev's attitudes towards Germany, it is particularly appropriate to try to assess its impact. "My generation," he wrote, "is a generation of the children of war. The war has left an imprint on us and shaped our character, even our world view."[30] During his talks with chancellor Kohl in Moscow in mid-July 1990, he reminisced that when the German offensive began in June 1941 he was ten years old, and that he could remember very well what had happened.[31] The events he remembers, as described in detail in his memoirs, were his father's temporary deferment because he was needed as a *kolkhoz* technician (the summer harvest had to be brought in) and his subsequent call-up for service at the front in August 1941; weary Red Army soldiers passing through Privolnoe after the evacuation of Rostov in August 1942; the occupation of the village by German troops for four and a half months; the collaboration of villagers with the occupation regime; and the restoration of Soviet control in January 1943.[32]

In the first phase of the German offensive, in the summer and fall of 1941, the southern army group (Heeresgruppe Süd) under General von Rundstedt made rapid advances, the Red Army retreating in disarray. Kiev, Kharkov, and the Donbas came

---

28 Ibid., pp. 38-42.

29 Interview with Gorbachev, *Komsomol'skaia pravda*, 7 November 1992; as quoted by Brown, *The Gorbachev Factor*, p. 30.

30 Gorbachev, *Zhizn'*, Vol. 1, p. 51.

31 Horst Teltschik, *329 Tage: Innenansichten der Einigung* (Berlin: Siedler Verlag, 1991), p. 320.

32 Gorbachev, *Zhizn'*, Vol. 1, pp. 42-51.

under German occupation and, for a short time, so did Rostov. In the second phase, beginning in the summer of 1942, German offensives were launched in two directions, one towards Stalingrad to cut the communications lines between North and South Russia, and a second towards Grozny in the North Caucasus and Baku on the Caspian Sea. "On 27 July 1942," to return to Gorbachev's recollections, "our troops evacuated Rostov. Completely disorganized they embarked upon retreat; somber looking and tired soldiers passed through. Their faces betrayed bitterness and feelings of guilt."[33] Stavropol was bypassed by both offensives, and the steppes to the north of the town where Privolnoe was located never became a major battle zone.[34] In August, however, German forces entered Privolnoe and established an occupation regime, initially consisting of regular German units, which were "then exchanged for other units of which I only remember the stripes on their sleeves and that they spoke Ukrainian."[35]

Several villagers collaborated with the occupation authorities, mostly people who had deserted the Soviet army and hidden for months. They were now cooperating with the Nazis, mainly as policemen. Gorbachev's grandmother was interrogated at the police station because her husband was a member of the communist party and chairman of a collective farm, and he and her son and son-in-law were serving in the Red Army. The house was searched. Rumors abounded about mass executions of Jews and communists. "We were conscious [of the fact] that the members of our family would be among the first to be on a list [of suspects] and thus my mother and grandfather Andrei hid me in a livestock compound behind the village. The action was to take place on 26 January 1943. But on 21 January 1943 Soviet troops liberated Privolnoe."[36]

According to Valeri Boldin, later Gorbachev's chief of staff and one of the conspirators in the August 1991 coup attempt against him, he (Gorbachev) did not "witness the kind of atrocities the Germans committed in Belorussia and many of the western regions of Russia."[37] This may be a fair observation. Later, however, Gorbachev did become quite conscious of the war's consequences and the large-scale destruction it had brought to Russia. He remembers that

> I travelled by rail from South Russia to Moscow [in 1950] to begin [university] studies. With my own eyes I saw the ruins of Stalingrad, Rostov, Kharkov, Orel, Kursk, and Voronezh. And how many other destroyed cities were there? Leningrad, Kiev, Minsk, Odessa, Sevastopol, Smolensk, Bryansk, Novgorod ... Everything was in ruins, hundreds and

---

33 Ibid., p. 45.

34 Medvedev, *Gorbachev*, p. 31.

35 Gorbachev, *Zhizn'*, Vol. 1, p. 45.

36 Ibid., pp. 45-46.

37 Valery Boldin, *Ten Years that Shook the World* (New York: Basic Books, 1994), p. 81.

> thousands of towns and villages, factories and enterprises. The most precious cultural monuments – art galleries, palaces, libraries and cathedrals – were plundered and destroyed.[38]

Such accounts are, indeed, personal reflections. No effort is made to deal with the broader issues of Russian-German relations and European security. The next section will attempt to reconstruct Gorbachev's thinking on these problems.

Another factor shaping Gorbachev's outlook on life and politics derives from the ethnic diversity of the region in which he grew up and where he worked most of his life. In his memoirs he asserts that Soviet patriotism was multifaceted and based on multiculturalism, multilingualism, and multiethnicity. He writes that in Stavropol krai, 83 percent of the population were Russian; other nationalities included Karachai, Cherkessians, Abasins, Nogai, Ossetians, Greeks, Armenians and Turkmen. He also mentions the region's Karachai-Cherkessian Autonomous Region and its radio and television programs as well as newspapers and books in five languages. "Life among so many nationalities made us tolerant as a matter of habit, and it taught us to meet each other with respect."[39] On the whole, then, he paints an idyllic picture of ethnic harmony.

On closer inspection of this picture, however, some blots do appear. One reads that starting with the rule of Catherine II, "border strongholds" were being constructed in the northern Caucasus; that "in the not all too distant past, [many] years of Caucasian wars cost numerous human lives"; and that society during the Civil War "was split not only in accordance with the class principle but also along national, religious, and territorial lines, at times even within individual families."[40] Such admitted blemishes, however, cannot dispel the impression that the artist, having first painted a picture of ethnic harmony, is either unaware of Russia's colonial and imperial past or deliberately attempting to conceal it. To the extent that the author displays cognitive dissonance, it is mitigated by nineteenth century romantic nostalgia, by references to novels by Mikhail Lermontov, and citations from verses by Nikolai Ogarev. "The vast steppe and the chain of mountains," he quotes from one of the verses, "the hidden belief in eternal union."[41] Russia is not seen by him as a conqueror but as a benevolent power *preventing* conquest: "The more the Russian state strengthened, the more insistent did the Caucasian peoples seek salvation in the relations with Russia from conquerors of all kind."[42] Although such notions may say little about Gorbachev's understanding of nationalism in Eastern

---

38 Gorbachev, *Perestroika*, p. 38; similarly Gorbachev, *Zhizn'*, Vol. 1, p. 57. The date Gorbachev gave for his train trip in *Perestroika* is "the late 1940s." However, his studies at university began in 1950. Hence, the insertion in square brackets provides the correct year.

39 Gorbachev, *Zhizn'*, Vol. 1, p. 35.

40 Ibid., pp. 32 and 36.

41 Ibid., p. 34.

42 Ibid., p. 32.

Europe, they reveal much about his lack of sensitivity to nationality problems in the Soviet Union. They also provide an important explanation of his inability effectively to deal with the issue when it became acute during his reign.[43]

To return to Gorbachev's career, the remainder of his teenage years was spent helping his father at the *kolkhoz's* machine-tractor station (MTS) and finishing high school. He then applied to Moscow State University to study law. He could not "claim that this decision had matured [sufficiently] ... but the rank of judge or prosecutor impressed me."[44] The choice was consistent with his ambition and outlook on life. In the Soviet era, and least of all under Stalin, there was no independence of the judiciary. Torture had become the usual method of obtaining grotesque confessions that served as formal accusation in secret, closed trials. Millions of people were sentenced without due process of law to execution or to the camps. Lawyers were needed to provide a legal veneer for these proceedings.[45] Not objectivity and impartiality were required of them but *partiinost'* – behavior in accordance with the interests of the party. But Gorbachev's image of the party and its policies as well as that of Stalin was essentially favorable. He had, as mentioned, no problem with the principle of collectivization, and he preferred not to probe too deeply to understand the rationale or ascertain the scale of the purges. He was by that time a candidate member of the CPSU. He had worked hard at the MTS and received the Order of the Red Banner of Labor. He had done well at school. With such achievements and his peasant background, he was accepted by the university.

In retrospect, Gorbachev discerns both positive and negative aspects of his university experience. The first three years of his studies, that is, the period from his enrolment until Stalin's death in March 1953, "coincided with a new wave of repression – with the notorious campaign against "rootless cosmopolitanism." Teaching amounted to nothing less than "ideological drill."

> It seemed as if from the very first day the learning process was designed to put shackles on the young spirit, to inculcate in the young heads a set of inalienable truth and to save them from the temptation of reasoning independently, analyzing and thinking. The iron brackets of ideology,

---

43 To take one of the many examples of Gorbachev's insensitivity to nationality problems, in 1984, upon the retirement of Dinmukhamed Kunayev, a Politburo member from Kazakhstan, Gorbachev ignored the tradition of naming a Kazakh to the post and instead appointed Gennadii Kolbin, a Chuvash, whom the Kazakhs regarded as Russian; see Robert G. Kaiser, *Why Gorbachev Happened: His Triumphs and His Failure* (New York: Simon & Schuster, 1991), pp. 150-151. As his three-day visit to Lithuania in January 1990 revealed, he also subscribed to the idea that it could be possible to assuage nationalism by appeals to economic rationality; see below, p. 477.

44 Ibid., p. 59.

45 Ruge, *Gorbachev*, pp. 33-34.

therefore, were always felt, in lectures, seminars, and discussions, sometimes more, sometimes less.[46]

A stifling atmosphere, then, that accurately reflected the comprehensive assault on creativity? Not quite. Gorbachev explains that the readings covered a broad range and included Western classics on constitutional law and government. He even goes so far as to say that "many problems notwithstanding, the democratic traditions of the Russian university remained alive. ... The spirit of scientific and creative work and sound criticism was maintained, even if for the most part this was without much awareness."[47] In reality, of course, only traces of the broad-mindedness and openness of the pre-1917 university had survived. Encouragement of independent thinking did not occur during Gorbachev's first years as a student but only after Stalin's death, as a thaw set in and political, cultural, and scientific conditions in the country eased.[48]

At the university, Gorbachev continued to pursue his political ambitions. He became leader of the law department's Communist Youth League (Komsomol) group and was granted full membership in the party. Friedrikh Neznansky, an émigré Russian now living in the West who was in Gorbachev's class, remembers him as a hard-liner who made speeches scolding the shortcomings and improprieties of fellow party members and recalls "hearing the steely voice of the Komsomol secretary, Gorbachev demanding expulsion from the Komsomol for the slightest offense."[49] Other students saw him and his behavior differently. Zdenek Mlynář thought that Gorbachev exercised "informal and spontaneous authority;"[50] Vladimir Kuzmin regarded him as "helpful and good-natured,"[51] Vladimir Liberman as "modest,"[52] and Rudolf Kolchanov as "intellectually curious," "tolerant," and not displaying "any signs of radicalism."[53] One of his professors thought that "he was a good companion, always ready for a joke" and that "he never really showed off, and even when he became the [department's] Komsomol chairman, he never gave himself airs."[54]

Gorbachev retained some independence of judgment and he showed courage. In one instance in 1952, when one professor was reading page after page from Stalin's *Economic Problems of Socialism in the USSR*, Gorbachev sent him a note, complaining that the students had read the book and that failure to discuss it showed a lack of respect for the students. When the faculty member ridiculed the anonymity of the note, Gorbachev admitted that he had written it. He was called to the dean's

46 Gorbachev, *Zhizn'*, Vol. 1, pp. 61-62.
47 Ibid.
48 Ruge *Gorbachev*, p. 33.
49 Remnick, *Lenin's Tomb*, p. 160.
50 Zdenek Mlynář, "Il mio campagno di studi Mikhail Gorbaciov," *L'Unità*, 9 April 1985.
51 As quoted by Ruge, *Gorbachev*, p. 37.
52 Ibid.
53 As quoted by Remnick, *Lenin's Tomb*, p. 159.
54 Ibid.

office but was probably saved from expulsion by his position at the time of deputy Komsomol secretary responsible for ideological questions.[55]

His courage is demonstrated also by the fact that among his closest student friends were Zdenek Mlynář, a foreigner, and Vladimir Liberman, a Jew. Another incident involved the latter. About a month after the newspapers had reported the arrest of a group of doctors who had allegedly tried to kill Stalin, most of them Jewish (the "doctors' plot"), Liberman was attacked in class by another student. Everybody was silent. Gorbachev, however, angrily came to his friend's defense, calling the perpetrator a "spineless animal."[56]

Gorbachev's friendship with Mlynář is of particular interest. The Czech student was to become one of the leading reformers of the Prague Spring and one of the authors of the Charter 77, which formed the basis of organized dissent in Czechoslovakia during the last twelve years of communist rule. It would, therefore, be reasonable to infer that Gorbachev and Mlynář, in their student days, developed concepts of reform socialism which they would later attempt to put into practice. Gorbachev, however, fails to confirm such inferences. He only goes as far as to say that "The more thoroughly I immersed myself in the works of Marx, Engels, and Lenin, the more deeply I thought about [the problem of] congruence between their notions of socialism and our reality."[57] Mlynář recalls that Gorbachev sharpened his (the former's) awareness of the discrepancies between the glowing portrayals and the sordid reality of Soviet life. This concerned in particular rural life and the enforcement of discipline on the collective farm through common violence.[58] The notion that the two students developed reform socialist ideas at this stage in their life must be doubted also because of the fact that ideological orthodoxy under Stalin and even the limited relaxation after his death were not at all conducive to the elaboration of such ideas. It was really only after Khrushchev's "secret speech" at the Twentieth Party Congress in February 1956 that a more wide-ranging discussion of the Stalin era became possible. "Stalinism," as another of Gorbachev's student friends has observed, "was something deep inside us. We were only lucky that we were young

---

55 Gorbachev, *Zhizn'*, Vol. 1, p. 64; the incident was reported earlier by Remnick, *Lenin's Tomb*, p. 160.

56 Liberman reported this incident to Ruge; see the latter's *Gorbachev*, p. 41. In his memoirs, Gorbachev does not mention the incident. He does say, however, that Liberman failed to appear in class one day because he was too upset to attend. People had ganged up, cursed, and maligned him, and finally thrown him out of a tram. Gorbachev was "shaken" by the incident; Gorbachev, *Zhizn'*, Vol. 1, p. 65.

57 Gorbachev, *Zhizn'*, p. 64.

58 Mlynář in *L'Unità*, 9 April 1985. Archie Brown, who interviewed Mlynář, provides additional information and competent interpretation of the relationship between Gorbachev and his Czech student friend; see Brown, *The Gorbachev Factor*, pp. 30-31.

and flexible enough to change later on." It is also for this reason that he thinks that Mlynář's influence on Gorbachev "is overrated."[59]

At university Gorbachev met his future wife, Raisa Maximovna Titorenko. The daughter of a Ukrainian father and a Russian mother, she was born in the small town of Rubtsovsk in the Altai region of southern Siberia. The family had suffered greatly during collectivization and the purges. Her grandfather, as mentioned, had been arrested and shot. Her grandmother, as Raisa Gorbachev recalled, "died of grief and hunger as the wife of an 'enemy of the people'" and her four children "were left to the mercy of fate."[60] The couple had more in common than the legacy of an "enemy of the people" family history. Like Mikhail Sergeevich, Raisa Maximovna was intelligent, hard working, did even better in school than her future husband (she received the highest mark in high school in every subject and was awarded a gold medal) and was accepted at MGU to study philosophy, not because of connections in Moscow but because of her achievements. She lacked Gorbachev's political ambitions but added to the relationship by her interest in philosophy, art, and literature. To the extent that this was needed, she also added to his awareness of problems of agriculture and rural life by her empirical sociological studies of the peasantry in the Stavropol region.

Upon completion of university studies, the question of what to do next arose for Gorbachev. He returned to his native region and, in August 1955, began working in the Stavropol region's prosecution office (*prokuratura*), but only for ten days. To his wife (who was still in Moscow and arrived in Stavropol shortly thereafter) he wrote that "working in the prosecutor's office is not for me."[61] One of the reasons why he decided to abandon law enforcement was the "unscrupulousness with which the USSR *prokuratura* officials were proceeding."[62] Yet as if more sensitivity and compassion or less party tutelage could be expected there, he joined the Communist Youth League. He himself notes: "Essentially, the political youth organization had no autonomy whatsoever; in practice, it acted as a 'recipient of instructions' of the CPSU." He also observes that "any attempt of the Komsomol to act independently was not only regarded [by the CPSU] as undesirable but as dangerous."[63] However,

---

59 Rudolf Kolchanov, as quoted by Remnick, *Lenin's Tomb*, pp. 159-60. Gorbachev mentions in his memoirs that in 1967 Mlynář visited Moscow and then came to see him in Stavropol'. "Zdenek asked me about the situation in the Soviet Union, in the Stavropol' region, and about our life. He in turn told us a lot about the processes going on in Czechoslovakia ..." (Gorbachev, *Zhizn'*, Vol. I, p. 119). Gorbachev doesn't say that this conversation had any impact on his thinking.

60 Raisa Gorbachev, *I Hope: Reminiscences and Recollections* (New York: Harper Collins, 1991), p. 14; for more detail on Raisa Gorbachev's family background and personality see Brown, *Gorbachev*, pp. 32-33.

61 Raisa Gorbachev, *I Hope*, p. 81; as quoted by Brown, *Gorbachev*, p. 36.

62 Gorbachev, *Zhizn'*, Vol. 1, p. 79.

63 Ibid., p. 82.

he makes no effort to explain why it would be preferable to work for one party-controlled institution rather than for another.

Gorbachev's rise in the Komsomol and party apparat was fast by Soviet standards after Stalin's death. In 1956, at the tender age of twenty-five, he became first secretary of the Komsomol for the city of Stavropol and quickly rose to the highest post in that organization for the entire Stavropol krai. In only fifteen years, at the age of thirty-nine, he became the most powerful person in the Stavropol region. His career in the *party* apparat began in 1962 and was advanced by Fedor Kulakov, the first secretary of the Stavropol regional party committee, an association that was to last (with Gorbachev's patron in the meantime having been promoted to full member in the Politburo) until 1977.[64] His initial position was that of party regional organizer and then, from 1963, head of the party organs department for the administration of collective and state farms, a new office created by one of the many administrative reforms under Khrushchev. "An outside observer," he wrote of his function, "may regard cadres work as scheming and paper shuffling, as dealing with intrigues in the apparat or as another dishonorable or unpleasant occupation, and up to a point this was true. In the [party] organs departments, intrigues were often spun and the fate of human beings decided."[65] He, however, had set himself a higher task, which consisted in the attempt at promoting the best people ("I met hundreds of communists who were faithfully doing their duty") in order to improve the performance of agriculture in the Stavropol region.[66]

Kulakov evidently considered his protégé's work to be effective. In 1966, at the age of thirty-five, Gorbachev was promoted to first secretary of the Stavropol city party organization, and he now had to deal primarily with urban problems. His next career advancements occurred two years later, when he was moved to the position of second secretary of the party organization of the entire Stavropol krai, and in 1970, when he became regional first secretary. Since important regional party positions carried with them a seat in the Central Committee, Gorbachev was elected to that body at the Twenty-fourth Party Congress, held in 1971, just one month after his fortieth birthday.[67] At the same congress, Kulakov had become a full member of the Politburo and was able to continue to act as a patron for Gorbachev. When Kulakov died in 1977, Gorbachev replaced him as Central Committee secretary in charge of agriculture. Two years later, he became a candidate member of the Politburo, and in

---

64 For the at first rocky establishment of the patron-client relationship between Kulakov and Gorbachev, see Gorbachev, *Zhizn'*, Vol. 1, pp. 99-101.

65 Ibid., p. 101.

66 Ibid., pp. 101-6; 118.

67 Brown, *Gorbachev*, p. 39.

the following year, in October 1980, at the early age of forty-nine, a full member of that body. For the Soviet Union under Brezhnev, this was a remarkable career.

This sketch of Gorbachev's political profile would be incomplete without consideration of his attitude towards the reform efforts undertaken by Khrushchev and Andropov. In one of his few reflections on fundamental problems of the Soviet system contained in his memoirs, he argues that the failure of Khrushchev's reform attempts was due to the fact that

> the system did not accept innovation – even more than that, it resisted it. One should have assumed that Khrushchev's experience would have reinforced him in his recognition that a transformation was not to be achieved by operating on individual limbs. The framework of the system should have been ruptured instead so that one could have made more progress. But Khrushchev himself was a prisoner of outlived structures and ideological dogmas, which made it impossible for him to transgress the narrow confines of the system. This dilemma may also have been the root cause of his style of leadership, his emotional fluctuations, and his impulsive upswings. Khrushchev's intellectual potential could not flourish in this environment.[68]

This, it would seem, is an accurate characterization not only of the basic dilemma that Khrushchev was facing and his shortcomings and failures in dealing with them but also an apt description of *Gorbachev's* dilemmas and deficiencies.[69] A similar reasoning can be applied to Andropov's failed reform efforts. "He [Andropov] knew the situation in our country better than anyone else and he also knew how much our society was threatened, but he shared the belief of many [communists] that one only had to take care of the cadres and create discipline, and everything would be fine."[70] An Andropov disciple and protégé, Gorbachev during his tenure in office as General Secretary initially very much adhered to this belief and acted accordingly.

Most of Gorbachev's career before he assumed the top Soviet leadership position was concerned with agriculture and organizational matters in the party. There are a few instances in his life and career, however, which can be said to have had some influence on his later conduct in *foreign* policy. Such instances are his visits abroad, including trips to East Germany in 1966; Bulgaria and Czechoslovakia in 1969 and 1970; Italy in 1971; Belgium, with a side trip to Amsterdam, in 1972; West Germany in 1975; France in 1976; Canada in 1983; and Britain in 1984. Gorbachev's visits to

---

68 Gorbatschow, *Erinnerungen*, p. 103.

69 To that extent, one would have thought it appropriate for Gorbachev's observation to be included in both the Russian and the German edition of his memoirs. This, however, is not the case. The Russian edition contains only the first sentence about the Soviet system's aversion to innovation (Gorbachev, *Zhizn'*, Vol. 1, p. 98) but omits the criticism of Khrushchev's shortcomings. Irredeemably suspicious Kremlinologists may be excused for assuming that the parallels between Khrushchev's and Gorbachev's failures were too close for comfort to be presented to Russian readers.

70 Gorbatschow, *Erinnerungen*, p. 151; Gorbachev, *Zhizn'*, Vol. 1, p. 148.

East Germany (which, as his trip to West Germany, will be dealt with later) and Bulgaria apparently did not contribute anything to awakening any awareness of the imperial nature of the relationship between the Soviet Union and Eastern Europe. His visit to Czechoslovakia was different.

The intervention of the Warsaw Pact had occurred only fifteen months prior to the arrival of a Soviet party delegation, which included Yegor Ligachev, then first secretary of the Tomsk region, and Boris Pastukhov, the CC secretary responsible for the Komsomol. Wherever the Russian visitors came into contact with ordinary Czechs and Slovaks, they were met with hostility. "If I were to say that we felt uncomfortable this would be an understatement," Gorbachev remembers. "We felt deeply that the people condemned and indignantly rejected this action [the intervention]." Prague, he thought, "appeared paralyzed and numb. [Our Czech] colleagues did not consider it possible to get us together with workers' collectives; they themselves decided not to meet with them." In Brno, the delegation visited a large enterprise but "the workers did not return our greetings and demonstratively turned away. In August 1969, mass actions had flared up again against the new régime and the Soviet intervention ... [The] situation was extremely tense and the delegation had to be guarded around the clock." In Bratislava, "almost all the buildings in the center of the city had bullet marks, and everywhere anti-Soviet slogans were written on the walls." When a member of the CPSU delegation pointed out in a meeting with party officials that Lenin had supported federalism in principle but not within the communist party, the first secretary of the Slovak branch of the Czechoslovak Communist Party, Slavik, "rose and left. On the following morning, no one from the leadership appeared." He also recognized that there was a direct connection between the August 1968 events in Prague and events in Moscow. "The developments in the ČSSR and the dynamics which it gained frightened the Soviet leaders to such an extent that they immediately abandoned their modest economic reform intentions and, in politics and ideology, hastened to tighten the screws."[71]

It would be inconsistent with Gorbachev's political philosophy and personality for him unambiguously to condemn the intervention. He finds extenuating circumstances. "To be sure, during the years of the Cold War the parties to the conflict looked at much of what was happening through the prism of bloc interests and acted accordingly, not shrinking from the adoption of extremely harsh measures."[72] He insinuates that Czechoslovakia wanted to leave the Warsaw Pact.[73] There is even a

71 Gorbachev, *Zhizn'*, Vol. 1, pp. 157-59.

72 Ibid., p. 157.

73 "The fact that, in the press of the ČSSR in mid-1968, there began to appear reports on the possible exit of the country from the WTO [Warsaw Treaty Organization] was the expression of the position of certain political forces, in other words, a result of the internal political development"; ibid., p. 158.

whiff of "all is well that ends well" in his treatment of the intervention. "When I was in Czechoslovakia in the following year, good relations had been established between the people in the countryside and our soldiers."[74]

Gorbachev's experience in the Western industrialized countries, as he acknowledges, also shaped his perceptions. The first and foremost realization was that Soviet propaganda had painted a skewed picture of life under capitalism. "Irrespective of their purpose, the visits were instructive for me above all because of the fact that the information which we received from abroad was meager and also carefully filtered."[75] He was surprised by the absence of border controls between Belgium and the Netherlands.[76] And he was completely unprepared for the openness of Western society and politics and the huge discrepancies in the standard of living and in the level of economic and technological development between East and West. His "*a priori* belief in the advantages of socialist as compared with bourgeois democracy was shaken." He also thought that "perhaps the most important thing which I brought back with me from my trips abroad was the realization that people there live in better conditions and have a higher standard of living. Why do we live worse than the other developed countries? This was a question which was persistently to occupy me."[77]

To sum up, the contours which emerge from the lines of Gorbachev's background and experiences before his becoming General Secretary add up to a very contradictory personality profile. Not that the observer is faced with a Dr. Jekyll and Mr. Hyde phenomenon. He rather has to contend with several different Dr. Jekylls. One of the keys to unlocking their essence can be found early in his memoirs where he remembers that in his maternal grandfather's house, "in a corner in the living room hung an icon with an oil lamp in front of it, because grandmother was deeply religious, and under the holy picture, on a small table made at home, [the room was] beautified by portraits of Lenin and Stalin. This 'peaceful coexistence' of the two worlds did not at all embarrass grandfather."[78] His approval of his grandfather's tolerant attitude is typical of his own attempts to reconcile the irreconcilable. Such attempts have had a positive and a negative dimension. Their positive features are his

74 Ibid.

75 Ibid., p. 168. Incongruously, however, he makes the West responsible for "lowering an 'Iron Curtain'" on the exchange of information (ibid., p. 157).

76 Ibid., p. 165.

77 Ibid., p. 169. Nothing, of course, as has by now become obvious, is ever unambiguous. He finds a few things to criticize in the West and things that the Soviet Union does better. This concerns, for instance, the treatment of "immigrants" (he probably meant the *Gastarbeiter*, or guest workers) and thinks that "public education and the provision of health services at home are built on more equitable principles" and that "public transportation in the cities deserved preference" (ibid., pp. 165 and 169).

78 Ibid., p. 38.

proclivity for compromise, his reluctance to condemn or rush to judgment, his preparedness to let things ripen and get more mature, his preference for persuasion rather than pressure, and his abhorrence of violence. Their negative qualities lie in his refusal firmly to take sides, his aversion to commitment, his proclivity for procrastination, and his tendency to talk rather than to act decisively.[79] These deficiencies were felt particularly acutely by those who expected effective political leadership in a difficult period of transition.

Gorbachev's disinclination to commit himself and act decisively is connected with his almost invariably indeterminate and inconsistent analysis. To review the evidence, in his university studies he felt attracted to the probing discussions with intelligent, open-minded classmates, but until the very end of his career he defended the basic tenets of Marxism-Leninism and socialism. In his search for a profession, he turned his back on the *prokuratura* because the state attorneys were too unscrupulous and the judiciary lacked autonomy, but he joined the Komsomol, another Soviet institution without scruples or autonomy. Dwelling on Russian history, he acknowledged past Russian colonization of the northern Caucasus but simultaneously discerned contemporary interethnic harmony in this region. Concerning collectivization, he decried its excesses but justified the changes in the countryside as objectively necessary. He saw no necessity for the purges but de-emphasized their scale. He took Khrushchev and Andropov to task for remaining shackled by obsolete ideological beliefs and trying to reform the system without rupturing its framework but, when in office, he embarked on the same road of "modernization," "acceleration," and "perfection," a disastrous anti-alcoholism campaign and other unworkable disciplinary measures.[80] In the political realm, as a Western biographer observed,

> As President he dismissed (in effect) a Politburo whose composition he could not control fully and substituted for it a Presidential Council, wholly appointed by himself – yet he did as good as nothing to build up his political support in place of the CPSU he had abandoned. He deprecated those who "claim the role of the messiah," yet there was an impatience of teamwork here, a deliberate self-isolation that suggests delusions of irreplaceability, if not vulnerability.[81]

---

79 "The only thing that is moving in the Soviet Union are Gorbachev's lips," was the memorable response by a (non-licensed) taxi driver on the way from the center of Moscow to Sheremetevo airport in early October 1988 to this author's question as to what changes he had seen."

80 "Noble intentions, deplorable results" is the title he gives to the chapter on his anti-alcoholism campaign – a characterization that may well be applied to domestic politics and economic affairs in general. In foreign policy, the epitaph could be "noble intentions and unintended results."

81 John Miller, *Mikhail Gorbachev and the End of Soviet Power* (New York: St. Martin's Press, 1993), pp. 72-73. Gorbachev's attack against those who "claim the role of the messiah" as published, according to Miller, in *Izvestiia*, 1 December 1990.

In the economic area, in 1990, when he finally appeared ready to abandon the framework of the system by seemingly endorsing the Shatalin plan for the transformation of the Soviet economy to a market economy within 500 days, he reneged on his promises and demanded the plan's harmonization with Prime Minister Ryzhkov's tired ideas for the retention of the centrally planned economy.

In Boldin's view, based on his observations as Gorbachev's chief of staff in charge of party affairs in 1987-91, there was no limit to his double standards.

> Gorbachev advocated democracy ... yet he decided people's fate as he alone determined the membership of the Central Committee and the Politburo, choosing first secretaries of republican parties, obkoms, and kraikoms according to his personal likes and dislikes. [He] fought to expand glasnost, yet he withheld from the people, the party, and even his own associates, vital information ... and threatened to dismiss newspaper editors who published material not to his liking, making good on his threats in several cases. ... He fought to protect the independence of the judiciary but instructed the procurator general on how to pursue certain investigations. [He] fought against administrative command methods of management, while keeping a tight grip on ministries and committees and setting policy on all economic issues from the center.[82]

Valentin Falin concurs with this view of Gorbachev's double standards and, coupled with the indecisiveness and incompetence he discerns in his former chief's personality, reflects on the consequences such features are likely to produce:

> One cannot be a democrat and at the same time fear democracy. One cannot pledge allegiance to freedom of thought and be intolerant of the opinion of others. One cannot with one hand abolish totalitarianism and with the other assert one's own authoritarian style of leadership. And, finally, one cannot make numerous promises without taking the time and care seriously to address the matters at issue.[83]

Both Boldin, a co-conspirator in the August 1991 coup attempt, and Falin, for reasons which will be explained below, cannot be considered unbiased observers. But even some of those (very few) close confidants and advisors who remained loyal to Gorbachev throughout his tenure in office and even beyond it have expressed frustration about their inability to fathom his genuine thoughts and convictions at any given time. Chernyaev, for example, has admitted to having felt "bitter about the discrepancy between the views he [Gorbachev] expressed and his actions" and about the fact that, "at times, his [public] declarations and actions deviated from what he told some of us close to him who sincerely sought to understand him, and even more so from what he told foreigners."[84]

---

82 Valery Boldin, *Ten Years that Shook the World: The Gorbachev Era as Witnessed by His Chief of Staff* (New York: Basic Books, 1994), pp. 298-99.

83 Valentin Falin, *Politische Erinnerungen* (Munich: Droemer Knaur, 1993), p. 44.

84 Chernyaev, *Shest' let s Gorbachevym*, p. 316.

Gorbachev's foreign policy notions were and on many issues are still today characterized by the same discrepancy between public and private views and the same mixture of candor and caveat, insight and ignorance, admission and retraction. He was sensitive to the Hitler-Stalin pact as a causal factor for the outbreak of World War II but defended the non-aggression treaty as necessary, preferring to ignore the secret protocols. He disapproved of the restrictive Soviet policy on the exchange of ideas between East and West, and lamented the skewed selection and scarcity of information in the Soviet Union prior to the advent of glasnost but charged that it was the West that had lowered the Iron Curtain on the free flow of ideas and persons. He realized the deep humiliation and injustice inflicted upon the Czechoslovak people in August 1968 but failed to question the legitimacy of Soviet imperial rule and, a year after the intervention, was able to discern a certain improvement in the relationship between Russians and Czechs.

There are, however, important differences in Gorbachev's approach to domestic as compared to foreign policy. It is also noteworthy that almost throughout his tenure in office he was regarded with much reservation by the population, resented by many reformers, and despised by hard-liners in Russia but generally well respected and often enthusastically celebrated in the West.[85] There are several reasons for this discrepancy. *First*, his policies abroad were characterized by more consistency in conceptual approach and more congruence between theory and practice than those in domestic affairs. This is true despite all of the linkages and interconnections between the two policy areas. *Second,* consistency in new thinking and practice – the reduction of global commitments, deceleration of the arms competition, withdrawal of forces and equipment, lowering of the Soviet threat profile, and abandonment of ideological stereotypes– paid off in the form of benevolent Western attitudes and policies towards Soviet imperial contraction. It set in motion a process of positive reinforcement in international affairs. There was nothing equivalent domestically. *Third*, his internal policies, particularly in the economic realm, were often indecisive and ineffective and produced a large and, after January 1987, rapidly widening rift between promise and achievement. This reinforced rather than detracted from the need to curtail imperial overcommitment and overengagement but did nothing to endear him to the Soviet public. *Fourth*, whereas fundamental change in domestic affairs required a substantial redistribution of power and resources, change in foreign policy tended to affect personnel and resources to a lesser degree, and structural impediments were more easily overcome. *Fifth*, it is easier to destroy and dismantle than to construct. In international affairs, the removal of the huge asymmetries in

85 An indication of the low popular esteem in which he is being held in Russia are the results of the first round of the June 1996 presidential elections. Gorbachev received a mere 0.51 percent of the vote.

intermediate-range nuclear forces and conventional military power as well as the termination of ill-advised imperial entanglements were instantly applauded. In domestic politics, deconstruction was bound to be resisted, and reconstruction could only be a long-term and much more difficult endeavor.

After this description of the basic features of Gorbachev's personality, his political philosophy and difference in his approach to domestic as opposed to foreign policy, it is possible now to turn to his perceptions and policies on the German problem.

3. Gorbachev's Perceptions of the German Problem

In his memoirs, Gorbachev has acknowledged that he was surprised by the course of events in Germany in the late 1980s.

> I would be lying if I claimed that I had foreseen the way in which the German problem would be decided and the problems that would arise in this connection for Soviet foreign policy. I doubt in this connection whether any politician (in the East or in the West) would have been able to envision one or two years beforehand what would happen [in 1989-90]. After the precipitous changes in the GDR, events developed at such a breathtaking pace that there was the danger that they would spin out of anyone's control.[86]

He moves on to criticize the approach adopted by his predecessors, saying that

> Brezhnev and Gromyko committed an error when they allowed themselves to be spoon-fed by the leading politicians in the GDR and, in the early 1970s, began to accept the official versions of events, which were impressive in their "simplicity." These myths were that there were two German nations, that the German problem was "closed," and that it would make no sense to reopen it. But the point was not Ulbricht's and Honecker's theoretical constructs on the national question. The main issue lay in the sincere conviction of the Soviet leadership that the security interests of the Soviet Union necessitated a perpetuation of the division of Germany at any price.

In fairness, Gorbachev does not claim that when he assumed office he was determined to change well-established policies or that he should even alter what he now criticizes as the simple myths and categorical imperatives of the past.

> I must confess that I, too, accepted these categorical imperatives, although I had doubts as to whether any circumstances could be preserved in perpetuity. The world is always in a state of flux, and if man ignores this objective law, it can only lead to defeat and loss. *When I embarked upon high politics, the existence of two German states was a fact and the question of reunification simply did not arise.*[87]

---

86 Gorbachev, *Zhizn'*, Vol. 2, p. 150; similarly Gorbatschow, *Erinnerungen*, p. 700.

87 Gorbachev, *Zhizn'*, Vol. 2, pp. 150-151; Gorbatschow, *Erinnerungen*, p. 701 (italics mine). With some poetic license, the Russian *kategorichnost'* has been rendered here as "categorical imperatives."

It is not surprising that Gorbachev, as he admits, shared the preconceptions of Brezhnev and Gromyko on the German problem. He had practically no exposure to the study of international relations at Moscow University. One of the subjects he took was diplomatic history,[88] but the teaching of the subject conformed to standard notions about the entirely peaceful character of Lenin's and Stalin's foreign policy. Even Khrushchev, in his "secret speech" to the Central Committee in February 1956, had – with the exception of Stalin's failure to anticipate the German attack of June 1941 and his post-war policy towards Tito's Yugoslavia – exempted this realm from criticism. Gorbachev not only seems to have believed and probably still believes the standard Soviet interpretation of the origins of World War II but also the Soviet version of the division of Germany. This is evident, among other things, in a conversation he had when he visited West Germany as a member of a CPSU delegation, led by his mentor Kulakov, in May 1975, on the thirtieth anniversary of the capitulation of Nazi Germany.

The visit apparently made a big impression on him. In particular, a brief and sharp encounter with a German citizen engraved itself deeply in his mind. He mentioned the encounter several times to high-ranking West German visitors, including Genscher in July 1986 and von Weizsäcker in July 1987. This is what happened, according to his own description. "At a filling station [at Mannheim] near Frankfurt, I talked with the owner. He told me: 'Stalin declared: The Hitlers come and go. But the German people remains. But then, at the end of the war, Stalin seized and divided the German people.'"[89] A discussion ensued, Gorbachev remembers, in the course of which he attempted to set the historical record straight. The plans for the division of Germany, he explained,

> had been worked out during the war years by Churchill and American politicians. We opposed these plans and advocated the creation of one single, sovereign, and democratic German state. [However] ... the Western powers supported the creation of a separate West German state, and only later did the GDR come into existence. We also advocated the creation of a single, sovereign, and above all peaceful German state on the basis of the de-Nazification, democratization, and demilitarization of

88 Gorbachev, *Zhizn'*, Vol. 1, p. 61. He also lists German language as one of his courses. There is no record, however, that he ever used any of it on his trips to East or West Germany or in his talks with German political leaders.

89 Gorbachev, *Perestroika*, p. 210. When Gorbachev told this story to Genscher, the German foreign minister smiled. He (Gorbachev) had been lucky that his German interlocutor was apparently not much of a historian because otherwise he would have quoted Stalin in full. The complete statement, importantly as Genscher thought, was as follows: "The Hitlers come and go but the German people and the German state remain;" see Hans-Dietrich Genscher, *Erinnerungen* (Berlin: Siedler, 1995), p. 500. "The experience of history shows that the Hitlers come and go but the German nation, the German state, remains" is the version of J.V. Stalin, *The Great Patriotic War of the Soviet Union*, 5th edition (Moscow: Foreign Languages Publishing House, 1950), p. 84.

> Germany. However, there were forces in the West which took the matter to where it is today. The Soviet Union, therefore, was not to be blamed (*ne vinovat*) for the division of Germany; one had to look elsewhere for the responsibility.[90]

The ordinary German citizen was apparently just as unconvinced by these arguments as the West German president more than a decade later.[91]

There is, however, an important unreported sequel to the Mannheim exchange. Gorbachev continued the discussion privately with Viktor Rykin, the accompanying translator, a German expert with a doctorate in German history and at that time a junior official in the Central Committee's International Department. Prompted by the conversation, Gorbachev predicted that the day would come when Germany would be reunified.[92] He was challenged on this point by Rykin. German unity, he told his chief, was a phenomenon of relatively recent origin. Several German states like Prussia, Bavaria, Saxony, Hesse, and others had existed separately, some of them for centuries. Furthermore, Austria – a much more homogenous country ethnically than, say, Switzerland – had evolved separately from the two Germanies after the Second World War and had developed a distinct national consciousness. Everyone seemed to accept this, including the Germans. So why shouldn't there be the possibility of the development of a separate *East German* national consciousness and the acceptance of two German states by the international community and by the Germans themselves?

Gorbachev stuck to his point. In his view, the difference between the two Germanys, on the one hand, and Austria and Germany, on the other, lay in the fact that German unity had been achieved at great cost. The division of Germany was artificial and considered to be so by most Germans. One only needed to think of the Berlin wall to understand the complete absurdity of the state of affairs in the center of Europe. But the wall could not and would not be there forever. It was only a temporary device. How, one had to ask, would the Russians react to a wall right through the heart of *their* capital? Would they put up with such a thing? Surely not.

Chernyaev was to say later that Gorbachev had an intuition "deep down" that the reunification of Germany was "inevitable."[93] But what was the significance of this

---

90 Gorbachev, *Perestroika*, p. 210. Gorbachev's report of this encounter can be found not only in *Perestroika* but also, with some variations, in his memoirs (Gorbachev, *Zhizn'*, Vol. 1, p. 166; Gorbatschow, *Erinnerungen*, pp. 167-168).

91 Unlike his book *Perestroika* (p. 210), which is neutral on this point, his memoirs suggest that his German interlocutor was inclined to accept what he (Gorbachev) considered to be the "historical truth," that is, that "the plans for the division of Germany had not at all been hatched in Moscow" (Gorbachev, *Zhizn'*, Vol. 1, p. 166; Gorbatschow, *Erinnerungen*, pp. 167-68). However, Viktor Rykin, his translator (see below), remembers the German's attitude as less agreeable and accommodating to the Soviet point of view. Interview with Rykin.

92 Ibid.

93 Interview with Chernyaev; see also Chernyaev, *Shest' let s Gorbachevym*, p. 304.

intuition for top-level decision making on the German problem? Are historians or political scientists justified in drawing a straight line from Gorbachev's 1975 perceptions of the artificiality of the division of Germany and the inevitability of German unity to his 1990 acceptance of German unification? This would be inappropriate. As the citations at the beginning of this section have demonstrated, he was still mired in conventional preconceptions and saw no need to change policies. It will be argued here that it was essentially the force of events that persuaded him to act as he did but even then, at no time during his tenure in office as party chief and executive president did he actively *promote* German reunification. On the contrary, the evidence is overwhelming that from 1985 through 1989 he himself, other chief policy makers, and his top political advisors as well as the most prominent experts on German affairs were quite *opposed* to putting it on the agenda.

The May 1975 visit to West Germany produced other impressions which may have had a bearing on how Gorbachev was to deal with the German problem when it became acute. In his memoirs, he writes that in meetings with professors and students in West Germany he "did not notice any hostility." He was "struck by a powerful anti-Fascist demonstration in Frankfurt, in which 250,000 people participated – communists, social democrats, representatives of the CDU, *Bundeswehr* soldiers, members of labor unions, and delegates from youth and veterans organizations." He and his colleagues thought that "overall, the attitude of the Germans towards the Soviet Union was changing in a positive direction and that a profound change was taking place in German thinking."[94] This reconstruction of his experience appears credible and, in addition to many meetings with West German government, party, and business leaders in 1985-89, may have made it easier for him to abandon the deeply engrained Soviet stereotypes on the German problem.

Yet it would seem that, upon assuming office in 1985, Gorbachev did subscribe to time-honored stereotypes and shared many popular Russian notions about Germany and the Germans. Such notions, as amply reflected in Russian literature and Russian sayings, include the idea that Germans are characterized by organizational ability, dedication to work, technological skill, punctuality, rationality and efficiency but that they are often overly meticulous, stuffy, and lack compassion and a sense of humor. At the risk of overstating the case, in contrast to his reminiscences about his visits to Italy, France, and Belgium in the 1970s, there is no empathy or warmth in his recollections on Germany. He speaks with some admiration of cultural and even environmental matters in the former countries but remains entirely within the political dimension in his treatment of the latter. Images of the German national character are often contrasted with presumed Russian national traits. Russian folk wisdom, for

---

94 Gorbatschow, *Erinnerungen*, p. 168; slightly different in the Russian edition – the "positive direction" is missing but the "profound change" is duly noted; Gorbachev, *Zhizn'*, Vol. 1, p. 167.

instance, holds that "the Germans arrive at things by their brains, the Russians through their eyes" (*nemets svoim razumom dokhodit, a russkii glazami*). "As for economic prowess and technological skills, another Russian proverb holds that "for everything the Germans have an instrument" (*u nemtsa na vsë instrument est'*). Yet another quips: "Next to a church, there is a priest; next to a machine, there is a German" (*gde tserkov', tam pop, a gde mashina, tam nemets*). In the post-war period, such images were applied also to East Germany. A standard Soviet joke explained the German acronym of DDR, or GDR in English, as meaning *davai, davai, rabotat'* (hurry up, hurry up, and work).

Gorbachev's recollections of his first trip to East Germany in June 1966 conform to popular Russian images of the Germans. At that time, he writes, Soviet "party officials were being sent [there] in order to study the [East German] experience in the implementation of reforms," that is, the harmonization of "new methods of planning and administration [with] a system of incentives and more economic leeway for enterprises."[95] The Soviet delegation appears to have been impressed because, after the completion of the trip, a memorandum was sent to the CC with the recommendation to study closely the East German reform efforts. "However," Gorbachev deplores, "the memorandum ended up no differently than many others during those years."[96] On that occasion, he also met Honecker who was then a full member of the SED Politburo and only a few years away from the top leadership position and who, according to Gorbachev's recollections, "already acted in a very self-confident manner."[97] Twenty years later, he was to reiterate his impressions in private conversation with the East German leader. The visit had been for him "a very important journey" and one that had "aroused deep emotions."[98] The reason for this emotional experience, he explained, lay in a comparison of the economic reform processes that had "begun at the same time in the Soviet Union and the GDR" (his reference was apparently to the reforms introduced by Prime Minister Kosygin). The "main question" which at that time had occupied both countries had been the problem as to "how one could avoid remaining behind the pace of scientific-technological progress in the world." East Germany, contrary to the Soviet Union, had looked at the highest world levels of production, drawn the appropriate conclusions for its own research and development, and succeeded "in rapidly increasing labor productivity"

---

95 Gorbachev, *Zhizn'*, Vol. 1, p. 155.

96 Ibid.

97 Ibid. Gorbachev, in contrast, was at that time only a junior party official and unlikely to have caught Honecker's attention.

98 Protocol (*Niederschrift*) of talks between Gorbachev and Honecker on 28 September 1988 in Moscow, SED Politburo, *Arbeitsprotokolle*, Central Party Archives, J IV 2/1/685 (indirect speech; this is to indicate hereafter that the original transcripts of the private conversations between Soviet and East German leaders are in indirect speech but that for better readability in the text *direct* speech was used. The transcipts sometimes alternate between the two forms).

and also "catching up in the quality [of production] in comparison with the advanced countries."[99]

What he didn't tell Honecker, of course, is what he noted in his memoirs. Although his meetings and conversations with East Germans had proceeded in a pleasant atmosphere, "they lacked warmth."[100] Specialists on Germany in the CPSU Central Committee who had contact with Gorbachev thought that, while he felt a "certain affinity" with Poland and the Poles and had cordial personal relations with Wojciech Jaruselski and Mieczyslaw Rakowski, his attitude towards East Germany and its official representatives was characterized by "indifference" and "psychological distance."[101] This was bound to affect the personal and political relationship between the two leaders – a factor that will now be examined in the context of East Germany's importance and its role in the Soviet Union's empire in Eastern Europe.

4. East Germany: Strategic Ally but Waning Economic Asset

Gorbachev inherited East Germany as an integral part of the Soviet empire. But his consent in 1990 to German unification meant abandoning a "strategic ally," as he called the GDR, and handing it over to what used to be an adversary alliance.[102] How could such vile treachery, in an orthodox communist and Russian nationalist perspective, occur? Part of the answer lies in the fact that in the period from 1985 to 1990 individual leaders had a major impact on history. The alienation, animosity, and antipathy that pervaded the personal relations between Gorbachev and Honecker contributed to the Soviet leader's sense of imperial malaise and his view of the Soviet possessions in Eastern Europe as a source of embarassment and a burden rather than an asset.

As in a marriage gone sour and drifting inexorably towards an uncivilized divorce, insinuations alternated with reproaches. Charges were met by countercharges. For some time, cutting remarks and cryptic allusions became the order of the day. But as the personal and political differences proved irreconcilable, open controversy and argument that might have cleared the air disappeared from the discourse. In the interest of self-preservation, to impress foes, and to reassure friends and neighbors, the two antagonists pretended that nothing was wrong. "Outwardly, everything looked normal: the embraces, the kisses, the awarding of medals, the cordial

99 Ibid. (indirect speech).

100 Gorbachev, *Zhizn'*, Vol. 1, p. 156.

101 Interviews with Tsipko and Rykin.

102 Gorbachev referred to East Germany as a "strategic ally" of the Soviet Union as late as December 1989, in his speech to the Central Committee of the CPSU after his return from the Soviet-American summit conference at Malta; see *Pravda*, 9 December 1989.

receptions, attendance of congresses – the almost ritual procession of the chosen."[103] But beneath the surface there was smoldering suspicion, resentment, and scheming.

It is probably true that even with the best of intentions and good will a cordial relationship was probably not to be expected. The personal chemistry of the two leaders was too different for this to happen. Gorbachev's flair, his spontaneous, outgoing, radiant, optimistic, often unconventional attitude and sense of humor contrasted sharply with Honecker's prim and proper appearance, the petty demeanor of a petit bourgeois and miserly bureaucrat, the impatience and intolerance, and the penchant for utterly humorless, schoolmasterly lecturing performed in an unpleasantly high-pitched voice. The personalities of the two leaders couldn't have been more mismatched. In the past, such mismatches between Warsaw Pact leaders had, of course, not been an obstacle to cooperation. However, in the present case, the personality problem was exacerbated by the political dimensions of psychology, notably Honecker's acute loss of a sense of reality concerning the true state of economic and political affairs in East Germany and Gorbachev's overestimation of the chances for a successful introduction of "democratic socialism" in the Soviet Union and Eastern Europe.

Another source of alienation lay in Soviet suspicions about Honecker's putative pan-Germanic, albeit socialist, pretensions. Honecker, as mentioned in the previous chapter, was born in 1912 in Neunkirchen, a town in the Saarland, one of the smaller German Länder, situated close to the German-French border. His career began with tasks in the communist youth organization and party work in the Saarland in the 1920s, continuing with agitprop training in Moscow in the 1930s. It was interrupted by a long prison term under the Nazis in World War II, resumed when Honecker became youth secretary and security chief of the SED Central Committee in the 1950s and 1960s, and culminated with his appointment as party chief in 1971. Not surprisingly, in the preparations for his visit to West Germany in 1987, Honecker insisted on returning to his birthplace in the Saarland and visiting the grave site of his father. As it happened, one of leaders of the West German Social Democratic Party, Oskar Lafontaine, was not only active in promoting the burgeoning SPD-SED exchanges but was also SPD chairman and prime minister of the Saarland. No wonder, therefore, that the *germanisty* in the international department of the CPSU Central Committee thought that Honecker represented the pan-German communist party tradition and that for him his contacts with the West German social democrats were a potentially fatal attraction.[104] Differences in education may also have played a certain role in fueling misunderstanding and distrust between the two leaders.

---

103 Shevardnadze in general terms about the relations between the reformist leadership in Moscow and the conservative leaders in Eastern Europe; *Moi vybor*, p. 199.

104 Interview with Rykin.

Whereas Gorbachev, as described above in detail, had an extensive university education, Honecker barely managed to finish basic education and never began an apprenticeship. His only work experience before becoming an apparatchik in the youth organization and in the party was that of a farmhand in Pomerania and helper to his uncle, a roofer, in the Saarland.

Further seeds for mutual suspicion and distrust were laid during the emergency meeting of Soviet and East German leaders in August 1984. Although the record, as noted, shows that Gorbachev merely adhered to the adamant position of the Politburo, Honecker returned from Moscow reportedly convinced that Gorbachev was a "*Scharfmacher*," that is, that he had taken a particularly hard line.[105] In Honecker's perceptions, that line seemed to continue when he was in Moscow on 12 March 1985 to attend the funeral ceremonies for Chernenko. Chancellor Kohl, who was also in Moscow on that occasion, had let it be known that he was keen to meet with the East German leader. Yet Gorbachev's suspicions of intra-German contacts had not been alleviated. Several of his advisors were trying to dissuade the SED chief from agreeing to such a meeting – to no avail. Kohl and Honecker met in what was an extraordinarily, perhaps demonstratively cordial atmosphere.[106]

Nevertheless, the two general secretaries seemed prepared not to start out their relationship as top leaders of their countries on a sour note. Gorbachev, in particular, wanted to reassure Honecker that there would be no major policy changes. After the arrival of the SED delegation at the airport in Moscow, he briefly talked with Honecker on the telephone and told him that the CC plenum, at its meeting of the previous day, had "*decisively come out for the consistent continuation of our political course. There is no necessity to change it. This concerns questions of domestic as well as foreign policy.*"[107] Similarly, the April 1985 CC plenum, which later assumed an almost mythical quality as having ushered in perestroika, did not provide any better clues as to what Gorbachev might have in mind. As Chernyaev, then still deputy head of the CC International Department, noted in his diary, on internal issues Gorbachev made some personnel changes and emphasized the need for "discipline, law and order, and decentralized decision making." On questions of foreign affairs, he was "flat, commonplace, and conventional" as if he "didn't want to touch the subject yet" or, worse, still "deferred to Gromyko." Overall, therefore, it did not seem that "Gorbachev had a more or less clearly defined concept as to how to advance the country to world levels."[108]

---

105 Interview with Krenz.

106 Ibid.; see also Egon Krenz, "Honecker und Gorbatschow," *Neues Deutschland*, 25 January 1993.

107 Gorbachev – Honecker telephone conversation, 12 March 1985, 3.35 p.m., SED Politburo, *Arbeitsprotokolle*, Central Party Archives, J IV 2/2A/2739 (italics mine).

108 Chernyaev, *Shest' let s Gorbachevym*, pp. 42-43.

Business as usual in the "socialist community" and Soviet-East German relations seemed to be indicated also in other fora. These included the meeting on 13 March of the first party secretaries of the Warsaw Pact countries held also on the occasion of the Chernenko funeral celebrations in Moscow; the extension of the Warsaw treaty for another twenty years at a meeting of the leaders of party and state of the alliance in Warsaw on 26 April; and the celebrations in Moscow and East Berlin on 8 May commemorating the fortieth anniversary of the Soviet victory over Nazi Germany. There were nevertheless a few indications of change in Soviet policy towards the *West*. These concerned Gorbachev's announcement of a moratorium on the stationing of intermediate range nuclear missiles and the halting of the "countermeasures" adopted after the deployment of INF in Western Europe.[109] But these announcements were not a problem for Honecker. They could be regarded as indicating that Moscow would now follow the course which he had charted earlier and for which he had been so severely reprimanded.

The first opportunity to talk in detail about international issues occurred on 5 May 1985 when Honecker was in Moscow on an official visit. The transcripts of the Gorbachev-Honecker meetings show that the Soviet party leader now did have more specific ideas about the directions and the methods to be employed to achieve change. They also demonstrate that up to a point he was intent on mending fences with his East German counterpart. Finally, they reveal an important paradox in Gorbachev's attempt at restructuring the Soviet system in 1985 and 1986. The fence-mending notwithstanding, the Soviet leader (mildly) criticized his East German counterpart despite the fact that the ideological basis and the foreign policy and economic strategies of perestroika were quite in conformity with East German preferences and practice.

Concerning the first, the ideological aspect of the paradox, Honecker could only have been reassured by the talks. The ideological basis of perestroika looked traditional, even orthodox. This was evident in Gorbachev's remarks to his East German counterpart on the tactics to be adopted by the communist parties in their struggle against imperialism:

> The fraternal countries charge ahead and often pose themselves new questions. There are differences in tactics, and in the solution of concrete problems. All the more necessary [therefore] is a more intensive exchange and closer coordination. Failing that, everyone looks for his own model. What would remain of socialism if everyone were to withdraw to his own national apartment? Imperialism would then pick off one [socialist

109 As announced by Gorbachev in an interview with *Pravda*, 7 April 1985.

> country] after another. ... *There is only one model, Marxist-Leninist socialism.*[110]

Honecker couldn't have put it more succinctly.

As for the foreign policy aspect of the paradox, Gorbachev's shift to a more flexible and conciliatory approach to the West, which was to bring him in line with previous East German approaches, was noted above. It is the economic aspect of the paradox that warrants analysis in more detail.

The GDR in Gorbachev's Economic Strategy

In May 1985, Gorbachev assured Honecker: "Between the Soviet Union and the GDR there is the broadest [possible] agreement on planning and guidance and on economic mechanisms."[111] Furthermore, he was "able to state with pleasure, after having listened [to you], that [we both] think along the same lines not only on general but also on specific questions."[112] Did the GDR really fit into Gorbachev's economic scheme?

In Gorbachev's view, the GDR, because of its scientific and technological potential, could make a significant contribution to the revitalization and modernization of the Soviet economy. In another round of confidential talks between the two leaders in February 1986, Gorbachev lamented in reference to the Soviet Union that "one should have begun with it [the emphasis on science and technology] twelve to fifteen years earlier, and one would be much further along. Now it is much more difficult to solve these tasks."[113] Honecker agreed and attempted to impress Gorbachev (successfully, it would seem) with the first in a seemingly never-ending series of East German progress reports on the improved relationship between science and production, the expansion of microelectronics and production automation, and the elaboration of new processes and materials in the GDR – all of which undertaken under the heading of creating in that country a "computer-based society."[114]

One of the best indications of what the two leaderships *specifically* had in mind can be found in the materials relating to the coordination of Soviet and East German national economic plans for the period from 1986 to 1990. The planning institutions of the two countries agreed on measures for the "acceleration of scientific-technological progress" and the "broadest application of the most modern results of

---

110 Transcript of the talks between Honecker and Gorbachev in Moscow on 5 May 1985 in Moscow, SED Politburo, *Reinschriftenprotokoll*, Central Party Archives, J IV 2/1/631 (indirect speech, italics mine).

111 Ibid. (indirect speech).

112 Ibid. (indirect speech).

113 Transcript of the talks between Gorbachev and Honecker on 27 February 1986 in Moscow, SED Politburo, *Reinschriftenprotokoll*, Central Party Archives, J IV 2/2/2156.

114 Ibid.

science and technology in the production process," the "rapid acceleration of labor productivity," and the "more effective and sparing use of material and labor resources."[115] Particular attention was to be given to the coordination of plans in microelectronics and computer technology and to "cooperation in the development of new basic technologies, the creation and production of electronic building blocks and microprocessors, as well as the necessary technological equipment and materials necessary for that purpose."[116] The plans for Soviet-East German trade were to reflect these priorities.

Table 3 – GDR-USSR Trade Projections, 1985-90 (in billions of rubles)[117]

	1985	1990	Annual Growth in %
Volume	14.80	17.80	3.70
GDR Exports	7.40	9.10	4.20
of which:			
Machinery	5.20	5.60	1.50
Chemical products	0.35	0.46	5.60
Consumer goods	1.10	1.60	7.80
USSR Exports	7.40	8.70	3.20
of which:			
Machinery	0.90	1.90	16.1
Energy, raw materials and chemical products	5.80	6.00	0.60

These and other data clearly reveal the intentions of the economic planners until the year 1990 and beyond. East German exports of microelectronic equipment were to increase more than twofold and those of microelectronic products almost fourfold. Moscow officials, as indeed Gorbachev, expected a significant breakthrough in the modernization of machine building in the USSR.[118] They thought it possible,

115 The basis for all this were decisions adopted at the June 1984 CMEA summit conference in Moscow and the draft of a Long-Term Program on the Development of Cooperation between the GDR and the USSR in Science, Technology and Production until the Year 2000, agreed upon on 6 October 1984.

116 Protocol on the Results of Coordination of National Economic Plans of the GDR and the USSR for 1986-1990 and Beyond, Attachment No. 2, SED Politburo, *Arbeitsprotokolle*, Central Party Archives, J IV 2/2/2127.

117 Ibid.

118 In fact, one of the most noteworthy features of the Soviet Union's five-year plan (1986-90) was that the planned average annual growth of investment in the machine-building sector amounted to no less than 12.5 percent.

consequently, to decrease East German machinery exports to a growth rate of only 1.5 percent per year and hoped that Soviet exports of this type of commodity would increase by 16 percent (!) annually.[119] Under the conditions of a "policy of increasing aggressiveness, boycott, and discrimination by the imperialist states" the two planning authorities of the two countries also agreed upon measures to reduce their dependency on the world market and to draw up a list of such products as were currently being imported and to substitute them by indigenous products.[120] Finally, in Gorbachev's opinion, East Germany could play an important role in countering Reagan's "Star Wars" initiative, or SDI.

East Germany and SDI. The perceived seriousness of the challenge of SDI can vividly be demonstrated by a letter Gorbachev sent to Honecker on 12 September 1985.[121] The Soviet party leader wrote that the "necessity of an intensification of socio-economic development" lay not only in the internal tasks which the CPSU had set itself. The "external factor" was also increasing in importance. "The West has emphatically embraced scientific-technological progress and in the struggle against socialism is putting [the emphasis] above all on technological warfare." He contended that SDI had "not only military but also great economic significance." Based on a policy of export restrictions, the "leadership of the USA is conducting a policy of a 'pre-programmed technological lag of the socialist countries.'"[122]

He also deplored the Reagan administration's attempt to enlist the support of the Western European countries and Japan for such a strategy. The West Europeans, he pointed out, had responded to SDI with Eureka, "a comprehensive program of coordinated efforts in the area of high technology." He admitted that "we are as yet unsure as to the balance between [its] military and civilian, that is, peaceful elements."[123] He also was ambiguous on the question as to whether the socialist countries should respond favorably to the invitation issued by the West Europeans to participate in the Eureka technolgy program.

Irrespective of how the issue of participation in Eureka was going to be resolved, it was clear that the United States' strategic design "poses in all sharpness the necessity for the member countries of CMEA to accelerate scientific-technological progress" and, in a foreseeable time frame, "to assume leading positions" in that sphere. He therefore suggested advancing the date for the adoption of CMEA's Comprehensive Program for Scientific-Technological Cooperation and, even before details of the program could be agreed upon, embarking immediately upon large-

---

119 Protocol on the Results, Attachment 2.

120 Ibid.

121 Gorbachev letter to Honecker, 12 September 1995, verbatim, SED, Central Party Archives, IV 2/2.035/58.

122 Ibid.

123 Ibid.

scale joint projects of scientific-technological cooperation and the creation of a common fund for the financing of such projects.[124]

Gorbachev also impressed upon other party leaders the gravity of the challenge. At the October 1985 summit meeting of the member states of the Warsaw Pact in Sofia, he told the assembled party chiefs that "*we clearly recognize the dangerous military-political consequences of SDI.*"[125] He again regarded Reagan's initiative as an "attempt to secure a permanent technological superiority of the West over the socialist community and, by the way, not only over it but also over the [United States'] own allies." Returning to a dialectic Marxist approach to the relationship between the United States and Western Europe, he interpreted Eureka both as a European response to SDI and an integral part of an "overall line of the West," with military industry in the United States and Western Europe seeking to maximize profit. Furthermore, he said: "We cannot but recognize [the fact] that the imperialist states create their own scientific-technological programs which are in many ways subordinated to the tasks of struggle against the socialist community." Again he saw the necessary Warsaw Pact response as consisting in "the fastest possible development of scientific-technological integration. We have to solve these problems more effectively than the capitalists."[126] The GDR and, to a lesser extent, Czechoslovakia were called upon together with the Soviet Union to play the most important part in countering the military-technological challenge emanating from the United States.

Deficiencies in the Economic Relationship. It was, of course, a serious error of judgment to assume that East Germany could play a significant role in countering SDI. It was equally erroneous to think that technological progress could be accelerated in Comecon in accordance with the Comprehensive Program. As Soviet prime minister Ryzhkov was to tell his CMEA colleagues in July 1988, "we have now been working for more than two years on the realization" of the program but "we cannot claim that we have made much progress"; the share of highly advanced technological products in CMEA economic exchanges remained "most insignificant."[127] The same applied to the expectation that the GDR could meaningfully contribute to the modernization of the Soviet economy. Soviet-East German economic exchanges were plagued by many problems, some of them specific to the bilateral relationship, others associated with the structural deficiencies of the

124 Ibid.

125 Gorbachev's speech at the meeting of the Warsaw Pact's Political Consultative Committee on 22 October 1985 in Sofia, SED, Central Party Archives, J IV,1/2A/2811 (italics mine).

126 Ibid.

127 Quoted from the speech by Nikolai Ryzhkov, the Soviet prime minister, at the 5-7 July 1988 meeting of CMEA, that is, the 44th council meeting, SED, Central Archives, J IV 2/2A/3141.

planning system in Comecon, the deteriorating overall performance of the economies, the burden of the arms competition and other growing costs of empire.

A first set of problems concerned exchange of information in science and technology. In his talks with Gorbachev on 20 April 1986, Honecker styled himself as an advocate of glasnost and dwelled on its virtues. He raised the subject by asserting that scientific-technological cooperation between the USSR and GDR should be improved by "de-bureaucratizing things" and by "solving certain questions of secrecy." Gorbachev replied that according to his information "some matters are being kept secret from the Soviet Union, too." Honecker rejected the charge but Gorbachev did not relent. He knew how much Honecker had done for the development of Soviet-East German scientific and technological cooperation. Yet a joint committee for economic relations established for the purpose of better information exchange had become an "amorphous and ineffective institution." He reiterated that he "was repeatedly receiving information to the effect that the comrades in the GDR keep this and that secret from the S[oviet] U[nion]." In his concluding remarks on this topic, Honecker professed some understanding for the Soviet need for secrecy in military affairs. "The thing, however, is that eminent GDR scientists often find it impossible to exchange information with their partners in the S[oviet] U[nion] and that their wishes are not being accommodated to the same extent as they would be in the GDR."[128]

A second set of problems was associated with the commodity composition of Soviet-East German trade. Major asymmetries existed and were confirmed in the national economic plans for 1985-90. The share of fuel and raw materials in the total East German imports from the Soviet Union was to amount to 70 percent in the planning period. This percentage would also be the share of metallurgical products, including technologies, in the total East German exports to the Soviet Union. As the GDR planning document states, the supply of the country "with raw materials and fuel to a large extent has to be paid by increasing GDR exports of machinery and equipment."[129] But Honecker complained to Gorbachev that "The Soviet Union is not prepared to import important machinery products from the GDR." The state of affairs in the coordination of plans thus far showed that "GDR machinery exports [to the USSR] in 1986 will *decrease* by 665 million rubles as compared to 1985."[130] This

128 Transcript of the conversation between Honecker and Gorbachev on 20 April 1986 in East Berlin, SED, Central Archives, Büro Honecker, 41666 (indirect speech).

129 Decision Concerning the Coordination of Plans with the USSR for the Period 1985-1990, adopted at its meeting of 27 August 1985, SED Politburo, *Arbeitsprotokolle*, J IV, 2/2/2A/2785. Attachment No. 7.

130 Protocol of the talks between Gorbachev and Honecker in Moscow on 5 May 1985, SED Politburo, *Reinschriftenprotokoll*, Central Party Archives, J IV 2/1/638 (italics mine). Honecker's complaint about the 1986 figures is not inconsistent with the above table on the five-

downturn could not be explained "by a lack of demand in the USSR or insufficient GDR production and delivery capacity."[131] He did not advance a theory as to the reasons for the projected decline, but economic planners in Moscow and East Berlin had a fairly good idea. Soviet officials had repeatedly protested against the East German practice of delivering industrial goods of low quality to the Soviet Union and of higher quality to Western industrialized countries. Moscow was also beginning to show a greater preference for more advanced and reliable Western technology and attempting to expand indigenous machinery production. Mutual recrimination did not end here. In the 1970s and early 1980s East Germany had become accustomed to both lavish supplies and the low cost of Soviet oil. In the second half of the 1980s, however, Soviet supplies were cut back, costs were rising, and East Berlin complained about alleged "violations of agreements."[132]

Third, hard currency was an issue. East Germany was contractually entitled to repair Soviet weapons systems, notably MiG aircraft, helicopters, jet engines, radar systems, and missiles in the armories of the Warsaw Pact and in several developing countries, including Egypt, Iraq, Syria, and Libya. The latter countries had to pay the GDR in hard currency. In top secret draft agreements, the Soviet Union now claimed a share of that money and began to demand full payment in hard currency for the Soviet spare parts to be used in the repair services in developing countries. It then lowered its demands to a share of 60 percent in hard currency, but this, too, was rejected by the SED Politburo.[133]

A fourth problem pertained to technology export controls. In what looked like a mirror image of Reagan's approach vis-à-vis his European allies to ensure compliance with economic sanctions towards the countries of the Warsaw Pact, in May 1985, Yuri Masliukov – a first deputy head of the state planning committee and chief of its military department – attacked GDR export policies. He told a high-ranking East German delegation in Moscow that the United States, its NATO allies, and Japan had strengthened their policies of "economic aggression and embargoes" and their

---

year (1985-1990) plan coordination, according to which GDR machinery exports were to grow on average by only 1.5 percent per year.

131 Ibid.

132 East German protests continued until 1989; for one of the many examples, see Politburo meeting of 10 January 1989, SED Politburo, *Arbeitsprotokolle*, Central Party Archives, J IV 2/2A/3186. The Soviet Union, in turn, had repeatedly called upon the GDR to participate more extensively in the construction of gas pipelines; see, for instance, [Politburo] Directive for the Preparations of the Participation of the GDR in the Construction of the Natural Gas Pipeline Yamburg-Western Border of the USSR, SED Politburo, *Reinschriftenprotokoll*, Protocol of 15 January 1985, Central Party Archives, J IV, 2/2/2094, Attachment No. 7.

133 Directives for the Bilateral Coordination with the USSR on the Shaping of Foreign Economic and Scientific-Technological Relations with Capitalist and Developing Countries, SED Politburo, *Reinschriftenprotokoll*, Protocol of 2 July 1985, Attachment 2, Central Party Archives, J IV, 2/2/2119.

attempts at "inflicting damage" on the socialist economies. The Warsaw Pact countries, on the other hand, were deliberately or unintentionally exporting strategically important "results of scientific research, advanced technologies, and scarce materials." The Soviet Union considered it necessary, therefore, "to unite the efforts of the Warsaw Pact member states for the protection of their military economic and scientific-technological potential."[134] To the amazement of the East German economic delegation, Masliukov produced a detailed list of technological manufactures and scientific processes subject to export control to non-socialist states but refused to hand it over, "pointing to its not yet final character." In its report, the East German delegation characterized the document it had seen as unacceptable because it was "unilaterally directed towards global export control." The Politburo agreed. It rejected the Soviet approach and in subsequent negotiations insisted on a "limitation [of export controls] to such products and technologies as are of strategic significance."[135] Nevertheless, at the end of the year, a Warsaw Pact convention on technology export controls was signed.[136] As was true of many other agreements, it failed to produce meaningful results.

Finally, there was a problem with a commodity that to both administrators and victims of empire provided relief and escape – alcohol. As all Soviet institutions, the Soviet armed forces in Germany were unable to evade the rigors of Gorbachev's anti-alcoholism campaign. The forces anticipated a reduction of 8,700 hectoliters of hard liquor, 3,100 hectoliters of wine, and 800 hectoliters of champagne and therefore sensibly requested substitution of these products by clothing, shoes, industrial products, and foodstuffs. This was apparently an item of utmost importance to be dealt with by the SED Politburo, which it did in its session of 27 August 1985. The deliberations were to provide yet another telling example of the absurdities of central planning and damaging interdependence on the basis of inflexible quotas. The Group of Soviet Forces in Germany was to be told that, unfortunately, the national economic plan had been completed and that, therefore, "additional provision of these products was impossible."[137] The end result was, one might have guessed, neither booze nor shoes.

Whatever the number and scope of Soviet-East German problems, they were probably in no way greater or smaller than those which the Soviet Union had with other CMEA countries. The main point here, however, is that the GDR was the most

134 Top secret agenda item prepared for the SED Politburo session of 2 July 1985, SED Politburo, *Arbeitsprotokolle*, Central Party Archives, J IV, 2/2A/2774.

135 Ibid.

136 For the text of the agreement, see SED Politburo, *Arbeitsprotokolle*, Central Party Archives, J IV 2/2A/2964.

137 Agenda item No. 34, Politburo meeting of 27 August 1985, SED Politburo, *Arbeitsprotokolle*, Central Party Archives, J IV 2/2A/2786.

important country of the bloc for Gorbachev's emphasis on science and technology as growth factors and his intended shifts from extensive to intensive development, from quantity to quality, and from coercion to incentives in economic management. Given Gorbachev's ideas about modernization of the economy, acceleration of growth, and improvement of scientific-technical cooperation, the last thing he would have wanted at that stage was for anyone to rock the rickety boat of the socialist community on the shoals of the German problem. He himself was to do so later for reasons which had as much to do with economics as with politics.

Political Aspects of Soviet-East German Relations

In preparation for his departure for East Berlin to attend the Eleventh SED congress, from 17 to 21 April 1986, Gorbachev agreed with the approach suggested by Chernyaev. His aide had proposed that

> in our talks with Honecker in Berlin we should not convey the impression that we want to "straighten him out" or influence him but [find ways] how jointly – philosophically and theoretically – to approach the problem of the "two Germanys" in the context of current world development.[138]

In private, as demonstrated above and as will also be explained further below, this was not quite how the Soviet leader chose to proceed. But publicly, at the Eleventh SED congress, he certainly reassured the East German leader. He reiterated his concern that "the ruling class of the FRG has not renounced its revanchist dreams and continues to speak of an 'open German question.'" The Soviet Union, he then went on to say,

> attaches much importance to the development of relations with West Germany as a major European state. What is more, we are prepared to develop these relations on an equal basis and for mutual benefit. But this first and foremost calls for Bonn's policy to meet in practice the interests of peace and security. We want to stress in that context that we unconditionally support the legitimate demand of the GDR to West Germany that relations between them be fully brought into accordance with the commonly recognized norms of international law.[139]

But differences in political perspective existed on several major issues. These included (1) Chinese-East German party relations; (2) East German criticism of Soviet domestic developments; (3) the political aspects of East Germany's economic relations with West Germany; (4) Honecker's refusal to inform his colleagues in the Politburo about emerging differences with Gorbachev; and (5) Honecker's persistent intention to pay an official visit to West Germany.

---

138 Chernyaev, *Shest' let s Gorbachevym*, p. 83.
139 Gorbachev's speech to the SED Congress, 18 April 1986, *Pravda*, 19 April 1986.

The Chinese Connection. The triangular relationship of Moscow-Beijing-East Berlin was one of the many factors putting strain on the difficult relationship between Gorbachev and Honecker. After Gorbachev's accession to power in March 1985, the process of rapprochement in Sino-Soviet relations had received a new impetus. In a speech to the CC, Gorbachev had assured the Chinese of his "serious interest" in an improvement of the relationship, listed China again as one of the "socialist states," and dispensed with the "third party" argument, that is, the theory according to which Moscow could not conclude agreements with China at the expense of other countries. What was meant in the circumstances was obvious. Beijing was constantly citing "three obstacles" which the USSR would have to remove before a "normalization" of relations could take place. Specifically, Moscow would have to reduce its military presence along the Chinese border to the level of 1964; end its support of Vietnamese expansionism in Southeast Asia, including in Cambodia; and withdraw its troops from Afghanistan. In previous Soviet interpretations, meeting any of these demands *would* have affected the interests of "third parties," notably Mongolia, Vietnam, Cambodia, or Afghanistan.

The Chinese reacted swiftly to the Soviet overtures. In their congratulatory telegram to Gorbachev upon his election as first secretary, and for the first time since the rupture of party relations in March 1985, they again addressed a Soviet party leader as "comrade." Chinese vice premier Li Peng, who headed the Chinese delegation at Chernenko's funeral, even handed a message to Gorbachev from the Chinese party chairman, Hu Yaobang.[140] But all these gestures were mere harbingers of a possible spring in the Sino-Soviet relationship. It was not until after the withdrawal of Soviet forces from Afghanistan in 1989 that a breakthrough in the relationship was achieved.[141]

East Germany, on the other hand, had already begun the process of "normalization" in 1983 and 1984 at both the state and the party level. Some of the momentum driving the improvement of Sino-East German relations derived from Honecker's previous close contacts with Hu Yaobang.[142] The Chinese, like the East German, party leader had made his career in the communist youth organization and in June 1981 had been elected party chief. This background notwithstanding, it is striking that the GDR commented favorably on the Chinese "four modernizations" and other reform measures adopted by Hu Yaobang and Deng Hsiaoping. This was

---

140 See Dieter Heinzig, "Soviet Policy Towards China," in Federal Institute for East European and International Studies, ed., *The Soviet Union 1984/85* (Boulder, Colo.: Westview, 1986), p. 288.

141 Ibid., pp. 286-287.

142 Honecker was to point out to Gorbachev that he "knew him [Hu Yaobang] from the youth movement and the WFDY [World Federation of Democratic Youth]" and agreed with the Soviet party leader that Hu had "more positive views than Deng Hsiaoping," SED, Central Party Archives, IV 2/1/638.

surprising given the SED's domestic orthodoxies and even more so because of its consistent criticism of Hungarian economic reforms. Thus, East German observers found "remarkable progress made by the People's Republic of China in its economic and social development" and noted the "visible improvement in living conditions" for the Chinese farmers,[143] who were raising their living standards more quickly than people in the cities, buying everything from washing machines to private cars.[144] The only reference to the ideological implications of the liberalizing agricultural and industrial reforms were quotations from Chinese decrees stating that China would "seek to counter the intrusion of bourgeois ideology."[145] Honecker seemed to believe that in China the dangers of "revisionism," let alone a restoration of capitalism, were slight.

Soviet-East German controversies over the Chinese issue after Gorbachev's accession to power in April 1985 started with a visit by East German planning chief and deputy prime minister Gerhard Schürer to Beijing in July 1985, and his favorable report on the state of affairs in China. A copy of the report had been dutifully transmitted to the CPSU. At the beginning of August 1985, Politburo member and secretary for security questions Egon Krenz received the first deputy chief of the Soviet embassy in East Berlin, who stated that he had a personal message from Gorbachev to Honecker. To Krenz's surprise, the Soviet envoy wanted to read out the message but retain the written text. Since the content of the message thus promised to be highly sensitive, Krenz insisted on having a stenographic record taken.[146] Posterity, therefore, became privy to yet another bizarre occurrence in "fraternal" intra-communist discourse.[147]

Gorbachev first politely thanked the SED for the Schürer report but immediately came to the point. Motivated by the importance of formulating coordinated actions by the fraternal socialist countries towards China, he wished to convey some considerations about certain aspects of the policy of the Chinese leadership. He charged, in essence, that Chinese policies were characterized by duplicity. As Chernenko had done previously concerning the GDR's policy towards West Germany, Gorbachev now implicitly accused Honecker of gullibility and naïveté on East Germany's policies towards *China*. He noted that "the Chinese in the talks with

---

143 Christa Runge, writing in *Horziont* (East Berlin), June and September 1984.

144 Werner Micke, a confidant of Honecker, writing in *Neues Deutschland*, 7-8 July 1984. The author was also deputy editor of the newspaper.

145 Article by Fritz Verner-Osten (pseud.) in *Horizont* (East Berlin), December 1984; for detail, see B.V. Flow, "Orthodox East Berlin Reacts Favorably to Major Reforms in China's Economy," *RFE / RL Soviet and East European Report* (Munich), Vol. 2, No. 12, 1 February 1985.

146 Interview with Krenz.

147 Stenographic record of the Gorbachev message to Honecker, as transmitted by Popov [first deputy chief of the Soviet embassy] to Krenz, SED, Central Party Archives, Büro Krenz, IV 2/2.039/280.

Comrade Schürer professed full understanding for the special relations" existing between the GDR and other socialist countries on the one hand, and the Soviet Union on the other. They had "said that 'We will never have insidious intentions.'" However, Gorbachev wanted to tell his "German friends that there are reasons for doubting the sincerity of such assertions." Deng Hsiaoping, for instance, one of the main architects of Chinese domestic and foreign policy, had stated that China's strategic interests "required that the Soviet Union be considered 'a political opponent'"; that the "Warsaw Pact and CMEA should 'not be strengthened but weakened'"; and that "a harsh policy of 'separating the socialist countries of Eastern Europe from the Soviet Union'" should be adopted. Chinese premier Zhao Ziyang had made essentially the same points when he had visited Turkey.[148]

Gorbachev also charged that "Hu Yaobang attempts to give assurances that China is pursuing a consistent line in support of the GDR on the so-called 'German problem.'" Such declarations would be welcome, Gorbachev continued, if they corresponded to the real state of affairs. In actual fact, however, the Chinese leaders had "several times publicly advocated the 'unification of Germany.'" As evidence for this allegation, he pointed to a visit by premier Zhao Ziyang to West Germany in June 1985 where he had assured his hosts that "China has 'understanding for the striving of the German people for unification.'" This position, the Soviet leader regretted, was not much different from what the G-7 leaders had stated at *their* meeting in Bonn in May 1985, namely, that they wanted to achieve a state of affairs "that would permit the German people to create 'unity by free self-determination.'" After mentioning several other examples of Chinese double-dealing, he denounced Beijing for supporting Bonn's position on the allegedly "unsolved German question."[149]

Quite in accordance with the Ideological and Imperial paradigm, Gorbachev thought that the West German class enemy was elated by such expressions of Chinese support. He reproached the East German leadership for having failed to realize that Chancellor Kohl had "declared during his visit to Beijing in October of last year [1984] that for the FRG 'it is of special significance that the Chinese People's Republic advocates the unity of Germany.'" He also indicted the SED for not realizing that "in June 1985, Bavarian prime minister Strauß warmly thanked the Chinese government for its constant support of the 'right of the divided countries to self-determination.'" In view of all this, Gorbachev said, there could only be one conclusion, namely, that "*the position of Beijing contradicts the vital interests of the German Democratic Republic as a socialist state.*"[150]

---

148 Ibid.

149 Ibid.

150 Ibid. (italics mine).

How is one to interpret these "confidential considerations"? Certainly, first and foremost, as a blunt criticism of East German foreign policy draped in thinly veiled charges of East German inexperience, ignorance, and gullibility. Their purpose evidently was to restore the proverbial "unity and cohesion of the socialist community." Gorbachev's attacks on GDR-Chinese relations were also a clear indication that there was as yet no deviation of the new Soviet leader from previous patterns of Soviet foreign policy. More fundamentally, they underline the deep foreign policy crisis in which the Soviet Union still found itself in 1985 but also the inability of the new leader to deal effectively with it.

To conclude this episode of imperial pressure on a strategically important actor at the periphery, Honecker found Gorbachev's information important or, more correctly, interesting enough to write on top of the document: "To the members and candidates of the Politburo." He also initialled the document ("EH") and dated it "2 August 1985." But this is apparently where the matter ended. In a personal conversation between Gorbachev and Honecker at the Warsaw Pact summit conference in Sofia later in the year, the East German party leader gave his critic the chance to expound on the theme of Chinese duplicity on the German problem by reminding him, in the context of a discussion of Chinese developments, that "we gave [you] the protocol on G. Schürer's trip to China."[151] Gorbachev, however, did not react. There is no further trace of any repercussions produced by the document. It thus remains buried in the archives, a sorry landmark on the road to the dissolution of empire.

Soviet and East German Domestic Policies. When Gorbachev visited East Berlin in April 1986 to attend the SED's Eleventh Party Congress, the still carefully concealed rift in his relations with Honecker was to widen. This occurred in private conversation between Gorbachev and Honecker on 20 April. The meeting got off to a bad start. After the usual opening formalities, invocation of the "vital necessity for the CPSU, the SED, the people of the two states and the General Secretaries personally to underline unity," and appeals not to provide "even the most minute cause for ambiguity" Gorbachev expressed displeasure. Although the "Twenty-seventh Party Congress of the CPSU [25 February - 6 March] was supported by the party and people of the GDR," he had the impression that "*Comrade Honecker was irritated by something*." He felt that the East German leader had "displayed a certain reserve" and had "reservations" concerning domestic developments in the Soviet Union.[152] For

151 Protocol (*Niederschrift*) on the meeting between Honecker and Gorbachev at the Warsaw Pact summit conference in Sofia on 23 October 1985, SED Politburo, *Reinschriftenprotokoll*, Central Party Archives, J IV 2/1/638.

152 Transcript of the conversation between Honecker and Gorbachev on 20 April 1986 in East Berlin, SED, Central Archives, Büro Honecker, 41666 (indirect speech, italics mine). Based on conversations with Honecker, the Soviet ambassador in East Berlin, too, concluded that the East German party leader "supported without qualification the *international* course" charted by the

instance, he (Honecker) had "spoken very extensively about international problems [and] how they had been dealt with at the Twenty-seventh Party Congress but not about their significance for socialism."[153] He had also "failed to mention anything about the fact that we are now [following the East German example] and pursuing the course of the unity of economic and social policy."[154]

Gorbachev evidently referred to the emphasis Honecker, after he had taken office in 1971, had put on the social dimension of the SED's policies, including an ambitious housing program and the "quality of life" as an important factor of production, but also to what under Ulbricht and in the first years of the Honecker era had been an important feature of economic and social life in East Germany: small-scale commodity production and the activity of private traders and craftsmen. However, another paradox in Soviet-East German relations is to be noted here. Gorbachev was apparently ignorant of the fact that in the second half of the 1970s small-scale commodity production and private economic activities had significantly been curtailed in conjunction with the establishment of large production associations, the *Kombinate*. This had occurred under the headings of rationalization, automation, standardization, and intensification of production.[155] This change in East German economic policy may have been the very reason why Honecker failed to compliment Gorbachev on his supposed imitation of the East German example and why the Soviet leader stubbornly continued to adhere to an outdated view of East German developments. It also raises the question of what it was that the Central Committee's specialists on East Germany, to the extent that they existed, were telling Gorbachev or whether he was interested in listening to them.[156]

If Gorbachev's complaints were meant to impress Honecker, they failed to achieve their purpose. The East German leader denied the Soviet allegations. He only went as far as to acknowledge, without further comment, that "the question is being posed, for instance, why Comrade Honecker previously said, 'To learn from the Soviet

---

Twenty-seventh Party Congress but "concerning the assessment of our concept for *domestic* development, he remained distant"; Wjatscheslaw Kotschemassow, *Meine letzte Mission: Fakten, Erinnerungen, Überlegungen* (Berlin: Dietz Verlag, 1994), p. 51 (italics mine).

153 Transcript of the conversation between Honecker and Gorbachev on 20 April 1986 in East Berlin, SED, Central Archives, Büro Honecker, 41666 (indirect speech). Gorbachev apparently referred to what Honecker had said in his report to the Eleventh Congress.

154 Ibid. (indirect speech). This was added by hand with a preface that the remark was made "in the car."

155 Bundesministerium für innerdeutsche Beziehungen, ed., *DDR Handbuch*, 2nd edition (Cologne: Verlag Wissenschaft und Politik, 1979), pp. 175-85.

156 Concerning the persistence of Gorbachev's erroneous notions about small-scale private production and trading in the GDR, including the idea that these features of East German life were "more democratic" than what existed in the Soviet Union, see *infra*, p. 291, n353.

Union means to be victorious,' but no longer says this today."[157] The effectiveness of Gorbachev's criticism was undermined further by his deference to Honecker and his praise for what he considered to be other achievements of socialism in the GDR. In an apparent prelude to a direct personal attack on the East German leader, Gorbachev deplored increasing dissension in the socialist community:

> Even when jokingly certain remarks are being made as, for instance, who ought to be considered the *doyen* among the General Secretaries in the socialist community, [I] am thinking about what may lie at the root of this. Are certain ambitions at issue here or efforts to appear infallible? Certain models [of socialism] are always being emphasized.

These remarks could have been taken as applying squarely to Honecker's pretensions. Yet Gorbachev *exempted* the East German leader from criticism. He spoke of "discussions of the Hungarian model" and "discussions in that direction also in Bulgaria" but complimented Honecker by saying: "In essence, only the Soviet Union and the GDR rest on firm foundations of socialism – and perhaps also the ČSSR."[158] He further undercut any case he might have wanted to make against East Germany by repeating what he told Honecker the previous year: "If one wants to talk about any model of socialism at all, there is only one and one only: the Marxist-Leninist model."[159]

Debts and Dependency. Another controversy was carried over from *before* Gorbachev's appointment as party chief. This concerned West German credits and alleged East German political dependency – an issue that had sharpened, as noted, in the spring and summer of 1984. In keeping with his general proclivity not to address contentious issues openly, Gorbachev raised the problem of debt and dependency but failed to discuss it in detail. He prefaced the topic by a review of "worrying" developments in Eastern Europe.[160] Poland was "lying flat on its back," Gorbachev said, and it was difficult to predict "when it would get up again." Hungary had recently received a letter from the International Monetary Fund outlining the measures that the country had to adopt in order to pay principal and interest, and this had been coupled with the "repressive demand that otherwise no [more] credit would be extended." As for East Germany, he had talked with prime minister Ryzhkov who had reported that "the FRG is attempting to buy up the GDR's obligations towards [foreign] countries in order to bind the GDR to the FRG."[161] Honecker, as previously, vehemently objected to the implication that the GDR was financially vulnerable.

---

157 Transcript of the conversation between Honecker and Gorbachev on 20 April 1986 in East Berlin, SED, Central Archives, Büro Honecker, 41666 (indirect speech)

158 Ibid. (indirect speech).

159 Ibid. (indirect speech).

160 Record (*Information*) of the meeting between Gorbachev and Honecker on 20 April 1986 in East Berlin, Central Party Archives, Büro Honecker, 41666.

161 Ibid. (indirect speech).

Indeed, "intensive efforts" had been made by the West to "cause difficulties" for the GDR but these efforts had been unsuccessful. This was due to the fact that the GDR had reduced its imports from hard-currency countries with the result that it now had "a surplus in its balance of trade amounting to between $3 and 6 billion per annum." He sought further to undercut Gorbachev's argument by saying that only a small portion of the foreign trade credit in the amount of DM 850 million available to the GDR had been called up – "only DM 170 million in the first quarter of the year." Finally, citing data released by the Bank for International Settlements in Basel, he asserted that the Soviet Union and East Germany were "considered to be among the financially most stable countries in the world," the latter's net debt amounting to only $3.5 billion.[162] The conclusion that Honecker wanted Gorbachev to draw was simple: the subject of political dependencies created by financial strings, at least in the East German case, was simply not worth discussing.

Secrecy and Lack of Trust. Another factor contributing to alienation in the relationship between Gorbachev and Honecker was the fact that the East German leader was keeping important matters not only from the "Soviet comrades" but also from the SED Politburo. In particular, in order not to weaken his position in the party leadership, he systematically suppressed information about Soviet-East German differences. This was well known in Moscow party circles long before Gorbachev's accession to power.[163] Kvitsinsky, speaking about the second half of the 1970s, has described the problem and the inability of the Soviet leaders to solve it:

> Since it had been reported to us that Honecker filed away all reservations and warnings conveyed to him from Moscow in his safe without informing even the Politburo about them, Gromyko expressed the wish that the other comrades also be given notice of the Soviet standpoint. Honecker gave the reply that this would be the last thing he would do; after all, he did not want to "undermine" the standing of the Soviet comrades in the eyes of the Politburo. The insinuation could not have been any clearer: "Your remarks, esteemed Soviet comrades, bear witness to such a lack of expertise that it is within your own interest that no one finds out about them."[164]

In the August 1984 Soviet-East German emergency meeting in Moscow, as noted, Chernenko had voiced his suspicion to Honecker that "your comrades are not properly informed about our positions" on matters of foreign policy.[165] In the private talks with Honecker in April 1986, Gorbachev (as noted) complained about the lack of exchange of information between the Soviet Union and East Germany on

162 Ibid.

163 Interviews with Tsipko and Maksimychev.

164 Kwizinskij, *Vor dem Sturm*, pp. 262-63.

165 Transcript (*Niederschrift*) of the August 17, 1984, meeting, SED, Central Archives, J IV 2/2.039/280; for the context and the full quotation see above, p. 176.

scientific-technological matters. However, on this point at least, he adhered to the line agreed upon in advance with Chernyaev that it would be better not to give the impression that he was attempting to "straighten" Honecker out. He refrained from extending the discussion of secrecy in the scientific-technological sphere to the political realm. Yet from Honecker's perspective, the transcript of the meeting would apparently contain too much evidence already of the emerging differences in the relationship between the two leaders for his colleagues in the Politburo to know about it. The transcript was, presumably for that reason, not included in the materials submitted to the SED Politburo for consideration at its session of 29 April but transferred to his (Honecker's) private files.[166]

The lack of glasnost in the political relationship between the GDR and the USSR and in the personal exchanges between the two leaders deepened mutual suspicions and undermined trust. Gorbachev, in retrospect, has acknowledged the existence of these interconnections:

> Soon after [in 1986], we began to address each other with the familiar form of "you." Yet a really open relationship, one of mutual trust, never did develop between us. Honecker, it seemed to me, was somehow tense and couldn't abandon the official manner. I was taken aback most of all, however, by [the fact] that he informed his colleagues about our talks only sparingly and selectively, whereas I always saw to it that the transcript of the notes of our meetings was transmitted without cuts to all the members of the Soviet leadership.[167]

Honecker's Plans to Visit West Germany . The most serious of the controversies, and one directly addressed by the two leaders, concerned yet again Honecker's persistent desire to visit West Germany. It was Gorbachev who introduced the issue in the context of a review of Soviet-West German relations. He made it clear that he himself had absolutely no intention to visit West Germany at this stage. This adamant position was, in part, based on the argument that the ruling coalition of conservatives and liberals would be rewarded for its policies and the chances of the social democrats in the upcoming state elections in Lower Saxony at the beginning of July would be hurt. In what can be considered a telling indication of the influence of the SPD in Moscow, Gorbachev admitted to Honecker that SPD presidium member Egon Bahr had "called upon [me] to promise not to go to the FRG this year. [I] thereupon communicated to Willy Brandt that [I] would not go this year." He

---

166 Büro Honecker, 41666; interview with Krenz; see also Egon Krenz, "Honecker und Gorbatschow," *Neues Deutschland*, 25 January 1993, and Küchenmeister, *Honecker – Gorbatschow: Vieraugengespräche*, p. 78.

167 Gorbachev, *Zhizn'*, Vol. 2, pp. 407-408. It is not entirely clear from the context whether the use of the second person singular in the conversations between the two leaders occurred "soon after" Gorbachev had attended the Eleventh SED Congress in April 1986 or after a visit by Honecker to Moscow in October of that year.

concluded by claiming that both "the SPD and the Greens do not want Gorbachev *and Honecker* to go to the FRG."[168]

Honecker flatly contradicted Gorbachev on that point. Brandt and the prime minister of North Rhine Westphalia, Johannes Rau, had "proposed to [me] that I go to the FRG in May." He conceded that it might perhaps not be a good idea to visit West Germany before the elections in Lower Saxony (not least, one might add, because this would not have fit his own schedule, which included his involvement in the East German parliamentary elections on 8 June, participation in the Warsaw Pact summit conference in Budapest 10-11 June, and a visit to Sweden at the end of June). But to visit the Federal Republic "between the beginning of July and 12 July," he thought, would "be useful for the SPD."[169] The tug of war continued, with mutual irritation and annoyance increasing in the process. Honecker, at one point in the conversation, snapped that "the games that are being played [in Moscow] in connection with [my] visit to the FRG have finally got to come to an end." At another point he insisted that it would be "good to accept the invitation now in order to get the thing off the table."[170] In a huff, he also refused to accept Gorbachev's invitation for dinner, only to relent shortly thereafter.[171]

On the day after the official end of the congress, Gorbachev told the SED leadership that he had asked Honecker what would happen if he were to travel to the FRG but he (Gorbachev) would not. "How should [we] explain this to the Soviet communists and to the Soviet people? This also would have to be explained to the party and the people of the GDR."[172] Gorbachev, to sum up, made it quite clear that he thought that the visit would not serve a useful purpose. Honecker, on the contrary, felt that the visit should be scheduled as soon as possible but again did not dare override the Soviet opposition. The plans for the visit were canceled accordingly, but the episode strongly reenforced Honecker's negative disposition towards Gorbachev.

---

168 Transcript of the conversation between Honecker and Gorbachev on 20 April 1986 in East Berlin, SED, Central Archives, Büro Honecker, 41666 (indirect speech, italics mine).

169 Ibid. (indirect speech).

170 Ibid. (indirect speech).

171 Interview with Krenz; see also Egon Krenz, "Honecker und Gorbatschow," *Neues Deutschland*, 25 January 1993.

172 Transcript of the meeting between Gorbachev and the SED Politburo on 22 April 1986 in East Berlin, SED, Central Archives, Büro Honecker, 41666 (indirect speech, italics mine). According to Krenz, on 22 April, at the meeting with the SED Politburo, Gorbachev adopted a "jovial" tone and, to Honecker's consternation, reported "full agreement between the two parties" on the main lines of policy, including "abandonment of comrade Honecker's plans for visiting the FRG." Honecker considered this to have been inexcusable double-dealing and never forgave Gorbachev for this (interview with Krenz and *id.*, "Honecker und Gorbatschow," *Neues Deutschland*, 25 January 1993). The official transcript of the 22 April meeting, however, does not note the "full agreement."

One of the reasons why the new Soviet leader, like his predecessor, was so adamant on the issue of Honecker's visit had much to do with Gorbachev's negative attitude towards Kohl and the West German government.

5. West Germany: Troublesome Tenant in Gorbachev's "Common House of Europe"

In his memoirs, Gorbachev glosses over Soviet-West German relations during the first two years of his tenure in office. This is perhaps because of some embarrassment. An honest appraisal would have necessitated acknowledging that, in essence, he was continuing the stale approach of "insulted giant" and "bear in hibernation" that Chernenko had adopted vis-à-vis Bonn. West Germany, he writes, "was our number-one trading partner in the West but in the military-political ranking order it figured as one of our 'potential adversaries.'" Furthermore, contrary to the grand fanfare about the Common House of Europe, in the period from his accession to power in March 1985 until October 1988, Gorbachev concentrated on the reordering of relations with the United States.[173] Western Europe played a subsidiary role in Soviet policy towards the West. West Germany fared even worse: it was given the cold shoulder. The "new page" in the book of Soviet-West German relations, a phrase used several times in that period, failed to be written.[174] Moscow, in essence, continued the previous policy of attempting to isolate and circumvent West Germany or, more specifically, the ruling center-right coalition in Bonn, and "punish" it for its role in legitimizing the stationing of U.S. medium-range missiles in Western Europe and supporting the idea of strategic defense.

In detail, it was no accident of diplomacy that in Western Europe, Gorbachev first visited Paris and not Bonn. Shevardnadze, in 1985 and 1986, held talks in Washington, Tokyo, and a number of European capitals, but he, too, studiously avoided the West German capital. It took one visit of the president of the Federal Republic (July 1987), three visits by Chancellor Kohl (July 1983, March 1985, and October 1988), five by Foreign Minister Genscher and one each by the prime ministers of Bavaria and Baden-Württemberg (December 1987 and February 1988) to Moscow as well as Honecker's visit to West Germany against unabated Soviet

---

173 "In the conditions of a general increase in tension," Gorbachev wrote, "the course of the FRG was primarily considered in Moscow in the context of Soviet-American conflict;" ibid. The emphasis on Soviet-American relations will be dealt with separately in the following section.

174 The metaphor was used for the first time by Gorbachev during West German foreign minister Genscher's visit to Moscow in July 1986; see Genscher, *Erinnerungen*, p. 501, and *Frankfurter Allgemeine Zeitung*, 22 July 1986.

opposition (September 1987) for Gorbachev to feel that the time had finally come to abandon his reservations.[175]

The lack of congruence between Gorbachev's rhetoric about the Common House of Europe and his policies towards West Germany is touched upon in his memoirs.

> My meetings with Reagan in Geneva and Reykjavik were already history, and we were in an active political dialogue with France, Italy, and Great Britain, but our relations with the FRG essentially remained unchanged. The abnormality of this situation finally became apparent for both sides, and it was becoming ever more evident to me that we would not be able, in the long term, to pursue a serious European policy without Germany. I spoke of this fact on several occasions during Politburo meetings and in the small circle of like-minded colleagues.[176]

Who was to blame for the "abnormal" state of affairs? In Gorbachev's view, the fault lay with Bonn. "The relaxation of Soviet-West German relations begun by Willy Brandt in the years of Ostpolitik," he writes in his memoirs, "yielded to a stiffening of positions at the beginning of the 1980s."[177] The extent to which this may have been the case will be examined later. At this stage it is appropriate to argue that the lack of progress in Soviet-West German relations had more to do with the *Soviet* stereotypes and clichés, inertia and objective difficulties of management of the contradictions in the Soviet empire than with West German intransigence. The argument can be supported by what Gorbachev told Honecker in private conversation on 20 April 1986.

In that conversation, the Kremlin leader introduced a discussion of Soviet-West German relations by saying that the federal government vacillated between acting insulted and attempting to blackmail the Soviet Union. Representatives of the ruling coalition of the CDU/CSU and the FDP, with Helmut Kohl as chancellor and Genscher as vice chancellor and foreign minister, had repeatedly argued that the government was going to be in office for a long time and that the Soviet Union would be making a mistake if it ignored that fact of life and continued to cultivate its relationship with the social democrats.[178] But Gorbachev showed himself unimpressed by these pleas. He clarified that the social democratic channels would be maintained. Furthermore, he contended, it would be pointless to take any initiatives

---

175 For a detailed treatment of the Gorbachev's failure to respond to West German overtures, see the series of articles by Hannes Adomeit, "Gorbatschows Westpolitik: 'Gemeinsames europäisches Haus' oder atlantische Orientierung?," *Osteuropa*, Nos. 6, 9, and 12 (1988).

176 Gorbachev, *Zhizn'*, Vol. 2, p. 152 (italics mine). The precise moment as to when *both* sides realized the "abnormality" of the situation remains unspecified.

177 Ibid., p. 151.

178 Transcript of the conversation between Honecker and Gorbachev on 20 April 1986 in East Berlin, SED, Central Archives, Büro Honecker, 41666. Gorbachev's point of departure was a visit by Horst Teltschik, Chancellor Kohl's foreign policy advisor, to the Soviet embassy in Bonn. In interviews with the author, Teltschik has confirmed that this is an argument he had made in talks with Kvitsinsky.

and useless to pay a visit to West Germany because one would only be hearing in Bonn what one was told in Washington. Kohl was so wedded to American policies that "he has already overtaken [Margaret] Thatcher. He not only moves in the wake of the USA but behaves like a lackey of the USA and completely associates himself with Reagan and the SDI plans." In the final analysis, the question arose "if we aren't facing here a cross breed of FRG revanchism with the course of social revenge of the USA."[179]

One could argue that Gorbachev's hard line vis-à-vis Bonn was motivated by his determination to dissuade Honecker from visiting West Germany. The argument may be valid, but only up to a point. The fact is that the Soviet leader did not deviate much from the tough line, neither at the Warsaw Pact summit conference in Budapest in June 1986 nor in his talks with Genscher in July of the same year. At the summit conference, Gorbachev adopted the traditional two-pronged approach in Soviet relations with West Germany. On the one hand, he acknowledged the "importance the role of the FRG in Europe and in the world. Our relations to the FRG are based on the positive experiences which significantly contributed to détente in the 1970s." He also saw "great opportunities which could open for the development of a political dialogue on broad problems as well as for the development of stable economic, scientific-technological and other relations." But, on the other hand, he regretted that in the last few years the FRG government had made the realization of these possibilities difficult to achieve.

> You know Kohl's policy. If it had not been for the support extended by the FRG, US missiles would not have been stationed in Europe. As regards SDI, the West German government not only associates itself with the American position but supplements it by a European variant of the militarization of space. Not to speak of the continued fanning of revanchism.[180]

After having taken note of the fact that parliamentary elections were soon (January 1987) to be held in West Germany and that the outcome of the elections was uncertain, he furnished one major rationale for his policy of watchful waiting on the German problem: "Our approach is the following: *In our contacts with the Kohl government for the time being [we will] not undertake anything beyond the necessary.*" As if in justification of his opposition to the Honecker visit, he applied this policy of deliberate distance to the question of a personal visit to West Germany:

> It is obvious what purpose the West Germans have in mind when they rather steadfastly are striving for a summit conference with us. They need it in order to improve their electoral chances. We [therefore] have arrived

---

179 Transcript of the conversation between Honecker and Gorbachev on 20 April 1986 in East Berlin, SED, Central Archives, Büro Honecker, 41666 (indirect speech).

180 Text of Gorbachev's speech at the Budapest PCC meeting, attachment for 18 June 1986 Politburo session, SED Politburo, *Arbeitsprotokolle*, Central Party Archives, J IV 2/2A/2897.

> at the conclusion that it is better not to proceed with such a meeting this year. *We do not want to support Kohl; on the contrary, it is necessary to let him and the West German public feel our attitude to his policy.*[181]

In continuation of the traditional policy of differentiation among the socio-economic and political forces in West Germany, he concluded that it was "useful to continue our active work with the Social Democrats, the Greens, and other circles of the opposition – perhaps also with Genscher."[182]

In the more restricted session of first party secretaries only, Gorbachev was even more blunt. He said that he was of the opinion that "the socialist countries have a *proven policy of pressure on the Kohl government*." The government was "beginning to feel this." The Soviet Union, in essence, had communicated to Kohl the following message: If Bonn had anything new to say, "then one would be thinking about inviting [sic] Kohl and talking with him about current problems." Kohl had reacted by "cursing a lot" and complained that Gorbachev was "meeting with Mitterrand, the demagogue, and with Craxi." But he (Gorbachev) refused to meet with him despite the fact that Kohl was advocating the continuation of the Ostpolitik and dynamic relations with the Soviet Union. Gorbachev also reported that he had answered Kohl that we "*would talk with him if he, as chancellor, were to show his own political profile*." Gorbachev concluded his account by telling his East European colleagues that he thought that "the FRG government had been given a lesson," which could also be useful "with regard to the upcoming elections and public opinion." All of this was not easy and he had talked about it "at length with Comrade Erich Honecker."[183]

Gorbachev's outline of the approach to be taken by Warsaw Pact countries towards Bonn did not remain unchallenged in the closed room. Honecker confirmed that he had talked about the German problem with Gorbachev. But he gave a different spin to the content of his meeting, evidently one that suited his unabated desire to visit West Germany. He had allegedly told Gorbachev that when one attempted to "create the Common House of Europe one had to be careful not to shunt the FRG to a siding. It is playing an important role in the EC and NATO. Such a policy could create an unwelcome effect of solidarity" in the West.[184]

Hungarian party leader János Kádár supported the Honecker line. He (like Honecker) thought that "the explanations on the FRG provided by Comrade Mikhail Gorbachev [should be put] in an all-European context." He elaborated that it was appropriate that Gorbachev had made his first international appearance in Paris. The

---

181 Ibid (italics mine).

182 Ibid.

183 Gorbachev's remarks to the restricted meeting at the Budapest summit conference; see protocol on the restricted meeting of the party chiefs of the Warsaw Pact member countries, attachment to 18 June 1986 Politburo meeting, SED Politburo, *Arbeitsprotokolle*, Central Party Archives, J IV 2/2A/2896 (italics mine).

184 Ibid.

fact that he had given hope to the Italian government for a visit and his contacts with Britain and the FRG also had to be seen in a positive light. He asked the Soviet Union not to rupture the relations with West Germany because experience showed that it was difficult to restore them later. Gorbachev, obviously taken aback, remarked that the Soviet Union "did not have such an intention and, of course, one could not approach the FRG like that." Kádár, undeterred, continued that "if a summit meeting with Kohl were not to take place it would be important to clarify that this was not the Soviet Union's fault." This elicited the (patently untrue) "opinion by Comrade Gorbachev that, on this question, the FRG was playing games. Erich Honecker was being invited to the FRG but others were not [sic]." But he did agree, gratuitously given his obstinacy on the West German issue, that one had to "take into consideration the weight of the FRG in international politics."[185]

It was in the circumstances of a clearly defined Soviet policy towards Bonn that Genscher paid his first visit to Moscow since the death of Chernenko. In comparison with visits by other foreign ministers, the late date of the visit (21 July 1986) in itself was a good indication of the abnormal state of Soviet-West German relations. Gorbachev, with Shevardnadze, Kvitsinsky, and Chernyaev present, told his visitor that the Soviet leaders did not always find West Germany's policy comprehensible.[186] A discrepancy existed in their view between Bonn's peaceful declarations and its actions. The federal government had been the most active advocate of the stationing of intermediate-range nuclear missiles. More importantly, it had tried to dictate terms to the Soviet Union and issue ultimatums. Efforts were now being made to search for solutions. He (Gorbachev) was able to understand why the United States had an interest in the stationing of missiles in Europe, but the German pressures for the deployment were difficult to comprehend.[187] The German foreign minister's explanations of the rationale of the coalition government's policies fell on deaf ears. Genscher even formed the impression that Gorbachev had wanted to end the talks after he had rehashed the Soviet argument on INF and had been told that his ideas about West Germany rested on misperceptions.[188]

The discussion revived when it turned to Europe and the German problem. Gorbachev provided the West German foreign minister with an opening when he asked what one should think of a recent statement by Reagan to othe effect that the conferences of Yalta and Potsdam had occurred a long time ago and that it was now time for Europe to be unified. Genscher replied that the federal government had

---

185 Ibid.

186 Genscher, *Erinnerungen*, pp. 495-496. German participants included the ambassador to Moscow, Jörg Kastl, and the Political Director in the German Foreign Office, Gerold von Braunmühl, who was assassinated by the Rote Armee Fraktion (RAF) only three months later.

187 Ibid.

188 Ibid., p. 498.

adopted a clear position on the inviolability of borders. But he could hardly imagine that the General Secretary, when he was speaking of the Common European House, wanted to preserve a *divided* house. President Reagan had wanted to clarify this. The Germans, because of the division of their country into two states, thought exactly the same way.[189]

Genscher had brought into the open a central contradiction in Gorbachev's conceptual approach. The continued existence of two separate German states, it would seem, was indeed part of the Soviet leader's design for Europe – at least for the foreseeable future. Only the forms of the division should be open to revision. East Germany, accordingly, would introduce reform socialism, West Germany would return to social democracy, and both states would establish a *modus vivendi* in their relations with each other. This is also, one may infer, the meaning behind Gorbachev's question to the German foreign minister whether the center-right coalition government was still adhering to the 1970 Soviet-West German treaty. Although the Federal Republic, in a separate Letter on German Unity, had declared for the record that its objective was still for "the German people to regain its unity, based on the principle of free self-determination," in Moscow's interpretation, the treaty was not designed to overcome the division of Germany but to make it acceptable.[190] The limited objective, first and foremost, of an improvement in Soviet-West German relations and only secondarily in intra-German relations, it would seem, was the context in which one must place the significance of what Genscher called Gorbachev's "decisive sentence" in the conversation: "*Let us open a new page in our relations*."[191] In the Soviet perspective of the mid- and late 1980s, one has to conclude, there could be new pages in Soviet-West German relations, but the book of divided Germany should remain closed.

The Soviet book on censorship rules also was not touched. The central newspapers expunged practically all the paragraphs and sentences from Genscher's dinner speech that described *his* vision of the Common House of Europe. They deleted his assurance that "through regular contacts with its eastern neighbors, including in the current year, the federal government has demonstrated its interest in a positive development between East and West." They omitted his statement that Bonn

---

189 Ibid., p. 499.

190 In more detail, the letter was handed by the German Foreign Office to, and was accepted by, the Soviet Ministry of Foreign Affairs at the signing of the 1970 Moscow treaty. It stated that "in connection with today's signing of the treaty" between the Federal Republic and the Soviet Union, the West German government declared that it interpreted the treaty "as not being in contradiction to the political goal of the Federal Republic of Germany to strive for a state of peace in Europe, in which the German people, in free self-determination, [can] regain its unity." *Dokumentation zur Ostpolitik der Bundesregierung: Verträge und Vereinbarungen*, 11th edition. (Bonn: Federal Press and Information Office, 1986), p. 15.

191 Genscher, *Erinnerungen*, p. 501.

advocated an end to the division of Europe and was, therefore, aiming at a state of affairs that "would make it possible for all the European peoples to shape their destiny autonomously without fear of threat and the use of force, that is, a Europe in which the right of self-determination will be safeguarded."[192] Typically, as indicated by the controversy over the deletions of text from the speech of visiting West German president von Weizsäcker almost exactly one year later (see below), in such cases of censorship high-level political approval was required. If so, a closer look at *Gorbachev's* concept of the Common House of Europe is warranted.

Before doing so, it is appropriate briefly to point to the reverberations of Genscher's visit in Soviet-East German relations. On 3 October 1986, in another round of talks between Gorbachev and Honecker, with West Berlin communist party leaders Herbert Mies and Horst Schmitt present, the East German leader reported that in talks with Otto Reinhold, the dean of the SED Central Committee's Academy of Social Sciences, Genscher had "talked very respectfully about the meeting that he had had here in Moscow." The West German foreign minister had emphasized that a new page had been opened in the relations between Bonn and Moscow. And he had stated that he would do everything possible in order to exert influence in Washington to improve the chances for successful Soviet-American negotiations.[193] In a reply reflecting superpower arrogance Gorbachev said that when Genscher was in Moscow "[w]e made him sweat a lot." He had brushed aside Genscher's declared preparedness to use his good offices in Washington with the remark that "in our relations with the FRG, we don't want any translation of the policy of the USA into German. What we have to say we will say directly, in Russian, to be translated into English."[194]

The Common House of Europe

On his visit to London in December 1984, in a speech before the House of Commons, Gorbachev for the first time referred to Europe as "our common house" (*nash obshchii dom*).[195] Soviet leaders had done so before. Brezhnev had used the term in November 1981 in a dinner speech during his visit to Bonn.[196] Gromyko, the Politburo member and foreign minister, had taken it up in January 1983 at a press conference in Bonn. "The Federal Republic of Germany as well as the Soviet Union,"

192 For the full text of Genscher's speech, see *Bulletin des Presse- und Informationsamts der Bundesregierung*, No. 89, 24 July 1986; for the Soviet version, see *Pravda*, 23 July 1986.

193 Verbatim record of the meeting between Gorbachev and Honecker (as well as Mies and Schmitt) on 3 October 1986 in Moscow, SED Politburo, *Arbeitsprotokolle*, Central Party Archives, J IV 2/2A/2937.

194 Ibid.

195 *Pravda*, 19 December 1984.

196 Ibid., 24 November 1981.

he said, "live in one common house, under one roof."[197] Traditionally, the term was reserved almost exclusively for *Western European* audiences.[198] It also had a decidedly anti-American connotation, its implication being that the United States, as a trans-Atlantic power, really had no business in that house. "Washington," as a *Pravda* editorial put it, is a stranger in that house."[199]

Gorbachev initially very much subscribed to such notions. In his speech to the House of Commons, for instance, he evidently had in mind the discussions during Reagan's first term in office, when he contended that Europe should not be regarded simply as "a theater of military operations."[200] In a speech before the elections to the Supreme Soviet in February 1985, he said the Soviet Union considered a normalization of relations with the United States to be important. However, he continued, "we are not forgetting for a single moment that the world is not limited to that country alone."[201] A few weeks later, in an interview with *Pravda*, he asserted: "The relations between the USSR and the USA are an extremely important part of international politics. But we are far from seeing the world through the prism of these relations." He then added, "We understand the weight which other countries have in international affairs and take this into account in our assessment of the overall situation in the world."[202]

What was the framework of reference Gorbachev used in his overtures to Europe? One set of ideas was historical and cultural, the other political and ideological. As for the former, Alexander Bovin (one of Gorbachev's foreign policy advisers and a frequent member of the party leader's entourage abroad) had first raised the theme of Europe linked by "historical ties" and a "common foundation of European culture."[203] This was a theme that could have and, as it turned out, *did* have disastrous consequences for Soviet imperial control and ideological cohesion in the bloc. The ideas of a Common European Home and common European cultural traditions were quite compatible with the Westernizing tradition in Russian historical development but *incompatible* with the Marxist-Leninist notions of antagonism and their

---

197 *Sowjetunion heute*, No. 2 (February 1983), Supplement, p. xiii.

198 To the author's knowledge, it was never used in any of the private conversations between Honecker and Gorbachev. It was Krenz who finally, on 1 November 1989, asked Gorbachev how he saw the role of the GDR in his Common House construct. The details will be discussed in the next chapter.

199 Literally, for Washington it is a "*khuzhoi dom*," that is, a house that belongs to others; "Evropa – nash obshchii dom," *Pravda*, 13 November 1985.

200 Ibid., 19 December 1984; similarly, the above-mentioned *Pravda* editorial claims that, for Washington, Europe is "a battlefield on the maps of [its] strategists;" ibid., 13 November 1985.

201 Ibid., 20 February 1985.

202 Ibid., 8 April 1985. Similar formulations were used by Gorbachev in his speech to the Twenty-seventh CPSU Congress in February 1986.

203 *Izvestiia*, 25 September 1985. The term "political culture" is used in his "Evropeiskoe napravlenie," ibid., 20 July 1986.

manifestation in the division of Europe along ideological, socio-economic, and military-political lines. The problem was made more acute by the fact that Western European political theorists and leaders, primarily those of a conservative persuasion, vehemently objected to the notion that Russia, and hence the Soviet Union, belonged to a common European tradition. In their view, there had been three major European currents of thought: the Renaissance, the Reformation and the Enlightenment. These currents had led to the emergence of a civil society and the codification of human and citizenship rights in the western and central parts of the continent. Russia and, *mutatis mutandis*, the Soviet Union, according to their argument, were not part of this tradition. Moscow had rejected the three major Western currents and embraced the Byzantine tradition: religious orthodoxy, absolutism, and despotism. "Europe" as an idea, therefore, did not stretch from the Atlantic to the Pacific and not even to the Urals but extended only from "Brest to Brest."[204] The idea of a special "Central European" tradition – the *Mitteleuropagedanke*, as not only German participants in the discussion called it – was a variation of the theme that was potentially particularly harmful to Soviet imperial control in Eastern Europe.[205] As a theoretical construct, it completely disregarded entities such as the Warsaw Pact and Comecon, included Catholic or Protestant Germany, Austria, Poland, Czechoslovakia, Hungary, Romania, the Baltic states, and the western part of Ukraine but excluded Orthodox Russia and Bulgaria.

Later in the controversy, and characteristic of his general political philosophy and practice, Gorbachev attempted to reconcile the irreconcilable. "In the Europe 'from the Atlantic to the Urals,'" he said in a speech in Prague in April 1987, "world civilization was enriched by the ideas of the Renaissance and the Enlightenment, and the humanist tradition and the teachings of socialism experienced a powerful development."[206] The replacement of the Reformation by socialist traditions was apparently meant to put Russia and, by extension, the Soviet Union, firmly back into the camp of "European" culture and civilization.

This definitional trick was bound to be regarded with some suspicion by most Europeans even in 1987. Prior to that, such suspicion was even more justified since Gorbachev in 1985 had provided a solidly *ideological* basis for his overtures to

---

204 Especially good examples of the discussion in the first half of the 1980s about Europe's identity were published by Werner Weidenfeld, ed., *Die Identität Europas*, Series of the Bundeszentrale für politische Bildung, Vol. 225 (Munich: Hanser, 1985).

205 Vice President Bush had forcefully made this argument on 21 September 1983 in a speech to the Austrian Association for Foreign Policy and International Relations; text in U.S. Wireless Bulletin, No. 175, 22 September 1983. In his speech, Bush expressly used the German term *Mitteleuropa*. The *Mitteleuropa* discussion that was taking shape beginning in the early 1980s and continued unabated until the fall of the Berlin wall can best be retraced in a special issue of *Daedalus* (Winter 1989); see esp. Timothy Garton Ash, "Mitteleuropa?," ibid., pp. 1-21.

206 *Pravda*, 11 April 1987.

Europe. He derived it from traditional Leninist concepts about "irreconcilable contradictions" and the incessant "redistribution of power" among the main imperialist rivals more often than not by military force. As set forth in Lenin's *Imperialism, the Highest Stage of Capitalism*, these processes were supposedly the inevitable result of severe competition among the imperialist states for colonies, markets, raw materials, and cheap labor. Gorbachev applied these notions to contemporary conditions. In December 1984, in an important speech on ideological matters, he noted "a general but increasingly pronounced loss of the previous economic and political preponderance of the United States and an erosion of its positions in comparison with the *new power centers, above all* the *Western European region and Japan*."[207]

When Gorbachev made that speech and for the first few months after having assumed office as General Secretary, he may still have been conscious of the intense controversies that had raged between the United States and Western Europe – about the "neutron bomb;" the stationing of INF; the scope of modernization of NATO's theater nuclear forces; the utility of arms control; burden sharing; East-West trade; the divisibility or indivisibility of détente; and the utility of sanctions in response to the Soviet intervention in Afghanistan and the imposition of martial law in Poland. Yakovlev may have been partially responsible for the persistence of Gorbachev's views about acute conflict between Western Europe and the United States. Writing in *Pravda* in March 1984, he claimed that the economic and political condition of the capitalist world system was characterized by a "sharpening of the imperialist contradictions between the USA, the Western European countries, and Japan, unprecedented in the post-war period." The dynamics underlying this sharpening, in his opinion, resulted from a "counteroffensive" conducted by the United States to regain the positions lost in the past decades. The means utilized by that "power center" to achieve this purpose, above all, was its predominant role in the military affairs of the Western alliance.[208]

What were the policy implications of such statements? One was sounded by Gorbachev in May 1985. In talks with Gianni Cervetti, the chairman of the communist section of the European parliament and member of the presidium of the Italian communist party, and later with Bettino Craxi, the Italian prime minister, Gorbachev advocated the expansion of economic contacts between the CMEA and the European Community as well as the establishment of official relations between these two organizations. While this approach was not new, he extended it by saying

207 *Pravda*, 12 December 1984 (italics mine).

208 Alexander Yakovlev, "Imperializm – sopernichestvo i protivorechiia," *Pravda*, 23 March 1985. At the time of his writing, Yakovlev was head of the Institute of World Economy and International Relations (IMEMO). See also Vladimir Lukin, "*Tsentry sily': Kontseptsii i real'nost*" (Moscow: Mezhdunarodnye otnosheniia, 1983).

that "to the extent to which the states of the EEC were to act as one single unit," he would be ready "to search for a common language with them on specific international problems."[209] Gorbachev, for the first time in Soviet attitudes and policies towards the European Community, was signalling a Soviet interest in some arrangement with that organization at the *political* level.

For the most part, however, Gorbachev's theme of the Common European Home found very little practical political application. In 1985-86 it had decidedly instrumental purposes. This was clearly stated by Bovin as early as September 1985. He was "not revealing any secrets by saying," he wrote, "that Soviet policy takes into account the differences of view between Western Europe and the United States. But it does so by no means in order to squeeze the United States out of Europe and gain political control of the continent. ... Our objective is much more modest. We would like to utilize Western Europe's [intellectual and political] resources to make good, via the trans-Atlantic channel, the obvious shortage of common sense in the incumbent US administration."[210] In other words, the preferential treatment of selected European countries, political parties and movements was to serve the purpose of changing the direction of American foreign policy. Similarly, in his speech to the French National Assembly in October 1985, Gorbachev declared as "absurd" the allegation that the Soviet Union wanted to drive a wedge between Western Europe and the USA. He also strictly denied any "anti-American" direction of Soviet policy toward the West and any Metternich-style "balance of power" tactics aimed at "inciting one state against the other."[211] "We are realists," he avowed, "and know how stable are the historical, political, and economic relations between Western Europe and the USA."[212] To that extent, one can very well consider the October 1985 French-Soviet summit to have been, from his viewpoint, both a rehearsal and preparation forthe more important Soviet-American summit in Geneva one month later.

Indeed, at the Twenty-seventh CPSU Congress in February 1986, Gorbachev failed to give more substance to his European visions. He and other speakers, while not entirely abandoning the "European direction," were focusing attention even more directly on the United States. The instrumental purposes of the Common House of Europe campaign remained unchanged. Speaking at the Tenth Congress of the Polish communist party in June 1986, Gorbachev said:

> The ancient Greeks have a myth concerning the rape of Europe. This fairy tale subject unexpectedly has received new significance in the modern

209 In his talks with Craxi, *Pravda*, 30 May 1985; see also the report on his discussions with Cervetti, *l'Unità*, 22 May 1985.

210 *Izvestiia*, 25 September 1985.

211 *Pravda*, 4 October 1985.

212 Ibid.

> age. Of course, Europe remains untouched in the geographical sense. But the impression arises that the independent policy of certain Western European states has been abducted and deported across the ocean and that the national interests of the peoples as well as the destinies of the 700 million inhabitants of our continent and the civilization which originated here a long time ago are being mortgaged under the pretext of safeguarding security.
>
> No one should misinterpret us: We do not intend to drive a wedge between the USA and its NATO allies. ... At the time [in the 1970s], the socialist countries welcomed the participation of the USA in the all-European process. ... But now it looks as if the American administration wants to pursue goals diametrically opposed to it [the CSCE process]: acceleration of the arms race and confrontation. Who can profit from this? Are the European peoples really interested in such a development of events?[213]

In 1985-86, to sum up, Gorbachev may have thought that appeals to separate European interests and promises of improved Soviet-Western European relations would induce the Western Europeans to exert more influence on US policies and, in turn, make the United States more amenable to compromise with the Soviet Union. "For us," as he put it euphemistically in retrospect, "the European direction was not only an independent good; it was also an important factor in the dialogue with the Americans."[214] It is for that reason and also because he regarded Kohl as Reagan's European bailiff that a closer look at the American dimension of Gorbachev's policies is warranted.

6. Priority for the Relations with the United States

Attempts to change American foreign policy had top priority in Gorbachev's international designs. This endeavor was evident at and after the Twenty-seventh Party Congress and characterized by astounding persistence. It was reflected in concessions to Washington and several reversals of positions to which Brezhnev, Andropov, and Chernenko had clung tenaciously. It was demonstrated by the unprecedentedly high number of Soviet-American summit conferences, a total of seven in five years, and even more frequent meetings at the ministerial level between Shevardnadze, on the one hand, and George Shultz and James Baker, on the other. And it manifested itself in the rise of the *Amerikanisty,* Soviet experts on American affairs, to influential posts in the central decision-making apparatus.

Foremost among them were Anatoly Dobrynin, former ambassador to the United States, who became secretary of the Central Committee, responsible for relations

---

213 Ibid., 1 July 1986.

214 Gorbachev, *Zhizn'*, Vol. 2, p. 152.

with non-communist parties and states;[215] Georgi Kornienko, a former first deputy foreign minister and formerly Dobrynin's right hand in Washington, who was appointed Dobrynin's new deputy in the Central Committee; Yuli Vorontsov, former deputy ambassador in Washington, who succeeded Kornienko in the foreign ministry and Viktor Karpov in his post as chief negotiator at the arms talks in Geneva; Alexander Bessmertnykh, also a former deputy ambassador to Washington, who was named deputy foreign minister; Alexander Yakovlev, a former student at Columbia University, ambassador to Canada, and director of the Institute of World Economy and International Relations, who was elevated to the post of secretary of the Central Committee responsible for propaganda; and Georgi Arbatov, who remained director of the Institute for the United States and Canada. As is particularly apparent in the case of Yakovlev and Arbatov, the impressive array of *Amerikanisty* in influential positions did not at all mean that Soviet policies were bound to move in a pro-American direction. What it did mean, however, was that the relationship with the United States was considered the main issue in Soviet foreign relations.

In his memoirs, Gorbachev is quite specific on this point.

> My supporters [favored] a forward movement in international affairs, but I thought that we had to begin with the *United States*. It was, after all, not only a superpower but also the recognized leader of the Western world. Without its consent any effort to achieve a turn in East-West relations was impossible; [if we had acted otherwise] we would even have been accused of attempting to "drive wedges" [between the United States and its allies] or of engaging in "intrigues."[216]

Shevardnadze agreed. He has acknowledged in retrospect that "by 1985, the situation was extremely gloomy," and "[w]e in the Soviet leadership were acutely aware of the need for fundamental changes in policy and a quest for alternatives. Naturally, Soviet-American affairs were our central concern."[217] He continues in his memoirs by providing some of the reasons why this was the case: (1) "American sanctions, which had been imposed because of our involvement in Afghanistan, were having their effect." (2) "The question of political dissidents in the Soviet Union and human rights practices in general was a sore point." (3) "Negotiations on nuclear weapons in space were stalled," and a "major controversy over the fate of the ABM Treaty" had broken out, with accusations flying that the Soviet Union had "violated agreements on strategic arms limitation." (4) "No solution was in sight concerning the deployment by both sides of medium-range nuclear missiles in Europe."[218]

---

215 As his visit to Kabul with foreign minister Shevardnadze in January 1987 showed, he also actively involved himself in policy towards communist states as long as the matter at hand was considered to be of vital interest.

216 Gorbachev, *Zhizn'*, Vol. 2, p. 11 (italics mine).

217 Shevardnadze, *Moi vybor*, p. 146.

218 Ibid., p. 147.

Shevardnadze summarizes: "No matter where we turned, we came up against the fact that we would achieve nothing without a normalization of Soviet-American relations."[219]

At the Warsaw Pact summit conference in Sofia in October 1985, Gorbachev painted the same gloomy picture as Shevardnadze. In open session, he said there was a fairly widespread opinion that the situation in the world was changing for the better and that everything was all right. One talked about a remarkable invigoration of the political dialogue between East and West. This was correct up to a point. Changes were obvious, and these had been achieved by the efforts of the socialist community for the support of forces and countries opposed to the aggressive course of the imperialist powers. However, one had to admit that, "without wanting to dramatize the situation, the state of affairs in the world continues to remain tense and in some aspects even explosive."[220]

In the closed session of the first party secretaries, he was even more blunt and gloomy. He discerned "massive pressure by imperialism, connected with its attempts at blackmailing us politically and economically and taking social revenge." The Soviet leadership had information to the effect that "everything in the current USA policy was aimed at achieving in one or another socialist country of Europe, or if possible in several of them, a political destabilization." The United States was endeavoring to "create constant sources of unrest in the Soviet Union and other socialist countries."[221] The remedies suggested to counter this threat, however, were *not* of the traditional Soviet variety. The struggle against imperialism, in Gorbachev's opinion, rather than calling for a redoubling of efforts in the military sphere, posed the "necessity of an acceleration of our development." It required at one and the same time "the growth of [our] economic potential, the improvement of the life of the people, and the maintenance of the military balance." The main and general line of the CPSU to meet these challenges was the "economic strategy of the CPSU" and the "comprehensive intensification of the national economy on the basis of scientific-technological progress and its acceleration." For these purposes to be achieved, implementation of the five-year plan for 1985-1990 would be decisive.[222]

In his private talks with Honecker half a year later Gorbachev was still mesmerized by the "question as to what one could expect from the main adversary.

219 Ibid.

220 Gorbachev's speech at the PCC meeting in Sofia, on 23 October 1985, SED Politburo, *Arbeitsprotokolle*, Central Party Archives, J IV 2/2A/2811.

221 Statement by Gorbachev at the closed session of first party secretaries at the PCC meeting in Sofia on 23 October 1985, SED Politburo, *Arbeitsprotokolle*, J IV 2/2A/2811.

222 Protocol on the closed session of first party secretaries at the PCC meeting in Sofia on 23 October 1985, SED Politburo, Arbeitsprotokolle, J IV 2/2A/2811.

Will it be possible to drive him into a process of disarmament?"[223] He thought that the CPSU and the SED were in "complete agreement" on how to assess the nature of American foreign policy. In vivid testimony to the persistence of outdated Leninist concepts on the nature of the opposed socio-economic system, he stated:

> Analysis in the Soviet Union proceeds from the principle that US imperialism cannot exist without the military machine. One-third of the national product of the USA derives from the exploitation of the Third World. In order to maintain this level, American imperialism cannot dispense with its military machine.[224]

Political logic would have it that if systemic imperatives really drove American arms production and foreign policy, the chances for the United States to change course without a systemic transformation would be non-existent. Logic would also have it that if it were true, as he asserted, that the "economic state of affairs in the United States is becoming ever more tense," tendencies for American expansion in the Third World would, for systemic reasons, be *strengthened* rather than weakened. Whatever the logic, Gorbachev advocated adopting a dual approach – to combine a conciliatory and accommodating stance vis-à-vis the United States with defense efforts (while at the same time maintaining the course on domestic economic development). He felt that it was necessary

> to conduct a realistic policy. Voices are being heard, especially in the USA, which demonstrate that Reagan will not last forever and that other forces will be at the helm. It is [therefore] definitely important to act serenely and sensibly, to keep a cool head, to develop initiative, if necessary, to give a rebuff to certain forces and, naturally, constantly to strengthen the defensive might.[225]

He also thought: "One cannot leave the fate of the world to Reagan and at the same time one *should not yield to provocation*."[226]

Gorbachev had consented to the summit meeting in Geneva in November 1985 despite his previous insistence that he would attend such a conference only if it were a serious and well prepared matter *and* clear beforehand that agreements in one or two important areas of arms control would be signed. In reality the summit was held according to an American agenda, no arms control agreements were concluded, and the United States subsequently adopted uncompromising and unyielding policies that could easily be characterized as provocative by critics in the Soviet Union. Such policies included the continuation of strategic modernization programs; the announcement by the Reagan administration in May 1986 that it no longer felt bound

---

223 Transcript of the conversation between Honecker and Gorbachev on 20 April 1986 in East Berlin, SED, Central Archives, Büro Honecker, 41666 (indirect speech).

224 Ibid. (indirect speech).

225 Ibid. (indirect speech).

226 Ibid. (indirect speech, italics mine).

by the SALT II treaty; the apparently unshakable support by Reagan and other leading administration officials not only for conducting research, developing and testing space-based defensive weapons but also for their deployment; the refusal to consent to a comprehensive nuclear weapons test ban and any limitation of anti-satellite systems; the adoption of a more assertive, militarily oriented policy of countering Soviet advances in the Third World, with money and weapons provided to the Contras in Nicaragua, the National Union for the Total Independence in Angola and the mujaheddin in Afghanistan; the dispatch of US naval vessels into the 12-mile zone off the Soviet Black Sea coast in March 1986; air attacks against Libya in April 1986; persistent demands for the curtailment of Soviet embassy, consular and United Nations personnel; continued restriction of East-West technology transfer; pressure on the Western allies to curtail their credit relations with Eastern Europe; opposition to most-favored nation status for the USSR and to Soviet membership in the General Agreement on Tariffs and Trade (GATT).

Some of Gorbachev's foreign policy advisors and propagandists did claim that they considered such policies "provocative." However, such challenges were portrayed by them, and by Gorbachev himself at the Twenty-seventh Party Congress, as a trap laid by the imperialists to induce the Soviet leadership to break off the dialogue with the United States rather than as a valid reason to do so.[227] As if in preparation and justification for the next Soviet-American summit meeting, Gorbachev reminded Honecker that in May 1972, even as the United States had imposed a blockade on North Vietnamese harbors and "were dropping bombs on Haiphong, Nixon was in Moscow."[228] Conciliatory responses were still the order of the day in June 1986. Talking about Soviet-American relations in a session restricted to the first party secretaries at the Warsaw Pact summit conference in Budapest, he reiterated that the fraternal countries were "*not to be nudged from political dialogue, irrespective of what the other side does*." He also reasserted: "Our constructive course will be continued." In sharp contrast to the negative and condescending attitude adopted vis-à-vis Kohl, he spoke almost warmly of Reagan and even showed himself well informed about the latter's health problems. He, Gorbachev, had recently received another personal message from the American president and, although it had contained nothing new, it had "a calm and casual tone." He had again been invited by

---

227 In his closing remarks to the Twenty-seventh Party Congress, Gorbachev briefly mentioned the lack of progress on arms control and other aspects of Moscow's relations with Washington. He spoke of the alleged fear by "someone there" in Washington of a radical, long-term improvement in Soviet-American relations. He then went on to say: "What are we to do comrades? Slam the door? It cannot be ruled out that this is exactly the sort of thing they want us to do;" *Izvestiia*, 7 March 1986.

228 Transcript of the conversation between Honecker and Gorbachev on 20 April 1986 in East Berlin, SED, Central Archives, Büro Honecker, 41666.

Reagan to a summit meeting. This, too, was "characteristic" for Reagan's approach. The Soviet Union was "still considering this. But the main formula is still the same." He would accept the invitation if it were possible "to consult about matters of substance."[229]

The October 1986 Gorbachev-Reagan summit meeting in Reykjavik did not produce any agreement on conventional, intermediate-range, or strategic nuclear weapons, and to that extent it could be considered a failure. Gorbachev, however, was intent on making the summit appear to have been successful. In a press conference in Reykjavik and two radio and television addresses in Moscow, Gorbachev called the meeting an "important stage" in the negotiating process that had created a "qualitatively new situation," deepened mutual understanding, and shown that "on the matter itself, agreements are possible."[230] Dobrynin, on the contrary, in a meeting with a group of representatives from a number of peace committees from Britain on 26 October 1986, stated that "it seems that the extremists are taking over in the U.S. administration, and they will do ... everything they can to negate and undermine the positive things that were achieved in Reykjavik. We will have to revise all aspects of our cooperation with the United States."[231] Arbatov was still to claim: "Attempts are being made to provoke us so that we will rupture the dialogue with our own hands, to bury the negotiations which have become an embarrassment to them [the Reaganites]." However, he continued, "the Soviet Union has learned something in the past years. There can be no doubt that the American administration will fail in provoking M.S. Gorbachev and the Soviet leadership."[232]

It is in the light of, in essence, negative American responses and operational problems in the Soviet Union that Gorbachev's overtures and concessions are of particular interest. Moves of this kind in the arms control sphere in 1986 and 1987 included, at the Stockholm Conference on Confidence Building and Disarmament in Europe (CDE), the abandonment of previously deeply ingrained and unwavering Soviet objections to on-site inspection by foreign observers of military moves and maneuvers. In the strategic arms control sphere the Soviet Union was prepared to

---

229 Gorbachev's remarks to a closed session of first party secretaries at the June 1986 Budapest summit conference; see the protocol on the restricted meeting of the party chiefs of the Warsaw Pact member countries, SED Politburo, *Arbeitsprotokolle*, Central Party Archives, J IV 2/2A/2896 (indirect speech, italics mine).

230 The press conference of 13 October as reported by *Pravda*, 14 October 1986; the radio and television addresses of 14 and 22 October 1986 in ibid., 15 and 22 October 1986. The direct quotes are from the latter sources.

231 Notes from personal diaries of Sergei Grigoriev.

232 Georgi Arbatov, "Ne ot khoroshei zhizni," *Pravda*, 21 November 1986. With characteristic modesty, Arbatov went on to say that he, too, had not allowed himself to become provoked when he wrote the article, even though he had felt like expressing himself more drastically. The immediate context of the quote pertains to Reykjavik. "But," he clarifies "the matter is not limited to Reykjavik."

make the "deep cuts" in offensive strategic missiles that Carter had proposed in 1977 and which Reagan had demanded in START; agree to count neither the US forward based systems (FBS) nor the French and British missiles and bombers against the total American strategic arsenal; accept rules for counting strategic bombers and cruise missiles that were advantageous to the US; and consent to the setting of sub-limits on heavy ICBMs. On intermediate-range nuclear systems, Moscow relinquished its demands for the full inclusion of the US Poseidon force, FBS, and French and British systems in the overall tally and no longer insisted on qualitative restrictions on the French and British force. Final agreement on the INF issue, so hotly contested in the late 1970s and the first half of the 1980s, was reached at the summit conference in Washington in December 1987. The noteworthy features of the accord were its applicability to both Europe and Asia; the exclusion of the British and French nuclear forces from its provisions; the scrapping of an entire category of modern weapons; the acceptance of significant asymmetrical cuts; and a comprehensive régime of on-site verification.

On other matters, too, Gorbachev was conciliatory. Concerning human rights issues and the development of contacts and communications between the East and the West, Moscow reduced the jamming of Voice of America broadcasts to the Soviet Union. After the resolution of the controversy over American correspondent Nicholas Daniloff, who had been imprisoned on false charges of espionage, it granted exit visas to dissidents Yuri Orlov, David Goldfarb, Viktor Flerov, and Irina Ratushinskaya. Finally, Andrei Sakharov was allowed to return to the Soviet capital from his exile in Gorky.

In addition to the arms competition and human rights, regional conflicts had been another major bone of contention in Soviet-American relations. On this issue, too, Gorbachev made significant concessions. Moscow agreed in the April 1988 Geneva accord to withdraw its troops from Afghanistan within nine months. In July 1988, it concluded a framework agreement with Washington providing for the withdrawal of an estimated 50,000 Cuban troops from Angola, the pull-back of about 3,000 South African troops from the south of the country, and the establishment of a timetable for the implementation of a ten-year-old United Nations plan for the independence of Namibia. It induced Vietnam to begin the withdrawal of troops from Cambodia. Its stance in the war between Iraq and Iran in the summer of 1988, including its support in the U.N. for a cease-fire, contributed to the cessation of hostilities between the two countries.

Given Gorbachev's determined and increasingly successful attempts to place Soviet-American relations on a new footing, it would seem that the stage was now set for a return to the Common European Home and the inclusion of West Germany in an overall improvement of East-West relations. This, however, did not occur until

October 1988. In addition to the more general reservations about Germany and the Germans, aversion to touching the German problem, suspicion about the budding intra-German contacts, and concern about rising West German influence in Eastern Europe there were several specific reasons for the long delay in the alignment of Soviet-American and Soviet-West German policies. One of these was the interview Kohl gave to *Newsweek* in October 1986.

7. German Unification in a "Hundred Years"

In the interview, published in *Newsweek* on 27 October 1986, Kohl had said: "I don't consider him [Gorbachev] to be a liberal. He is a modern communist leader who understands public relations. Goebbels, who was one of those responsible for the crimes in the Hitler era, was an expert in public relations, too."[233] This was a serious gaffe that should never have been allowed to appear in print. But it did. In the embarrassing circumstances, all the usual efforts at damage-limitation were made. The chancellor's office paraphrased Kohl to the effect that his remark had "not been rendered correctly"; that "erroneously, the impression has arisen that he had compared the General Secretary of the CC of the CPSU, Mikhail S. Gorbachev, with Goebbels"; and that it had not been his "intention to insult the General Secretary."[234] But the damage was done. When Genscher in Vienna on 4 November dutifully conveyed the chancellery's authorized explanations to Shevardnadze, the Soviet foreign minister replied that Moscow had initially believed that the remarks lacked a factual basis and that the matter had been a provocation. It had, therefore, made inquiries with *Newsweek*. On the basis of its tape recordings, the journal had confirmed the accuracy of the quote. Furthermore, after the chancellor, through a spokesman, had distanced himself from the remarks, Moscow had contacted the editor-in-chief of the weekly, who had also rejected the German contention that he had been misquoted.[235]

No matter how many times one may re-read and twist and turn the remark, one is left to conclude that Kohl did believe, or profess to believe, that a fundamental

233 *Newsweek*, 27 October 1986, p. 29. As is customary with such interviews, the transcript of the tape recording was submitted to the interviewee for verification and, if necessary, revision. Kohl's press spokesman, Friedhelm Ost, had received the transcript. He made things worse. Rather than recognizing the seriousness of the comparison and suggesting to delete the Goebbels remark, he *inserted* – presumably for the benefit of the American public – the clarification of Goebbels as being "one of those responsible for the crimes of the Hitler era"; see ibid., 17 November 1986, p. 58.

234 The "clarification" was provided in Kohl's interview with *Die Welt* (Hamburg), 2 November 1986. On 4 November, the German foreign minister read the full text of the chancellor office's explanations, including the reference to the interview in *Die Welt*, to Shevardnadze; Genscher, *Erinnerungen*, p. 518. For the Soviet foreign minster's reactions, see below.

235 Ibid.

political change had not taken place in Moscow; that some or all of Gorbachev's initiatives were exercises in propaganda; and that the Soviet leader was quite skillful at the game – as skillful, indeed, as Goebbels. One could, charitably, interpret the remark as having been directed at a domestic rather than an international audience.[236] This notion could be regarded as being supported by his barb, also published by *Newsweek*, about the Social Democrats as being "more Russian than the Russians." But the interview was granted to an American, not a German news magazine. And, conversely, the unkind characterization of both Gorbachev and the SPD could be regarded as an expression of his frustration at the Soviet leader's apparent view of the West German government as a disagreeable and uncooperative tenant in the Common European Home and his annoyance with Gorbachev's preferential treatment of the opposition. The matter was made worse by the impression that was being conveyed, if not by the fact itself, that Kohl was too proud and stubborn to express regret or retract the remark and too keen to brush things aside with "quoted erroneously" and "taken out of context" excuses.[237]

What was the impact of Kohl's blunder in Moscow? Most of all, the remarks were met with incomprehension among the German experts at the Central Committee and the foreign ministry. The authenticity of the remarks having been established beyond reasonable doubt, the assumption of the officials was that there must have been a purpose behind them. However, no one could convincingly explain what it was.[238] Publicly, Gorbachev chose not to react to the remarks. But Chernyaev has credibly stated that the Soviet leader felt "deeply offended" by them,[239] and Shevardnadze charged that they "angered us to the depth of our souls."[240] They reinforced Gorbachev's negative predisposition toward Kohl and the CDU-CSU as well as his

---

236 The idea that Kohl's remarks were related to the German electoral campaign has been expressed by David H. Shumaker, *Gorbachev and the German Question: Soviet–West German Relations, 1985-1990* (Westport, Conn.: 1995), p. 36.

237 Speaking to the Bundestag in November 1986, Kohl insisted that the printed portion of the interview "does not correctly reflect the meaning or the context of the one-and-a-half-hour conversation ..." He also said that he had not intended to compare Gorbachev to Goebbels: "I regret that this impression was given and distance myself from it emphatically." (*Newsweek*, 17 November 1986, p. 58.) In his memoirs, perhaps too tactfully, Genscher merely reiterates the lame excuses of the chancellor's office; Genscher, *Erinnerungen*, pp. 517-522. President Richard von Weizsäcker, if the source is accurate, was more blunt. Honecker had reportedly mentioned to Dobrynin, who was in East Berlin in January 1987, that in a conversation with the permanent representative of the GDR in Bonn he (Weizsäcker) had called Kohl a "fool" (*Dummkopf*); Record (*Niederschrift*) Talks Between the General Secretary of the SEC Central Committee, Comrade Erich Honecker, with the Secretary of the CPSU Central Committee, Comrade A.F. Dobrynin, on 20 January 1987, in the Central Committee Building, SED Politburo, Central Party Archives, J IV/2/2A/2976, pp. 36-37 of the typed transcript (indirect speech).

238 Interview with Rykin.

239 Interview with Chernyaev.

240 TASS, 10 November 1986.

tendency to differentiate between the chancellor and Genscher. And although the remarks did not change Moscow's policy towards Bonn – as mentioned, the course towards "minimum contact" had already been set – they delayed even further the inclusion of West Germany in Moscow's evolving efforts to improve relations with other Western European countries and the United States. "Gorbachev," to quote his foreign policy advisor, "intensified contacts with Britain, Italy, and the United States, and in that way wanted to 'teach the Germans a lesson.'"[241] Several visits by West German ministers to Moscow had to be canceled. Even more demonstratively than before, Moscow's representatives were by-passing Bonn by in a wide arc, and the Soviet ambassador in Bonn was instructed to avoid talks with the chancellor.[242] The remarks also revealed internal controversies about Moscow's relations with Bonn. Based upon talks with Gorbachev, Deputy Foreign Minister Yuli Vorontsov recommended to the Soviet ambassador in Bonn (Kvitsinsky) that he try gradually to bury the issue. "After all," Vorontsov asked, what is Kohl supposed to do now, "get a rope and hang himself?"[243] Kvitsinsky took this to mean that there was a struggle in Moscow between two opinions and that Gorbachev himself appeared to be wavering.[244]

In Moscow, the gaffe also brought into sharp focus the question as to who should be the proper partner in Bonn. This concerned in particular the problem of the appropriate status and role to be allocated to the SPD. In East Berlin on 20 January 1987, Dobrynin (in his capacity as head of the Central Committee's International Department) in private conversation agreed with Honecker, who lamented the fact that all the support one had attempted to give to the SPD in the electoral campaign had been in vain. "We wanted to help them but they can't be helped. No one really seriously believes that they want to govern. They are a true social democratic party; they are afraid of government responsibility."[245] The chances of that party in the elections, then only a few days away, looked bleak. "The danger exists," Honecker lamented, "that the SPD will not receive 40 percent of the votes but only 37 percent."[246] Dobrynin thought that the "SPD is playing a weak game."[247] The CDU, in contrast, had the upper hand. Many representatives of that party, as he acknowledged, now wanted to visit the Soviet Union. "No one was willing to admit

---

241 Chernyaev, *Shest' let s Gorbachevym*, p. 261.

242 Kwizinskij, *Vor dem Sturm*, p. 416.

243 Ibid.

244 Ibid.

245 Record (*Niederschrift*) Talks Between the General Secretary of the SEC Central Committee, Comrade Erich Honecker, with the Secretary of the CPSU Central Committee, Comrade A.F. Dobrynin on 20 January 1987 in the Central Committee Building, SED Politburo, Central Party Archives, J IV /2/2A/2976 p. 35 of the typed transcript (indirect speech).

246 Ibid., p. 36 of the typed transcript (indirect speech).

247 Ibid., p. 34 (indirect speech)

that they would be acting as an envoy of Kohl, but they were asking what could be done in order to rectify what has happened."[248] Dobrynin then revealed his own and perhaps a more widespread dissatisfaction in Moscow with the negative and unproductive approach taken vis-à-vis West Germany by saying: "*After the elections [we have] to approach [the relationship with West Germany] differently.*"[249]

The CDU, as Dobrynin had correctly observed, was intent on changing Gorbachev's mind about the West German government's policy. Its determination increased almost in direct proportion to the progression of his New Thinking after the important January 1987 Central Committee plenum, which introduced *demokratizatsiia*. It also began to subscribe to the (erroneous) belief that the New Thinking would spawn a major Soviet initiative on the German problem. One of the earliest examples of this belief was expressed in a working paper by CDU parliament member Bernard Friedmann and presented to the party for discussion in early 1987.[250] More senior representatives of the governing coalition took up the topic, including FDP presidium member Otto Graf Lambsdorff; the prime minister of Rheinland-Pfalz, Bernard Vogel; and the chairman of the CDU in the Bundestag, Alfred Dregger. They argued that the federal government should not simply sit back and wait for a Soviet proposal on German unification, and then improvise a response, but that it should take the initiative itself and suggest a new security architecture in Central Europe.[251] In September 1987, in a speech to the Kurt Schumacher Foundation, the secretary of state for intra-German relations, Ottfried Hennig asserted that there were "reports in Moscow" according to which Gorbachev had told "top party officials" Falin, Arbatov, Melnikov, and Portugalov to prepare new policy options on Germany. On the basis of these studies, the leadership in Moscow wanted to formulate a concept that it would then present to the Western powers as a draft basis for a solution of the German problem.[252]

---

248 Ibid., pp. 34-35 (indirect speech).

249 Ibid., p. 35 (italics mine; indirect speech). Nevertheless, Dobrynin cautioned that one should not be too much in a hurry to alter the approach because "if change were to take place too rapidly, the impression would be conveyed that [we] had not expected an electoral victory by Kohl."

250 See the report on the working paper in *Frankfurter Allgemeine Zeitung*, 21 May 1987.

251 Ibid.

252 Kurt Schumacher Foundation, press release, as quoted by Fred Oldenburg, "Sowjetische Deutschland-Politik mit neuen Perspektiven? Mutmaßungen über Moskauer Studien und Dobrynins Antworten," *Aktuelle Analysen*, Bundesinstitut für ostwissenschaftliche und internationale Studien (Cologne), No. 37 (1987). Only three of the four persons mentioned (Valentin Falin, Danil Mel'nikov, and Nikolai Portugalov) could be considered experts on Germany. None qualified as a "top party official." Falin was head of the foreign correspondents' office at the *Novosti* press agency; Portugalov a consultant for the propaganda department of the Central Committee; Mel'nikov a researcher at the Institute of World Economic and International Relations (IMEMO); and Arbatov director of the Institute for USA and Canada. For more data on these officials and their possible role in the intra-Soviet discussions on German policy, see below, the chapter on Soviet domestic politics and the German problem.

The impression in Bonn about impending policy changes in Moscow's German policy was reinforced by remarks made by CPSU Central Committee advisor and German expert Nikolai Portugalov. The parliamentary elections in West Germany in January 1987, in his view, had revealed a "concrete and dynamic process of [rising] national self-confidence among the West Germans."[253] This process was taking place not only among revanchist, chauvinist, and military circles and a hard-line "*Stahlhelm*" (steel helmet) faction in the CDU/CSU alliance. It could also be "noted among left and liberal forces," in whose opinion "West German national confidence and legitimate national pride should be in harmony with the postwar realities of Europe." Portugalov even called the representatives of this view "patriots," who recognized that today's Germans still had to bear responsibility for Hitler's crimes. Portugalov *de facto* rejected the idea advanced by Honecker at the East German SED Party Congress in 1971 that the GDR had become a separate German nation. "Certainly, for all Germans, including socially progressive West Germans," he argued in a reversal of traditional Soviet positions, "*the people of the GDR will always be Germans who belong to one and the same nation.*"[254]

Closer to the official Soviet view, Portugalov attributed to "left and liberal Germans" the idea that "life of the Germans as one nation could only be achieved within the context of two independent and sovereign states with different political systems." In a follow-up article, he predicted the expansion of German-German relations within this framework and finally the construction and completion of the Common European Home. One could, for example, "imagine without any difficulty that the citizens of both of the sovereign and independent 'German apartments' would live in their own way yet maintain close relations with one another, particularly since they speak a common language." Equally in line with traditional Soviet positions, he predicted that "the time will finally come to terminate the foreign military quartering in the apartments of the central part of the home."[255] He also studiously avoided adopting the position that a *unified* Germany should be part of the Common European House.

There was also no change in the Soviet position on the Berlin problem – Gorbachev's ruling on "minimum contact" was extended to that city. As if in preparation for his twice-postponed visit to West Germany, Honecker appeared keen to accept an invitation by the West Berlin senate to take part in the city's 750th anniversary celebrations. Shortly before the visit was to take place, in April 1987, the

---

253 *Moskovskie novosti*, 2 February 1987; Portugalov's views on the German issue were cited in the German press, including *Frankfurter Allgemeine Zeitung*, 23 February 1987.

254 Ibid. (italics mine).

255 *Neue Zeit*, No. 22 (May 1987), pp. 10-12.

East German party leader declined the invitation.[256] Did Honecker yet again yield to a Soviet veto? There is no direct evidence to that effect. However, Vadim Medvedev, the head of the CPSU Central Committee secretariat responsible for relations with the ruling communist parties, clarified what *he* at least thought of the celebrations. Speaking at the party congress of the Unity Party of West Berlin (SEW) in mid-May 1987, he deplored that the events in West Berlin were being "abused for propaganda purposes to spread outdated slogans and revanchist ideas" and that Bonn and West Berlin apparently regarded the city as a "kind of Trojan horse of the West in the socialist East."[257] Surely, no decent person would have wanted to lend support to such purposes.

As the attacks against Bonn and West Berlin demonstrated, Gorbachev's professed desire to see a "new page" opened in Soviet-West German relations was counteracted and contradicted by phraseology from the rubbish bin of Soviet history. He himself failed to open a new page when President von Weizsäcker, accompanied by Genscher, visited the Soviet Union from 6 to 11 July 1987.

German Unity: In a Hundred Years?

In the year after Genscher's talks in Moscow Gorbachev had refused to receive any high ranking representative of the Federal Republic. Given the federal president's high international standing, his sensitivity to the damage done to Germany's reputation in the Second World War, and his commitment to German-Russian reconciliation the opportunity presented itself to break the ice in Soviet-West German relations. The chance was used only up to a point. To the extent that cordiality characterized the conversations between Gorbachev and von Weizsäcker, this was probably a tribute to the visitor's reputation and an indication of the mutual compatibility of personalities rather than the "opening of a new page" in Soviet-West German relations. There is a reflection of this in Gorbachev's memoirs where he acknowledges that the German president had "very cautiously and tactfully touched upon the question of the unity of the German nation."[258] Yet Genscher's account is also credible. "The conversation between Federal President von Weizsäcker and General Secretary Gorbachev was occasionally quite pointed, in fact, at times harsh."[259]

---

256 Honecker's refusal to attend the anniversary celebrations was approved by the SED Politburo on 14 April 1987 (see SED Politburo, *Arbeitsprotokolle*, J IV 2/2/2214) and published in *Neues Deutschland* on the same day.

257 Quoted in *Frankfurter Allgemeine Zeitung*, 18 May 1987.

258 Gorbachev, *Zhizn'*, Vol. 2, p. 152.

259 Genscher, *Erinnerungen*, p. 543. The terms Genscher used were *deutlich* and *hart*.

Genscher's characterization of the talks is also to some extent confirmed by the account Gorbachev has provided in his memoirs. In reply to the president's evident wish to raise the topic of German unity, he had said:

> Today the two German states are a reality from which one must proceed. The [1970] Moscow treaty and [West Germany's] treaties with Poland, Czechoslovakia and the GDR as well as with other states are also a reality. It is on this basis that the effective development of political, economic, cultural, and human contacts is possible. Any attempts to undermine these treaties, however, must be sharply condemned. The Soviet Union respects the post-war realities and respects the German people in the FRG and the Germans in the GDR. It is on this basis that we intend to build our relations in the future. History *will give its judgment* in the future.[260]

What is missing in the memoirs – understandably, given the achievement of German unification within little more than three years – is what Gorbachev thought about the likely time-frame in which history might decide: in "a hundred years," he had told the West German president. Soviet ambassador Kvitsinsky and German ambassador Blech both confirm that this was indeed the time horizon that was mentioned by Gorbachev.[261] Von Weizsäcker expressed disappointment about the relegation of the issue to an almost indefinite future.[262] A TASS report issued after the meeting also contains the reference to a hundred years, and it conveys the harshness remembered by Genscher.[263]

How is one to interpret Gorbachev's remarks to von Weizsäcker? One way is to emphasize the apparent openness of the German problem from the Soviet leader's perspective. The argument can be made that by saying that history would decide, Gorbachev proceeded from the idea that there *was* something to be decided – an

---

260 Gorbachev, *Zhizn'*, Vol. 2, p. 152 (italics in original). The term used is *nas rassudit*, literally, history "will judge between us" or "will judge who is right." Erroneously, the memoirs refer to June as the month in which Gorbachev made this statement.

261 Interviews with Kvitsinsky and Blech; see also Kwizinskij, *Vor dem Sturm*, p. 421.

262 Genscher, *Erinnerungen*, p. 544.

263 According to the TASS report, when the West German president raised the issue of "one German nation," TASS reported, Gorbachev replied that he did not wish to "theorize" about the topic. To him, only the "political aspect, the existence of two German states with different socio-economic systems" was relevant. What things would look like "in a hundred years, history will decide." If, furthermore, one could "hear time and again" that the "'German problem' remains open," this gave rise to doubt as to whether the Federal Government was still thinking about adhering to the 1970 Moscow treaty; TASS report, as published in *Pravda*, 8 July 1987. The tougher – Genscher and TASS – versions of what the Soviet party leader told von Weizsäcker are also contained in his book (Gorbachev, *Perestroika i novoe myshlenie*, pp. 208-10). The elaborations there, however, are not characterized as a direct response to what the West German president had said but as general reflections arising from the conversation. Falin (*Politische Erinnerungen*, pp. 483-84) asserts that "I recommended to the General Secretary to delete the half a century [sic]. The reference to history would have been enough. He did not accept this advice." There is no confirmation that the fifty years had ever been mentioned by Gorbachev.

obvious deviation from the position the Soviet Union had stubbornly adhered to from Khrushchev to Chernenko. As potentially with Soviet and Russian policy towards Japan on the Kurile islands or the "Northern Territories" in Tokyo's political geography, to continue the argument, by acknowledging the existence of an unresolved problem, Gorbachev met an inalienable prerequisite for future negotiations. Genscher and other West German officials looked at the proverbial glass as being half full rather than half empty. They chose to ignore the extraordinarily long time frame and pretended to, or actually did believe that for Gorbachev the German question was still unresolved. This fit squarely into Genscher's overall approach towards the new Soviet leader and his new foreign policy slogans and concepts. As the German foreign minister had stated in a speech in Davos on 1 February 1987, the West had no reason meekly to shun talks and negotiations. "Our motto can only be: Let us take Gorbachev seriously; let us take him at his word. ... Let us not sit there with folded arms and wait what Gorbachev will present to us! Let us rather try to influence developments from our side, to advance and shape them."[264]

In July 1987, however, Gorbachev's glass was not really half full regarding the German problem. It contained only a few drops of stale political rhetoric. By handing to impersonal and unpredictable "history" the responsibility for solving what he, at least openly, did not even recognize as a problem, he *de facto* rejected the idea that any initiative was required. European statesmen could, indeed should sit back and see what might happen in a century. This interpretation is corroborated by the possible origin of Gorbachev's "history will decide" phrase. In April 1986, Gorbachev had told Honecker about a conversation he had had with Egon Bahr. The SPD leader, according to Gorbachev, had stated that "*the existence of two German states now is advantageous for peace*" and that everything else would "*be decided by history*" – a phrase which to the Soviet leader showed how "cunning" the social democrats were but which he found convenient enough to adopt as his own position.[265] His book *Perestroika*, which went to the publisher in June 1988, confirms the interpretation that Gorbachev was averse to taking any initiative on the German problem. It took the conversations with von Weizsäcker as a point of departure and scathingly called "all these declarations on the restoration of 'German unity' as far removed from *Realpolitik*, to use the German term." No matter what Reagan and other politicians were saying, the West could "not make the FRG a realistic offer on the so-called 'German problem.' What has developed historically should also be left to history." The reality was "the existence of two German states with different social and political

---

264 As quoted in Genscher, *Erinnerungen*, p. 527.

265 Transcript of talks between Gorbachev and Honecker on 20 April 1986 in East Berlin, SED Politburo, *Arbeitsprotokolle*, Central Party Archives, Büro Honecker, 41666 (italics mine).

systems. ... Both [states] can make a contribution to the cause of Europe and the world. What will be in a hundred years history will decide."[266]

Gorbachev's unwillingness substantially to revise the Soviet position on the German problem was underscored by several Soviet reports on the visit that often adopted an unfriendly and schoolmasterly tone.[267] Perhaps predictably, the attitudes of disapproval and condescension were most pronounced in the treatment of the visit by Gromyko, who by that time, had been shunted from the post of foreign minister to the largely ceremonial position of president. Putting the Federal Republic on the defensive on *moral* issues, he charged that Bonn was guilty of sheltering war criminals who had committed atrocities in the Soviet Union. Moscow had given the German president a list of persons, demanding their extradition, and he hoped that appropriate action would soon be taken. Regarding the *Berlin problem*, he asserted that there were countries that wanted "to use West Berlin as a detonation charge and a source of provocation in Europe"; the Federal Republic apparently had to be admonished to ensure strict adherence to the existing "agreement on West [sic] Berlin." Concerning *military* affairs, he still decried Bonn's position on intermediate range nuclear missiles and warned the coalition government not to insist on the stationing of Pershing I-a missiles. And with regard to the Federal Republic's stated desire for an improvement of *political* relations and cooperation in *economic, technical, and cultural* matters, Gromyko expected the German side to show the same "spirit of favorable disposition with due observance of mutual interests" as had already been displayed by the Soviet Union.[268]

The von Weizsäcker visit, then, was not a turning point in Soviet-West German relations. Gorbachev confirmed this publicly at the time. In reference to Genscher's visit in the preceding year, he said that agreement "seemed to have been reached on 'opening a new page' in the relations between the two countries." However, so far, the page had "remained empty." Alluding to the Goebbels remark, he continued that "at one time there was even a threat that [the book] would be closed. Fortunately, this did not happen."[269]

Privately, too, Gorbachev had not revised his negative image of West Germany. His attitude of superpower arrogance and condescension toward that country persisted. This can be demonstrated, among other things, by the following event: Gromyko had invited von Weizsäcker to an official luncheon. Speeches were given on that occasion. When *Pravda* and *Izvestiia* appeared on the following day,

---

266 Gorbachev, *Perestroika i novoe myshlenie*, p. 209.

267 For instance, *Pravda*, 8 July 1987.

268 *Pravda*, 9 July 1987. As for Gromyko's warning on the Berlin problem, an agreement on *West* Berlin was never concluded. All four-power agreements applied to Berlin as a whole.

269 *Pravda*, 8 July 1987.

however, important sections of the German president's speech had been excised. This included references to Kant and Königsberg, the existence of an all-German national consciousness, the wish of the Germans to be united in free self-determination, and pleas for liberalized emigration procedures for ethnic Germans living in the Soviet Union. The pattern of censorship set during Genscher's visit one year earlier was repeated and, as on the previous occasion, it was probably not the result of standard operating procedures but occurred upon authorization by the top political leadership. Immediately after the banquet, Gromyko, Shevardnadze, Yakovlev, and Ryzhkov had discussed the problem. The latter three advocated publication of the full text. Earlier speeches by Thatcher and Mitterrand had, after all, been published unabridged. But Gromyko disagreed and left the meeting, sulking. He then called Gorbachev and successfully persuaded him to authorize the cuts. Gromyko then gave ambassador Kvitsinsky instructions "to delete those parts which 'the Soviet people dislike.'" Chernyaev was courageous enough to call Gorbachev and tell him that the cuts had been a mistake. Gorbachev answered angrily: "I don't care. You have to treat the Germans that way. They love order – *Ordnung*!"[270]

Until October 1988, in accordance with Gorbachev's persisting negative perceptions of West Germany, examples of change in Moscow's policies were scarce. In 1987, the number of emigrants of German descent from the Soviet Union rose considerably as compared to the previous year, from less than 1,000 to 14,000 persons. At the beginning of that year, cooperation agreements on nuclear energy, health care, and research in agriculture were signed by German ministers Riesenhuber and Süssmuth and Soviet deputy prime minister Murakhovsky. The Soviet leadership lauded West Germany for its contribution to the agreement on the dismantling of intermediate range nuclear weapons as codified at the Washington summit in December 1987.[271] The prime ministers of Bavaria (Franz-Joseph Strauß) and Baden-Württemberg (Lothar Späth) visited Moscow in December 1987 and February 1988, respectively. There was some, although not much traffic in the other direction. Dobrynin visited Bonn at the beginning of October 1987, as did Shevardnadze in mid-January 1988. On the latter occasion, some more agreements were signed. These applied to political consultation at governmental level, the establishment of consulates general in Kiev and Munich, and long-term economic cooperation.

Yet the ambiguities and contradictory attitudes towards Bonn also continued. In his meeting with Späth, Gorbachev provided the usual rationale for the necessity of

---

270 Chernyaev, *Shest' let s Gorbachevym*, p. 155.

271 Gorbachev intimated this for the first time in his article about world security in *Pravda,* 17 September 1987; see also Shevardnadze's press conferences in Washington, 18 November 1987, *BPA Ostinformationen*, No. 179, 21 November 1987, and Geneva, ibid., 26 November 1987.

change in the Soviet approach to Bonn. He even made it appear as if a shift of tack had already taken place. The Soviet leadership, he said, had reconsidered its relationship with the Federal Republic of Germany. Without an independent European role international relations could never be freed "from the military strategic constraints of security." A new role for Europe could not be imagined "without the FRG and an improvement in its relations with the USSR." It was encouraging, therefore, that the time of "hostility and estrangement" between the two countries was receding into the past and that "the century-old linkages between our peoples and cultures are being restored." But he also warned Bonn that it would commit a grave mistake if it tried to circumvent the Washington agreement on the removal of intermediate range weapons by arms "compensations" – an obvious reference to the Pershing I-a issue. Furthermore, he reproached the German government for having reacted with "hesitation and vacillation" to appeals from Moscow for more extended cooperation.[272]

But hesitation and vacillation were more characteristic of Moscow's attitudes. Thus, Dobrynin's speech on 8 October 1987 at the Friedrich Ebert Stiftung, a research foundation under the auspices of the SPD, contained nothing more than relatively general and noncommittal phrases on German issues. As if the notion of the Common European House had not remained diffuse enough, it was blurred even further by his wish for cooperation in "our common home, the planet earth"![273] To the disappointment of those who had expected Dobrynin's visit to produce an announcement concerning a visit by Gorbachev to Bonn, nothing was said on the issue. In January 1988, in talks between Chancellor Kohl and Foreign Minister Shevardnadze a "possible meeting" between the chancellor and the general secretary was discussed again. But to little avail. Bonn acknowledged that any decision on the visit would be taken only in the "second half of the year."[274]

Disregarding customary diplomatic protocol and considerations of prestige, the German chancellor took the initiative and visited Moscow in October 1988. On that occasion, the Soviet position of principle was again stated without ambiguity. Gorbachev rejected the West German idea that the status of (West) Berlin should be improved and that it should be made the "touchstone" of Soviet-West German relations. Regarding larger issues, he complained that he had already "*spoken several times about the so-called 'German problem'*" but that the matter apparently still needed clarification: "*The current situation is the result of history. Attempts at*

---

272 Ibid.

273 Text of his speech according to the official press release by the Soviet embassy in Bonn.

274 Information provided to this author by government officials in Bonn.

overturning what has been created by it or to force things by an unrealistic policy are an incalculable and even dangerous endeavor."[275]

Kohl's visit nevertheless proved to be a "turning point" in Soviet-West German relations.[276] On 23 October, when Gorbachev and Chernyaev had discussed the materials for the upcoming summit meeting, the latter had expressed the following concern: "'I assess the situation as follows. The country (FRG) is willing to support us energetically but he (Kohl) is not.' Gorbachev answered: 'It is the opposite with us. The leadership is willing but the country is not.' Luckily, we were both mistaken."[277] Personality factors played a large role. The personal chemistry between the two leaders turned out to be much more compatible, and Kohl appeared much more flexible and sensitive to Soviet interests than Gorbachev had expected. Soon after the meeting, in Chernyaev's opinion, "mutual trust [between Kohl and Gorbachev] increased rapidly and they moved to a first name basis."[278] Equally important, the leaders' personal aides, Chernyaev and Teltschik, had a strikingly similar psychological and political make-up. Both of them approached politics without ideological preconceptions and stereotypes and both of them were conscious of this very fact. Writing in reference to the October 1988 talks, Chernyaev observed in retrospect:

> We sat opposite each other [in the Kremlin], and I looked the chancellor's extraordinary advisor in the eye. He was a man with a sharp practical sense who played an important role in German politics at the time, in particular with regard to Soviet-German rapprochement. Our press and the foreign ministry officials [had] painted a rather "unpleasant" picture of this official but as in so many other cases that proved to be wrong.[279]

Teltschik, in turn, has attributed the same non-ideological outlook, sharp intellect, and keen practical sense to his counterpart.[280] When the time arrived for Moscow to abandon previous principles and preferences and deal with the practical issues of

---

275 At the dinner speech of 24 October 1988, *Pravda*, 25 October 1988 (italics mine).

276 Chernyaev, *Shest' let s Gorbachevym*, p. 261.

277 Ibid.

278 Ibid.

279 Ibid., pp. 261-62; interviews with Chernyaev. I very much share these perceptions. I've known Teltschik since my student days at the Freie Universität Berlin in the late 1960s. When he was Kohl's personal assistant, I was a senior research associate at the Stiftung Wissenschaft und Politik in Ebenhausen. During that time, we exchanged views on German-Soviet relations and, more specifically, cooperated on the content and wording of the Soviet-West German Joint Declaration of June 1989.

280 Interview with Teltschik. Despite the friction that was to develop between Gorbachev and Chernyaev on the one hand, and Falin on the other, the latter was to acknowledge in an interview in 1993: "Chernyaev was a genius and definitely a sincere and very honest person [who] developed his own ... ideas in his work [as advisor to Gorbachev] and made sure that speeches and documents would be written properly"; interview series conducted by Ekkehard Kuhn, *id.*, *Gorbatschow und die deutsche Einheit*, p. 97.

united Germany's status and role in Europe, the smooth working relationship between these officials proved to be of considerable importance.

Several agreements were signed during the October 1988 visit – on cooperation in space, environmental protection, prevention of accidents at sea, food processing, construction of a high-temperature nuclear reactor, and cultural programs. The most important agreement signed, however, was that on the extension of a credit of DM 3 billion. On 17 October, after five months of negotiations, a consortium of West German banks led by the Deutsche Bank and the Soviet Bank for Foreign Trade had finalized the agreement. This was a low-interest commercial credit to be used for the modernization of the Soviet light and food industry. Despite the fact that the credit was not guaranteed by the West German government, it had very much encouraged and facilitated the deal. Its political importance was underlined by the fact that it was officially signed during Kohl's Moscow visit.[281]

For reasons to be explained in the next chapter, the credit accord was connected with a shift in Gorbachev's perceptions of the relative role of the two Germanies and the fate of perestroika. Contrary to his praise of the GDR's achievements in the private conversations with Honecker, it was beginning to dawn on Gorbachev that he had gravely overestimated the importance of East Germany or, for that matter, of the Soviet bloc, for the modernization of the Soviet economy.

8. Gorbachev and Eastern Europe: Decline of the Will to Empire

Chernyaev has described Gorbachev's attitudes and policies towards Eastern Europe as follows: "It seems to me that at first subconsciously and then consciously he considered the role [of the Soviet Union] as the 'leading and directing force of socialism' to be a burden. It interfered with his embarking with full sincerity upon a world policy in line with the New Thinking." The only thing that he hoped for, Gorbachev's foreign policy advisor continues, was to be understood and that the East European party leaders would embark upon changes akin to what he was trying to do in the Soviet Union.[282] He has gone even further and suggested that Gorbachev "did not have any particular interest in the socialist community" and that he "maintained contacts with the leaders of the socialist countries without any particular interest, only

---

281 Information as supplied by Deutsche Bank officials in Moscow in October 1988; see also *Handelsblatt*, 10 October 1988, *Süddeutsche Zeitung*, 11 October 1988, and *Frankfurter Allgemeine Zeitung*, 18 October 1988. It is characteristic for an emerging pattern of West German and, later, united Germany's determination to support economic reform in the Soviet Union but Moscow's inability to use it productively and efficiently that by mid-March 1989 *not a single Pfennig of the available DM 3 billion had been called up*. Leonid Abalkin, one of the chief economic advisors to Gorbachev, confirmed this to the author at the first session of the newly founded German-Soviet Forum, 13-15 March 1989.

282 Chernyaev, *Shest' let s Gorbachevym*, pp. 81-82.

grudgingly agreed to visits, and was clearly disinclined to demonstrate a 'leading role.'"[283]

This disinclination developed only gradually. As Georgi Shakhnazarov, Gorbachev's advisor on East European affairs, has stated, three stages can be distinguished in Soviet relations with Eastern Europe.[284] In the first stage "there were hardly any changes; [our policy] remained within the traditional framework and was carried out by relying on conventional and ingrained methods, even though the dynamic personality of the new leader here, too, injected some original elements." The second stage was marked by the impact of perestroika on the relationship. But this did not occur as a result of a deliberate attempt by Gorbachev to put pressure on the dependencies and impose his will. "On the contrary, ... he thought that changes were entirely the subject of the sovereign choice of the parties and peoples." The third stage was characterized by a sharp decline in the intensity of cooperation, the rupture of the bonds of the socialist community, and ultimately the dissolution of the Warsaw Pact and Comecon. The new governments which replaced the communist regimes in Eastern Europe "began to orient themselves towards the West, and the Soviet leadership, in the conditions of a mounting crisis in the country and occupied by acute forms of political struggle, had neither the strength nor the means to counteract this [development]."[285]

To use the present conceptual framework and terminology, it would seem that Gorbachev intended to restructure the Soviet-East European relationship from that of imperial domination to that of hegemony. This intention existed irrespective of the fact that he either lacked awareness or was purposely denying that he was presiding over an imperial construct. As mentioned above, Gorbachev – in conversation with Havel – resented the characterization of the relationship with Czechoslovakia as colonial.[286] Even in retrospect, his terminology on Soviet relations with Eastern Europe remained euphemistic and apologetic. Generalizing about the difficulty of restructuring these relations, he writes:

> Stubborn resistance in the system of the socialist community had to be overcome – a system that since the Stalin era had hardly experienced change. Only the forms, the decorum so to speak, had become more decent. The essence and the methods, however, with some rare exceptions, had remained the same. ... The [Soviet] cadres were, after all, used to a certain style. It took a long time until they renounced arrogance and conceit towards the *allies*.

---

283 Ibid.

284 Georgi K. Shakhnazarov, *Tsena svobody. Reformatsiia Gorbacheva glazami ego pomoshchnika* (Moscow: Rossika, Zevs, 1993), p. 100.

285 Ibid.

286 See *supra*, p. 28.

He also deplored that "[t]he inertia of *paternalism* made itself felt for a long time."[287]

As defined earlier, however, an imperial or "colonial" relationship is more than an alliance and governed by more than benevolent paternalism. It is characterized by the penetration of the internal system and control over the domestic and foreign policy of the dependencies.[288] This had been the nature of the relationship between the center and the periphery in the Soviet bloc prior to Gorbachev's ascent to power. The major difference between Gorbachev and his predecessors in the Kremlin was his gradual *loss of will* to maintain the imperial relationship. His goal, to use a term much decried in the West in the mid-1970s, was the establishment of an "organic" relationship between the metropole and the satellites.[289] It was to be a hegemonial system that would not have to be based on the threat or use of force in order to keep unpopular communist governments in power.[290]

Concerning the use of force, Shevardnadze has written that after the April 1985 CC plenum which ushered in the Gorbachev era, "military interference [in the socialist countries] was completely ruled out."[291] This decision raised the question of the continued presence of Soviet armed forces in the area.

> Our military presence in Eastern Europe was questioned long before the start of events in 1989-90. And it was not just the governments that came to power in those years that demanded the withdrawal of Soviet troops, but their predecessors as well. Some of them told us in strictest confidence, using very cautious formulations, that the continued presence of Soviet troops in their countries would create serious problems for them. It would be better for us to take steps ourselves in this direction, they said, than to be forced later to move in haste under the pressure of events.[292]

In the summer of 1987, Yakovlev had specifically raised the question of Soviet troop withdrawals from *East Germany* in a conversation with ambassador Kochemasov. "*What do you think, isn't the Group of Soviet Forces in Germany too large? What*

---

287 Gorbachev, *Zhizn'*, Vol. 2, pp. 312-13 (italics mine).

288 See above, p. 25.

289 In December 1975, at a conference of American ambassadors, U.S. State Department advisor Helmut Sonnenfeldt had stated that the relationship between the USSR and Eastern Europe was "unnatural." The United States should "strive for an evolution that makes [that] relationship ... an *organic* one." It should support the "visible aspirations in Eastern Europe for a more autonomous existence *within the context of a strong Soviet geopolitical influence*"; "State Department Summary of Remarks by Sonnenfeld," *New York Times*, 6 April 1976 (italics mine). This definition of American policies came to be called the "Sonnenfeldt Doctrine."

290 Support for this assessment can also be found in a conversation between Gorbachev and Vadim Medvedev shortly after the appointment of the latter to the post of chief of the Socialist Countries Department in March 1986. Interference in the internal affairs of these countries had to stop and a fresh look at the problems that had accumulated was necessary, Gorbachev told Medvedev; see Medvedev, *Raspad*, pp. 7-8.

291 Shevardnadze, *Moi vybor*, p. 206.

292 Ibid.

would happen if we were to accede to its – even unilateral – reduction?"[293] It is doubtful, however, that a formal decision was ever taken on the matter of military intervention. It is more likely that the general aversion to the use of force in Eastern Europe evolved in conjunction with an emerging consensus among the top decision-makers in 1985-88 that the reapplication of such methods would destroy the credibility of the New Thinking and seriously damage relations with the United States and Western Europe.[294]

To provide some detail about the evolution of Gorbachev's attitudes and policies in the first phase of the process, there is no evidence that he was disinterested in the fate of the Soviet bloc. On the contrary, he attempted to achieve much closer cooperation and coordination among its members. This was apparent in the line he adopted at the Warsaw Pact summit conferences in the first two years of his tenure of office as Soviet party chief. This included his role at the meetings of the alliance in Moscow in March 1985, informally convened on the occasion of Chernenko's funeral; in Warsaw in April 1985, scheduled in order to renew the Warsaw Treaty for another twenty years; in Sofia in October; in Moscow in December, to discuss economic cooperation; and in Budapest in June 1986.

Gorbachev's intentions were clearly stated at the first ordinary summit in Sofia, where he emphasized the need for more coordination and expressed the thought that there was "general agreement" among the participants that Warsaw Pact summit meetings should "take place not less than once a year."[295] He also suggested that cooperation should be made more effective by instituting the practice of sessions restricted to the party first secretaries, the idea being that "each comrade could present the considerations dear to his heart."[296] The meetings should proceed "without an agenda."[297] Kádár agreed and called them a particularly appropriate forum for the consideration of economic issues, including basic structural changes in CMEA since its institutions were "relatively independent and not very effective;" if the first secretaries agreed on any particular question "this would carry at least as much weight as the decision of any other body."[298]

---

293 Kotschemassow, *Meine letzte Mission*, pp. 62-63.

294 Interview with Tarasenko.

295 Gorbachev's speech at the Warsaw Pact summit meeting in Sofia, 22 October 1985, SED Politburo, *Arbeitsprotokolle*, Central Party Archives, J IV 2/2A/2811.

296 Opening remarks at a closed session of first party secretaries at the June 1986 Warsaw Pact summit conference in Budapest; see the protocol on the restricted meeting of the party chiefs of the Warsaw Pact member countries, SED Politburo, *Arbeitsprotokolle*, J IV 2/2A/2896.

297 Protocol of the closed session of first party secretaries at the PCC meting in Sofia on 23 October 1985, SED Politburo, *Arbeitsprotokolle*, J IV 2/2A/2811.

298 Kádár, final remarks at a closed session of first party secretaries at the June 1986 Warsaw Pact summit conference in Budapest; see the protocol on the restricted meeting of the party chiefs of the Warsaw Pact member countries, SED Politburo, *Arbeitsprotokolle*, J IV 2/2A/2896.

Gorbachev's idea reflects a certain amount of naïveté. Considering the career patterns as well as the psychological and political make-up of the majority of the participants and the long history of secrecy and distrust among them, it was strange to assume that glasnost would suddenly arise and permeate the small circle of the chosen few. Leaders like Jaruzelski and Kádár did not need the restricted forum because they were prone to address issues "dear to their heart" irrespective of the venue in which they appeared. In contrast, leaders such as Ceauşescu, Honecker, Husák, and Zhivkov who were disinclined to show their cards would hardly be swayed suddenly by a new forum and engage in glasnost. In fact, a cursory comparison of the content of the leaders' public speeches and their remarks in the restricted meetings reveals no significant discrepancies between the public and the private stance. Gorbachev's presentation at the closed session in Sofia was even *less* open and controversial, and more conservative, than his public statement. Perhaps to the surprise of his colleagues, he declared communism still to be the goal of the CPSU. The Soviet Union, he told them, was engaged in constructing "mature socialism" (Brezhnev had invented this term), and the important thing now was to advance towards "the highest stage, that of the communist social formation." When exactly this goal would be achieved was difficult to say. This was "not a question of arithmetic but of politics."[299]

At the summit meeting in Warsaw, Gorbachev had used the catchwords for Soviet intervention – the claim that relations in the bloc were "based on the full equality and comradely mutual assistance of sovereign states" and the "principle of socialist internationalism."[300] In fairness, however, he cannot be blamed for the notorious "Vladimirov" article that appeared in *Pravda* three months later and created quite a stir among Western Sovietologists.[301] The article, written by Oleg Rakhmanin, the deputy head of the CC department for the relations with the ruling communist parties, contained all of the stereotypes of "socialist internationalism," "common interests of the socialist community," and "observance of the fundamental principles of socialist economic management," and it viciously attacked "anti-communist theoreticians and opportunists," "revisionist, nationalist, and clerical concepts," "national models of socialism" and ideas about the specific nature and special role of individual members of the socialist community. "Did you know," Gorbachev asked Konstantin Rusakov, the head of the department, in the Politburo meeting of 29 June, "that this kind of article [was] prepared in your department? The author is Rakhmanin, your second in command." Rusakov claimed that he had not known. "And you," turning to

299 Statement by Gorbachev at the closed session of first party secretaries at the PCC meting in Sofia, 23 October 1985, SED Politburo, *Arbeitsprotokolle*, Central Party Archives, J IV 2/2A/2811.

300 *Pravda*, 28 April 1985.

301 Ibid., 21 June 1985.

Zimyanin, the secretary for propaganda, "did you know that this article was received by *Pravda*, the central organ of the Central Committee?" Again the answer was no. "And you," he asked Yuri Afanasev, the *Pravda* editor-in-chief, "didn't you understand what you were doing? Why didn't you send it to the Politburo or at least to the [CC] secretariat?" Afanasev mumbled something in defense about Rakhmanin's influence and powers of persuasion.[302] The editor-in-chief could also have argued in his defense that Gorbachev's own – at least his publicly stated – views on Soviet-East European relations were at that time conservative enough for such an article not to be out of place.

Gorbachev's approach of non-interference and disinclination to involve himself actively in the affairs of Eastern Europe emerges more clearly in the second stage of the center-periphery relationship. A crucial juncture in the process of reconsideration of the relations, as he himself has written, was the Central Committee plenum of January 1987 that introduced democratization and broadened openness.[303] This meeting heralded a fundamental and, as it turned out, fateful shift from economic to political reform in the Soviet Union. It increased differentiation in the bloc or, more to the point, sharply divided its members. It also shaped Gorbachev's attitudes and policies towards individual leaders and countries, depending on the degree to which they were prepared to follow the Soviet lead.

Honecker, as noted, had made his "reservations" about Soviet domestic developments known as early as the preceding year; how he reacted subsequently will be explored below. Ceauşescu, as Gorbachev deplores, "declared unambiguously that he could not agree with what had been said at the plenum; the CPSU was entering upon a dangerous path." Zhivkov adopted a contradictory stance, at first rejecting the new concepts, then "reorganizing the political system of his country with all its mechanisms of economic administration and management" but failing to introduce "real democratization, which would have required an unfettered public opinion." Husák, as usual, "displayed common sense and circumspection." His reactions, for the most part, were positive. "The practice of the C[ommunist] P[arty], however, was mainly determined by [Vasil] Bi'lak, [Jan] Fojtík, and [Miloš] Jakeš [party leader after 1987], who still vividly remembered 1968 and therefore didn't think about 'loosening the reins.'" Kádár "wholeheartedly welcomed the changes in the Soviet Union since they presented him with the opportunity to proceed more consistently" with reform. Jaruzelski, too, endorsed the changes in the Soviet Union because they

302 Politburo proceedings of 29 June 1985, as quoted by Chernyaev, *Shest' let s Gorbachevym*, p. 50. Chernyaev errs concerning the month. The Vladimirov article was published and the Politburo meeting took place on 21 and 29 *June* 1985 repectively – not in July. In his memoirs, Medvedev has criticized Rakhmanin as having been "hopelessly wedded to the stereotypes of the past;" Medvedev, *Raspad*, p. 23.

303 Gorbachev, *Zhizn'*, Vol. 2, p. 318.

reenforced his reformist course in Poland and because "he knew very well that the problems of any country cannot be solved by the method of force – at least not the basic ones."[304]

Medvedev has observed that the attitudes of the socialist countries and leaders towards perestroika were "the main criterion of differentiation in [their] political positions."[305] In turn, Gorbachev's attitudes and behavior towards individual East Eruopean countries and leaders were shaped by his awareness of this differentiation, as Chernyaev has explained.[306] The most cordial personal rapport, according to his observations, existed between Gorbachev and Jaruzelski. This was not only a matter of personal compatibility but also because of Gorbachev's conviction that the Polish leader, by imposing martial law in December 1981, had acted not as a traitor to Poland but as her savior. His policies of "socialist renewal" (*obnovlenie*) preceded and, after Gorbachev's accession to power, coincided with perestroika. Gorbachev also had a deep respect for Kádár and always had great pleasure communicating with him. Concerning his attitudes towards the Czechoslovak communists, he "had a certain amount of respect only for Husák." His relations with Zhivkov, too, were difficult, partly because the Bulgarian leader arrogated to himself the right to act as doyen of the "socialist community" and partly because of his proclivity for lecturing Gorbachev on both ideological and political questions. His relations with Honecker were also strained. The worst rapport existed between Gorbachev and Ceauşescu, "to whom he sometimes referred as the *Führer*." He ridiculed and contemptuously dismissed his maneuvers as a nuisance and contrary to *Realpolitik*.[307]

The Demise of the Brezhnev Doctrine

In practice, then, ideological *Gleichschaltung* and military-political coordination in the bloc were being replaced by a colorful but fading patchwork of bilateral relations. The Brezhnev doctrine of limited sovereignty was being abandoned in favor of what in 1988 came to be called Freedom of Choice (*svoboda vybora*), which supplemented the concepts of the New Thinking and the Common House of Europe and transformed the Soviet role in Europe. Gorbachev and his closest advisers and colleagues were later to convey the notion that this principle existed and was communicated to the East European party leaderships and peoples at the very beginning of his rule. This, however, was not the case. The principle began to take root firmly, and essentially only in the mind of Gorbachev and his closest advisors, at

304 Ibid., pp. 318-19.
305 Medvedev, *Raspad*, p. 34.
306 Chernyaev, *Shest' let s Gorbachevym*, pp. 81-82.
307 Ibid.

the second stage of Soviet-East European relations. Uncertainty about likely Soviet reactions in case of anti-communist and anti-Soviet upheavals persisted until 1989.

To trace the application of the new principle to bloc relations, at the Twenty-seventh party congress Gorbachev refrained from mentioning socialist internationalism or any of the other code words for Soviet interventionism. Instead, he emphasized "unconditional respect in international practice for the right of every people to choose the paths and forms of its development" and averred that "unity has nothing in common with uniformity, with a hierarchy."[308] At the February 1988 Central Committee plenum, at the Nineteenth Party Conference in June 1988, and in his speech on 7 December 1988 at the United Nations Gorbachev elaborated on the new concept. For the Soviet Union, he said, "the obligation of the principle of freedom of choice is above every doubt. Freedom of choice is a general principle which does not know any exceptions."[309] Several specialists at the Institute for the Economics of the World Socialist System and in Central Committee departments were even more radical in their break with past approaches, denouncing "domineering methods," "great power ambitions," and "hegemonial pretensions" and, in a direct attack against the Brezhnev doctrine, denied that "respect for national sovereignty could be subordinated to some higher principle governing their relations – that of unity."[310]

Yet there were several reasons why in 1985-88 skepticism was warranted among Eastern European leaders, parties, and citizens about the scope and durability of Soviet adherence to the principle of non-intervention.[311] First, it was unclear whether Gorbachev would be able to hold on to power for long. Whereas his more daring supporters were concerned that perestroika would turn into a *perestrel'ka* (a mass execution by the firing squad, liberally translated), conservatives in the bloc like Czech Politburo member Vasil Bilák were saying: "Let's wait and see! Ultimately,

---

308 Speech by Gorbachev at the Twenty-seventh party congress, *Pravda*, 26 February 1986.

309 Speech by Gorbachev to the UN, *Pravda*, 8 December 1988.

310 Yurii Novopashin, "Politicheskie otnosheniia stran sotsializma," *Rabochii klass i sovremennii mir*, No. 5 (September 1985), pp. 55-65. Details about this and other criticism by academic specialists and Central Committee officials of the imperial Soviet approach to Eastern Europe and the Brezhnev doctrine as provided by Karen Dawisha, *Eastern Europe, Gorbachev and Reform: The Great Challenge*, 2nd edition (Cambridge: Cambridge University Press, 1988), pp. 201-205.

311 An excellent analysis of the ambiguities of Gorbachev's statements and policies within the bloc, which has inspired the present discussion, is Charles Gati, *The Bloc that Failed: Soviet-East European Relations in Transition* (Bloomington, Ind: Indiana University Press, 1990), pp. 65-103.

those who let themselves get carried away by perestroika will break their necks. New people will then appear."[312]

Second, even if Gorbachev were not replaced by a coup, there was no guarantee that he would not yield to hard-line domestic pressures and reverse his permissive stance. Some lessons of the past were perhaps applicable. At the Twentieth party congress in February 1956, Khrushchev, too, had promulgated the principles of non-interference in the internal affairs of socialist countries, respect for their independence, equality in inter-state and party relations, and the legitimacy of different roads to socialism only to disregard such commitments a few months later in Hungary.

Third, it was uncertain whether Gorbachev really meant what he said. Did he really mean *peoples* rather than communist *parties* when he had supported – at the Twenty-seventh party congress – the right of the former to choose their preferred paths and forms of development? In his speech in Prague in April 1987, it was evident that he meant the latter. "We consider the independence of every *party*, its responsibility to the people of its own country, and its right to decide the questions of the country's development to be unconditional principles."[313] In his programmatic *Perestroika*, he reiterated that the freedom of choice was limited to the communist parties and their leaders:

> The entire framework of political relations between the socialist countries must be strictly based on absolute independence. This is a view held by *the leaders of all fraternal parties*. The independence of each *party*, its sovereign right to decide the issues facing its country, and its responsibility to the nation are unquestionable principles.[314]

Fourth, although the traditional code words for Soviet intervention had been omitted at the Twenty-seventh party congress, they resurfaced subsequently. This applied to terms such as "socialist community," the "common interests" and "common responsibility" of the communist parties, and the requirement of "unity." The ominous flavor of interventionist terminology, despite all of the assurances of Soviet non-interference, was contained, for instance, in his speech in Prague.

> At the same time [while upholding the right of each party to be independent], we are of the firm conviction that the *community of socialist nations* will be successful only if every party and country is concerned not only about its own interests and only if every party and country treats its friends and allies with respect and is sure *to take their interests into account*.[315]

---

312 Gorbachev told Alexander Dubček in Moscow in May 1990 that Vasil Bilák had made this statement. He (Gorbachev) had heard it in connection with Husák's impending replacement by Jakeš, which took place in December 1987; Gorbachev, *Zhizn'*, Vol. 2, p. 362.

313 Speech by Gorbachev in Prague, *Pravda*, 11 April 1987 (italics mine).

314 Gorbachev, *Perestroika i novoe myshlenie*, p. 170 (italics mine).

315 *Pravda*, 11 April 1987 (italics mine).

The same flavor permeates *Perestroika*.

> We are also convinced that the socialist community will be successful only if every party and state cares for both its own and *common interests*, if it respects its friends and allies, heeds their interests and pays attention to the experience of others.
>
> Awareness of this relationship between domestic issues and the *interests of world socialism* [is typical of the countries of the socialist community. We are united, *in unity resides our strength,* and from unity] we draw our confidence that we will cope with the issues set forth by our time.[316]

Fifth, there was little uncertainty that in Gorbachev's mind the right of every people or party to choose the paths and forms of its development meant *socialist* development. But what would happen if anti-communist and anti-Soviet forces were to become ascendant and wanted to establish a multi-party system, abandon central planning, and introduce a market economy? And even if political and socio-economic changes transcending the parameters of Soviet perestroika were deemed acceptable in Moscow, what would be its reaction to demands for an exit from the Warsaw Pact?

Sixth, about 575,000 Soviet troops were still deployed in Eastern Europe – more than 400,000 in East Germany, 75,000 in Czechoslovakia, 65,000 in Hungary, and 40,000 in Poland – embedded in an offensive military doctrine.[317] Revision of the doctrine occurred even more haltingly than that of other aspects of theory. The new concepts, which will be described below in more detail, included "reasonable sufficiency" (*razumnaia dostatochnost'*) of military forces; the superiority, under some conditions, of strategic conventional defense over offense; and the restructuring of the armed forces of NATO and the Warsaw Pact towards their mutual "structural inability" to launch a surprise attack.

It was not until December 1988, however, that Gorbachev – in his speech at the United Nations – launched a major initiative that would, for the first time since the end of World War II, significantly and *unilaterally* reduce the huge Soviet preponderance in conventional forces in Europe, curtail the Soviet Union's offensive capabilities, and impair the role of the Soviet armed forces as the guardian of

---

316 Gorbachev, *Perestroika i novoe myshlenie*, p. 170 (italics mine). The text in square brackets is missing in the Russian version but can be found in both the English and German versions of his book. In 1985-88, the code words for interventionism could be replicated many times. In his speech commemorating the seventieth anniversary of the Bolshevik revolution in November 1987, for instance, he said that "we also know what damage can be done by weakening the *internationalist principle of mutual benefit and mutual aid* and by a lack of attention to the *general interests of socialism;*" *Pravda*, 3 November 1987 (italics mine).

317 The distribution of troops according to Western estimates; Douglas L. Clarke, "Soviet Troop Withdrawals from Eastern Europe," *Report on Eastern Europe*, (Munich, Radio Liberty / Radio Free Europe), 30 March 1990, pp. 41-49; Robert E. Harkavy, *Bases Abroad: The Global Military Presence* (Oxford: Oxford University Press, 1989), pp. 114-15.

Moscow's imperial position in Eastern Europe.[318] Six tank divisions of the 28 Soviet tank and motorized rifle divisions based in East Germany, Czechoslovakia, and Hungary were to be disbanded. Fifty thousand troops and 5,000 tanks were to be withdrawn, including assault landing formations and river-crossing units which, in the NATO perspective, had been designed for offensive operations in West Germany.[319] Also to be withdrawn from this region were one in four Soviet artillery pieces in Europe and one in eight combat aircraft.[320] An additional 5,000 tanks were to be pulled back from the western Soviet Union. Such measures were a dramatic departure from the prior stubborn Soviet refusal to contemplate anything but symmetrical reductions. They also enhanced confidence that Gorbachev was serious about the achievement of a military balance at lower levels of armament. But even after full implementation of the announced measures in the course of 1989, the strength of the Soviet armed forces in Eastern Europe would remain sufficient for military intervention, if such intervention was considered necessary.

Finally, perhaps most importantly, in 1985-88 Gorbachev failed to take a step that more than any other would have removed doubt that a clean break with the Soviet Union's imperial past had been made: a clear and unequivocal condemnation of the Warsaw intervention in Czechoslovakia. The opportunity to do so presented itself in April 1987 when the Soviet party leader visited Prague. "What, then, did the year 1968 mean, when [we look] at it from the perspective of 1987 and 1988?," Gorbachev asked. "It meant that perestroika had been delayed by twenty years."[321] He did ask that question, but only in retrospect, in his memoirs, not in 1987 or 1988. In Prague, he said: "An honest admission of [our] own errors and mistakes and the determination to eliminate them strengthen the prestige of socialism."[322] This pertinent observation, however, was made in general but failed to be applied to the Warsaw Pact intervention.

To look more systematically at the problem of the demise of the Brezhnev Doctrine, three possible forms of revision can be distinguished. First, revision could

---

318 *Pravda*, 8 December 1988. Gorbachev had told members of the communist youth organization only several weeks before his speech to the United Nations that unilateral troop reductions were not on the Soviet agenda. "You understand, we cannot come along just like that and dissolve (*rasputit'*) our army at a time when all the others maintain an army and arm themselves. To do that would be wrong. We will for that reason set out on the road of reducing armies and armaments [only] together with other states;" *Pravda*, 1 November 1988.

319 As for precise modalities, according to confidential information provided by civilian Soviet arms control experts, the 5,000 tanks to be withdrawn from Eastern Europe were to replace older models in the western parts of the Soviet Union; in this region a total of 10,000 tanks were to be dismantled.

320 The percentages as calculated by Western military experts; see *Financial Times*, 9 December 1988.

321 Gorbachev, *Zhizn'*, Vol. 2, p. 354.

322 Text of the speech as published in *Pravda*, 10 April 1989.

have been initiated by not only calling the intervention – euphemistically – a political mistake but indadmissible in principle and reprehensible on moral grounds. Second, since Soviet forces were still stationed in Czechoslovakia as a result of the intervention, eradication of the doctrine from the political fabric of the bloc could have taken the form of raising the question of the legitimacy of the Soviet military presence in that country. Third, since the doctrine's main content was that of the postulate of limited sovereignty of the members of the "socialist community," restoring the right of these members to decide matters on their own would also have meant abandoning the doctrine. Gorbachev addressed neither the principle and morality of military intervention nor the presence of Soviet forces in Eastern Europe. It was only on the third issue where some movement was noticeable, although – as noted *supra* – still qualified by references to "general interests" of the "socialist community" and the unconditional right for each "party" to solve questions of the country's development.

In politics as in life there are sins of commission and omission. Condemnation of the intervention in principle and on moral grounds would have discredited those Czechoslovak leaders who had come to the top as a result of the intervention and it would have generated pressures for the reinstatement of those half a million party members who had been purged. Gorbachev received reformist prime minister Lubomír Štrougal in November, but in the following month the predominantly conservative Czechoslovak Politburo and Central Committee replaced Husák by Jakeš, one of their own, as general secretary of the party. Almost immediately thereafter, in January 1988, the new leader went to Moscow. "If the Soviet leaders were to acknowledge that its action [the military intervention] had been a mistake," he told Gorbachev, "the CPCz [Communist Party of Czechoslovakia] would inevitably be weakened considerably, and the opposition, on the other hand, would be strengthened."[323] He begged his Soviet counterpart not to hurry but to delay reassessment of the intervention until the situation in Czechoslovakia had stabilized – a request that was granted.[324] "Non-interference" in this way turned into interference. It went beyond that to active interference, when the Soviet media joined the Jakeš leadership in condemning demonstrations against the new regime in mid-January 1989.[325]

To summarize, the Gorbachev factor in Eastern Europe in 1985-88 was important in delegitimizing communist rule, but it was not a source of intellectual or political inspiration. The enthusiastic popular welcome Gorbachev invariably received during his visits to Eastern Europe was as much a tribute to his courage for trying to reform

323 Gorbachev, *Zhizn'*, Vol. 2, p. 358.

324 Ibid.

325 The reports and commentary in *Pravda*, 20 January 1989, are a good example of this.

the Soviet Union as a declaration of no-confidence in the conservative regimes of the bloc. The models of change which inspired intellectuals and ordinary citizens, particularly in Hungary, Poland, Czechoslovakia, and East Germany were not reform socialism led by the communist parties but the political and economic system of neighboring West Germany, Austria, and Scandinavia. The motive forces were not utopian "socialism with a human face" and "market socialism" but Western-style political pluralism, social democracy, and market economy. As Moscow's loss of will to empire became more apparent and its disinclination to use force in order to uphold conservative regimes in the bloc more credible, it was only a matter of time before the limits of Soviet tolerance would be tested. But this did not occur in all seriousness and with repercussions unforeseen by Gorbachev until the third phase of Soviet-East European relations. In the interim, assumptions were widespread in both Eastern and Western Europe that the sparks of change would spread from Hungary and Poland to Czechoslovakia and only from there to East Germany. Surprisingly, the sparks were to ignite East Germany first and only then Czechoslovakia. The following section examines in more detail why this fateful sequence occurred by reverting to the events taking place in the GDR and in Soviet-East German relations.

Soviet-East German Relations: Defiance versus Deference

In his memoirs Gorbachev states tersely that after the January 1987 CPSU Central Committee plenum the differences between the Soviet and the East German leadership could no longer be concealed.

> Honecker personally gave instructions no longer to publish in the GDR any materials of our [Central Committee] plenary meetings. ... Thereafter, news and documents from the Soviet Union were subjected to political censorship, cut extensively, or held back entirely. The distribution of German language periodicals published in Moscow, such as *Sputnik* and *Neue Zeit*, was outlawed [in November 1988 and February 1989 respectively]. Mutual misunderstanding, in fact alienation, increased.[326]

He also notes that Honecker, as well as other SED leaders, became "critical of me in the same measure as our perestroika and glasnost unfolded; and although he visibly displayed moderation in our talks, it was impossible not to notice his rejection of [our] democratic changes."[327]

In ordinary circumstances, that is, in a normally functioning empire, one would have expected its chief representative to take the recalcitrant provincial governor to task. In the Soviet empire after 1987, however, this was no longer the case. A strange anomaly arose and became the order of the day. As tension between the two leaders

---

326 Gorbachev, *Zhizn'*, Vol. 2, p. 408.
327 Ibid.

increased and Soviet and East German policies drifted apart, a reversal of traditional imperial roles took place: the exponent of the most exposed part of the imperial periphery was lecturing, admonishing and criticizing the head of the imperial center rather than *vice versa.* Even more astonishingly, the latter reacted to the criticism with lame excuses, apologies, disclaimers, retractions, and promises to take remedial action. *Passé* was the refreshing atmosphere of the August 1984 emergency meeting in Moscow where both sides had openly and confidently presented their case and attempted to convince each other of the validity of their arguments.

To revert to the analogy of a disintegrating marriage, it was almost as if, after every reasonable effort had been made to achieve reconciliation, the erstwhile partners felt that there was nothing more to say, with one partner withdrawing in silence, the other engaging incessantly in gratuitous bickering. Not that there was no opportunity to talk. At the end of May 1987, Gorbachev attended a Warsaw Pact summit conference in East Berlin, mainly to discuss problems of European security; Honecker attended the seventieth anniversary celebrations of the Bolshevik revolution in Moscow in November; and the Soviet party leader again traveled to East Berlin in December to report on the Soviet-American summit and explain his rationales for agreeing to the Washington treaty on the abolition of intermediate-range nuclear forces. Yet these opportunities failed to be used for a fresh start.

To provide some evidence, Dobrynin had been given the assignment by Gorbachev "confidentially to inform comrade Honecker" about the impending January 1987 plenum of the CPSU Central Committee.[328] Although the Politburo still had to finalize the proceedings, the main outlines of a program of political democratization and economic reform had more or less taken shape. They concerned (1) a new law on enterprises, providing for more autonomy in the production process; (2) democratization of the electoral process by allowing choice among several candidates; and (3) democratization of the party by mitigating the time-honored *nomenklatura* system (appointment in accordance with party lists), letting lower-level entities propose their own candidates and abandoning the practice of determining in advance who would be allowed to speak at Central Committee meetings. When Honecker – in reference to the last point – interjected, "[w]e do it like this," Dobrynin replied: "*[I] am not saying this [in order to make recommendations] but rather think that much of what is now intended in the Soviet Union is already being done in the GDR.*"[329] But the point about the plenum was precisely the opposite! The CPSU was *departing* from the neo-Stalinist system to which the GDR was tenaciously clinging,

328 Protocol (*Niederschrift*) of a meeting between Honecker and Dobrynin on 20 January 1987, SED Politburo, *Arbeitsprotokolle*, Central Party Archives, J IV 2/2A/2976. Also present at the meeting on the Soviet side were the Soviet ambassador in East Berlin, Vladimir Kochemasov, and Viktor Rykin as translator.

329 Ibid., p. 12 of the typed transcript (indirect speech, italics mine).

and by asserting that this was not the case, Dobrynin was handing Honecker the very argument he and other top SED officials were already making, that is, that everything was fine in the GDR and change unnecessary.

On behalf of the SED, Kurt Hager was to reiterate this stance. A veteran of the Spanish civil war and a long-time friend of Honecker, Hager was responsible for ideology in the Politburo where he had sat as a full member since 1963.[330] When he was asked in April 1987 whether the SED would eventually emulate Soviet-style reforms in the GDR, he snapped: "Just because your neighbor puts up new wallpaper, does that mean that you would feel obliged to do the same?"[331] Not quite as insulting as Kohl's remarks about Gorbachev and Goebbels, the Hager comment was similarly irritating from the Soviet leader's perspective since it implied that the changes he was introducing in the Soviet Union were not fundamental but merely superficial.

To take another example of East German assertiveness and Soviet deference, at the bloc conference of secretaries for ideology in Warsaw in January 1987, Yakovlev told his colleagues that Moscow had received complaints from some comrades in the fraternal countries about certain interviews and articles by Soviet citizens, who had expressed opinions with which they disagreed. The first thing he wanted to say about this was that "we, too, [sometimes] disagree with such remarks and particularly with the way in which they are presented in the West. *But on this issue there should be complete clarity. If we are talking about democracy and publicity, one has to take these [concepts] seriously, not treat them as empty phrases.*"[332]

It is almost certain that Yakovlev's remarks were prompted by an extraordinary exchange that took place between Honecker and Gorbachev on 3 October 1986 in Moscow.[333] The private conversation, among other topics, had concerned glasnost and the role of intellectuals in promoting change. Honecker had taken the initiative and commented about a recently held congress of Soviet film producers. The Soviet comrades obviously had their problems, he mused condescendingly. However, the problems of the Soviet Union should not be exported to the GDR. He then exemplified what he had meant by this cryptic comment by two events.

---

330 Jeffrey Gedmin, *The Hidden Hand: Gorbachev and the Collapse of East Germany*, For the American Enterprise Institute (Washington, D.C.: The AEI Press, 1992), pp. 56-57.

331 "Jedes Land wählt seine Lösung," interview with Kurt Hager, *Stern* (Hamburg), 9 April 1987.

332 Speech by Aleksandr Yakovlev at the conference of ideological secretaries of the Warsaw Pact countries, Warsaw, 23 January 1987, SED Politburo, *Arbeitsprotokolle*, Central Party Archives, J IV 2/2A/2976, p. 8 of typed transcript (italics mine).

333 Transcript (*Niederschrift*) of the talks between Honecker and Gorbachev on 3 October 1986 in Moscow, SED Politburo, *Arbeitsprotokolle*, Central Party Archives, J IV 2/2A/2937, Supplement No. 2, pp. 35-43 of the typed transcript. Except for the identification of the speakers at the beginning of the quoted paragraphs, all italics are mine. The transcripts alternate between direct and indirect speech; the quotations have been rendered here consistently in direct speech.

> West Berlin television and radio stations [recently] broadcast a question-and-answer game with [Yevgeni] Yevtushenko. Yevtushenko spoke of [the existence] of a single body of German literature. This is also what the official circles of the FRG are saying. However, the fact is that since the Weimar Republic a single body of German literature has never existed, only a bourgeois and a proletarian body. [I would like to] mention only [Bertold] Brecht, [Willi] Bredel, [Thomas] Mann, [Lion] Feuchtwanger, and [Erich] Weinert. *Yevtushenko said he is for German unity. This is a provocation.* West Berlin television is broadcasting, above all, with the GDR in mind. Such a statement is directed against the GDR. He also talked other nonsense.[334]

Honecker buttressed his argument against glasnost by a second example of Soviet provocation:

> West Berlin television also broadcast a conversation with three other Soviet writers. In that broadcast, [Andrei] Voznesensky stated that the writers are the conscience of the nation. One cannot in the least agree with that. The radio and television stations in West Berlin, furthermore, are financed by the US Congress. *The appearance by Voznesensky and others is directed against the general line of the [East German] party and state.*[335]

The criticism betrayed an unreconstructed Stalinist mind-set about the legitimacy of censorship and it provided the Soviet host with a golden opportunity to educate his guest about the function of glasnost in the impending program of democratization in the Soviet Union. Instead, Gorbachev embarked upon what can only be called an undignified, even degrading, apologia. He stated that

> Comrade Kochemasov [the Soviet ambassador in East Berlin] reported to the [CPSU] Central Committee on Yevtushenko's statements and a discussion with him. In the discussion Yevtushenko had said [to Kochemasov] that no one really could tell the German people anything different than that it is for unity. Naturally, he had had unity on a socialist basis in mind. Comrade Kochemasov had then pointed out to him that perhaps he had said one thing but meant another. *As for the above-mentioned writers, they are, in principle, not bad people.*[336]

Honecker then brought up the biggest gun in the arsenal of communist invective and fired it directly at Gorbachev: "[I] ask for forgiveness, if [I] have to say this. But the appearance of such writers on television and radio financed by the USA is counterrevolutionary."[337] The Soviet leader failed to react to this charge.

> *Comrade M. Gorbachev:* We have done everything in the past and will continue to do so in the future so that the GDR as a state of German workers and peasants and as an independent socialist state will strengthen and develop.

---

334 Ibid., pp. 35-36 of the typed transcript (italics mine).

335 Ibid., p. 36 of the typed transcript (italics mine).

336 Ibid. (italics mine).

337 Ibid., pp. 36-37 of the typed transcript.

Comrade E. Honecker: This is why the comrades of the SED and the citizens of the GDR have good relations with the Soviet Union and also a reason why [we] cannot argue with people who come here from the Soviet Union. Polemic [arguments] against citizens from the S[oviet] U[nion] can always be interpreted as anti-Soviet. *One should let those people appear in Siberia but not in West Berlin.* What is being said in West Berlin can't be irrelevant to us. [But] [w]e don't have any influence on that.

Comrade M. Gorbachev: When a Soviet citizen commits a lapse and does so in the GDR [sic], then the comrades in the GDR can also tell him their opinion directly. That is their duty and their right. We will naturally tell this to our people, too.

Comrade E. Honecker: What was said in West Berlin can't be helped now. If it is being said now that the writers in the Soviet Union are the conscience of the nation, deviationists in the GDR will very quickly use that [for their own purposes]. That would be consistent with FRG propaganda.[338]

Later in the conversation, Honecker returned to the subject and complained that the GDR didn't "want to fight on two fronts" (that is, presumably, against Western bourgeois propagandists and Soviet intellectuals). Gorbachev replied that he would "give the highest priority" to this question and "instruct Yakovlev to talk to Yevtushenko."[339] Finally, he regretted that "several writers, for a number of years, have not accepted invitations to visit the GDR. Statements about freedom, censorship, etc. have been uttered by Yevtushenko for the past thirty years. These people like publicity. [I] think that one has to talk to them about this [too]."[340] One is left to wonder whether Honecker's perceptions of Gorbachev's ineffectiveness as a political leader and his deviation from socialist principle were not being nourished by the Soviet leader's failure to assert himself firmly and decisively in the bloc. Loss of respect is probably an apt description of Honecker's reaction to this and other episodes. In the circumstance, Yakovlev's above-mentioned exercise in damage-limitation was bound to be fruitless.

Honecker's perceptions of Gorbachev as both ineffective and unprincipled may explain why he finally decided to ignore the unabated Soviet opposition to his unchanged desire to visit West Germany.[341] In April 1987, he had the SED Politburo

---

338 Ibid. (italics mine).

339 Ibid., pp. 42-43 of the typed transcript.

340 Gorbachev made these remarks at a dinner conversation with Honecker, Mies, and Schmitt; SED Politburo, *Arbeitsprotokolle*, Central Party Archives, J IV 2/2A/2937, Supplement No. 3, p. 41 of the typed transcript.

341 Kochemasov (*Meine letzte Mission*, pp. 136-37) cursorily describes the history of the Soviet-East German controversy over the Honecker visit and writes: "Finally, I was instructed [by Moscow] to transmit to Honecker the agreement of the Soviet leadership to an official visit to the FRG." No date is provided for the receipt of the telegram.

endorse his travel plans.[342] At the end of May, a summit conference of the Warsaw Pact countries took place in East Berlin which produced no record as to whether Honecker's plans were approved or even discussed. In September, the twice postponed (vetoed) visit to the Federal Republic finally took place. From Honecker's perspective, the visit was a resounding success. Although billed by the West German government as a visit by a head of government, the visit unfolded as a state visit with all the appropriate trappings and protocol. Honecker met with President von Weizsäcker, Chancellor Kohl, the prime ministers of North Rhine Westphalia, Bavaria, and Saarland – Johannes Rau, Franz-Josef Strauß, and Oskar Lafontaine respectively – the leaders of the major political parties and, indeed, rock star Udo Lindenberg. Perhaps the most symbolic part of his visit was his stay in the Saarland where, as noted, he was born and had acquired his leftist credentials, where he still had friends and relatives, and where he now laid a wreath at his father's grave. It was to little avail that he reiterated his often quoted phrase that "to unite socialism and capitalism was as impossible as it is to unite fire and water." Internationally, suspicions arose that what Kohl and Honecker were "really" trying to do was to lay the groundwork for the achievement of "reunification on the sly."[343]

Apart from real or apparent symbolism, what about the more tangible results of the visit? To Dobrynin, Honecker had boasted that the GDR "annually receives 3 to 4 million Western visitors" and that in 1986, "1.773 million GDR citizens travelled to the FRG and other Western countries."[344] Such visits, as Honecker agreed with Kohl, were to be increased. There was also to be an expansion of relations between the two German states in other dimensions of policy. This was evidenced by a number of agreements concluded in Bonn. These pertained to the environment; protection from radiation exposure; scientific and technical cooperation; easing of travel; sister-city partnerships; the improvement of existing and construction of new train connections between Berlin and the Federal Republic; and the establishment of a joint electricity network between the two German states.

Despite the fact that the five-day visit received wide international press and television coverage, officially the event was almost completely ignored in Moscow. One day after the end of the visit, a short article appeared in *Pravda* written by its

---

342 On the Politburo decision see SED Politburo, *Arbeitsprotokolle*, Central Party Archives, J IV 2/2/2214.

343 This suspicion was, in fact, expressed by William Safire, "The Germanys: Reunification on the Sly," *International Herald Tribune*, 14 August 1984.

344 Dobrynin was apparently duly impressed and commented: "That's a lot." Honecker-Dobrynin talks, SED Politburo, *Arbeitsprotokolle*, Central Party Archives, J IV 2/2A/2976. These figures, however, are misleading. Honecker was using the term visitors. However, individual visitors were not recorded, only *visits*. Since many persons, above all functionaries on official business, were traveling to the West several times a year, the actual number of visitors was less than the figure suggested by Honecker.

correspondent in *East Germany,* who reported disparagingly that "an interesting event" had taken place. "Official talks" had been held in Bonn and a "joint statement" had been issued.[345] No details were given about the broad scope of the East German leader's visit, including Honecker's side-trip to his native Saarland and his laying a wreath at his father's grave. No statistics were provided about visits by East Germans to West Germany. Not a word was expended on the easing of travel restrictions, the joint electricity network, the transportation agreement, or the sister-city partnerships.[346]

Superficially, Soviet-East German business continued as usual, and so did the rituals. When Honecker visited Moscow in November 1987 on the occasion of the seventieth anniversary of the Bolshevik revolution, he received yet another Soviet decoration, the Order of Lenin. In private conversation with Honecker on 4 November, however, a new practice was instituted by Gorbachev.[347] In what must again be considered highly unusual in the history of empires, the Soviet leader reported extensively on the metropole's internal problems and was to continue to do so until the collapse of the communist regime in the GDR. Intra-party life was beginning to acquire greater dynamism, he told Honecker. A new consciousness was starting to develop; citizens were becoming more active; private initiative was on the rise; cooperatives were being founded; and much progress was being made in agriculture. However, on many issues society was more advanced than the party. "Scum," which had been submerged, was drifting to the surface. "Nationalist sentiments" were on the increase. There were "certain difficulties in the struggle against alcohol[ism]." He then went on to describe at length the controversies in the top Soviet leadership. On 21 October, Politburo candidate and head of the Moscow city party organization Boris Yeltsin had severely criticized the slow pace of change and asked to be relieved of his duties (a request retracted some days later); in the Central Committee, there had been heated discussions which had lasted approximately five hours but had failed to resolve the matter.[348]

Honecker graciously refrained from commenting directly on the Soviet internal problems. His criticism was indirect and it was contained in his customary progress report on East German economic affairs. As on previous occasions, he underlined East Germany's apparent importance to the USSR in high technology, telling Gorbachev that every third employee in East German science and technology was now involved in one or several of the more than 170 projects agreed upon between

---

345 M. Podkliuchnikov, "Glavnoe – uprochenie mira," *Pravda*, 12 September 1987.

346 Ibid.

347 Notes (*Aktennotiz*) on the talks between Honecker and Gorbachev on 4 November 1987 in Moscow, SED Politburo, *Arbeitsprotokolle*, Central Party Archives, J IV 2/1/627.

348 On 11 November 1987, Yeltsin lost his position as Moscow party chief and in January 1988 his candidacy in the Politburo.

the two countries. He sparkled with some data and much new-fangled terminology about micro-electronic processors, memory bits, lasers, digitalization, image resolution of satellite photography, precision surfacing of materials, optical sensors, new measuring instruments in medicine, fermentation in biotechnology, and nuclear fusion. He reminded his host, since he seemed to have forgotten, of the "May 1985 agreement for the strengthening of the scientific-technological positions of socialism against the acceleration of the arms [race] in space." He claimed that by the progress the GDR was making "we are counteracting the strategic embargo of the United States and other imperialist states." He even went as far as asserting that the production of micro-electronic equipment in the GDR was being organized in such a way "that the requirements of the USSR can be met." How was all this possible? "Strict state control" was the answer. This observation reinforced one of his very few earlier responses to Gorbachev's report on the controversies in the top Soviet leadership: "[I] agree with [you] that the decisive question is [how] to increase the role of the party because otherwise one cannot make progress."[349]

To characterize the meaning of the November 1987 talks, it appears that Gorbachev's concern about domestic problems was beginning to mount and that in his perceptions the burden of empire was getting heavier. He certainly did not want to deal with Soviet-East German relations as a problem. "[T]he [class] adversary contends that the leadership of the SED and Comrade Honecker allegedly do not understand the policy of the Soviet Union," he said. "On the other hand, the adversary is trying to tell the GDR that there is ambiguity in the attitude of the Soviet Union towards the GDR." However, nothing had changed in Soviet-East German relations. "All the sworn commitments are being adhered to. The relations with the GDR continue to be a [top] priority for the Soviet Union. There will be no deviation from this whatsoever. If problems arose, one should always discuss them openly."[350]

Problems did continue to arise but they were not discussed openly. At their meeting in the Polish capital in July 1988 on the sidelines of the Warsaw Pact summit conference, Gorbachev had suggested another meeting with Honecker. It would be "important," he thought, "for Comrade Honecker to come to Moscow prior to Helmut Kohl['s]" planned visit in October.[351] Coordination of Soviet-East German

---

349 Ibid. (indirect speech).

350 Ibid. (indirect speech). As these remarks would seem to show, it was Gorbachev who was trying to avoid controversy. His memoirs (*Zhizn'*, Vol, 2, p. 409) convey a different impression. He writes that a "temporary 'detente'" occurred in their relations when Honecker visited Moscow on the occasion of the seventieth anniversary celebrations of the Bolshevik revolution, and he attributes this relaxation to a change in *Honecker's* attitude. "After he had familiarized himself with my speech, he remarked that all differences had now been removed. In fact, the speech was published shortly thereafter in the GDR, unabridged."

351 Notes (*Aktennotiz*) of a meeting between Honecker and Gorbachev on 15 July 1988 in Warsaw, SED Politburo, *Arbeitsprotokolle*, Central Party Archives, J IV 2/2A/685.

policies towards Bonn seems to have been the reason for Gorbachev's suggestion. When Honecker visited the Soviet capital in September, however, such coordination did not appear to have been an important part of their talks – at least the transcripts of their private conversation contain nothing about it. One also might have expected by now to discern an increase in Soviet criticism of East German policies. There is no evidence of this either. What the transcripts do show, however, is Soviet praise for the GDR and a continuing pattern of East German assertiveness and Soviet deference.[352]

First, Gorbachev told Honecker, whereas the Soviet Union under Brezhnev had failed to draw the appropriate lessons from the scientific-technological revolution, the GDR "succeeded in rapidly accelerating labor productivity and also the quality [of production], catching up with the advanced countries." Second, "the conditions in the economy of the GDR are also significantly more democratic. There are even private craftsmen and traders. All this existed in the Soviet Union under Lenin. But later it was abolished."[353] Third, and most astonishingly, in comparative perspective the overall development of socialism in the GDR had much to recommend itself. There were "many negative and critical facts" in the socialist development of "the Soviet Union, Hungary, and Poland but far fewer in the GDR."[354]

Honecker, as usual, accepted the compliments in good grace but complained about glasnost. He returned to the problem of his ideological war on two fronts. It was one

---

352 Transcript (*Niederschrift*) of the talks between Honecker and Gorbachev on 28 September 1988 in Moscow, SED Politburo, *Arbeitsprotokolle*, Central Party Archives, J IV 2/1/685.

353 Ibid. (indirect speech). Gorbachev's favorable view of what in Soviet parlance was called *melko-tovarnoe proizvodstvo*, or small commodity production, has been confirmed by Aleksandr Tsipko, a Central Committee official in the department for relations with communist and workers' parties and a specialist on the GDR and Poland. In Tsipko's opinion, Gorbachev's view played an important role in the origins of both the January 1987 program of democratization and marketization of the economy and the frictions with Honecker. In 1985, the journal *Sotsiologicheskie issledovaniia* had published an article by Richard Kosolapov, chief editor of *Kommunist*, in which he had sharply criticized small commodity production and the SED for supporting it. Honecker was offended and took up the matter in the SED Politburo. In January 1986, Tsipko and Oleg Bogomolov, the head of the Institute on the Economy of World Socialism, wrote a report for Gorbachev, arguing that such "leftist" outbursts not only undercut moves towards the market economy in the Soviet Union but also soured Soviet-East German relations. Shakhnazarov supported this argument. When small commodity production became part of the Soviet Union's reform program in 1987, Gorbachev expected Honecker to respond enthusiastically to it but was "bitterly disappointed" and "irritated" when the opposite occurred. This enhanced his "psychological estrangement from the GDR and Honecker," which later turned into "hostility." Interview with Tsipko.

354 Transcript (*Niederschrift*) of the talks between Honecker and Gorbachev on 28 September 1988 in Moscow, SED Politburo, *Arbeitsprotokolle*, Central Party Archives, J IV 2/1/685 (indirect speech, italics mine). The transcripts use the acronyms of HPR (Hungarian People's Republic) and PRP (People's Republic of Poland). The criticism of the two countries contrasts sharply with what Gorbachev was saying in internal discussions at the time and later in his memoirs where he portrays and praises the two countries as being pioneers of reform.

thing, he said, that two dozen radio and ten television stations of the class enemy were directing their broadcasts against the GDR, spreading hostile propaganda in German. One could cope with that. But it was "intolerable" that journals such as *Literaturnaia gazeta*, the literary journal, and the weekly magazine *Ogonek* were allowed to carry articles purporting to demonstrate the failure of socialism as an historical experiment, and that such views and articles were disseminated in East Germany through Moscow's German language publications *Neue Zeit* and *Sputnik*.

Gorbachev, as previously, was apologetic. He knew that "the mistakes that are being made in the Soviet Union worry the comrades in the GDR. The Soviet comrades, too, are worried when the pace is too fast and excesses occur." He could assure Honecker, however, that "these negative phenomena are not being looked upon with indifference" and one would "deal with them." He extended this promise to cover glasnost. "As for the publications mentioned by Comrade Honecker, we won't put our hands into our lap, but we will continue to work with these press organs." He also appealed to the East German party leader to keep things in perspective. The GDR, as he (Honecker) had mentioned, was struggling on the most forward ideological front and had to cope with bourgeois propaganda twenty-four hours a day. "What difference, then, can a few Soviet publications, which are met with disapproval also by the Soviet comrades, make to the SED? They will certainly not cause an upheaval in the GDR, which has stood fast against more serious attacks."[355]

Gorbachev's appeal to Honecker not to worry too much about the effects of Soviet glasnost on the GDR implied that the problem would not disappear. Indeed, it erupted again only one month later. Among other materials offensive to the GDR, the November 1988 issue of *Sputnik* featured an article about one of the "blank spots" in the history of German communism. "The German communists," the author correctly wrote, "refused to join the social democrats in their struggle against Hitler. Had they done so, Hitler would not have been able to win the [1933] *Reichstag* elections and European history would probably have run a very different course."[356] The suggestion that the KPD was co-responsible and culpable for the rise of Hitler struck a raw nerve of its successor organization, the SED. It banned *Sputnik* and adodpted other protective measures on the ideological front. It ordered the withdrawal of five films,

355 Ibid. (indirect speech). In his memoirs, Medvedev claims that during his visit to East Berlin and in his talks with Honecker on 24 August 1988 he had asserted the Soviet point of view more forcefully: "Concerning the measures by the GDR authorities prohibiting [Soviet periodicals I] had to reemphasize the astonishment we had expressed earlier and point out again that the limitation of glasnost and the ban on Soviet periodicals and on the publication of Soviet materials in the GDR did not serve to strengthen our relations and in my view did not enhance the authority of the SED;" Medvedev, *Raspad*, p. 164.

356 As quoted in *Neues Deutschland*, 24 November 1988.

among them Tengiz Abuladze's anti-Stalinist satire "Repentance," from East German movie theaters. In December 1988, because of a "paper shortage," it suspended publication of *Freie Welt,* the weekly magazine of the East German-Soviet Friendship Society. In February 1989, it stopped distribution of *Neue Zeit* because the journal had included an interview with Polish Solidarity leader Lech Wałesa. And in April 1989, it refused permission to stage an art exhibition on "Glasnost and Perestroika in the Name of Gorbachev."[357]

The East German regime found itself increasingly isolated in the bloc. This was demonstrated, among other events, by the third follow-up conference of the CSCE, held from 4 November 1986 to 19 January 1989 in Vienna. East Germany was forced to accept, as a basis of discussion and final agreement, a draft document on human and citizens rights submitted by the neutral and non-aligned countries. The document included many provisions abhorrent to the East German representatives but, with the exception of Romania, acceptable to every other delegation in the bloc. As the GDR delegation lamented in an internal report, the "Soviet Union is increasingly prepared, in the interest of concluding the Vienna meeting soon, to accept the ... [Western] demands. Hungary and Poland support this position. The ČSSR and Bulgaria only point to difficulties on religious and minority issues." This only left Romania, which, according to the report, "continues to reject the draft of the neutral and non-aligned states and NATO's supplementary proposals."[358]

The proposals to which the GDR objected pertained to the detailed publication of balance of payment and trade statistics; unrestricted institutional and personal contacts between universities and other educational and research establishments; the right of citizens to freedom of movement; and the obligation of states to provide written justification for the rejection of applications for travel and emigration.[359] Most objectionable, however, were two "basket 3" draft provisions, which both Honecker and Ceauşescu, during the latter's visit to East Berlin in November 1988, rejected outright in a joint statement: the legalization of "Helsinki watch committees" that had been formed in Eastern Europe in order to check on the implementation of commitments made by their governments and the abolition of requirements for minimum currency exchanges for visits in CSCE countries.[360]

Honecker appeared adamant on these two points. On 5 January 1989, he warned Yuri Kashlev, the head of the Soviet delegation to the CSCE follow-on conference in

---

357 The above examples of East German *Abgrenzung* from Soviet glasnost are from Gedmin, *The Hidden Hand*, pp. 59-62.

358 SED Politburo, *Arbeitsprotokolle*, Central Party Archives, J IV 2/2/2295.

359 These and several other provisions were enumerated in the new directives for the GDR delegation to the CSCE on 15 September 1988; see SED Politburo, *Arbeitsprotokolle*, Central Party Archives, J IV 2/2/2295.

360 SED Politburo, *Arbeitsprotokolle*, Central Party Archives, J IV 2/2/2505.

Vienna, that even to mention anything about the Helsinki watch groups in the final document would amount to a "*legalization of counter-revolutionary activities*."[361] As for the abolition of minimum exchange requirements, the GDR had no intention to lose money and co-finance West German "capitalist exploitation." He asked Kashlev to tell Gorbachev that if these two points were not changed, the GDR would use its veto and thereby conceivably prevent the adoption of a final document. He certainly had no intention "to carry out an agreement on these two points."[362]

The alarm with which Honecker treated the "basket 3" provisions of the CSCE follow-up conference was commensurate with the threat they posed to the legitimacy of his regime. In the final analysis, they amounted to the legitimation of the pernicious influence of transnationalism in the Soviet empire. They also helped produce an entirely new phenomenon in the GDR: demonstrations were beginning to occur in a country where a revolution could allegedly not take place because people would refuse to step on the lawn, and this phenomenon was to continue and gain momentum in the fall of 1989 despite the state's massive security presence, arrests, and intimidation.[363] Honecker's alarm and his futile threat to exercise a veto in Vienna were seemingly contradicted by his characterization of the contrast between favorable conditions in the GDR and mounting instability in the other countries of the Soviet bloc. There were lots of problems in several socialist countries, he lectured Kashlev. The problems included "the unsatisfactory development in Poland, the processes in Hungary, the increasing controversies in the ČSSR, and the unsettled situation in Estonia, Lithuania, Azerbaijan, Armenia, and Georgia." East Germany, as opposed to these countries and Soviet republics, constituted "an island of tranquility".[364] He also reminded Kashlev that, because of its geostrategic location, the GDR's stability was "important for the socialist world as a whole."[365]

Honecker's alarm was coupled with defiance. The CSCE follow-up conference had put the spotlight on the main symbol of the division of Europe, the Berlin wall. In a speech in East Berlin, he repeated some of the standard arguments that he and Ulbricht had made in defense of construction of the wall in 1961, including the charge that the West was intent on "plundering" the GDR by an artificial exchange rate.[366] The wall was necessary to prevent the West from exporting its "society on

---

361 Ibid. (italics mine).

362 Ibid.

363 On 15 January 1989, the same day the CSCE final document was adopted in Vienna, some 190 people demonstrating for democratic change were arrested in Leipzig.

364 Talks between Honecker and Kashlev on 5 January 1989, SED Politburo, *Arbeitsprotokolle*, Central Party Archives, J IV 2/2A/2310.

365 Ibid.

366 To the extent that there was hypocrisy, it was not limited to the West. Honecker chose to ignore that the free-market rate of one West German Deutschmark to seven East German marks was

drugs" (*Drogengesellschaft*) to the GDR. He also discerned a good deal of hypocrisy in the Western wailing at the wall. West Germany, for instance, was quite satisfied to see the wall kept in place because it wanted to safeguard itself against "asylum seekers from distant countries." Therefore, he concluded, notwithstanding the "vigorous advocacy" of the abolition of the Berlin wall by "*Herr* Genscher and *Herr* Shultz" at the final session of the January CSCE follow-on conference in Vienna,

> *the wall will remain for as long as the conditions have not been altered which led to its construction. It will still be there in 50 and also in 100 years if the reasons for [its existence] have not been abolished.*[367]

Since the present account has been brought up to the beginning of East Germany's terminal illness and established that Soviet policies played a large role in triggering it, it may be useful to provide an interim assessment of the rationale of Gorbachev's approach in the period from his assumption of office as General Secretary in March 1985 until his visit to West Germany in June 1989. Gorbachev's images of and objectives in East Germany within the context of his overall definition of Soviet interests in Eastern Europe will be employed as a framework of analysis.

Interim Assessment

Gorbachev's goal was the creation of a reform socialist East Germany that would remain an integral part of the Soviet sphere of influence in Eastern Europe and continue to be an active member of a reformed Warsaw Pact and CMEA. The method to be applied in order to achieve this goal was not pressure but persuasion. East Germany was not to be forced to copy Soviet developments. It should voluntarily emulate them. The likelihood of a successful reformist transformation was, in his perceptions, greater in the GDR than in other countries of the bloc (including in the Soviet Union) because of East Germany's comparably modern infrastructure, the superior organizational abilities of its personnel, and its high levels of education and scientific-technological development. If this is an accurate reconstruction of Gorbachev's framework, it had several weaknesses.

The first was the idea of reform socialism. Such a system has never existed, and it is doubtful that such a model as it existed in Gorbachev's mind – that is, as a harmonious combination of the plan and the market, capable of adapting rapidly to innovation – could ever be realized. A second weakness was the notion that the ruling communist parties of Eastern Europe could transform themselves into a reform

---

almost precisely the rate applied to West German consumer goods in GDR chain stores Exquisit and Delikat.

367 "Schlußbemerkungen Erich Honeckers auf der Tagung des Thomas-Münzer-Komitees," *Neues Deutschland*, 20 January 1989 (italics mine). The Vienna follow-up conference had ended only a few days prior to Honecker's remarks.

socialist vanguard. Such a metamorphosis was perhaps possible in a democratic environment, such as in Western Europe but hardly in Eastern societies where civil society had to be rebuilt from the bottom up. A third weakness was connected with the specific nature of the GDR as the smaller part of a divided nation. Gorbachev failed to address the fundamental question which Otto Reinhold, rector of the Academy of Social Sciences at the SED Central Committee and one of the main party theorists, was to put as follows in August 1989: East Germany, he said, "is thinkable only as an anti-Fascist and socialist state, as a socialist alternative to the FRG. What rationale would there be for a capitalist GDR next to a capitalist FRG?"[368]

In addition to these fundamental conceptual weaknesses, there were glaring inconsistencies in Gorbachev's practical approach. The first is directly related to the last structural deficiency mentioned above and concerns his attitudes towards intra-German relations and policies towards West Germany. Gorbachev was intent on limiting West German influence in the GDR. This aim was predicated upon the idea, adhered to no less by Gorbachev than by Khrushchev, Brezhnev, Andropov, and Chernenko, that rising West German economic power and GDR indebtedness translated into increasing West German influence in East German affairs. How could such influence be measured? Perhaps the best indicators are East German deviation from Soviet foreign policy and domestic politics.

In *foreign policy*, however, there should have been, and for the most part there was, no major disagreement between the GDR and the USSR. Honecker had refused to subscribe to the hard-line policies towards the United States and Western Europe as determined principally by Gromyko. Gorbachev, in essence, had brought Soviet foreign policy in line with East Berlin's approach. Indeed, in June 1989, he acknowledged in private conversation with Honecker that Soviet-East German "cooperation in the foreign policy sphere is especially close."[369] His concern that the GDR was veering towards unification was also unwarranted. Honecker remained as closely wedded to the theory of the long-term existence of two independent and sovereign states as Gorbachev. In *domestic politics*, one of the main yardsticks of dependence would have been the degree to which East Germany was moving towards the West German model, including democratic elections, free speech, political pluralism, a multi-party system, and a market economy. This was definitely *not* the policy direction that Honecker was choosing. His concessions to West Germany were only at the margins of the traditional communist model of the one-party state, controlled elections, censorship, and a command economy. Where

---

368 Otto Reinhold on Radio DDR II, 19 August 1989; Bundespresseamt (BPA), *DDR Spiegel*, 22 August 1989.

369 Transcript (*Niederschrift*) of talks between Gorbachev and Honecker on 28 June 1989 in Moscow, SED Politburo, *Arbeitsprotokolle*, Central Party Archives, J IV 2/2A/3228 (indirect speech).

Gorbachev, to the extent that he recognized this as a problem, did have a point was the erosion of the communist system at the societal level as a result of the access of the vast majority of East Germans to West German television and radio broadcasts and the increasing number intra-German visits and exchanges, which sharpened perceptions in the GDR of the tremendous discrepancy in the quality of life between East and West Germany and increased popular pressures for liberalization in the GDR. Yet this very fact points to other contradictions and inconsistencies in Gorbachev's approach. If limitation of West German influence was his goal, he should have encouraged Honecker to curtail the intra-German contacts and exchanges. Yet in the interest of reaching agreement on a final document at the CSCE follow-on conference in Vienna, he put pressure on East Berlin to agree to the very human rights provisions that had the strongest potential for undermining the "socialist foundations" in the GDR. At the very least, Gorbachev was pursuing mutually exclusive objectives. A confident and consistent implementation of his reform socialist objective in the GDR would have required a trilateral approach: the coordination of Soviet, West German, and East German policies. Not even the hint of such an approach can be discerned before it was too late.

Finally, it is difficult to form a definite opinion as to whether Gorbachev really believed the incessant East German progress reports and his own remarks, repeated many times in conversation with Honecker, that the GDR had already taken the direction of socio-economic development that the Soviet Union belatedly was only beginning to pursue and that the GDR was a bedrock of stability that could easily afford reform. If so, he would have been in good company. Many Western observers, including many specialists on East Germany, were thinking along similar lines. As the year 1989 progressed, however, such perceptions became untenable. This raises the problem of what it was that Gorbachev's own German specialists were telling him. Is it fair to conclude that many of the inconsistencies in his approach were due to conflicting advice and perhaps bureaucratic conflict among the *germanisty* involved in policy-making? And who was instrumental in changing established policies and charting an entirely new course from the adherence to the concept of two separate German states to the acceptance of German unification? These questions will be addressed in the next chapter.

Chapter 5: Domestic Implications of Gorbachev's German Policy

1. The Institutional Setting

The inquiry thus far has been conducted at two levels of analysis. The first has been that of Gorbachev as a political leader and has focussed on his personality and political philosophy. The second has treated the Soviet Union as a "rational actor" in the international system and has been concerned with Moscow's problems of maintaining and then modifying its global influence in relation to the scientific-technological revolution, the mounting costs of empire, and the emancipatory aspirations of its dependencies. The examination in this chapter proceeds at a middle level of analysis. It is concerned with the question of what was happening *inside* the "black box" of decision-making, that is, with the impact of group, elite, bureaucratic, and "non-rational" factors on foreign policy. It features an analysis of the role of the CPSU, the Politburo, and the Central Committee Secretariat with its various subordinate departments; the Soviet foreign ministry and its subdivisions; the defense ministry and the armed forces; the KGB; and the academic institutes specializing in international affairs. This level is particularly relevant in the Soviet imperial context, where internal party politics were typically transnational, with various leaders and groups of the CPSU maintaining manifold contacts with the communist parties of the dependencies. But it also raises the question of how the center's institutions with their own vested interests in confirming the legitimacy and effectiveness of four decades of policy on the German problem could change course so abruptly and completely.

To provide an overview of the main argument and the main stages of development, Gorbachev's initial idea – as noted earlier – was to reinvigorate and revitalize the party, increase its power and authority, create a strong reformist core, appoint competent and dedicated leaders at its middle echelons, and use it as an instrument with which to modernize the country. By the end of the Twenty-seventh CPSU congress in late February and early March 1986, a nucleus of reformist leaders had been formed in the Politburo and was beginning to consolidate its power; there were now twelve new faces out of twenty-seven in the Soviet top leadership (full and candidate members of the Politburo and secretaries of the Central Committee).[370] However, whereas personnel change-over at the top was rapid, the transmission of changes *from the top* was painfully slow. This was due to half-hearted and often ill-advised measures conceived at the highest levels of decision-making, but also to bureaucratic inertia, procrastination, and resistance at the lower and middle echelons of the party.

---

370 Brown, *The Gorbachev Factor*, p. 160.

Beginning with the January 1987 Central Committee plenum, the paradigm for change was substantially revised. Its central element came to be *demokratizatsiia*, the main purpose of which was the supplementation of change at and from the top with changes *from below*. The bloated and inefficient party apparatus was to be put under pressure not only by a reformist leadership but also by a politically conscious and socially active citizenry. Within the party, recalcitrant segments were also to be pressured by greater openness of discussion, transparency of decision-making, and choice among several candidates for election to party offices. The vivid and often acrimonious exchanges at the Nineteenth Party Conference in June 1988, originally conceived of as a forum at which to effect further personnel changes, were the high point of intra-party discourse but also the beginning of a new tack decided upon by Gorbachev – the weakening of the central party apparat, which still constituted a formidable barrier to radical reform, and the establishment of new state and legislative bodies to assume some of the CPSU's functions. These objectives were met, in part, by the comprehensive reorganization of the Central Committee departments at its September 1988 plenary meeting, which decreed the merger of the three departments dealing with foreign affairs and created six Central Committee Commissions. Legislative and executive power were strengthened by Gorbachev's assuming the presidency of the Supreme Soviet and by elections to the first Congress of People's Deputies from March to May 1989. The democratic credentials of this "outer" parliament that was to elect an "inner" parliament – a new Supreme Soviet – were still questionable. One-third of the 2,250 deputies were to be delegates from various "public organizations," of which the CPSU and the Trade Unions had a hundred seats each, but the other two-thirds were to elected directly by territorial constituencies. The elections for the vast majority of the latter seats (73 percent according to some calculations) were multi-candidate, genuinely contested, by secret ballot, and preceded by vigorous debate.[371] The period just before and after the first Congress was a time of euphoria. These were the days when radical democrats thought that reform of the party was not only possible but the only route to change.[372]

The logic of comprehensive and radical transformation necessitated action in six dimensions of policy. The first was the *political* realm, the direction of change required to proceed from a totalitarian one-party state to a parliamentary democracy. The second lay in the *legal* system, which had to move from arbitrary and voluntarist party rule to a system based on the rule of law. The third was in the *economic* area and provided for shifts from a command economy and state ownership of the means of production to private property and the market. The fourth concerned *defense and*

371 Miller, *Gorbachev and the End of Soviet Power*, pp. 114-120; Brown, *The Gorbachev Factor*, p. 156.

372 Remnick, *Lenin's Tomb*, p. 220.

the military-industrial complex, the movement here envisaging the establishment of civilian control over the armed forces, defense conversion, and the curtailment of the power and influence of the military. The fifth was the *nationality and federative* problem, the logic of change in this area being the restructuring of the unitary, centralized state and the establishment of a genuine federation with new arrangements for power sharing. The sixth concerned *foreign policy*, the transformative dynamics in this realm aiming at the replacement of imperialism and the ideology of antagonism by a cooperative mind-set and institutions attuned to interdependence and international integration.

The difficulty and complexity of successfully managing this multifaceted transformation were enormous. The time frame in which it could be achieved would not be years but decades. This Gorbachev knew perfectly well. But the interconnectedness of issues was not always clearly comprehended by Gorbachev or, when it was, was often understood too late.[373] Most importantly for the ultimate outcome of the process, practically from the very beginning of "radical reform" he permitted severe imbalances to develop among the various dimensions of the required transformations. These imbalances concerned a rate of change in foreign policy that was much more rapid than in the domestic sphere; in internal affairs, political change that outpaced economic transformation; and evisceration of the party apparat and its authority that failed to be matched by the establishment and consolidation of new institutions. Most importantly, in an in principle laudable but in the circumstances ill-advised untiring attempt to build consensus, Gorbachev declined to split the party, shed the orthodox and conservative elements, form a new reform socialist or social democratic organization, and invest his power and authority with a new source of popular legitimacy. He never campaigned at the head of a new party on a platform of comprehensive and coherent political and economic reform. Until the end, his position as leader of the country derived not from popular elections but from the very institution which he was enervating – the CPSU.

This book is about the *foreign policy* dimension of change, rather than about domestic politics. But this focus requires reconstruction of a dialectic relationship between internal and external change. Its essence rests in the fact that transformative change domestically was inconceivable without repudiation of the internationalist precepts of Marxism-Leninism and the imperial legacy and, conversely, that the dismantling of empire and consent to German unification were impossible without emasculation of the institutions wedded to the old thinking. What will not be

373 This interpretation is controversial in the literature. Archie Brown, in particular, has persuasively argued that Gorbachev was quite conscious of the interrelatedness of change in all dimensions and that his aim, developed through a learning process, was social democracy in the Soviet Union. The counterargument here is that, although Gorbachev used the term, he saw its content differently than, say, West German social democrats.

attempted here is a detailed chronological account of the changes in all dimensions of policy. Instead the major events and trends in the international dimension affecting the German problem will be highlighted.

Some explanation of the structure of this chapter may also be appropriate. The structure replicates the process of radical change in the Soviet Union under Gorbachev. *Ideas* in that process came first. They were, predictably, not generated within the party apparat but by academic specialists. The latter were first to break new ground, and in many instances were deliberately asked to do so by members of the small core of reform-minded political leaders. This had the dual advantage of testing reactions and the strength of resistance in the party apparat and the military. Once the philosophical terrain had suitably been prepared, the reformist core would publicly and authoritatively associate itself with hitherto heretical positions. Given the fact that the Soviet system was built on ideology and that power, institutions, and ideology were inseparable, conceptual change was followed by replacement of personnel, institutional changes, and reallocation of resources. It is for this reason that the role of academic institutes and specialists will be examined first. Since the unconventional ideas were first endorsed by Shevardnadze, who was appointed foreign minister early in the reform process, in July 1985, and disseminated in the foreign ministry, his role and that of the ministry will be dealt with next. The major losers in the struggle for ideas and influence were the party apparat, to be reformed thoroughly or, more accurately, severely weakened in autumn 1988, as well as the defense ministry and the armed forces. The curtailment of their power in foreign policy will be analyzed next. It is the contention of this book that, contrary to the opinion held by some Western observers and Russians with a predilection for conspiracy theories, the KGB did not play an important part in either promoting or resisting change. Its role will be analyzed last.

2. The Academy of Sciences: International Relations Institutes and Specialists

Except for the Kennedy administration, it is difficult to find any political system and time period in which the influence of academic specialists on foreign policy-making was as significant as in the Soviet Union under Gorbachev. This phenomenon was particularly astounding if measured against past practice. Academic specialists had previously been constrained by censorship and the narrow parameters of Marxist-Leninist ideology. Their access to the top political leadership under previous leaders, with the partial exception of Andropov, was practically non-existent. Such influence as they were able to exert was through party channels, which often diluted and distorted their input. Nevertheless, the institutes on international affairs under the

USSR Academy of Sciences, with their contacts and exchanges with counterparts in Western countries, represented "oases" of independent thinking.[374]

The biggest, most prestigious and best connected of the former was (and still is) the Institute of World Economy and International Relations (IMEMO) at the USSR Academy of Sciences. Nikolai Inozemtsev had been its director in the 1970s and early 1980s. After his death, he was succeeded by Alexander Yakovlev in 1983, followed by Yevgeni Primakov in 1985. The institute played an important part in the conceptualization of Soviet foreign policy and was invariably involved in the preparation of the reports of the Central Committee delivered by the General Secretary to the CPSU party congresses, and it participated in the drafting of party documents and speeches by party leaders. IMEMO also spawned several specialized regional institutes, including the Institute for the Study of the USA and Canada (ISKAN) at the USSR Academy of Sciences, founded in 1967, with many of the researchers transferring from the former to the latter institute, including its first director, Georgi Arbatov.[375]

Important and influential as IMEMO may have been, the institute did not lend itself to a comprehensive reassessment of the German problem. The ideologically ordained assumption of the division of the world into two fundamentally opposed socio-economic systems, capitalism and socialism, was reflected in the separation of academic institutes dealing with either the politics and economics of the Western industrialized countries or that of the socialist community. IMEMO dealt with the former. IMEMO also did not have *Germanisty* that were politically well connected and influential. This was true for Danil Mel'nikov, an affable, competent, and well respected generalist on German affairs and Danil Proektor, a retired army officer, whose specialization were military and security issues.[376]

East Germany fell under the purview of the Institute for the Economics of the World Socialist System (IEMSS), headed by Oleg Bogomolov. This institute dealt not only with economic but also with political affairs pertaining to socialist countries. Even well before Gorbachev's ascendancy to power it was a repository of unconventional thinking. In 1979, for instance, it issued a report advising against military inter-

---

374 Arbatov (*The System*, pp. 63-93) used this metaphor to describe the role of academic specialists in various institutions, including the institutes at the USSR Academy of Sciences.

375 Arbatov had worked at IMEMO. In 1967, when he founded ISKAN, he was working for Andropov at the CC as a member of a Group of Consultants.

376 I had the opportunity to discuss German issues with both researchers – at IMEMO, at the Stiftung Wissenschaft und Politik in Ebenhausen, and at international conferences. Mel'nikov struck me as having a far more independent mind than Proektor. What was particularly vexing and disappointing was the fact that the latter, in frequent discussions at SWP, would express understanding for West German views on European security, while the articles he published subsequently lacked any such understanding.

vention in Afghanistan.[377] On its staff were also some of the most radical critics of Soviet policy on the German problem – Viacheslav Dashichev, head of IEMSS's foreign policy section, and Alexander Tsipko, a specialist on Poland and East Germany. Their inputs to policy-making on the German problem will be discussed later.

It was not until January 1988, with Gorbachev's Common European Home firmly established as a slogan, that an Institute on Europe was founded. Vitali Zhurkin, a specialist on U.S. and arms control matters, was its founding director and Vladimir Shenaev, an expert on German economic affairs, was its deputy director, the directing staff later to be joined by Sergei Karaganov.[378] The foundation of the institute presented the opportunity to integrate research, conferences, and policy advice on both Western Europe and Eastern Europe as well as on East and West Germany, but the opportunity was missed. The research and policy-making agenda remained focussed on Western Europe.

Independent minds could be found not only in institutes on international relations but in some of the Central Committee departments (these will be dealt with later), as well as in some newspapers and journals. For instance, the *World Marxist Review*, with its head offices in Prague, was one of the breeding grounds of non-conformist thought. Given its intended function – to spread the CPSU's interpretation of Marxism-Leninism in the international communist movement – the journal may seem even in retrospect a rather unlikely place for relative intellectual autonomy. And indeed, the articles it published were for the most part uninspiring, rehashing the CPSU's line. But, as occasionally happened in the Soviet system, the special position it enjoyed depended less on the purposes of its foundation and the institutional setting than on its personalities and *their* power and influence. In this case, its importance as an oasis of independent thought derived in large measure from Alexei Rumyantsev, its editor-in-chief, who attracted talented and creative writers to the journal and was not afraid to defend them.[379] Among these were Chernyaev, Shakhnazarov, and Ivan Frolov (all three were subsequently to become personal assistants to Gorbachev), and Georgi Arbatov, later the head of the Institute of the USA and Canada.[380]

---

377 Bogomolov confirmed this in conversation with this author, as did Dashichev and Tsipko. The point that the Institute of Economics of the World Socialist System advised against intervention, but that the advice was disregarded, was also made in various articles and interviews by other staff members of the institute.

378 Shenaev wrote his doctoral thesis on the West German currency reform in 1948. In contrast to Zhurkin, he harbored deft anti-American sentiments. When I visited the institute in October 1988, I had a heated exchange with him on the role of the United States in Europe. The discussion ended – abruptly – when he slammed his fist on the table and exclaimed that the United States had "absolutely no business in Europe."

379 Arbatov, *The System*, p. 80.

380 Chernyaev was appointed advisor on foreign policy in February 1986; Shakhnazarov, to deal with Eastern Europe, in October 1988; and Ivan Frolov, to advise on ideological issues, in January 1987.

Perhaps even more paradoxically, another oasis in the intellectual desert under Brezhnev was the Socialist Countries Department under Andropov in the 1960s.[381] The Group of Consultants he gathered around him reads almost like a Who's Who of advocates of an improvement in Soviet relations with the West and of theoreticians of the New Thinking. They included Arbatov, Bogomolov, and Shakhnazarov, who have already been mentioned; Fyodor Burlatsky, an eminent political scientist and head of one of the sub-departments; Alexander Bovin, who later became a well known journalist writing as political commentator for *Izvestiia*; Nikolai Shishlin, a political scientist and publicist; and Gennadi Gerasimov, who later became spokesman for the foreign ministry.[382] Since Gorbachev was an Andropov protégé, it is not surprising that all of them were to play a role in one capacity or another when the former came to power.

The outlines of the New Thinking were drawn in the previous chapter. What is necessary here is to reconstruct in more detail and more precisely the major departures from old thinking, to associate them with personalities and institutions, and to identify the main institutional targets or victims of the new thought. To emphasize the main point of this endeavor, since ideas and ideology and the Soviet system were intimately connected with power and resources, the challenge to traditional Soviet thinking on foreign policy and international security issues was bound to detract from the power and authority of the institutions that were the mainstays of empire – the party apparatus and the military.

Erosion and Collapse of Ideology. Concerning Marxist-Leninist ideology, as on all other major issues, the Gorbachev era began with modest revision, produced a chain reaction that spun out of control and ended in collapse. This process in the international dimensions of ideology began with a reinterpretation of "peaceful coexistence." Previous attempts at expanding cooperative relations with capitalist states had been hampered by the dogma about "irreconcilable contradictions" between the two world systems. Even in the era of significant revision of the dogma under Khrushchev, peaceful coexistence was still regarded as a "special form of class struggle," and this was also the main emphasis given to the concept under Brezhnev, Andropov, and Chernenko. As the Gorbachev era progressed, it was not capitalism that was "buried" but the very idea of class struggle. "Marxism as such," claimed Yakovlev, "is the understanding of *common interests* from the viewpoint of history and the perspective of the development of *all humanity* and not just certain of its countries and classes."[383] Peace was declared to have priority over the class struggle. The indivisibility of international security was underlined, and the way to achieve

---

381 Andropov was head of the department from 1962 to 1967.

382 Arbatov, *The Soviet System*, p. 88.

383 Speech in Vilnius, *Pravda*, 13 August 1988 (italics mine).

security was said to be not by military-technical means but by political efforts. War in the nuclear age was proclaimed to be "inadmissible" (*nedopustimyi*), a statement with which the theoreticians of the New Thinking made short shrift of the previously elaborate distinctions between "just" and "unjust" wars.

Formalized perceptions of the basic structural features of the opposed socio-economic system were also revised. The orthodox Leninist view of imperialism ("the highest stage of capitalism") as inherently and irrevocably aggressive, structurally incapable of disarming, and therefore attempting to solve its deepening systemic crisis by militarism was first put in doubt and then abandoned. One IMEMO analyst even engaged in the time-honored practice of nonconformist analysts in the Soviet era to discredit orthodox Marxist-Leninist notions by attributing them to Western theorists. "It is inadmissible," he wrote, "to agree with the assertions by certain Western [sic] politicians and researchers to the effect that disarmament inevitably leads to economic decline and an increase in unemployment." Past experience had shown that conversion of military resources was "achieved without serious negative consequences both in socialist and in capitalist countries."[384]

Military Power as a Questionable Means to Achieve Political Influence. On the practical issues of foreign policy, academic specialists expressed doubt as to both the effectiveness and the legitimacy of the use of military power for political ends, and they thereby questioned the rationale of the Soviet attempt to maintain parity in the military-strategic realm and preponderance in conventional weapons. They certainly, not least through their contacts with Western colleagues, were conscious of both the costs of empire and the "paradox of superpower" – enormous military power but a weak and declining socio-economic base. They argued for a better balance between military and other means of exerting influence in world affairs; improvement of the Soviet record on human rights; enhancement of the Soviet Union's diplomatic, political and cultural presence in countries and organizations in which it had been underrepresented or not represented at all; participation at the international economic level in organizations such as General Agreement on Tariffs and Trade (GATT) and the International Monetary Fund (IMF); and the construction not only of legal, organizational ties but also of *political* arrangements with the European Community. In order to reduce the costs of empire, contain the political repercussions over relations with the United States and other countries, and lessen the risk of counter-intervention or counterrevolution supported by the USA, they advocated scaling down existing international involvements, above all in Afghanistan, and avoidance of new commitments, in particular *military* engagements. The Soviet Union, as

384 R. A. Faramazian, *Gonka vooruzhenii v stranakh NATO*, published under the auspices of the Scientific Council for Research on Problems of Peace and Disarmament at the Institute for World Economy and International Relations (IMEMO) (Moscow: Nauka, 1988), pp. 184-85.

Primakov argued in June 1988, "has taken the firm decision to scale down its military presence abroad."[385]

Foreign Policy Decision-Making. In accordance with the criticism of the over-emphasis on the military instrument in foreign policy, academic specialists attacked the previous predominance of military rationales. The Soviet intervention in Afghanistan and the decision to station SS-20 intermediate-range nuclear missiles in Europe and Asia were mentioned as particularly glaring examples of such a mistaken approach to international security affairs.[386] "Overcentralization" in foreign policy-making was assailed as one of the many "deformations" that did "great harm to Soviet national security interests."[387] Decisions, as Dashichev deplored, were made by the "elite," by a few leaders, by Brezhnev, Suslov, Ustinov, perhaps also Gromyko. "Unfortunately, the experts' voices did not have any influence. And the public received no information at all."[388] Concerning the INF issue, they said that the decision to produce and deploy the SS-20 missiles and to do so rapidly and in great numbers was motivated by an erroneous definition of security interests; by a false sense of needing overinsurance and superiority in numbers ("the more missiles, the more stable [Soviet] security");[389] and "by technological advances rather than political analysis."[390]

Redefinition of Threats. The theoreticians of New Thinking also redefined the nature of threats facing the USSR. They pointed out that in the past, notably in the "period of stagnation" under Brezhnev, a number of factors had contributed to the construction of certain stereotypes of the enemy (*obrazy vraga*). These had included the "consideration of the differences and contradictions between the two social systems and between individual countries as an absolute given;" the adherence to "ideological remnants of the theory of 'world revolution;'" and the "clinging to secretiveness, suspicion, and impenetrable 'monolithism.'"[391]

---

385 Yevgeni Primakov, "USSR Policy on Regional Conflicts," *International Affairs* (Moscow), No. 6 (June 1988), p. 7.

386 A good example of this were the replies to questions from viewers by Nikolai Shishlin, deputy chief of the CPSU Central Committee's propaganda department, Moscow television service, in Russian, 26 July 1988.

387 Viacheslav Dashichev, "Vostok–Zapad: poisk novykh otnoshenii: O prioritetakh vneshnei politiki Sovetskogo gosudarstva," *Literaturnaia gazeta*, 18 May 1988; see also his interview with the West German news magazine, *Der Spiegel*, 4 July 1988, p. 124.

388 Dashichev, interview in *Der Spiegel*.

389 Igor Malaschenko, "Warum bauen wir mehr Raketen ab?," *Neue Zeit* (Moscow), No. 7 (1988), p. 21.

390 Sergei Vybornov, Andrei Gusenkov, and Vladimir Leontiev, "Nothing Is Simple in Europe," *International Affairs* (Moscow), No. 3 (March 1988), p. 41.

391 A. Iu. Mel'vil, "'Obraz vraga' i novoe politicheskoe myshlenie," *SShA*, No. 1 (January 1988), p. 34.

They also asked whether "our orthodox social scientists, armed with quotations, have not painted the world in extreme moralistic colors as an arena in which 'good' and 'evil' are struggling with each other."[392] In their view, it was necessary to dispose of the idea that a competitor invariably had to be considered an "enemy." One had to embark on a "radical departure from the traditions of the past," on a "de-escalation of political rhetoric" and the "emancipation from those of its forms which are most strongly ideological and portraying matters as absolute."[393] Zhurkin admitted that "you, me, political commentators, scientists as well as the military press overstated the threat of war ... at a time when a rationally organized nuclear attack on the Soviet Union was impossible because a retaliatory response would have followed."[394]

Public opinion polls were one of the important facets of glasnost and were used to support rethinking in international politics. A case in point was the publication of a survey of threat perceptions of West Germany and the Germans conducted in May 1989 (see Table 4).[395] The timing is important since this was a period before discussion about German unification had affected Russian opinion. The survey revealed a wide discrepancy between decades of hostile anti-West German propaganda and public perceptions. Only a small minority felt threatened by the Federal Republic. To the extent that threat perceptions existed they were of a "theoretical" nature or most likely derived from the view that West Germany could be *drawn* into a war by the United States (about a quarter of the respondents felt that the Soviet Union was threatened by the other superpower).

Reconsideration of the Content and Importance of the "Correlation of Forces." Another important change in thinking on security matters was the strong emphasis on economic components in the "correlation of forces." Views were expressed to the effect that "in our contemporary world the parameters of world power are determined first and foremost by economic, scientific, and technical indicators;"[396] that after the advent of mutual deterrence the imperialist countries, notably the United States and its Defense Department, had changed tack and devised a new strategy aimed at "economically exhausting the USSR through a lengthy arms race" and "formulating

392 Ibid.

393 Ibid., pp. 30 and 39.

394 In a discussion on Soviet television with Deputy Minister of Foreign Affairs Vladimir Petrovsky and V. S. Zorin, political observer of Soviet TV and moderator of the discussion, 30 July 1988, *FBIS*-SOV-88-148, 2 August 1988.

395 "Obraz nemtsa i FRG v SSSR," *Moskovskie novosti*, No. 25, 18 June 1989, p. 7. The poll was conducted by telephone between 12 and 14 May 1989. There were 851 respondents.

396 Vitali Zhurkin, Sergei Karaganov, and Andrei Kortunov, "Vyzovy bezopasnosti – starye i novye," *Kommunist*, No. 1 (January 1988), pp. 47-48; see also their "O razumnoi dostatochnosti," *SShA*, No. 12 (December 1987), pp. 13-14.

Table 4 – Threat Perceptions of Germany

1. Do you personally feel that the USSR is threatened by West Germany?

Yes, strongly	3
Theoretically there is a threat, but for all practical purposes it does not exist	20
No, I don't feel that it is	54
There is no threat whatsoever	17

2. Do you think that war with West Germany in this century is possible?

Practically impossible	66
Not very probable but I don't exclude such a possibility	29
The possibility of war with the FRG is quite high	1

3. From which country or region do you feel the USSR is threatened most?

USA	19
FRG	3
Near East	2
Asian Countries	2
Britain, France	0.6
Don't feel threatened by any country	54

military programs, 'to which an effective Soviet response would be substantially more costly than the programs themselves,'"[397] so that what was needed were "real results from perestroika and in particular an equalization of the balance between military and nonmilitary opportunities in international affairs."[398] Since the end of the 1970s, the military had warned that modern, technologically sophisticated armed forces could only be maintained on the basis of a modern, efficient economy. They had also asserted that it was the aim of NATO to redirect the arms race into the technological sphere and thereby impoverish and defeat the Warsaw Pact countries.[399] But academic specialists and the military had different views as to how the Soviet Union should cope with such a challenge. The idea of the civilian specialists was to reform and modernize the economy rather than to continue pouring resources into the

397 Zhurkin et al., "Vyzovy bezopasnosti," pp. 47-48.

398 Vladimir Lukin in discussion with Alexander Bovin, "Na poroge novogo veka," *MEMO*, No. 12 (December 1987), p. 53.

399 For a statement to that effect see, for instance, the Warsaw Pact commander in chief, Marshal V. G. Kulikov, *Doktrina zashchity mira i sotsializma. O voennoi doktrine gosudarstvuchastnikov Varshavskogo Dogovora* (Moscow: Voenizdat, 1988), p. 83.

military-industrial sector. Gorbachev and the foreign ministry agreed with the civilian rather than the military viewpoint.[400]

Military Doctrine. The challenge of academic specialists was extended to one of the most sensitive and most jealously guarded preserve of the military – military doctrine. Military parity in the past had been measured against the sum total of the military capabilities of all the major potential adversaries combined, that is, the USA, Western Europe, Japan, and China. Military strategy had to meet the criterion of the armed forces' ability successfully to conduct offensive operations and to inflict "annihilating blows" on the enemy. Civilian analysts explicitly attacked such wide definitions of security requirements as militarily unnecessary and economically damaging and advocated instead the construction of military forces that would meet the requirement of "reasonable sufficiency" (*razumnaia dostatochnost'*).[401] They ventured into the history of warfare and tried to show that strategic conventional defense often proved superior to offense. Vitali Shlykov, a free-lance journalist, engaged in a particularly scathing and uncompromising attack on military incompetence and the military's predilection for quantitative superiority. Whereas the World War II tank battle of Kursk had been used by other writers to demonstrate the advantages of defense over offense,[402] Shlykov demonstrated that on the eve of World War II the Soviet tank forces had been quantitatively superior to those of the Germans,[403] and he chastised as obsolete the "pre-nuclear thinking" (still rampant in the military) that tanks were a "kind of universal equivalent of military power" that could make up for the lack of combat skill.[404] This reinterpretation of military history justified force reductions and emphasis on quality rather than quantity. It also posited as an important aim in conventional arms control negotiations the restructuring of the armed forces of NATO and the Warsaw Pact so that they would have a mutual "structural inability" to launch an attack, and in particular a surprise attack.[405] Move-

---

400 See, for instance, Gorbachev's speeches at a meeting in Vladivostok on 28 July 1986, *Pravda*, 29 July 1986, and at the Eighteenth congress of the Soviet trade unions on February 25, 1987, *Pravda*, 26 February 1987. The MFA's support of these views was expressed by Deputy Foreign Minister Petrovsky in a discussion on Soviet television on 30 July 1988, *FBIS*-SOV-88-148, 2 August 1988.

401 See V. Zhurkin, S. Karaganov and A. Kortunov, "Vyzovy bezopasnosti" and id., "O razumnoi dostatochnosti."

402 Kokoshin and Larionov, "Kurskaia bitva."

403 Vitalii Shlykov, "On the History of Tank Asymmetry in Europe," *International Affairs* (Moscow), No. 10 (1988).

404 Vitalii Shlykov, "'Strong Is the Armor:' Tank Asymmetry and Real Security," *International Affairs* (Moscow), No. 12 (1988), p. 39.

405 Andrei A. Kokoshin and V. Larionov, "Kurskaia bitva v svete sovremennoi oboronitel'noi doktriny," *MEMO*, No. 8 (August 1987), pp. 32-40; id., "Protivostoianie sil obshchego naznacheniia v kontekste obespecheniia strategicheskoi stabil'nosti," *MEMO*, No. 16 (June 1988), pp. 23-31.

ment towards such objectives was clearly reflected in Gorbachev's announcement of December 1988 to withdraw 6 tank divisions and other forces and equipment from Eastern Europe.

To return to the question of why the New Thinking could be to be put into practice and how it was possible to ignore or overrule the most powerful vested interests in the Soviet national security bureaucracy, it is useful to refer to decision-making on the December 1987 Washington INF treaty. Policy-making on the treaty was one of the earliest examples of the effective interplay between the foreign ministry and academic specialists. It set a pattern that was to be repeated on several important foreign policy and international security issues, including the German problem. Alexei Arbatov, at the time of the INF negotiations head of IMEMO's arms control and disarmament section and member of an advisory group on arms control at the foreign ministry, has aptly summed up the pattern. An initial negotiating position would be formulated by an interagency commission consisting of the Defense Ministry, as represented by the General Staff; the Central Committee's Department for Defense; the Military-Industrial Commission (VPK); the Ministry of Foreign Affairs; and the KGB. The first three institutions formed a powerful coalition whose positions were coordinated from the very beginning and were not easily reversible by the top party leadership. Indeed, when presented with a consensus decision by this or other important commissions, Gorbachev would usually approve it. How, then, was it possible to overcome military opposition? The answer that Arbatov gives to this question is the close cooperation between the academic institutes and the foreign ministry and "back-channeling."

> Shevardnadze very often used the tactic [of back-channelling] if he could not [openly] oppose the opinion of other agencies. Being in a minority of one, he would accept [their opinion] for some time, even knowing that it would not be accepted at the negotiations. Then he would get reactions from the West, and then he would bring those reactions back to Gorbachev, and give him his consideration. Shevardnadze was not permanently at the negotiations and he brought these reactions, and arguments and counterarguments, to the attention of Gorbachev and Yakovlev. In this process the Academy of Sciences, with its conferences, which were regularly – actually permanently – going on, either between East and West or between Americans and Soviets on a bilateral basis, was very active. In particular, there were two institutes at the Academy, the Institute on the Study of the USA and Canada and the Institute on World Economy and International Relations (IMEMO) ... which very closely cooperated with the Foreign Ministry. I would even venture to say that the Foreign Ministry on its own would not have been capable of withstanding the pressure of all the other agencies in the establishment.[406]

406 "Policy Formation in the USSR on the INF Treaty: An Interview with Alexei Arbatov," Nuclear History Program (NHP), Oral History Transcript, Center for International Security Studies at

The portrayal reveals that the practice of decision-making by a small circle of leaders, a practice decried so much by the academic specialists, was *not* broken. However, the previous small circle of leaders, such as Brezhnev, Suslov, Ustinov, and Gromyko, was replaced by another, consisting of Gorbachev and his personal assistants, Shevardnadze and Yakovlev. There were two more differences. In contrast to the preceding period, civilian institutions – the MFA and the academic institutes – were being involved more prominently in international security affairs, and the content of policy was different. Obviously, not all radical advice was deemed acceptable or practical. Not all academic specialists were equally influential or had equal access to the top decision-makers. But almost invariably their input had *some* impact. This applies even to some of the most controversial advice on one of the most sensitive topics – the German problem.

An example of this is the role of Dashichev. In January 1987, in his capacity as IEMSS *sektor* head, he wrote a critical analysis of Soviet foreign policy in the 1970s and early 1980s.[407] He radically attacked the whole conceptual basis of Soviet policy and, in particular, decried the expansion of the Soviet sphere of influence by military means; the pretension to be militarily equal to all other powers; the build-up of a blue-water navy that exceeded any reasonable definition of security needs; the deployment of the SS-20 intermediate-range nuclear missiles; overemphasis on the "peace movement" in Western Europe; and risky guarantees to shaky Third World regimes. He also made some policy recommendations, suggesting democratic legitimation and parliamentary control of foreign policy and the establishment of foreign affairs committees that would have both controlling and advisory functions in relation to the foreign ministry.

The report was forwarded by IEMSS director Bogomolov to Shevardnadze. In contrast to the state of affairs under the *ancien régime*, the report elicited a positive response. In March 1987, Dashichev was appointed chairman of the Scientific Advisory Council at the MFA's socialist countries' department, a body founded to contribute to the solution of foreign policy problems and, after Shevardnadze's appointment, to promote the New Thinking in the foreign ministry. Upon Dashichev's initiative, on 27 November 1987 – for the first time since the 1950s! – the council dealt with the German problem. Various options for change in intra-German relations were being discussed, including the possibility and desirability of German

---

Maryland School of Public Affairs, University of Maryland, NHP Transcript No. 3 [n.d]. Alexei Arbatov is the son of ISKAN Director Georgi Arbatov.

407 Dashichev's analytical report or memorandum was dated 4 January 1987. The text was published in German translation in *Osteuropa* (May 1993), pp. 485-90. The subsequent portrayal of how Shevardnadze and the MFA bureaucracy treated the report is based on Wjatscheslaw Daschitschew, "Wie das Umdenken in der sowjetischen Außenpolitik begann," *Osteuropa* (May 1993), pp. 482-83.

unification. Dashichev argued that the division of Germany harmed Soviet national interests and that it was necessary to change Soviet policy on the German problem and direct it towards closer relations between the two Germanys and eventual reunification. This heretical idea, as he has written, was rejected by the participants in the meeting but a taboo was broken.[408]

One of the questions that has puzzled Western scholars is Dashichev's putative impact on Soviet or, more precisely, Gorbachev's, Shevardnadze's, and Yakovlev's thinking. Addressing this issue, Karaganov has explained that in the Soviet foreign policy establishment there were four schools of thought on the German problem.[409] The first was that of *No Change and Don't Touch It*. The second could be described as *Let's Appear Flexible But Adhere to the Status Quo*, its rationale being that such a stance would provide the Soviet Union with leverage over West German and East German policies. The third could be labelled *Let's Be Flexible and Keep an Open Mind*. This openness extended to the possibility of eventual German reunification. The fourth was that of *Take the Initiative Now* and actively work towards German unification rather than be faced with unplanned and unmanageable conditions later. Adherents for the first position could be found in the foreign ministry and the party apparatus. Majority opinion was that of schools two and three. The last school, according to Karaganov, had only *one* advocate – Dashichev.

Kvitsinsky has dryly remarked that Dashichev "elevated himself to the role of an advisor to Gorbachev, which was untrue but was not refuted by anyone."[410] It was refuted. When German unification was on the international agenda, but its status in European security undecided, MFA spokesman Yuri Gremitskikh asserted that "Professor Dashichev and his political allies are not members of the expert community participating in working out Soviet policies."[411] Similarly, Tsipko has confirmed that Dashichev "supported the idea of the German unification and united Germany's membership in NATO" but called the idea that he may have had significant influence on Soviet policy-making on the German problem a "myth."[412] But he has also made an observation that may shed some light on why it is that so many of Dashichev's contemporaries have deprecated his role. Tsipko has stated that in the period until the fall of 1989 he read many documents compiled by various

---

408 Ibid.

409 Karaganov in conversation with the author (Moscow, May 1990). For the four schools of thought in the context of four stages in the evolution of Soviet policy on the German problem, see Sergei Karaganov, "Implications of German Unification for the Former Soviet Union," in Paul B. Stares, ed., *The New Germany in the New Europe* (Washington, D.C.: Brookings Institution, 1992), pp. 331-64. The labels of convenience used here for the schools of thought are my own, not Karaganov's.

410 Kwizinskij, *Vor dem Sturm*, p. 13.

411 TASS, 4 April 1990.

412 Interview with Tsipko.

institutes at the Academy of Sciences advocating the idea that we need to support closer relations between the two German states. "However, none of these documents considered the possibility of German unification and NATO membership. This was lacking."[413] Dashichev, in contrast, *had* considered this possibility and supported turning it into reality. He had, thereby, committed an offense, serious even in the era of New Thinking. He was right – but too early.

But why was there no comprehensive reconsideration and implementation of change in Soviet policy on the German problem in 1985-89? The reasons for this failure, to be explored further in the following sections, are not that Gorbachev and his associates were frustrated in any attempt to embark on new initiatives by a determined party and military opposition, and not that advice to depart from previous approaches was lacking. They themselves *and* the majority of academic specialists thought it expedient to stay the traditional course and were not to be deflected from it by counsel provided by a minority of one. This interim conclusion can be confirmed by an analysis of the role of the foreign ministry in policy-making on the German problem.

3. The Ministry of Foreign Affairs

In the period of Soviet imperial construction and decline the role of the foreign ministry in the Soviet Union, in comparison to that in other communist systems, was an anomaly. Its influence on policy-making was far greater in Moscow than in other communist capitals. Although, as noted, the Soviet Constitution allocated to the CPSU the "leading role" in politics and society, including in foreign policy, in practice the foreign ministry held a preeminent position in its functional realm. This was due in large measure to the authority and power which Gromyko had acquired in his almost forty years as foreign minister. Chernyaev has even characterized Gromyko as having exercised a "monopoly" in foreign policy.[414] This was to some extent the result of the specific features of his career. Gromyko was appointed chief of the American desk at the foreign ministry in 1939. He participated in his capacity as embassy counselor and then as ambassador to Washington in the war-time conferences in Teheran, Yalta, and Potsdam, and he headed the ministry starting in 1957. In the various capacities, he had dealt with each and every American president from Roosevelt to Reagan! Given the fact that Soviet-American relations had been a central concern of Soviet diplomacy in the Cold War and that Gromyko embodied the institutional memory of the ministry, he had an important competitive advantage in domestic power struggles over foreign policy. This is indicated, for instance, by his

---

413 Ibid.

414 Chernyaev, *Shest' let s Gorbachevym*, p. 49.

promotion to full membership in the Politburo in 1973, whereas another long-serving head of a rival party institution, chief of the Central Committee's International Department (ID) Boris Ponomarev, was able to advance only in 1971 to the position of candidate member, his further advancement being blocked by Gromyko.[415] He remained "perennially first among the second."[416]

New thinking or new policies were hardly to be expected from Gromyko. This was true most of all with regard to the German problem. He was thoroughly preoccupied with Soviet-American relations and preferred to deal with European affairs over the heads of the Europeans. The rising international influence of West Germany he regarded with as much suspicion and irritation as Honecker's policy of making political concessions in exchange for West German credits.[417] But it was Gromyko's conservative attitudes and policies in general, not his central focus on the United States or his stance on the German problem, that induced Gorbachev early in his tenure as General Secretary to appoint a new head of the foreign ministry. To almost everyone's surprise, the person to succeed him was not one of the professional diplomats preferred by the incumbent – Georgi Kornienko, Anatoli Dobrynin, or Yuli Vorontsov – but Eduard Shevardnadze, an "outsider."[418] Gromyko "initially almost seemed shocked."[419] Shevardnadze, too was unprepared: "To say that I was surprised would be an understatement," he has written about the telephone call in which the party leader asked him to take the MFA position. Gorbachev notes in his memoirs that the appointment both "nationally and internationally was met with immeasurable astonishment" and goes on to say: "Many people expressed incomprehension and disapproval because a non-Russian was given responsibility for this extraordinarily important function."[420] However, the ethnic factor was neither a salient criterion for Shevardnadze's appointment nor the primary reason for the consternation and concern among MFA officials at his appointment.

---

415 Interview with Zagladin; Chernyaev, *Shest' let s Gorbachevym*, p. 12.

416 The characterization of Ponomarev as "perennially first among the second" is Chernyaev's; ibid.

417 Some of the evidence presented here of Gromyko's uncompromising attitudes on the German problem and his annoyance and irritation with both West German and East German policies has included his attempt to force Honecker to inform his Politburo colleagues about Soviet-East German differences; his criticism of Honecker on the debt and dependency issue; his hard line towards Bonn on the stationing of intermediate-range nuclear missiles; his stance in the August 1984 emergency meeting in Moscow on all major issues of both East German and West German foreign policy; and the catalog of complaints and grievances handed to visiting West German president von Weizsäcker in July 1987.

418 Chernyaev, *Shest' let s Gorbachevym*, pp. 48-49; Chernyaev also puts Chervonenko on the list of possible replacements for Gromyko. Kornienko, Vorontsov, and Dobrynin were specifically mentioned by Gromyko when he and Gorbachev discussed the issue in a Politburo meeting at the beginning of July 1985. The meeting included Shevardnadze, who had been asked to attend; Gorbachev, *Zhizn'*, Vol. 1, p. 288.

419 Ibid.

420 Ibid.

Gorbachev justified his choice by claiming that the *party* should be in charge of foreign relations.[421] After the October revolution, Soviet foreign ministers had belonged to one of two categories. In one group were those, like Chicherin, Litvinov, and, at the time of his appointment, Gromyko, who had relatively little political power but were chosen for their professional skill. In the second category were those, notably Trotsky, Molotov, and to some extent Shepilov, who enjoyed a certain stature in the party or had close personal ties to the party leader. Shevardnadze clearly belonged to the second group.[422] In choosing an outsider as foreign minister and having the Central Committee elect him as a full member to the Politburo, Gorbachev was applying the same logic that he would later, in 1989, apply to the CPSU: that it would be difficult, if not impossible, for an institution and its personnel with vested interests to embark on fundamental organizational and conceptual change.

There were other reasons for Gorbachev to opt for Shevardnadze: "He successfully contended with difficult circumstances in Georgia; he is courageous, has a sense of what is new and [is able to] develop new approaches."[423] Discussing his plans with KGB chief Chebrikov and party secretary Ligachev, he also argued: "The future [foreign] minister should, in my opinion, be an eminent political personality."[424] Experience in foreign affairs was not a criterion for his choice. This he clarified in conversation with Shevardnadze. "No experience? Well, perhaps that's a good thing. Our foreign policy needs a fresh eye, courage, dynamism, and innovative approaches.[425]

Gorbachev had developed a favorable opinion of Shevardnadze through contacts with him dating back to the December 1956 plenary meeting of the Committee of the Komsomol when he was first secretary of the Central Committee of the Komsomol in Georgia and Gorbachev first Komsomol secretary in Stavropol.[426] "At that time," as he writes in his memoirs, Shevardnadze "did not yet speak Russian quite fluently." He was also "not a 'pace setter for youth,' as it was then called," and he didn't seem to possess many leadership qualities. But there was something in his psychological and

421 Chernyaev, *Shest' let s Gorbachevym*, p. 49.

422 This categorization was suggested by John Van Oudenaren, *The Role of Shevardnadze and the Ministry of Foreign Affairs in the Making of Soviet Defense and Arms Control Policy*, Rand Research Report R-3898-USDP, Prepared for the Under Secretary of Defense for Policy, July 1990, p. 4.

423 As quoted by Chernyaev, *Shest' let s Gorbachevym*, pp. 48-49.

424 Gorbachev, *Zhizn'*, Vol. I, p. 288. In his memoirs (ibid., pp. 287-289), Gorbachev fails to emphasize the aspect of party affiliation and control as a criterion for choosing Gromyko's successor.

425 Shevardnadze, *Moi vybor*, p. 81.

426 There is a minor discrepancy here between Shevardnadze's and Gorbachev's account. Gorbachev (*Zhizn'*, Vol. 1, pp. 287-88) writes that he met Shevardnadze for the first time at the Twelfth Congress of the Komsomol (n.d.). Shevardnadze (*Moi vybor*, p. 58) states that they met at a Komsomol Central Committee plenum in Moscow, presumably the 26-27 December 1956 plenary meeting.

political make-up that recommended him to Gorbachev. A relationship of trust was established and confirmed subsequently when they were party secretaries in neighboring Georgia and Stavropol' *krai* respectively, and when Gorbachev advanced to the position of secretary of the CPSU Central Committee.[427] They met frequently, not only on official party business but also privately, at Gorbachev's *dacha* at the Black Sea resort town of Pitsunda, in Abkhazia.

Despite their similarity in outlook, foreign observers have commented on salient differences in the personality of Gorbachev and Shevardnadze. Based on his many meetings with both leaders, Secretary of State James Baker described Gorbachev as always beaming with energy and confidence, as someone who had an actor's gift to fill a stage with his presence, who exuded an upbeat attitude and optimism, and who was invariably positive. While the task the reformers faced was daunting, it was not hard to feel – Baker thought – that Gorbachev's confidence alone might carry perestroika to success. Less kind critics, particularly in the Soviet Union, were to go one step further and chastize the Soviet leader for naiveté. Shevardnadze, in contrast, according to Baker,

> carried an aura of wisdom and insight into just how difficult the task was before them. Sometimes it seemed such wisdom carried a psychological cost. As reform became more difficult, his shoulders seemed to carry the burdens of the world, his grandfatherly hair made him look older than he was, and the patches under his eyes semed to darken and lengthen, reflecting, it seemed, the true tragedy of Soviet history. The more I would work with these two men, the more I would see this difference – and the more I came to believe that Shevardnadze was perhaps the more realistic of the two.[428]

It was Shevardnadze's status as an outsider that was a source of irritation and annoyance at the MFA. The mentality pervading this institution was aptly summed up in its strident slogan of *MID dlia midovskikh*, or the "MFA for foreign ministry officials only."[429] His political background and the reputation which preceded him before his arrival at the ministry was a cause of apprehension. In Georgia, from 1965 to 1968, Shevardnadze had been minister of the interior and, starting in 1972, first secretary of the party. In both capacities, he had made valiant and, considering the firmly rooted racketeering and protection networks and free-wheeling black market activities in that southern republic, futile attempts to weed out corruption. (Presumably these were the "difficult circumstances in Georgia" to which Gorbachev had referred.) The form that the attempts had taken were extensive personnel changes and

---

427 Gorbachev, *Zhizn'*, Vol. 1, pp. 287-88. Similary, Shevardnadze (*Moi vybor*, pp. 59-60) speaks about "three decades of friendship" and a relationship of "trust" that existed between them.

428 James A. Baker, III, with Thomas M. Defrank, *The Politics of Diplomacy: Revolution, War and Peace, 1989-1992* (New York: G. P. Putnam's Sons, 1995), p. 79.

429 Interviews with Grigoriev. The "only" is not a literal translation but conveys more accurately the meaning of the slogan.

prosecution for illegal activities. No wonder that the MFA expected Shevardnadze uncompromisingly to wield the broom to clean up the ministry's Augean stables. Kvitsinsky has vividly described such concerns:

> At the foreign ministry in Moscow there was an atmosphere of tense expectation. Hardly anyone of the foreign ministry officials knew Shevardnadze. No one was able to say anything specific about his foreign policy concepts. Rumors persisted stubbornly to the effect that he would turn the whole foreign ministry upside down and fundamentally reorganize it. Such prospects initially terrified and paralyzed the foreign ministry.[430]

What about the political philosophy behind the anti-corruption campaign? There are different interpretations of the extent to which Shevardnadze, in his position as first party secretary in Georgia, can be considered to have steered a "liberal" or "reformist" course. In the party apparat in Moscow, there were many who looked at him merely as a "tough policeman, not as a man of ideas and certainly not of liberal ideas; some officials made unkind allusions to Stalin and Beria as also having been Georgian, and rumor abounded that after the war he had been a commandant of a Stalinist labor camp."[431] Other observers, mostly Western, regarded him as having been an "unusually successful first secretary in Georgia, improving the republic's agriculture and industry while conducting a quiet but effective liberalization campaign to loosen political controls."[432] The truth lies probably somewhere in the middle. Shevardnadze, at the time of his appointment to the foreign ministry, was in all likelihood someone who looked at the Soviet system essentially through the same lenses as did Andropov and Gorbachev, and probably would have agreed very much with what the latter once explicitly asserted, that "only 20 percent of the potential of the socialist order is being effectively utilized at present in the areas of the economy, politics, science, and culture."[433] In that view, the combination of setting a personal example of self-discipline, hard work, honesty, and flexibility and conducting a sound personnel policy to elevate like-minded leaders to responsible positions would transform the Soviet Union into a modern country. Gorbachev was convinced that he and Shevardnadze were like-minded. By bringing the latter into the foreign ministry and the Politburo, he acted on the idea of creating a strong "reformist" center in the party and of having someone at his side whom he could trust and on whom he could rely in the domestic power struggle.

Looking at the period 1985-89, how justified was the MFA officials' anxiety about large-scale personnel changes? For the most part, it turned out to be unwarranted.

---

430 Kwizinskij, *Vor dem Sturm*, p. 371.

431 Interviews with Grigoriev.

432 Kaiser, *Why Gorbachev Happened*, p. 105.

433 Transcript of the conversation between Honecker and Gorbachev on 20 April 1986 in East Berlin, SED, Central Archives, Büro Honecker, 41666 (indirect speech).

There were some transfers and institutional changes. New departments and sections were created. New concepts and ideas were implemented in accordance with the New Thinking. However, the vast majority of foreign ministry officials emerged from the ordeal perhaps scarred but essentially intact. As in many other institutions, the inertia of the system was to triumph.[434]

Institutional impediments to change were particularly strong in the MFA departments dealing with Eastern Europe and East Germany. In his memoirs, Shevardnadze laments the mentality of the officials responsible for this area at MFA headquarters and the type and quality of the ambassadors posted there. He deplores interference of the party in the ministry's affairs and decries the congruence of outlook of both party officials and MFA personnel.

> Fed on the dogma of the division of the world into 'coexisting systems,' our party officials and diplomats could not conceive of any major changes. Practically speaking, the party official and the diplomat spoke as one person, because the ideological and political 'kinship' of party-state hierarchies in the countries of the former socialist community presupposed unquestioning subordination of diplomats to the nomenklatura.[435]

He also regrets a specific feature of Soviet-East European relations: "Top *party officials* were appointed to ambassadorial posts in Eastern Europe, and those appointments were made exclusively by the Politburo."[436] The officials chosen were often first secretaries of important *oblasts*. This practice betrayed a *deeply rooted imperial mind-set*. It indicated that the working assumption of the Politburo and the message accordingly conveyed to local potentates was that Moscow considered the countries in which its ambassadors would be stationed not as independent and sovereign states but as *administrative* entities of the same order as those existing in the Soviet Union itself.

But this practice had its costs. Communist party transnationalism severely undercut diplomacy.

> The subordination [of diplomats to the nomenklatura] determined the way decisions were made. Former party officials appealed to higher party levels in all questions, bypassing the Ministry of Foreign Affairs. And in the countries where they were posted they would often act in a similar way, going directly to the top and ignoring the foreign ministries of the host country.[437]

Transnationalism also worked in the opposite direction. After having established relations of trust with the new reformist foreign ministers in Eastern Europe, Shevardnadze was told by them that "'a number of influential people in our countries

434 Interview with Tarasenko.

435 Shevardnadze, *Moi vybor*, p. 194 (italics mine).

436 Ibid.

437 Ibid.

critically inclined toward perestroika find allies among your emissaries who come from Moscow or work in your embassies.'"[438] Confirming the point made here about the paucity of personnel changes during his tenure in office, Shevardnadze acknowledges that the way of doing things could not be changed immediately. Ambassadors of a "new type and caliber" were appointed beginning only in 1989, after the creation of parliamentary structures in the Soviet Union and the onset of the East European revolutions.[439]

The subordination of diplomacy to transnational party interests was also standard practice in Soviet-East German relations. In 1971-75, Pyotr Abrasimov was Soviet ambassador in East Berlin.[440] But since he had been, inappropriately from the center's perspective, too closely involved in Ulbricht's removal from office and too closely associated with the ascendancy of his successor and was therefore regarded as unsuitable to assert unquestioningly and unconditionally the center's interests in the periphery, he was replaced by Mikhail Yefremov. By making this decision, however, the Politburo was merely exchanging one problem for another. Yefremov had been first party secretary of the Saratov *oblast'*. In that position, according to Kvitsinsky, he had acted according to the axiom – advantageous for his relations with the center – that in his own area of competence everything was in order.[441] Transferring this *modus operandi* to East Berlin, he didn't report a word about Honecker's deviations from the Moscow's line. In reply to concerned inquiries from Moscow, he only said that he had close contact with Erich, and that there was full mutual understanding. However, as Kvitsinsky continues,

> East Berlin was not Saratov. Yefremov did not take into consideration that, apart from him, there were still many other Soviet 'scribes,' through whom Moscow would find out what was actually happening in the GDR. Among such 'scribes' were members of the GDR's leadership, who reported to Moscow via their channels that Honecker practically wrapped our ambassador around his finger. Since Honecker knew only too well that the people in Moscow were not enthusiastic about his high-handedness and criticized his German policy, he performed a clever move by sending Paul Markowski, the head of the Department for International Liaison at the Central Committee of the SED, to Moscow as an intermediary. In one of those evenings of convivial drinking with members of the CPSU Central Committee, Markowski lamented that the Soviet

---

438 Ibid., pp. 197-98.

439 Ibid., p. 195.

440 Although Abrasimov had been first secretary of the Smolensk *oblast'* in 1961-62, his career was associated more with state than with party institutions. Positions in the former included, at the beginning of his career, the vice-chairmanship of the Belorussian Council of Ministers (government), 1948-50 and 1952-55. The latter part of his career was spent primarily in the foreign ministry, with ambassadorial assignments in Poland (1957-61) and France (1971-73), and as head of the MFA's Department for Liaison with CP's of Socialist Countries (1973-75).

441 Kwizinskij, *Vor dem Sturm*, p. 263.

ambassador was not very helpful to Honecker regarding German policy. He repeated [this charge] the next day, in a sober state, and asked urgently for the replacement of the ambassador.[442]

Yefremov was duly replaced and the Politburo now adopted a new line of reasoning. Precisely because his predecessor Abrasimov seemed to have Honecker's confidence perhaps *he* would be able to persuade the recalcitrant East German leader to heed Moscow's advice. Predictably, as has amply been documented here, nothing changed. As Soviet-East German relations deteriorated, and with it the relationship between Abrasimov and Honecker, the East German leader in 1983 demanded the ambassador's recall.[443]

Viacheslav Kochemasov, appointed by Andropov, became the new ambassador. He proved equally unable to assert the center's interests but was able to remain in this post until the collapse of the GDR.[444] The continuing ineffectiveness of the relationship between the MFA and the Soviet party leadership on the one hand, and between Moscow and the embassy in East Berlin on the other, is indicated by Chernyaev's reaction to a telegram sent by Kochemasov in preparation for Gorbachev's participation in the Eleventh congress of the SED. Chernyaev told Gorbachev: "The ambassador expresses suspicion and enumerates and exaggerates the dangers of 'German-German' relations. But he doesn't have a single idea as to how he pictures the long-term development and how we should conduct our policy."[445] But the strained relations between the ambassador and the East German party leader also undercut the effectiveness of Soviet policy on the German problem.

To take one of the many examples, in 1989 Soviet embassy official M. Loginov was called to the propaganda department of the SED Central Committee and, based on the allegation that he had been in West Berlin and talked to members of the CDU leadership, was charged by party officials with "interference in the internal affairs of the GDR." In a tense exchange with the Kochemasov, Honecker repeated and amplified the accusation, stating that the official in question had "criticized the policy of the SED." Unmoved by Kochemasov's explanations that there had been a mix-up, that it had not been M. Loginov but O. Loginov, third secretary in the embassy, who had been on perfectly legitimate business in the western part of the city, and that one should try to "discuss the nature of the question calmly and objectively," Honecker

442 Ibid., pp. 263-64.

443 Kotschemassow, *Meine letzte Mission*, pp. 57-58.

444 Prior to his appointment to the Soviet embassy in East Berlin, Kochemasov's career, unlike that of most other ambassadors in Eastern Europe, had been entirely with state institutions. After various MFA appointments, including counselor in the embassy to the GDR (1955-60), he had been deputy chairman of the presidium of the RSFSR Council of Ministers (1962-83).

445 Chernyaev, *Shest' let s Gorbachevym*, p. 83.

threatened in allusion to Yefremov's recall: "I would like to tell you frankly that the same question can arise as in the case of your predecessor."[446]

To return to the evolution of events at the center, in his criticism of Shevardnadze's stance on the German problem, Kornienko refers to one of his former chief's many interviews on the topic. He quotes him as having predicted as early as 1986 that the problem of German unification would very quickly be put on the international agenda.[447] Kornienko then proceeds to challenge this assertion. He explains that throughout the post-war period, the department dealing with German affairs at the MFA was one of the most important. After the formation of two separate Germanys, all questions concerning bilateral relations with the two states as well as the German problem as a whole were dealt with in a single branch of the ministry – the Third European Department. In addition to the two Germanys, its sphere of responsibility included West Berlin and Austria. The department's experts, according to Kornienko, held many different opinions on the directions the two German states were taking but "none of the professional diplomats doubted that the German question as such was still far from being closed and that it demanded a complex approach."[448] This was also the "rationale behind maintaining a single department in the Ministry of Foreign Affairs dealing with the FRG, the GDR, and West Berlin."[449]

What about the new foreign minister? Did he use the opportunity presented by the existing institutional structure and its apparent underlying rationale and link up the common home for German affairs at the MFA with Gorbachev's concept of the Common House of Europe? On the contrary, to continue with Kornienko's account, "Shevardnadze found it perplexing that the same department that dealt with the capitalist FRG also dealt with the questions pertaining to the communist GDR. He decided to clean up this 'mess.'"[450] At the beginning of 1986, he removed the GDR and West Berlin from the jurisdiction of the Third European Department and allocated them to a new Department for European Socialist Countries (analogously, he also established a new department for the socialist countries of Asia). Alexander Bondarenko, a veteran of the Great Patriotic war and head of the Third European Department since 1971, remained chief of the truncated department. Gorald

446 Kotschemassow, *Meine letzte Mission*, pp. 57-58.

447 *Literaturnaia gazeta*, 10 April 1991, as quoted by Kornienko in [Marshal] Sergei F. Akhromeev and Georgi M. Kornienko, *Glazami marshala i diplomata* (Moscow: Mezhdunarodnye otnosheniia, 1992), p. 262. Kornienko was first deputy foreign minister from 1977 to 1986.

448 Ibid., p. 263.

449 Ibid. It is doubtful that this was the rationale. The continued existence of all the German entities under one roof at the MFA was in all likelihood one of the many examples of bureaucratic inertia.

450 Ibid.

Gorinovich became head of the new department of European socialist countries.[451] Kornienko scathingly comments:

> It is not surprising, perhaps, that he [Shevardnadze] himself did not have at that time (contrary to what he says now) an understanding of the entire complexity and gravity of the German problem. What is unforgivable is that even in this case he exhibited a complete disregard for the professional knowledge and opinions of those people who had spent decades studying the German problem. They – with the exception of those who are always ready to be the 'yes men' to any leadership – to a man were against the 'division' of the two German states into different branches at the Ministry of Foreign Affairs.
>
> The Minister did not even listen to questions such as how, if this measure were adopted, one would deal with West Berlin. To leave it in the department dealing with West Germany politically would not have addressed the goals which concerned us, since this would have watered down the quadripartite agreement on Berlin, according to which West Berlin was not to be a part of West Germany and not to be administered by it. To move West Berlin along with East Germany to the department dealing with the European socialist states was also inadequate; the professionals immediately recognized that, in a practical sense, with regard to questions of West Berlin, Western representatives would not deal with this department.[452]

Germany was finally "divided" in the foreign ministry. Problems pertaining to relations with East and West Germany were allocated to different departments. West Berlin was transferred first, along with East Germany, to the directorate dealing with Eastern Europe. Since this seemed to be a symbolic gesture of West Berlin's incorporation in the Soviet bloc, "it evidently made the Western states unhappy." But then, in the summer of the same year, West Berlin was "tacked on to West Germany, as a gift of sorts to Hans-Dietrich Genscher, who was coming to Moscow for a visit."[453] It was only much later, *after* the transformation of the socio-economic systems in Central and Eastern Europe and the disappearance of one country after another from the department's roster of socialist European states, that the division at the foreign ministry finally gave way to the Common House of Europe as manifested

---

451 Interview with Bykov.

452 Kornienko in Akhromeev and Kornienko, *Glazami marshala i diplomata*, pp. 263-264. Other former and current Soviet foreign ministry officials have confirmed that there was considerable opposition in the MFA to the proposed organizational changes. These include Kvitsinsky and Bykov (in interviews conducted by the author) and Kochemasov. The Soviet ambassador wrote: "I twice voiced opposition when this question was being decided by the new minister, who called me twice in [East] Berlin. I told him that this would be artificially "tearing apart" the whole German question. One would lose sight of the interconnectedness [of issues] and lose specialists." Kotschemassow, *Meine letzte Mission*, p. 23.

453 Kornienko in Akhromeev and Kornienko, *Glazami marshala i diplomata*, p. 264.

by the merger of the Third (FRG, West Berlin and Austria) and the Fourth (Poland and Czechoslovakia) European departments.[454]

The consequences and lessons to be derived from this Quixotic, almost Khrushchevian, administrative reorganization are perhaps fourfold. First, Shevardnadze at that time was still insensitive to the rationale of treating Germany as one entity, most likely because he, too, assumed that German unity was a thing of the past and that the German problem would *not* very soon be put on any international agenda. Second, the reorganization demonstrated that Shevardnadze was conscious of the need for change in the foreign ministry but did not really know how to go about implementing it. Third, the reorganization changed nothing in substance. The two department heads dealing with the German problem – Bondarenko and Gorinovich – were impediments to rather than agents of change; they both subscribed to conservative positions and were to establish a good working relationship on that basis.[455] Fourth, the 1986 reorganization points to a larger problem: the organizational changes were, in essence, *not* followed by a comprehensive personnel *revirement*. As if in a modified game of musical chairs, a known set of participants was simply rotating among various positions but staying in the game.[456] Bondarenko, for instance, not only survived the MFA's reorganizations and revirements but, his conservative views on Germany and political differences with Shevardnadze notwithstanding, was to represent the Soviet position in the Two Plus Four negotiations in 1990.[457]

But what about Gorbachev? How sensitive was *he* to the issues of MFA reorganization? Was he even aware of the strange administrative gyrations and contortions on German affairs? There is direct testimony to the effect that he not only knew about but *approved* of the changes. In remarks to a closed session of first and general secretaries, who had gathered for the Warsaw Pact's summit meeting in Budapest in June 1986, he reported (evidently with some enthusiasm) that a conference had taken place recently in the Soviet foreign ministry, "unprecedented in the history of Soviet diplomacy." The CPSU had recognized that in the foreign policy sphere "a greater degree of party control" and "stronger party spirit" were necessary. He himself had spoken for two and a half hours at that meeting, and an open and very thorough discussion had taken place. Musing about the background for the meeting, he stated that the "main problem" with the foreign ministry had been the fact that there was "still a lot of inertia and old thinking" in the ministry and that Soviet

454 Interview with Bykov, former section head in the Fourth and then the reorganized Third Eastern Europe Department.

455 Interviews with Kvitsinsky and Bykov.

456 Interview with Tarasenko.

457 This may have been due in part to the fact that Shevardnadze personally respected and liked Bondarenko; interview with Tarasenko.

diplomacy was "insufficiently paying attention to the challenges of the current dynamic developments." Decisions had consequently been taken to "modernize" this sphere of activity.[458] As part of this modernization, what had come to pass was a "reorganization of the structure of the foreign ministry and of all the territorial directions of foreign policy." This had applied, "in particular to the European direction, for which a specific structural entity had been created." New entities had been created for the "Warsaw Pact, CMEA, and scientific-technological cooperation." He deplored that there was still "no organic link between the foreign ministry" and the various institutions "responsible for economic cooperation." However, the functional divisions in the foreign ministry had been overhauled. A department for arms control and disarmament had been created because this was an area that "requires professionals with expert knowledge." New departments concerned with nuclear energy, space, international economic relations, and human rights had also been established.[459]

To return to Kornienko and his criticism of Shevardnadze and, by implication, of Gorbachev, he is almost charitable in his concluding assessment. From the point of view of the subsequent more far-reaching changes which were to take place in Germany, the episodes he had mentioned seemed to him almost "inconsequential." What he decries more than the ill-advised organizational changes is that "this kind of unprofessionalism and improvisation by Shevardnadze on German affairs, as on many others, became apparent later on as well, when the German question became a truly critical aspect for our government."[460] The reader might ask, as indeed Kornienko realizes, why he and his co-author "did not come out earlier with public criticism of those serious miscalculations in our German policies [committed then and] at the end of 1989 and the beginning of 1990." His reply is that

> It is not easy to answer this question. Much can be explained here, first, that in many cases we as well as others were faced with *faits accomplis* for, as time went by, the development of foreign policy became ever more secretive. Second, we understood the futility of criticism; as in previous times, the leadership paid little attention to anyone's opinion if that opinion differed from its own.[461]

These observations are valid only up to point. They accurately reflect the evolution of decision-making but are self-serving as to its rationale. The rapid and unforeseen events in 1989-90 required the very qualities which were almost entirely lacking in

---

458 Gorbachev's remarks to a closed session of first party secretaries at the June 1986 Budapest summit conference; see the protocol on the restricted meeting of the party chiefs of the Warsaw Pact member countries, SED Politburo, *Arbeitsprotokolle*, Central Party Archives, J IV 2/2A/ 2896.

459 Ibid.

460 Kornienko in Akhromeev and Kornienko, *Glazami marshala i diplomata*, p. 264.

461 Ibid.

the MFA – new approaches, new thinking, flexibility and, indeed, improvisation. Similarly, there is merit in the criticism that the 1986 reorganization of the departments dealing with the German problem was ill-advised and can serve to refute Shevardnadze's assertion that he had known from the very beginning that the German problem would soon be put on the international agenda. But, as will be demonstrated later in more detail, if he had listened to the "professionals" in 1989-90, he would have been locked into conservative policies, obstructionism, procrastination, and delay. Nothing would have changed. It is for this reason that the "professionals" were simply ignored and bypassed, and that two major developments took place as a consequence. (1) The head of the institution would choose a team of trusted, competent and, in his understanding of the term, "professional" *personal assistants*. In the case of Shevardnadze and the MFA, this process is mirrored by the remarks he made to his two chief aides, Sergei Tarasenko and Teymuraz Stepanov: "I expect you to tell me the truth. No one else will."[462] (2) Decision-making on important issues shifted to a small circle of leaders *outside* the established institution who would act independently and according to their best judgment. The estrangement of the top leader from his institutional base and the transfer of decision-making away from the institution traditionally empowered to deal with issues under its purview to outsiders happened not only in the MFA. It also occurred, and even more so, in the various branches and organs of the Communist Party.

4. The CPSU: Politburo, Secretariat, and Central Committee Departments

The role of the Communist Party of the Soviet Union (CPSU) in both domestic and foreign policy changed radically between 1985 and 1989. When Gorbachev became General Secretary, the party was the dominant institution of the country. Both the Soviet Constitution adopted in 1977 and the party rules of 1986 described the CPSU not only as the "leading and guiding force of Soviet society" but also called it the "nucleus of the political system of Soviet society, the state, and public organizations." The party, with the Politburo at its apex and "armed with Marxist-Leninist theory," was responsible for "determining a general perspective on the development of the country, including the domestic and foreign policy of the USSR."[463] Until the September 1988 Central Committee plenary meeting and in the absence of serious efforts to reorganize the central party apparat, Gorbachev's approach to party affairs involved mainly personnel changes at the top.

---

462 Interview with Tarasenko, conducted by Lis Bernstein, Russian Research Center, Harvard University.

463 "Kommunisticheskaia Partiia Sovetskogo Soiuza," in Vadim Zagladin and Gennadi Kiselov, eds., *Politicheskie partii: Spravochnik* (Moscow: Politizdat, 1986), p. 21.

In the period from Gorbachev's election as General Secretary until the September 1988 reorganization of the party apparat, five full members had been dismissed from the Politburo and eight new leaders appointed – the majority of the total membership of thirteen in that body.[464] In the secretariat, six of the nine members in March 1985 had left and ten had been newly appointed. More importantly, eight of the thirteen secretaries had been elected since the Twenty-seventh party congress. By no means could it be argued, however, that the majority of the new appointees to the Politburo were committed to radical reform. They can most appropriately be called "Andropovian" in outlook. They included two leaders, Mikhail Solomentsev and Vitali Vorotnikov, who were promoted to the Politburo during the brief tenure of Andropov as General Secretary between November 1982 and February 1984, but also several others who, while reaching Politburo status later, had their main promotion during the same period. These were Yegor Ligachev, appointed chief of the party cadres' department and secretary in 1983; Nikolai Ryzhkov, chief of government under Gorbachev and selected by Andropov in 1983 to become party secretary in charge of the economy; Nikolai Slyunkov, promoted in 1983 to become party chief in Belorussia; Lev Zaikov, secretary in charge of defense industry under Gorbachev, chosen by Andropov in 1983 to replace Romanov in Leningrad; and Victor Chebrikov, appointed KGB chairman in 1982. Two holdovers from the Brezhnev era were also still in the Politburo – Andrei Gromyko, president of the Soviet Union, and Vladimir Shcherbitsky, the party chief of Ukraine.

There were, therefore, only *three* supporters of radical reform in the Politburo in September 1988 – Alexander Yakovlev, Secretary of the Central Committee and head of its propaganda department; foreign minister Shevardnadze; and Alexander Nikonov, the party secretary in charge of agriculture. Other leaders then considered supporters held important jobs but were not full Politburo members. These included defense minister Dmitri Yazov; party secretary Anatoli Lukyanov; and first deputy prime minister Vselovod Murakhovsky. Before his dismissal as alternate Politburo member and first secretary of the Moscow party organization, Boris Yeltsin had also belonged to this group. Thus the personnel basis of radical reform had remained slim. Considering Yazov's and Lukyanov's participation in the August 1991 coup attempt, the review of personnel changes at the top also demonstrates that, with the exception of Yakovlev and Shevardnadze, it was difficult to ascertain who would be prepared

464 This summary of personnel changes in the Kremlin leadership is based on *The Gorbachev Challenge and European Security*, Report by the European Strategy Group (ESG), (Baden-Baden: Nomos, 1988), pp. 85-89. Michel Tatu was the author of the report's section on Soviet domestic developments.

and to what degree to support the reform process. The Nina Andreeva affair in March 1988 had, alarmingly for Gorbachev, underlined this very fact.[465]

This state of affairs had several consequences.[466] *First*, the revamping of personnel at the higher and middle levels of the party adversely affected the expectations and behavior of the party officials and led to the gradual erosion of the General Secretary's authority in that institution. Confronted with uncertainty and concerned about possible demotion or transfer, many party executives continued to dispatch distorted information about their performance to the center. The internal cohesiveness and the effectiveness of work was disrupted by the practice of the new appointees to bring their own proteges into the Central Committee secretariat and departments.

Second, Gorbachev's growing disappointment with the performance of the central party apparat induced him, until the publication of the Andreeva letter, to rely on Ligachev to remedy the lagging performance of the apparat. As informal "second party secretary," Ligachev was in charge of the day-to-day operations of the Central Committee's Secretariat, and in that capacity he maintained close contact with the heads of the various CC departments and the republican and regional party secretaries. As Andrei Grachev has observed, until the reorganization in autumn 1988, Ligachev "remained an unchallenged authority for the whole of the gigantic party apparat, and Gorbachev wanted to believe that as long as Yegor Kuz'mich [Ligachev] was with him he need not be afraid of an organized Fronde or Vendée."[467] Yakovlev has confirmed that "Gorbachev still needed Ligachev. He thought that Ligachev was compensating for the lack of a 'strong hand.'"[468]

Third, Gorbachev came to put ever more trust in a small circle of associates and personal assistants in order to advance the cause of radical reform. One of his close associates was Shevardnadze, whose role has already been mentioned. Another was Yakovlev. His background, political philosophy, and importance for perestroika will be dealt with immediately below. Gorbachev's personal assistants were Anatoli Chernyaev, who was appointed foreign policy advisor in February 1986; Georgi

---

465 The reference is to a letter drafted by an until then unknown lecturer at a Leningrad chemical institute, Nina Andreeva, and professionally rewritten as an article by a *Sovetskaia Rossiia* journalist in consultation with officials in the Central Committee apparat. The letter appeared in that newspaper on 13 March 1988. The letter amounted to a vicious attack on the reform process. In subsequent Politburo discussion, it was in varying degrees supported by Ligachev, Gromyko, Chebrikov, Lukyanov, Nikonov, Solomentsev, and Vorotnikov. The members who criticized the letter were Yakovlev, Shevardnadze, Ryzhkov, and Medvedev.

466 The discussion of the consequences of the slim personnel basis for radical reform is based on Sergei Grigoriev, "The International Department of the Central Committee of the Communist Party of the Soviet Union and Gorbachev's Attempts to Reform the Party Apparat: A Case Study of Disintegration of Authority," unpublished Ph.D. dissertation, Tufts University, May 1996, pp. 235-39.

467 Andrei Grachev, *Kremliovskaia khronika* (Moscow: EKSMO, 1994), p. 120.

468 Yakovlev, manuscript (unplished) for *Gor'kaia chasha*, p. 8.

Shakhnazarov, who in October 1988 became advisor on Eastern Europe and from autumn 1989 also on domestic political and legal reform; and Ivan Frolov, who starting from early 1987 dealt with ideology and had the unenviable task of trying to reconcile Marxism-Leninism with the New Thinking. The effect of Gorbachev's reliance on a small circle of aides and associates was a policy-making process that not only cut across traditional institutional lines but undercut the authority of bureaucracies and their leaders. *Ad hoc* policy-making groups were being formed to deal with urgent business as it arose. This, as will be argued *infra*, included the German problem when it became acute.

Fourth, disappointed with the lagging performance of the party apparat and the persisting conservatism at all its levels, but also faced with deteriorating economic conditions and an erosion of his support in the country, Gorbachev turned to foreign policy as an area in which tangible success could be demonstrated. The seeds of this development were sown as early as June 1984, when he visited Italy to participate in the funeral celebrations for Italian communist leader Enrico Berlinguer.[469] As Gorbachev acknowledged, the visit made "a deep and lasting impression on us."[470] He was warmly received by the Italian Communist Party leadership and enthusiastically welcomed by huge crowds. At one point, when he went out on the balcony together with CPI leader Giancarlo Paetta, thousands of people exuberantly incantated "Gorbachev! Gorbachev!," and "*Viva* Gorbachev!"[471] Such demonstrative expressions of support for him personally and the policies he came to represent were to be repeated when he was General Secretary and visited other countries in Western and Eastern Europe and the United States and established close personal contacts in the plethora of meetings with Western political leaders.

Fifth, the difficulties and disappointments with the party apparat finally persuaded Gorbachev to reorganize it and weaken its influence on policy-making. The measures taken in the pursuit of this purpose had a profound impact on how, institutionally, the imperial legacy in Eastern Europe and the German problem would be dealt with. The two departments of the party apparat that were most closely and directly involved with foreign policy-making were the Central Committee's International Department (ID) and the Department for Liaison with Communist and Workers' Parties of the Socialist Countries. They therefore deserve close scrutiny. Since Yakovlev was one of the main architects of their reorganization, was involved in determining important personnel changes in the process, and was one of its main beneficiaries, it is

---

469 Interview with Zagladin, who was a member of the CPSU delegation to Italy.

470 Gorbachev, *Zhizn'*, Vol. 1, p. 255.

471 Chernyaev, *Shest' let s Gorbachevym*, p. 15, based on what Gorbachev told him personally at the airport after his return from Italy and on conversations with Zagladin.

appropriate to examine his personality, political philosophy, and relationship with Gorbachev.

Yakovlev and the Party Apparat

Alexander Yakovlev was born in 1923 in the village of Korolyovo, near Yaroslavl. In the Second World War he was a marine attached to the Baltic fleet command, was badly wounded in a battle near Leningrad and since then has had to struggle with the effects of his injuries. After the war, he became a Komsomol leader and journalist, graduated from Higher Party School and held a succession of party posts. In 1959, he attended Columbia University as a mature student, an experience that provided a basis for a better understanding of the United States but did not transform him into an ardent admirer of the American way of life and culture.[472] The first harbingers of a non-conformist political philosophy in the *Soviet* environment became public in the early 1970s, when he was acting head of the Central Committee's Propaganda Department. At a time when Brezhnev was tolerating or encouraging Soviet and Russian "great power" tendencies he wrote an article attacking Russian nationalist writers for chauvinism, thereby incurring the wrath not only of Russian nationalists but also of communist party officials.[473] In light of this, he asked for an ambassadorial posting to an English-speaking country and in 1973 was sent to Canada.[474] In the Soviet political context at the time, the ambassadorial appointment amounted to a dignified demotion which, however, was to have important consequences. It marked the beginning of a relationship of trust between Gorbachev and Yakovlev when the former visited Canada for seven days in 1983, with ample opportunity provided to exchange views.[475] Yakovlev recalls: "We were telling each other that the system was so rotten that it would be difficult to save it; that the party stagnated; and that something had to be done, and done urgently."[476] It was also during the

---

472 Conversation with Columbia University alumni who knew Yakovlev when he was a student there. This author attended Columbia in 1970-73 and received his Ph.D. from that institution in 1977.

473 Brown (*The Gorbachev Factor*, p. 74) credits Yakovlev with "vigorous opposition" to the often chauvinistic views of Russian nationalists. This may be somewhat of an overstatement.

474 Ibid.

475 In his memoirs (*Zhizn'*, Vol. 1, pp. 237-39), Gorbachev does not specifically mention that a close relationship with Yakovlev was established during his trip to Canada. He does, however, write favorably about the Canadian trip and its having been "thoroughly prepared" by Yakovlev. Chernyaev (*Shest' let s Gorbachevym*, p. 26) has confirmed that it was in Canada that Yakovlev "became friends with Gorbachev."

476 Yakovlev, *Gor'kaia chasha*, pp. 4-5. It is doubtful that Gorbachev at that time would have agreed with Yakovlev that the system was so rotten that it would be difficult to save it. Such a view is in stark contrast to Gorbachev's conviction, expressed three years later (as quoted in the previous section), that only 20 percent of the potential of the socialist order was effectively being utilized.

Canadian trip that Chernyaev and Yakovlev, as the former has averred, realized that they "were of the same kind" (*rodnye dushi*), and that they became "good friends."[477] In the same year Yakovlev was brought back from "exile," with Gorbachev's help, by party chief Andropov, who placed him in the position of head of the Institute for World Economy and International Relations.[478] From then on, his contacts with Gorbachev were continuous, the latter in his capacity as party leader coming to rely increasingly on Yakovlev's theoretical abilities and practical organizational skills.

In July 1985, when Shevardnadze was appointed foreign minister, Gorbachev elevated Yakovlev to a more influential position. He was transferred from IMEMO to head the Central Committee's Agitation and Propaganda Department. In March 1986, he became a member and Secretary of the Central Committee, and began playing an active role in broadening Soviet information policy, reinvigorating cultural life, enlightening the party with the New Thinking, disseminating new ideas in the apparat, and making sure that they were being implemented in the party's foreign relations. He also became involved in the management of a crucial issue where internal and international dimensions of policy intersected – the nationality problems of the Soviet Union. New Thinking also required addressing the "blank" or – more appropriately – *dark* spots in Soviet history, foremost among them the secret protocols of the Hitler-Stalin Pact, the forcible incorporation of the Baltic states, and the "liquidation" of thousands of Polish military officers at Katyn. This raised sensitive moral and political issues directly impinging on the legitimacy of the Soviet internal and external empire and Moscow's relations with Eastern Europe and the Baltic states. At the same time, Yakovlev's responsibilities in this area produced an important feature of the Gorbachev era. The three closest and most influential

---

477 Chernyaev, *Shest' let s Gorbachevym*, p. 26.

478 I first came to know Yakovlev or, more appropriately, one aspect of his political personality, when I participated in the April 1984 Moscow conference between IMEMO and the Deutsche Gesellschaft für Auswärtige Politik. The meetings were co-chaired by Yakovlev and DGAP director Karl Kaiser. The former demonstrated on that occasion that he was perfectly able uncompromisingly to represent the official party and government line of the day. That line was rabidly anti-American – so much so, in fact, that one of the senior German participants, at the end of the first day, exclaimed in dismay that as a social scientist he had kept track of the proceedings and could confidently assert that more than 80 percent of what he had heard from the Soviet side had been anti-American innuendo and slander. Apart from the content, the emphasis on Soviet-American relations was in complete disregard of the agenda, which was concerned with Soviet-*German* relations. If the following day were to begin on the same anti-American note, his suitcase was packed and he would leave instantly for Sheremetevo airport to take the next available flight to Frankfurt. When I confidentially asked a senior IMEMO researcher whether he had not been embarrassed by Yakovlev's performance and the new head was not doing IMEMO a disservice by engaging in cheap party propaganda, the reply was that privately Yakovlev was quite different; that he was only doing what was required of him; and that it was much more important for IMEMO's role in policy-making to have someone as a director who had good party connections than someone who was able to make a good impression on foreign visitors.

associates and advisors of the General Secretary – Shevardnadze, Yakovlev, and Chernyaev – were all primarily concerned with *foreign policy*. To the extent that differences existed among them, they were less severe than those that separated the three aides from other competitors.

In 1986, Yakovlev's formal position had still lagged behind his political influence. This was to change rapidly. In January 1987, he was made a candidate member of the Politburo and in June 1987 a full member. After the September 1988 reorganization of the party apparat he replaced Ligachev in his role as *kurator* for the departments dealing with the party's foreign relations and thus became responsible in the Politburo for all foreign policy issues. By that time, however, the powerful role of the Politburo and the party apparat, including that of the Central Committee Secretariat and Departments, had already been eviscerated, and Yakovlev was exerting influence on policy-making primarily through his direct association with Gorbachev.

A first telling indication of Yakovlev's unconventional views on the German problem came in January 1989, when he visited West Germany on the invitation of the minuscule and uninfluential German Communist Party (DKP) to attend its Ninth Party Congress. The main purpose of his having accepted the invitation, it would seem, had not been any inclination to lend support to the party but to get a better grasp of the German problem and to establish contact with mainstream political forces in West Germany. In fact, he had scarcely arrived at Frankfurt airport when he treated his ostensible hosts with a dose of irony and sarcasm. Ignoring, knowingly in all likelihood, the stubborn refusal of the SPD to align itself in any way with the DKP, Yakovlev claimed that things had much changed for the better since he had last visited West Germany in 1970 and that this concerned in particular the improvement of cooperation between the German Communists and Social Democrats in the struggle for peace and democratic transformation.

As a tribute to his stature and his influence on Soviet policy-making, and quite in contrast to previous heads of CPSU party delegations attending DKP congresses, Yakovlev was received by the German chancellor. He told Kohl that the Soviet leadership wished speedy and comprehensive negotiations on the realization of the projects that were discussed during the latter's visit to Moscow in October 1988. All agreements reached at that time were valid "in their full scope." In a lecture at the Deutsche Gesellschaft für Auswärtige Politik, he addressed the German problem. He spoke of the political, territorial, and historical reality of the existence of two German states. The New Thinking could not abolish this reality but it could help people to live better with the conditions it imposed. As for the future, history would decide. Most importantly, he distanced himself from the East German regime and from the Berlin wall and even denied Soviet responsibility for its construction. In private, he asked ambassador Kvitsinksy whether the wall was really necessary.[479] Publicly, when he was asked whether "restructuring" in Europe could be effective despite the wall and the East German standing orders to shoot at would-be border crossers, Yakovlev replied: "*I do not represent a German state, but the Soviet Union.*"[480] Even more strongly, on West German television, he said that *the wall "was not built by us. That's not our wall.*" The Soviet Union had to "*liberate itself from the illusion of blind allegiance*" to East Germany.[481]

After this portrayal of Yakovlev, his political philosophy and importance for perestroika, it is now appropriate to focus on the decline, in 1985-89, of the role of the two main Central Committee Departments directly involved in the policy-making process on European affairs.

The Central Committee Departments and Commissions

At the Central Committee, the party had organized a twentieth century surrealist version of Rudyard Kipling's "East is East, and West is West, and never the twain shall meet." In contrast to the MFA's Third Department until 1986, the division of Europe was replicated organizationally at Central Committee headquarters at Staraia ploshchad'. After reorganization of the International Department in the wake of the 1956 Hungarian revolution, all matters pertaining to Eastern Europe, including East Germany, were dealt with in the Department for Liaison with Communist and Workers' Parties of the Socialist Countries; subject matter concerning Western Europe remained under the ID's auspices.[482] There was practically no cooperation between the two departments on the German problem – an absurd state of affairs that *de facto* did not change for almost a year even after the merger of the departments in September 1988. It was only in preparation for Gorbachev's visit to East Berlin in October 1989 to participate in the celebrations for the fortieth anniversary of the foundation of the GDR that specialists on the two Germanys cooperated.[483]

The nature of functions performed, the type of official and organizational ethos were different in the two departments. As Vadim Medvedev, CC secretary and head of the department for liason with the socialist contries from March 1986 to September 1988, has stated, in the late Brezhnev era the functions of the department were to observe, discipline, and control the countries under its purview. Its internal

---

479 Kwizinskij, *Vor dem Sturm*, p. 13. Kvitsinsky replied that the existence of the wall was, of course, unpleasant but that to remove it would mean the end of the GDR.

480 In the question and answer part at the end of his lecture to the DGAP, *Frankfurter Allgemeine Zeitung*, 10 January 1989 (italics mine).

481 Yakovlev interview with ARD (West German television), *Süddeutsche Zeitung*, 10 January 1989 (italics mine).

482 Medvedev, *Raspad*, p. 20.

483 Interview with Tsipko.

organization was not problem-oriented but country-specific: a special section existed practically for each and every country. "It was therefore not surprising," in his view, "that its character was shaped by stalwart *apparatchiki* and that the efforts of a sizable number of independently thinking people were unwelcome."[484] As described earlier, first deputy head Oleg Rakhmanin was one of those stalwarts who remained stuck in the orthodox and dogmatic mold. The same applied to Martynov, the head of the section that dealt with East Germany. Since the majority of the party leaderships in Eastern Europe, including the Czechoslovak leadership after 1968, had a neo-Stalinist outlook, the department officials received hardly any impulse in their contacts and exchanges so that they would adapt their political philosophy to the challenges of the modern world.[485] And since communist parties were in power in Eastern Europe and claimed the same "leading role" in politics and society as the CPSU in the Soviet Union, the interaction between them and the socialist countries' department in Moscow essentially had the quality of *state-to-state* relations. Indeed, as Shevardnadze pointed out in retrospect, from the perspective of the MFA the functions of Soviet diplomats and Soviet party officials in Eastern Europe were practically interchangeable.[486]

The beginning of a shift in the balance between orthodox and more innovative officials in Moscow began in 1986 when Shakhnazarov was promoted from deputy to first deputy department head and when in November Alexander Tsipko was made *konsultant* on questions relating to East Germany and Poland.[487] Since the latter's appointment was characteristic for the process of personnel changes under Gorbachev and his attempt to transmit new impulses to the established Central Committee departments, the circumstances of the appointment shall be recounted briefly. Tsipko, an expert on Marxism-Leninism and political philosophy, had shifted emphasis in the Institute of Economics of the World Socialist System to concentrate on Poland after the eruption of the Solidarity crisis in 1980. In July-August 1985 and January 1986, he had visited the GDR, commissioned by the All-Union Society for Relations With Foreign Countries, and lectured on the beginning of perestroika and

484 Medvedev, *Raspad*, p. 20. The former department head conveys the dubious notion that things were different before the late Brezhnev era .

485 Interview with Shakhnazarov.

486 Shevardnadze, *Moi vybor*, p. 194.

487 Since the role of Nikolai Portugalov, another Central Committee *konsultant* (in the International Department) in policy-making on the German problem will be dealt with below, it may be useful to explain that the position of *konsultant* was by no means unimportant. Consultants dealt with all documents and compiled analytical reports relating to the country concerned, and they prepared memoranda for talks with foreign officials visiting Moscow and speeches for party leaders going on trips abroad. They were also authorized to see all telegrams about the situation in the country concerned, including secret reports by the embassy, KGB, and GRU. Only the telegrams destined for Politburo members were unavailable to consultants.

political developments in the USSR. To his surprise, SED officials and members of the GDR-USSR Friendship Society openly told him about the existence of an ideological crisis in the GDR. On the basis of questions asked at his lectures and subsequent conversations, he concluded that this was indeed the case. In his own words: "I came to understand that the idea that the GDR was the most reliable member of the world socialist system was a myth and that its citizens lived in two entirely different worlds – mentally in West Germany and physically in East Germany. In my report, I predicted that this bubble [GDR] would soon burst."[488] The report made a strong impression on Shakhnazarov and provoked Martynov's ire.[489] But since it was issued by the Institute for Economics of the World Socialist System and duly signed by Oleg Bogomolov, the institute's head, it was forwarded to Gorbachev. Furthermore, Shakhnazarov suggested that Tsipko be made *konsultant* to deal with East Germany.

Differentiation of outlook and opinion was greater in the Central Committee's International Department.[490] This was in part due to the fact that the department's contacts were with the non-ruling Western communist, socialist, social democratic, and labor parties and so-called "progressive movements," in Western Europe and the United States as well as with the communist parties and the "national-liberation movements" in Asia, Africa, and Latin America. Yet in 1985, the institutional ethos was still shaped to a large extent by Ponomarev, who after several decades at the Comintern and at the helm of the ID since 1949 (!) could hardly be expected to introduce new thinking and practices in that organization. Perhaps to a lesser extent, this applied also to Vadim Zagladin, first deputy head since 1975.

A first attempt to revamp the organization was made by Gorbachev in March 1986, when he appointed Anatoli Dobrynin Central Committee Secretary and head of the International Department. The appointment produced as much consternation in the ID as Shevardnadze's elevation to the MFA in the preceding year. (President Reagan was surprised, too. "Is he really a communist?" he asked when he was told that Dobrynin was leaving Washington for his new position.)[491] Several mutually

---

488 Interview with Tsipko.

489 Interview with Shakhnazarov.

490 On the role of the International Department see Grigoriev, "The International Department: A Case Study;" id., "The International Department of the CPSU Central Committee: Its Functions and Role in Soviet Foreign Policy-Making and Its Rise and Fall Following the Major Reorganization of the Central Party Apparatus under Gorbachev," Strengthening Democratic Institutions Project, Harvard University, John F. Kennedy School of Government, December 1995; Mark Kramer, "The CPSU International Department: Comments and Observations," ibid., pp. 99-122; id., "The Role of the CPSU International Department in Soviet Foreign Relations and National Security Policy," *Soviet Studies*, Vol. 42, No. 3 (July 1990), pp. 429-48; and Robert W. Kitrinos, "The International Department of the CPSU," *Problems of Communism*, Vol. 33 (September-October 1984), pp. 47-76.

491 Dobrynin, *In Confidence*, p. 594. Reagan was informed of the transfer by Secretary of State Shultz.

reenforcing reasons can be adduced for Dobrynin's transfer. *First*, Gorbachev applied a logic similar to the one that had pertained to Shevardnadze's appointment to the MFA: that an outsider would feel less constrained by institutional pressures to effect changes in personnel and policy. *Second*, given Dobrynin's background as a career diplomat and his more than twenty years of experience as Soviet ambassador to the United States, the appointment held the promise of greater professionalism in the ID and improved cooperation between the department and the MFA. *Third*, the ID would not only be strengthened by professional expertise and induced to cooperate with the MFA but also to compete with it by assuming tasks previously the exclusive preserve of the foreign ministry. These purposes would also be served by another transfer from the foreign ministry – first deputy foreign minister Georgi Kornienko, who was made Dobrynin's first deputy head at the ID. (The latter's expertise was in arms control, and he had good contacts with the military and a long-standing friendship with the head of the General Staff, Marshal Sergei F. Akhromeev.)[492] *Fourth*, Yakovlev had supported Dobrynin's nomination. One of the reasons for this lay in the fact that in the ten years that they were ambassadors to Canada and the United States respectively they had forged good contacts and come to respect each other. With Dobrynin as head of the ID, Yakovlev was hoping to continue their mutually beneficial cooperation and play a more important role in foreign policy-making.[493]

Dobrynin did introduce some changes. He pioneered the practice of including public figures – eminent scientists, journalists, writers, and artists – in summit delegations. Some staff changes were also made. Two new sections were added to the ID in November 1986, the section for military-political problems, headed by Lt. Gen. Victor P. Starodubov, and the section for international economic cooperation, chaired by Mikhail Pankin.[494] In essence, however, Dobrynin was unable to meet the high expectations placed on him. This was in part due to the very lack of familiarity with the organization and its tasks. He failed to take into account that the ID was integrated in a complicated network of the CC CPSU apparatus where different mechanisms of interaction obtained, and he ignored the basic functions of the agencies run by the department.[495] He also, as Chernyaev has observed, "continued to

492 This was part of abolishing, as Chernyaev put it, the "monopoly" of the MFA in foreign policy-making that had evolved under Gromyko (Chernyaev, *Shest' let s Gorbachevym*, pp. 35-36). As Grigoriev has pointed out, there may have been a supplementary purpose for the transfer – to separate Shevardnadze from Kornienko, with his deep roots in the MFA and facilitate the new foreign minister's tasks in the MFA (interview with Grigoriev).

493 Ivan Frolov had made this point confidentially (Grigoriev, "The International Department: A Case Study," p. 243).

494 Kramer ("The Role of the International Department," p. 454) aptly calls it the "arms control section."

495 Interview with Grigoriev.

behave like an ambassador."[496] These deficiencies coincided with Gorbachev's general disappointment with the performance of the party apparatus and the shift in the main repository of foreign policy-making to the Shevardnadze-Yakovlev-Chernyaev axis. The reorganization of the ID in September 1988, therefore, was not only to be more fundamental than previous efforts but it was also to form part of an overall design to enervate rather than invigorate the apparat and its components.

Comprehensive Reorganization of the Party Apparat

According to material published in the first issue of *Izvestiia TsK KPSS*, the decision to reorganize the party apparatus was taken at a session of the Politburo on 8 September 1988.[497] At the meeting the Kremlin leadership approved a draft that Gorbachev had presented in a special note on 24 August. The decision of the Politburo was not disclosed to the public until the special Central Committee plenum on 30 September. No communiqué was published about this particular session of the Politburo – an indication of the fact that only some of its members were present when the decision was made and that the reorganization plan had been opposed by some members of the leadership. In his note of 24 August, Gorbachev complained about the latter:

> To be frank, we started to think about how to solve these problems [restructuring of the party organs] immediately after the April 1985 plenum of the Central Committee in connection with preparations for the Twenty-seventh Party Congress. We formulated an unanimous standpoint on these issues, which was outlined as a set of principles on the eve of the Nineteenth All-Union Party Conference and presented to the conference in a Central Committee report. These questions were a central theme of discussion in the party and in society. Nevertheless, it turns out now when we come to the practical implementation of this task that *there are certain differences about the approach to the reorganization of the party apparatus. I see this from the notes by some of the comrades on this question.*[498]

The "certain differences" about party restructuring apparently caused a serious clash in the Politburo that was resolved in Gorbachev's favor. At the plenum in September 1988, Gorbachev removed Gromyko and Solomentsev from the Politburo

---

496 Interview with Chernyaev.

497 "Zapiska t. Gorbacheva, M.S., 'O reorganizatsii partiinogo apparata' ot 24 avgusta 1988 goda," and "Postanovlenie Politburo TsK KPSS ot 8 sentriabria 1988 goda," *Izvestiia TsK KPSS*, No. 1 (1989), pp. 81-86. This discussion of the origins and consequences of the reorganization of the party apparat is based on Alexander Rahr, "Who Is in Charge of the Party Apparatus?," *Report on the USSR* (RFE/RL, Munich), 14 April 1989. The present and the following three paragraphs have been shortened here and supplemented by information that has become available since Rahr published his analysis, but *for the most part they are a verbatim reproduction.*

498 *Izvestiia TsK KPSS*, No. 1, 1989, p. 83 (italics mine).

and stripped Ligachev of his position as supervisor of the party apparatus. The departure of Gromyko and Solomentsev and the demotion of Ligachev – the "hard core" of the Soviet leaders who had initially backed Gorbachev's election as General Secretary but later lost enthusiasm for reform – smoothed the way for the restructuring of the apparatus.

In line with Gorbachev's proposal, the Politburo decided to set up nine CPSU Central Committee departments with the following hierarchical order – party work and cadres policy; ideology; socioeconomic policy; agriculture; defense; state and legal policy; international relations; general affairs; and administrative matters. Gorbachev stressed that the main object of the changes was to stop the Secretariat and the CC departments from interfering in government business.[499] He also said that the decision to retain the Agrarian and Defense Departments was necessary at the current stage of reform, but that these departments might easily be dissolved in the future. Gorbachev's note indicated that the creation of the Commission for Agriculture was intended as a temporary measure and that the days of Ligachev, the party secretary for agriculture, were numbered.

Close scrutiny of the work of the party apparatus after its reorganization suggests that the changes were not aimed primarily at streamlining its structure. It seems more likely that Gorbachev's main goal was to deprive the Secretariat of much of its tremendous power. As mentioned earlier, the Secretariat had, in fact, been run by Ligachev rather than by the General Secretary.[500] By the summer of 1988, Ligachev, as the real master of the party machine, was said to have become a threat to his nominal chief. Consequently, Gorbachev took away the power of the Secretariat and restricted the influence of Central Committee secretaries to specifically defined areas by appointing them chairmen of new Central Committee Commissions. In the past, Central Committee secretaries virtually ruled the country through the Central Committee departments, and the central party apparatus was completely subordinated to them. After the September 1988 reorganization, however, Central Committee secretaries were placed under the control of the Politburo and, in theory, became answerable to the members of the Commissions they headed. However, the work of

---

499 In an otherwise uninspiring account of the reorganization, Gorbachev writes in his memoirs that, for him, the "most important" purpose of the reorganization was not to "deprive Ligachev of his power" but to "change the function[s] of the organ [Secretariat], which had duplicated the function[s] of the Politburo and the government;" Gorbachev, *Zhizn'*, Vol. 1, p. 410. Interestingly, the German version of his memoirs is much more assertive and more to the point. Far more important than the "neutralization of Ligachev, for me ...," he writes, "was the [purpose] of *finally putting an end to [the practice of] the Secretariat undercutting the competency of the Politburo and the government*," Gorbatschow, *Erinnerungen*, p. 399 (italics mine).

500 This was confirmed by the stenographic record of the October 1987 Central Committee plenum, *Izvestiia TsK KPSS*, No. 2 (1989), p. 239.

the commissions failed to be organized in such a way as to make them an effective substitute for the Secretariat in supervising the party machine.[501]

How, then, did the comprehensive reorganization of the apparat affect the party's international activities? The Politburo decision of 8 September 1988 had stated that "at present, there are three departments at the CC CPSU concerned with international affairs [International Department, Socialist Countries Department and the Department for Travel and Cadres Abroad]. ... *The preservation of such a structure is inappropriate and has to be changed by the creation of a single International Department, within which sub-departments should be created to deal with the major directions of its activities.*"[502] This decision was put into effect, and Valentin Falin was appointed head of the new ID. Karen Brutents, Rafael Fyodorov and Viacheslav Morozov became first deputy department heads, responsible respectively for the non-communist world, the socialist countries, and trips abroad.[503]

Several new sections were being created, including a section for contacts with parties and international organizations of non-communist orientation, such as the Socialist International and the Liberal International. This section was headed by Rykin who had played an active role as head of the Central European section, comprising the German speaking non-communist countries and entities in Europe – West Germany, West Berlin, and Austria. Rykin's removal from the "German direction" was largely viewed in the ID as an expression of Falin's professional jealousy. Rykin, as described above, had known Gorbachev since the mid-1970s, had close contacts with Chernyaev, and was a personal friend of Willy Brandt and other German social democratic leaders and thus a strong competitor to Falin. But Rykin's job was given to his former subordinate and protégé, Igor Shmatov, who, like Rykin, had started his career as an interpreter at the International Department. Thus, unofficially, through his connections with Shmatov, Rykin continued to play a role in German affairs.[504]

---

501 This was quite contrary to what Gorbachev had promised the Central Committee members when he set up the new *Commissions*. The resolution of the November 1988 plenum that established the commissions had stated that one of their purposes was "to facilitate the involvement of Central Committee members and candidate members in active work on major directions of domestic and foreign policy" and that they should meet "when required but not less often than once every three months;" *Pravda*, 29 November 1988.

502 "Postanovlenie Politburo TsK KPSS," *Izvestiia TsK KPSS*, No. 1 (1989), p. 85 (italics mine).

503 Gorbachev's memoirs utterly confuse the issues of reorganization of the foreign policy activities of the party apparatus. He writes that "the question arose whom to appoint [head of] the International Department (*mezhdunarodnyi otdel*) – Dobrynin, Yakovlev, Medvedev? I then decided on Yakovlev, ...;" Gorbachev, *Zhizn'*, Vol. 1, p. 409). Falin is never mentioned in this context. Later, when he discusses the establishment of the Commissions (p. 410), he states that Yakovlev became responsible for the "international direction."

504 Interviews with Rykin and Grigoriev.

Another part of the restructuring of the party's apparat in foreign policy-making was the creation of Central Committee Commissions. The resolution that established the six commissions had stated that one of their purposes was "to facilitate the involvement of Central Committee members and candidate members in active work on major directions of domestic and foreign policy."[505] Their purposes appear to have been the dilution of the party's dominant role in decision making and revitalization of the party's activities by the inclusion of leading non-party experts and non-party groups in the decision-making process.[506] In the foreign policy area, a Commission on International Policy (CIP) was formed. Its chairman was Yakovlev. Its twenty-four members were leading experts in foreign and foreign economic policy.

There was also an important change at the pinnacle of the party structure. Yakovlev was elevated to the position of Politburo member responsible for the party's international activities (*kurator*) and thus, in addition to being chairman of the Commission on International Policy, was empowered to supervise Falin and the International Department.

What about the impact of the restructuring of the CPSU's foreign policy? If the purpose of the changes had been enervation of the party's dominant role in foreign policy-making, as has been argued here, the objective was certainly achieved. As almost any reorganization of a large bureaucracy, the revamping of the ID, with the creation of new sub-departments and sections, and the replacement or and transfer of personnel to operate new cogs in the party machine, led to uncertainties and inefficiencies. The reorganization also carried with it substantial cuts in staff. The number of employees in the three sub-departments was to be reduced within a year and not to exceed 300, which meant fewer functionaries than in the old ID alone. Yakovlev, in his position as Politburo *kurator*, adopted a dual role. On the one hand, presumably in the interest of enhancing his own power and strengthening the analytical potential of the ID, he promoted or transferred several officials. But, on the other, he failed to involve himself actively in its affairs. Only twice, in March and June 1990, did he address the new department's employees.

In theory, the merger of the Central Committee's three foreign affairs departments permitted a more comprehensive view of and policy towards the outside world. One could also argue that, to some extent, there was advance unification on German affairs since the relations with East Germany's SED were now put under the same roof as those with the political parties and movements in West Germany.[507] In practice, however, there was little change. Now it was the *sub*-departments and their

505 *Pravda*, 29 November 1988.

506 Grigoriev, "The International Department: A Case Study," p. 301.

507 Interview with Zagladin.

heads who jealously guarded their turf, with Brutents generally adodpting a tougher position than Fyodorov.[508]

What about the Commission on International Policy? The list of its members had been approved at the CC's November 1988 plenum, but its first meeting was to take place only in March 1989.[509] Altogether, in 1989-90, only four meetings of the CIP were held. The scarcity of meetings was matched by their lack of importance. In contrast to CC Secretariat decisions, CIP resolutions were non-binding. Analytical reports failed to reach the leaders at the apex of power, with little harm done, since the rapid pace of events in Central and Eastern Europe between 1988 and 1990 quickly rendered the reports obsolete.

To reflect on the restructuring of the foreign policy components of the party machine, analysts have debated whether its purpose was to eviscerate the apparat or to make it more effective.[510] It is unclear, however, why one objective should contradict the other, or why, for that matter, the two aims should exclude still others. Restructuring was in all likelihood designed to achieve four interrelated purposes, the first three pertaining to the ID and the fourth to the CIP: (1) to weaken the apparat by organizational changes and staff reductions; (2) to make a smaller entity more effective by the elimination of bureaucratic overlap, retirement of aging officials, and appointment of new functionaries; (3) to subordinate it more closely to the reformist core in the Politburo and its foreign policy *kurator*; and (4) to make the party more responsive to an informed public by the inclusion of non-party experts. In a convenient phrase, restructuring was meant to make the party's foreign policy apparat not only *lean* but also, in accordance with the New Thinking, *less mean*.

It might seem that Falin's appointment to the position of head of the new ID was both an auspicious and fortuitous move directly related to his credentials as a German expert, occurring precisely at a time when the latent German problem was beginning to become acute. This, however, was not the case. In fact, his views and intention to

---

508 Interview with Grigoriev.

509 *Izvestiia TsK KPSS*, No. 9 (1990), p. 24.

510 The two positions have aptly been argued by Sergei Grigoriev and Mark Kramer in the former's monograph, "The International Department of the CPSU Central Committee: Its Functions and Role in Soviet Foreign Policy-Making and its Rise and Fall Following the Major Reorganization of the Central Party Apparatus under Gorbachev," Strengthening Democratic Institutions Project, Harvard University, John F. Kennedy School of Government, December 1995. In Grigoriev's view, Gorbachev did not have a "secret plan to destroy the CC CPSU apparatus from the inside." The ID could have been "transformed into a viable structure" comparable to the U.S. National Security Council. He regards the fact that this transformation did not come about as a "failure," for which Gorbachev and his top aides must bear "their share of responsibility" (p. 87). Contrary to that, Kramer argues (on p. 118) that, by autumn 1988, "Gorbachev had come to believe that a radical restructuring of Soviet society would be impossible unless he weakened and even undermined the central party apparatus, which had been such a formidable barrier to reform. ... The old system had to be weakened and, eventually, dismantled."

play a determining role on the German problem were one of the reasons why the ID, in the policy-making process on that issue, *failed* to be more directly involved in 1989-90 than one might have expected at the time of the ID's reorganization. It is appropriate, therefore, to focus more closely on the Falin's role in foreign policy-making, in particular on the German issue, and his relationship with the reformist inner core of the Politburo.

Falin's Role in Policy-Making

One of the main formative experiences in Falin's life, as he writes in his memoirs, was the German attack against the Soviet Union in June 1941, which occurred when he was fifteen years old.[511] The war struck his family with full force and in all its brutality. His grandmother and his father's sister and her five children were its victims, as well as three of the four children of his other sister, their husbands, and near and remote relatives on his mother's side who lived in Leningrad and its suburbs. The war not only shaped his emotions but also his educational and career preferences. He found it almost incomprehensible that a nation that had been regarded in Russia as a model of culture, organization, and order and had produced eminent philosophers, scientists, writers, and composers could create such "an ocean of evil and suffering."[512] The urge to comprehend the German national character, whether it was shaped by "the spirit or the iron studded boot," also determined his choice of university. In 1946 he enrolled in the Moscow State Institute for International Relations (MGIMO) with a concentration on German language, history, culture, politics, and economics. After his graduation in 1950, he was posted to the Soviet Control Commission in Berlin, which, after the foundation of the GDR, was the successor institution of the Soviet Military Administration in Germany. His responsibilities were to collect and analyze information pertaining to developments in West Germany. In that capacity, he also forged contacts with officials of the emerging political parties, trade union representatives, and businessmen in both East and West Germany.[513]

Typically for career patterns of officials in the Soviet period, Falin alternated between state and party jobs. After his return to Moscow in 1951, he was posted to the Committee on Information at the foreign ministry and the CC's Information Department. For a number of years thereafter, he held executive posts in the Soviet Ministry of Foreign Affairs. In 1959, he was told by Gromyko to assume responsibilities in the Third European Department. In 1961, after the summit meeting

511 Falin, *Politische Erinnerungen*, p. 21.
512 Ibid.
513 Ibid., pp. 25-29.

between Khrushchev and Kennedy in Vienna, he was transferred to the Council of Ministers to act for Khrushchev as adviser and speech writer on German affairs, but he also continued to cooperate closely with Foreign Minister Gromyko. Their working relationship deepened in 1965, when he advanced to the position of head of the Group of Advisers at the foreign ministry. One of his tasks was to analyze information reaching the ministry and twice daily report to Gromyko. He also was entrusted to write speeches for Gromyko.[514]

In August 1968, at the time of the Warsaw Pact intervention in Czechoslovakia, he was made head of the Third European Department. In that capacity and as Soviet ambassador to West Germany in 1971-1978, he became one of the main advocates of Soviet-West German rapprochement. In 1978, he was transferred to the party apparat to become first deputy head of the Central Committee's International Information Department and served under Brezhnev, Chernenko, and Andropov. But in 1983, his until then smooth career was severely set back. His stepson, a Soviet diplomat who had served in Vienna, had chosen not to return to the Soviet Union. A cloak of secrecy was thrown over the defection because of the father's prominence. But moralist and disciplinarian Andropov apparently held the father accountable for the sins of the son. What also did not help Falin's career was the fact that he married his own secretary, a woman from Soviet Central Asia, several decades younger than he. It was his third marriage. In October 1983, he was demoted to the humble position of *Izvestiia* political analyst or "observer" (*obozryvatel'*).[515]

In December 1985, Shevardnadze offered him the post of planning chief at the foreign ministry, which he declined. He did agree, however, to Yakovlev's request to become part of a team of writers, including Arbatov and Anatoli Kovalev (a writer turned deputy foreign minister), to participate in drafting Gorbachev's speech to the Twenty-seventh Party Congress. At that congress, he was elected alternate member of the CPSU Central Committee and shortly thereafter, in March 1986, appointed chief of Novosti, the official Soviet information agency. In October 1988, he was named chief of the CC's International Department and, finally, in July 1990, at the last CPSU congress – the Twenty-eighth – appointed to the once powerful Secretariat of the Central Committee.

What about Falin's standing in the foreign policy establishment, his political philosophy, and his attitudes towards the German problem? There is no evidence that his life-long interest in German affairs and his experience in Berlin and Bonn had

---

514 Ibid., pp. 29-37.

515 In his memoirs, Falin makes no reference to these two possible reasons for his demotion – the defection, which had occurred in 1981, and his unconventional marriage. In his version, he fell victim to "intrigues" by Leonid Zamyatin, his chief at the CC's International Information Department. Zamyatin's maneuvers supposedly "created my conflict with Yuri Andropov, who in the meantime had become General Secretary;" Falin, *Politische Erinnerungen*, p. 38.

elicited much empathy with or sympathy for Germany, East or West.[516] However, in the opinion of foreign ministry and party officials, his active involvement in Soviet-German relations in the 1970s had shaped basic preconceptions which he was unable to overcome.[517] As one of the chief architects of the August 1970 Moscow Treaty and the September 1971 Quadripartite Treaty on Berlin, he viewed the arrangements and the *modus vivendi* reached between West Germany and the Soviet Union, and between the two German states, as the main pillar of European security. He clearly had a vested interest in the continuation of the conceptual and practical approach he had developed on the German problem. As his voluminous memoirs underline, his views essentially did not deviate from those held by Gromyko, except on a rather more theoretical than practical matter. He severely criticizes Gromyko for having, in conversation with him, "put the cards on the table" and expressly "abandoned the perspective of a united socialist Germany."[518] As his clinging to an unrealistic policy goal demonstrates, Falin, although times have changed, has been unable or unwilling to change with them.

In 1988-90, Falin's approach towards emerging German unification was distinctly more conservative than that of Yakovlev, Shevardnadze, Chernyaev, or Gorbachev. This, among other factors, was connected with his close ties to the leadership of the German Social Democratic Party (SPD), whose attitudes towards German unification were different from those held by chancellor Kohl and the ruling coalition. His ties became "institutionalized" when he assumed the office as head of the International Department. In this capacity he had to deal with the complaints and pressures generated by the embattled SED and its successor party, the PDS. As the German problem moved from the "hundred years" horizon to the current agenda, Shevardnadze and Chernyaev, in contrast, had to cope with the practicalities of its solution in cooperation with the Kohl government. From their institutional perspective, they felt that they could not afford the luxury of theoretical discussion with opposition parties and forces.

Anti-American tendencies also played a certain role in Falin's conservative approach to the German issue. Talking to executives in the ID, he often characterized Americans as "pushy, arrogant, and overconfident," criticized the Soviet preoccupation with American affairs, and demanded that equal attention be paid to relations with European and Asian countries.[519] Since a viable NATO seemed to depend on

---

516 This is not contradicted by the fact that he went to Hamburg after German unification to live and teach there, a move facilitated by Egon Bahr. His *de facto* emigration was in all likelihood not because of a special fondness for Germans and Germany but the result of what he considered humiliating treatment by Gorbachev and lack of career opportunities in the new Russia.

517 Interviews with Kvitsinsky, Maksimychev, and Bykov.

518 Falin, *Politische Erinnerungen*, p. 239.

519 Personal notes by Grigoriev.

the continued presence of American forces in Europe, he also strongly opposed membership of Germany in NATO, remarking scathingly in his book that "somehow, one would not have suspected that 'all-human values' are identical with Atlanticism."[520]

Conservatism on the German problem did not extend to all political issues. As Chairman of APN, the Novosti news agency, he had been instrumental in the foundation of the progressive *Moscow News*, which continued to be financed by the agency until 1989. Yakovlev has acknowledged that he admired Falin's position vis-à-vis Ligachev's demands to shut down *Moscow News*. This was probably also one of the reasons why Yakovlev strongly supported Dobrynin's replacement by Falin as head of the ID.[521] In his position of Chairman of APN, which engaged in foreign policy propaganda, Falin had closely cooperated with Yakovlev, who was then in charge of the CC CPSU Agitation and Propaganda Department. The two officials also shared disrespect, if not disdain, for certain leaders of communist countries – for Ceausescu, first and foremost, but also for Honecker and Zhivkov. Finally, they derided the idea that it was necessary or useful to maintain contact with and finance even the most minute and uninfluential parties in the international communist movement.[522]

To summarize, given the emergence, *nolens volens,* of the German issue on the Soviet foreign policy agenda, Falin's appointment as head of a reorganized International Department seemed both an auspicious and fortuitous move. Theoretically, the most eminent expert on Germany was elevated to a position which would permit effective management of a complex issue. Falin was certainly prepared to assume such a role. In practice, however, his intention to play the first fiddle did not coincide with the score and composition of the orchestra as determined by conductor Yakovlev. His appointment to the position of department head, while he was not even a full member of the Central Committee, let alone CC Secretary, meant that he was expected to play a less prominent role.[523] Falin was not prepared to reconcile himself with a more modest position. This in itself was bound to lead to conflict between him and Yakovlev. But the struggle over power and influence became intertwined with both differences over policy and a clash of personalities. Whereas Falin's intellect may be incisive, his bearing was detached and impersonal. These traits stood in marked contrast to those of Gorbachev, Shevardnadze, Yakovlev, and Chernyaev. From 1988 to 1990, therefore, differences of personality and conflict over power and

520 Falin, *Politische Erinnerungen*, p. 497.
521 Interview with Grigoriev.
522 Interview with Zagladin.
523 Unlike Ponomarev and Dobrynin, who had held the position of head of the ID before him, Falin did not become CPSU CC Secretary upon appointment. He was elected to that position only after Yakovlev had announced in July 1990 that he did not want any leading role in the CPSU hierarchy.

policy combined not only to deny the foremost German expert center stage in the resolution of the German problem but progressively to relegate him to an isolated position.

As amply demonstrated here, Falin's subordinate role in foreign policy-making was intimately connected with the decline in the power of the party and its apparat. A similar development occurred in the role played by one of the mainstays of the Soviet empire – the Soviet armed forces.

5. The Ministry of Defense and the Armed Forces

In the comparative history of imperial collapse the Soviet empire represents an anomaly. The Roman empire, the nineteenth and early twentieth century Czarist, Ottoman, and German as well as twentieth century British, French, and Portuguese colonial empires came to an end only after military convulsions – a series of uprisings, local or regional wars, or a world conflagration, or a combination of internal and external conflict. Typically, the ruling elite, with the assistance of the security apparatus and the armed forces on which it depended, made a determined effort to prevent or postpone imperial decline and collapse. Furthermore, in several cases, military governors on the periphery, on their own or in cooperation with factions in the metropole, took matters in hand and actively resisted imperial devolution. None of these phenomena could be observed in the Soviet case. The Soviet empire did not disintegrate as a result of catastrophic war. No resolute action was taken by the institutions of imperial power – the party apparat, the armed forces, and the internal security services – to resist the demise. The August 1991 coup attempt, with all the power institutions represented in the Emergency Committee, occurred only *after* the external empire had already collapsed and was also a less than determined effort to keep the *internal* empire intact.

To summarize the main arguments of this section, the Soviet military grudgingly and resentfully but, in the final analysis, without open resistance accepted imperial decline and disintegration. This was due to a combination of factors. Foremost among them were (1) the lack of a Bonapartist tradition in the armed forces; (2) strict subordination to and control by the CPSU; and (3) a precipitous decrease in the party's power and influence. An inner logic linked the last two factors. Since the party had penetrated and was in control of the armed forces, the erosion of the CPSU's power and authority was bound to erode the military's equally prominent and privileged position. In fact, the defense ministry, the armed forces, and the "military-industrial complex" essentially suffered the same fate as the party apparatus: a significantly reduced access to, if not exclusion from, policy-making on central issues. Within a very short time, they had to adjust to the progressive devolution of empire, including the withdrawal of forces from Eastern Europe; a severe decline of their role in economic affairs; deep cuts in forces and expenditure; shifts in resource allocation from military to civilian uses; fundamental change in military doctrine and security concepts; increased access of civilians to hitherto closely guarded secrets; and a significant drop in prestige and social status. Presentation of some detail is necessary in order to appreciate the enormity of these developments, which in their impact went beyond the Gorbachev era to affect deeply Russia's conduct in world affairs under Yeltsin.

As in other dimensions of policy under Gorbachev, change in military affairs was gradual at first, became more radical and eventually led to the abandonment imperial thinking and policies. This process can be divided into three major phases. The first phase extended from Gorbachev's election as party chief in March 1985 to the January 1987 Central Committee plenum. In this period, there was little criticism of the military, some personnel and no institutional change, and an economic development strategy that seemed to serve both civilian and military requirements. One might have thought initially that the armed forces were to be exempted from restructuring. A second period lasted from the January 1987 CC plenum to the "Rust affair" in May of the same year. This short time interval is characterized by a more vigorous advocacy of restructuring, not solely in the economy and society, but also in politics and military affairs. The third phase began with the Rust incident and included the ouster of the defense minister, extensive personnel transfers and demotions in the defense ministry and the armed forces, revisions of international security concepts and military doctrine, and a greater role than hitherto for the foreign ministry and academic institutes and specialists in security decision-making.[524]

Perestroika, Democratization, and Glasnost in the Armed Forces

The three-stage process of change was facilitated by developments prior to Gorbachev's election as General Secretary but after he had already acquired an important role in policy-making. Beginning in the fall of 1984, the military was subordinated more strongly to party control, as evident in the removal of Marshal Nikolai Ogarkov, a strong advocate of modernization and increased resource allocation to the military, from his posts as Chief of the General Staff and First Deputy Defense Minister.[525] Curtailment of the military's influence on policy-making

---

524 The ordering of phases draws on Marion Recktenwald, "Perestrojka in den sowjetischen Streitkräften," *Research Report*, Bundesinstitut für ostwissenschaftliche und internationale Studien (Cologne), No. 10 (1987), p. 27; see also Dale R. Herspring, "On Perestroika: Gorbachev, Yazov, and the Military," *Problems of Communism*, Vol. 34, No. 4 (July-August 1987), pp. 99-107.

525 Ogarkov's dismissal was in all likelihood connected with disagreements between him and the top party leadership about the level of resources to be allocated to defense; see Azrael, *The Soviet*

continued after defense minister Ustinov's death in December 1984 and the appointment of Sergei Sokolov as his replacement. The important role of the military had been based to a considerable extent on the influence Ustinov had exerted on Brezhnev and the top ruling circle.[526] His successor, Sokolov, was bound to be in a weaker position not only because of his 73 years of age but also his rather uninspiring, colorless personality. Furthermore, in contrast to his predecessor, he was not a full member of the Politburo.[527]

The turnover of top military officers and party officials concerned with defense issues gained momentum after Gorbachev's accession to power. In the first two phases of change, this process included the removal in July 1985 of Grigori Romanov, one of Gorbachev's main rivals, from his posts as full member of the Politburo and CC secretary responsible for the arms industry; the replacement of Sergei Gorshkov (Navy), Vladimir Tolubko (Strategic Rocket Forces), Vasili Petrov (Ground Forces), Alexander Altunin (Civil Defense), Pavel Kutakhov (Air Force), Ivan Shkadov (Cadres), and Alexei Yepishev (Main Political Administration).

Several measures which Gorbachev adopted in the military sphere had a symbolic and demonstrative character. In May 1985, conservative forces had wanted to use the fortieth anniversary of the Soviet Union's victory and the renewal of the Warsaw Treaty as an occasion for patriotic mobilization in grand style, but both were celebrated on a more modest scale. On such occasions in Red Square, the military under party leaders Brezhnev and Andropov had prominently been placed atop the Lenin mausoleum at the right hand side of the General Secretary, and they had taken up half the rostrum. Starting with Chernenko's funeral in February 1985, the senior military figures were shunted to a less prominent position. By 1986 only four senior officers were allowed on the rostrum, and only at some distance from the top political leader.[528]

Nevertheless, in the first two phases of perestroika in the armed forces, there were several demands for change with which the military was able to agree, or at least with

---

Civilian Leadership and the Military High Command, The RAND Corporation, R-3521-AF, June 1987, and Dale R. Herspring, "Nikolay Ogarkov and the Scientific-Technical Revolution in Soviet Military Affairs," *Comparative Strategy*, Vol. 6, No. 1 (January 1987), pp. 29-59.

526 Testimony to Ustinov's influence has been provided, for instance, by Khrushchev's son, Sergei, in his memoirs, published in a four-part series, "Pensioner soiuznogo znacheniia," *Ogonek*, Nos. 40-43 (October 1988).

527 Sokolov was elected candidate member of the Politburo in April 1985.

528 See the corresponding photographs, *Pravda*, 14 November 1985, and ibid., 8 November 1986. The demonstrative diminution of the military's standing has been described in detail by Hans-Henning Schröder, "Gorbatschow und die Generäle: Militärdoktrin, Rüstungspolitik und öffentliche Meinung in der 'Perestrojka,'" Bundesinstitut für ostwissenschaftliche und internationale Studien (Cologne), *Research Report*, No. 45 (1987), and Astrid von Borcke, "Militär und Politik in der Sowjetunion: Zur Rolle des Militärs im politischen Entscheidungsprozess," in Hannes Adomeit et al., *Die Sowjetunion als Militärmacht* (Stuttgart: Kohlhammer, 1987), pp. 73-89.

which it was unable to disagree. Such demands included the rejuvenation of cadres, the more careful utilization of economic resources, eradication of corruption, the encouragement of initiative, greater combat effectiveness, and the more rapid and effective introduction of science and technology in the armed forces.[529] The military was to have greater problems only with the pressures generated in the next phase of change, which aimed at democratization and openness in the armed forces.

The third phase of restructuring in military affairs was ushered in by the landing of Mathias Rust, a young West German pilot, with a single-engine Cessna aircraft in Red Square, at the end of May 1987. Given that Gorbachev was embarking on more radical reform in domestic politics, the Cessna's landing was almost literally a gift from Heaven. The demonstration of gross ineptitude by the Soviet air defense forces in tracking and bringing down the intruding aircraft was used by the party leader to oust Marshal Sokolov, replace the chief of the Air Defense Forces, and demote and expel from the party's ranks several other air defense officers. In replacing the defense minister, Gorbachev bypassed the more senior military contenders – Akhromeev, Lushev, Kulikov, and of course Ogarkov – and appointed Dmitri Yazov, a general almost unknown in the West. Changes in the top military leadership in 1987, as Table 5 shows, were especially numerous.[530]

Another major departure from traditional approaches was the attempt to introduce democratic principles in the armed forces. This was an aspect of military reform which, under the heading of *innere Führung*, had formed a central part in the foundation of the West German Bundeswehr and which was now, like the Prussian military reforms after the Napoleonic wars, used by civilian experts in the Soviet Union as a model for change. Predictably, given centuries of harsh authoritarianism in both the Imperial Russian and the Soviet army, the military establishment failed to understand how "civilian" principles, such as of voluntary participation, due process, and criticism could be brought in line with the "military" requirements of subordination, discipline, and command and control. "How can democracy be reconciled with one-man command (*edinonachalie*)?" was the question which the editors of *Krasnaia zvezda* allowed readers to ask in letters to the editor.[531] The new defense minister did his duty to explain that the two principles were not mutually exclusive

529 Agreement with several of these demands was expressed, for instance, at a meeting of party activists in the armed forces, "Perestroika – delo kazhdogo. Sobranie partiinogo aktiva Ministerstva oborony SSSR," *Krasnaia zvezda*, 18 March 1987.

530 Adapted from Naomi Koizumi, "Perestroika in the Soviet Military," Paper Prepared for the European-Japanese Symposium on Soviet Perestroika: Security and Foreign Policy Dimensions, London, RIIA, 14-16 December 1988.

531 "Demokratizatsiia i Vooruzhennye Sily. Kandidat v chleny Politburo TsK KPSS, ministr oborony SSSR general armii D. T. Yazov, otvechaet na voprosy chitatelei 'Krasnoi zvezdy,'" *Krasnaia zvezda*, 18 November 1988.

but *complementary*.[532] But such explanations never found practical support and application in the services.

Table 5 – Personnel Changes in the Military Leadership, 1985-88

Year	Defense Min	Cs-in-C of Forces	MPA	General Staff	Mil Distr	GF	Navy	ThF
	15[a]	5[b]	4[c]	8[d]	16[e]	4[f]	4[g]	4[h]
1985	2	2	2	0	3	1	2	0
1986	2	0	0	1	1	0	1	1
1987	4	1	0	3	7	3	1	1
1988	1	0	1	2	3	0	0	1
Total	9	3	3	6	14	4	4	3
Percent	60	60	75	75	88	100	100	75

Notes

a Ministry of Defense: defense minister, 3 first deputies, and 11 deputies.
b Commanders in Chief of the five services of the armed forces.
c Main Political Administration: chief, 1 first deputy, and 2 deputies.
d General Staff: chief, 3 first deputies, and 4 deputies.
e Heads of the Military Districts.
f Chiefs of the Group of Forces.
g Commanders of the four fleets.
h Chiefs of the Theater Forces.

Another reform attempt in security affairs was glasnost in defense expenditures. In August 1987, Deputy Foreign Minister Vladimir Petrovsky had laid the groundwork for more realistic provision and international comparison of data when he acknowledged that outlays for research, development, testing, and procurement were not included in the official Soviet defense budget.[533] One month later, Gorbachev suggested that the major powers should provide each other with reliable figures on military expenditures.[534] The intention was laudable but the results disappointing.

532 The examples which Yazov used to demonstrate the complementarity of the two principles were rather limited. They included constructive criticism within the appropriate party and other channels, greater participation in the evaluation of training exercises, and more reporting of accidents, corruption, and other forms of dereliction of duty.

533 "Razoruzhenie i razvitie. Na mezhdunarodnoi konferentsii v N'iu-Iorke," *Pravda*, 27 August 1987; on the need for political and planning purposes to provide more credible figures on military expenditures, see, for instance, G. Khanin and V. Seliunin, "Statistika znaet vse," *Novyi mir*, No. 12 (1987), p. 257.

534 In an important article on problems of world security that departed from many other traditional Soviet approaches, *Pravda*, 17 September 1987.

The Soviet budgets for 1988 and 1989 still contained the unrealistic official figures. Petrovsky and academic specialists regretted that the publication of more detailed data on defense outlays had to await implementation of a comprehensive price reform envisaged under the next (1991-95) five-year plan.[535] American Defense Secretary Frank Carlucci was informed in August 1988 that the Soviet government was unable for technical reasons to provide exact data because Soviet military expenditures were scattered across several different government departments, making it difficult to produce a budget breakdown resembling that of the U.S. defense budget.[536] However, the West German defense minister, in talks with his Soviet counterpart in Moscow in October 1988, was told that figures on the Soviet military effort *did* exist but that the ministry was against publication of such figures at present.[537]

Legislative control of security policy and the armed forces was yet another intended reform measure. According to the draft provisions for the reform of the constitution, as outlined by Gorbachev at the June 1988 Nineteenth party conference and endorsed by the Supreme Soviet in November 1988, the legislative organs (Soviets) at all levels of government were to receive greater powers. At the national (all-Union) level, a newly constituted Supreme Soviet, with the help of a standing committee, was to exert control over all the main bodies involved in military and military-industrial activity. As explained by Shevardnadze at the Soviet foreign ministry's "all-Union scientific-practical conference" in July 1988, legislative control was to extend to "questions concerning the use of military force across the national borders of the country, the plans for defense construction, and transparency of the military budgets and their connection with the problem of national security."[538]

Finally, the changes that had the most profound impact on European security and that most profoundly affected Moscow's policy on the German problem concerned nuclear and conventional arms control, armed forces reductions, and disarmament. Gorbachev's initiative of January 1986 that had called for the abolition of *nuclear weapons* as well as the October 1986 Reykjavik summit meeting at which the "deinvention" of nuclear arms had been discussed had raised concern among the military. But then, to their relief, no agreement had been concluded. The negotiations on intermediate-range nuclear missiles, however, were different. They *did* produce an agreement, and one that was very much resented by the military establishment. MFA

---

535 Petrovsky at a press conference in Moscow, as quoted by *Süddeutsche Zeitung*, 20 August 1988.

536 On a visit to Moscow, *Wall Street Journal*, 31 August 1988, p. 6. Marshal Akhromeev had made similar statements during his visit to Washington in July 1988; see *Time*, 8 August 1988, p. 6.

537 Interview with the West German defense minister, Rupert Scholz, on the *Zeitspiegel* program of the *Bayern 3* television channel, 2 November 1988.

538 Speech by Member of the Politburo of the CC of the CPSU, Minister of Foreign Affairs, E. A. Shevardnadze, at the Scientific-Practical Conference of the MFA of the USSR, 25 July 1988, *Mezhdunarodnaia zhizn'*, No. 9 (September 1988), p. 20.

officials and academic specialists apparently felt that they had to justify themselves and explain to the military the rationale of asymmetrical cuts. This Shevardnadze did at the historic "scientific-practical conference" in July 1988 and on many later occasions with the argument that the asymmetry of cuts created an asymmetry of advantages.[539] The treaty "removed from our borders American rockets which literally in a few minutes could be fired and reach vitally important facilities on the territory of the USSR," he said in an interview. "What difference does it make if it happens that we destroy more rockets than the Americans? We put more of them in place, so let us remove more of them. The main thing is that we are better off."[540]

Even more damaging and devastating to military thinking was the whole process of first unilateral and then asymmetrical cuts in *conventional weapons* begun by Gorbachev's announcement at the United Nations General Assembly in December 1988 of plans to cut the overall size of the Soviet armed forces by 500,000 officers and men, and to withdraw troops from Eastern Europe and Mongolia. According to Western estimates, the Soviet armed forces at that time consisted of 3.5 million officers and men, of which 800,000 were stationed abroad.[541] Military leaders had stringently warned against downsizing *per se* but especially against unilateral and asymmetrical reductions. For instance, Gen. Ivan Tretiak, commander of the Soviet air defense forces, had called Khrushchev's troop reductions a "hasty step" and "a terrible blow to our defense capacity" and now demanded that unilateral cuts be examined "a thousand times over."[542] Defense Minister Yazov, Soviet Chief of Staff Akhromeev, and Warsaw Pact armed forces Chief of Staff Gribkov had all, with minor variations, made the point that "the limits of sufficiency are defined not by us but by the actions of the United States and NATO."[543] Akhromeev also opposed unilateral downsizing; in fact, his resignation was made public on the very day on which Gorbachev had announced the military cuts and withdrawals.[544] There was

---

539 At the July 1988 conference he said that it was one of most basic interests of the Soviet Union "to have the military activity of all countries confined to their national boundaries" and that, as regards INF, it "took into account that these missiles are of different value from the standpoint of Soviet and American security. ... Thanks to it, the American nuclear presence has been moved away from our borders;" *International Affairs* (Moscow), No. 10 (1988), p. 19.

540 Interview with *Argumenty i fakty*, No. 18 (1989).

541 See Robert E. Harkavy, *Bases Abroad: The Global Military Presence* (Oxford: Oxford University Press, 1989), pp. 114-115. At a press conference at the United Nations in December 1989, Deputy Foreign Minister Vladimir F. Petrovsky disclosed that the Soviet Union still had a total of 627,000 troops stationed abroad and that the Soviet aim was to bring "all our troops stationed abroad back by the year 2000"; Reuters, 15 December 1989.

542 TASS, 17 February 1988.

543 D. T. Yazov, "O voennom balanse sil i raktno-iadernom paritete," *Pravda*, 9 February 1988; S. F. Akhromeev, "Shto kroetsia za briussel'skim zaiavleniem NATO?," *Krasnaia zvezda*, 20 March 1988; A. I. Gribkov, "Doktrina sokhraneniia mira," ibid., 25 September 1987.

544 The timing of his announcement to coincide with Gorbachev's speech may not have been deliberate. Akhromeev reports in his memoirs that he asked Yazov in September 1988 to report

also considerable anxiety in the military industry, in particular among the more highly paid production engineers and managers, that defense expenditure and troop cuts would jeopardize their jobs and privileges. As one of them exclaimed in exasperation after the signing of the Washington INF agreement: "May God [sic] save us from further disarmament measures."[545] The appeals to divine intervention, however, were to no avail.

Since Marshal Akhromeev can be considered representative of the moderately conservative, professionally competent, and politically loyal type of military officer in the Soviet armed forces, his views are of particular importance. In his memoirs, he gave the following interpretation of the 1988 reorganization of the party apparatus and its consequences. "The Soviet people," he said,

> will yet have to analyze this historic period [the end of 1988]. Precisely at this time, there started a carefully planned attack of the antisocialist forces and the party's own defectors on the communist party. Their aim was to discredit and destroy the party. As a communist veteran, I had a hard time watching what was happening to the country. It was especially hard for me until I finally realized that we were dealing with real ideological opponents. We should have fought them without making any concessions or compromises.[546]

He then explains why he resigned. He turned 65 in 1988, and at such an age he found it "appropriate for a prominent military leader to leave his post. ... Certainly, one can still work productively and apply the richness of one's experience." However, he thought, it "becomes difficult to maintain one's creativity at its peak, to develop new initiatives, and to control a large staff. No one can fight his age." He also had to think about his worsening state of health: His war-time wounds had started to bother him again. Most important in the present context, he was tired of the many differences with the political leadership, notably "my frequent fights with Shevardnadze ... about his independent moves during the negotiations on conventional and nuclear arms reductions." He deplored that

> my positions and views were almost certainly misrepresented or amended with certain comments. This resulted in two or three quite poignant talks with the General Secretary of the CPSU. [Gorbachev] reprimanded me and I in turn tried to justify my position, which was not appreciated by the leadership. I was never shy to express my unflattering observations on the

---

his resignation request to Gorbachev. At the end of October 1988 he was told that his request would be accepted. At the beginning of November Gorbachev called him to the Kremlin office, where he confirmed the acceptance of his resignation but asked him to stay on as military adviser; Akhromeev and Kornienko, *Glazami marshala i diplomata*, pp. 215-216. For further detail on the reasons for his resignation, see below, pp. 353-54.

545 The head of a weapons laboratory, as quoted in a letter sent by a 25-year old engineer, identified as Sergei Sukharev, to *Literaturnaia gazeta*; see "Ne dai bog, poteriaem nomenklaturu," ibid., 4 May 1988, p. 14.

546 Akhromeev in Akhromeev and Kornienko, *Glazami marshala i diplomata*, p. 214.

> work of the Ministry of Foreign Affairs in the intra-departmental circles. I knew at that time that this would be reported to the leadership. I wouldn't characterize the situation around me as tense but found it uncomfortable.[547]

A final reason for his resignation was acute concern about developments in the Warsaw Pact.

> The Soviet Union started to experience very difficult relations with many of the [Warsaw Pact] countries. I saw all this happening but couldn't help it. This deeply frustrated me. Some readers perhaps don't understand this, but I found it impossible to participate myself in destroying the alliance that had been created by the efforts of Zhukov, Konev, and Rokossovsky, by the efforts of officers, generals, and admirals of several generations.[548]

Akhromeev's request to be relieved of his duties as chief of staff was accepted, but Gorbachev asked him to act as his military adviser, "to prepare suggestions on major military issues, especially on negotiations on nuclear and conventional arms."[549]

Akhromeev's account is of some importance not only because it sheds light on the circumstances of his resignation and – after the collapse of the Warsaw Pact and the August 1991 coup attempt – his suicide. It is valuable also because it corroborates the existence of sharp disagreements between the MOD and the MFA over security matters and the rejection of the former's point of view on practically all of the contentious issues of Soviet security policy. The account also poses both an important and intriguing question: who was primarily responsible for the major departures from traditional Soviet approaches to security affairs and foreign policy, including on the German problem – Gorbachev, Yakovlev, or Shevardnadze? Institutionally, was it the party chief and president with his personal assistants and staff, or the MFA? Akhromeev's "unflattering" view of the MFA's work and his acceptance of the offer to become military advisor to Gorbachev clearly point in the direction that he, at least, thought *Shevardnadze* to have been the main agent of change and the chief culprit in the demise of the Soviet empire.

After having highlighted the curtailment of influence of the military establishment in the center of the Soviet empire and Akhromeev's answer to the perennial Russian question of Who is to Blame? (*kto vinovat?*), the following sub-section seeks to illuminate the role played by the military establishment at the periphery of empire, the Soviet armed forces in East Germany.

---

547 Ibid., p. 215. He also mentions controversies "with the chiefs of other services in relation to the Afghan problem." Although Akhromeev speaks of these controversies and those with Shevardnadze over arms control issues as "rumors" (*slukhi*), it is clear from the context that these rumors were well-founded but, in his view, misrepresented to Gorbachev.

548 Ibid., pp. 215-16.

549 Ibid., p. 216.

The Soviet Forces in the German Democratic Republic

On 10 June 1945, the Red Army units stationed on the territory of the Soviet Occupation zone in Germany were transformed into the Group of Soviet Occupation Forces in Germany.[550] According to the Declaration Regarding the Defeat of Germany and the Assumption of Supreme Authority with Respect to Germany of 5 June 1945, supreme authority in the country was assumed by the Four Powers. The Soviet armed forces that had conquered Berlin (largely consisting of the First Belorussian Front) became an occupation force under the Soviet Military Administration and Marshal Zhukov, its commander in chief. Its headquarters were originally in Potsdam but later moved to Wünsdorf, south of Berlin. When the occupation regime was formally terminated in 1949, Moscow changed the name of its forces to Group of Soviet Forces in Germany; it denied East Germany's request to substitute "German Democratic Republic" for "Germany."[551] In fact, retention of the original term for the forces was one of the few tangible signs that Stalin insisted on maintaining Soviet rights and responsibilities with respect to Germany as a whole and that, unlike Ulbricht, he refused to regard the German question as settled. On 29 June 1989, only a few months before the East German regime collapsed, a new designation was introduced: the Western Group of Forces (WGF). The statement issued on this occasion clarified that this alteration again did not affect Soviet post-war rights and responsibilities.[552]

Before the unilateral reductions announced by Gorbachev in his speech at the UN General Assembly in December 1988, the Soviet ground forces in Germany consisted of the 2nd Guards Army (with headquarters in Fürstenberg), the 3rd Assault Army (Magdeburg), the 8th Guards Army (Weimar), and the 20th Guards Army (Eberswalde, surrounding Berlin), with 4 divisions each, plus the 1st Guards Armored Army (Dresden), with 3 divisions. The Soviet Air Force embraced the 16th Front Air

---

550 The following four paragraphs of this section on the Soviet forces in East Germany are a revised and shortened but essentially *verbatim* summary of the comprehensive analysis by Ulrich Brandenburg, "The 'Friends' Are Leaving: Soviet and Post-Soviet Troops in Germany after Unification," Bundesinstitut für ostwissenschaftliche und internationale Studien (Cologne), *Research Report*, No. 33 (1992). For a less comprehensive treatment, see Claus J. Duisberg, "Der Abzug der russischen Truppen aus Deutschland: Eine politische Erfolgsbilanz," *Europa-Archiv*, No. 16 (1994), pp. 461-469.

551 The other Groups of Forces in the European theater were the Northern Group (NGF) of forces based in Poland, the Central Group (CGF) in Czechoslovakia, and the Southern Group (SGF) in Hungary.

552 Details on this and other issues of the presence and status of the GSFG/WGF can also be found in Karl-Wilhelm Fricke, "Okkupanten oder Waffenbrüder? Die Gruppe der Sowjetischen Streitkräfte in Deutschland," *Deutschland-Archiv*, Vol. 15, No. 3 (March 1982), pp. 269-276; Christian Raap, "Truppenstationierung in Deutschland nach der Wiedervereinigung," *Monatsschrift für Deutsches Recht*, No. 12 (1991), and id., "Die Stationierung von Streitkräften in fremden Staaten unter besonderer Berücksichtigung Deutschlands," *Archiv des Völkerrechts*, Nos. 1-2 (1991), pp. 53-84.

Army with a network of air bases throughout the former GDR. Except for a small support unit (not under GSFG/WGF command) there was no Soviet naval presence in the territory. The 1,026 Soviet military installations covered 243,015 hectares (about 2.25 percent of the GDR territory) and included 110 airfields and helicopter bases, 100 training and firing ranges, 70 radar and radio transmitter stations, 8 ammunition depots (the largest of which covered nearly 3.5 square kilometers), and 400 barracks and housing compounds. The full extent of the Soviet military presence and the area covered by the GSFG/WGF installations were not disclosed even to the East German authorities until a few months before unification.[553]

At the time when Gorbachev announced impending troop and equipment cuts in December 1988, the Soviet military presence in East Germany amounted to more than 400,000 servicemen with about 200,000 dependents and civilian employees. After the cuts in 1989 there were still about 550,000 persons associated with the renamed Western Group of Forces (WGF), including 337,000 servicemen and 200,000 dependents and civilian employees. In conjunction with East Germany's National People's Army (NVA), the Polish and Czechoslovak armed forces, and Soviet units based in the western military districts of the Soviet Union, the Group of Soviet Forces in Germany formed the 1st Strategic Group of the Warsaw Treaty Organization. All of the GSFG/WGF units were classified as category A, with 90 percent of personnel at wartime strength. Service in East Germany was considered prestigious because it appeared to be an indispensible rung on the career ladder. Most of the commanders in chief of the GSFG became commanders in chief of the Warsaw Pact armed forces, six were appointed Marshal of the Soviet Union, and two – Zhukov and Grechko – Minister of Defense.

Both the Declaration on Sovereignty of the German Democratic Republic, issued by the Soviet government on 25 March 1954, and the Treaty on Relations between the GDR and the USSR of 20 September 1955 considered the presence of Soviet troops on East German territory to be temporary. But neither of the two treaties nor the Agreement on Questions Related to the Temporary Stationing of Soviet Armed Forces of 11 April 1957 provided a legal basis for the presence of the Soviet forces other than that they had a right to be there as an occupation force until the conclusion of a German peace treaty. Article 18 of the 1957 agreement stipulated that, "in case of a threat to the security of the Soviet forces," the Supreme Command of the GSFG upon consultation with the GDR government had the unrestricted right to take measures in order to "eliminate such a threat."[554] In June 1953, the Soviet military

553 *Der Spiegel*, 13 May 1991.

554 The agreement was published in *Gesetzblatt der Deutschen Demokratischen Republik*, Part 1, No. 28 (1957).

had asserted such a right when it cracked down on the popular revolt in East Germany and East Berlin.

In the 1957 agreement, the Soviet Union had reserved for its forces a large measure of extraterritoriality. Military personnel, civilian employees, and family members travelled in and out of the country effectively without East German control. Soviet troops enjoyed essentially unfettered freedom of movement, indifference of the GDR authorities to the violation of environmental regulations, almost complete absence of restrictions on low-level flights by military aircraft, and training unhampered by GDR civilian interference. Military officers had access to special hunting preserves. Contacts between Soviet soldiers and their East German counterparts, let alone the civilian population, were not allowed to develop other than in a carefully staged setting. Soviet conscripts remained isolated even when the GDR could be considered politically "safe" – a state of affairs that was not helped by the introduction of openness and democratization in the Soviet Union.

Some contact, however, did exist at higher military levels. In his memoirs, Marshal Akhromeev remembers large-scale military maneuvers that were held in East Germany in 1988, and he reflects in that context on Soviet-East German political and military relations.[555] In the course of the exercises he met with the defense minister, Army General Hans Kessler, he wrote.

> We were old friends. For a long time, he had occupied the post of chief of the general staff of the National People's Army of the GDR, and during this time we had frequently worked together. This was a person of true honesty. I believed him wholly. We were of the same age. He was born and raised in a family of communists. In the years of his youth, fascism had ruled Germany. In July 1941, in the most difficult time for us, as a soldier of the *Wehrmacht*, he had crossed the line of the German-Soviet front and immediately joined us in the battle against the fascists. After victory, as a member of the Communist Party and later the SED, he diligently and wholeheartedly worked for the benefit of the German people. Hans Kessler was a real friend and ally. He was one of those people who fought for communist ideals to the end. I never believed and don't believe even now that he was capable of committing any kind of inappropriate deeds or the abuses of which he was accused during the fall of Erich Honecker and the establishment of the new regime. [...] I just want to say that we owe a debt to people like him.[556]

The Chief of the General Staff of the National People's Army, Col. Gen. Fritz Strelitz, was also present at the training exercises. Akhromeev knew him well, too, and had also "developed a friendly rapport" with him. However, despite the friendships he had forged, he writes, he was "leaving the GDR with a heavy heart, with a feeling of alarm and uneasiness." Kessler and Strelitz

555 Akhromeev and Kornienko, *Glazami marshala i diplomata*, p. 182.
556 Ibid.

> had expressed concern and a lack of understanding of certain aspects of our foreign policy as well as the relations between the Soviet Union and the GDR. They openly told me that certain Soviet newspapers and magazines were writing articles that could undermine socialism in East Germany. I was forced, in turn, to tell them that we did not understand Erich Honecker's conservatism. Couldn't they see that the pressures within the GDR were mounting, the people were demanding change and that it was impossible to ignore this? *But it was impossible to have a truly honest discussion with my German friends since both they and I were constrained by the positions of our respective political structures and therefore had to maintain loyalty and correctness first and foremost with regard to our leaders.*[557]

Such a mind-set of self-imposed constraints obviously did not lend itself to independent action by the Soviet armed forces in Germany. Nor was there any proclivity in Moscow to involve the WGF in the stabilization of the Honecker regime. To the extent that controversy exists, it concerns the question whether the Soviet armed forces intervened in order to *dissuade* the East German regime and its security apparatus from using force to prevent political change. This problem will be examined next.

The Controversy Over the Use of Force

Several occasions for violent confrontation and intervention presented themselves. On 6 and 7 October 1989 unauthorized demonstrations were planned in Berlin to counter the official celebrations for the fortieth anniversary of the foundation of the GDR. Other demonstrations were scheduled for 9 October, when the customary manifestations against presumed fraud committed on that day of the month in the May 1989 local elections were to be held in Berlin and other East German cities.[558] Since this date fell on a Monday, the by then equally traditional demonstrations in Leipzig – the *Montagsdemonstrationen* – were also going to take place on that day.

Rumors abounded. Their origin, in part, lay in the SED's Chinese connection. The East German leadership had reacted with a mixture of equanimity and approval to the merciless repression of the student dissidents at Tiananmen Square in June 1989. A parliamentary resolution, for instance, the draft of which Honecker had personally signed, noted that the efforts

> steadfastly pursued by the party and state leadership of the People's Republic of China at achieving a political solution of domestic problems have been thwarted due to violent, bloody riots by anti-constitutional elements. As a result, the people's power was forced to restore order and

557 Ibid. (italics mine).

558 According to the GDR's electoral commission chaired by Egon Krenz, 98.77 percent of the electorate had exercised their right to vote; 98.85 percent of the votes had been cast for the candidates of the National Unity Front.

security by the use of the armed forces. In that context, unfortunately, numerous people suffered injury, and deaths also occurred.[559]

The terse statement also considered "the events in Beijing exclusively a [Chinese] domestic affair" and opposed "any foreign interference."[560]

Furthermore, Krenz had returned on 2 October from an official visit to China, and Yao Yilin, a high-ranking Chinese Politburo and Communist Party member, was scheduled to attend the anniversary celebrations in East Berlin. Krenz was later to deny any empathy or sympathy with the Chinese crackdown. However, the internal Politburo record on his meeting with the General Secretary of the Chinese Communist Party on 26 September 1989 notes that Zhiang Zemin was "grateful" for the solidarity which the SED had extended to the party "in the complicated situation of a counterrevolutionary uprising."[561] Krenz was apparently proud of this solidarity, and certainly uncritical, when he replied that " for communists such class solidarity [is] a matter of class honor and class obligations. Whoever, like the People's Republic of China and the GDR, is pursuing the same social goals in the interest of the people is also facing the same adversary on the barricades of socialist revolution."[562] Krenz also did not object to Zhiang Zemin's apodictic statement that with increasing distance from the "June events" there was ever more clarity about the "intentions which the imperialist circles are pursuing with their concept of so-called peaceful change." They had an "aggressive program for undermining socialism."[563] In talks with Chinese Politburo member Qiao Shihe, Krenz went so as far as to say that the East German support was based on the communist principle that "wherever the power of the people has achieved victory, no one will be allowed to touch this power."[564] Wide-spread concern in East Germany and East Berlin that the SED leadership was planning a *chinesische Lösung* – a Chinese-style solution – to its problems was therefore not unfounded.

The security services of the party were meticulously watching, recording developments, and keeping the top echelons informed. The Leipzig regional party office, for instance, sent a detailed report on the *Montagsgebet* (Monday prayer) in Nikolai church and the subsequent demonstrations to Honecker. Krenz, too, read the report

559 Draft Declaration of the Volkskammer of the GDR Concerning the Current Events in the People's Republic of China, personally approved by Honecker in his own handwriting on 8 June 1989; SED Politburo, *Arbeitsprotokolle*, Central Party Archives, J IV 2/2A/3221.

560 Ibid.

561 Notes on the talks between Krenz and Zhiang Zemin on 26 September 1989 in Beijing, attachment 1 for agenda item 5, Politburo session of 17 October 1989, SED Politburo, *Arbeitsprotokolle*, Central Party Archives, J IV 2/2A/3247.

562 Ibid.

563 Ibid.

564 Notes on the talks between Krenz and Qiao Shi on 25 September 1989 in Beijing, attachment 2 for agenda item 5, Politburo session of 17 October 1989, SED Politburo, *Arbeitsprotokolle*, Central Party Archives, J IV 2/2A/3247.

and summarized it for the party. Honecker, who took careful note of the number of participants (6,000-8,000), had both Krenz's summary and the full report from Leipzig distributed to the members of the Politburo.[565] The report had referred to the peaceful demonstrations as a "provocation" and attacked the church as the "starting point of all of these hostile activities" and a "hotbed of anti-socialist and hooligan elements." It concluded by expressing support for the "readiness of the communists and [their] demand to act more decisively and to take action against the hostile elements."[566]

Rumor was rampant also in West Berlin. Its mayor, Walter Momper, had told Falin in conversation that he had heard that demonstrators from Leipzig were planning a massive breach of the borders, presumably in Berlin. Falin considered this information important enough to report it to the head of the communist party of West Berlin (SEW), who relayed it to SED Politburo member Hermann Axen, who in turn lost no time in informing Honecker.[567] The message Falin wanted to convey to the SED leadership was that in view of the "wide international attention" which the anniversary celebrations would command the East German leadership should "think carefully about how to react" to possible demonstrations.[568]

If Falin had implied that the GDR authorities should exercise restraint, his advice fell on deaf ears. On 27 September, Honecker issued a directive which proceeded from the assumption that "certain circles in the FRG and West Berlin as well as groups supported by them" in East Germany were intent on abusing the fortieth anniversary celebrations for a "slanderous campaign against the socialist order and social conditions" and the "disruption of normal life in the GDR" and that measures had to be taken to maintain law and order.[569] Kochemasov, the Soviet ambassador to East Berlin, claims to have seen this or perhaps another directive signed by Honecker to use force against the demonstrators.[570]

---

565 Report by the Leipzig Regional Party Office to Honecker and Internal Central Committee Note by Egon Krenz to Erich Honecker, both dated 3 October 1989, read and forwarded by Honecker (marked with his own handwriting) to the Politburo, SED Politburo, Central Party Archives, IV 2/2039, 317. Krenz's note to Honecker also refers to a telephone conversation in the evening of 2 October in which he had informed Honecker about developments in Leipzig.

566 Leipzig report, ibid.

567 Hermann Axen to Erich Honecker, Internal Central Committee Memorandum, Secret, Eyes Only, 3 October 1989, Central Party Archives, Büro Axen, IV 2/2035.

568 From a report on a conversation between Falin and the head of the SEW, Dietmar Ahrens, Hermann Axen to Erich Honecker, Internal Central Committee Memorandum, Secret, Eyes Only, 3 October 1989, Central Party Archives, Büro Axen, 2/2035.

569 According to an official investigative report by the city parliament of East Berlin, "'Chinesische Lösung:' Wollten Stasi-Leute ein Blutbad unter Demonstranten provozieren?," *Der Spiegel* (Hamburg), 18 December 1989.

570 As quoted by Stanislav Kondrashov, "Nashe mesto v mire," *Izvestiia*, 29 April 1990.

It is doubtful that such a directive would have been specific as to implementation. It is an incontrovertible fact, however, that the state security service, or Stasi,[571] in Leipzig and Berlin did use excessive force against demonstrators on 7 and 8 October. This included the merciless beating of unarmed demonstrators with truncheons and the arrest of more than one thousand people, many of whom were subjected to police brutality while in detention. All this was considered shocking enough later to lead an official investigation by the East Berlin city parliament to conclude that "certain forces [had] wanted an escalation" so as to justify "the total use of all the available combat means and force potential against the demonstrators."[572] The police brutality substantially increased anxiety among members of the opposition movement and heightened their fear as to what would happen on Monday, 9 October, when even larger demonstrations were scheduled in Leipzig. To their relief there was no repetition of the violence of the preceding days. But plans and instructions for the demonstrative use of force had undoubtedly existed. The problem is only to decide at what *level* such plans were made, *who* was to be in charge of implementation and under what *circumstances*, and whether the *Soviet armed forces* had any role in staying the arm of the GDR's internal security services.

One of the accounts purporting to shed light on this problem is a report by Rainer Wiegand, a former director of East German counterintelligence, who has said that the Stasi had been told to use all the force necessary short of shooting to stamp out dissidence, and he attributed to Krenz an order to "shatter counterrevolutionary structures in the GDR."[573] But Krenz and Schabowski strictly deny such allegations; the former even contends that there was no contingency planning for 9 October. "It is an error to assume," he stated,

> that the demonstrations scheduled for Monday, 9 October 1989, had – in a timely fashion and for a long time – been the center of attention of the leaders of party and state of the GDR. Neither the leadership of the GDR nor that of the USSR were at that point fully conscious of the fundamental nature of the processes taking place in the GDR. The loss of a sense of reality among the SED Politburo members close to Erich Honecker was so profound that such large-scale political demonstrations as would occur in Leipzig so shortly after the fortieth anniversary of the GDR were deemed not to be possible. The leadership of the GDR, for that reason, also had no prepared political concept as to how to react to an internal crisis in the country.[574]

---

571 Stasi is short for Staatssicherheitsministerium or Ministry for State Security.

572 Excerpts from the city parliament's investigative commission report, as quoted in "'Chinesische Lösung,'" *Der Spiegel*, 18 December 1989.

573 In a ten-part series in *Die Welt* (Hamburg), 21 May to 13 June 1990; see also "'Chinesische Lösung'" (1989); for further detail, see Elizabeth Pond, "A Wall Destroyed: The Dynamics of German Unification in the GDR," *International Security*, Vol. 15, No. 2 (Fall 1990), pp. 42-43.

574 Krenz, "Anmerkungen zur Öffnung der Mauer," p. 366.

Both former East German leaders even contend that they had not heard anything about the police brutality on that evening – and not even on the morning of 8 October, when they met at Stasi headquarters with the minister of the interior, the minister and several generals of state security, and the chief of police. Mielke, the Stasi chief, is said to have reported on this occasion that the provocateurs had not achieved their goals. They had been dispersed. This had been done without major complications. However, one had to count on further demonstrations for which it was necessary to keep the security forces in a state of readiness.[575]

Since Krenz and Schabowski were determined to bring about reformist change in the GDR, if need be without Honecker, any bloodshed in the streets would have been counterproductive. Contrary to all the verbal support he gave to the Chinese, it is credible that Krenz told Schabowski after his return from the visit to China: "Whatever may have happened at Tiananmen Square, nowhere should we to act with military force against demonstrators. That would be the political and moral end for us."[576] It is also believable that the demonstrations in Leipzig came to be the "*center of attention*" of the SED leadership only in the morning of 9 October; that Krenz was informed only on that day by the director of the Leipzig Youth Research Institute about "measures taken by the security organs, anxieties among the population, and the possibility of clashes during the demonstrations;" and that he was concerned enough not to leave security matters to the specialists but to intervene and to make sure that the "authorities in Leipzig and the security ministries issue orders to avoid violence at any price."[577] All of this does not exclude the possibility that local officials and institutions in Leipzig and Dresden also acted to stave off the blows prepared by security officials.[578]

What about the role of the Soviet Union and the Soviet armed forces? Shevardnadze asserted in an interview that the danger of Soviet military intervention existed, "for instance, during the demonstrations in East Germany in 1989."[579] If such danger existed, it was extremely remote and lessened even further by political action. According to Soviet embassy sources in East Berlin, the increasing instability of East Germany in the summer of 1989 had prompted the Soviet leadership through various

---

575 Schabowski, *Das Politbüro*, pp. 78-79; id., *Der Absturz*, p. 237; Schabowski is paraphrasing here, not quoting directly.

576 Schabowski, *Der Absturz*, pp. 236-37.

577 Ibid. (italics mine). In essence, Krenz's account is confirmed by Schabowski, *Das Politbüro*, p. 80. Markus Wolf, too, is "convinced" that the "Beijing variant did not correspond to his [Krenz's] preconceptions;" Wolf, *In eigenem Auftrag*, p. 195.

578 Hans Modrow, for instance, in his then capacity as first party secretary of Dresden, in conjunction with mayor Wolfgang Berghofer has taken a large part of the credit for successfully persuading both sides, the chiefs of police and the demonstrators, to refrain from violence; Hans Modrow, *Aufbruch und Ende* (Hamburg: Konkret Literatur Verlag, 1991), pp. 14-15.

579 Shevardnadze interview in *Der Spiegel*, No. 22 (1991), p. 166.

channels to impress upon the party leaders in East Berlin that it regarded any "interference in the affairs of other parties and states" as "unacceptable" and ruled out "the use of military force under any circumstance."[580] On 8 October, in anticipation of a confrontation between the security forces and the opposition on the streets of Leipzig on the following day, Ambassador Kochemasov ordered General Snetkov, the Commander in Chief of the Western Group of the Soviet Forces, "under no circumstances to intervene in the events." The troops under his command were to "remain in their barracks, not to participate in any military exercises" and like their families "not to leave their military compounds."[581] According to Kochemasov, he had acted upon his own initiative. On the following day, he claims, Moscow – presumably the defense ministry – sent corresponding instructions to the WGF command.[582]

Krenz is emphatic that the Soviet side was not included by the SED leadership in decision-making on that issue, and not even consulted. Any possible or potential assistance to be extended by the Western Group of the Soviet Armed Forces "was not considered at any point in the fall of 1989."[583] As for any specific Soviet order not to intervene, he asserts that he had had many meetings with Kochemasov and Snetkov. But an order not to intervene

> never became known to the political leadership of the GDR. Had it been given, Army General Snetkov would certainly have informed me about it. Our long-standing personal acquaintance prohibits me from doubting the honesty and candor of the former commander in chief. An order from Moscow to the Soviet armed forces to stay out of the internal conflicts of the GDR would have required that 'somebody' thought it possible that the Soviet army would intervene. I do not know of anyone who would have made such a suggestion to the [Soviet] army command in Wünsdorf.[584]

The facts of the matter may very well be that neither the Soviet embassy nor the WSG command discussed the intricacies of how to react to the East German demonstrations, but that they *did* discuss how to react to another event that touched their interests much more directly: the opening of the Berlin wall on 9-10 November.[585]

---

580 I. Maksimychev and P. Menshikov, "Edinoe germanskoe gosudarstvo?," *Mezhdunarodnaia zhizn'*, No. 6 (1990), p. 45. Both authors were officials in the Soviet embassy in East Berlin. Maksimychev confirmed the point about the warnings to this author, personal interview in Moscow, 2 June 1993; similarly Soviet ambassador Kochemasov in his interview in *Tribüne* (East Berlin), 8 May 1990, as quoted by Gerhard Wettig, "Die sowjetische Rolle beim Umsturz in der DDR und bei der Einleitung des deutschen Einigungsprozesses," in *Der Umbruch in Osteuropa* (Stuttgart: Franz Steiner Verlag, 1993), p. 41.

581 As quoted by Stanislav Kondrashov, "Nashe mesto v mire," *Izvestiia*, 29 April 1990; this version of events was confirmed by Kochemasov (*Meine letzte Mission*, p. 169); see also Oldenburg, "Sowjetische Europa-Politik," p. 758.

582 Kotschemassow, *Meine letzte Mission*, p. 169.

583 Krenz, "Anmerkungen zur Öffnung der Mauer," p. 366.

584 Ibid.

585 Given the fact that Kochemasov is not always reliable on dates and often fails to indicate any dates at all for the information he provides, it is probable that the telephone conversation

Rainer Eppelmann, a former Protestant clergyman appointed East German minister for defense and disarmament after the collapse of the GDR, asserted in an interview that on 11 November his predecessor, Kessler, had ordered an army division into action to close the borders but that this order had been refused.[586] Assuming that there is some truth to this and that the order was really an order and not part of some contingency planning, one could further assume that Kessler had backing in Moscow for this move. Shevardnadze's frequently expressed dark allusions to the military's opposition against German unification could be cited in support of such backing.[587] However, Shevardnadze's statements have always been of a general nature. He never described any specific contingency in response to which troops were to be dispatched, nor has he provided evidence as to which military leaders or units were allegedly involved at which time. It would seem, therefore, that intentions or plans to undo the opening of the wall by military force existed neither at the political nor at the military level and neither in Moscow nor at Soviet military headquarters in Wünsdorf.[588] What in all likelihood did exist, however, was concern that matters could get out of hand and *nolens volens* involve the Soviet armed forces. Unless one chooses to dismiss Kochemasov's account as a fabrication, his telephone conversation with Snetkov as well as instructions by the Soviet defense ministry to the WSG command are most appropriately placed in the context of overinsurance, that is, to make absolutely sure that neither active intervention nor inadvertent involvement would occur. This conclusion is not necessarily contradicted by Krenz's assertion that he had not been informed. Had he asked, he might have been told.

6. The KGB

According to popular preconceptions, internal security and foreign intelligence services – the guardians of the *arcana imperii* – are behind everything important that is happening in the world. Such perceptions often spring from fairly simple minds with a predilection for conspiracy theories. Given the closed nature of the Soviet system and the vast size of the KGB, or Committee for State Security, Western (and Russian) public opinion was particularly prone to suspect that the agency exerted significant influence on Soviet politics. Western analysts have proclaimed that because of the organization's unrestricted access to open and secret information the KGB "enjoyed the best insight into the real situation at home and in the Soviet

---

between him and Snetkov did not take place on 8 October but on 10 November. The latter date for the conversation is provided by *Der Spiegel*, 2 October 1995.

586 Rainer Eppelmann interview, *Die Welt*, 10 July 1990.

587 For instance, in an interview with Fedor Burlatsky in *Literaturnaia gazeta*, 10 April 1991.

588 This conclusion coincides with the analysis by Wettig, "Die sowjetische Rolle beim Umsturz in der DDR," pp. 55-56.

empire."[589] In its dealings with the outside world, the agency has been regarded as having been "even more omnipresent than in Soviet domestic life" and as the "primary executor in foreign policy."[590] The officers of the First Chief Directorate (FCD), responsible for Soviet clandestine activities abroad, have been portrayed as having been particularly effective, as "highly skilled professionals and members of an elite cadre"[591] and as "the Soviet regime's most urbane, cosmopolitan, and educated functionaries."[592] Liberal inclinations, too, have often been imputed to them, and first and foremost to Andropov and to officers at the organization's middle and lower echelons. Concerning the role of the KGB in the Soviet empire and German unification, perceptions of the ubiquitous presence and effective activities of the KGB have unequivocally been expressed in a book with the catchy title of *Conspiracy: How German Unity Was Really Achieved.*[593] "I am certain," writes Yevgenia Albats, "that the KGB was behind the overthrow of Honecker in East Germany."[594]

However, to summarize the main argument of this section, the author confesses to be impressed less by the KGB's analytical foresight, efficient organization, and effective operations than with its parochialism and preposterous pretensions, and the many instances of bungling and blundering. To be rejected is the notion that Andropov was some sort of closet liberal and that he and the KGB put Gorbachev in power and engineered perestroika.[595] The agency from 1985 to 1989 did not, either at the senior or middle-echelons of power, suddenly burst in full bloom with reformist zeal. The "Chekists," as KGB officers often refer to themselves, certainly sought to convey the impression that they were fully in tune with the new spirit of the time, but essentially they did not deviate from the agency's more nationalist than ideological

589 Astrid von Borcke, "The KGB and Perestroika," in Federal Institute on Soviet and International Studies, ed., *The Soviet Union 1988-1989* (Boulder, Colo.: Westview, 1990), p. 64. To avoid misunderstanding, except for some overstatements of the kind quoted, von Borcke's work is scholarly and her conclusions balanced. This applies in particular to her book *KGB: Die Macht im Untergrund* (Stuttgart: Hänssler, 1987).

590 John Barron, *KGB: The Secret Work of Soviet Secret Agents*, A Corgi Book (London: Transworld, 1974), p. 23.

591 Rose E. Goettemoeller and Paul F. Langer, *Foreign Area Studies in the USSR: Training and Employment of Specialists*, The Rand Corporation, R-2967-RC, January 1983, p. 99.

592 Astrid von Borcke, "KGB International: The Role of the Secret Service in Soviet Foreign and Security Policy," in Federal Institute on Soviet and International Studies, ed., *The Soviet Union 1986-1987* (Boulder, Colo.: Westview, 1989), p. 313.

593 Ralf Georg Reuth and Andreas Bönte, *Das Komplott: Wie es wirklich zur deutschen Einheit* kam (Munich: Piper, 1993).

594 Albats, *The State within a State*, p. 199.

595 This is not contradicted by the above-mentioned fact that Andropov in his position as head of the Central Committee's Socialist Countries Department, after having left the KGB, cultivated relations with eminent academic specialists and protected them from KGB and party harassment and persecution. This benevolent intervention would seem to have been predicated less on any liberal inclinations on Andropov's part than on his proclivity to seek the best available expertise in the interest of perfecting and modernizing the Soviet system.

and authoritarian, repressive, xenophobic, antisemitic, and anti-Western institutional ethos.[596] Whereas every other institution forming an integral part of the *ancien régime*, notably the party and the armed forces, as we have seen, had to accept in the course of the radicalization of reforms extensive personnel changes and had to suffer through revelations of internal mismanagement, corruption, and past crimes, the KGB was largely exempted from such ignomies. The vast majority of its officials remained unreconstructed, unrepentant, and unavailable for comment. The few exceptions – whistleblowers and defectors – were shunned and reviled by the organization.

The agency, then, was not in the forefront of reformist change. But until 1990 it also did not actively conspire to turn back the transformation processes in the internal empire. In the external empire, notwithstanding the agency's special powers and privileges, its pervasive network of informers at home and missions (*rezidentury*) abroad, and the secret activities of myriad officers thinly disguised as diplomats, foreign trade representatives, and journalists, the KGB was unprepared to act in a determined fashion to try to prevent the collapse. It was included in decision-making on the central issues of internal and external empire but more as a matter of bureaucratic routine and political reassurance than as a competent actor whose counsel was deliberately elicited. To return to the metaphor of the decision-making orchestra used above, the clandestine fiddle played by the KGB was only of *secondary* importance. The following sub-sections seek to substantiate these sweeping assertions.

The Impotence of Omnipotence

The inability of the KGB to control the course of events is nevertheless astounding, considering its tremendous material and personnel resources. Organized into four Chief Directorates (foreign operations, internal security and counterintelligence, communications and cryptography, and command of the border troops) and nine Directorates (military counterintelligence, ideological counterintelligence and dissidents, economic counterintelligence, security of government installations, government security, communications interceptions and signal intelligence, surveillance, transport, and military construction), the KGB combined the functions of both the CIA and the FBI.[597] But it exceeded both American agencies in the number of employees and the scale and type of operations, and it differed from them in the nature of its tasks. As for its size, when Gorbachev was elected party chief, the KGB was

596 Cheka is short for *Vserossiiskaia cherezvychainaia komissiia*, or All-Russian Extraordinary Commission, the name for the secret police founded by Felix Dzerzhinsky in 1917.

597 Albats, *The State within a State*, pp. 26-27. The Fifth Directorate, which had monitored dissent, was dissolved in October 1989. Its responsibilities were reabsorbed by the Second Chief Directorate and a new Directorate for the Defense of the Soviet Constitutional System.

estimated to have 25,000 officers and some 40,000 administrative personnel on its central staff in Moscow, in the provinces about 50,000 to 100,000 officials and a vast network of informers, some 300,000 to 350,000 border troops, and up to 30,000 agents abroad, who cooperated to varying degree with 100,000 members of the "allied" services in Eastern Europe.[598] Former KGB Maj.-Gen. Oleg Kalugin has claimed that more people worked in the KGB than in all the security agencies of Europe put together.[599] Albats places the total number of KGB employees prior to the August 1991 coup attempt at 720,000 people, or one Chekist for 428 Soviet citizens.[600] (In comparison, the CIA in the 1980s was said to have about 15,000 employees on its payroll and the FBI about 21,000 agents.)[601]

The KGB's main function was also quite different from that of Western intelligence agencies. As the "sword and shield" of the revolution, it was extensively used by the communist party to establish, consolidate, and expand Soviet power. In performing these tasks it left a wide trail of blood and human misery. Robert Conquest estimates the number of victims of the Great Purges alone at 15 million;[602] Alexei Myagkov speaks of a total of 20 million KGB casualties;[603] Roy Medvedev cited 40 million victims;[604] and Alexander Solzhenitsyn holds the organization responsible for the death of 60 million people.[605] Medvedev, whose estimates lie in the middle range, included the following victims in his count:

---

598 Von Borcke, "The Role of the Secret Police," p. 56. The figure of 65,000 officers in KGB headquarters is identical with that provided by former KGB Col. Oleg Gordievsky; see his interview with Natalya Gevorkian, *Moskovskie novosti*, 3 March 1991. Yevgenia Albats says that she was "able to glean a more exact figure of 89,000 Chekists in the capital;" Albats, *The State within a State*, p. 24.

599 In an interview with Yevgenia Albats and Natalya Gevorkian, *Moskovskie novosti*, 3 March 1991; see also his "Ne perekhodit' na lichnosti," *Komsomol'skaia pravda*, 3 July 1990. Kalugin was a specialist in foreign intelligence and as an exchange student at Columbia University had become acquainted with Yakovlev. In the agency he rose to the position of chief of foreign counterintelligence. He broke with the KGB in 1987, when he wrote a letter to Gorbachev warning him that the KGB was out of control.

600 Albats, *The State within a State*, p. 23. "The total number of people it employs," she cautions, "is the KGB's most closely guarded secret. And for good reason, since if they were to answer the question truthfully, they would immediately be faced with the far more challenging question: What exactly does this vast army of people *do*?"

601 Christopher Dobson and Ronald Payne, *The Dictionary of Espionage* (London: Harrap, 1984), p. 21; Albats, *The State within a State*, p. 24.

602 Robert Conquest, *The Great Terror* (London: Macmillan, 1968), p. 533.

603 Aleksei Myagkov, *Inside the KGB* (New York: Ballantine, 1983), p. 29.

604 In articles in *Moskovskie novosti* in November 1988 and *Argumenty i fakty* in February 1989, as quoted by Bill Keller, "Major Soviet Paper Says 20 Million Died as Victims of Stalin," *New York Times*, 4 February 1989. The term "victims" is broader, covering those people who did and those who did not survive arrest, deportation, imprisonment, and forced labor (40 million in Medvedev's accounting).

605 Alexander Solzhenitsyn, *The Oak and the Calf* (New York: Harper and Row, 1980), p. 536. In his speech on the seventieth anniversary of the 1917 revolution, the reader may remember,

- One million imprisoned or exiled from 1927 to 1929, falsely accused of being saboteurs or members of opposition parties.
- Nine to eleven million of the more prosperous peasants driven from their lands and another two to three million arrested or exiled in the early 1930's forced collectivization campaign. Many of these are believed to have been killed.
- Six to seven million killed in the punitive famine inflicted on peasants in 1932 and 1933.
- One million exiled from Moscow and Leningrad in 1935 for belonging to families of former aristocrats, merchants, capitalists, and government officials.
- About one million executed in the Great Terror of 1937-38, and another four to six million sent to forced labor camps from which most did not return.
- Two to three million sent to camps for violating absurdly strict labor laws imposed in 1940.
- At least ten to twelve million "repressed" in World War II, including millions of Soviet Germans and other ethnic minorities forcibly relocated.
- More than one million arrested on political grounds from 1946 to Stalin's death in 1953.

It would, of course, be unfair to taint every KGB officer with the brush of collective guilt for the immense human misery caused by that institution. In particular, it would be inappropriate not to draw a distinction between officers engaged in analytical work and those responsible for *mokrye dela*, the wet or bloody affairs. One may want to differentiate between officers involved in the task of maintaining a repressive system in the Soviet Union itself and those active in foreign intelligence, the latter as a rule being relatively more sophisticated and engaged in more analytical work than the former. And one may also find differences in the personality profile and world view of KGB career officers and those *komitetchiki* who had begun their career in other Soviet institutions, e.g., the party or the diplomatic service, and were then transferred to the agency. Nevertheless, in order to make it in the KGB it was useful to be or at least appear dedicated to the organization, indifferent to its sordid past, and impervious to moral issues.

To turn to the role of the KGB in the Gorbachev era, some analysts have considered the secret service not only as the "sword and shield" of perestroika but also as the "power behind the throne." They argue that Andropov as party chief had remained loyal to the agency. He had promoted Gorbachev to the number two position in the party hierarchy during his tenure in office, and after his (Andropov's) death the organization had continued its support for the heir apparent. Under the assumption that Gorbachev would provide the discipline and dynamism necessary to modernize

---

Gorbachev had spoken only of "thousands and thousands of party members and non-party people;" see above, p. 197.

the Soviet economy and improve the country's defense capabilities, the KGB threw its support behind him in the Kremlin succession struggle. For instance, the First Chief Directorate (FCD) for foreign intelligence, headed at that time by Vladimir Kryuchkov, in close cooperation with the *rezidentura* in Britain took great pains to make sure that Gorbachev's visit to London in December 1984 would be a success and enhance his foreign policy credentials.[606] In some versions of the argument, an "unholy trinity – the KGB, the CPSU, and the MIC [military-industrial complex] – cooked up the plan for perestroika"[607] and in another the KGB had stopped believing in Marxism-Leninism and conspired to replace it by nationalism.[608] Whereas Gorbachev's election as party chief was not due entirely or even mainly to support from the KGB, the agency nonetheless saw the election as a major victory.[609] Gorbachev, the argument continues, repaid the KGB for its support. He agreed to an expansion of the retaliatory powers of the security forces to expel foreign representatives in response to expulsions of Soviet spies, consented to a substantial increase in KGB representation in the party organs at the Twenty-seventh party congress and exempted the agency from the rigors of perestroika. He made Victor Chebrikov a full member of the Politburo in April 1985 and also conferred this status on his successor Kryuchkov as head of the KGB in October 1988.[610]

This interpretation does have some validity. However, it ignores Gorbachev's ambiguous attitude towards the KGB and fails sufficiently to take into account the fact that perestroika was a dynamic process with distinct phases of development as described in previous sections. Ample evidence has been presented here to confirm that Gorbachev shared some of Andropov's beliefs and continued some of his policies

---

606 Interview with Grigoriev; Christopher Andrew and Oleg Gordievsky, *KGB: The Inside Story of Its Foreign Operations from Lenin to Gorbachev* (London: Hodder and Stoughton, 1990), p. 606. Gordievsky was a KGB foreign intelligence officer recruited in 1974 as a double agent by the British secret service. In 1982-85 he was the KGB's deputy *resident* in London.

607 Albats, *The State within a State*, p. 197. It is unclear in her chapter entitled "Who Was Behind Perestroika?" whether she identifies with this argument or is simply telling a "fascinating story" (p. 202) for effect. At the end of the chapter she cautions against "oversimplification" by saying: "The story is more complex than that: it's about subtle timing and overlapping interests."

608 This version is expounded by Victor Yasmann, "Red Religion: An Ideology of Neo-Messianic Russian Fundamentalism," *Demokratizatsiya*, Vol. 1, No. 2 (1993), pp. 20-39.

609 Ibid., p. 608. The more outlandish statements about the KGB being behind Gorbachev's appointment and perestroika typically come from Russians living and writing in the West, including Albats, Gordievsky, and Yasmann; similarly, Abdurakhman Avtorkhanov, *Ot Andropova k Gorbachevu: dela i dni Kremlia* (Paris: YMCA Press, 1986). In the jointly authored book by Andrew and Gordievsky it would seem that the Western scholar was valiantly attempting to tone down some of the more radical assertions of his Russian co-author. For instance, it is incorrect to quote the book to the effect that "the KGB had stage-managed perestroika" (Albats, *The State within a State*, p. 168). Andrew and Gordievsky write on p. 608 that Gorbachev's election "was not, of course, due wholly or even mainly to support from the KGB."

610 Ibid., pp. 608-609. The argument about the KGB as a motor driving perestroika can also be found in J. Michael Waller, *The KGB in Russia Today* (Boulder, Colo.: Westview Press, 1995).

in the "modernization" and "acceleration" phase of his tenure in office. Furthermore, he had to rely extensively on the agency's internal affairs directorates for implementation of his anti-corruption and anti-alcoholism campaigns. Similarly, his attempts at introducing science and technology to the production process, staying in the military-technological competition with the West and undercutting Star Wars, and acquiring foreign technology for these purposes also made extensive KGB involvement necessary. Not surprisingly, then, as late as June 1988 – at the Nineteenth party conference – he praised the "purposeful work" of the leadership of the KGB and GRU (military intelligence), "aimed at improving their activities in the conditions created by the present stage of the development of our society and the unfolding of democratic processes."[611]

However, in the radicalization-of-reform, openness, and democratization phase with its new directions in Soviet ideology and foreign policy, the KGB was bound to be more of a liability than an asset. Furthermore, the argument can be made, although not conclusively be proven, that in this phase (lasting until autumn 1990, when he began actively courting the conservative forces), Gorbachev considered the KGB a *threat* to his reform program. There would have been a compelling logic to such a perception. This logic would have consisted of the following elements. (1) As the party's authority was weakening and its power after the 1988 reorganization deliberately being curtailed, its control mechanisms in the KGB were also being eroded. This process was enhanced by the progressive dismantling of the ideology upon which the party's power and authority had rested. The KGB, in contrast, did not suffer commensurately from the deideologization of Soviet politics and society. Its institutional ethos, as mentioned, was much more technocratic and nationalist than ideological. In a disoriented and disintegrating system this would have enhanced the agency's relative autonomy and elevated its status as a repository of law and order. (2) In the CPSU, notably in the International Department, but also in other Soviet institutions, there was some differentiation and a fair number of officials who could be persuaded actively to join in the reform effort. A similar state of affairs did not exist in the KGB. (3) The defense ministry and the armed forces bore the full brunt of perestroika. Although not in a mutinous and insurrectionist mood, they certainly had to be a source of concern for the political leadership. Since the new presidential and parliamentary institutions formed after May 1989 never became rooted and politically effective, it could have been a disastrous mistake for Gorbachev to confront the KGB head-on and precipitate a powerful anti-reform coalition of Chekists, orthodox party officials, and disgruntled military officers. In this interpretation, then, the caution Gorbachev displayed in his attitudes and policies towards the KGB was neither predicated on ideological affinity with the agency nor on gratitude for past favors. For

611 *Pravda*, 29 June 1988.

him, it would seem, the KGB was simply one powerful Soviet institution too many to take on.

This is not to say that no attempt at all was made to bring the KGB in line with perestroika and openness and to change its personnel and operations. In 1985-89, eight of fourteen union republic KGB chiefs were relieved of their duties. The officers included, with the likely reasons for their replacement in parenthesis hereafter, the top Chekists of the Central Asian republics of Kazakhstan, Kirgizia, and Tadzhikistan (corruption or inability to stamp out corruption); Lithuania, Azerbaijan, and Armenia (failure to control ethnic and inter-republican unrest); Georgia (age); and Ukraine (maltreatment of an investigative journalist who died in detention).[612] At the end of September 1988, the personnel changes reached the very top. Chebrikov, who had been first party secretary of Dnepropetrovsk *oblast'*, KGB cadre chief from 1967 to 1982, and chief Chekist since 1968, and whose career profile reflected the conservative and provincial outlook of the agency, was ostensibly promoted. He was made a CC Secretary and head of one of the newly established Commissions, the Commission for Legal Policy.[613] The commission was to oversee the work of the CC's State and Legal Policy Department which had traditionally exercised a degree of control over the administrative organs – the armed forces, the KGB, the Ministry of Internal Affairs, the Prosecutor's Office, the trade unions, and the Komsomol. On paper, the functions of the Commission for Legal Policy were broader than those of the other commissions, and thus Gorbachev seemed to have made a deal with Chebrikov in order to whittle away at Ligachev's power. He appeared to have *gained* Chebrikov's support and not, as many observers thought, lost it. The former head of the KGB also still ranked high on the CPSU's "popularity scale." In the election of the party candidates for the Congress of People's Deputies from March to May 1989, he – together with Gorbachev and Ryzhkov – was among the Politburo members receiving the highest number of votes.[614] In practice, however, since the party was losing power, any previously important party position was being devalued, and thus Chebrikov's promotion was in essence a demotion. At the same time, the trend lines pointed in the direction of more pressure on the KGB. In conjunction with the attempt to exert parliamentary control over the armed forces, the KGB, too, was to be supervised – by a Supreme Soviet Committee on Defense and State Security.

One KGB officer's loss was another officer's gain. Kryuchkov was appointed chairman of the KGB, promoted over the heads of two first deputies, and he was the first chief of foreign intelligence ever to reach the top position in the agency. His

612 Von Borcke, "The KGB and Perestroika," p. 62.

613 This description and analysis of Chebrikov and the Commission on Legal Policy is based on Rahr, "Who Is in Charge of the Party Apparatus?," pp. 21-22.

614 Ibid.

career had been closely tied to that of Andropov, beginning in Hungary when the former was posted to the *rezidentura* and the latter ambassador in that country. Kryuchkov followed Andropov to Moscow and worked for him in the CC Socialist Countries Department and later, when his mentor became KGB chief, as head of his secretariat. Kryuchkov was thus privy to the agency's most sensitive secrets. In 1971 he was promoted to deputy head and, three years later, head of the FCD. In December 1987, Kryuchkov – traveling incognito – was included in the Soviet delegation going to Washington to sign the treaty on the elimination of intermediate-range nuclear missiles. Never before had a Soviet leader been accompanied on a visit to the West by the head of the FCD.[615]

When he became chairman of the KGB, Kryuchkov was hailed by Western analysts as an "expert with modern ideas, at least in foreign policy" and an "ally" of Shevardnadze and Yakovlev.[616] Gordievsky, however, who knew him well, has painted a different picture. He has described him as single-minded, self-confident, intolerant of differing viewpoints, and utterly humorless, as someone who never strayed from a prepared text and never tried to coin a striking phrase. A workaholic, he shunned alcohol, and even before Andropov and Gorbachev launched *their* anti-alcoholism campaigns, he banned drinking parties where he had the power to do so. When he became FCD chief he had absolutely no experience of foreign intelligence operations or of life in the West. His world view was "shaped by ideological stereotypes and conspiracy theories" and by "paranoia about the threat from the West."[617] This was not, one would have thought, the kind of personality and political profile conducive to the pluralization and liberalization of Soviet society, abandonment of empire, and cooperation with Western countries. It was a profile that fit much more closely his later role as one of the main organizers of the abortive August 1991 coup. In fact, he never repented his role in it. The only regret he had was that he and his co-conspirators had let themselves be deceived and that they had not acted more decisively. When asked later about the reason why he, as head of such a powerful organization as the KGB, could have let the collapse of the Soviet Union happen, he replied: "We were hostages of our own illusions. ... We obeyed the law and the president, and Gorbachev had one quality: his hypocrisy was so great that it was not easy to tell the difference between truth and lies."[618] What precisely it was that recommended Kryuchkov to Gorbachev or someone close to him is unclear and will probably remain so.

---

615 Andrew and Gordievsky, *KGB: The Inside Story*, p. 625.

616 Von Borcke, "The KGB and Perestroika," p. 64.

617 Andrew and Gordievsky, *KGB: The Inside Story*, pp. 534-35, 602.

618 David Remnick, "Letter from Russia: The War for the Kremlin," *The New Yorker*, 22 July 1996.

Perhaps it was relative flexibility and adaptability. Kryuchkov did introduce some cosmetic and operation changes and thereby conveyed the impression – to some – that the KGB was now in step with openness. As aptly described by Remnick, Kryuchkov tried to "personalize" himself and the institution he represented. He confessed to the press his admiration for Van Cliburn and Bellini's *Norma*.[619] He fielded (carefully screened) questions on a television show. He allowed (carefully chaperoned) tours of Lubyanka. Comrade Katya Mayorova was crowned Miss KGB – probably the only security services beauty queen in the world. "Violence, inhumanity, and the violation of human rights have always been alien to the work of our secret services," he told the Italian paper *L'Unità*.[620] To the parliament's Committee on Defense and State Security he revealed: "The KGB has no secret informers, only assistants."[621] In November 1989, Sergei Kuznetsov, an active member of the Democratic Union Party, had been sentenced to three years' imprisonment for civil rights activism. One month later, Kryuchkov presided over a meeting with the International Women Journalists' Press Club where he clarified for the record that "the security organs did not combat "dissent", only specific unlawful activities."[622] As for the future work of the *komitetchiki*, he said, "our actions must protect human rights."[623]

There were a few changes at the operational level. "Active measures," *desinformatsiia*, cooperation with and financing of "peace movements" and various front organizations – work that had traditionally been coordinated with the CC's International Department – were being deemphasized. Officers that had been trained for work abroad were being reassigned to the Baltic republics, Armenia, Azerbaijan, Moldova, and other areas in which independence movements and ethnic unrest were erupting. Finally, prompted by the embarrassment which terrorists armed with Soviet weapons and explosives were causing in Moscow's diplomatic relations with the West, the hijacking of an Ilyushin transport plane from the northern Caucasus to Israel in December 1988 and, as Kryuchkov said, the disappearance not of "several tons of enriched uranium in the world but ... of several hundred tons," the KGB was by 1989 ready for (limited) cooperation with Western intelligence agencies to combat

619 The enumeration of measures designed to enhance the KGB's image draws on Remnick, *Lenin's Tomb*, pp. 342-44.

620 Ibid., p. 342.

621 Supreme Soviet Hearings, 14 July 1989, BBC, SWB, SU/0513 C/1-6, 20 July 1989; as quoted in Andrew and Gordievsky, *KGB: The Inside Story*, p. 627.

622 Transcript of the December 1988 meeting (Stenogramma vstrechi Predsedatelia KGB Vladimira Kriuchkova s chlenami Mezhdunarodnogo press-kluba zhenshchin-zhurnalistok), Yevgenia Albats's personal archive; Albats, *The State within a State*, p. 206.

623 Ibid.

international terrorism.[624] However, to the extent that it is known, there were no concomitant personnel cuts in the KGB and no significant organizational changes.[625]

After this survey of the functions of the KGB in the Soviet political system and the ambiguous relationship between Gorbachev and the KGB, the question about the likely role of the agency on the German problem can now be addressed.

KGB Operations in Germany

What follows closely from the cosmetic character of the changes in the KGB is the fact that access to the agency's archives on its operations in Germany remains closed. Some interesting and intriguing information, however, *is* available, suggesting some plausible lines of interpretation. There is, first and foremost, little doubt about the KGB's concern about developments in East Germany. Like the armed forces, the security agency's largest base abroad was in the GDR, and to lose it would have meant major disruptions of its intelligence operations in West Germany and NATO. Organizationally, one of the FCD's deputy heads, Gen. Victor Grushko, had nominal responsibility for West European affairs but *de facto* for the German problem as a whole since – as in the MFA before 1986 – one of his departments, the Fourth Department, dealt with both West and East German affairs as well as with Austria. General Anatoli Novikov was the chief of this "German" department.[626]

Even before the rapid erosion of the GDR's stability in 1989, the FCD and the German department in Moscow as well as the *rezidentura* in East Berlin (Karlshorst) were facing the same problem Gorbachev had to contend with at the political level: East German arrogance and condescension; disdain for the changes occurring in the Soviet Union; criticism about their possible repercussions in the GDR; and failure to inform Soviet counterparts about sensitive developments in the GDR. The harbingers of change became briefly visible in the mid-1970s, when a KGB officer from the Karlshorst *rezidentura* was arrested for drunken driving and its chief, Gen. Anatoli Lazarev, complained about "the use of Nazi methods against a fraternal power."[627] Honecker vigorously rejected the complaint, and at his insistence – along the Yefremov-Abrasimov pattern – Lazarev was recalled to Moscow.[628]

---

624 For the changes in KGB operations see Andrew and Gordievsky, *KGB: The Inside Story*, pp. 635-36 and Albats, *The State within a State*, p. 235.

625 The dissolution of the Fifth Directorate was noted above, n. 597.

626 The data on the organizational structure concerning the KGB and Germany and on Gen. Grushko are from Andrew and Gordievsky, *KGB: The Inside Story*, pp. 3-4, 565, 641, 653; on Novikov, see Reuth and Bönte, *Das Komplott*, p. 211.

627 Andrew and Gordievsky, *KGB: The Inside Story*, p. 640.

628 Ibid.

When Kryuchkov moved up to become top Chekist in October 1988, he was succeeded in his post as FCD head by Leonid Shebarshin.[629] Unlike his predecessor, Shebarshin had extensive international experience. He was a professional diplomat who had been posted twice to Islamabad, transferred to the KGB, and worked for the agency in New Delhi and Teheran. There is little direct evidence of his relations with the East German state security ministry or his attitudes towards developments in the GDR. A rare exception are the transcripts of his talks with Stasi chief Mielke in East Berlin in April 1989. Also present at the meeting were Lt. Gen. Grushko, Col. Novikov, and the head of the *rezidentura* in East Germany, Gennadi Titov.

Mielke lived up to the Russian proverb, "Where there is the khan, there goes the horde." He followed closely in Honecker's footsteps. In an extraordinarily tedious and pretentious briefing, Mielke showered his colleague with the usual statistics about the GDR's achievements and concluded: "As a matter of principle, it can be stated that the situation in our republic is characterized by great political stability. State security is at all times reliably safeguarded."[630] He then verbally flogged and flailed Shebarshin, vehemently complaining about an article in *Moskovskaia pravda* ("circulation about 1 million") that had revealed to Soviet readers that Stalin had at one time worked as an agent for the Czarist secret police, the Okhrana.[631] He pierced him with questions: Had the KGB not placed the archives under its control? Are there still any archives that are not under KGB control? If Stalin had liquidated the people who knew about his past, why hadn't he destroyed the archival evidence? Could it now be said that it had been Stalin, the Okhrana agent, who had defeated fascism? Had he built socialism and the international communist movement in that capacity? If that were true, he, Mielke would also be an agent of the Okhrana. In fact, "all of us would be Okhrana agents because we worked under Stalin." The blistering attack culminated in a thinly veiled threat: "I have to be afraid that you will expose our agents if there is a possibility to look at the archives. ... You hurt yourself, and we are put in the uncomfortable position [to have to decide] whether we can still tell you where we are getting [our] information from." Shebarshin interrupted Mielke at that point, the only time he did so in the course of the harangue, to state the obvious: "*I sit here like a defendant. I am not responsible for this article.*"[632]

Several other gems refract both the secret service mind-set and the state of Soviet-East German relations. After his lecture, Mielke asked his guest's forgiveness for its

629 Shebarshin has published a book about his work as head of foreign intelligence; Leonid V. Shebarshin, *Iz zhizni nachal'nika razvedki* (Moscow: Mezhdunarodnye otnosheniia, 1994). It does not, however, contain anything of value on the issue of KGB operations in Germany.

630 "Top secret" notes (*Notiz*) about the talks between Mielke and Shebarshin on 7 April 1989, SE, Central Party Archives, ZAIG 5198, Bl. 100-39.

631 The article had appeared in *Moskovskaia pravda* on 30 March 1989.

632 "Top secret" notes (*Notiz*) about the talks between Mielke and Shebarshin (italics mine).

length. However, they had not been meeting all that often. Furthermore, "I thought that Comrade Shebarshin would report it [the content of Mielke's statement] to Comrade Kryuchkov, and that Comrade Kryuchkov will transmit it in an appropriate form to Comrade Chebrikov, who would inform Comrade Gorbachev." One almost has to admire the pathetic if not pathological sense of self-importance of the Stasi chief, his apparently unshakable belief in the free flow of information in and the unbroken importance of the Soviet Politburo as a decision-making body. Mielke evidently assumed that Kryuchkov, not being as yet a full member of the Politburo, would have no direct access to Gorbachev, but that Chebrikov, by virtue of his full membership, *did* and would have the time and interest to listen to a rehash of Mielke's innuendos. Nevertheless, what Mielke specifically had in mind was stated at another place with similarly disarming simplicity as his explanation of the purposes of his elaborations. Since Gorbachev's visit to West Germany was at that time only a few weeks away, he warned against "détente euphoria," falling victim to "human rights demagoguery" and other "imperialist intrigues," and allowing "interference in the internal affairs of socialist countries." In that context he exclaimed: "*The FRG is playing a dual game! To know that is important for Comrade Gorbachev's trip to Bonn.*"[633]

A final gem is an exchange about the role of the security agencies in political and social change. In the process, Shebarshin – in stark contrast to his own superior and to his East German counterpart – emerges as an essentially sensible observer and politically loyal official. After a poignant and fair presentation of both the risks and benefits of perestroika and glasnost, he dismisses his East German host's evident proclivity for the eradication of problems such as the emergence of nationalism and excesses of glasnost by traditional administrative measures: "It would not be realistic to hope that [these problems] can only be solved by state security means, albeit the state security organs have to make a corresponding contribution." He also tells his host that whether anybody liked it or not: "We are carrying out the orders and instructions of the party. We don't make policy, but we are implementing it." Mielke disagreed. In another example of his exaggerated sense of self-importance and of the manipulative role of the security agency Mielke countered: "*It isn't entirely true that we are only implementing party policy. Our information must find expression in party policy.*" He begged his interlocutor "not to be too modest" about this.[634]

As in the Gorbachev-Honecker private conversations, several sensitive subjects in the Shebarshin-Mielke exchange were either missing or only cryptically alluded to. The most important of the these was the systematic attempt made by Honecker to increase, with the assistance of Mielke, his own control in the domestic system and

633 Ibid. (italics mine).
634 Ibid.

the Stasi's autonomy vis-à-vis the KGB. As Gordievsky has confirmed, both attempts had begun well before Gorbachev's ascent to the highest office in the Kremlin. He also provides an interesting twist to this confirmation when he reports that Mielke and Markus Wolf, the Stasi's chief of foreign intelligence, were complaining at the KGB's Lubyanka headquarters that "Honecker was restricting the intimacy of Soviet-GDR intelligence operations."[635] It is difficult to say whether these complaints were genuine or disingenuous, a ruse or trap laid by one or the other to ascertain how the KGB would react, or both. Whatever the case may be, the "endless discussions in the [KGB] center, some of them witnessed by Gordievsky in Grushko's office, on how to strengthen Mielke's and Wolf's hands against Honecker," would have been utterly pointless.[636] In Gordievsky's view, the "situation was further complicated by the fact that Mielke and Wolf themselves were scarcely on speaking terms."[637]

Missing in the "top secret" conversation of the secret service officers was also a KGB operation in East Germany that was so secret that it was kept not only from the Stasi but out of normal KGB channels – the Luch (ray of light) operation. According to a report by the German Federal Agency for the Protection of the Constitution, and replicated by Soviet sources,[638] "Luch was removed from the ordinary hierarchical structure of the official *rezidentura* and was known only to members of the Fourth ['German'] Department directly concerned and the top level of the FCD."[639] It is plausible to assume that Titov was also informed about the operation and provided staffing for it. That is, Shebarshin, Grushko, Novikov, and Titov were almost certainly aware of the operation in their meeting with Mielke in April 1989 but chose to keep quiet. What about Luch's functions? The Bundesamt report states:

> The establishment of this group had been considered necessary in the course of the growing tendencies of emancipation of the MfS [Ministry for State Security] in relation to [its] KGB 'mentor' and doubts about the unconditional loyalty of the leading SED cadres in that connection. ... Starting from the mid-1980s, the Luch group had been instructed to persuade citizens of the ... GDR in leading positions of science,

---

635 Andrew and Gordievsky, *KGB: The Inside Story*, p. 640.

636 Ibid.

637 Ibid. In his book, Markus Wolf, *In eigenem Auftrag: Bekenntnisse und Einsichten* (Munich: Schneekluth, 1991), refers neither to the differences with Mielke nor to Soviet-East German controversies over the breakdown of cooperation.

638 Evgeni Bovkun, "'Luch' KGB v svetlom tsarstve kapitalizma" [Luch in the Bright Czardom of Capitalism], *Izvestiia*, 22 September 1993. The title of Bovkun's article is evidently derived from Russian literature, from *luch sveta v temnom tsartstve* [ray of light in the dark Czardom] used in a literary critique by Nikolai Dobrolubov in reference to a nineteenth century play by Alexander Ostrovsky, *Groza* [Thunderstorm]. Dobrolubov called the heroine of this play, a progressively-thinking woman, a ray of light in the darkness.

639 A summary of and excerpts from the report by the federal agency (Bundesamt für Verfassungsschutz) can be found in Reuth and Bönte, *Wie es wirklich zur deutschen Einheit kam*, pp. 210-12.

technology and politics to cooperate with the KGB and thereby influence socially relevant processes.[640]

This poses the interesting question whether Gorbachev was playing a dual game, asserting publicly and in conversation with Honecker the principle of "non-interference" but authorizing clandestine operations for the destabilization of the Honecker regime – an effort, furthermore, that turned out to be successful when Honecker was forced to resign on 17 October 1989. The story sounds interesting but has no basis in fact. In reality, the Luch operation was more limited in scope and politically ineffective. It also changed over time, as the West German report states. Whereas, from the mid-1980s until 1988, "priority was given to persuade high-level GDR leading cadres" to cooperate with the KGB, Luch subsequently concentrated on the establishment of contacts with "experts at the mid-level of management" and "members of the [old] bloc parties, parties newly founded in the process of systemic change, and youth organizations."[641]

There may have been two interrelated reasons for the change in approach. The first is high-level political intervention. Several instances are known in which high-ranking members of the SED Politburo had contacted Soviet representatives about the possibility of assistance in the replacement of Honecker. SED Politburo member and First Deputy Prime Minister Krolikowski had approached Ambassador Kochemasov and told him that for a long time he had looked for a pretext under which to talk to him. A very difficult state of affairs had arisen in a party rife with dogmatism, centralization, and curtailment of discussion. Everything was being painted in rosy colors. Something needed to be done. When Kochemasov asked what it was he had in mind, he received the following reply: "*The leadership has to be replaced.*"[642] The ambassador was also told that there were other members in the Politburo who shared this point of view. In accordance with Gorbachev's stance of non-interference and referring to the circumstances of Ulbricht's replacement, Kochemasov explained that the times of Soviet involvement in East German leadership changes were over. Kochemasov nevertheless sent a telegram to Moscow reporting the conversation.[643]

Kochemasov was similarly approached, as he writes in his memoirs, by Prime Minister and Politburo member Willi Stoph.[644] Even prior to that, Stoph had taken the "extreme risk" of establishing contact with the KGB *rezidentura*. According to Ivan Kuzmin, the head of its Information Department, the East German premier had transmitted material to the KGB residency, some of which in his own handwriting.

640 Ibid., p. 210.
641 Ibid., p. 211.
642 Kotschemassow, *Meine letzte Mission*, p. 59 (italics mine).
643 Ibid.
644 Ibid., p. 60.

The material described the precarious state of the East German economy, the state of affairs and distribution of power in the party, and Honecker's dishonesty in his relations with the Soviet Union. Stoph's approach, in Kuzmin's interpretation, allowed only one simple conclusion: unless Honecker was replaced the GDR would collapse.[645] To that extent, it was a "direct appeal to Mikhail Sergeevich [Gorbachev] for [his] support" in an attempt to force the East German leader from office.[646] How did Gorbachev react? He responded, according to the KGB officer, in line with a "personal trait of his character. As usual, he said nothing. He didn't take any decision."[647]

It is reasonable to infer from all this that the political leadership in Moscow *could* have cooperated with a faction in the East German leadership trying to unseat Honecker, but deliberately desisted from making such an attempt. The change in the level of contacts Luch was seeking to establish may have been directly connected with this approach. The political leadership in Moscow appears to have reasoned that sooner rather than later, somehow, Honecker would be forced out of or die in office. In that event, it was expedient to have in place contacts with mid-level cadres for the post-Honecker era. Gorbachev thus declined to authorize the KGB to give history a push. He decided to let things drift or, if one prefers to use his terminology, to let history decide. And decide it did. But in ways neither predicted nor desired by him.

This chapter was intended to examine the domestic setting, the major institutional actors, and the main political leaders determining policy on the German problem. Except for some glances ahead where it seemed appropriate, the period covered was from Gorbachev's ascent to power in March 1985 to the elections to the Congress of People's Deputies in March 1989. This period was characterized by first gradual and then progressive radicalization of change in domestic and foreign policy. Developments in that period were still mainly of an evolutionary nature. But the seeds for *revolutionary* change had been planted. In the next and final phase the seeds bore fruit.

---

645 Interview with Ivan Kuzmin, conducted by Mikhail Karpov, "Padenie Berlinskoi steny," *Nezavisimaia gazeta*, 5 November 1994.

646 Ibid.

647 Ibid. Kuzmin obviously thinks that the political leadership *should* have taken action – and earlier than 1989. Starting in the second half of 1988, he wrote in an article, the *residentura* reported more frequently and more strongly about the GDR's growing indebtedness, deterioration of economic conditions, dissatisfaction among the population, and the emergence of "*irreversible structures*" which pointed to an "*objective process towards the restoration of German unity*;" Ivan Kuzmin, "Sekretnye sluzhby mnogo znali – no resheniia prinimali politiki," *Novoe vremia*, No. 20 (1993), pp. 28-29 (italics mine).

Chapter 6: The Last Crisis

1. The Transformed Internal and International Setting

Gorbachev's attitudes and policies on the German problem evolved on three interacting levels: (1) radicalization of political change and mounting economic and nationality problems in the Soviet Union; (2) redefinition of the Soviet-East German relationship in a new context of Soviet-East European relations; and (3) a shift in the perceived importance of West Germany for the mitigation of Soviet economic problems and the reordering of European security. Change that had been initiated "from above" was now driven "from below," and this applied to both the Soviet Union and Eastern Europe.

Mounting Domestic Problems

To turn to the first level, in his account of the Gorbachev era, Chernyaev dwells on the acute frustration he felt with the evolution of domestic political and economic affairs in 1989. He sensed a "crisis of leadership" and harbored an "inner discomfort" and "dissatisfaction with Gorbachev that resulted from the great gap between domestic and foreign policy developments." He calls that year a "year lost."[1] Leonid Abalkin, deputy prime minister and chairman of a newly founded Commission on Economic Reform, in a speech to the Supreme Soviet on 29 June 1989, considered the Soviet economy to be in a "state of emergency." He deplored that for one and a half years economic conditions in the Soviet Union had "deteriorated further every month."[2] Gorbachev, at the Congress of People's Deputies, on 30 May 1989, regretted that the general public had not felt any major beneficial effects of perestroika. Whereas, previously, he had characterized the economy as being "on the verge of crisis," he now thought that the Soviet economy was "in a state of crisis."[3]

The economic crisis had acute social repercussions. The growing gap between popular expectations raised by promises for the improvement of the economy and the acute supply problems in the agricultural and consumer goods sector created "strong tensions," made people "insecure," and even led to "embitterment," as Gorbachev confided to Honecker in June.[4] In the following month, a wave of workers' strikes broke out in the Soviet Union. They began in the coal mines of the Kuznetsk Basin of Siberia and then spread to Vorkuta in the far north, to the Don Basin in Ukraine,

1 Chernyaev, *Shest' let s Gorbachevym*, pp. 264, 315-316.
2 Central Soviet Television, 29 June 1989.
3 Central Soviet Television, 30 May 1989.
4 Transcript (*Niederschrift*) of the talks between Gorbachev and Honecker in Moscow, 28 June 1989, SED Politburo, *Arbeitsprotokolle*, Central Party Archives, J IV 2/2.035/60.

Karaganda in northern Kazakhstan, and Sakhalin in the far east. After that month, the Kremlin could never again have confidence that it was the master of events. Links were being forged between the radical reformers among the intelligentsia in the cities, nationalists in and between the republics, and the political uprising of workers across the country.[5]

There was perhaps only one way to avoid shipwreck: not to try stem the tide or steer against the powerful currents but to navigate with them. A passionate plea not to battle the currents was made by Andrei Sakharov in private conversation with Gorbachev in May 1989, after a heated and unpleasant exchange at the first session of the Congress of People's Deputies. "It is not for me," Sakharov said,

> to tell you how serious things are in the country, how dissatisfied people are, and how everyone expects things to get worse. There is a crisis of trust in the country towards the leadership and the party. Your personal authority and popularity are down to zero. People cannot wait any longer with nothing but promises. A middle course in situations like these is almost impossible. The country and you are at a crossroads – either increase the process of change maximally, or try to retain the administrative command system with all its qualities. In the first case, you must use the support of the "left" [the reformers]; you can be sure there will be many brave and energetic people you can count on. In the second case, you know for yourself whose support you will have, but you will never be forgiven the attempt at perestroika.[6]

But three years later, after the collapse of the Soviet Union, speaking in reference to the constitutional changes Sakharov had suggested, Gorbachev was to lament: "*If we had only listened more carefully to Andrei Dmitrievich [Sakharov] ...* "[7]

The catharsis of vigorous political debate, demonstrations, more democratic elections, and the workers' strikes interacted with another factor that would be of crucial importance in the demise of both the internal and the external empire: the proliferation of ethnic conflicts and the upsurge in independence movements throughout the Soviet Union. The most determined national revival threatening the survival of the Soviet Union developed in the Baltic republics. What had begun as a drive for more autonomy for Estonia, Latvia, and Lithuania within the constitutional framework of the Soviet Union, in 1989 turned into a powerful independence movement with torrents of demonstrations and protests against the Hitler-Stalin pact, the forcible incorporation of the three countries into the USSR, the subsequent

---

5 Remnick, *Lenin's Tomb*, p. 233.

6 Ibid., p. 281. Earlier, at the congress session, Sakharov had taken the floor, imploring Gorbachev to endorse a "decree on power" that would end the communist party's monopoly. Gorbachev had reacted angrily. He had unceremoniously cut Sakharov off and proceeded to lecture him, adopting, as Remnick observes, an attitude of "haughty disdain" and a "peremptory, bullying tone." It was because of this treatment that Sakharov had requested a private audience.

7 Ibid., p. 282 (italics mine). The full sentence reads: "If we had only listened more carefully to Andrei Dmitrievich [Sakharov], we might have learned something."

executions and deportations, and the imposition of a system that had left the Baltic states far behind their Scandinavian neighbors in socio-economic development. Management of the nationality problems was not helped by Gorbachev's inability to understand that national emancipation movements have hardly ever been deflected from their drive towards independence by arguments of economic rationality. Even after the realization of Baltic independence, Gorbachev has chastized the Baltic peoples for ingratitude and allegedly jeopardizing their prosperity. They forgot, he writes in his memoirs, that their well-being and the higher labor productivity in the Baltic republics as compared to other Soviet republics had been "created by immense investments financed from the Union budget and of course also by qualified specialists and workers who had come to the Baltic area from Russia and other Union republics" and by the "supply of fuel and energy free of charge (*darovomu*)."[8]

In another European part of the Soviet Union, unrest occurred in Moldova, with demonstrators demanding independence and reunification with Romania. Most sensitive for the whole character and cohesion of the Soviet Union and Russia's identity, however, was the emergence of Rukh, a powerful independence movement in Ukraine. Many Russians could conceive of a Soviet Union without the Baltic states and Central Asia. However, the Kievan Rus had been the precursor of the Russian state, and "Little Russia" (as Ukraine historically was called), was being regarded in Moscow as an integral part of a Slavic Union. The idea of two separate Slavic states was simply anathema to most Russians; hence, the political survival of Gorbachev and the reform course crucially depended on the prevention of Russian-Ukrainian separation and divorce.

The Pandora Box of nationalism, ethnic conflict, and secessionism was opened also in Central Asia and the southern republics of the USSR. In April 1989, large demonstrations for autonomy and independence took place in Tbilisi, the Georgian capital. They were brutally suppressed by Soviet troops, with the use of spades and poison gas. In July, with the situation in the Georgian capital ostensibly defused, the sparks of ethnic strife ignited another fire in the area, in Georgia's Abkhaz Autonomous Region. In neighboring Armenia and Azerbaijan, the upsurge of nationalist sentiment locked the two republics into conflict over Nagorno-Karabakh. In June, more than 50 people were killed and at least 500 injured in the Soviet Union's worst ethnic bloodshed in decades in Uzbekistan, as Uzbeks turned against the Meshketians, a Turkic minority in Central Asia. The uncertainties created by ethnic conflicts and the reassertion of Muslim identity induced many Russians to leave the area. Those remaining behind were organizing and demanding that the center intervene on their behalf. In September a special Central Committee plenary

---

8 Gorbachev, *Zhizn'*, Vol. 1, p. 511.

meeting on nationality problems finally took place. But its decisions and resolutions had practically no impact on the course of events.

The Soviet leaders' preoccupation with internal affairs and their felt necessity to try to extinguish the flickering ethnic fires limited their ability effectively to manage foreign policy. For instance, in preparation for Gorbachev's planned visit to Bonn, 12-15 June, Shevardnadze was scheduled to visit the West German capital on 16 April. However, because of his involvement in Moscow's efforts to defuse the nationality conflict in Georgia, the foreign minister felt constrained to postpone the visit. Similarly, on 7 June government spokesmen in Bonn let it be known unofficially that Gorbachev's program in West Germany would have to be curtailed due to domestic political problems in the USSR, including the outbreak of violent nationality conflicts in Uzbekistan and the on-going session of the Congress of People's Deputies. Soviet foreign ministry spokesman Gerasimov surmised that the session might be interrupted for the duration of Gorbachev 's visit. Meetings with the chairmen of the four parties represented in the West German parliament were first removed from the program and then reinstated, but a planned interview for the two main West German television channels was canceled. Gorbachev also asked that several hours daily be kept free of any engagements so that he would be able, from the Soviet embassy in Bonn, to deal with reports from the USSR.[9]

Eastern Europe: Breaking Through the Socialist Framework

To turn to the second level of analysis, the drive for national emancipation in Eastern Europe: a pivotal role here was played by the increasing realization among both party leaderships and popular movements that Gorbachev was disinclined to use force in order to prevent change. Nationality conflicts and independence movements in the Soviet Union and the way the center attempted to cope with them forcefully interacted with the movements for national emancipation in Eastern Europe: as with regard to the German problem, the leadership's intense preoccupation with nationality issues in the Soviet Union was a drain on Gorbachev's time and energy; it reinforced his aversion to intervention in the internal affairs of the dependencies; and it eroded even further Gorbachev's will to empire. Clearly recognizable for everyone concerned, his attempt to safeguard the integrity and viability of the USSR took precedence over maintaining control and cohesion in the bloc.

This was reflected in the evolution of the principle of Freedom of Choice. In February 1989, in Kiev, Gorbachev elaborated on that theme, stating authoritatively

9 *Süddeutsche Zeitung*, 8 and 9 June 1989. The talks with the chairmen of the four parties represented in parliament took place after a formal dinner on 12 June. The session of the Congress of People's Deputies ended on 9 June, a few days prior to Gorbachev's arrival in Bonn.

that Soviet relations with the socialist states should be based on "unconditional independence (*bezuslovnaia samostoiatel'nost'*), full equality, [and] strict non-intervention in internal affairs."[10] This, in turn, presupposed "responsibility of the party and government of each socialist country to its own people."[11] In other words, the local party leaderships could no longer rely on the Brezhnev Doctrine and Soviet military intervention to keep them in power. They themselves had to provide for their own political legitimacy and viability.

In the countries to which the principle of Freedom of Choice applied, the most important changes occurred in Hungary and in Poland. In November 1988, in *Hungary* the Social Democratic Party, outlawed since 1948, reconstituted itself and at the beginning of March 1989 held its first national party congress. In the communist party – the Hungarian Socialist Workers' Party (HSWP) – quite in contrast to the CPSU, radical reformist strands became ascendant This state of affairs, also unlike in the Soviet Union, later in the year led to the split of the party into a conservative and radical reformist wing. Parliament adopted a new constitution which abolished the monopoly of a single political party; codified human and civil rights, the separation of powers and equality of several forms of ownership; and opened the way to a market economy. In domestic affairs, the new government under Prime Minister Miklós Németh and Foreign Minister Gyula Horn, was thoroughly committed to a reform socialist program and, in foreign policy, to a reorientation away from the Warsaw Pact and Comecon towards cooperation with Western European countries, notably West Germany (see below).[12] The new government, therefore, reinstated the two main objectives promulgated by Prime Minister Imre Nagy that had prompted Soviet intervention in 1956: the establishment of a multi-party system and the declaration of neutrality.

On domestic issues, however, it was *Poland* which, seen from the traditional Soviet perspective, broke through the limits of acceptable change in the bloc. The forces of radical change lay in an accelerating political and economic crisis. In April 1989 the "round-table" talks on constitutional reform were successfully concluded with an agreement on comprehensive parliamentary and electoral reform, later approved by the Sejm. In June the Polish United Workers' Party (PUWP) suffered a crushing defeat. Solidarity received 99 of the 100 seats in the Senate, the newly created upper house of parliament. In the lower house, the Sejm, the communist party also found itself in a minority after the elections. The party had compiled a national

10 "Perestroika - delo vsekh narodov strany. Rech' M.S. Gorbacheva na vstreche s trudiashchimisia v.g. Kieve," *Pravda*, 24 February 1989.

11 Ibid.

12 The new constitution was adopted in March 1989, and the election of a new government occurred in March 1989. The first national conference of the reformist wing of the HSWP was held in May 1989 in Szeged.

list of 35 candidates, including such ostensible party reformers as Prime Minister Mieczyslaw Rakowski and Interior Minister Czeslaw Kiesczak as well as other members of the Politburo and top leaders of the communist coalition parties. All of these candidates failed to receive the necessary 50 percent of the vote and thus were unable to run in the second round of the elections. This stood in stark contrast to the votes cast for Solidarity. All of its candidates received more than 50 percent of the vote, and all of them were represented in parliament without having had to stand in the second round of elections. As a result, the PUWP lost its monopoly on power. Solidarity and the parties allied with it became the dominating force in the Sejm.

The stunning defeat of the communist party raised the question as to the legitimacy of its rule. President Wojciech Jaruzelski nevertheless appointed Kieszcak prime minister – a choice unacceptable to Solidarity since he had been one of the architects of the December 1981 state of emergency and the subsequent suppression of the labor organization. Unable to form a government, he resigned on 19 August. This raised a prospect unprecedented in the history of the Soviet bloc: the formation of a non-communist, in fact, *anti-communist* government. No surprise, then, that the PUWP made a last-ditch effort to prevent that prospect from becoming reality.[13] Party chief Rakowski tried the traditional ploy of the "Soviet card," asserting that a grand coalition was needed in order "to dispel fears of allies and partners abroad." He declared that the party had "entered a period of open struggle for power and [was] threatened by a breach of agreements signed at the Round Table. He went on: "The situation is dangerous, but this is not the time to give up. The party should not commit suicide."[14]

In these conditions, Moscow's attitudes were crucial. Press reports mirrored the PUWP's concern, calling the situation in Poland "dangerously aggravated." But at the official level more restrained counsel prevailed. A foreign ministry statement said: "The Soviet Union is vitally interested in what happens in a neighboring friendly country which is a member of the Warsaw Pact ... but [the Soviet Union] has no intention of interfering."[15] On 20 August, Gorbachev did intervene, but *de facto* in support of Solidarity. He called Rakowski and in the course of a 40-minute telephone conversation, the Soviet party leader – according to PUWP spokesman Jan Bisztyga – encouraged the communist party to take part in the new government.[16] The

13 The following summary of events draws on Philip Zelikow and Condoleezza Rice, *Germany Unified and Europe Transformed: A Study in Statecraft* (Cambridge, Mass.: Harvard University Press, 1995), pp. 69-71.

14 *Pravda*, 21 August 1989, as quoted by Zelikow and Rice, *Germany Unified*, p. 70.

15 As reported by Warsaw Television Service, 17 August 1989, quoted by Zelikow and Rice, *Germany United*, p. 70.

16 Francis X. Clines, "Gorbachev Calls, Then Polish Party Drops Its Demands," *New York Times*, 23 August 1989.

spokesman did not offer a precise summary of the phone call. Neither did Gorbachev, despite the fact that his telephone call was probably the only example of direct intervention in Eastern Europe between 1985 and 1990 in favor of radical change.[17] However, the subsequent alteration in the tone and content of statements by the Polish Communist Party in favor of cooperation with non-communist parties and the designation of Tadeusz Mazowiecki, a longtime leading member of Solidarity, for the post of prime minister would seem to have been the result of Gorbachev's involvement.

Addressing Solidarity's parliamentary caucus, the prime minister designate stated obliquely that his government would take immediate steps to "make it possible for different economic organizations to be formed in the direction of the reform of the system of property."[18] In an interview with an Italian newspaper, Solidarity leader Lech Walesa put the point more bluntly. He said that the government intended to embark upon the road from a communist system of ownership to capitalism. Echoing, probably unwittingly, a then current popular East European joke about socialism as constituting "the longest and most painful transition phase from capitalism to capitalism," he added: "Nobody has previously taken the road that leads from socialism to capitalism. We are setting out to do just that, to return to the prewar situation when Poland was a capitalist country, after having gone through a long period of socialism."[19]

What about East Germany? Was the Honecker regime to be *exempted* from the need to establish its own legitimacy and viability? Did Gorbachev disingeniously imply that the Freedom of Choice should be granted to the East German state and government but not to the *people*? The Soviet leader's reaction to the rapidly unfolding events in that country will be examined below in detail. As for the conceptual and declaratory level, ambiguity was dispelled in June 1989, during Gorbachev's visit to West Germany. The Joint Soviet-West German Declaration, signed on that occasion, acknowledged the "right of all *peoples* and states freely to determine their destiny."[20] It went even further by endorsing the "precedence of

---

17 In his memoirs, Gorbachev fails to reflect on the first transgression of the parameters of the socialist framework of change in the bloc, nor does he report the telephone conversation with Rakowski. After having mentioned the election of Jaruzelski to the post of president and Rakowski to that of head of the PUWP, he merely muses that the "constellation of political forces [in Poland] continued to remain unfavorable for the party that had ruled the country [Poland] for almost forty-five years. However, the labor organization Solidarity, *which now assumed political responsibility, at the same time did not achieve greater popularity.*" Gorbachev, *Zhizn'*, Vol. 2, p. 347 (italics mine).

18 John Tagliabue, "Wider Capitalism Encouraged by Polish Leaders," *New York Times*, 24 August 1989.

19 *Il Messagero* (Rome), 22 August 1989.

20 "M.S. Gorbachev v FRG. Sovmestnoe zaiavlenie," *Izvestiia*, 15 June 1989 (italics mine).

international law in domestic and international politics" and "unqualified respect for the norms and principles of international law, *especially respect for the right of peoples to self-determination.*"[21] According to West German understanding, this term was the international legal counterpart to Gorbachev's Freedom of Choice. As interpreted in four decades of political and legal discussion in the Federal Republic, the right of self-determination was denied to East Germans. It could be exercised only in free elections, which would also be the precondition for the re-establishment of German unity. The Joint Declaration was carefully prepared and extensively discussed point by point over a period of six months.[22] Thus there was agreement between Moscow and Bonn on the principle of popular legitimacy. Yet there was no Soviet position, and there would never be official clarification as to whether that principle was compatible with the one-party state in the GDR and whether it was being violated in that country through undemocratic elections.

The dramatic internal changes in Eastern Europe had fateful consequences in the international realm. On 2 May 1989, an event of world historic significance took place when border units of the Hungarian armed forces began to dismantle obstacles along the Austro-Hungarian border.[23] This was not the first time that the Iron Curtain was dismantled in Hungary. In 1955, in the era of Soviet acceptance of Palmiro Togliatti's idea of "diversity in unity" in international communism and the first major post-World War II thaw in East-West relations, Hungary had torn down the border obstacles. This was one of the main reasons why hundreds of thousands of Hungarians were able, in the aftermath of the November 1956 popular revolt, to cross the borders into Austria. In 1957, as a result of Soviet intervention, a new protective fence had been erected. In the second half of the 1960s and early 1970s, mines were cleared from the security zones, but an elaborate electric warning system was installed and new lanes for border patrols were added. The measures adopted in May 1989 reestablished the permissive regime of the fall of 1956, and they were more than a simple demolition job. They were political symbolism, marking the disappearance of the Iron Curtain. Reporters from both East and West were invited to witness the event, and to underline its significance, special equipment from Austria

---

21 Ibid. (italics mine).

22 Interviews with Teltschik and Chernyaev; Helmut Kohl, *Ich wollte Deutschlands Einheit*, as portrayed by Kai Diekmann and Ralf Georg Reuth (Berlin: Propyläen, 1996), pp. 40, 47-49; Genscher, *Erinnerungen*, p. 625.

23 The significance of the dismantling of the Iron Curtain in Hungary for triggering a process that was to lead in the final analysis to German unification, beginning on 2 May with the first physical measures at the borders and culminating in Budapest's authorization of the exit of thousands of East Germans to Austria on 11 September (see below) has been emphasized by Kohl, *Ich wollte Deutschlands Einheit*, pp. 65-85, and Genscher, *Erinnerungen*, pp. 637-42. In contrast, Gorbachev in his memoirs fails even to mention Hungary's decision.

was used to extract the concrete posts from the soil. Pieces of barbed wire were distributed as souvenirs.[24]

The dismantling of the border obstacles had primarily an internal rationale. Since most Hungarians were permitted to travel freely to Austria and only very few of the travelers had used the opportunity that presented itself to stay abroad, the border regime was – as Prime Minister Németh thought – a "cruel anachronism." He also considered the border obstacles to be like a "second Berlin wall."[25] Yet when the Hungarian government adopted the decision on the opening of the borders, it was still willing to adhere to a 1968 agreement and the previous practice according to which only East Germans with valid GDR exit stamps in their passports would be allowed to cross the Hungarian-Austrian border. East Germans trying to cross illegally would continue to be arrested and sent back to the GDR.[26] But the dismantling of the border obstacles was bound to create severe complications for East Germany and evoke concern in Prague and Bucharest. What actually began to happen was that East German travelers, principally in Hungary but in other East European countries as well, would attempt to leave and then, frustrated in their effort, would seek refuge in West German embassies. In the summer, more than 200,000 East Germans were on vacation in Hungary, many of whom on camping sites close to the borders and waiting for an opportunity to travel west. The number of would-be emigrants in the West German diplomatic representations in Budapest, Prague, Warsaw, and East Berlin was rising. On 9 August, Hungary stopped enforcing the return of GDR citizens. Its border authorities kept turning back thousands of East Germans, but hundreds were slipping through the net each week. By late August thousands of East Germans were awaiting their fate in Hungarian detention camps and several hundred in the West German embassy compound in Budapest. On 25 August, Németh and Horn held secret talks with Kohl and Genscher at Schloss Gymnich near Bonn. The Hungarians informed the West German chancellor and the foreign minister that they were prepared, as Horn later wrote, to embark on the risky and "illegal" step to open the Hungarian-Austrian border on a specified date at night until early morning so that several thousand GDR-citizens could escape.[27]

---

24 Michael Frank, "Ungarische Grenzaktion: Ein erstes Loch im Eisernen Vorhang," *Süddeutsche Zeitung*, 3-4 May 1989. The measures were taken in implementation of a Hungarian government decision adopted in February 1989.

25 Németh in an interview with Friedrich Kurz, "Ungarn 89," in Dieter Grosser, Stephan Bierling and Friedrich Kurz, *Die sieben Mythen der Wiedervereinigung: Fakten und Analysen zu einem Prozeß ohne Alternative* (Munich: Ehrenwirt, 1991), p. 130.

26 Ibid., pp. 37-39, 123-130. This summary of the Hungarian decision to open the borders and its international repercussions also draws on Zelikow and Rice, *Germany Unified*, pp. 63-64.

27 Gyula Horn, *Freiheit, die ich meine: Erinnerungen des ungarischen Außenministers, der den Eisernen Vorhang öffnete*, trans. Angelika and Péter Máté (Hamburg: Hoffman and Campe, 1991), pp. 319-320.

Implementation of a corresponding decision occurred in the night of 10-11 September.[28]

Several observations are appropriate. First, the events in Hungary were an early indication of uncontrolled and uncontrollable dynamics becoming dominant in the bloc. Leaders in both East and West were forced to react to unforeseen events, in the process altering and often abandoning altogether well established policies and preferences. As for the West German government, its attitudes and policies had been governed by the then still valid principle of Ostpolitik, that is, to avoid undercutting the Honecker regime while attempting to alleviate the hardships of the division. In fact, in the Schloss Gymnich talks the German chancellor had characterized the position of the government in Bonn as a balancing act: to avoid destabilizing the GDR but at the same time not to strengthen it.[29] But the increasing popular pressures "from below" in East Germany and the Hungarian decisions on emigration led to a shift in Bonn's attitudes. Starting from August and September 1989, the West German government was less inclined to take the vulnerabilities and sensitivities of the Honecker regime into consideration and more prone to pursue a new agenda of pressure for change in the GDR.[30]

Second, governments and communist party leaderships in the bloc were increasingly acting in accordance with their own definition of interests and taking fateful and far-reaching decisions without consultation of the imperial center. As amply demonstrated, for instance, by East Berlin's credit deals with Bonn and its refusal to "change the wallpaper," independent action in the bloc was certainly not unprecedented. But in 1989, the tendency grew in direct proportion to Gorbachev's manifest disinclination to involve himself actively in bloc policy. In Horn's view, Gorbachev and Shevardnadze would most likely have "consented to our decision" to let the East Germans leave *if* they had been asked. But they were not. The Hungarian leaders proceeded from the – in all likelihood correct – assumption that their Soviet counterparts knew about the Hungarian plans through their contacts with East Berlin and that they were being pressured to intervene on its behalf. There was another, more unlikely, source of information for the impending Hungarian move: the West German chancellor. In a telephone conversation shortly after the Schloss Gymnich talks, Kohl told Gorbachev what the Hungarian government was planning and asked him whether it had his support. The Kremlin leader had only one comment: "The

---

28 Kohl says that more than 6,000 people crossed the borders from Hungary into Austria on 10-11 September and that – presumably prior to the opening of the Berlin wall – more than 100,000 East Germans were to follow; Kohl, *Ich wollte Deutschland's Einheit*, p. 84.

29 Horn, *Freiheit, die ich meine*, p. 319.

30 This change has been described in more detail by Zelikow and Rice, *Germany Unified*, pp. 65-67).

Hungarians are good people."[31] It appears that Budapest, of all the major players in the event, was the last source of information for Moscow. According to Horn, "we informed the Soviets only on the last day" before adopting the measures of 10-11 September.[32]

Third, the Hungarian events brought into sharp focus an accelerating East German malaise. Conditions were beginning to resemble those obtaining in the months of crisis before the building of the Berlin wall. In fact, the main function of the wall as compelling the East German population to cooperate with the regime was superseded by the Hungarian decisions. As in the spring and summer of 1961, the East German regime was now again being faced with the syndrome of *Torschlußpanik*, the concern among the GDR citizens that to leave the country was a matter of now or never because, either as a result of a conservative backlash in Moscow or an SED decision to outlaw travel to Czechoslovakia, the gates would soon be closed. As in the spring and summer of 1961, this concern enormously swelled the number of would-be emigrants and produced an exodus of mostly young and enterprising citizens. This, in turn, exposed the tenuous legitimacy of the communist regime, the glaring gap between the quality of life in the two Germanys, and the wide gulf between an entrenched party leader and a restive society. It also threatened to have negative repercussions on East German economic development.

Fourth, the Hungarian decisions on emigration and Soviet reactions illuminated East Germany's increasing isolation in the bloc. This was the major difference in conditions between 1961 and 1989. Given the fundamental congruence of Soviet and East German interests in the early 1960s, the unbroken will to empire in Moscow, and tight bloc discipline, Ulbricht had been able to muster collective Warsaw Pact support for the building of the wall. In the late 1980s, however, except on the issue of the continued existence of the GDR, Soviet and East German interests and policies diverged; the will to empire no longer existed in Moscow; bloc discipline had evaporated; and East Berlin was able to draw support only from like-minded orthodox party leaderships in Prague and Bucharest. Its pressures on Budapest to comply with the 1968 agreement, therefore, were to no avail. Informed by Horn of the Hungarian decision on 31 August in the GDR capital, Foreign Minister Fischer exclaimed in a rage: "This is blackmail! In fact, this is treason! Don't you realize that you are thereby abandoning the GDR and joining the other side? This will have grave consequences for you."[33] SED Politburo member and CC Secretary Günter Mittag, in a meeting later in the day, according to the East German transcript, "strictly opposed

---

31 Kohl, *Ich wollte Deutschlands Einheit*, p. 75. The exact date of the telephone conversation is unclear.

32 Horn, *Freiheit, die ich meine*, p. 326.

33 Ibid, p. 324.

[the Hungarian government's] intention to ignore agreements concluded with the GDR" and "demanded of Comrade Horn to reconsider the position which he had taken."[34] On 9 September, Honecker personally intervened and in a telegram to Hungarian party leader Rezsö Nyers, attempted to reverse the Hungarian government's decision. But this effort, too, was wasted.[35]

Fifth, the Hungarian government's actions underlined the crucial importance of West German economic leverage in the disintegrating bloc. As Fischer's rage indicated, the Hungarian government had made a deliberate decision to give preference to the relations with West Germany over those with East Germany and to reorient itself away from the bloc towards, as Horn put it, "Europe."[36] The reason for this had much to do with economics. In their memoirs, Kohl and Genscher have emphatically rejected Western news reports and East European rumors that there was a direct linkage between West German money and the Hungarian decisions. In the secret talks at Schloss Gymnich, Kohl asked Németh several times whether the Hungarians expected West German concessions (*Gegenleistungen*) in exchange for their refusal to return would-be East Germans refugees to the GDR, and each time the Hungarian prime minister had replied: "Hungary will not sell people."[37] But although the assertions of the absence of a direct linkage in the Gymnich talks are credible, neither the West German nor the Hungarian leaders have denied that linkage was *implicit* on a more general level. Kohl, in his own words, considered it simply a matter of fact, or self-evident (*selbstverständlich*), that "we would help those who help us. The Hungarians could have acted quite differently. It was not an easy decision for the government in Budapest in this situation, despite valid agreements with the GDR government simply to say: We let the Germans go."[38] It is for this reason that the negotiations in progress for the extension of a West German credit to Hungary in the amount of DM 500 million were successfully concluded shortly after the Gymnich talks and that Bonn vigorously supported Budapest in its endeavor to become a member of the European Community. "I am convinced," Horn has acknowledged, "that the Hungarian reform forces, above all at the time of change in 1988-89, would not have managed to stay on top without practical [West German-

34 Notes (*Vermerk*) on the meeting between Mittag and Horn, SED Politburo, *Arbeitsprotokolle*, Central Party Archives, J IV 2/2A/3238. Fischer was present at the meeting. Judging from Horn's report on the talks, despite the clarity of Mittag's demand (*Aufforderung*), the latter tried a more conciliatory and diplomatic tack than the one Fischer had adopted earlier; Horn, *Freiheit, die ich meine*, p. 324.

35 Ibid., pp. 325-26.

36 Ibid., p. 322.

37 Kohl, *Ich wollte Deutschland's Einheit*, p. 74. The West German foreign minister has similarly contended that "Our Hungarian guests did not make financial demands"; Genscher, *Erinnerungen*, p. 640.

38 Kohl, *Ich wollte Deutschlands Einheit*, p. 74.

Hungarian] cooperation and [West German] credits."[39] As will be argued below, similar implicit linkages, rather than specific and direct conditionalities, applied to the nexus between West German economic incentives and Gorbachev's later consent to German unification and united Germany's membership in NATO.

West Germany: The New Soviet Priority

To turn to the third dimension of the transformed domestic and international setting, Soviet policy towards *West* Germany: in May 1989, as we have seen, the Hungarian leadership had begun to reorient its foreign policy toward that country and Western Europe. A convincing case can be made for arguing that the Soviet leadership followed suit only one month later. The occasion for Moscow's reorientation was Gorbachev's long delayed visit to West Germany. Chernyaev has unequivocally made that very point. Speaking about the visit and its results, he concludes: "Even in the GDR, at top and bottom levels, it was [now] understood that the Federal Republic was to be given priority in Soviet policy towards Germany. [West Germany] would also be the main partner for the construction of a new Europe."[40] What are the reasons that would justify such a far-reaching conclusion?

One of the reasons is of a general nature and lies in the international political realm. Genscher has pertinently observed: "In retrospect, one can say ... that German foreign policy immediately prior to entering into the most dramatic phase of post-war policy had reached the pinnacle of its international influence."[41] This fact of international life was reflected not only in Gorbachev's reorientation of priorities but also in President Bush's invitation to West Germany to join the United States in a "partnership in leadership."[42]

A second, more specific factor can be found in the removal of one of the major obstacles to a rearrangement of Soviet-West German relations: NATO's decision at the Brussels summit meeting on 30 May not to insist on the immediate modernization of short-range nuclear missiles. It is difficult in retrospect to comprehend the highly emotional character of the controversies which preceded the decision, both within the Western alliance and between the Soviet Union and NATO. Indeed, the acrimonious debate from January to May 1989 about theater nuclear weapons appears quite incongruous in view of the fact that three years earlier Reagan had acceded to Gorbachev's vision of a nuclear-free world, scholars had been talking about a "post-nuclear era," agreement had been reached on the abolition of both long-range and medium-range nuclear missiles, and proposals for comprehensive disarmament

39 Horn, *Freiheit, die ich meine*, p. 318.
40 Chernyaev, *Shest' let s Gorbachevym*, p. 291.
41 Genscher, *Erinnerungen*, p. 626.
42 In a speech in Koblenz on 30-31 May 1989.

in conventional weapons were seriously being discussed. Finally, the conflict seems even more incomprehensible considering the rapidly changing political context in 1989. Given the New Thinking, with its by then clearly demonstrated implications for a reduction of the East-West military competition in Europe, it was no longer appropriate, if it ever had been, to look upon nuclear weapons as a primarily military issue. Genscher recognized this with great clarity and was determined to prevent an SNF modernization decision – as was the Soviet Union.

Briefly to remind ourselves of the heated controversy, in April 1989 Marshal Akhromeev had claimed that the Oka (SS-23) missile had a range of *less* than 500 kilometers and should thus be considered a short-range system. He had also asserted that "its range was no secret to US representatives at the [INF] talks" and objected to United States plans to deploy a new missile, the Lance, with a range of close to 500 kilometers.[43] Two weeks prior to the NATO summit, on 12-13 May, Shevardnadze had reiterated the viewpoint of the Soviet chief of staff when he visited Bonn in preparation of Gorbachev's visit. At a press conference, he deplored that NATO wanted to deploy a new missile with a range comparable to that of the Soviet Oka missile, which was being abolished in accordance with the December 1987 Soviet-American INF treaty. He pointedly asked:

> Why, then, should we destroy the SS-23 missiles if the other side is creating and will deploy an analogous missile? By engaging in scholastic exercises one cannot resolve the problem. The fact is that there would be two identical types of missile. But whereas the Soviet one would be destroyed, the American one would be produced.[44]

When he was asked whether that statement should be interpreted in such a way that, if NATO were to take a decision on modernization, the Soviet Union would halt the withdrawal of the SS-23 and their destruction, he replied: "One would have to think about this. Would it [after a decision by NATO to develop a follow-on system to Lance] make sense to destroy these [our] missiles? Or would it be possible that in that circumstance we would be forced to create new systems and respond in kind to the NATO decision?" Pressed further, he continued: "We either will have to arrest the destruction of the SS-23 missiles or create new systems."[45]

Although Shevardnadze's reply was interpreted by members of the Western defense community as a "throwback to cold war tactics" and "blatant extortion,"[46] and despite the fact that such tactics in the past had often had a tendency to backfire, Genscher's determination to prevent an early SNF modernization decision prevailed

---

43 "Takticheskie iadernye oruzhiia - preimuzhestvo ili balans?," *Pravda*, 19 April 1989.

44 "Press-konferentsiia v Bonne," *Pravda*, 14 May 1989.

45 Ibid.

46 Richard Perle, "Moscow's Threat: A Bluff the West Should Call," *International Herald Tribune*, 18 May 1989.

at the Brussels summit.[47] NATO was committing itself to "partial reductions," thereby implying that there was a minimum number of SNF that was non-negotiable. But since the existing Lance system was soon to become obsolete and further arms control and disarmament measures (including Bush's proposal for the limitation of Soviet and American troops in Europe to 275,000 officers and men) were being discussed, it was, as Genscher realized, highly likely that the Lance would never be modernized and that there would be a "triple zero" solution for nuclear missiles.[48] Undoubtedly, to conclude the consideration of this issue, the successful West German opposition to SNF modernization contributed significantly to the acceleration of the arms control and disarmament process in Europe and removed a major impediment to a productive Soviet-West German summit.

A third reason for the shift of priorities in Soviet policy on the German problem and, more generally, in Europe lay in the strengthening of the "relationship of trust" between Kohl and Gorbachev that had been established in October 1988.[49] To the detriment of an accurate understanding of international affairs, political scientists often tend to downplay the importance of personality factors. One may suspect that this has something to do with the difficulty of measuring, or "operationalizing," such intangible "variables" as sympathy and empathy. Political leaders and diplomats, on the contrary, have generally been less averse to admitting their importance. In this writer's view, too, such factors matter a great deal. Judging from the personal accounts of the two leaders and their entourage, Gorbachev's opinion of Kohl improved during and after his visit to West Germany in June 1989. This, in turn, affected his thinking and behavior – as Gorbachev publicly admitted. At the July 1990 press conference where he and Kohl announced details of their agreement on the external aspects of German unification, he said that he considered the "personal factor highly important" and that the agreement they were announcing would not have been possible if it had not been for the close relations that had developed between him and the German chancellor and also among other Soviet and German officials. After his visit to Bonn in June 1989, but before the rapid changes on German soil, he continued, a "reserve" of trust and good will had been built, which had helped "us deal responsibly and constructively" with those changes."[50]

---

47 In his memoirs, Genscher has described at length the circumstances and the dramatic proceedings at the Brussels summit; *Erinnerungen*, pp. 614-21.

48 Ibid., pp. 618-19. The first two "zeroes" were on intermediate-range and medium-range nuclear missiles.

49 For the establishment of a "relationship of trust" during Kohl's October 1988 visit to Moscow, see above, p. 270.

50 Joint press conference in Zheleznovodsk, in the northern Caucasus; "Press konferentsiia M.S. Gorbacheva i G. Kolia," *Pravda*, 18 July 1990. Analytically, however, it is still an interesting problem to consider what came first, Gorbachev's realization of the expediency, if not political necessity, to establish a better personal rapport with Kohl or the "establishment of trust" that led

During Gorbachev 's visit, the two leaders met privately on three occasions, twice at the chancellery and once at the chancellor's home.[51] At their meeting in Kohl's villa on the banks of the Rhine, they talked extensively about their personal background and life, with mutual understanding facilitated by the fact that they are part of the generation that had consciously experienced World War II. Gorbachev told Kohl about his childhood, his grandfather as a victim of Stalinism, his father's work on the collective farm, and his own experiences during the war, including the German occupation. Kohl reciprocated and told his guest about his own parents, his father having been drafted to the war, the allied air raids on his native Ludwigshafen, and about his brother, who was killed at the front. After the conversation about both personal and political matters and when Gorbachev and his wife were leaving the chancellor's villa, they embraced each other. "For me," Kohl has said, "this evening was a pivotal experience, and I believe for Gorbachev too."[52] Gorbachev, in his memoirs, remains non-committal about what *he* felt. This is presumably for the reason that he has been keen to dispel the notion that his policies on German unification were in any way governed by emotion rather than reason. However, there is nothing in his account that would contradict the favorable impression which the chancellor had received.

In contrast to the treatment accorded to Kohl, Gorbachev in his memoirs is explicit on what he felt about von Weizsäcker. He writes that he understood why the German people had such great admiration for their president, considering his "comprehensive knowledge, intelligence, natural poise, and good will," attributes which contributed to the fact that "since that time, we have kept in contact and that our conversations each time became more sincere and characterized by more trust."[53] It was, however, not only between the chancellor and the Kremlin leader and at the very top level that an atmosphere of friendship prevailed. The advisers on foreign policy to the two leaders and the two foreign ministers also built on their good previous contacts and strengthened their personal relationship.[54]

The impact of personal experiences on Gorbachev's perceptions and behavior can also be found in another dimension: the enthusiastic welcome he received from the

---

to a reorientation of the Kremlin leaders's policies toward West Germany. In this writer's view, it was the former that came first. Furthermore, it would seem that distrust and suspicion in the Soviet leader's view of Kohl was never far below the surface. An indication of this is his rapid return to decidedly negative perceptions after the chancellor's announcement of his Ten Points on 28 November 1989, when a furious Gorbachev (and Shevardnadze) turned the tables on the chancellor's Goebbels remarks and compared Kohl's behavior with that of the Nazis; see *infra*, pp. 449-52.

51 Kohl, *Ich wollte Deutschlands Einheit*, p. 40; Gorbachev, *Zhizn'*, Vol. 2, p. 159.

52 Kohl, *Ich wollte Deutschlands Einheit*, p. 47.

53 Gorbachev, *Zhizn'*, Vol. 2, p. 156.

54 Genscher, *Erinnerungen*, pp. 627-32; interviews with Teltschik and Chernyaev.

German population and from labor union, business, and public opinion leaders. In his memoirs, he reports:

> The program for the visit was extraordinarily varied. I had the opportunity to visit many Bundesländer and numerous cities and villages as well as to meet with politicians, entrepreneurs, artists, workers, and representatives of political parties and social groups. ... We also came in contact with the inhabitants of the German capital. ... The scenes at the square of Bonn's city hall were truly unforgettable. In the street below there was an overflowing wave of well-wishers and people expressing their friendship. Calls and wishes of luck like, "Gorby! Make love, not walls!" and "Keep it up, Gorbachev!" accompanied us. As we stepped out onto the balcony of the City Hall, thunderous applause surged forth from the crowd.
>
> In the course of the visit, we also met with metal workers in a factory of the Hoesch corporation in Dortmund. When we stepped out of the car, we ended up in a row of thousands of people who welcomed us. An enormous factory room was filled to the last seat. People stood on an improvised parquet floor and on workbenches, climbed onto scaffolding and moving equipment and alternately lifted each other onto their shoulders.[55]

Gorbachev summarizes these experiences by comparing them with those gained during his visit to West Germany fourteen years earlier, acknowledging that in June 1989 he was "moved by the wave of sympathy from these people who had received us so warmly and welcomed us so sincerely."[56]

It would seem that the encounters had impressed Gorbachev not only because they did not fit the stereotypes implanted in his mind. Speaking about a similarly warm welcome Gorbachev had received in Washington in December 1987, former American ambassador to Moscow Jack Matlock has observed that Gorbachev enjoys the pomp and circumstance of power and thirsts for public acclaim. At home, to continue the ambassador's account, he was beginning to bridle at indications that his popularity was less than universal and to contain politicians like Yeltsin, who exhibited more charisma than he with people in the street. In Washington, as later in the capitals of Western Europe, he found what he was denied at home: worship of an adoring crowd. His evolving personal relationships with Reagan, Bush, Kohl, Thatcher, Mitterrand, and other Western leaders reinforced the important insight that he no longer dealt with hostile forces that had to be managed, fended off, or appeased. The focus shifted to how common interests could be served.[57]

A fourth reason for the priority accorded to West Germany in Soviet policy in Europe after June 1989 was connected with the content of the talks, the agreements

---

55 Gorbachev, *Zhizn'*, Vol. 2, pp. 156-57.

56 Ibid., p. 159.

57 Jack F. Matlock, Jr., *Autopsy of an Empire: The American Ambassador's Account of the Collapse of the Soviet Union* (New York: Random House, 1995), p. 152.

reached, and the prospects for future cooperation. It is not possible to prove but proper to conjecture that in his conversations with Gorbachev about the German problem, Kohl had struck a responsive cord. On a walk along the Rhine in the early morning hours on the third day of the visit, the German chancellor outlined his vision of a comprehensive reordering of Soviet-German relations and their codification in a Grand Treaty. Such a treaty, Kohl said, would be inadequate as long as Germany remained divided. The division of Germany was the most important impediment to an improvement in the relations among the two peoples. Gorbachev responded by reiterating the Soviet position about the division as being the logical result of a historic development. Kohl resumed the argument. Pointing to the Rhine, he said that the river symbolized history. A dam could be built across its path but the river would overflow and still find its ordained way to the sea. It was similar with German unity, which was sure to come. The only question was whether it should be addressed by the present generation or whether one should continue to wait, with all the problems that this would pose. The Germans would never reconcile themselves with the division. Gorbachev no longer contradicted.[58] Although he failed to draw any practical conclusions, but considering what he had told Rykin fourteen years earlier, it would seem that he fundamentally agreed with the German chancellor.

As for the Grand Treaty, the outlines of its probable provisions were visible in the Joint Declaration issued at the end of the talks. In a similar document, the 1972 Basic Principles of Relations Between the United States and the Soviet Union, Washington had unwisely deferred to traditional Soviet language. The first principle of the agreement had stated that the United States and the Soviet Union would "proceed from the common determination that in the nuclear age there is no alternative to conducting their mutual relations on the basis of peaceful coexistence."[59] Thus, on the face of it, the Nixon administration had agreed to class struggle as the governing principle in Soviet-American relations. West German negotiators in 1988-89, in contrast, succeeded in committing Moscow to several concepts and norms favored by Bonn. As described above, this applied to the principle of self-determination. It was extended to the precedence of international law in domestic and international politics and included the West German concepts of *Gemeinsame Sicherheit* (common security) and *Europäische Friedensordnung* (framework, structure, or architecture of peace in Europe) which supplemented Gorbachev's idea of the Common European House.[60] On the German problem, the Joint Declaration also contained language

58 Kohl, *Ich wollte Deutschlands Einheit*, pp. 43-44.

59 *Department of State Bulletin*, Vol. 66 (26 June 1972), pp. 898-99. National Security Advisor Henry Kissinger had negotiated the text of the Basic Principles.

60 Text in Press and Information Office of the Federal Republic of Germany, *Bulletin*, No. 61 (15 June 1989). Several of the principles under this heading conformed to the New Thinking but

supporting Bonn's viewpoint. The document deplored that the European "continent has been divided for decades" and that both countries considered it "their paramount objective ... to contribute to overcoming the division of Europe." In the Russian version, it also featured a terminological innovation conforming to West German preferences. In the first sentence, the declaration refers to the Federal Republic of Germany as *Federativnaia Respublika Germaniia*, rather than *Germanii*, the alteration implying that there is or should be one single Germany – *Germaniia* – with a federal structure rather than two or more German entities.[61]

As for a Grand Treaty and the comprehensive reordering of Soviet-German relations, perhaps their most important component was the idea of a significant expansion of Soviet-German economic cooperation and West German economic and financial assistance for the modernization of the Soviet economy.[62] However, since this was a long-term proposition and depended on both West German private investors and traders to take risks as well as on the kind of radical structural reforms that Gorbachev was not as yet prepared to undertake, there was little the West German government could do beyond committing itself to short-term assistance (*Sofortmaßnahmen*) to help alleviate the acute supply problems in the Soviet Union.[63] For the time being, cooperation in the economic and other spheres had to remain limited. What could be achieved was set forth in eleven agreements signed during Gorbachev's visit. They concerned the protection of German investments in the Soviet Union; the opening of cultural institutes; exchange programs involving scientists, youth, high school students, and teachers; the training of qualified workers and management personnel in commerce and industry; joint measures against drug traffic; information exchange on nuclear energy; and the opening of a "hot line" – an encoded telefax connection – between Bonn and Moscow.

West Germany thus became the Soviet Union's most important partner in Europe. But this was not, it would seem, because of Gorbachev's personal preferences but because of objective conditions. His liaison with Kohl, to use a convenient metaphor, was not one of the heart but of the mind.[64] His true preference, one suspects, really lay with other European countries – with France, for instance. This is indicated by statements he made at the Warsaw Pact summit conference in Bucharest, on 7-8 July, shortly after his return from a visit to Paris "W*e have to devote primary attention to France,*" *he* told the assembled party chiefs. "That is a country of developed political thinking and with a developed culture. France is listened to not only in Europe but

---

these, in turn, were significantly influenced by West German, above all Social Democratic, concepts.

61 "M.S. Gorbachev v FRG. Sovmestnoe zaiavlenie," *Izvestiia*, 15 June 1989.

62 Interviews with Teltschik and Chernyaev.

63 Kohl, *Ich wollte Deutschlands Einheit*, p. 42.

64 This is to reinforce the point made supra, p. 395, n. 50.

also in many other extremely important regions of the world."[65] The fact that West Germany nevertheless had become the Soviet Union's most important partner in Europe in practice meant that Gorbachev was prepared to cooperate more closely with that country than with any other in Europe, including East Germany. Cooperation with West Germany, however, meant within the framework of two separate German states. It did not mean that he accepted Kohl's idea of actively working toward ending the division of Germany. This was shown, among other things, by continuing Soviet-West German differences over the Berlin problem. Two agreements had been ready for signature at the summit, one on maritime shipping and the other on shipping in internal waters, but both failed to be signed because Moscow, to underline its legal position that West Berlin was a separate political entity, insisted on the city flying a separate flag. This demand was rejected by the Federal government.

The thinly veiled euphoria in Bonn about the Joint Statement and about having committed Moscow in that document to the idea that overcoming the division of Europe was in the paramount interest of both West Germany and the Soviet Union would have dissipated somewhat if the West German negotiators had known what Gorbachev told Honecker only two weeks after its publication. In private conversation, the Kremlin leader assured his East German counterpart that there had been no horse trading and that the Soviet Union had made no concessions. He had sensed that attempts had been made to set him and Honecker and the GDR and the Soviet Union against each other. In response, he had emphasized that the Soviet Union maintained close relations with the GDR but that it also wanted to improve relations with West Germany. He had portrayed this as being quite normal. Prospects for an improvement of Soviet-West German relations were significant if the transformation process in the Soviet Union were to be successful. As for the problems raised by Kohl (that is, German unification), he had replied that history had decided. Nothing could be changed about that. The course of history might change; one would have to wait and see. However, one always had to proceed from existing realities.[66]

If what Chernyaev has stated is correct, namely, that – in the wake of Gorbachev's visit – West Germany was to be given priority in Soviet policy towards Germany and that Bonn rather than East Berlin was to be the main partner for the construction of a new Europe, nothing was said about this to Honecker. In the private talks, Gorbachev

65 Speech by Gorbachev at the Warsaw Pact summit conference in Bucharest, 7-8 July 1989, SED Politburo, *Arbeitsprotokolle*, Central Party Archives, J IV 2/2/2336 (italics mine).

66 Transcript (*Niederschrift*) of talks between Honecker and Gorbachev in Moscow on 28 June 1989, SED Politburo, *Arbeitsprotokolle*, Central Party Archives, J IV 2/2A/3228. Kohl had indeed raised the issue of Honecker's recalcitrance and commented that it was now easier to talk with Moscow than with East Berlin; Kohl, *Ich wollte Deutschlands Einheit*, pp. 41-43.

also did not attach any special significance to the Joint Declaration. In fact, he failed to mention that document. No wonder, then, that Honecker acted as if everything was back to normal in Soviet-East German relations. "Comrade Honecker emphasized," the transcript says, "that we consider the complimentary words [sic] which Comrade Gorbachev uttered in Bonn about the GDR and its policies to be an endorsement of the line pursued thus far [by the GDR] and an encouragement unwaveringly to adhere to it."[67]

In view of the serious differences in political philosophy and policy between the GDR and the USSR, it may almost seem absurd to raise the question whether Honecker was simply speaking tongue in cheek, being perfectly conscious of the lack of Soviet endorsement for his policy line, or whether he genuinely believed that he had Soviet support. Controversial as the proposition may be, it would seem that on balance he was more sincere in his belief than ironic, let alone sarcastic. Until that time, in all the private conversations recorded in the East German archives, Gorbachev had *never* directly criticized Honecker or his policies, and he would continue to refrain from open criticism until the very end of the Honecker regime. He had, contrary to that, been *complimentary* about both the East German leader and East German policies (although not in conversation with Kohl), even deferential. The objective divergence of Soviet and East German policies could be, and in all likelihood *was*, interpreted by Honecker along the lines of what is good for the Soviet goose had already been digested by the East German gander (Gorbachev had consistently encouraged this very notion) and that the changes that he considered to be bad for the Soviet Union should not be imitated by East Germany. In the circumstances, it is hard to blame him for believing that Soviet endorsement of his policies should unambiguously be reiterated at the forthcoming celebrations on the fortieth anniversary of the foundation of the GDR. This was not to be. In essence, the celebrations turned into a *marche funèbre* for the Honecker regime. They were also another step forward along the path towards the collapse of East Germany and the Soviet empire in Eastern Europe.

2. The Demise of the Honecker Regime

The anniversary celebrations from 6 to 8 October and Gorbachev's visit to East Berlin on that occasion could not have failed but take place in an atmosphere of heightened tension and apprehension. First, in response to the Hungarian government's decision to let East Germans leave without valid travel documents, the East German

---

67 Transcript (*Niederschrift*) of talks between Honecker and Gorbachev of 28 June 1989. There is nothing in the transcript nor in Kohl's memoirs that would convey the idea that in his talks with the chancellor Gorbachev had said anything complimentary about East Germany.

authorities had severely restricted travel to Hungary. But this had failed to produce the – from the GDR's perspective – desired effect of closing all loopholes: the flow of people intent on leaving the country was simply diverted to Western, and primarily West German, embassies, first and foremost the Federal Republic's embassy in Prague but also those in East Berlin and Warsaw. In the Hungarian capital, thousands of East Germans had scaled the walls of the West German embassy and found themselves stranded on its muddy grounds. Honecker was averse to abandoning the official East German position that the "illegal presence of some [sic] GDR citizens in the representations of the FRG can only be interpreted as blackmail;" that there was "no special road (*Sonderweg)* around GDR emigration laws;" and that the only thing the East German government would be prepared to do was to "give assurances that those who return will not be punished."[68] But considering that the festivities in East Berlin could be marred by an unresolved and embarrassing problem, he relented. At the end of September, that is, only little more than a week prior to the beginning of the celebrations, he yielded to West German pressures and let the East Germans leave Czechoslovakia – by special trains and on a circuitous route from Prague *via Dresden* to Hof in Bavaria in order to convey the notion that the East Germans were leaving their country legally. By that time, since the beginning of the summer, about 45,000 East Germans had left the GDR, legally, semi-legally, or illegally. On 3 October, the GDR authorities attempted to prevent a repetition of East Germans scrambling into the Prague embassy by closing the border with Czechoslovakia. However, unless there was a fundamental resolution of the problem, either by more far-reaching East German restrictions and repression or by a rapid and comprehensive liberalization of emigration laws, it was obvious that the exodus would continue.[69]

Second, the official celebrations were to coincide with unofficial demonstrations scheduled to take place in East Berlin on 7 October. The unauthorized demonstrations, held on the seventh of every month, were also commemorative. But they were not designed to celebrate GDR achievements but to remind the ruling party of the electoral fraud which the demonstrators were conviced the party had committed in the May 1989 local elections. Krenz had been the chairman of the electoral commission. On 9 October, the by then equally traditional demonstrations held every Monday of the week in Leipzig (*Montagsdemonstrationen*) were also

---

68 Protocol of the meeting between GDR state secretary and first deputy minister of foreign affairs, Herbert Krolikowski, and the chief of the Federal Republic's chancellery's office, Rudolf Seiters, on 18 August 1989 in East Berlin, Central Party Archives, Büro Axen, IV 2/2035.

69 For details about the East German refugee problem, the West German pressures on East Germany to consent to their exodus from the embassies and Soviet reactions: for primary sources, see Genscher, *Erinnerungen*, pp. 643-45, 650-51; Horn, *Freiheit, die ich meine*, p. 327; for secondary sources, see Elizabeth Pond, *Beyond the Wall: Germany's Road to Unification*, A Twentieth Century Fund Book (Washington, DC: The Brookings Institution, 1993), pp. 97-98; and Zelikow and Rice, *Germany Unified*, pp. 73-76.

planned to take place. Restiveness and rumors abounded. Krenz, the SED Central Committee secretary in charge of security, was to be back in time for the celebrations from a visit to China. Members of the democratic opposition, as noted *supra*, feared that he would return as an advocate of a "Chinese solution" to the East German regime's troubles and that a crackdown on demonstrations and dissent would begin as soon as the anniversary celebrations were over.[70]

For Honecker, the celebrations were of symbolic importance to show once again how far the GDR had traveled since 1949. They presented an opportunity to remind his detractors that the state had weathered several crises before and that, if need be, it would overcome many more. Yet this time Honecker faced three problems that were linked with external difficulties: deterioration of his health; increasing intra-party rivalries and dissatisfaction; and a widening gap between the party and the people. The East German leader, then 77 years of age, had undergone surgery in the preceding year and in the period from 12 August to 25 September 1989 had been absent from public life for health reasons. His political health had also deteriorated, both inside the party and the bloc. In these circumstances, he and the dogmatic party stalwarts needed Soviet support more than ever. But they were unsure whether they would receive it. Such support was perhaps not unlikely. Gorbachev may have been warned and chastened by the developments in Poland and Hungary.

For Gorbachev, too, much was at stake. The first question that had to be decided was whether to accept Honecker's official invitation to attend the anniversary celebrations. The SED chief had put pressure on him to attend. In private conversation, on 28 June 1989 in Moscow, Honecker had explained:

> In the GDR, we now focus on the fortieth anniversary of the foundation of the republic on 7 October. We want to celebrate this jubilee together with our allies and friends all over the world, whose support, empathy, and solidarity we have felt in all these years of socialist construction. More than seventy delegations from socialist countries, fraternal and avant-garde parties, and national-democratic movements are expected in Berlin. *We would be pleased if we could, on that occasion, welcome Comrade Gorbachev at the head of the delegation of the Soviet Union.* One could arrange things so that Comrade Gorbachev could, with his delegation, before and after the celebrations, visit a few important places in the GDR.[71]

Gorbachev was non-committal. He thanked Honecker for the invitation and stated that, "in principle, participation at the fortieth anniversary would be very desirable.

70 For the discussion of East German fears, the Stasi's plans to use force, and the role of the Soviet armed forces, see pp. 358-64.

71 Transcript (*Niederschrift*) of the talks between Honecker and Gorbachev on 28 June 1989 in Moscow, SED Politburo, *Arbeitsprotokolle*, Central Party Archives, J IV 2/2A/3228 (direct and indirect speech is used in the original; italics mine).

[We will] think about it."[72] Honecker seemed to be taken aback by this tepid response and reiterated his invitation. Indeed, he said,

> one should think carefully about it; [the event] will have great resonance in the GDR and in the whole world. ... The participation of Comrade Gorbachev would, in effect, be [putting] a seal [of approval] on socialism on German soil [and on the GDR] as being a cornerstone of peace and socialism in Central Europe. It would at the same time be an expression of solidarity with restructuring in the Soviet Union.[73]

The Soviet leader still refused to commit himself and continued to do so throughout the summer. In mid-September it seems that Honecker, through Ligachev, was trying to force Gorbachev's hand. Ligachev, as noted, had been shunted to a political siding (the Central Committee's agricultural commission) but was unwilling to reconcile himself to a secondary role in the affairs of state. On 12 September, he traveled to East Berlin, purportedly to discuss agricultural issues but more likely to shore up the SED's sagging morale. He spoke warmly of the Soviet Union's "forty years of indestructible friendship" with East Germany, went on to say that Gorbachev and the USSR condemned the provocative West German campaign against East Germany and, apparently without the Soviet leader's knowledge and permission, announced that Gorbachev would visit East Berlin to participate in the anniversary celebrations. On the following day, a Soviet foreign ministry spokesman limited himself to acknowledging that the visit was "perfectly possible" and said that "a delegation at the highest level" had not been ruled out.[74]

The reason for Gorbachev's reluctance to commit himself was rooted in a dilemma. Not to attend could have been interpreted as an affront and a signal that Honecker no longer had his confidence. Even worse from the Soviet leader's vantage point, it could have been regarded as a sign that he had written off the GDR altogether – a message which he was not prepared to convey. But attendance could have been misinterpreted as endorsement for Honecker, which he was equally determined to avoid. Reformist forces in East Germany, both inside and outside the party, expected the Soviet visitor to exert pressure on Honecker, preferably publicly, to change his policies and persuade him to step from office.

Gorbachev's ultimate decision was influenced by advice provided by the CC's International Department that he should attend but make it a point to talk not only to

72 Ibid. (ind. sp.)

73 Ibid. (ind. sp.).

74 Zelikow and Rice, *Germany Unified*, p. 72; author interviews as well as the interview conducted by Condoleezza Rice (September 1994) with Chernyaev. The agro-business part of Ligachev's trip was tersely reported by *Pravda* and *Izvestiia*, 13 September 1989. Western diplomats said that Ligachev had participated in the weekly SED Politburo meeting and that he had admonished his East German colleagues that, even if they were not to institute Gorbachev-style reforms, they should at least try to respond better than before to the needs and grievances of the people; *Die Welt*, 14 September 1989.

Honecker but also to meet with the whole East German leadership.[75] The officials of the department thought, correctly, that Gorbachev had "conducted his educational work with the East German *primus* only" who, in turn, had "not been telling his colleagues the whole truth."[76] They advised him, therefore, that in closed session with the entire top SED leadership he should, more forcefully than previously, make a case for comprehensive reform in East Germany.[77] The difficulty of charting a course between the Scylla of attendance and putative endorsement of Honecker, and the Charybdis of blunt criticism and destabilization of East Germany, was apparent in last minute changes in the preparation for the visit: "The size of the delegation was significantly reduced, the schedule of the meetings altered, and language somewhat more critical of East German policies included for his meetings with Honecker and the SED leadership."[78]

Considering the extraordinary importance of the anniversary celebrations, it is appropriate to provide some detail, beginning with a reconstruction of the schedule of events. On Friday morning, 6 October, Gorbachev would arrive and be welcomed by the East German leadership at East Berlin's Schönefeld airport. He would then travel by car to Niederschönhausen palace where the Soviet delegation was to stay. In the afternoon, the celebrations would officially begin with a gala meeting in the Palast der Republik (Palace of the Republic), with public speeches to be delivered, among others, by Gorbachev and Honecker. In the evening, there would be an officially sponsored *Fackelzug*, or torch-light procession. The Soviet delegation would then return to Niederschönhausen, with opportunities provided for its members to relax and prepare for meetings on the following day. On Saturday, 7 October, the celebrations were to continue with the laying of wreaths at Treptow cemetery; a military parade in downtown East Berlin; private talks between Honecker and Gorbachev and a meeting with the participation of the two party leaders, the Soviet delegation, and the full and candidate members of the SED Politburo, both to take place in Niederschönhausen palace; a reception and dinner later in the afternoon; and Gorbachev's departure to Schönefeld airport for a plane scheduled to depart for Moscow at 8:00 p.m. The impression which various aspects of the events made on the main protagonists can now be reconstructed with some confidence from archival materials, memoirs, and interviews.

Gorbachev's perceptions of political conditions in East Germany began to be shaped on the car trip from the airport to the palace. The streets along the way were lined with people, many of whom young, who were enthusiastically and

75 Falin, *Politische Erinnerungen*, p. 484 (italics mine).

76 Ibid.

77 Interviews with Zagladin and Rykin.

78 Interviews with Grigoriev (the *verbatim* quote) and Tsipko..

demonstratively welcoming the Soviet president with shouts of "Gorby! Gorby!" The outburst of popular enthusiasm visibly annoyed Honecker who sat stone-faced in the car next to the Soviet guest who noticed that his host felt quite uncomfortable. Along the way to Niederschönhausen, Falin saw only one placard supportive of Honecker, carried by a middle-aged man, which read: "*Mach weiter so, Erich*!" (Carry on, Erich!). The outbursts of popular enthusiasm were repeated during the evening torch light procession, despite the fact that the 40,000 to 50,000 participants had been carefully selected from party activists and affiliated organizations, notably the communist youth organization (FDJ).[79]

In his speech at the gala meeting in the Palace of the Republic on 6 October, Honecker defiantly repeated formulas that confirmed to everyone present that far-reaching reforms were not on his agenda. "Forty years of the GDR have meant forty years of heroic labor, forty years of successful struggle for the construction of our socialist republic and the welfare of our people," was the main theme pursued by him.[80] In the social sphere, everyone in the GDR had his place, independent of *Weltanschauung* and religion. Socialism, with its humanistic aspirations, was creating space for the development of the personality of each and everyone. The GDR had risen to be one of the top ten industrial nations in the world and was strengthening its economic potential by the introduction of modern technologies. The country had enhanced its international prestige and influence and become a member of the United Nations and its specialized agencies. One hundred and thirty-five states had established diplomatic relations with it. The GDR was also a reliable guarantee against neo-Nazism and chauvinism and would remain firmly anchored in the Warsaw Pact. No one could doubt that East Germany, as the other socialist states, would step over the threshold of the year 2000 in the certain knowledge that the future belongs to socialism. Honecker's few references to the Soviet Union almost exclusively concerned economic and technological cooperation. "In the meetings I have held in the past few years with our friend and comrade, Mikhail Gorbachev," the possibilities for a more productive division and labor and cooperation had been "ever more deeply explored" and "corresponding steps" had been initiated.[81]

Gorbachev, in his public speech, struck fairly traditional and conservative notes. He rejected accusations that the Soviet Union had been responsible for the division of Germany and Europe. He reprimanded West Germany for allegedly seizing on the reforms to "reanimate" dreams of a German *Reich*. With the leaders of the Warsaw

---

79 The description of events and of Gorbachev's observations and reactions according to Gorbatschow, *Erinnerungen*, pp. 934-35, and Falin, *Politische Erinnerungen*, p. 484.

80 "Ansprache des Generalsekretärs des ZK der SED und Vorsitzenden des Staatsrates der DDR, Erich Honecker, auf der Festveranstaltung zum 40. Jahrestag der Gründung der DDR," *Neues Deutschland*, 9 October 1989.

81 Ibid.

Pact countries arrayed behind him, Gorbachev assailed demands to dismantle the Berlin wall.

> We are constantly called upon to liquidate this or that division. We often have to hear, "Let the USSR get rid of the Berlin wall, and then we'll believe in its peaceful intentions." We don't idealize the order that has settled on Europe. But the fact is that until now the recognition of the postwar reality has insured peace on the continent. Every time the West has tried to reshape the postwar map of Europe it has meant the worsening of the international situation.[82]

In another indication of support for the GDR and of his opposition to putting the German problem on the international agenda, he thought that he "should tell our Western partners that matters relating to the German Democratic Republic are *decided not in Moscow, but in [East] Berlin*."[83]

He alluded only slightly to East German problems, and this was coupled with reassertion of the Soviet position of non-interference in the internal affairs of socialist countries and parties. "The GDR," he said, "of course has its problems that demand solution. They arise from the internal demands of a society moving towards new horizons and the gradual process of modernization and renewal in which the socialist world now finds itself." But, he added, the East German communists "will know how to find answers to the questions on the agenda of the day in cooperation with all the forces of society."[84] Another allusion to the necessity of change in the GDR was his remark that "history has its own laws of development (*zakonomernosti*) and its own tempo and rhythm, that are determined by the ripening of objective and subjective factors of development. To ignore this is to invite further problems."[85] The potential impact of the latter allusion was limited, however. Gorbachev had not referred specifically to East Germany – his remark had prefaced the part dealing with perestroika in the Soviet Union – and "ripening" was by then a well-known Gorbachevian metaphor for internal inaction and external non-intervention.

---

82 Gorbachev's speech at the fortieth anniversary of the founding of the GDR in East Berlin on 6 October 1989, "Prazdnik sotsializma na nemetskoi zemle. Rech' M.S. Gorbacheva," *Pravda*, 7 October 1989.

83 Ibid. (italics mine).

84 Ibid. This allusion to East German problems that demanded solution had traveled a strange and tortuous path through Soviet bureaucratic channels. Perhaps unbeknownst to Gorbachev, it was suggested by a *West German political leader*. Shortly prior to Gorbachev's departure to East Berlin, Prime Minister Björn Engholm (SPD) of the Land Schleswig-Holstein, on a visit to Moscow had proposed to Portugalov that Gorbachev include in his GDR anniversary speech a statement supportive of the GDR's putative reformists. For reasons that are unclear, Portugalov asked Tsipko to ask Shakhnazarov to suggest it to Gorbachev. Portugalov may already have begun to suspect that Falin's standing with Gorbachev had declined and that Shakhnazarov had a better chance to win Gorbachev's ear; interview with Tsipko.

85 Ibid.

The evening in Niederschönhausen presented the opportunity for walks in the park and for Gorbachev and his delegation to review the events of the day. The Soviet leader had been conscious of difficulties in East Germany. But he had apparently underestimated the width of the gap that separated the SED from the population. "What shall we do?", he asked. "We can't force the people to be silent. Honecker is beside himself. If he can't manage to get along with his own party activists, one can well imagine the mood among the masses. There is something we didn't understand."[86] The remarks were made to fellow party members Falin and Shakhnazarov, who consoled themselves by thinking that Gorbachev's presence in Berlin was a guarantee of sorts that the dissatisfaction with the regime would not take aggressive forms and rupture the political framework.[87] They also expected that the following day would bring some "clarification" as to what could or should be done. If at all, such clarification would be obtained in two meetings, the first restricted to Honecker and Mittag on the East German side, and Gorbachev and members of his delegation on the Soviet side,[88] the second with the entire SED Politburo.

The meetings of 7 October indeed brought clarification but not of the kind desired by the Soviet delegation. According to the East German transcript of the meeting between Honecker and Gorbachev, the Soviet leader continued to take a conciliatory and deferential attitude, saying that

> what unites us today [is] not accidental but based on firm principles. Everything else are specific questions. Occasionally, some problems arise about domestic conditions and foreign policy. We need constant exchanges about that. I find that to be normal. We understand each other better now than before, and that gives us the possibility better to discharge our role and responsibility. [We] harbor no suspicion towards other countries [and our] relations are characterized by *mutual trust*. We are able to speak of mature relations between our peoples and states.[89]

After this blatant misrepresentation of the actual state of affairs in Soviet-East German relations and some platitudes about the difficulties of socialist transformation, Gorbachev cautiously alluded to the desirability or expediency of unspecified change in the GDR. These allusions were preceded and followed by complimentary remarks about Honecker's public speech of the preceding day. He

---

86 Falin, *Politische Erinnerungen*, p. 485.

87 Ibid.

88 Günter Mittag, *Um jeden Preis* (Berlin: Aufbau Verlag, 1991), p. 18. There is, for the present purposes, a rather inconsequential controversy as to whether Mittag was present. Mittag has written: "I participated in both talks which Gorbachev conducted on 7 October in Berlin – initially with Erich Honecker and then with the whole Politburo." Falin (*Erinnerungen*, p. 485) confirms that Mittag was present at both meetings but Schabowski (*Der Absturz*, p. 241; *Das Politbüro*, pp. 73-74), based on what he was told by a TASS correspondent, denies that he was.

89 Transcript (*Niederschrift*) of the meeting between Honecker and Gorbachev of 7 October 1989 in East Berlin, SED Politburo, Central Party Archives, J IV, 2/2.035/60 (direct speech, italics mine).

(Gorbachev) was "very pleased" with that speech because it had "clearly shown the path traveled by the GDR and very convincingly demonstrated [the GDR's] success" and also because it had 'honestly and correctly stated what needed to be done." He also wanted to say in a spirit of

> friendship that [I] am pleased that the sights have been directed towards the future. There is no need on a day like this to develop these ideas further but [I] have understood this to mean that the SED will deal with [them] shortly after the celebrations, on the road towards the Twelfth Party Congress. The fact that concerns which had arisen recently had been dealt with proved the necessity and accuracy of the ideas of E. Honecker. E. Honecker and the party should take the initiative lest demagogues suggest other ideas. *From [my] own experience [I] know that one must not be too late.*[90]

The remainder of his remarks again addressed problems of transformation in the Soviet Union.

In his reply, Honecker reiterated the themes he had struck in his official speech about friendship between the GDR and the USSR, new life that had sprouted from the ruins of World War II, and content citizens who now had running water, showers, and baths. He boasted yet again about East German progress in microelectronics and plants which had achieved an astonishing increase in labor productivity of between 300 and 700 percent as a result of the introduction of new technology. "The GDR," he concluded the portions of the speech dealing with internal issues, "is a modern industrial state with a high research potential."

What about problems? To the extent that they existed, perhaps with the exception of the activity of the churches, they all had an external origin. They were due, in Honecker's view, to a sharpening of the class struggle.[91] First, there were economic pressures. Chancellor Kohl had declared that Bonn would extend economic assistance to the GDR if it embarked on reform. He (Honecker) had rejected this offer because the GDR refused to accept any conditionality. Bonn and Washington, however, had a broad agenda and in their economic strategy were concentrating their efforts on Hungary. Kohl had offered to extend a credit of DM 500 million to that country if it opened its borders and Bush had tied his credit offer to the election of a new party leadership in Budapest.

Second, there was the issue of open borders, a topic that Honecker had introduced by reporting Kohl's credit offer. He complained that the West German chancellor had the same aim as Reagan, who (in June 1987, at the Brandenburg Gate) had demanded not only the abolition of borders between the GDR and the FRG but in all of Europe. The Hungarian border issue, he thought, was particularly complicated.

---

90 Ibid. (ind. sp., italics mine).

91 The ordering and numbering of the issues is the author's, not Honecker's.

Seven million GDR citizens annually visited Czechoslovakia and many vacationers heading for (the Black Sea coasts in) Bulgaria and Romania traveled through Hungary. This "forced us temporarily to stop visa-free travel to Czechoslovakia."

Third, there were the military-political pressures. NATO had scheduled maneuvers with a planned participation of 250,000 troops. On the basis of previous maneuvers and of documents in the possession of the GDR he was able to state that "'erosive tendencies'" in socialist countries were meant to serve as a pretext "to deal a blow to the GDR and the ČSSR."

Fourth, in line with his past complaints to Gorbachev about the unpleasant necessity for GDR to defend itself on two fronts, he incongruously agreed "with the CPSU that no more ground should be yielded to demagogues, since such demagogues have their say in Soviet newspapers, too." He also emphasized the crucial importance of strengthening the Soviet communist party so that it could cope with the transformation process in that country.

Finally, Honecker's *exposé* included some gratuitous and injurious remarks about supply problems in the Soviet Union. The background to the remarks was his 28-30 June 1989 visit to Magnitogorsk, on the occasion of the sixtieth anniversary of the city's foundation. The city administration had invited him to take part in an excursion in order to show him something about the living conditions of the people. He himself had not accepted the invitation, he said, but the comrades accompanying him had done so. When they had returned they had reported to him what they had seen. He then commented to Gorbachev and the members of the Soviet delegation present in the meeting: "*It [is] incomprehensible that, despite voluminous production, salt, soap, flour, and other things have disappeared from the shops.*"[92]

There can be little doubt that the exchange was considered artificial and unproductive by both sides. This was immediately obvious even to outsiders. An East German television correspondent reported that she had been asked to cover the press conference which Gorbachev and Honecker were scheduled to hold after their meeting. However,

> a press spokesman appeared and announced that there would be no briefing. Shortly thereafter Honecker came out alone. With his hands in his pockets, he went across the park to the Politburo meeting [with Gorbachev] that was to become so famous later. Then Gorbachev came

92 Ibid., (ind. sp., italics mine). According to Falin's recollections (*Politische Erinnerungen*, p. 486), Honecker said that "the shops were lacking even salt and matches." Falin, however, while generally rendering the content and atmosphere of the meetings accurately, confuses the sequence of events. He ascribes much of what was said in the first -- more restricted -- meeting, including Honecker's remarks on the supply problems in Magnitogorsk, to the second session. The transcripts of both meetings clarify that Honecker made this comment in the restricted meeting. Falin has acknowledged that his account is based on memory, not on notes he took.

out, also alone. I clearly understood: This is it. There will be no perestroika in the GDR.[93]

The subsequent meeting between Honecker and Gorbachev in the presence of the full and candidate members of the SED Politburo and the Soviet delegation was essentially a replay of the more restricted session.[94] But there were also some important differences. Gorbachev's allusions to the necessity of change in the GDR were somewhat more forceful. Honecker refrained from reiterating the notion of the "sharpening class struggle" and chose not to repeat the review of internal problems caused by external interference. Gorbachev again spoke first, for fifty minutes, "in the extraordinarily sympathetic way so typical of him,"[95] "coherently, convincingly, and emotionally."[96] He paid homage to the achievements of the GDR and its positive role in the socialist community, in Europe, and in the world. He complimented the East German communists, who had given everything so that the dream of the working class, which had inspired several generations of Germany's working people, could assume concrete form. The SED could now justifiably have a feeling of satisfaction. Turning to Soviet-East German relations, he still asserted: "*For us, the German Democratic Republic is the most important partner and ally. This provides the guideline in our policy.*"[97] The time horizon for the continuation of a Soviet-East German special relationship at the state and party levels had to be measured not in years but in centuries. "*We have talked about this [and other matters] with Comrade Erich Honecker and realized that we are in complete agreement [sic] as regards the assessment of processes occurring in our countries and in the socialist world as a whole.*"[98]

To the participants in the meeting it looked as if there was going to be no end to the praise of East German achievements and not even a hint to the serious differences between the two leaders and parties. This was not to be. By reinterpreting, in essence, Honecker's public speech, he attempted to commit the East German leader(ship) to embark on comprehensive change:

> The question arises, of course: What next? What Comrade Erich Honecker said in his speech [yesterday] in reply to this question naturally could not be complete. This was, in fact, only an anniversary address, in which he expressed very important thoughts also for the long term. What

---

93 As quoted by Maksimichev, *Rekviem po GDR*, p. 47.

94 Stenographic record (*Niederschrift*) of the meeting between Honecker and Gorbachev on 7 October 1989 in East Berlin, SED Politburo, Central Party Archives, J IV, 2/2.035/60. The meeting lasted from 1 p.m. to 2:30 p.m.

95 Schabowski, *Das Politbüro*, p. 74; id., *Der Absturz*, p. 241.

96 Falin, *Politische Erinnerungen*, p. 486.

97 Stenographic record (*Niederschrift*) of the meeting between Honecker and Gorbachev on 7 October 1989 in East Berlin, SED Politburo, Central Party Archives, J IV, 2/2.035/60 (italics mine).

98 Ibid. (italics mine).

> was dealt with only briefly was the necessity of further thorough and fundamental changes in society, its basis, superstructure, and democracy, with the emphasis on a more comprehensive inclusion of people in the processes that are occurring. I have concluded this from the fact that work for the next party congress is in full progress – a party congress that will have to be a turning point in the development of the country and that will have to determine the perspectives of the further development of society. It was very important for me to hear this.

There had, of course, been nothing in Honecker's public address about fundamental change or any turning point in the development of the GDR, and to that extent Gorbachev's remarks, although they did not contain direct criticism of the Honecker regime for its failure to outline a reform program, can be regarded as a strong appeal for change. The appeal was strengthened by his saying that he had "just told Erich Honecker that it will be easier for you to carry out transformations because you don't have such [high] tensions in the socio-economic area [as we do in the Soviet Union]." Furthermore, after a detailed discussion of transformation problems in the USSR, he repeated his philosophical statement about the necessity of change but again without directly linking it to the GDR: "If we were to remain behind, history would punish us immediately." And later, in reference to the demise of the communist parties in Poland and Hungary, he said: "If the party does not react to history, it [the party] will be condemned."[99] He concluded his speech with an appeal and a promise: "We are ready to act jointly with you, to cooperate. We are open to everything, without reservation."

Honecker had listened to Gorbachev's speech with a "slightly reddish face and, perhaps to be polite, cut a contorted smile."[100] In a voice that was faint but more high-pitched than usual, he expressed gratitude for what Gorbachev had said. Without hinting at the political problems in East Germany and the disintegrating bloc, he again lectured on the country's achievements in microelectronics and space technology. There was now a deafening silence in the room. Gorbachev turned

---

99 The Russian *zhizn'* and German *Leben* – literally "life" – has been rendered here as "history." The remark about "those being late will be punished by history" came to assume an almost mythical quality. This memorable phrase came to be widely disseminated because Gorbachev used it on more than one occasion, for instance, on 7 October at the Memorial for the Victims of Fascism and Militarism; Wolf, *Im eigenen Auftrag*, p. 139. It was used by Gerasimov in an interview on Radio GDR II, 19 October 1989. Later, however, Gorbachev denied that his remark was meant to apply to Honecker and the GDR. When Krenz, in his capacity as new party leader, visited Moscow on 1 November 1989 to coordinate policies with the Soviet Union, he conveyed "cordial greetings from all of the comrades of the Politburo of the CC of the SED" and expressed gratitude for the talks he (Gorbachev) had held with the full Politburo, in which "many things had been mentioned," and that this applied "above all to the remark that those being late would be punished by history." Gorbachev interrupted him and said that in making this remark he "*had really talked about himself*"; transcript of the talks between Krenz and Gorbachev, SED Politburo, Central Party Archives, IV, 2/1/704, p. 3 of the typed transcript.

100 Schabowski, *Das Politbüro*, p. 74.

around to members in his delegation. With a forced smile and puzzled look he uttered a "sss," perhaps a short substitute for: "Well, comrades, that's it then. There is nothing more to say."[101]

There was a brief exchange immediately after this meeting between Gorbachev and Polish communist leaders Mieczyslaw Rakowski and General Jaruzelski. The Soviet leader told them: "Well, the German comrades are optimists, and they have interesting concepts." But he failed to explain what he meant, pointing instead to the ceiling of the room to indicate that the Stasi had probably planted listening devices and that it would be inopportune to discuss matters in detail.[102] There were also brief exchanges between Gerasimov and Schabowski, and between Falin and Krenz, in the course of which the East Germans expressed their disappointment with Honecker's speech and gave cryptic assurances that matters in East Germany would take their inevitable course, that is, presumably, that the replacement of the top leader was imminent.[103] The subsequent dinner confirmed that Honecker was unrepentant, and perhaps even determined to embarrass and humiliate Gorbachev. The seating order at table number one placed Gorbachev next to Ceausescu. PLO leader Yasir Arafat, too, was seated at that table, as was Krenz.[104]

Truth and Consequences

The visit to East Berlin made a deep and lasting impression on the Soviet participants. Disappointment, disbelief, frustration, and resignation were their main reactions. In his memoirs, Gorbachev writes that

> my careful attempts to convince [Honecker] of the necessity of not delaying the start of reform in the country as well as in the party led to no concrete results whatsoever. Each time, I ran into a wall of incomprehension. After our last meeting in October 1989, when I was taking part in the celebrations of the fortieth anniversary of the founding of the GDR, I went home in a particularly uneasy frame of mind. It was painfully obvious that the country resembled nothing so much as a simmering kettle with a tightly shut lid.[105]

On separate occasions, he told Krenz and Kochemasov that talking to Honecker and the Politburo had been like "*throwing peas against a brick wall*."[106] To Willy Brandt

---

101 Ibid., pp. 74-75; id., *Der Absturz*, pp. 241-42.

102 *Polityka* (Warsaw), No. 16, 18 April 1992.

103 Schabowski, *Das Politbüro*, p. 77; Falin, *Politische Erinnerungen*, p. 487.

104 Interview with Krenz.

105 Gorbatschow, *Erinnerungen*, p. 711.

106 Transcript of the meeting between Krenz and Gorbachev in Moscow, 1 November 1989, SED Politburo, Central Party Archives, IV 2/1/704, p. 39 of the typed transcript (italics mine); Kotschemassow, *Meine letzte Mission*, p. 111. In keeping with the appropriate English idiom, I have added the "brick" to the "wall" of the transcript and Kochemasov's report.

he confessed: "I returned from the GDR *worried and alarmed*."[107] "If it still needed confirmation," Gerasimov observed, "Gorbachev now knew that there was never going to be any far-reaching reform in the GDR under Honecker."[108] Similarly, Falin and Shakhnazarov concluded that "the days of the Honecker regime are numbered."[109] They were indeed. Honecker was forced to step down from office just ten days after Gorbachev had departed from East Berlin. But how is one to evaluate Gorbachev's behavior? What was his contribution to Honecker's downfall?

Upon his return to Moscow, at the airport, Gorbachev remarked to members of the Politburo that in front of the rostrum at the Platz der Republic groups of young people had marched by, protesting against Honecker and the SED leadership, and claimed that he had turned to Honecker and said: "You won't be able to stay [in power] unless you start reforms immediately."[110] Two questions arose from these remarks for the Soviet ambassador in East Berlin:

> First, why didn't Gorbachev speak about this during his meeting with the members of the leadership of the CC of the SED on 7 October in order to buttress his argument with newly won impressions? Second, at our get-together in the palace [Niederschönhausen] in the evening of 6 October, after the torch light procession of youth, Gorbachev didn't mention anything about such observations. On the contrary, he spoke of an impressive manifestation. Where, then, lies the truth?[111]

The truth is probably to be found in Gorbachev's continuing approach of persuasion and restraint. The peas he threw at Honecker were of the mushy and overcooked kind. Despite the fact that his remarks in the 7 October meetings about the necessity of change and about history being a stern judge were stronger than what he had ever stated before, they were made only after he had let Honecker throw sticks and stones at him for several years. Furthermore, nothing has come to light and no one in Gorbachev's entourage has ever suggested that he ever raised the subject of reform and the kinds of reform supposedly necessary *directly* with Honecker; that he at any time advised him to *step down* if he were unwilling to comply with his suggestions; and that he was actively encouraging or authorizing anyone in the East German leadership or in the Soviet imperial establishment in the GDR to seek ways to *replace* Honecker.

A good case can be made for the argument that, if Gorbachev wanted to maintain some semblance of cohesion and commonality in the "socialist community," he now

---

107 Transcript of meeting between Brandt and Gorbachev, Moscow, 17 October 1989, M.S. Gorbachev, "Iz Arkhiva Gorbacheva: M. S. Gorbachev – W. Brandt," *Svobodnaia mysl'*, No. 17 (November 1992), p. 27 (italics mine).

108 Interview with Gerasimov.

109 Falin, *Politische Erinnerungen*, p. 487.

110 Kotschemassow, *Meine letzte Mission*, p. 113.

111 Ibid.

needed to interfere more vigorously on behalf of processes of change in the GDR and elsewhere in Eastern Europe, and that it was simply not enough to try to change Honecker's siege and bunker mentality and the policies conducted on that basis by cautious pleading and persuasion. One of the possible ways to bring pressure to bear on Honecker would have been a public campaign. But there was none. Soviet reports on the anniversary did not even hint at dissonance and dissatisfaction, and failed to mention the demonstrations against the SED regime. They trumpeted the traditional line that "the historic anniversary of the German socialist state" had proceeded "in an atmosphere of optimism."[112] Those who had seen the torch light procession on 6 October had realized that East German youth had "taken over the banner of socialism and peace on German soil from the older generation and were carrying it forward into future decades." The military parade on the following day had emphasized that "the GDR remains a reliable member of the Warsaw alliance."[113]

As noted above in reference to the KGB and its Luch operation, there was also no coordinated and consistent attempt at rearing a party faction in the SED that Moscow could have relied upon to remove the recalcitrant party leader from office. As Schabowski has stated: "The Soviet ambassador was not allowed to interfere as in former times." When Walter Ulbricht was forced to resign, "everything was discussed in Moscow. But now there was no Brezhnev Doctrine."[114] Gorbachev confirmed publicly on 6 October and reiterated privately to Krenz on 1 November that "matters relating to the German Democratic Republic are decided not in Moscow, but in Berlin."[115] It may be credible, as Krenz has said, that Gorbachev's parting remark at the Schönefeld airport to a small group of "trusted East German comrades" had been "*deistvuite*" (take action), but it would be quite erroneous to draw from this the conclusion that Gorbachev had thereby given an opposition faction in the party a signal to act.[116] Schabowski calls this idea "simply a pathetic myth."[117] The Soviet party leader could not in the least have considered "Politburo members Mittag and Axen, who were also at the airport," to "have been possible conspirators" against Honecker.[118] Yet if Gorbachev *had* wanted to promote the

---

112 S. Baigarov, B. Ovchinnikov, and M. Podkliuchnikov, "Nash orientir - druzhba," *Pravda*, 8 October 1989; similarly their earlier report, "Znamia truda i mira. Spetsial'nye korrespondenty "Pravdy" peredaiut iz Berlina," *Pravda*, 6 October 1989.

113 *Id.*, their report of 7 October, *Pravda*, 8 October 1989.

114 Schabowski interview with Serge Schmemann, *New York Times*, 17 October 1989.

115 The 6 October remark, as quoted above, p. 407; for Gorbachev's reiteration of the point, see Krenz, "Anmerkungen zur Öffnung der Mauer," p. 366.

116 Krenz, *Wenn Mauern fallen*, p. 96.

117 Schabowski, *Das Politbüro*, p. 77.

118 Ibid.

removal of Honecker, his ability to do so may have been limited, but corresponding possibilities certainly existed.[119]

In accordance with the inner logic of the new paradigm, he emphasized instead the need for events to run their course. Autonomy of national decision makers, non-interference, and freedom of choice were the new operational principles which he applied. As he told Krenz in Moscow, he had "always exercised the greatest degree of restraint towards the comrades in the GDR." He had, of course, known "very well the situation in the GDR." But his goal had been "*not to let disharmony arise* in the relations" between the CPSU and the SED. He had been patient because he "understood that the [East German] *party and the whole society had to mature for these changes*."[120] Thus, in Gorbachev's design, rather than taking the initiative himself to impose change, he left it up to the East German reformist leaders to take charge. Falin put it succinctly when he told Krenz after the 7 October banquet that Gorbachev, as a guest in East Berlin, "has done and said more than could be expected from a guest. Everything else now depends on you."[121] The anti-Honecker conspirators were left to their own devices and reduced to keeping Gorbachev informed of their progress.

This process began at the end of the anniversary celebrations, when Krenz and Schabowski made some cautious attempts to convey to various members of the Soviet delegation, including Falin and Gerasimov, the notion that some leaders in the SED top echelons were dissatisfied with Honecker's disastrous course.[122] Krenz told Falin: "Your [party leader] has said everything there was to say. Ours didn't understand anything."[123] As the details of the plan for Honecker's involuntary resignation were taking shape, Harry Tisch, a full member of the SED Politburo and chairman of the trade unions, who had traveled to the USSR on 16 October on a routine visit, informed Gorbachev about the planned move. The Soviet party leader reportedly "took note" of this information "with satisfaction and without losing many words over it."[124]

The information was apparently not lost on Gorbachev. On the following day, when the SED Politburo met in East Berlin to depose Honecker, he reassured Willy Brandt (and probably also himself) that

> serious changes are beginning to take place [in the GDR]. A meeting of the [SED] Politburo will take place today to be followed by a plenary

---

119 For details see pp. 378-79.

120 Transcript of meeting between Gorbachev and Krenz, in Moscow, 1 November 1989, SED Politburo, Central Party Archives, J IV, 2/1/704, p. 37 of the typed transcript (italics mine).

121 Falin, *Politische Erinnerungen*, p. 487 (italics mine).

122 Schabowski, *Das Politbüro*, p. 77.

123 Falin, *Politische Erinnerungen*, p. 487.

124 Schabowski, *Der Absturz*, p. 262.

> meeting of the CC. At issue will be the [establishment of] a broad dialogue of the party with society and the population.[125]

But what were Gorbachev's options if these serious changes were not to materialize in the East German communist party and the broad dialogue between the SED and the population failed to occur? They would then be quite limited. In essence, he would find himself not simply on the proverbial horns of a dilemma but tossed in the air by "history" as if on the horns of a bull in the streets of Pamplona. For his approach of non-interference to work in favor of the Soviet Union and the creation of a reform socialist East Germany, he needed the cooperation of both the West and the population in the GDR. A separate reform socialist GDR, however, was neither in the interest of the West German government nor of the East German population. This would be revealed unequivocally after the collapse of the Berlin wall and through the official West German and popular East German reactions to that momentous event.

3. Gorbachev and Krenz

With the replacement of Honecker, Gorbachev finally appeared to have achieved a major unspoken objective: the establishment of a reform socialist system under a new leader. Yet Krenz's regime was only transitional and it was to last only until 3 December. In a repetition of patterns observable in many previous revolutions, he and the demoralized representatives of the *ancien régime* were retreating step by step in front of ever more insistent and more far-reaching demands for change. The pressures were transported to the top like on a conveyor belt: popular opinion influenced the attitudes and actions of the rank and file of the party, who in turn exerted pressure on the top party leaders. They, like the troubled imperial center, were unwilling to use force and lost control over the course of events.

In his attempt to construct reform socialism in East Germany, Krenz faced major problems. One was that of political legitimacy. When Honecker had resigned, he had suggested Krenz as his successor, thereby conveying a perhaps not too erroneous notion of continuity. Krenz, after all, had for a long time been considered Honecker's heir apparent, the *Kronprinz*, or crown prince, of the regime.[126] In the perceptions of the members of the democratic opposition, he was considered a careerist capable of making tactical adjustments but not of carrying out strategic change. As chief of internal security in the party, he was held responsible for many years of repression and for having ordered the violent dissolution of the 7 October demonstrations in

---

125 Transcript of meeting between Brandt and Gorbachev in Moscow, 17 October 1989, M. S. Gorbachev, "Iz Arkhiva Gorbacheva: M. S. Gorbachev – W. Brandt," *Svobodnaia mysl'*, No. 17 (November 1992), p. 28.

126 This problem was referred to by Schabowski as the "curse of the Pharao"; Schabowski, *Der Absturz*, p. 271.

East Berlin, Leipzig, Dresden, and other East German cities. As head of the electoral commission, he was seen as having been responsible for rigging the May local elections. And as head of the delegation that had traveled to China after the June crackdown in Tienanmen Square to congratulate the Chinese, he was regarded as not being averse to a "Chinese solution" in East Germany. Many observers, including members of the SED, were appalled by his hour-long television speech, a repetition of his address to the earlier CC session, with which Krenz had begun his rule on 18 October.[127] Matters were not helped either by the fact that Krenz assumed all of Honecker's political functions and adorned himself with his regalia.. He allowed himself to be crowned party chief, head of state, and chairman of the national defense council. Furthermore, several of the discredited members of the old Politburo and the Central Committee apparatus, including Horst Dohlus and Hans-Joachim Böhme, some the most pliant of the Honecker leadership, were reappointed to their positions.[128]

It was obvious that the CC, as it was then constituted, was unwilling and incapable of confessing to the fundamental errors of the past and meeting the new challenges. Furthermore, an internal Politburo report (compiled by Dohlus) still observed with opprobrium that the Neue Forum was continuing "to develop broad activity in all social areas" and that the church institutions were continuing "to serve the opposition forces in their activity."[129] At the same time, the report was optimistic that the ground could be cut from under the opposition movement and that a greater degree of trust could be established between the SED and the population if the party entered upon the road to democratization and openness jointly with Gorbachev. In implementation of the report, the Politburo decided to permit again the sale of *Sputnik* magazine. On 1 November it also reopened the borders with Czechoslovakia and three days later announced that its citizens would be allowed to leave through Czechoslovakia upon

---

127 Schabowski is scathing in his criticism of the speech, saying that Krenz, appearing in front of millions of people in East and West Germany, "simply repeated what he had told the highest party organization a few hours earlier ... as if he was speaking in front of a gigantically enlarged Central Committee"; Schabowski, *Der Absturz*, p. 272. In fairness, however, many parts of the speech were *not* couched in the party jargon; see Wolfgang Oschlies, "Egon Krenz: 'Mut zur Wahrheit': Sprachliche Anmerkungen zur Antrittsrede des neuen SED-Chefs," *Gelesen, kommentiert* (Bundesinstitut für ostwissenschaftliche und internationale Studien), No. 19, 19 October 1989.

128 The mixture of the old and the new and differences over how to deal with the mounting problems in East Germany were evident also in the fact that the East German security agencies were still plotting and scheming to carry out all sorts of, as they called it, Measures for the Prevention of the Further Formation and for the Roll Back of Anti-Socialist Movements; heading of an agenda item prepared by Mielke and others for the SED Politburo session of 24 October 1989, SED Politburo, *Arbeitsprotokolle*, Central Party Archives, J IV 2/2A/3250.

129 Information Concerning the Current Political Situation after the Ninth Meeting of the Central Committee of the SED, internal paper for the SED Politburo session of 23 October 1989, SED Politburo, *Arbeitsprotokolle*, Central Party Archives, J IV 2/2A/3250.

simple presentation of personal identity cards. This had the immediate and, from the SED's viewpoint, disastrous effect that over the weekend when the announcement was made a record 23,500 East Germans left for West Germany. This was a higher rate of emigration than during the peak periods in August 1961, when East Germany had closed the borders and built the wall.[130]

Another record was broken on 4 November. The largest demonstrations in the GDR since 1953, with about half a million people participating in the event, took place on Berlin's Alexanderplatz. For many participants the demonstrations were a moving experience. Organized by the opposition movement, the speakers included dissidents of dubious political conviction, such as Markus Wolf, the former intelligence chief, and Gregor Gysi, later to become head of the PDS, the renamed SED. None of the speakers' placards and banners called for reunification as yet. The demands were for freedom of speech, freedom of assembly, freedom of travel, and accountability of government officials. The *volonté général* ("*We* are the people!") was set against the no longer credible claim of the party to be the people's vanguard. Clearly, the framework for the changes envisaged was a socialist East Germany with a human face. In fact, the representatives of the Neue Forum and other alternative and opposition forces in East Germany now began to call more persistently and vigorously on their compatriots to remain in their own country rather than look for a brighter future in West Germany.

Among many other inalienable conditions, Soviet support for the reform socialist experiment was seen as crucial by the new regime. This was evident in the internal report for the Politburo meeting of 23 October which had asserted that "the telephone conversation between Comrades Egon Krenz and Mikhail Gorbachev [see below] elicited great satisfaction among the population" and that the citizenry was "looking forward to the imminent visit by Comrade Krenz in Moscow," which they "understood to be significant for the closing of ranks between the SED and the CPSU."[131] It was indicated also by Krenz's later statement that he would never have accepted the job of party leader if he had not been convinced that he would receive Gorbachev's backing.[132] On 21 October he called the Soviet leader and informed him about the leadership change. In the conversation, according to Krenz, he did receive the Soviet leader's "full support;" nothing was said that would have led him to believe

130 The figures on emigration according to ADN, the East German news agency, 6 November 1989.

131 SED Politburo, *Arbeitsprotokolle*, Central Party Archives, J IV 2/2A/3250. The content of the telephone conversation was reported in *Neues Deutschland*, 23 October 1989. Schabowski has reported that Krenz, in a Politburo meeting on 29 October, had explained that, in his first meeting as party chief with Gorbachev to take place in Moscow, he wanted to have the party's "blessing" for his policies; Schabowski, *Der Absturz*, p. 299.

132 Interview with Krenz.

that Gorbachev was "anything but sincere in his backing for a reform socialist East Germany."[133]

Reports in the Soviet press also connveyed the notion that there was support in Mosow for a reform socialist East Germany. As noted in the context of the October celebrations in East Berlin, the central Soviet papers and national television had essentially failed to paint an even vaguely accurate picture of Honecker and the deteriorating state of affairs in the GDR. Now, after the leadership change, Soviet newspapers launched attacks on Honecker, saying that with the help of the news media he had erected a "wall of silence cut off from reality and trumpeted the GDR's success and the overfulfillment of the annual plans not very different from the way our dispatches used to be."[134] As a complete surprise to most Soviet readers, their newspapers now reported that since August alone, more than 60,000 East Germans had fled to the West. Krenz, according to the press reports, had much to recommend him. He belonged to a new generation of East German leaders, had visited the Soviet Union several times in the past, spoke Russian fluently, and was ready to engage in dialogue with the democratic forces of his country.[135]

In private conversation with Krenz on 1 November in Moscow, Gorbachev reiterated his support for Krenz. According to the transcript of the talks, the Soviet leader took note of the fact that the East German people and party were about to embark on fundamental reform and wished Krenz success in this endeavor. East Germany was, after all, the Soviet Union's "closest friend and ally."[136] He also reflected on the importance of their meeting.

> Your visit, Comrade Krenz, so shortly after your election to the highest offices of the GDR, is of extraordinary significance for mutual coordination [of our policies] at the beginning of a new stage in our relations. The point [now] is jointly to demonstrate that we stand together and that the development in the Soviet Union is very close to that in the GDR and *vice versa*. This is also important for the other socialist countries and for the whole world. The FRG, too, will be interested in

---

133 Ibid.

134 *Trud*, 22 October 1989, in an article by its correspondent in East Berlin, V. Nikitin.

135 Ibid.

136 Transcript (*Niederschrift*) of the talks between Krenz and Gorbachev on 1 November 1989 in Moscow, SED Politburo, *Arbeitsprotokolle*, Central Party Archives, IV 2/1/704, pp. 2-3 (ind. sp.); see also the supplementary Politburo materials on the visit, J IV 2/2/2358 and J IV 2/2A/3255. Krenz also took notes, to which he referred in his "Anmerkungen zur Öffnung der Berliner Mauer im Herbst 1989," *Osteuropa*, No. 4 (1992), pp. 365-369. *All subsequent citations from the transcript are in indirect speech (ind. sp.) in the original, rendered here for better readability in direct speech. For the same reason, the first person singular has been used for the "Comrade Honecker" and "Comrade Gorbachev" in the original.* The subsequent page numbers are those of the typed manuscript. Zelikow and Rice quote from an essentially identical, albeit longer, transcript kept in the Bundesarchiv Potsdam, E1-5630; see Zelikow and Rice, *Germany Unified*, pp. 87-91. The reasons for the existence of two versions are unclear.

> what it is that Gorbachev and Krenz have agreed to. In principle, I share all the thoughts that you, Comrade Krenz, have expressed.[137]

As Krenz later said, since he was concerned about East German instabilities on the one hand, and the widening discussion in the West about German unification on the other, the central purpose of his visit was to establish whether Gorbachev was still committed to the idea of the continued existence of two German states and what role, if any, he saw for East Germany in a new Europe.[138] The transcript reflects this concern. Krenz asked his host "to outline more clearly the place which he [intended] to allocate to the FRG and the GDR in the all-European house."[139] Gorbachev prefaced his reply by saying that he welcomed the fact that Krenz had raised this question and continued:

> On this problem [German unity] the GDR, the Soviet Union, and the other socialist countries have until now pursued a correct line. [This line] has led to the recognition of the existence of two separate German states, to the international recognition of the GDR, to its active role in the world, to the conclusion of the [1970] Moscow treaty as well as other treaties, and to the Helsinki conference.

He then proceeded to dismiss the talk about German unification. There was nothing to worry about. "There is no reason," he told Krenz, "to surmise how the German question will be solved some time [in the future]. The current realities have to be taken into account. This is the important thing." Typically, he left open the possibility of reunification at some time in the future:

> Should the tendency of rapprochement in Europe endure *for several decades* and the process of integration continue – irrespective of the social systems and with a separate evolution of politics, culture, paths of development, and traditions – then, *perhaps*, the question could be different. But this is *not a problem of current politics.*[140]

What is it that gave Gorbachev the confidence so close to the collapse of the GDR and the Soviet empire to believe that the question of German unity might "perhaps" arise in "several decades"? Internationally, he argued, there was no support for it. It had become clear to him

> in recent talks with Margaret Thatcher, François Mitterrand, but also with Jaruzelski and Andreotti, that all of these political leaders proceed from the [necessity of] safeguarding the post-war realities, including the existence of two German states. Posing the question of the unity of Germany is regarded by all of them as extremely explosive for the current situation. They also do not want the Warsaw Pact and NATO to be dissolved, and it is for this reason that they are for continued membership of Poland and Hungary in the Warsaw Pact. The balance [of power] in

137 Transcript, pp. 33-34; Krenz, "Anmerkungen zur Öffnung der Mauer," p. 367.

138 Interview with Krenz.

139 Transcript, p. 19; Krenz, "Anmerkungen zur Öffnung der Mauer," p. 367.

140 Transcript, p. 24 (italics mine).

> Europe [they argue] should not be disturbed because no one knew what the consequences might be.[141]

As for the United States, he thought that they had "until now taken a similar position." He reported that in a meeting between Yakovlev and former national security advisor Zbigniew Brzezinski the question had been discussed "whether one could imagine a situation in which the reunification of Germany became a reality." Brzezinski had replied that "for him, this would be a calamity."[142] Nevertheless, Gorbachev thought that there were "some nuances" in the American attitude, which still had to be examined. This idea, however, was dismissed by Shakhnazarov, present at the meeting in his capacity as Gorbachev's adviser on Eastern Europe: to the extent that nuances existed, they were most likely designed for "the broad public."[143]

The exercise in mutual reassurance continued with evidence derived from Gorbachev's talks with West German social democratic leaders. Gorbachev told Krenz that Willy Brandt, chairman of the SPD and the Socialist International, had said that he considered East Germany an enormous achievement of socialism. Its disappearance would be a shocking defeat for social democracy. Although Brandt was putting himself at a distance from communists, he nevertheless considered social democracy a branch of the workers' movement and continued to adhere to the socialist idea. Bahr, the Soviet leader went on, had unequivocally made this very point.[144] There is additional evidence for the opinions Brandt shared with Gorbachev. On 17 October, in private conversation with the General Secretary, the SPD party chairman had outlined common views and interests on the German problem between Western European social democrats and socialists, on the one hand, and between Soviet and Eastern European reform communists, on other. He regretted that young people were leaving the GDR despite the "new self-awareness" that was being born there. The remedy he suggested was for the SED leadership "to begin a dialogue not

141 Transcript, p. 20; Krenz, "Anmerkungen zur Öffnung der Mauer," p. 367. Gorbachev had expressed these views about what Western leaders really thought about the prospect of German reunification in private conversation with Willy Brandt, chairman of the SPD and the Socialist International; "Iz Arkhiva Gorbacheva: M.S. Gorbachev – W. Brandt" (transcript of a meeting between Gorbachev and Brandt, held in Moscow on 17 October 1989), *Svobodnaia mysl'*, No. 17 (November 1992), pp. 22-29.

142 Transcript, p. 19. A note on translation is appropriate here. The East German record uses *Zusammenbruch*, which could be rendered as "collapse." But this could give the idea that Brzezinski, as reported by Yakovlev and Gorbachev, had simply referred to the collapse of the post-war order. But the thought to be rendered here is probably that of a strongly undesirable development, that is, a "calamity," "catastrophe," or "disaster."

143 Transcript, p. 20.

144 Ibid.

only with the bloc parties but also with society at large."[145] Importantly, Brandt outlined an alternative to German unification in the form of increased cooperation between West Germany and a reformed East Germany. He told Gorbachev:

> One cannot separate German from European affairs. If this is the case, and if the rest of Europe will keep moving towards closer relations and integration, then both German states may discover more similarities in different spheres between themselves than with other countries. Maybe it makes sense, then, to draw before them the perspective of getting some "common roof" for cooperation in those spheres.[146]

It is precisely such a "common roof" in the form of a community governed by treaties across various dimensions of policy (*Vertragsgemeinschaft*) that reformist GDR Prime Minister Hans Modrow would propose only several weeks later.

To return to the Krenz-Gorbachev exchanges, there is a second reason why the Soviet leader thought that German unification was not on the international agenda and why East Germany would and should continue to occupy an important room in the Common House of Europe: the by now familiar idea that democratic socialism in the GDR not only had a chance but more of a chance in that country than elsewhere in the socialist bloc. According to Gorbachev, this was true, in particular, because of the "social orientation" of GDR's economy – a strong asset "that should not be abandoned." Although he considered it "too early" for the SED, just a few days after the replacement of Honecker, to present a "detailed plan" of change, he was nevertheless heartened by the fact that the "main directions of a program of action have clearly been outlined – more socialism, renewal, and democratization."[147]

But what kind of socialism? If the GDR were to introduce democratic socialism and a market economy and present a human face, what would be the difference between such a system and the West German *Sozialstaat*? Krenz, probably in contrast to Gorbachev, who never addressed this issue publicly and (to the extent that this is known) privately, was conscious of a basic problem. Echoing Reinhold's conviction, expressed a few months earlier, that East Germany was thinkable only as socialist alternative to West Germany,[148] Krenz considered de-ideologization (*Entideologisierung*) of the relations between the two German states to be a "very complicated question" and a problem "quite different than what is [normal] in the relations among other states." Deideologization in the German-German relationship would mean "abandoning the defense of socialism" in East Germany and would raise questions as

---

145 "Iz Arkhiva Gorbacheva: M.S. Gorbachev - W. Brandt" (transcript of a meeting between Gorbachev and Brandt, held in Moscow on 17 October 1989), *Svobodnaia mysl'*, No. 17 (November 1992), p. 28.

146 Ibid.

147 Transcript of the Krenz-Gorbachev meeting, p. 35.

148 See above, p. 296.

to the rationale of the Berlin wall and the border regime between East and West Germany.[149]

Furthermore, did reform socialism in the GDR mean that the SED should abandon its claim to the monopoly on power? Apparently not, in Gorbachev's view. Only a few weeks earlier, he had rejected this idea. To revert briefly to the private conversation between him and Brandt, the latter had asked him for advice on what he considered to be a difficult problem with which he had been confronted:

> A group of Social Democrats has been formed in the GDR. They consider themselves not a party but an association. I don't know them personally. But I have heard that they don't want to be an appendage of the SED. Recently, I received a letter from them in my capacity as chairman of the Socialist International and was put in an awkward position. On the one hand, we can't admit this association to the Socialist International. On the other hand, I can't just refuse to react to this approach.

The CPSU General Secretary replied by saying,

> I would advise, in order not to do any harm to the processes taking place there, to wait some time and particularly now to show caution and restraint. Later, after reassessing the situation and the on-going processes, it may be possible to work out a reaction.[150]

To return to Krenz and Gorbachev, a large part of their conversation consisted of a diagnosis of East Germany's economic malaise and its political implications. Quite in contrast to the pattern of the Honecker-Gorbachev talks, the two leaders now soberly and at times somberly addressed what they acknowledged to be a precarious state of affairs – and one at variance with Gorbachev's optimistic assessment at the meeting that, if Honecker had adopted a reform program just "two or three years ago," the ensuing development "could have been the culmination of his life."[151] Given the importance of the topic, it is appropriate to link it up with the "debt and dependency" problem that had plagued Soviet-East German relations in the Honecker era.[152]

By 1989, the economic plight of the GDR was not only serious but desperate. Due to the secrecy and compartmentalization of functions endemic to communist systems, few members even at the top echelons of the SED were aware of this fact. The extent of the economic malaise was revealed to them only in a watershed analysis of the economic situation of the GDR, presented by Gerhard Schürer, the chairman of the State Planning Commission, and one of the chief economic advisors to Honecker. The report was presented to Krenz and most of the members of the SED Politburo on 31 October and to the Tenth Conference of the SED Central Committee from 8 to 10 November 1989. When Krenz discussed East Germany's predicaments with

---

149 Transcript, p. 25.

150 Transcript of meeting between Brandt and Gorbachev, p. 28.

151 Transcript, p. 40.

152 On the "debts and dependency" issue, see above, pp. 167-72 and pp. 237-38.

Gorbachev, he was not only aware of the content of the report but several times used data it contained.[153]

The Schürer report concentrated on three major deficiencies of the East German economy: (1) the decline in the "rate of accumulation" in the productive sector from 16.1 percent in 1970 to 9.9 percent in 1988, which had led to obsolescence of much of the industrial equipment and declining rates of growth in national income; (2) the financing of economic growth through external and internal credit; and (3) the inability to meet the planning targets for exports in the 1986-1990 Five-Year Plan. The overall picture painted by the report was that of a society living far beyond its means. Honecker had blatantly disregarded what he had said in 1971, that "our society can never borrow more than it produces."[154] The violation of this common economic sense was amply reflected in the data that Schürer submitted. These included a reported increase in the GDR's indebtedness to the "non-socialist world" from 2 billion Valutamarks, or hard currency marks, in 1970 to about 49 billion marks in 1989; the growth in the regime's internal debt from 12 billion East German marks in 1970 to 123 billion marks in 1989; a debt-to-export ratio of 150 percent, rather than the 25 percent that Schürer considered economically sensible; subsidization of the microelectronic industry to the tune of 3 billion East German marks annually; and labor productivity that was 40 percent lower than in West Germany.[155] Perhaps the most shocking revelation to the party was the report's assessment that, if merely an increase in the level of hard-currency indebtedness was to be avoided, the rate of consumption would have to be curtailed by 25 to 30 percent.[156]

One of the many reasons for the mounting debt and economic decline lay in the difficulties experienced by the Soviet Union, upon which the GDR had long relied for much of its economic activity, including the import of raw materials at cut rates and, early in the Honecker era, the financing of credit. But in 1989 the Soviet Union itself, as mentioned, was experiencing acute financial distress and was no longer able

153 Gerhard Schürer *et al.*, "Analyse der ökonomischen Lage der DDR mit Schlußfolgerungen," dated 27 October 1989, submitted to the Politburo for its meeting of 31 October 1989, SED Politburo, *Arbeitsprotokolle*, Central Party Archives, J IV 2/2/2356. The co-authors were Gerhard Beil, Alexander Schalk-Golodkowski, Ernst Höfner, and Arno Donda. The Politburo endorsed the report without changes. For a detailed discussion of the report and its repercussions, see Hans-Hermann Hertle, "Staatsbankrott: Der ökonomische Untergang des SED-Staates," *Deutschland-Archiv*, Vol. 25, No. 10 (October 1992), pp. 1019-30, and his interview with Schürer, "'Das reale Bild war eben katastrophal!': Gespräch mit Gerhard Schürer," ibid., pp. 1031-39.

154 Information Concerning the Current Political Situation after the Ninth Meeting of the Central Committee of the SED, internal paper for the SED Politburo session of 23 October 1989, SED Politburo, *Arbeitsprotokolle*, Central Party Archives, J IV 2/2a/3250.

155 Schürer report, pp. 4 and 10-11.

156 Ibid., p. 11.

and no longer willing to sustain the GDR in the way to which the latter had become accustomed. The metropole was looking after its own interests rather than those of the periphery.

The political implications of the dismal economic state of affairs were considerable. East Germany in the late Honecker era had led a kind of dual existence. On the one hand, it had stridently affirmed its sovereignty and rejected any attempt, implied or explicit, by West Germany, to erode its political or social autonomy. On the other hand, it had begun to undermine this very autonomy by allowing its indebtedness to Western banks and governments to increase. The GDR, as a result, became economically most dependent on that state from which it most wanted to remain apart. But West Germany's willingness to continue to finance much of the debt in exchange for making the division of Germany less painful for the East Germans (*menschliche Erleichterungen*) and a lessening of tensions between the two Germanys changed during the Krenz interregnum: it was progressively raising the price tag for economic and financial assistance. Within a few days after the opening of the wall, it would no longer be content with piecemeal concessions but demand fundamental systemic change. Given the severity of the GDR's economic problems, something had to give, and that something would turn out to be the regime itself. In Hertle's words, "No other state in the world [other than West Germany] would have been ready to relieve the GDR of its debts, and its allies were in no position to do so. Thus, the political and economic destruction of the GDR was preordained."[157]

To resume the description and analysis of the private exchanges between Krenz and Gorbachev, it was Krenz who introduced the topic by saying that the day before the SED Politburo had received and discussed an unadulterated report of a kind that had never been submitted to that body. He was concerned, he said, that when the report would be brought to the attention of the Central Committee, it "could produce a shock with detrimental consequences."[158] In reply, Gorbachev claimed (not very credibly) that

> the Soviet Union has been aware of the real state of affairs in the national economy of the GDR ... and has always endeavored to meet its obligations towards the GDR. Except for the fact that, due to domestic problems, 2 million tons of projected oil deliveries had to be canceled, [we] always understood that the GDR cannot function without the Soviet Union. Such support was the internationalist duty of the Soviet Union. At the same time, [we] asked ourselves, why, given this state of affairs, were we constantly being showered in such an aggressive way with GDR success stories? This was hard to bear since [we] knew the real condition of the GDR. [I] tried once to raise this issue with Comrade Honecker and

157 Ibid.

158 Transcript of the Krenz-Gorbachev exchanges, pp. 9-10.

to discuss the GDR's indebtedness. But he strongly objected to this since such problems [supposedly] did not exist.[159]

Krenz repeated (without direct attribution) some of the salient data of Schürer's report, saying that the GDR at present had to pay interest in the amount of $4.5 billion, which amounted to 62 percent of annual export revenue; that it had to raise new credit in order to meet its credit obligations; that the electronics industry was being subsidized with 3 billion marks per annum; that the economy was facing new challenges; and the population had new expectations, but if one were to match productive capacity and consumption, the standard of living would have "to be lowered immediately by 30 percent."[160] At one point during Krenz's presentation of economic data, Gorbachev interjected and admitted that he had "not imagined the situation to be that precarious."[161]

What, then, was to be done? What policies should be adopted, individually and jointly, to meet the precarious situation? Even a benevolently inclined reader of the record can only conclude that the Krenz-Gorbachev policy prescriptions fail to add up to a coherent plan of action. They constitute instead a hodgepodge of inadequate measures, obsolete remedies, contradictory preferences, and vague commitments.[162] A first set of measures discussed concerned *economic assistance*. If East Germany was to survive as a state, let alone be transformed into a showcase of reform socialism, a massive rescue operation was immediately required. But the Soviet Union was neither prepared nor able even to begin thinking about such an operation. At one point, after having admitted earlier that, for domestic reasons, the USSR had to cut oil deliveries to the GDR by 2 million tons (see above), Gorbachev assured Krenz that "things would remain unchanged [sic], that the GDR would receive raw materials from the Soviet Union."[163] At another point, he promised that the Soviet Union "will do everything in order to meet the obligations it has assumed" but

---

159 Ibid., p. 10. Gorbachev may have alluded to his talks with Honecker on 20 April 1986 in East Berlin; see above, pp. 237-38.

160 Transcript, pp. 9-10, 13-16.

161 Transcript, p. 15. The transcript of the Krenz-Gorbachev talks found in the Bundesarchiv in Potsdam, E1-56320, has the East German leader put the projected GDR debt at the end of 1989 at $26.5 billion and the estimated current account deficit at $21.1 billion. The note taker recorded: "Astonished, Comrade Gorbachev asked whether these numbers are correct." For a summary of the talks, including the above citation, see Zelikow and Rice *Germany Unified*, p. 87.

162 This author, therefore, disagrees with Zelikow and Rice, who write that "Krenz and Gorbachev had agreed on a detailed plan of action"; ibid., p. 91.

163 Transcript, pp. 10 and 22. The reality was, however, that – as Schürer had revealed in an earlier report (May 1989) – it had *not* been "possible to conclude an agreement in the 1986-1990 Five-Year Plan ... for the delivery of certain raw materials [from he USSR], such as lead, zinc, apatite concentrate, ammonium phosphate ..."; cited in Hertle, "'Das reale Bild war eben katastrophal,'" p. 1034.

acknowledged that this would only "alleviate the situation in the GDR somewhat."[164] It is only in relation to the socialist bloc as a whole and Polish indebtedness to the West in particular that Gorbachev explicitly and unequivocally stated: "*The question is often posed what the Soviet Union can do in this situation. Economically, it can do very little.*"[165]

A second circle of problems touched upon several times in the conversation were the relations between the Soviet Union and *West Germany*. The record clearly reveals, as the Germans would say, *Ratlosigkeit,* or not knowing what to do. At one point in the talks, Gorbachev suggested that Moscow should seek to "bind the partner FRG more closely" to the Soviet Union because this would give East Germany a better position in the triangular relationship USSR-GDR-FRG.[166] At another, he thought that "now is the time to exert more pressure on Chancellor Kohl," presumably for the reason that "there are people in the governing parties who would like to get rid of Kohl," despite the fact (presumably advantageous for him in the CDU) that he had "put his money on the nationalism horse."[167] And at yet another point, he declared that it was important to continue "the principled and flexible policy" and to make sure that West Germany would "not be able to exert pressure on the GDR through the known [economic and financial] mechanisms."[168]

A third set of policies discussed concerned the relationship between the *two Germanys*. Both leaders were acutely aware of and anxious about West German attempts to use economic leverage for political purposes but also conscious of the fact that East Germany now needed West German financial assistance more than ever. Furthermore, curtailment of the links between the two German states would have contradicted Gorbachev's New Thinking and his concept of the Common House of Europe. He therefore acknowledged that "manifold human contacts exist between the two German states;" that "it would be detrimental to reduce the relations between the GDR and the FRG or even to rupture them;" and that it was "important for the GDR to maintain and further develop its relations with the GDR."[169] Yet at the same time, the contacts had to "be kept under control and managed;" it was necessary "to exercise caution so that the ideological opponent would not gain positions that he could exploit."[170]

---

164 Transcript, p. 17.

165 Transcript, p. 23 (italics mine). "It is absurd to imagine," Gorbachev continued, "that the Soviet Union could subsidize 40 million Poles."

166 Transcript, p. 22.

167 Transcript, pp. 22, 25.

168 Transcript, p. 17.

169 Transcript, pp. 21, 22.

170 Transcript, p. 21.

A fourth set of measures dealt with the *political dimensions of Soviet-East German cooperation*. As in his private talks with Honecker, he pleaded for more coordination and less secrecy. He also made it clear that he considered the party to be the main agent of change – a surprising and incongruous idea considering his own disappointments with the CPSU, his move away from that institution to an executive presidency and the fact that East Germany was not Hungary or Poland, that is, that the SED had neither a strong tradition nor a significant reservoir of reform socialism. Nevertheless, he advised Krenz to do what essentially amounted to copying major elements of the October 1988 CPSU reform: to replace party cadres at the forthcoming SED Central Committee plenum and to "elect some smart and original people from the CC to the Politburo as well as prominent representatives from the cultural and scientific community to the Central Committee. That would improve the prestige of these bodies." At the plenum "one could certainly continue to defend Honecker" although it was "doubtful whether this would still be possible in relation to society." He agreed with Krenz that Soviet-East German cooperation should now "be brought more strongly under the control of the parties;" that the "exchange of experience should be intensified between the departments of the Central Committees;" and that the same applied to contacts between "the CC secretaries."[171]

Fifth, the new East German leader provided his Soviet counterpart with information about some measures that had been taken and were being prepared in *East Germany* itself. The use of weapons at the borders to prevent would-be refugees from escaping would be stopped, Krenz told Gorbachev. The border troops had been instructed accordingly. The travel and emigration regime would be liberalized. Since this issue was the most important change coveted by the East German population and the most vexing for the SED and was to become a bone of contention between Moscow and East Berlin only a few days later, it is appropriate to quote verbatim. This is what Krenz said:

> The draft of the new Law on Travel (*Reisegesetz*) has been adopted in the Politburo and has been passed on to the Council of Ministers, which will put it up for public discussion. It is scheduled to be adopted by the Volkskammer [parliament] before Christmas. Each GDR citizen, according to the law, will have the possibility to acquire a passport and an exit visa for travel to all countries. The circle of those exempted from this [new rule] will be kept very small.

Krenz also mentioned that the GDR was not in a position to supply those who wanted to travel abroad with hard-currency funds. This inability would be made public.[172]

---

171 Transcript, pp. 35-36.
172 Transcript, pp. 25-26.

In conclusion a careful reading of the record of the conversation reveals not only a lot of wishful thinking and much uncertainty about what to do but also concern about future developments. Speaking about the mass demonstrations in the GDR, Krenz said that the party leadership would use political means to solve political problems. The demonstrations would be legalized and the police would not intervene. But he also acknowledged that "the situation is developing according to its own dynamics."[173] Gorbachev had similar concerns:

> The processes now develop very dynamically and could further accelerate. The leadership of the party must react accordingly. If the processes were to gain in spontaneity or lose their political orientation, this would be a disaster. An unmanageable situation could thereby arise.

Gorbachev added that he had seen this happening in the Soviet Union.[174] Concern about the likely course of events was evident also among his advisers.[175] Chernyaev, for instance, remembers that, as Krenz's plane was leaving Moscow, several officials joked ominously: "There goes the committee for the dissolution of the GDR."[176]

Such comments raise the question as to whether Krenz really had Gorbachev's backing or whether he and the *germanisty* advising him would have preferred someone like Modrow, with better reform socialist credentials, to be at the helm in East Germany. As for these credentials, Modrow had become chief of the regional party organization in Dresden in 1973 and almost immediately gained respect and trust among party reformers and the population by his self-confidence, relaxed style, and openness to discussion and new ideas. For instance, in interviews prior to his nomination to full Politburo membership on 3 November and prime minister on 8 November, he had described the country as "ruined" and said that, without new leaders, East Germany would be "lost." Not surprisingly, in East Germany and abroad he was often described as a possible "East German Gorbachev."[177] Krenz, in contrast, upon his appointment to the top leadership positions in the GDR – and in conformity with a pattern typical of many revolutions, where conservative reformers had first been replaced by more radical figures and then by revolutionaries – was widely considered a transitional figure.[178]

In Gorbachev's talks with Krenz, there is a slight hint to the former's preferences. The Soviet party leader regretted that Honecker had "blindly supported Comrade

---

173 Transcript, p. 29.

174 Transcript, p. 34.

175 Interviews with Shakhnazarov and Grigoriev.

176 Rice interview with Chernyaev, Moscow, June 1994, as quoted by Zelikow and Rice, *Germany Unified*, p. 91.

177 Ferdinand Protzman, "From Dresden, Torchbearer for Change," *New York Times*, 11 November 1989.

178 This is, for instance, what Hungarian prime minister Németh told Kohl on 19 November in Bonn; Kohl, *Ich wollte Deutschlands Einheit*, p. 155; Teltschik, *329 Tage*, p. 40.

Mittag" and that he had humiliated and failed to consult with other SED leaders. Gorbachev had been struck "especially negatively" by how Modrow had been dealt with.[179] Furthermore, almost immediately after Krenz had taken office, Ambassador Kvitsinksy confidentially conveyed Moscow's preference for Modrow to a high-ranking official in the West German government.[180] On 21 November, Portugalov mentioned to Teltschik that he doubted whether Krenz would outlast the next SED Party Congress, scheduled to begin on 8 December, and that Modrow would be his successor in the position of party leader.[181] But while it is appropriate to infer from these remarks that the Soviet leadership and the Kremlin's *germanisty* would have preferred Modrow to Krenz as party chief, it would again be wrong to conclude that they conspired in his replacement or, for that matter, that they would have acted differently if Modrow had been elected party chief by the CC in mid-October. As with Honecker, the center dealt with whoever happened to be the chief paladin at the periphery of the crumbling empire.

4. The Collapse of the Berlin Wall

In Moscow, Krenz had defended the wall as historically necessary, as a "border between two social systems, a border between two military blocs ... a kind of protective shield." He had rejected the idea to tear it down, saying: "We should not live in a world of dreams."[182] Little more than a week later, a "minor error" turned the world of dreams into reality.[183] Liberalization of travel and emigration was one of the

179 Transcript, p. 11. Krenz, in response, told Gorbachev that two years earlier Honecker had instructed him to intervene in controversies that had broken out in the Dresden party disctrict and to engineer Modrow's replacement. Honecker's disapproval of Modrow is reflected also in the conclusions of an internal SED Central Committee inquiry. The party leadership of the Dresden region, the concluding report said, had allowed severe deficiencies in industry and construction to develop and showed a lack of offensive orientation "in the struggle against bourgeois and hostile (*feindliche*) views"; *Neues Deutschland*, 23 June 1989.

180 Interviews with Kvitsinsky and Teltschik.

181 Teltschik, *329 Tage*, p. 44.

182 Wire reports from Moscow, 1 November 1989; David Remnick, "Krenz Hints at East German Perestroika," *Washington Post*, 2 November 1989.

183 "Kleiner Irrtum, Große Wirkung" (Small Error, Big Repercussions) is the title of the chapter in Krenz's book that deals with the collapse of the Berlin wall; *Wenn Mauern fallen*, p. 176. Several accounts of the main actors involved in the drama have been published, making it possible to reconstruct with some confidence the circumstances leading to the opening of the wall. The accounts include Krenz, *Wenn Mauern fallen*, pp. 176-82; *id.*, "Anmerkungen zur Öffnung der Mauer," pp. 365-69; Schabowski, *Der Absturz*, pp. 302-11; *id.*, *Das Politbüro*, pp. 134-39; and Kotschemassow, *Meine letzte Mission*, pp. pp. 184-87. The extent to which Soviet leaders and officials were informed about the Law on Travel and how they reacted to the opening of the wall has best been described by Igor Maksimychev, Kochemasov's deputy, who was privy to the exchanges between Moscow, the Soviet embassy in East Berlin, and the East German government. The present account draws extensively on his testimony, notably his article, with Hans-Hermann Hertle, "Die Maueröffnung: Eine russisch-deutsche Trilogie," *Deutschland-*

main points on the agenda of the new regime in East Berlin. The matter had become more urgent, however, as a result of external pressures. On 1 November, as mentioned, the East German government had reopened the borders with Czechoslovakia, and three days later it announced that its citizens would be allowed to leave through Czechoslovakia using only personal identity cards. As in September, thousands of East Germans crowded Czechoslovak roads and the West German embassy compound in Prague. On 7 November, Foreign Minister Fischer summoned Kochemasov and informed him that the Czech leadership had requested to free it from the nuisance of having to deal with the East German refugees *per se* but also to prevent repercussions on the Czechoslovak population. If appropriate measures were not taken, the *Czechoslovak* government would be forced to close the borders with East Germany. Since such a turn of events, Fischer continued, could have unpredictable consequences, the SED Politburo was inclined to make the following decision: to formulate language in the new version of the Law on Travel under preparation to permit East German citizens to exit directly to West Germany. Permissible points of exit would be certain border crossing points in East Germany and in Czechoslovakia. Only GDR citizens who had applied for exit in East Germany would be allowed to leave through Czechoslovakia in transit to West Germany but not if they applied *in* Czechoslovakia. The East German foreign minister wanted the ambassador to establish the reaction of the Soviet leadership concerning the proposed measures.

Kochemasov immediately called Shevardnadze for instructions. The reply he received was that, "If [our] friends consider such a decision to be feasible, there will in all likelihood be no objection." But he would nevertheless tell the MFA bureaucracy to formulate an answer, which would be supplied to the East German leaders no later than 9 November. The Soviet foreign minister also asked the embassy to formulate a position.[184] On 8 November, Kochemasov accordingly called a meeting of the leading embassy staff, including KGB and GRU representatives, in which he outlined the problem. The reaction of the participants in the meeting was unanimous: The GDR is a sovereign country, and the Soviet Union should not

---

Archiv, Vol. 27 (November 1994), pp. 1137-58; his "Possible 'Impossibilities'," *International Affairs* (Moscow), No. 6 (June 1993), pp. 108-17; "Krushenie. Rekviem po GDR," in *id.* and Hans Modrow, *Poslednii god GDR* (Moscow: Mezhdunarodnye otnosheniia, 1993), pp. 9-156; and his two-part series, "Berlinskaia stena. Ee padenie glazami ochevidtsa," *Nezavisimaia gazeta*, 10 and 12 November 1993. Maksimychev clarified some ambiguities in an interview with me on 2 June 1993 in Moscow.

184 Kotschemassow, *Meine letzte Mission*, pp. 185-86. According to Falin, another telephone call was made by Shevardnadze's first deputy, Anatoli Kovalev. He had called Kochemasov and, like his superior, told him that the Law on Travel should be treated as an East German decision. The Soviet ambassador had not considered the oral instructions to be sufficient and asked for written confirmation; Falin, *Erinnerungen*, pp. 488-89.

instruct it how to act. The East German leaders possessed the most accurate information on the internal political situation. *They* should know how to find a way out of the crisis. But they also should bear responsibility for the measures they adopted, not, as previously, the Soviet Union. As one of the embassy counselors pointed out, since the planned step *de facto* meant the opening of the borders, an obviously risky step, East Berlin evidently wanted to share responsibility with Moscow for the possible consequences. The Soviet foreign ministry was informed of the embassy's views.[185]

Simultaneously with Fischer's request to the Soviet ambassador, Krenz had instructed Stoph to work on an executive decree as the basis for a law on travel and emigration to be adopted later. (On 7 November, the government had resigned because parliament had rejected a rather restrictive cabinet draft law on exit, but it continued to handle affairs until the formation of a new government.) Stoph transmitted these instructions to Mielke. In the morning of 9 November, two colonels of his ministry for state security, together with two interior ministry department heads, began drafting a text in accordance with the new instructions. The limited character of the instructions was, in the Soviet embassy's view, confirmed by the fact that the working group did not include representatives of the East German foreign ministry's department on West Berlin, which, because of its special significance, had at some point come under direct control of the head of party and state.

However, either for the reason that the drafting committee did not understand the instructions or because it deliberately chose to ignore them, the draft prepared by the four officials was strikingly different from what Fischer apparently had intended. The draft referred to all types of travel, including short-term visits, and to all of East Germany's borders, including the borders with West Berlin. Although it is more than doubtful that the drafting committee did not know the quadripartite status of Berlin and the duty of East Germany to consult the Soviet embassy on all questions affecting this status, it seems that their members failed to direct the attention of their superiors to the latitude they had allowed themselves.

Starting on the morning of 9 November, the phone connecting the Soviet embassy directly with the East German government hardly ceased ringing. East German foreign ministry officials requested information about Moscow's response. But Kochemasov could not reach anyone in the Soviet capital to give an authoritative answer. Finally, Ivan Aboimov, deputy foreign minister and head of the MFA's department for European socialist countries – at his own risk – instructed the ambassador to tell Krenz that Moscow had no objections. Any other response was

---

185 This account draws in particular on Maksimychev, "Berlinskaia stena" and "Krushenie"; see above, n. 183.

hardly possible. But both Kochemasov and Aboimov naturally assumed that the East German authorities would act in accordance with the intentions conveyed by Fischer.

In the meantime, a political storm had broken loose in the GDR. A three-day plenary meeting of the SED Central Committee had begun on 8 November with the resignation of the full Politburo (practically unchanged since Honecker had been forced to step down) and continued in an atmosphere of popular distrust in the party and the new leadership. On the following day, shortly prior to the resumption of the CC plenum at 3:30 p.m., outgoing Prime Minister Stoph handed the draft of the new Law on Travel to Krenz. Since the latter realized that the law was of crucial importance for the future of the country and should not be a matter determined only by the Politburo and the government, he decided to deviate from the agenda and familiarize the 213 members of the Central Committee with the text of the draft.[186] The draft decree provided that, "effective immediately," the following new "temporary regulations" would apply to travel and permanent exit abroad. (1) There would no longer by any requirement to present supporting documents (e.g., government orders for business trips, private invitations, or proof of family connections); (2) no more reliability checks would be performed by the regional offices of the Volkspolizei; (3) the offices issuing the visas had to provide the travel documents without delay (*unverzüglich*); and (4) any exit point between East and West Germany, and East and West Berlin could be chosen. The new regulations, according to the draft, would terminate the previous practice of GDR embassies to issue the appropriate travel documents for permanent exit through other countries to East German citizens possessing an identity card. In the discussion at the Central Committee plenum, it was pointed out that the "temporary" validity of the draft would lead to a flood of travel and exit applications, and that it would be better to delete this provision. A corresponding proposal was adopted and the draft approved without any further changes by the Central Committee.[187]

Schabowski, the SED secretary for Berlin, had not been present at the discussion of the draft decree. Shortly before 6 p.m. he returned to the CC meeting, was given a copy of the draft and told by Krenz to announce the new regulations at the 7 p.m.

---

186 Interview with Krenz. For the text of the draft as presented to the Central Committee, see Krenz, *Wenn Mauern fallen*, pp. 180-81.

187 There is some controversy here about the extent to which the draft was discussed. Krenz conveys the notion that there was ample discussion; Krenz, *Wenn Mauern fallen*, p. 181. Schabowski, based on what CC members told him, thinks that Krenz refrained from pointing out the enormity and the likely consequences of the changes that were envisaged and that he may have done so deliberately in order not to provoke unwelcome questions or criticism by what was still a conservative body; Schabowski, *Der Absturz*, p. 306. Maksimychev goes even further (too far, in this writer's view), asserting that the draft was presented "during a break" in the CC proceedings; that it was hardly discussed because "everyone was busy doing other things"; and that, consequently, the decision which put an end to the Berlin wall "was taken hastily and as a result of several misunderstandings"; Maksimychev in *Nezavisimaia gazeta*, 10 November 1993.

press conference. He was conscious of the fact that the draft had been approved by party bodies, the Politburo and the Central Committee, but not by the government, the Council of Ministers, and that his primary task was to explain the proceedings of the CC plenary meeting. It was only at the end of the press conference that a question was put to him concerning travel and permanent exit. Schabowski explained the new provisions as best as he could, wondering, when he came to the part of the text that dealt with the applicability of the decree to the borders in Berlin, whether all of this had been coordinated with the Soviet authorities. However, despite the fact that he was explaining only *draft* provisions, and that cabinet approval was only pending, he announced the regulations as being "effective immediately."

The combined effect of the announcement that the GDR authorities had been instructed to issue travel and permanent exit visas without delay and without the usual prerequisites, that the regulations also applied to the borders in Berlin and that the provisions were effective immediately, propelled thousands of Berliners into action. They wanted to verify for themselves whether all of this could be true. Confused security guards at the checkpoints, as a consequence, were faced with growing crowds of people. Overwhelmed, the local commanders decided on their own simply to open the borders. At 11 p.m. a bewildered minister of the interior ratified the *fait accompli* and confirmed the commanders' desperate decisions with an official order.[188]

To return to the Soviet dimension, embassy officials in East Berlin were unpleasantly surprised by the statements which Schabowski had made at the press conference, above all by the fact that the checkpoints in West Berlin had been included as possible exit points.[189] They could not imagine that this could have occurred without Gorbachev's specific approval and assumed that Krenz had contacted the Kremlin directly without their knowledge. But doubts as to whether such approval had, in fact, been given arose early in the morning, on 10 November, before the official beginning of the working day at the embassy. The embassy received a call from the MFA's European socialist countries' department: "What is happening at the wall? The world's telegraph agencies have gone crazy." After having

---

188 An excellent description of the events, based on extensive interviews, can be found in Pond, *Beyond the Wall*, pp. 1-6. Krenz has pointed out that in the evening hours of 9 November, the question was whether to open the borders or use military force. There was no time left for Soviet-East German coordination and to decide which border crossings were to be opened, and when. Action had to be taken swiftly and responsibly in order to avoid bloodshed and civil war. "I was aware of the fact that Allied interests were touched. It was also clear to me that our unilateral action in the GDR annulled the 1961 joint resolution of the member states of the Warsaw treaty on the joint securing of borders. But in the evening of 9 November, I saw no other possibility"; Krenz, "Anmerkungen zur Öffnung der Mauer," p. 369.

189 The account on Soviet reactions to the opening of the Berlin wall is based on Maksimychev, "Krushenie," pp. 56-59, and "Berlinskaia stena," for the most part *verbatim*.

been provided with an explanation of the events, the department followed up with a second question: "Was all this discussed with us?" Erroneously, the Fourth Department thought that it would be easier to get an answer to this question in East Berlin rather than in Moscow. Nevertheless, it persisted in its attempts at clarification and a few minutes later the ambassador received a request to demand explanations from Fischer, whom he immediately called. The East German foreign minister, referring to apparently more pressing business (the continuation of the SED plenary meeting) only remarked: "What's the point of talking about it now?" Unable to receive a satisfactory reply from Fischer, the embassy called the head of the West Berlin department at the East German foreign ministry, Walter Müller, who provided the following explanation:

> We ask you to understand that the decision taken last night on exit without visas to West Berlin and West Germany was a forced one. Any hesitation would have had very dangerous consequences. There was no time for consultation. Today, we will directly inform Gorbachev about everything. Starting from 8:00 this morning, the regular border crossing regime will be reestablished [sic!]. The GDR government requests the embassy to influence the occupation authorities of the three Western powers in West Berlin with the purpose of maintaining public order at the wall on the West Berlin side.[190]

Kochemasov also talked to Shevardnadze, who approved the position of the embassy and said that, according to his information, "there appear to be movements of the [Soviet] military [in East Germany]. It is necessary to make sure that there is full compliance with Moscow's instructions as to "No action!" The ambassador at once contacted the chief commander of the Soviet armed forces in East Germany and told him not to move and to avoid contact with the German population. This occurred despite the fact that neither the embassy nor the secret services, then or later, had any information about any action supposedly intended by the Soviet forces. Shevardnadze's concerns were apparently more of a precautionary character. As Müller's communication to the Soviet embassy implied, East German foreign ministry officials – and perhaps others in the party and security services – thought that "order" would somehow be reestablished at the crossing points. If so, these ideas turned out to be erroneous. East German officials also requested that the Soviet embassy address the Western powers with regard to preventing attempts by West Berliners to besiege and cross the wall without any authorization, also to no avail.[191]

Krenz has asserted that he had informed Gorbachev about the GDR government's plans for the liberalization of travel; that there had been consultation and coordination on the issue; and that the Soviet leadership, therefore, "could not have

190 Maksimychev, "Berlinskaia stena."

191 Ibid. On the controversy about Soviet military intervention in the fall of 1989, see above, pp. 358-64.

been surprised by the opening of the border."[192] He also thought that Moscow was divided on the question as to how to react to the opening of the wall and infers this from two telephone conversations with the Soviet ambassador. The first telephone call came shortly after 9.00 a.m. on 10 November.

Kochemasov: Comrade Krenz, Moscow is concerned about the situation at the Berlin wall as it has developed last night.

Krenz: That surprises me. In principle, we only moved up by a couple of hours what was scheduled for today anyway. Our foreign minister had coordinated [in advance] the travel decrees with the Soviet side.

Kochemasov: Yes, but this is only partly true. It only applied to the opening of border crossings to the FRG. The opening of the border in Berlin affects the interests of the allies.

Krenz: That was not my understanding of the matter. But this is now merely a theoretical question. Life gave a different answer last night. The opening of the border could only have been stopped by military means. That would have caused a terrible bloodbath.

Kochemasov, according to Krenz, briefly remained silent and then remarked: "You are right. I see it the same way." Krenz later said that he was "angry about the content of the phone call. I asked myself who was playing with marked cards here. On the very 9 November, it had been explained to me that the draft decrees on travel had been coordinated with the Soviet side."[193]

Shortly before 10.00 a.m., Kochemasov called a second time. This time, he conveyed a personal message from Gorbachev.

Kochemasov: Comrade Krenz, on behalf of Mikhail Gorbachev and on behalf of the Soviet leadership I congratulate you and all [our] German friends on your courageous step of opening the Berlin wall.

Krenz: I sincerely thank you and ask you to thank Mikhail Sergeevich for this solidarity. Convey to him that we are very happy that our views coincide.[194]

German Unification on the National Agenda

The process of German unification began in earnest after the collapse of the wall, and it began immediately and spontaneously in Berlin. As a sign of the accelerating dynamics, without consultation of the sector commandants in Berlin and the inter-allied *Kommendatura*, the mayors of East and West Berlin met and began discussing

192 Krenz, "Anmerkungen zur Öffnung der Mauer," p. 368.

193 Quoted by Krenz according to his personal notes of the telephone conversation with Kochemasov on 10 November 1989; Krenz, "Anmerkungen zur Öffnung der Mauer," pp. 368-369.

194 Ibid.

the practical consequences of a now, in essence, undivided city. Students from East Berlin and East Germany began enrolling in classes at universities in West Berlin; the prestigious West Berlin *Tagesspiegel* newspaper more than doubled circulation in response to a dramatic increase in demand from East Germany and East Berlin; Lufthansa and Interflug began making arrangements for new routes; the Volkswagen company, without waiting for new laws on joint ventures, prepared to build a new car with the makers of the East German Trabant; the West German political parties began looking for counterparts in the East to build up party organizations; and the harbingers of monetary integration appeared in the form of the West German Deutschmark becoming the *de facto* tender among people in East Berlin.

For the East German regime, the collapse of the wall opened a vicious circle. Contrary to expectations, the new regulations on travel and emigration failed to stem the westward exodus of East Germans. Since May, when Budapest had begun dismantling the Iron Curtain, about 60,000 East Germans had left through Hungary. From 3 to 9 November, about 65,000 had emigrated through Czechoslovakia. Before 9 November, a total of 220,000 East Germans had registered in West Germany and West Berlin. After 9 November, in less than two weeks, the number of East Germans registering to remain in West Berlin was 12,500 and, in West Germany, 42,200 people.[195] As in 1953 and 1961, the majority of the emigrants were young and enterprising members of society, and as in the two previous years of crisis, the downward spiral of the East German economy was thereby accelerated. This, in turn, persuaded even more East Germans to seek a better future in West Germany. It also changed the mood and political direction at the mass demonstrations in East Germany. On 20 November, at the demonstrations in Leipzig, Dresden, Chemnitz, and other East German cities, the defiant slogan of "*Wir sind das Volk*" (We are the people) was being replaced by "*Wir sind ein Volk*" (We are one people, or one nation).[196]

The fact that Kohl had abandoned the strictures of German Ostpolitik had become obvious even before the opening of the wall. In the traditional state of the nation address, on 8 November, he said: "We have less reason than ever to be resigned to the long-term division of Germany into two states." Without, at this stage, explicitly outlining how the division could be overcome, enough was said for anyone to know the general direction: through systemic change in East Germany. This was indicated by his calls for an East-West German dialogue "with all political forces in the GDR" and his promise of a "completely new dimension of our economic assistance" if the new regime in East Berlin embarked not merely on "cosmetic corrections" but

195 *New York Times*, 25 November 1989.

196 Pond, *Beyond the Wall*, p. 135. The change in mood was duly noted by Teltschik, *329 Tage*, p. 42.

instituted "fundamental reforms" (*grundlegende Reformen*). "The SED," he said, "must give up its power monopoly, allow independent parties and assure binding free elections."[197] To the chagrin and then the fury of both East German and Soviet communist party leaders, the demands were repeated by Kohl in the Bundestag on 16 November and became more insistent as the SED regime became more shaky and vulnerable.[198] On 17 November, Prime Minister Modrow countered the German chancellor's demands by the announcing a program of internal reforms and outlining a concept on the national question. He rejected as "unrealistic, as well as dangerous, speculation about reunification" and proposed instead wide-ranging cooperation between the two German states governed by a series of bilateral treaties – a *Vertragsgemeinschaft*, or treaty community.[199]

Kohl and his advisers considered it important to prevent Modrow's idea from gaining international acceptance. Furthermore, they thought that the time was ripe to present *their* ideas about the path to German unification more clearly and comprehensively than before. Parliamentary elections were scheduled for the following year; taking the initiative now on a vital national issue could serve to differentiate the CDU from both the opposition Social Democrats and the junior partner in the ruling coalition, the Liberals.[200] It was primarily the last purpose that accounted for the fact that the initiative was being prepared in secrecy. This, in turn, had the effect of not only excluding Genscher (FDP) and the foreign ministry from the drafting process but also of surprising West Germany's Western partners and the Kremlin when the initiative was launched by the chancellor on 28 November in a speech to the Bundestag.[201] Since his program for the achievement of German unification (Ten Point Plan) was to lead to a major crisis of confidence in Soviet-

---

197 Text in *Stenographische Berichte des Deutschen Bundestages*, 8 November 1989, pp. 13010-18. For the origin of Kohl's demand for fundamental political change in the GDR, see Pond, *Beyond the Wall*, p. 131.

198 "Erklärung der Bundesregierung zur Lage in der DDR," Vol. 7 (Bonn: Bundesverlag, 1990), pp. 412-21.

199 Text in *Neues Deutschland*, 18 November 1989.

200 The first and second of the three purposes have been described by Kohl, *Ich wollte Deutschlands Einheit*, p. 159 and Teltschik, *329 Tage*, pp. 46-53. The third purpose was only hinted at by Teltschik, who has reported opinions expressed in the CDU presidium to the effect that one had to watch out that the SPD would "not steal this subject" (German unification) from the CDU; ibid., p. 53.

201 As a tribute to the special role of and strong support extended by the United States on the unification issue, an exception of sorts was made. Bush was informed by Kohl in general terms on 17 November that an initiative would be forthcoming. The American president was also to receive the text of Kohl's speech together with an explanation of the West German position and interests to be considered in preparation for the Malta summit; Kohl, *Ich wollte Deutschlands Einheit*, pp. 158 and 167-68. But this was only on 28 November, as the Ten Point plan was announced to the Bundestag.

West German relations and prompt Gorbachev savagely to attack Genscher when he visited Moscow, it is appropriate briefly to summarize it.[202]

Point 1. Practical measures should be adopted to deal immediately with some of the issues that had arisen from the opening of the wall. These included the proposal to East Berlin to share the burden for financing the flood of East German visitors to West Berlin and West Germany.

Point 2. There should be a significant expansion of cooperation between the two German states on economic, technological, environmental, and cultural matters; emphasis was put on the improvement of telecommunications and railway connections between the two parts of Germany.

Point 3. West German economic assistance to East Germany would be significantly expanded *if* the new regime would commit itself "irrevocably" to a "fundamental change of the political and economic system." Specifically, the GDR had to change its constitution, admit multiple parties, introduce free elections, and abandon central planning. Such demands were described as not being preconditions (*Vorbedingungen*) but objectively necessary so that economic aid could produce the desired effects.

Point 4 explicitly endorses Modrow's concept of a *Vertragsgemeinschaft*. This is understood by Kohl as the establishment of a close net of contractual relations through inter-governmental cooperation, including the forging of common institutions across all dimensions of policy. The "treaty community," however, is not considered to be a goal in itself but a transitory form of intra-German relations.

Point 5 introduces the next stage. It provides – after free elections in East Germany – for the creation of "confederative structures" between the two German states with the ultimate goal of the creation of a federation.

Points 6-9 deal with the international conditions necessary for the process of German unification to succeed. These include placing the process into the context of European integration; the opening of the European Community to the countries of Central and Eastern Europe; the broadening of cooperation within the CSCE, with the possible creation of new institutions for East-West economic cooperation; and further progress in conventional and nuclear arms control.

Point 10 merely restates the goal of the government as being reunification, that is, the reestablishment of German unity at the state level.

The Ten Points contained little that had not been stated in Kohl's previous two speeches to the Bundestag on 8 and 16 November. Their novelty, as well as their impact lay in the fact that they were presented as a *plan* for the achievement of German unity in several stages of development. Kohl had refrained from indicating a

202 Text in *Stenographische Berichte des Deutschen Bundestages,* 28 November 1989, pp. 13508-14.

time frame, saying in his introduction to the program that "The road to German unification, we all know that, cannot be planned at the drawing board or with a calendar in hand."[203] (Privately, he thought that German unity might be achieved within five to ten years.)[204] But the failure to consult or inform domestic and international partners conveyed the notion that West Germany was now determined to speed up the process towards reunification. It reinforced the concern abroad that a unified Germany would be prone to act unilaterally; that it would be the dominant country in Europe; and that it would return to Great Power policies. The German problem, therefore, yet again became the central issue on the international agenda.

5. German Unification on the International Agenda

The prospect of German reunification had been a topic of international discussion in the fall of 1989. But the opening of the Berlin wall advanced the discussion of reunification from a mere theoretical possibility to the single most important topic on the agenda of international politics. This was evident in the preparations for and discussions at the summit conference of the European Community leaders in Paris on 18 November; the Soviet-American summit in Malta on 2-3 December; the summit meetings of the two military alliances, of NATO in Brussels and of the Warsaw Pact in Moscow, both on 4 December; the meeting between Gorbachev and Mitterrand in Kiev on 6 December; and the summit conference of the EC's European Council in Strasbourg on 8 December. The most important features of these meetings and of the private exchanges between its major participants were the reservations and hesitations by Prime Minister Thatcher and President Mitterrand on the one hand, and the determined drive towards the achievement of German unity by both Chancellor Kohl and President Bush on the other.

As for the Soviet Union, Gorbachev and his supporters have argued that – in the period from the opening of the wall on 9-10 November until the end of January 1990 – their primary concern was not the prevention of unification but the management of a process that could have gotten out of control and led to unpredictable consequences. Support for this argument could be found in the fact that Gorbachev refrained from adopting the kind of forceful measures at the military level but also at the political and diplomatic level that would have been necessary in order to arrest the inexorable movement towards German unity. The means to do so were still available to him in the form of the presence of substantial Soviet military forces in East Germany. But the Gorbachevian interpreation is credible only up to a point.

203 In German, "*ist nicht vom grünen Tisch oder mit einem Terminkalender in der Hand zu planen.*"

204 Teltschik, *329 Tage*, p. 52.

After all, his preferences were clear: East Germany's transformation from a moribund, orthodox system to a viable, reform socialist country. To that extent he was *against* unification. It is, therefore, not convincing to argue that his negative attitude towards German unification was essentially tactical and temporary, embarked upon under the assumption that the GDR and with it the Soviet empire in Eastern Europe were irretrievably lost. Until the end of 1989 it was still unclear, certainly to Gorbachev, whether the reform experiment in the GDR would fail. If it had succeeded, the purportedly provisional support for a reformist GDR could have lasted a long time. It could have turned the wide-spread idea in both Eastern and Western Europe of the 1970s and 1980s that the division of Germany was here to stay from a possibility into reality.

In detail, as for the Soviet leadership's reactions to the opening of the wall, it was (predictably) Yakovlev who adopted the most advanced position. On 15 November, he called the accelerating democratization movement in Eastern Europe, including the dismantling of the Berlin wall, moves in the right direction. The Soviet Union, he told the Japanese prime minister, would not interfere in the processes of change. In conversation with Japanese Socialist Party (JSP) Chairwoman Takako Doi, he went even further and said that the Soviet Union would not interfere with moves by East and West Germany to reunite. "*The decision is for the Germans themselves to make.*" He also indicated that Britain, France, and the United States were wary of reunification and were trying to persuade the Soviet Union to slow down the process, thereby *de facto* cautioning his colleagues in Moscow not to lend a helping hand to such Western efforts.[205]

Shevardnadze and the foreign ministry, in contrast, *were* attempting to slow down the momentum towards German unification. In talks with Roland Dumas, the French foreign minister, on 14 November in Moscow, he said:

> Great anxiety is caused by attempts being undertaken by certain circles in West Germany to place the issue of reunification of Germany on today's political agenda. What we have here is a matter that affects the vital interests of many European countries. We are seeing a desire to question the existence of a sovereign state, the German Democratic Republic, and also the territorial and political structure of the continent as a whole.[206]

The principal means to assure stability on the continent, in his view, was "the gradual rapprochement of the eastern and western parts of Europe."[207] Soviet foreign ministry spokesman Gerasimov also propagated this line. Furthermore, he provided one of the first negative, perhaps anticipatory or preemptive reactions to possible

205 "Soviets Won't Oppose German Reunification," Jiji Press Ltd., Tokyo, 15 November 1989 (italics mine).

206 Bill Keller, "Gorbachev Urges West to Show Restraint on Turmoil in Eastern Europe," *New York Times*, 15 November 1989.

207 Ibid.

changes in the alliance systems and the balance of power in Europe. "Politically," he warned, "now is not the time to talk about reunification. The two Germanys belong to two different military blocs." It was impossible to talk realistically about reunification as long as there were "American, British, French, even Canadian troops in West Germany." Conversely, Gerasimov continued, the GDR is a "strategic ally" of the Soviet Union and certainly "more important geographically than Hungary." To convert the GDR into a neutral Austria was just hypothetical. "Why should East Germany be considered an Austria when this is our firm ally? The NATO forces are dangerous and to compensate we should count on the Warsaw Pact."[208]

Gorbachev shared these viewpoints. This is reflected in a plethora of public and private statements. These included letters sent to Bush, Thatcher, and Mitterrand on 10 November. In the letter to the American president, he expressed the fear that "a chaotic situation may emerge with unforeseeable consequences" and warned against the danger of "political extremism" in West Germany. In particular, he thought that

> when statements are made in the FRG designed to stir up emotions, in the spirit of implacable rejection of the postwar realities, that is, the existence of two German states, then such manifestations of political extremism can only be seen as aimed at undermining the current dynamic processes of democratization and renewal of all aspects of the society's life. And, looking ahead, this can bring about a destabilization of the situation not only in Central Europe, but on a larger scale.[209]

The practical political consequence he derived from such dangers was to call for the immediate convocation of a Four Power meeting.

The appeal to Four Power action and his concerns about political extremism in West Germany, however, were lacking in a telephone conversation with Chancellor Kohl, on 11 November. The German chancellor, in his rendering of its content, assured Gorbachev that the government had no interest in chaos in the GDR; that it did not want to deplete the GDR of its population because this would lead to severe economic problems; the people should stay in their homeland and this they would do if conditions in the GDR were to change fundamentally.[210] Gorbachev acknowledged that the changes that had occurred in Eastern Europe since they had last met (in June 1989) had been much more rapid than expected. Differences were evolving in the speed, depth, and form of the changes. As for the GDR, it needed more time for its

---

208 At a press briefing in Moscow after the GDR's lifting of travel and emigration restrictions, as quoted by Esther B. Fein, "The Kremlin Reacts Calmly, But Says Border Must Stay," *New York Times*, 11 November 1989, and David Remnick, "Soviets Warn Against Reunification," *Washington Post*, 11 November 1989.

209 State Department document 363047, 11 November 1989, cited by Zelikow and Rice, *Germany Unified*, p. 107.

210 Kohl, *Ich wollte Deutschlands Einheit*, p. 141. Later in the conversation, Kohl also expressed understanding for the difficulties of the new leadership in East Berlin and acknowledged that reforms could not be achieved overnight.

transformation in the direction of freedom, democracy, and economic viability. He then continued:

> Instability is inherent in any change. This is why, when I talk about maintaining stability, I mean that in every respect we should take well-thought out steps in relation to each other. Today, an historical turn is taking place towards new relations and towards a different world. We should take care not to put this turn at risk by awkward (*neukliuzhimie*) actions. I hope, Helmut, that you will use your authority and your political weight and influence, that other political leaders will remain within the framework appropriate for the present time and its demands.[211]

Kohl, in Gorbachev's version of the conversation, had replied that a cabinet meeting had just been concluded in Bonn and that if he (Gorbachev) had been present, he would have realized that he would "probably have been surprised by how much our assessments coincide."[212] The congruence of views, however, is not confirmed by Kohl and Teltschik. *They* report the chancellor as having told Gorbachev that if he had been present at the meeting, "you could have convinced yourself that policy on Germany in the Federal Republic is being conducted with a sense of measure."[213]

Gorbachev, indeed, would most likely *not* have found a congruence of views. Differences of perception and policy, as it turned out, remained hidden – despite or perhaps because of the cordiality of the conversation. First, whereas Gorbachev's main concerns were stability, socialism, and change in the GDR, Kohl's parameters of change were broader and transcended the division of Germany. Second, whereas Gorbachev may have thought that he had received commitments by the German chancellor to the effect that he would cooperate in slowing down the momentum of change, Kohl apparently concluded from the conversation that Gorbachev had agreed to let the people of the GDR decide their own fate, no matter what the speed of change. Third, whereas the two leaders had indeed agreed to consult each other if required by the circumstances, it was unclear what such circumstances might be.

Gorbachev's reactions, furthermore, were shaped by wishful thinking and an astounding misreading of developments. This became apparent in a meeting on 16 November with the parliamentary leaders of West Germany and France that lasted several hours and dealt almost exclusively with events in Germany. There was no

---

211 Gorbachev, *Zhizn'*, Vol. 2, p. 164. This part of the conversation was recorded essentially identically by Kohl, *Ich wollte Deutschlands Einheit*, pp. 141-43; Teltschik, *329 Tage*, p. 28, and Chernyaev, *Shest' let s Gorbachevym*, p. 305.

212 Gorbachev, *Zhizn'*, Vol. 2, p. 164.

213 Kohl, *Ich wollte Deutschlands Einheit*, pp. 141-43; Teltschik, *329 Tage*, p. 28. The term used is *Augenmaß*. Similarly, the record of the conversation transmitted to East Berlin stated only that "Kohl agreed with Gorbachev's point of view [literally: Ausführungen]. According to him [Kohl] this problem was discussed along these lines at the cabinet meeting"; Information über den Inhalt des Telephongesprächs zwischen Michail Gorbatschow und Helmut Kohl, 13 November 1989, SED Politburo, *Arbeitsprotokolle*, Central Party Archives, J IV 2/2A/3258.

reason to dramatize things, Gorbachev mused. He was, of course, aware of the never-ending procession of cars (the East German Trabants or Trabbies) streaming across the various border checkpoints in Berlin. But this was only natural given the fact that travel and emigration had been denied to the East Germans for such a long time and that the decision by the new leadership in East Berlin to open the borders had been long overdue. No state should deny rights of free movement to its citizens. However, he continued, the East Germans simply wanted to get an impression of what things were like in the West. They were *not* going to turn their backs on the GDR. The novelty of their being able to exercise new rights and the attractions of the West would wear off.[214]

The next opportunity for Gorbachev to shape the debate and decisions on the German problem presented itself in Italy, at the end of November, en route to the Malta summit. Soviet-American relations would obviously be the central focus of the discussions. But Gorbachev and his entourage, both prior to and during the summit, were very much under the impression of the rapidly unfolding "velvet revolution" in Czechoslovakia. In mid-November, demonstrators in Prague had brutally been beaten. Undeterred, the anti-communist opposition had formed the Civic Forum and over the next two weeks had organized a series of mass demonstrations and strikes that quickly swept away the orthodox communist party leadership under Miloš Jakeš in both Eastern and Western Europe and forced the government to agree to round-table discussions with the Civic Forum, to expunge the communist party's monopoly from the constitution, and to embark on comprehensive political and economic reform.

To put the events in context, Poland and Hungary were well on the road to rejecting rather than reforming socialism. The mood in East Germany, as noted, was changing accordingly, with the added complication of the increasing demands for unification. Czechoslovakia was following the very same pattern observable in the neighboring countries, with evolution turning into revolution. It appears, however, that Gorbachev failed to understand the inexorable drift in Eastern Europe towards

---

214 Participants in the meeting included, in addition to Gorbachev, the presidents of the Bundestag, Rita Süssmuth; of the Assemblée Nationale, Laurent Fabius; of the Supreme Soviet, Anatoli Lukyanov; and of the Union Soviet, Yevgeni Primakov. Information on the meeting was provided to this author by Wolfgang Ischinger, present at the meeting in his capacity as German foreign service official responsible for parliamentary liaison. It is possible that Gorbachev developed this unrealistic notion in part as a result of his telephone conversation with Kohl on 11 November. The record of the conversation transmitted to East Berlin stated: "Chancellor [Kohl] admitted that the majority of the GDR citizens, which had crossed the borders to the FRG did not want to stay there permanently [and] avowed that the leadership of the FRG was not striving for that to happen. In his words, a mass resettlement in the FRG would be an absurd development. 'We want the Germans to build their future in their own home.'" Information über den Inhalt des Telephongesprächs zwischen Michail Gorbatschow und Helmut Kohl, 13 November 1989, SED Politburo, *Arbeitsprotokolle*, Central Party Archives, J IV 2/2A/3258.

the collapse of communism. In Czechoslovakia, he thought, the conditions for the successful introduction of reform socialism were promising since that country was not encumbered by external debts and, in contrast to the Soviet Union, did not suffer from food supply problems.[215] Hence, it was not only for tactical political reasons but also because of genuine conviction that, on 30 November in Rome, he publicly dismissed the Western raptures about the alleged victory of capitalism in the cold war as mere anti-communist propaganda and rudiments of old thinking. Socialism was not coming to an end but taking various forms in its further evolution. The dramatic processes of change were only now "unleashing the tremendous human and democratic potential inherent in that system." It was fitting to remember, he said, that the history of capitalism had encompassed many centuries and had known bloody revolutions, terrible wars, sharp political crises and economic depressions, even fascism. Socialism, contrary to that, had existed only for a few decades.[216] The implication of this defiant reaction to Western glee was obviously that socialism had several more centuries ahead of it.

Gorbachev also outlined how the processes of change should be managed. He restated his vision of the Common European Home and, in order to strengthen pan-European cooperation, proposed to convene a summit meeting of the leaders of the thirty-five CSCE member states (a "Helsinki 2"), to be held in 1990. Should the CSCE, then, be empowered to deal also with the vexing German problem? Perhaps this was the implication of the proposal. But Gorbachev refrained from establishing such a link.[217] In his prepared speeches – in Rome and, on the following day, in Milan – he studiously avoided mentioning Germany. It was only at the press conference in Milan, and only in response to a question by an Italian journalist about German reunification, that he repeated the familiar contradictory refrain: history had already decided but history might decide otherwise. Political leaders, however, should not touch the issue: "*Today, to put the problem of reunification on the agenda of international politics would be inappropriate. Moreover, it would complicate the situation.*"[218]

Prior to the Malta summit, then, Gorbachev had conveyed three different notions about how he might perhaps deal with the German problem: (1) manage the process in a Four Power framework; (2) discuss the problem at a CSCE summit conference;

---

215 Interview with Shakhnazarov; see also *id.*, *Tsena svobody*, p. 109.

216 Speech in Rome on 30 November, "Za meniaiushchiisia is stabil'nyi mir. Rech' M.S. Gorbacheva," *Pravda*, 1 December 1989.

217 Zelikow and Rice speak of a "major proposal," and they convey the notion that Gorbachev directly linked the CSCE and the German problem; Zelikow and Rice, *Germany Unified*, pp. 126-27. The former opinion is debatable but the latter is erroneous.

218 "Press konferentsiia v Milane," *Pravda*, 3 December 1989 (italics mine). He also said: "One should not push and force processes that have not ripened."

and (3) not do anything at all. At the summit, to the extent that there was clarification, it was that there was no Soviet concept on how to manage the German problem and that the third course of action, that of *inaction*, was the option preferred by Gorbachev. This impression, formed by both Soviet and American participants at the summit, was reinforced by the fact that the German topic, its central objective importance notwithstanding, was only one of many others discussed. These included the issue of Western versus all-human, democratic values; political developments in the Soviet Union; the situation in the Baltic states; East-West economic relations; conventional and strategic arms control; chemical weapons; the US "open skies" proposal; and regional conflicts (Afghanistan, Central America, and the Middle East).[219] In fact, Gorbachev made a deliberate attempt to *downplay* the German issue. This is also evident in his memoirs. He writes that he had told Bush that there was too much haste in connection with the events in Germany. Reunification was a very serious matter and hence it was necessary to act with care. The process could perhaps not be stopped. But it should also not be artificially accelerated.[220] Bush had replied that even the most conservative Western political leaders agreed with such an approach and that he would "not jump on the wall because too much is at stake in the situation." He (Gorbachev) had reiterated his "Helsinki 2" proposal in order to deal with a new phase in East-West relations and to turn NATO and the Warsaw Pact into political rather than military organizations.[221] His account, as well as that of other participants in the conference, shows that he refrained again from establishing a direct link between this proposal and the German issue. To that extent, it is fair to conclude that the most important feature of the Malta summit lay in the *absence* of any decision on the German or any other major international problem and in the congenial atmosphere of the discussions – in mutual assurances to exercise restraint and, as Baker summarized, in enabling Bush and Gorbachev "to establish a personal bond," which became critical as "through the spring of 1990 we worked to bring a unified Germany into NATO."[222]

Two members of the Soviet delegation would severely criticize Gorbachev for this off-hand and hands-off attitude: ambassador Dobrynin and Marshal Akhromeev. According to the former Soviet ambassador's observations, President Bush had "cautiously sounded out Gorbachev on reunification in casual conversation," and the

---

219 According to the extensive account of the Malta summit in Gorbachev, *Zhizn'*, Vol. 2, pp. 142-49, and *id.*, *Gody trudnykh reshenii*, pp. 173-76. Other primary sources used for this part are the accounts by Chernyaev, *Shest let s Gorbachevym*, pp. 301-10; Akhromeev and Kornienko, *Glazami marshala i diplomata*, pp. 253-54, 259; and Dobrynin, *In Confidence*, p. 630. The best secondary source is Zelikow and Rice, *Germany Unified*, pp. 127-31.

220 Gorbachev, *Zhizn'*, Vol. 2, p. 146.

221 Ibid.; similarly, Chernyaev, *Shest' let s Gorbachevym*, p. 310.

222 Baker, *The Politics of Diplomacy*, pp. 169-70.

latter had "responded in a general way" that Soviet policy was founded on adherence to an all-European process and the construction of a Common European Home, in which the security interests of all countries should be respected. But he had not specified how this could or should be done, although he had with him a confidential MFA memorandum outlining a concrete policy: German reunification should be the final product of a gradual transformation of the political climate in Europe, in the course of which both NATO and the Warsaw Pact would shift their orientation from military to political purposes and be dissolved by mutual agreement.[223]

Akhromeev was even more critical.[224] He noted that the "discussion of what may very well have been the most important question at that time, the situation in Europe and Germany, was scheduled for the final stage of the negotiations." He also reflected on the reason why this may have been the case: "On our part, I think, this was *due to the fact that our position on the question of German unification had not yet been formulated*."[225] Little more than a month had passed since the departure of Honecker and his closest advisors from the leadership of the GDR, he continued. Events in the GDR had developed rapidly, and no less rapidly was the Soviet Union losing its influence in that country. Despite that, "Mikhail Gorbachev arrived at the Malta meeting *without a defined long-term plan for dealing with the German problem*."[226]

He thought that the absence of a Soviet position and a long-term plan on the German problem was causing some problems for the United States because

> understanding the posture of the Soviet Union towards the emerging idea of union between East and West Germany was one of the foremost [American] goals of the Malta summit. Because of this, George Bush, while expressing satisfaction as well as awe at the rapid changes taking place in the countries of Central Europe, and in East Germany in particular, spoke of the United States' satisfaction with the moderation of the position of the Soviet Union with regard to these changes. He relentlessly grilled Gorbachev as to which position the Soviet Union would take with regard to the possible unification of Germany. It was clear that the answer to this question would, in large part, determine the future US policy toward the problem of German unification as well as the relations with the Soviet Union in 1990.

Akhromeev concluded by saying that Gorbachev avoided giving a definitive answer to this question and explains why.

---

223 Dobrynin, *In Confidence*, p. 630. The confidential foreign ministry memorandum, to which Dobrynin referred, has not been published. Nevertheless except for the suggestion that German reunification *should* be the end result of the evolution of the CSCE process (it is doubtful that the MFA had, in fact, put it that way), all the other ideas were mentioned by Gorbachev.

224 Akhromeev and Kornienko, *Glazami marshala i diplomata*, p. 253.

225 Ibid. (italics mine). It is unclear what Akhromeev meant by "scheduled." To the extent that Germany was discussed at all, it was also discussed on the first day.

226 Ibid.

> His [Gorbachev's] reasoning stemmed from the belief that it was necessary to resolve European problems as a whole within the framework of the Helsinki accords of 1975, which guaranteed the sanctity of borders in Europe, including the borders between the GDR and the FRG. He proposed, due to the fact that the situation in Europe was unclear, to have Eduard Shevardnadze and James Baker work on the European question more substantively and thus also to tackle the German problem.[227]

The criticism is taken one step further in the joint analysis by Akhromeev and Kornienko. They enumerate various opportunities missed by the foreign ministry and other agencies, and that these included the failure by Gorbachev to discuss the question of Germany with Bush at the Malta summit and shortly thereafter at the meeting with Mitterrand in Kiev. But they consider it even more inexcusable that there was no defined Soviet position on this topic even at the meeting with Chancellor Kohl in Moscow in February 1990.[228]

Gorbachev, Genscher, and Kohl's "Diktat"

It is a matter of political preference whether one should interpret Gorbachev's attitude on the German problem as a laudable policy of non-interference or a deplorable lack of defined position. Whatever the preference, on 5 December the Soviet president abruptly abandoned the philosophical musing on the German issue. This occurred in talks with Genscher in Moscow, described by the German foreign minister as the "most unpleasant meeting" he had ever had with the General Secretary. "Never before or thereafter had I seen Gorbachev so agitated and bitter."[229] Chernyaev has concurred, saying that the meeting "went far beyond the bounds generally accepted in the relations among government leaders of that rank."[230] The bone of contention were Kohl's Ten Points.

The Malta summit had presented Gorbachev with the opportunity to discuss and, if necessary, to criticize Kohl's initiative. Gorbachev had not used that opportunity. This had been the case despite the fact that, as he has written, he had considered the Ten Point plan an inappropriate response to the requirements of the times because the impression was being created that the German chancellor was subordinating interests of historic significance to the exigencies of the upcoming parliamentary elections in West Germany, an impression which Gorbachev regarded as having been confirmed by Kohl's failure to inform not only his European allies but also his own foreign

---

227 Ibid. To comment again on Akhromeev's portrayal, the author accurately speaks of a general belief by Gorbachev to solve European issues in the Helsinki framework but not of a specific corresponding proposal tied to the German problem.

228 Ibid.

229 Genscher, *Erinnerungen*, p. 684.

230 Chernyaev, *Shest' let s Gorbachevym*, p. 308. For reasons difficult to fathom, his account of the Gorbachev-Genscher exchanges were not included in the German version of his memoirs.

minister.[231] Prior to the Gorbachev-Genscher exchanges, the Soviet foreign minister had prepared his German counterpart for things to come, warning him that Gorbachev was very upset and predicting that the upcoming meeting was hardly likely to be pleasant.[232] As the meeting was to confirm, the Soviet president was well briefed by the then still influential *germanisty* of the foreign ministry and the Central Committee.[233]

Gorbachev welcomed Genscher, saying that events had given the visit a particular coloration.[234] He called his guest a privileged discussion partner and said that he knew him well and regarded him highly, and that it was precisely for that reason that he felt he could speak openly and directly, and raise difficult subjects. Genscher conveyed regards from the German president and from the chancellor, and proceeded to dwell on the transformation that had occurred in East-West relations, the irreversibility of the changes, and the necessity for policy-makers to proceed carefully and responsibly. West German policy was based on the treaties concluded with the Soviet Union, Poland, and Czechoslovakia, the Basic Treaty with East Germany, and the (June 1989) Soviet-German Joint Declaration. The Federal Republic was not entering upon a separate German road, he said, but was fully integrated in the European Community.[235]

---

231 Gorbachev, *Zhizn'*, Vol. 2, pp. 163-64.

232 Genscher, *Erinnerungen*, p. 683.

233 Interview with Zagladin. Kvitsinsky remembers that, at the end of November or the beginning of December, he had briefly been recalled from Bonn to help prepare an interdepartmental paper on upcoming negotiations with the East German government; Kwizinskij, *Vor dem Sturm*, p. 17. Falin was responsible for the Central Committee input.

234 Present at the meeting were, on the Soviet side, Gorbachev, Shevardnadze, and Zagladin, and, on the German side, in addition to Genscher, the foreign ministry's political director, Dieter Kastrup, and the West German ambassador to Moscow, Klaus Blech. This account of the meeting is based on what is apparently a transcript of the meeting in possession of the Gorbachev Foundation, "Zapis' besedy M.S. Gorbacheva s ministrom inostrannykh del FRG F.-D. Genscherom, 5 dekabria 1989 goda," Hoover Institution Archives, Box 3, Zelikow-Rice Project on German Unification; the memoirs by Gorbachev, Genscher, and Chernyaev; and personal interviews with Zagladin and Blech. Zelikow and Rice, *Germany Unified*, pp. 135-37, have aptly summarized Gorbachev's attack on Kohl's ten-point program based on these sources, with the exception of Gorbachev's and Genscher's memoirs, which were unavailable to the authors at the time of their writing.

235 There are two major discrepancies here between the Soviet transcript and Genscher's memoirs. The *first* concerns the terms "stability" and "stabilization." Whereas Genscher fails to mention these terms even once, the Soviet transcript shows five usages. Genscher allegedly had spoken of West German policy as being aimed at the (1) "creation of a stable framework for reform in Central and Eastern Europe"; (2) the "stabilization of the situation by means of the development of relations with the Soviet Union, Poland, Hungary, and the GDR; (3) turning the Helsinki process into a "guarantee of stability on the continent"; (4) "enhancing stability in Europe and the rapprochement of its states and peoples"; and (5) allocating a "stabilizing function" to the two military alliances; "Zapis besedy s Genscherom," p. 33. The *second* is about German unification. Genscher asserts that he had spoken of the necessity of the two states to grow together (*Zusammenwachsen*) within European structures and developments; that the Letter on

Gorbachev replied that a difference needed to be made between political philosophy and practical steps. Concerning the latter, he failed to understand Chancellor Kohl and his intentions towards East Germany as expressed in the Ten Points. "One has to conclude, frankly speaking, that they are demands having the character of an ultimatum put to an independent and sovereign German state." [236] Kohl had assured him in the telephone conversation (on 11 November) that he did not want to destabilize the situation in the GDR and that he would act with circumspection and only after consultation. Now it seemed that the German chancellor no longer needed this understanding. "Perhaps he thinks that his melody, the melody of his march, is already playing and he is already marching to it." There was no point to engage in diplomatic niceties. "If you want to cooperate with us, we are ready for it. If not, we will draw the appropriate conclusions."[237]

Gorbachev in particular objected to two points of the Ten Point program. The first was the idea of establishing a confederation. Only yesterday, he said, Kohl had asserted that Bush supported the idea.

> What next? What is meant by confederation? Does confederation envisage a common defense, a common foreign policy? Where would the FRG be – in NATO or in the Warsaw Pact? Or will it perhaps become neutral? But what would NATO be without the FRG? And, in general, what will happen further? Have you thought all of this through?

Shevardnadze interjected, saying that "Today, this style is being adopted [in West German policy] towards the GDR, tomorrow perhaps towards Poland and Czechoslovakia, and then – towards Austria."[238]

The second point that Gorbachev fiercely attacked, quoting verbatim from Kohl's speech to the Bundestag, was the idea that West Germany would be prepared to embark on an entirely new dimension of aid if East Germany irrevocably changed its political and economic system. This he considered to be quite unacceptable. "What else is that but the most blatant interference in the internal affairs of a sovereign state?" he asked. Shevardnadze again interjected: "Even Hitler didn't permit himself this." Gorbachev resumed the attack and, among other things, called Kohl's demand for the liquidation of the bureaucratic command economy and the opening of its doors to Western investment "simply double-dyed revanchism."[239] Gorbachev's perceptions of Kohl, it would seem, had reverted to the period after the latter's

---

German Unity (August 1970) had unambiguously posited the West German goal as being German unification; and that Moscow could at no time have been in doubt about this goal. Neither the transcripts nor Gorbachev's and Chernyaev's memoirs make any reference to this.

236 "Zapis' besedy s Genscherom," p. 34. Contrary to what he was to claim later (see *infra*), at least according to the transcript, Gorbachev did not explicitly use the term *diktat*.

237 "Zapis' besedy s Genscherom," pp. 34-35.

238 Verbatim quotes in "Zapis' besedy s Genscherom," p. 34.

239 Ibid., pp. 34-35.

Goebbels remark and before the meetings of October 1988 and June 1989. In fact, the deliberate display of irritation with Kohl and the irksome German problem found its expression in similar reactions to the German chancellor's attempts, for instance, in a lengthy letter of 14 December, to clarify the Ten Points and his suggestion "to meet soon in the new year in an informal setting and at a place of your choosing."[240] In a letter of his own to Kohl, Gorbachev reiterated his position, without referring to the clarification and the invitation.[241]

How is one to interpret the vehement attack on the Ten Points and the demonstrative displeasure with Kohl? One possible explanation is that of a spontaneous emotional outburst. It could be argued that Gorbachev was lashing out at Genscher in frustration and anger caused by the convergence of mounting political problems, deterioration of economic conditions and rising nationality conflicts in the Soviet Union, and uncontrollable events in Eastern Europe. As his former chief of staff has observed, "Gorbachev was increasingly tired and irritable during the last two years of his tenure, losing his temper often."[242] Such outbursts by top leaders, furthermore, were not uncommon in the internal intercourse in the Soviet era, and Gorbachev had permitted himself on several occasions to follow the pattern.[243] But they were quite uncommon in talks with Western leaders. Nevertheless, in the international domain, too, examples of excessive and unreasonable behavior by Gorbachev can be found. For instance, when he and Shevardnadze had met with Canadian Prime Minister Brian Mulroney in Moscow, shortly prior to Kohl's speech to the Bundestag, the Soviet leader had accused the American ambassador in Bonn (Vernon Walters), an outspoken supporter of German unification, of "acting like a German gauleiter."[244] But whereas frustration about loss of control domestically and internationally may have played a role in Gorbachev's behavior, the outburst in conversation with Genscher was by no means spontaneous. The Soviet leader, as noted, was not only well briefed, quoting verbatim from the Ten Point plan, but also – judging from Shevardnadze's advance warning to Genscher – determined to dispense with the customary diplomatic conventions and convey a strong message.

240 Cited by Kohl, *Ich wollte Deutschlands Einheit*, pp. 193-94.

241 This was interpreted in Bonn as the letters having crossed each other; ibid., p. 209, and Teltschik, *329 Tage*, p. 85. Neither Kohl nor Teltschik mention the date of Gorbachev's letter, only that they saw it on 18 December, after their return from Hungary. However, the interpretation of the letters having crossed each other is not very convincing: Kohl's letter was dispatched on 14 December and he then left for a three-day visit to Hungary on 16 December. No letter had arrived in Bonn before his departure. Thus, the time interval of two days should have been sufficient time for Gorbachev in *his* letter at least to acknowledge receipt of the letter from Kohl.

242 Boldin, *Ten Years That Shook the World*, p. 262.

243 One of the examples, Gorbachev's rude treatment of Sakharov, was mentioned above; see p. 382.

244 Zelikow and Rice, *Germany United*, p. 124, based on a memcon of a dinner between Bush and Mulroney, 29 November 1989.

Even if the eruption was deliberate, the question still needs to be answered what prompted it.

One possible explanation is to be fond in the Gorbachev-Kohl telephone conversation of 11 November and the genuine or pretended differences in interpretation of its content. The emphasis Gorbachev chose to put on the telephone conversation was that there was a congruence of views and a mutual commitment to consult each other, to act responsibly, to exercise restraint, and to contribute to the stabilization of conditions in the GDR. Kohl had concurred with the necessity to prevent chaos in East Germany, but he had also contended that this was possible only if fundamental reforms were to be adopted by its new leadership.[245] To highlight the difference of view, whereas Gorbachev wanted to stabilize the new regime, Kohl aimed at stable *conditions* in East Germany under a *new system*.

Another reason for the acrimonious exchanges lay in Gorbachev's perceived link between West German domestic politics and change in East Germany. On this issue, too, he was well briefed. His attack on Genscher is littered with references to Kohl's initiative as having been motivated by the upcoming parliamentary elections and as demonstrating the subordination of responsible international conduct to the electoral campaign. In allusion to presumed or genuine policy differences between the CDU and the FDP, he professed to be astonished that Genscher, not having been informed of the initiative by Kohl, would act as a policy advocate for the chancellor. The Ten Points, of course, had an important domestic political dimension. But Gorbachev chose to disbelieve Genscher's explanation that Kohl's initiative had found wide-spread support not only in the Bundestag and among the West German public but also in East Germany, and that at issue was not the subordination of national interests to party politics but their *alignment*.

Yet another reason for the fierce attack may lie in Soviet internal politics and, more broadly, future perceptions of Gorbachev's role in history. By December 1989, his position as master of the Kremlin notwithstanding, Gorbachev had to cope with the Sorcerer's Apprentice syndrome, with the increasing perception domestically that he had set in motion processes that he was unable to control – an extremely dangerous image to present in the Soviet context. The consistent pattern of non-interference was making him vulnerable to charges of inactivity and incompetence, to having liquidated the GDR either by criminal design along the lines of Beria or, equally damaging, by criminal neglect. Concern about such perceptions had briefly surfaced in his remark to Mitterrand that the day Germany was unified, "a Soviet

245 Gorbachev, *Zhizn'*, Vol. 2, p. 164; "Zapis' besedy s Genscherom," p. 34; Kohl, *Ich wollte Deutschlands Einheit*, pp. 141-43.

marshal will be sitting in my chair," and to Kochemasov that "Our people will never forgive us if we lose the GDR."[246]

If domestic purposes were one of the factors underlying the harsh line Gorbachev had taken with Genscher, one would expect to find indications of such purposes in the Soviet leader's public statements. But a delicate balance had to be struck. To convey the new image of being tough on Kohl and seemingly in control of events was certainly advantageous politically, but revelation of the full extent of the acrimonious exchanges with Genscher and the intended pressures on Kohl could have *reinforced* rather than mitigated domestic perceptions that his policies had been ineffective and that he had indeed lost control – and his composure. To complicate matters, a decision on how to proceed had to be made on the spot since Genscher had asked him directly at the end of the meeting how both sides should characterize the talks. The Soviet transcript and Genscher's memoirs provide different accounts of the reply. The German foreign minister's memoirs have the general secretary answering that the time for making his assessment public had not yet arrived.[247] According to the Soviet transcript, Gorbachev suggested specific language that recurs almost verbatim in the subsequent TASS report. This includes the wording that the talks had been "frank and comprehensive," as well as "open and direct," and that Gorbachev had emphasized that "the Soviet Union considers the German Democratic Republic a reliable ally and an important guarantor of peace and stability in Europe and will extend to it solidarity and support."[248] Corroborating the interpretation of domestic purposes, the ringing declaration of support for East Germany was repeated by Gorbachev in a speech to the Central Committee on 9 December. "We would like to emphasize with all determination," he said, "that *we will let no harm come to the GDR. It is our strategic ally and member of the Warsaw Pact.*" To ignore the realities that had developed after the Second World War carried the risk of a "destabilization of Europe."[249]

---

246 The remark to Mitterrand, as quoted by Zelikow and Rice, *Germany Unified*, p. 137. The remark to Kochemasov as reported by Maximychev, "Possible 'Impossibilities,'" pp. 112-13; similarly Kotschemassow, *Meine letzte Mission*, p. 110. There are some discrepancies as to the date when the latter remark was made, whether in October or November. The date, however, is immaterial. The concern about the likely domestic consequences of the loss of the GDR was a constant preoccupation.

247 Genscher, *Erinnerungen*, p. 686.

248 "Vstrecha M.S. Gorbacheva s G.-D. Genscherom" (TASS report), *Pravda*, 6 December 1989, and "Zapis besedy s Genscherom," p. 36. There are only slight variations in the wording. The TASS report uses the wording "direct, frank and comprehensive," and Gorbachev's suggested "true" (*vernyi*) ally was turned into a "reliable" (*nadezhnyi*) ally.

249 Gorbachev delivered two speeches to the Central Committee, one dealing primarily with domestic affairs, the other with the results of the Malta summit. The quotation can be found in the former, "Vystuplenie M.S. Gorbacheva na Plenume TsK KPSS po voprosam II S"ezda narodnykh deputatov SSSR," *Pravda*, 10 December 1989 (italics mine). The Russian term used for "strategic ally" was *strategicheskii soiuznik*.

A probable contributory factor for such a seemingly unequivocal commitment to the GDR was the summit meeting of the Warsaw Pact that had taken place in Moscow on the preceding day and the separate talks between Gorbachev and Modrow on that occasion.[250] The composition of the East German delegation reflected the accelerating pace of change in East Berlin – and put the Soviet leadership in a quandary. Krenz and the SED Politburo had been forced to resign on 3 December. Krenz was still included in the delegation but no longer in his capacity as party chief but as head of state and chairman of the defense council, positions from which he would step down immediately after his return from Moscow. Thus, pending the election of a new party leadership and program at an extraordinary congress, to begin on 8 December, the SED was in a state of disarray. In the circumstance, the Soviet leaders decided to treat Modrow, the prime minister and simultaneously their preferred candidate for the top party position, as the head of the delegation. In consequence, *he* rather than Krenz was given the floor at the Warsaw Pact summit and identified in the press as the main discussion partner in private conversation (arranged by Falin) with Gorbachev.[251]

The purpose of the meeting, according to Modrow's later account, was to discuss the character of the democratic changes in East Germany and to coordinate Soviet-East German policies. Characterizing the meeting, Modrow stated that

> It became apparent that Gorbachev still harbored illusions. I did not dissuade him in this regard because I, at least in part, still believed in this idea as well: democratization as a process that would strengthen socialism in the GDR. Indeed I had the fear – he had no idea – that [the process would lead] to a gradual disintegration of socialism in the GDR. [But] Gorbachev thought that now the path was free for perestroika in the GDR.[252]

The fact that Gorbachev still harbored illusions was apparent also a few days later, in a meeting with Mitterrand in Kiev. The Soviet leader ruminated: "The situation in the GDR is difficult. But it is not catastrophic. The people are working, and there are

---

250 In fact, as Genscher was being driven from the airport to Moscow, he saw the caravan of vehicles with the East German delegation stopped close to the airport, on the opposite side of the road. Shevardnadze, apparently still involved in the wrap-up of the Warsaw Pact summit but perhaps also as a sign of displeasure with the West German government, had failed to appear at the airport. Instead, it was Deputy Foreign Minister Anatoli Adamishin who had met the West German foreign minister and who had pointed out the caravan with the East German leadership. Genscher surmised that the vehicles had deliberately been halted in order to preclude that he would meet, or meet with, the East German leadership; Genscher, *Erinnerungen*, p. 682.

251 Hans Modrow, *Aufbruch und Ende* (Hamburg: Konkret Literatur Verlag, 1991), pp. 48, 92; *id.*, "Abschied von der zweiten Heimat," *Die Zeit*, 27 April 1990. Modrow only cursorily refers to the Warsaw Pact summit and his conversations with Gorbachev. The TASS report isued at the time was equally brief. It stated that talks had been held on 4 December between Gorbachev and Prime Minister Modrow, and that "Chairman of the State Council of the GDR E. Krenz and Foreign Minister of the GDR O. Fischer" had attended the meeting; *Pravda*, 5 December 1989.

252 Ibid.

fewer demonstrations." Mitterrand asked him whether he thought that the East Germans were responding favorably to the idea of reunification. Gorbachev replied that there was such a response. "However, you know, more than half of the population of the GDR wants to keep the present make-up of their country."[253] In conformity with such convictions, Gorbachev had not drawn the conclusion from the resignation of the SED Politburo that the center of gravity in the GDR had irrevocably shifted away from the SED to the coalition government, the opposition parties, and the East German population. He still considered the SED (to be renamed PDS, or Party of Democratic Socialism at the party's upcoming extraordinary congress) to be the agent of change in East Germany.[254] He also retained an ambiguous attitude to the ideas of *Vertragsgemeinschaft*, confederative structures and confederation, no matter whether in the Modrow or the Kohl versions. An interdepartmental paper, in the drafting of which Kvitsinsky was involved, included the suggestion to the SED to refurbish its proposal, first made by Ulbricht in the 1950s, of a German confederation.[255] A *limited nature* of intergovernmental cooperation was envisaged by its authors. Portugalov had hinted at such purposes earlier, when he had spoken of "federative structures in areas such as the economy, ecology, culture, and many other things."[256] Similarly, in his meeting with Genscher, Gorbachev had attacked the idea of a common defense and security policy of a German confederation.[257] Limited intergovernmental cooperation, however, was not what the West German government or the East German population wanted. Kvitsinsky, therefore, considered the interdepartmental paper to be dead on arrival even if it were to receive endorsement by the Soviet Politburo, formally still empowered to approve the draft.[258]

The apparent or real abandonment of the nonchalant and noncommittal attitude towards the erosion of imperial control and influence in East Germany and Eastern Europe in December 1989 raises the question as to whether Gorbachev was now prepared to take tough practical measures and, if so, what options he still had available. One possible course of action was to play on the keyboard of Western European, and particularly British and French, concerns about the emergence of a

---

253 "Zapis' besedy M.S. Gorbacheva s prezidentom Frantsii F. Mitteranom, Kiev, 6 dekabria 1989 goda," p. 39.

254 The TASS report provides an indication of this belief. The report states that Gorbachev gave assurances that the "SED and our German friends can always count on our solidarity and support by the CPSU and the whole Soviet people" and that he wished "the communists of the GDR success in the preparation of the [extraordinary] party congress."

255 Concerning the origins of the interdepartmental paper, see above, n. 233.

256 Interview with *Frankfurter Allgemeine Zeitung* on 17 November, FBIS-SOV-89-222, 20 November 1989, p. 34, quoted by Gedmin, *The Hidden Hand*, p. 114.

257 This was mentioned above; "Zapis' besedy s Genscherom," p. 34.

258 Kwizinskij, *Vor dem Sturm*, p. 17.

strong Germany – a Fourth Reich – in the center of Europe and, for that purpose, to revive Four Power control mechanisms.

European Concerns and the Four Power Card: Four Minus Two?

The opportunity to play the card of European apprehensions certainly existed. It presented itself not only because Kohl's Ten Point plan had been as much of a surprise to West Germany's European allies as to Gorbachev, but also because it had been received by them with as much dismay. This was evident at the summit meeting of the European Community on 8 December in Strasbourg. "In all the years that I had been chancellor," Kohl was to write in retrospect, "I had never experienced an EC summit held in such an icy atmosphere." Now *he*, in turn, was surprised about his partners' reactions – the "interrogative questioning almost resembling that of a tribunal."[259]

The primary reason underlying the dismay lay in an apparent paradox. Western European leaders had reiterated their commitment to German reunification in the belief that this topic would forever remain theoretical, while privately adhering to the view that the division of Germany served European security interests. The latter sentiment, like the little boy's revelation about the emperor's new clothes in Andersen's fairy tale, had publicly been expressed in September 1984 by Giulio Andreotti, then Italy's foreign minister. In the context of blossoming intra-German contacts but frigid East-West relations and prompted by the cancellation of Honecker's visit to West Germany, he had stated: "We all agree that there should be good relations between the two Germanys ... but one should not exaggerate things in this direction. ... Pan-Germanism has to be overcome. There are two German states, and two they shall remain."[260] Unrepentant, he had later added that he didn't understand the commotion caused by his remarks. He had not been the only Western leader who in the past twenty years had objected to German reunification. "Who," he asked, "has ever asserted that Ostpolitik means reunification?"[261] Unlike in the fairy tale, however, the little boy of the twentieth-century real-life story incurred the wrath of the emperor and was severely taken to task; his parents profusely apologized and

---

259 Kohl, *Ich wollte Deutschlands Einheit*, p. 195.

260 "Genscher: Andreotti hat die Bundesrepublik gekränkt," *Frankfurter Allgemeine Zeitung*, 17 September 1984.

261 Ibid. Confirming Andreotti's allegation, former Austrian chancellor Bruno Kreisky commented: "Mr Andreotti had the mishap to express somewhat more clearly what everyone is thinking." For this quote and other European reactions see "'Dem Herrn Andreotti ist es halt passiert': Wer denkt was über den Wunsch der Deutschen nach Einheit?," *Frankfurter Allgemeine Zeitung*, 29 September 1984, and Eberhard Schulz and Peter Danylow, *Bewegung in der deutschen Frage? Die ausländischen Besorgnisse über die Entwicklung in den beiden deutschen Staaten*, 2nd ed., Research Paper No. 33, Research Institute of the Deutsche Gesellschaft für Auswärtige Politik, Bonn, April 1985, pp. 164-54.

in the end the public reasserted that the emperor wore clothes after all.[262] Yet despite the reassertion of reunification as an agreed-upon goal, European – in particular, French, Italian, and Dutch – apprehensions had not been assuaged. This was evident at the Strasbourg summit.

Thatcher was to take the lead in the "interrogation." The German chancellor thought that her negative attitude in Strasbourg, like that of many other leaders and among the public in Britain, was predicated, at the psychological and emotional level, upon "deep distrust" vis-à-vis Germany and the Germans and, at the political level, based on categories prevalent before Churchill and on "nineteenth-century "balance of power" thinking." Kohl also imputed to her the idea that Britain still played first fiddle in Europe.[263] Genscher, not usually given to dramatization, in retrospect characterized Thatcher's demeanor at the meeting as "blustering," motivated, in his view, by the fact that the prime minister only "hesitatingly adjusted to the inevitability of Germany unity."[264] But there was more to her attitude than mere adjustment problems. She was not only concerned about the speed with which German reunification was being put on the international agenda but about the very *principle.* In September, returning via Moscow from a visit to Japan, she had confided to Gorbachev that "although NATO had traditionally made statements supporting Germany's aspiration to be reunited, in practice, we were rather apprehensive."[265] (This echoed a statement made by French political scientist Alfred Grosser to the effect that West Germany's Western allies were all in favor of reunification as long as they knew that it was not a realistic prospect.[266]) The West, she had told Bush in November, should "respect Gorbachev's wish to keep the Warsaw Pact frontiers."[267] She also questioned whether self-determination should be the central principle to govern the German problem. There were other important issues to consider, she said, including the role of the Four Powers in Berlin, the CSCE commitment to the inviolability of the European borders, continuation of change in Eastern Europe and the very fate of Gorbachev and perestroika.[268] At the Strasbourg summit, however,

262 The Italian ambassador in Bonn was called to the West German foreign office for an explanation of Andreotti's statement. In a letter to chancellor Kohl, Italian prime minister Benedetto Craxi disavowed his foreign minister; see *Frankfurter Allgemeine Zeitung*, 17 September 1984.

263 Kohl, *Ich wollte Deutschlands Einheit*, p. 196. Genscher similarly has stated that "The British prime minister, it seemed, had political and emotional reservations"; Genscher, *Erinnerungen*, p. 691.

264 Genscher, *Erinnerungen*, p. 690.

265 Margaret Thatcher, *The Downing Street Years* (New York: HarperCollins, 1993), p. 792.

266 Cited in *Le Monde*, "La question allemande: ouverte ou fermée?," 30 September 1984.

267 Memcon of a telephone conversation between Bush and Thatcher, 17 November 1989 (note taker was Philip Zelikow), quoted in Zelikow and Rice, *Germany Unified*, p. 406.

268 In talks with Bush at Camp David, on 24 November 1989; Thatcher, *The Downing Street Years*, p. 794, and the memcon of the meeting (note taker Brent Scowcroft), quoted in Zelikow and Rice, *Germany Unified*, pp. 115-16.

the principle of self-determination was formally reasserted, and the summit, in consequence, was interpreted by Genscher as a "great success."[269]

On the surface, Thatcher's attitude seemed to coincide with that of François Mitterrand, and it is for that reason that the former thought that "If there was any hope now of stopping [sic] or slowing down reunification, it would only come from an Anglo-French initiative."[270] The latter's reservations, however, were much less fundamental than that of the former: the French president was thoroughly committed to his country's reconciliation with Germany and to European integration. The strong personal bonds that existed between Kohl and Mitterrand were also very much an expression of several decades of close French-German cooperation in the European Community on Coal and Steel and the European (Economic) Community and the two countries' mutual commitment to European integration. To that extent, as Kohl realized, Mitterrand shared the West German government's view that European integration and German unification should not be contradictory but *complementary* processes.[271] Similarly, Genscher thought that "Mitterrand, through the Europeanization of the German problem, wanted to prevent a repetition of the previous mistakes on both banks of the Rhine." The German foreign minister also understood the importance which the French leader attached to an unequivocal codification of Poland's borders.[272]

A first major test as to whether Gorbachev intended to play the anti-Hitler coalition card and, if so, whether he would be able to do so came in the meeting between him and Mitterrand on 6 December in Kiev. The (Soviet) transcript of the meeting demonstrates both the ambiguity of Gorbachev's intentions and the limited possibilities to instrumentalize French concerns.[273] Certainly, there were similarities in perception between the two leaders. These pertained to Kohl's initiative.

> F. MITTERRAND. ... Kohl's speech, his Ten Points, turned everything upside down. He confused all the factors. He is hurrying. I told Genscher that, and he didn't very much contradict my conclusions.
>
> M.S. GORBACHEV. This is very interesting! I also told him that. ... [He] is formulating his theses in such a form that they practically amount to a *diktat*.
>
> F. MITTERRAND. You said that explicitly? *Diktat* – that is a German word.

269 Genscher, *Erinnerungen*, p. 690.

270 Thatcher, *Downing Street Years*, p. 796.

271 Kohl, *Ich wollte die deutschen Einheit*, pp. 197-99.

272 Genscher, *Erinnerungen*, pp. 691-92.

273 All subsequent citations from the meeting according to "Zapis' besedy M.S. Gorbacheva s prezidentom Frantsii F. Mitteranom. Kiev, 6 dekabria 1989 goda."

> M.S. GORBACHEV. I spoke even more sharply. And E.A. Shevardnadze [in reference to Kohl's demands for fundamental change in East Germany] said that even Hitler did not always speak in such a tone.

French and Soviet views also coincided on the relationship between German reunification and the processes of both Western and pan-European integration.

> F. MITTERRAND. ... It is necessary to make sure that the all-European process develops more rapidly than the German question and that it overtakes the German movement. We have to create all-European structures. The German component must only be one, and by no means the dominant or leading element of politics in Europe.

The similarities in interpretation extended to the importance of codifying the Polish borders as final and alleged ambiguities in the American attitude on this issue.

> F. MITTERRAND. ... I have to acknowledge that I remarked to my German friends and expressed my astonishment that when they put forward their considerations they failed to mention the frontiers of Poland. This is a serious problem. All the countries of the European community approach this the same way even though the sharpness with which they express this may vary.
>
> M.S. GORBACHEV. I have the feeling that the United States are not quite open about their position, they don't explain it fully.
>
> F. MITTERRAND. This is true. ...

What about the practical consequences of this congruence? Mitterrand put that very question to Gorbachev. "What, concretely, are you planning to do?," he asked. "Above all, to continue the line of peaceful changes," Gorbachev replied. "May each country decide its directions for itself." Perhaps taken aback himself by the lack of concreteness, the Soviet leader added: "You are right, one should not simply observe, one has to act." However, according to the Soviet transcript, the suggested action extended to nothing more than such generalities as "building trust" and "broadening cooperation." It was *Mitterrand* who made a specific suggestion. Speaking about his forthcoming visit to the GDR, agreed upon with Honecker and scheduled for 20 December, and asserting that cancellation of the visit would have political significance (that is, presumably, that it could be considered a declaration of no-confidence in the Modrow government), with Gorbachev interjecting that he, too, should probably visit the GDR, the French president suggested: "Well, then, let's go together." Nothing, however, came of this suggestion.

To generalize from the meeting with Mitterrand, the two leaders shared interpretations, sentiments, and concerns, and agreed that *something* should be done. But they had no plan of action and, at least as far as bilateral relations were concerned, no intention to develop a plan. It was in all likelihood in consequence of the mutually perceived need to do something and be seen as doing something that, on 8 December, Gorbachev reverted to the Four Power proposal.

The idea to convene a Four Power meeting at the ambassadorial level to discuss the German problem had apparently been developed in the Soviet embassy in East Berlin. In a telegram to Moscow, Kochemasov had emphasized that the very convocation of such a meeting would serve to emphasize the continued responsibility of the Four Powers for the German problem and that it would be advisable to hold meetings on a regular basis, that is, to institutionalize the process. Presumably conscious of the likely Western, certainly American, objections to a reactivation of the Four Power mechanism on Germany, the embassy suggested using the Western allied Berlin initiative of December 1987 as a frame of reference.[274] This found acceptance by his superiors despite the fact that the Western initiative, which had envisaged an expansion of contacts and exchanges between East and West Berlin and authorization for Lufthansa to institute a regular service to Berlin, had been rejected by Moscow with the argument that Four Power discussions could only pertain to *West* Berlin, and that matters of civil aviation could not be discussed in that framework because they touched upon the sovereignty of the GDR.[275] Now, however, not only Berlin as a whole but the German problem, according to Soviet intentions, was to be the subject matter of discussion.

The Four Power meeting took place on 11 December in the building of the Allied Control Council in the American sector of Berlin.[276] If symbolism was the intended effect of the meeting, no better venue could have been chosen. The ACC, defunct since Marshal Sokolovsky had left it in protest in March 1948 at the onset of the Berlin crisis, had been the collective repository of interallied sovereignty in and instrument of control over defeated Germany. Now, after the passage of more than four decades, the widely disseminated picture of the four ambassadors – Walters, Kochemasov, Mallaby, and Boidevaix – in front of the Control Council headquarters building was bound to create the impression that the wartime coalition was determined to reassert its interests in Germany and give corresponding notice to Bonn. To that extent, it superbly served the purpose of a warning shot and proof of interallied activity. If, however, the meeting was designed by the Soviet leadership as a serious effort to prevent or delay German unification, or to reestablish the anti-

274 Kotschemassow, *Meine letzte Mission*, p. 196.

275 Soviet and East German decision-making processes and the rationales for the objections in Moscow and East Berlin to the Western initiative, including talks between Bondarenko and SED Politburo member Krolikowski and Honecker's consent to the Soviet reply, can be found in SED Politburo, *Arbeitsprotokolle*, Central Party Archives, J IV 2/2/2A/3146.

276 Mitterrand, at the Strasbourg summit, had reported as a matter of fact that the Soviet Union had asked to convene a meeting of the four guarantors of the 1971 Berlin Agreement, adding that France, as a matter of course, would accede to the request; Teltschik, 329 Tage, p. 72; Kohl, *Ich wollte Deutschlands Einheit*, p. 201. It is unclear from Kochemasov's account where the suggestion came from to choose the ACC building as the venue for the meeting. The Soviet ambassador had suggested to hold the meeting "in the FRG"; Kotschemassow, *Meine letzte Mission*, p. 196.

Hitler coalition framework for managing the German problem, it turned out to be a resounding failure. Although the British and French had readily agreed to the meeting, and the Americans reluctantly, all three powers had insisted on an agenda limited to *Berlin*. Kochemasov did not respect that limitation, repeating the then current Gorbachevian litany about the GDR as a strategic ally of the Soviet Union and member of the Warsaw Pact and criticizing certain persons or circles who would like to interfere in the internal affairs of the GDR. The three Western ambassadors, however, opposed the broadening of the agenda and objected to the Soviet proposal for an institutionalization of the interallied process. The meeting also evoked strong reactions in Bonn. At the NATO foreign ministers' conference on 13 December in Brussels, Genscher wanted to achieve "absolute clarity" on that matter and bluntly warned: "You have to decide between cooperation with us in NATO and the European Community or with the Soviet Union in the Control Council."[277] If, to reiterate, the Soviet leadership had regarded the Four Minus Two venue as an appropriate forum for asserting its interests, it failed in that purpose.

To summarize, utilization of Western European concerns and Four Power machinery to arrest or delay German unification was never a viable Soviet option. Little could by gained by attempts to turn the anti-Hitler coalition into an anti-Kohl coalition. Such attempts continued to be made after 11 December, but they lacked conviction and determination. There were several mutually reinforcing reasons for Gorbachev to refrain from playing the interallied card. (1) The *Western powers* were not prepared to join the Soviet Union in such an attempt. For several decades, as mentioned, they had formally committed themselves to the principle of German unification to be achieved through self-determination, which in turn was to be exercised through free elections. For these powers now to admit openly that their support of these principles was a charade would seriously have eroded the credibility of Western diplomacy. (2) Even the *Soviet Union* was committed to self-determination through the assertion of the principle of the Freedom of Choice and, more specifically, the June 1989 Joint Declaration. On a practical level, the anti-Hitler coalition option carried serious risks. West Germany's power and influence in Europe had steadily increased; the United States regarded that country as its most important ally in Europe and solidly supported Bonn's position; France was inextricably linked to West Germany in the European Community and unwilling to jeopardize progress on European integration; and Britain on its own was too weak to be an effective Soviet ally. (3) None of the Western leaders, ideologically least of all Thatcher, but also Mitterrand, as his performance in Kiev showed, had any serious interest in stabilizing a reform socialist *East Germany* of dubious legitimacy, nor did they have the means to do so. In addition, the Four Minus Two framework meant

277 Genscher, *Erinnerungen*, p. 696.

exclusion not only of West Germany but also of East Germany from the negotiation process – a step that would have counteracted any policy aimed at upgrading the international stature and internal legitimacy of the GDR. (4) The stabilization of the *reform process* in the Soviet Union had top priority for the Soviet leadership, and for that purpose a cooperative, rather than an ostracized West Germany was an important precondition. For the Soviet Union to join Bonn's partners in an attempt to stop German unification, as Chernyaev has written, would have meant that "the cold war would have broken out again" and that this was something the Western European "alliance partners [themselves] did not want."[278] Soviet policies on Germany, therefore, continued to be constrained by severe internal and international circumstances, by lack of vision, and by bureaucratic confusion. This applies also to Gorbachev's acceptance of German unification.

6. Gorbachev's Acceptance of German Unification

Theoretically, one of the central analytical tasks in the reconstruction of the collapse of Soviet empire could be the attempt to pinpoint the precise date when the Soviet leadership consented to German unification and decided on the basic outlines of united Germany's international status. Ideally, one would be able to identify one or more Politburo meetings where the internal and external aspects of German unification were put on the agenda, discussed, and then resolved. In practice, however, both the internal and external aspects were never formally discussed and decided simultaneously. A formal meeting of the Politburo to consent to German unification or to decide the Soviet position on Germany's international status was never held. A meeting that was held at the end of January 1990 and that involved a selected circle of decision-makers, including several Politburo members, simply took German unification for granted. Its participants decided a few procedural questions for negotiations with West German and East German leaders but failed to address, let alone resolve, the principles of the Soviet negotiation position on the external aspects of German unification. A formal Politburo meeting on the German problem took place at the beginning of May 1990, but it continued to treat the internal and international problems of the German problem as separate, and the majority of its participants, including Gorbachev, were adamantly opposed to united Germany's membership in NATO. This apparently firm position was reversed less than four weeks later by Gorbachev, single-handedly, at the Soviet-American summit in

278 Chernyaev, *Shest' let s Gorbachevym*, p. 310. He expressed this opinion in reference to the Malta summit and Bush's comment to Gorbachev that "Kohl knows that some Western alliance partners verbally support reunification, which the German people want, but are concerned about this perspective," and that it was "strange that the Soviet Union was sitting in the same boat with our European NATO allies."

Washington – to the surprise of the American and the consternation of the Soviet participants, without prior consultation of other Politburo members and top decision-makers, and contrary to the advice of all the senior experts on Germany.

How is it possible to explain this extraordinary state of affairs? Part of the answer has been provided in the previous chapter, which dealt with the relegation of the traditional mainstays of the imperial system to a secondary role; the shift in decision-making authority to a small circle of top leaders and their advisers and personal assistants; the exacerbation of conflict between the broad base of conservative bureaucracies and the thin layer of advocates of the New Thinking at the top; and an increase in pressure for more radical reform exerted by the newly created legislative bodies and the politically aware segments of public opinion. Another explanation lies in the interaction of the disintegration of the traditional decision-making institutions and machinery and the disintegration of empire.

In detail, the consent to German unification began with bureaucratic confusion. One of its noteworthy examples was the speech Shevardnadze delivered on 19 December to the Political Commission of the European Parliament. Not unlike the main report by the general secretary to party congresses in the past, including Gorbachev's address to the Twenty-seventh congress, the foreign minister's speech constituted a compromise between different positions of various institutions. In the present case, in addition to embodying the vested interests of the foreign ministry and the Central Committee's International Department, it represented a split between the top and the middle echelons *within* the foreign ministry. Shevardnadze, conscious of the inexorable drift towards German unity on the one hand, and the stale and ineffective Soviet approach to the German problem on the other, had wanted to set new directions in his speech in Brussels. That objective, in essence, failed to be achieved because of blatant inconsistencies and contractions, and the unhealthy mixture of the old and the new that characterized the speech.[279]

The problem had begun with a draft submitted by Bondarenko and the Third European Department that reflected both the traditional Soviet position on Germany and the hard line Gorbachev had adopted vis-à-vis Genscher on 6 December and at the 9 December Central Committee meeting. The draft contradicted Shevardnadze's purposes of flexibility. In consequence, he asked Tarasenko (as noted, one of his chief personal aides but not an expert on Germany) to rewrite it and to focus on the conditions that the Soviet Union should attach to German unity if and when it occurred. The revised draft was returned to the Third Department and produced a severe conflict between Tarasenko and Bondarenko, the latter demanding that the

279 The following account of the background of the speech is based on this author's interviews with Tarasenko and Kvitsinsky; see also, based on the same sources, Zelikow and Rice, *Germany Unified*, pp. 149-50.

line authoritatively laid down by Gorbachev be adhered to and that the draft be kept intact. Upon Shevardnadze's insistence, the revisions remained in the draft document. However, it would seem that the foreign minister himself was by no means as unequivocally committed to an entirely new approach as his aide has made it appear in retrospect: the Foreign Minister had the draft submitted to Ambassador Kvitsinsky in Bonn, who bent it away from the implicit acceptance of unification and hardened the conditions to be attached to it. Shevardnadze received Kvitsinsky's revised revisions after he had arrived in Brussels and, Tarasenko's protest notwithstanding, accepted them for the final version.

Shevardnadze, *ex post facto*, sought to impute clarity of purpose to the speech. "In Brussels," he wrote in his memoirs, "I carefully outlined our position."[280] However, given the conflicting inputs, the speech contained major contradictions. One of the most glaring concerned the fact that Shevardnadze dealt with the possible implications of German unification but, at the same time, stated that the Soviet position had been expressed by "Gorbachev at the CPSU Central Committee plenum" to the effect that the GDR was the Soviet Union's "strategic ally and a member of the Warsaw Pact;" that one had to take these "realities" into account; and that any departure from the existence of two separate German states would threaten "destabilization in Europe."[281] The Helsinki process of pan-European cooperation should not "be ruined on German soil," he warned. That was "impermissible." He also reminded his listeners that the Four Powers had legal rights in Germany and "have at their disposal a considerable contingent of armed forces equipped with nuclear weapons on the territory of the GDR and the FRG."

The central part of Shevardnadze's speech was a barrage of questions, formally separated as a bloc of seven, with several sub-questions. "Where are the legal and material guarantees," he asked, that German unity would "not create a threat to the national security of other states and to peace in Europe?" Would Germany recognize the existing borders in Europe? What place would it take in the military-political structures existing on the continent? What would be its military doctrine and the structure of its armed forces? Would it be prepared to take steps toward demilitarization and adopt a neutral status? What would be its attitude toward the presence of allied troops and the continued operation of military liaison missions of the Four Powers? What would be the status of the Quadripartite Agreement of 1971 on Berlin? How would German unification tie in with the Helsinki process? Would a united Germany radically restructure its economic and other links with Eastern Europe? Would the two German states, if they expressed themselves in favor of

280 Shevardnadze, *Moi vybor*, p. 230.

281 "Evropa – vremia peremen. Vystuplenie E.A. Shevardnadze v politicheskoi komissii Evropeiskogo parlamenta," *Pravda*, 20 December 1989.

starting to move toward the unity of the Germans, consider the interests of other European states and be ready to conclude a European peace settlement? "The peoples of the Soviet Union," Shevardnadze concluded, "have a right to know what any changes in Central Europe might mean for their future and their security. We paid for today's European stability with the lives of 20 million people."[282]

The hybrid nature of Shevardnadze's speech was evident not only in its contradictory substance but also in the fact that some of the questions appeared in the future tense ("will Germany ...?"), others were expressed in the future conditional ("would Germany ...?"), thus leaving the audience to wonder whether its author(s) proceeded from German unity as inevitable or hypothetical. Nowhere, however, was German reunification mentioned as a potentially positive contribution to European security. Several of the questions were almost indistinguishable from conditions, but they failed to add up to a consistent Soviet position or international framework in accordance with which German reunification could be achieved. Shevardnadze's preferences as to how individual questions should be answered also remained vague. Since a united Germany was apparently considered undesirable, the continued existence of two German states could be interpreted as being his main preference. If German unity were to come nevertheless, his preference then appeared to be a demilitarized, neutral country. NATO membership seemed to be definitely out of the question: one could "not seriously think that the status of the GDR will change radically while the status of the FRG will remain as it was," Shevardnadze said. This, however, was precisely what was to happen. In fact, as the Soviet foreign minister was speaking, the internal conditions in the GDR *were* changing radically and eroding even further Moscow's remaining influence in that country.[283]

Acceleration of the Demise of the GDR

The primary instrument of Soviet control in East Germany had been the East German communist party. That control, as reconstructed here in detail, had substantially weakened as a result of policy differences between the CPSU and the SED and, at the personal level, between Honecker and Gorbachev. After the involuntary resignation of both Honecker and Krenz, one of the issues that would determine the fate of the residual Soviet influence in East Germany was the degree to which the SED would be successful in transforming itself into a viable reform socialist party. An attempt to achieve this metamorphosis was made at the party's extraordinary

282 Ibid.

283 Shevardnadze talked to Genscher after he had delivered the speech. The conversation appears to have been uneventful and uninspiring. The West German foreign minister formed the impression that Moscow would accept the course of events, provided they proceeded in an orderly fashion; Genscher, *Erinnerungen*, p. 703.

congress that began on 8 December and lasted, with one week of intermission, until 17 December. The party changed its name to Socialist Unity Party–Party of Democratic Socialism (SED-PDS, later only PDS); elected as party chief Gregor Gysi, a flamboyant defense lawyer, who had made a name for himself in political trials; gave prominence to reform communist leaders such as Wolfgang Berghofer, the mayor of Dresden, and Prime Minister Modrow; and promised to pursue a new path between Western-style capitalism and command-bureaucratic socialism, that is, the road of democratic socialism. The effort, however, was in vain. Several factors contributed to this failure.

First, revolutions, as perceptive observes have noted, often follow a cycle. The *ancien régime's* repression provides cause for grievances and gives rise to demands for reform; a new leadership takes heed of the demands and embarks upon a reformist course, which in turn is interpreted as weakness, fueling a revolution; radicalization sets in, and the cycle ends in a return to reform or in reaction.[284] In late 1989 and the first half of 1990, East Germany, neighboring Czechoslovakia and Poland, as indeed the Soviet Union itself, were in the middle of a phase of *radicalization*. In such a phase, the discredited mainstays of the old regime, including its reformist vanguard, usually have little chance to recapture the trust and goodwill of the population.

Second, the SED lacked a reform socialist tradition. Its possible emergence had been suppressed first by Ulbricht after the forced merger of the KPD and SPD in April 1946 and then by Honecker, most recently in his "two-front" struggle against Gorbachev-style *demokratizatsiia* and West German social democracy and *soziale Marktwirtschaft*. Conceivably, there was a reform socialist base among the rank and file members. That possible base, however, was rapidly melting away. In the three months preceding the congress, the party lost over half a million of its 2.3 million members – a process that showed no sign of being arrested, let alone reversed, as 1989 drew to a close. The majority of those who were leaving the party, one would suspect, were turning their back not only on past neo-Stalinism but also on possible future reform socialism in the GDR.[285]

Third, the SED-PDS's association with the Soviet Union and the CPSU was a serious liability. The disadvantages of the link had by no means been removed by Gorbachev's reform attempts, which in both Soviet and East German perceptions had yet to produce tangible economic benefits. To the extent that the enthusiastic welcome that the Soviet party leader had received in East Berlin two months earlier

---

284 See, for instance, Alexis de Tocqueville, *L'ancien régime et la révolution* (Paris: Gallimard, 1979), and Crane Brinton, *The Anatomy of Revolution*, rev. ed. (New York: Vintage Books, 1965).

285 For the statistical data and their interpretation see David Binder, "At Confessional East Berlin Congress, an 'Absolute Break' with Stalinism," *New York Times*, 18 December 1989.

could have been interpreted as a popular endorsement for the introduction of reform socialism in the GDR, rather than a tribute to Gorbachev's courage and personality and a demonstration of no confidence in Honecker, the popular mood had substantially changed after the opening of the wall. Due in part to the realization, both in East Berlin and in Moscow, of the possible problems that could be caused by an emphasis on close party links, the CPSU delegation attending the congress was small and kept a low profile. Previously, the CPSU General Secretary would have attended such a congress. At the SED-PDS's extraordinary congress, however, the Soviet delegation was led by Yakovlev and included Ambassador Kochemasov and CC International Department officials Falin, Kopteltsev and Portugalov. It did not include Gorbachev: his personal assistants and ID officials thought that his participation could have been interpreted as old-style interference in internal party affairs and would have committed the prestige of the Soviet Union to a political process and a leadership struggle whose outcome was indeterminate.[286] The role of the delegation, too, was minimal. In the view of Markus Wolf, one of the officers of the congress, that role consisted for the most part of the "delegation conveying to the party chairman and his deputies the official greetings of the Central Committee of the CPSU."[287]

Fourth, the establishment of trust between the new party and the population was hampered by the stream of revelations about party corruption and the activities of the state security ministry.[288] Most East Germans had apparently adhered to the notion that the GDR party elite had been inured against the temptations of the perks and privileges enjoyed by the "new class" in other communist countries. Such comforting notions about austere lifestyles of the elite, however, were shattered starting in early December after the submission to the *Volkskammer* of a parliamentary committee's report investigating the party's abuse of power. Independent investigations also revealed the shadowy business activities of Schalk-Golodkowski's Coordinating Committee (Ko-Ko), including the plundering and sell-off of treasures from East German art and natural history museums. The damaging revelations extended to the involvement of the Stasi in sheltering West German terrorists, as well as training and financing terrorist activities abroad. The vast network of Stasi informers also began to be uncovered. At the same time, evidence came to light about systematic attempts made by state security personnel to destroy files, tapes, and videos that presumably contained incriminating evidence about Stasi activities, full-time agents, and

---

286 Interview with Zagladin.

287 Wolf, *In eigenem Auftrag*, p. 313.

288 The description of party corruption and Stasi activities follows Pond, *Beyond the Wall*, pp. 140-44.

collaborators. In response, also at the beginning of December, irate citizens began to occupy Stasi offices in order to prevent the burning and shredding of records.

Fifth, the repository of radicalization was irrevocably shifting to an amorphous Roundtable of social and political forces and to an even more amorphous, but ultimately more powerful population. Typically for the vagaries of revolution, a wide rift was opening between the two agents of radicalization. The Roundtable, which in addition to the purportedly "new" communist party and its vacillating allies of the "democratic bloc" included a colorful spectrum of social and political opposition groups – the Protestant and Catholic churches, human rights activists, peace advocates, feminists, and ecologists – stood firmly on the ground of building a *separate* and socialist East Germany; some of its members even expressed regret that the wall had come down because it hindered such a development.[289] The majority of the population, in contrast, was increasingly embracing the goal of *unification* which, in essence, meant introduction of the West German political, economic, and social system in East Germany.

In their attempt to construct a socialist utopia, it was not only the SED-PDS but also the more radical opposition democrats temporarily allied with it in the Roundtable that faced severe handicaps in their attempt to shape the destiny of a separate East Germany. The latter's main problems consisted in internal dissension, political ineffectiveness, and lack of administrative experience. Their common denominator had been opposition to the Honecker regime, but their social and professional backgrounds as well as their political and philosophical persuasions were extremely diverse.[290] The artists, writers, bards, pastors, and scientists that made up the opposition groups were, for the most part, only loosely organized. They subscribed to a wide range of ideas, including those expressed by Mahatma Gandhi, Catholic Latin American liberation theologists, Martin Niemöller and Dietrich Bonhoeffer of the Protestant anti-Nazi Confessing Church, American civil rights activists as well as the West German Greens and the "peace movement." Some of the groups shared a strong sense of "anti-politics," with an emphasis on *Kultur* and society rather than on the acquisition and management of power. Furthermore, in contrast to Poland and Czechoslovakia with their Lech Wałesa and Vaclav Havel, East Germany lacked a prominent anti-establishment figure who could have united the various currents of the opposition movement and given them purpose and direction. The Roundtable, then, acting in many ways as a second parliament, was

289 For instance, Friedrich Schorlemmer, one of the opposition leaders, had expressed the following view: "The coexistence of two political and social systems will create great problems. Therefore I would prefer that the wall, where there are no holes, remains a while longer"; quoted in Daniel Hamilton, *After the Revolution: The New Political Landscape in East Germany*, German Issues, No. 7 (Washington: American Institute for Contemporary German Studies, 1990), p. 12.

290 See Hamilton, *The New Political Landscape*, pp. 8-9.

bound to be yet one of those transitional institutions that tend to spring up in times of revolutionary upheaval but disappear as it progresses. Its most important achievement, perhaps, was the agreement to hold free elections in May 1990, later advanced to 18 March.

Given the inability of the SED-PDS to win the trust of the population and the ineffectiveness of the democratic opposition, the West German government and West German political parties became the most important driving force in East German internal affairs. A Hegelian approach or, in its material version, a Marxist view may help in understanding the ensuing process. Its objective nature – deteriorating East German political and economic conditions – was supplemented by a dialectic relationship between two subjective factors: the West German government's determination to maintain the momentum towards *unification* and its interest in a *stabilization* of conditions in East Germany. This necessitated reconciliation of seemingly contradictory purposes. (1) While unification implied abolition of the GDR, stabilization necessitated some degree of assistance; but that assistance should not serve to preserve what was, after all, still a communist regime without popular legitimacy. (2) The commitment to reunification had to be credible, but it should not precipitate a collapse of law, order, and administrative structures in the GDR.[291]

One of the main reasons for the West German government's interest in a modicum of stabilization lay in the unabated outflow of East Germans. In mid-December 1989, the Federal German government reported that, in the period from 1 January to 13 December 1989, a total of 324,776 East Germans had registered to resettle in West Germany.[292] In November, 133,429 *Übersiedler* had registered. In the period between 1 and 13 December, 24,143 East Germans had done so, that is, East Germans were still leaving the GDR at the rate of 2,000 a day – a rate that was maintained in January 1990.[293] This state of affairs caused problems for both the Kohl and the Modrow government. As for East Germany, given essentially the same composition of the emigrants in 1989 as in 1953 and 1961, the disruptive effects for the economy were considerable. But West Germany was negatively affected, too, since it was saddled not only with the administrative cost and effort of attempting to integrate the large influx of Germans from the GDR but also of the German *Aussiedler* from Eastern and South-eastern Europe (foremost from Romania) and the

291 The West German government's perceptions of conflicting policy preferences became evident in the government's preparations for Chancellor Kohl's visit to Dresden; see Wolfgang Schäuble, *Der Vertrag: Wie ich über die deutsche Einheit verhandelte*, with an introduction by Dirk Koch and Klaus Wirtgen (Stuttgart: Deutsche Verlags-Anstalt, 1991), pp. 21-22.

292 Figures of the Federal Republic's ministry of the interior, as quoted in *New York Times*, 16 December 1989.

293 Shortly before the building of the Berlin wall, East Germans were leaving the GDR at the rate of about 3,000 a day; for details about the earlier emigrations trends, see above, p. 105.

Soviet Union (the Volga Germans), expected to reach about 350,000 by the end of the year. As the chief West German manager of the difficult technicalities of unification has stated, Bonn was concerned that "the national problem could turn into a social problem."[294] There was, of course, a theoretical possibility of stopping the flow: the government could introduce a law on a separate West German citizenship in the Bundestag. From a practical perspective, however, this avenue toward the solution of the refugee problem was blocked. It could have been argued that such a step would be a violation of the constitution and that, to provide clarification and legitimacy to such a measure, a decision of the constitutional court would be required or a two-thirds majority in parliament to change the Basic Law. Whatever the legal implications of the government's intentions, the political controversies that would have been produced by the introduction of a new citizenship law would have been enormous, and even raising the issue would have transformed the flow of East Germans into a torrent.

The shift of political dynamics away from GDR party and government institutions to the West German government and East German popular movements was amply demonstrated by Genscher's and Kohl's visits to East Germany. On 16-17 December, the West German foreign minister had visited several East German cities, including his native Halle. His primary contacts there were with representatives of the democratic opposition, in particular with leaders of the Protestant Church, and with leaders of the liberal democratic bloc party, the LDPD, thereby heralding both the drift of the "democratic bloc" parties away from communist tutelage and the beginning of attempts by the more powerful parties in West Germany to build up corresponding party structures in the east. The most memorable event was Genscher's address in Halle's Market Church, which he had attended with his parents until he left the GDR in 1952. Politically the most important feature was the warm and at times exuberant reception he received in the East German cities and towns he visited.[295] Kohl's visit to Dresden on 19 December confirmed the pattern of close interaction between the West German government and the East German population. Like his foreign minister, the West German chancellor was enthusiastically greeted by tens of thousands of East Germans, waving black-red-and-gold flags without the communist regime's hammer-and-sickle emblem. The green-and-white flag of the former state of Saxony was also in evidence, a harbinger of yet another development to come: the abolition of the GDR's administrative districts, modeled along Soviet oblasts, and the reconstitution of the *Länder* structure in East Germany.[296]

---

294 Schäuble, *Der Vertrag*, p. 22.

295 Genscher, *Erinnerungen*, pp. 697-702.

296 Modrow, in retrospect, has acknowledged that there was only "a small number of people who courageously demanded a continuation of the process of democratization and of the existence of

The degree to which East Germany, at any time in the past, had been dependent on West Germany is still debatable. For the most part, there had been a gap between Soviet perceptions and reality, with the imperial center exaggerating that dependence. There can be little doubt, however, that the gap had closed by the end of 1989.[297] This was dramatically underlined by Kohl's talks with Modrow on 19 December in Dresden. The almost complete exchange of the GDR's dependence on the Soviet Union for that on West Germany was palpable in Modrow's demeanor. As described by Teltschik, the East German prime minister opened the talks between the two delegations, reading at a hectic pace from a typewritten text, his "face pale and contorted, his fuzzy hair in a mess. He avoids eye contact, hardly shows any emotion ... and doesn't smile." He was visibly concerned about the accelerated drift towards German unification and domestic instability in the GDR and complained about West German interference in East German internal affairs.[298] The central East German demand in the negotiations was the request for West German financial assistance in the amount of DM 15 billion for the year 1990. Modrow justified this demand not only by pointing to the acute problems caused by the opening of the borders, the *de facto* introduction of the West German mark as a second currency in the GDR, and the need to finance the modernization of East German industry and agriculture. He also regarded it as just compensation for the reparations that the GDR had paid to the Soviet Union on behalf of all of Germany.[299] Kohl rejected the – in his view – unacceptably high sum of the aid request with the argument that the "framework conditions" for the extension of large-scale assistance had to be created first. He did, however, agree to the creation of a joint hard currency fund in the amount of DM 2 billion for the purpose of facilitating travel between the two parts of Germany; to increase the credit line under the European Recovery Program by DM 2 billion; to raise the credit ceiling for East German exports to West Germany from DM 1.5 to 6 billion; and to elevate the amount of compensation for postal charges in intra-German exchanges from DM 100 to 300 million. Following the established practice

---

the GDR," but that a "large majority wanted the unification of the two German states"; Modrow, *Aufbruch und Ende*, p. 100.

297 For details about the deteriorating economic conditions in the GDR and the degree of East Germany's dependency on West Germany, see above, section 3 of the present chapter.

298 Teltschik, *329 Tage*, p. 88; similarly Kohl, *Ich wollte Deutschlands Einheit*, p. 215.

299 According to internationally recognized estimates, Modrow wrote in his memoirs, the GDR had paid reparations in the amount of DM 99.1 billion, the Federal Republic only DM 21 billion. Furthermore, West Germany had benefitted from the Marshall Plan; Modrow, *Aufbruch und Ende*, p. 98. Modrow as well as Kohl and Teltschik also report the West German chancellor's objection to the use of the term *Lastenausgleich*, or burden sharing. The term was used in West Germany for compensating claimants in that part of the country who had suffered economic losses in the Second World War, including those who had lost properties in the east. The term implied a moral obligation to pay damages. Kohl rejected such an implication and suggested instead the term *Solidarbeitrag*, or solidarity contribution.

of such generosity, political conditions had to be met by the GDR. These included further commitments by the Modrow government to liberal and market-oriented reforms; a change in the exchange rate of the East German and the West German mark to reflect more closely their market value; in preparation of the *Vertragsgemeinschaft,* the creation of a plethora of joint commissions with the purpose of synchronizing and harmonizing communications, environmental, legal, and law enforcement activities; and finally, as a symbolic gesture, the opening of the Brandenburg Gate as an exit point for pedestrians.[300]

Kohl's visit to Dresden and his talks with Modrow created yet another of the many paradoxes described here. The wide-spread popular support for German unity and the weakness of the Modrow government amounted to a revelation for the West German chancellor that significantly influenced his thinking.[301] It reinforced his disinclination to support a government in East Berlin that had not been legitimized by free elections and persuaded him to push more vigorously and directly for German unification than before. The joint declaration signed in Dresden on the establishment of a *Vertragsgemeinschaft* and good-neighborly relations between the two states as part of a "new European architecture" was already obsolete when it was signed.[302] Modrow later was to complain bitterly, but accurately that Kohl reneged on almost all of the financial commitments; that "as early as January, [the chancellor] no longer had any interest in negotiations about a *Vertragsgemeinschaft*"; that for him "I soon became no longer a responsible partner for talks"; and that, based on the enthusiastic popular reception he had experienced in Dresden, he abandoned the policy of gradualism and decided on "unification in quick step."[303] Kohl, however, still envisaged a five-year time frame in which unification could be achieved *if* the Soviet Union consented to it. He was still conscious of the fact that the "key to German unity" lay in the Kremlin.[304] That key was to be handed to him in February 1990. The reasons for this fundamental change in Soviet policy lay not only in the loss of control over events in

300 Kohl, *Ich wollte Deutschlands Einheit*, pp. 215-16; Teltschik, *329 Tage*, pp. 89-90; and press reports; for the text of the joint declaration on the talks between Kohl and Modrow, see "Gemeinsame Mitteilung über die Gespräche des Bundeskanzlers mit dem Ministerpräsidenten der DDR in Dresden," Press and Information Office of the Federal Government, *Bulletin*, No. 148, 20 December 1989, pp. 1249-52.

301 In his memoirs, Kohl called it a *Schlüsselerlebnis*, or key experience, on the road to national unity; Kohl, *Ich wollte Deutschlands Einheit*, p. 213.

302 "Gemeinsame Mitteilung," p. 1249.

303 Modrow, *Aufbruch und Ende*, pp. 99-100.

304 Interview with Teltschik. On 21 December Mitterrand visited East Berlin. The French president's ambiguity about the purpose of the visit was described *supra*, in the context of his talks with Gorbachev on 6 December. The unfolding events had made the visit even more problematic. Since there was neither a French attempt nor indeed the possibility for France to stabilize the Modrow government and delay German unification, there is no point here to dwell on the visit.

the GDR but in the close interaction of the accelerating collapse of the center's empire in Eastern Europe – the external empire – with the increasing likelihood of a disintegration of the *internal* empire, that is, of the Soviet Union itself. That interaction occurred, as mentioned, in conditions of a radicalization of Soviet domestic politics.

Yielding the Key to German Unity

The radicalization of Soviet domestic politics in the winter of 1989 and 1990 – a winter of discontent – occurred at four different levels: the top political leadership; the USSR Congress of People's Deputies and the Supreme Soviet; the communist party; and among public opinion in Moscow, Leningrad, and in other cities and parts of the country. The move towards more radical reform included economic components but its primary rationale was *political*. As a result, the gap between political liberalization and economic restructuring became wider and domestic political conflicts more acute. These conflicts were exacerbated by nationality conflicts and independence movements in the Baltic states and Azerbaijan.

The form which the new dynamics took centered on the question as to whether the Soviet Union should and, indeed, could achieve a transition from a totalitarian one-party state to a pluralist democracy; from a system dominated by a leader appointed by a party holding the monopoly of power to one with a popularly elected president; from a unitary, centralized state to a genuine federation with power allocated to the union republics; from a command economy and state ownership to private property and the market; from the privileged role of the military in politics and society and resource allocation favoring the military-industrial complex to civilian control of the armed forces and defense conversion; and from arbitrary and voluntarist party rule to a system based on the rule of law. The process, as described earlier, had been set in motion by Gorbachev's campaign for glasnost after the Chernobyl disaster in April 1986. It continued at the January 1987 Central Committee plenum and the June 1988 Party conference, with their emphasis on democratization, the October 1988 emasculation of the central party apparatus and the March 1989 elections to the First Congress of People's Deputies. The course of action to be decided by Gorbachev and his advisors in 1990 was whether he should (1) take the lead in this historic change and replace his power and authority derived from the communist party by popular legitimacy, expunge article 6 from the Soviet constitution that enshrined the CPSU's monopoly of power, force a split of the party, lead a new radical reform-socialist or social-democratic movement and, with its backing, contest free elections for the presidency, (2) stand aloof from party politics and popular elections and shift the center of gravity to an executive presidency elected by the Congress of People's

Deputies or (3) retain his office of General Secretary of the CPSU and continue to work for reform within the party and, through it, in the country.

"What on earth should I do?," Gorbachev asked Yakovlev in exasperation on 26-27 January, "Azerbaijan and Lithuania, [right-wing] radicals, on the one hand, and social democrats, on the other. The blows are becoming ever more painful. The economy is adrift. The people are at the end of their rope."[305] Yakovlev replied that the time for decisive action had come and that Gorbachev should take charge of a comprehensive reform effort in political, economic, and nationality affairs.[306] This was essentially the course of action favored by many participants at the founding conference of the Democratic Platform of the CPSU, held on 20-21 January, with 405 party members from 78 cities attending, including the leaders of the Interregional Group from the Congress of People's Deputies; representatives of strike committees from mining areas; Yakovlev and Yeltsin; presidential advisor Shakhnazarov; political scientist Fyodor Burlatsky; sociologist Tatyana Zaslyavskaya; economists Nikolai Shmelev and Gavril Popov; historian Yuri Afanasiev; legal scholar and (later Leningrad mayor) Anatoli Sobchak; and the future leader of Russia's Democratic Party, Nikolai Travkin.[307] In the Politburo meeting of 29 January, the CC secretary for economic administration Nikolai Slyunkov proposed reform measures along the lines of Stanislav Shatalin's plan for the radical reconstruction of the Soviet economy.[308] However, as on almost any other question of domestic politics and economic affairs, Gorbachev adopted a middle course of action.

In the political domain, prior to a crucial Central Committee meeting, first scheduled for the end of January and then held on 6 February, Gorbachev endorsed the abolition of article 6; objected to the postponement of a party congress to be held in July 1990 for the adoption of a new party program; replaced several regional party bosses; met with a group of militant miners; and permitted the largest-ever rally to take place in the Soviet Union on the day before the CC plenum in the large square around Hotel Moskva, with more than 200,000 people demonstrating for reform. However, he rejected the idea that a new executive president be elected by direct popular elections, opting instead for elections to that office by the *Congress of People's Deputies*. In the economic realm, he instructed Prime Minister Ryzhkov to

305 Chernyaev, *Shest' let s Gorbachevym*, p. 330. "What on earth should I do?" Literally, Gorbachev had asked: "What should I do? What should I do?"

306 Ibid.

307 Brown, *The Gorbachev Factor*, p. 404; on the organization and composition of the conference, see Matlock, *Autopsy of an Empire*, pp. 306-7.

308 Chernyaev, *Shest' let s Gorbachevym*, p. 333.

supplement essentially traditional government reform measures by some "elements" of Slyunkov's reform program.[309]

The sense of malaise and apparent intractability of mounting problems in the winter of discontent was deepened by the nationality problem. In Azerbaijan, the National Front, legalized by party secretary Abdul Rakhman Vezirov a few months earlier, took advantage of the Nagorny Karabakh issue to gain a mass following and began to force out communist officials in several cities.[310] On 13 January, in a repetition of the massacres that had taken place in the industrial city of Sumgait two years earlier, mobs attacked apartment houses in which Armenian families were living and killed the occupants. Women and children were thrown from upper-story windows to their death on the pavement below. The National Front took control of key points in Baku and, in effect, began to seize control of the republic. On 15 January, Moscow ordered troops into the area and, starting on the night of 19 January, entered Baku and used force to restore both law and order and the communist party to power, arresting the leaders of the National Front and dissolving informal organizations. The intervention, however, neither succeeded in suppressing the drive for independence in Azerbaijan nor did it stifle unrest in its Nakhichevan enclave in Armenia or mitigate the conflict between the two Transcaucasian republics. Civil unrest and independence movements also continued in neighboring Georgia.

The problem in the Baltic states could not be defused in the same manner, not even temporarily: in contrast to the violence in Azerbaijan, the mass demonstrations in the Baltic states were peaceful, providing no obvious pretext for military intervention. Its moral and legal basis would have been extremely shaky because of the secret protocols attached to the 1939 Hitler-Stalin pact and the accession of the Baltic states to the Soviet Union in 1940 under duress. The United States had never recognized their incorporation in the USSR. Public opinion in that country and in Western Europe might look with equanimity upon the use of force against "uncivilized" Moslem nationalists in the distant Transcaucasus but certainly not in a Western-oriented part of Europe. However, a decision in Moscow about what, if anything, to do about the Baltic problem had to be taken in the winter of discontent

309 Ibid. It is difficult to say, of course, what the outcome of popular elections for a presidential contender campaigning on a radical reformist platform would have been. At that crucial juncture of Soviet history, Gorbachev's popularity was on the decline, but the argument can be made that this was due primarily to perceptions of his indecisiveness. According to polls conducted by the reputable VTsIOM polling organization, it was not until May 1990 that Yeltsin, his likely main competitor, moved ahead of him in the popular standing; *Reitingi Borisa El'tsina i Mikhaila Gorbacheva po 10-bal'noi shkale* (Moscow: VTsIOM, 1993); as quoted by Brown, *The Gorbachev Factor*, p. 203.

310 This summary of the events in Azerbaijan follows the account by Matlock, *Autopsy of an Empire*, pp. 301-4.

after the Lithuanian CP had declared its independence. Given the monolithic, vertical structure of both the Soviet Union and the CPSU, that is, the lack of a genuine federalism in the state and the party, such a declaration by a republican CP was tantamount to a declaration of independence of the country. This was clearly recognized by the center.

On 3 January Vadim Medvedev went to Vilnius to prepare a three-day visit, with Gorbachev and Yuri Maslyukov at the head of a 40-member CC delegation. Their purpose was to persuade the Lithuanian CP and to reverse its secession from the CPSU and to retract its demands for Lithuanian independence. The Soviet party chief's mission to Vilnius from 11 to 13 January predictably failed to convince the Lithuanians that their future would be better served by staying in the union – a failure made even more complete by his utter incomprehension of the very essence of nationalism. "Gorbachev," as Chernyaev observed, "deep down could not reconcile himself to a secession of the Baltic states [from the union]. He sincerely believed that in particular, the population of the [Baltic] republics would suffer. He was therefore convinced that extremists and separatists had turned the people's heads."[311] In his memoirs, Gorbachev still betrays utter incomprehension of Baltic nationalism, repeating the same arguments he had made in Vilnius. He scornfully dismisses the Balts' economic grievances, saying that, in comparison to the rest of the Soviet Union, the superior labor productivity of the Baltic states had been made possible by "immense investments from the union budget" and by "qualified specialists and workers from Russia and other union republics," and that the three republics' economic development had been assisted by "the delivery of fuel and energy free of charge [sic]."[312] Against the background of a general economic crisis in the Soviet Union and with the people of the Baltic countries comparing their economic fortunes with that of the neighboring Finns and Swedes, the appeals to economic rationality remained unconvincing. The drive for Baltic independence thus remained and thereby the threat to the existence of the Soviet internal empire.

On 22 March, this threat was considered serious enough for the Politburo to discuss the Lithuanian problem and to support a plan by Gen. Valentin Varennikov that closely resembled the script for the Warsaw Pact's intervention in Czechoslovakia: appeals for help by pro-Soviet factions, invasion of Lithuania by three regiments, isolation of the legally elected leadership in Vilnius, and the creation of a presidential regime with emergency powers. For reasons that are still unclear, the apparent Politburo consensus on the use of force ("Yakovlev and Medvedev said

---

311 Chernyaev, *Shest' let s Gorbachevym*, p. 339.
312 Gorbachev, *Zhizn'*, Vol. 1, p. 511.

nothing") failed to be implemented, and military intervention as a means for bringing the Baltic states to heel was temporarily replaced by severe economic pressure.[313]

To return to the center's problem of external empire, the acceptance of German unification, was – figuratively speaking – squeezed in between the use of force in Baku and contemplation of the use of force in Vilnius and between pressures for more radical democratic political and economic reform and reinstitution of the old methods to maintain Soviet power. It would be an exaggeration to say that the German problem had become a side issue, but it certainly was not on top of the Soviet leaders' agenda in the winter of discontent. Nevertheless, on 26 January, Gorbachev convened a small circle of top decision makers in his Central Committee office to discuss it. In addition to the Soviet party chief and Chernyaev, his personal aide on foreign policy, the participants included Prime Minister Ryzhkov; Foreign Minister Shevardnadze; Politburo international affairs *kurator* Yakovlev; KGB chief Kryuchkov; arms control adviser to Gorbachev and former chief of staff Akhromeev; ID head Falin; personal aide to Gorbachev for relations with the socialist countries Shakhnazarov; and ID deputy head Fyodorov, responsible for these countries at the ID. The discussion, "tough" at times, lasted four hours and a "number of most important decisions were adopted."[314]

One of the questions to be decided was the problem as to who, in the conditions of an accelerated drive towards German unity, should be the Soviet leadership's main addressee for the management of the problem, East Germany or West Germany; if the former, who in that country – the Modrow government, Gysi's PDS, or the Roundtable?; if the latter, Chancellor Kohl and the ruling coalition of CDU/CSU and FDP, or the opposition SPD? Chernyaev was the first to speak, emphasizing that the Soviet Union no longer had any influence or political forces in the GDR on which it

---

313 Chernyaev, *Shest' let s Gorbachevym*, p. 337. Chernyaev was present at the Politburo meeting. Soviet ground forces commander Varennikov can be considered as one of the most uncompromising generals in favor of the use of force in order to maintain the internal empire. He was in charge in January 1991 when an attempt was made to overthrow the legitimately elected Lithuanian leaders and institutions. On that occasion, soldiers fired on demonstrators at the Vilnius television tower. At least fourteen people were killed and hundreds injured: they were shot, beaten, or crushed under tank treads. Varennikov was also solidly behind the August 1991 coup attempt, again advocating the use of force to dislodge Yeltsin from the White House; see Brian Taylor, "The Soviet Military and the Disintegration of the USSR," paper presented in the Olin Critical Issues Series, The Collapse of the Soviet Union, Harvard University, 11 February 1997.

314 Alexander Galkin and Anatoli Chernyaev, "Pravdu i tol'ko pravdu. Razmyshleniia po povodu vospominanii," *Svobodnaia mysl,* No. 3 (1994), p. 26; Chernyaev, *Shest' let s Gorbachevym*, p. 346; interviews with Chernyaev and Shakhnazarov. In his memoirs, Falin (*Erinnerungen*, p. 489) lists Yazov as one of the participants, but in his interviews with this author Chernyaev has emphatically denied that this is correct. Shakhnazarov (*Tsena svobody*, p. 125) lists Ivashko (presumably Vladimir Ivashko, the party chief in Ukraine), as one of the participants, but this, too, appears to be incorrect. As usual, the written account and later oral clarifications by Chernyaev are more reliable.

could count. Thus, *West Germany* should be the main addressee of Soviet policy. And in that country, he continued, one should deal with the chancellor but not with the opposition. His rationale was that the social democrats were politicizing and using the issue in their electoral campaign. Kohl, on the other hand, was aiming at German unification as part of a European process, was in close association with his NATO partners and more reliable in his personal relations with Gorbachev. He even went as far as arguing against inviting Modrow, the East German prime minister, for a visit to Moscow, let alone SED party chief Gysi, the head of a "party that *de facto* no longer exists and that has no future."[315] Falin, Fyodorov, Yakovlev, and Shakhnazarov disagreed and opted for political contacts and cooperation with the SPD. Shevardnadze and Ryzhkov (with the reservation of "let's not give everything to Kohl") in essence supported Chernyaev. Kryuchkov was prepared to align himself with the opinion of the majority but agreed that the state structures of the GDR were dissolving and that there was no one on whom the Soviet Union could base its policies.

An important decision adopted at the meeting, in accordance with a corresponding proposal by Chernyaev, was the creation of a negotiation framework of six countries, comprising the two Germanys and the four occupation powers with special rights and responsibilities in Germany: the Soviet Union, the United States, Britain, and France. A final decision was to have Akhromeev draw up plans for the withdrawal of troops from Germany.

Gorbachev summarized the results of the meeting as follows:

- To form a Group of Six.
- To orient policies toward Kohl but not to ignore the SPD.
- To invite Modrow and Gysi.
- To maintain close contact with London and Paris.
- To prepare the withdrawal of forces from the GDR.[316]

In the context of decision-making theory at the micro-level and searching for an understanding of the collapse of empire at the macro-level of analysis, three aspects of the meeting deserve emphasis. First, the decisions that, in essence, amounted to the consent to German unification were made by an *ad hoc* committee, not by one of the established institutions, such as the Politburo or the Defense Council. Second, as corroboration of the first point and as an indication of the severe internal crisis and the preeminence of domestic politics over foreign policy, two Politburo meetings held at about that time did *not* address the German problem: the only agenda item of the PB meeting of 22 January was the draft of a new CPSU platform, and the two

---

315 Chernyaev, *Shest' let s Gorbachevym*, p. 346.

316 Ibid., p. 347. Contrary to the assertion by Zelikow and Rice, *Germany Unified*, p. 163, the issue of united Germany's membership in NATO does not appear to have been discussed.

most important items of the PB session of 29 January were the precarious state finances and the creation of a presidential office.[317] Third, one of the institutions that, in the era of the dominance of the ideological and imperial paradigm, would have been represented first and foremost, was missing altogether at the meeting: the defense ministry. There has been controversy as to whether the *ad hoc* group, or any other group, was institutionalized to deal with the German crisis. Falin unambiguously states that, as early as at the time of the opening of the Berlin wall, an executive, emergency or crisis committee (*Krisenstab*) had been "formed upon my initiative."[318] He claims that the following leaders participated in its first meeting: Gorbachev, Shevardnadze, Yakovlev, Chernyaev, Shakhnazarov, Kryuchkov, *and* Defense Minister Yazov. He also states that the committee met only once more in its entirety. However, no date is given for the first or any subsequent meeting, and it is likely that the ID chief got confused here. In a stinging rebuttal of Falin's portrayal, Chernyaev denies ("does not remember") the existence of such a *Krisenstab* and correctly states that Gorbachev's memoirs contain no reference to it.[319]

What is most likely behind the controversy over the emergency committee is, to put it in precise political science terminology, sour grapes. The decisions adopted by the *ad hoc* committee and subsequent decisions on the German problem were a direct challenge to the once influential *germanisty* and the once so powerful International Department of the Central Committee. Falin happened to be an exponent of both. They contradicted the interests and advice of ID first deputy head Fyodorov, another specialist in German affairs, who was untiring in his effort to get a campaign under way in the Soviet Union and abroad against German unification[320] and who, in the *ad hoc* meeting, still declared: "*No one in the Federal Republic wants reunification.*"[321] They also ran counter to the positions adopted by Bondarenko, the chief of the MFA's Third Department, and Gorinovich, the head of the Fourth Department (restructured to deal with the dwindling number of socialist countries), all of whose caution and conservatism was disregarded by Gorbachev and Shevardnadze.[322] "It was exasperating," Falin later complained bitterly, "to see how Gorbachev would express his definitive agreement with a particular issue in my presence while his foreign

317 Ibid., pp. 327 and 332.

318 Falin, *Politische Erinnerungen*, p. 489.

319 Galkin and Chernyaev, "Pravdu i tol'ko pravdu," p. 25. The fact that Gorbachev's memoirs contain no reference to a crisis committee, however, is not surprising since they draw heavily on Chernyaev's *Shest' let s Gorbachevym*.

320 Interview with Grigoriev.

321 Chernyaev, *Shest' let s Gorbachevym*, p. 346.

322 Interviews with Kvitsinsky and Tarasenko.

minister would do exactly the opposite, without Gorbachev putting him into place."[323]

Gorbachev's acceptance of German unification became a matter of international public record four days after the *ad hoc* meeting, when Modrow visited Moscow, and was confirmed in the Soviet leader's talks with Baker on 9 February, and Kohl and Genscher on 10 and 11 February. Both privately and publicly, Gorbachev no longer referred to the GDR as the Soviet Union's strategic ally and reliable member of the Warsaw Pact to which no harm would be done. That subject was irrevocably closed. In private conversation with Modrow, Gorbachev instead endorsed the East German government's hastily construed plan to lead from a treaty on cooperation and good neighborliness between the two German states to a confederation and ultimately to a unified federal state.[324] Only some faint echoes of the previous hard-line approach reverberated in the meeting. He would not permit Kohl to destabilize the situation in the GDR. Apart from that, the conversation had a more philosophical – typically Gorbachevian – rather than practical content. "Unfortunately," Modrow complained in retrospect, "Gorbachev is not the kind of man who would delve deeply into economic problems. In our consultations on economic problems he always avoided this issue and transferred it to Ryzhkov. But in doing so, he didn't in the least commit himself and failed to provide instructions that Ryzhkov would have to carry out."[325] As the talks underlined, his endorsement of the Modrow plan was at least in part predicated on the idea that the SPD would support it.[326] Whereas this notion was not far-fetched, Gorbachev still harbored illusions about the 18 March elections, assuming that the East Germans would vote for the continued existence of the GDR.[327]

Publicly, Gorbachev went on record after the meeting with the acknowledgment that pressure was building up for German reunification: "*Time itself is having an impact on the process and lending dynamism to it.*"[328] Asked about the question of German reunification by an East German television reporter, Gorbachev replied:

> *Basically, no one casts any doubt upon it.* However, the development of events in the world, in the German Democratic Republic, and in the Soviet Union requires profound assessment and an analytical approach to

---

323 Falin, *Politische Erinnerungen*, p. 491.

324 Modrow, *Aufbruch und Ende*, pp. 119-23. In addition to Gorbachev, the Soviet participants in the meeting were Ryzhkov, Shevardnadze, and Falin.

325 Ibid. Modrow, in this context, specifically mentioned the problem of Soviet oil deliveries to the GDR. Gorbachev evaded the issue.

326 Modrow confirmed this in the interview series conducted by Ekkehard Kuhn in 1993, *id.*, *Gorbatschow und die deutsche Einheit*, p. 101.

327 Ibid.

328 Francis, X. Clines, "Gorbachev Sees a German Union But Warns of 'Chaos of Nihilism,'" *New York Times*, 31 January 1990.

a solution of an issue which is an important aspect of European and world politics.

It was "essential," however, "to act responsibly and not seek a solution to this important issue in the streets." He elaborated on that point and warned that the "chaos of nihilism, the *diktat* of the crowd" remained dangerous obstacles to the East European processes of democratization. He also warned of the danger of "neo-Nazi excesses" in the GDR. "Attempts by radical right-wing forces to incite neo-Nazi attitudes in the republic are among the most dangerous obstacles" to increasing democratization, he thought. Finally, he invoked "Four Power obligations" for Germany.[329]

Gorbachev's remarks on 30 January were correctly interpreted in West Germany as removing Soviet objections as the single most important impediment to reunification. Probably in reaction to this, Shevardnadze, in an interview with Soviet reporters, attempted to tone done the repercussions of the Gorbachev statements and again to slow down the momentum towards reunification, saying that "It is not the idea of reunification itself but the revival of the sinister shadows of the past associated with it as well as a possible growth of militarism that are met with apprehension in the world."[330] "All peoples", he said, "especially those of the Soviet Union, must have a guarantee that the war threat will never come from German soil." How was this to be achieved? A "*European-wide referendum with the participation of the United States and Canada*" should be held, he suggested, or at least matters should be decided "by broad discussion in the parliaments".[331] It is difficult to say why Shevardnadze tabled the referendum proposal. Not only was such an idea hardly workable, but it was sure to be rejected, first and foremost by the West German government.

The consent in principle to German unification immediately raised the problem of a unified Germany's international status. Shortly after his return from Moscow, at a press conference in East Berlin, Modrow presented some guidelines. Alluding to the image of a common European house, Modrow stated that his plan was "founded on the idea that already in the stage of confederation, both German states will step by step *detach themselves from their alliance obligations toward third countries and attain a state of military neutrality.*" He later reiterated that several conditions had to be met on the way to unity, including "maintenance of the interests and rights" of the Four Powers in both Germanys and "*military neutrality of both the GDR and the FRG.*"[332] Modrow's remarks, coming so soon after his Moscow visit, implied that the

---

329 Ibid.

330 "Po povodu pozitsii pravitel'stva GDR," *Pravda*, 3 February 1990.

331 Ibid. (italics mine).

332 "Hans Modrow unterbreitet Konzept 'Für Deutschland, einig Vaterland,'" *Neues Deutschland*, 2 February 1990.

idea of a neutral Germany had been discussed with and approved by the Soviet leadership.[333]

Soviet acceptance of German unification formed the basis of discussion in the meetings between Gorbachev, Shevardnadze, and Baker on 8-9 February.[334] Shevardnadze regretted that unification was arriving faster than anyone had expected. In fact, it was already a fait accompli: "I am afraid that's the case, and I'm not sure of any way to avoid it." He nevertheless supported the Modrow plan for the process to take place gradually and in distinct phases. In accordance with his pessimistic view of both history and world affairs (and perhaps to buttress his ideas for Four Power negotiations, a peace treaty, a European-wide referendum, or CSCE involvement, whatever the West would accept) he expressed worries about domestic developments in Germany. The neo-Nazis might gain power. The right-wing *Republikaner* were a serious force in the country and might receive as much as 20 percent of the vote, he thought. In *his* talks with Baker, Gorbachev adopted a much more unconcerned and cooperative stance than his foreign minister. "There is nothing terrifying in the prospect of a unified Germany," he said. He knew that some countries, such as France and Britain, were concerned about who would be the major player in Europe. But this was not a Soviet or an American problem: "We are big countries and have our own weight." He also referred to a "mosaic" of opinion in West Germany about unification. Some wanted confederation; others wanted a federation. Opinion was also divided on NATO membership, some supported it; others favored neutralism; yet others preferred a confederation wherein both countries would retain their alliance memberships until the current alliances were replaced by new CSCE structures.

Soviet acceptance of German unification as a fait accompli also posed the problem as to the relationship between its internal and external aspects. Two interconnections had to be addressed, one concerning the West German constitutional provisions for such a contingency, the other the question as to which of the two aspects should be decided first. On the first issue, German unity could be achieved on the basis of two constitutional provisions. Article 23 of the Basic Law provided for accession, that is, there would be no necessity for constitutional revision. The existing West German political and socio-economic system would simply be

---

333 Modrow confirmed this in the interview series conducted by Ekkehard Kuhn in 1993, *id.*, *Gorbatschow und die deutsche Einheit*, p. 101. The issue of German neutrality, or neutralization, versus membership of a united Germany in NATO will be discussed in the next section.

334 The account of the meetings between Gorbachev, Shevardnadze, and Baker is based on the American memcons of the talks, as summarized by Zelikow and Rice, *Germany Unified*, pp. 179-85. Note taker was Dennis Ross. Confirmation of several points was provided also by Ambassador Jack Matlock, who was present at the talks, in conversation with this author on 10 February 1997 in Cambridge, Mass.

extended to East Germany. A West Germany writ large would be created. Unification in accordance with article 146, on the other hand, necessitated convocation of a new constitutional assembly and the adoption of a new constitution by referendum; this would conceivably have given East Germany and, by extension, the Soviet Union a chance to influence the direction and outcome of the process.[335] On the second issue, the question to be decided was whether the internal or the external aspects of German unification should take precedence, or whether both should be resolved simultaneously. Falin's position and that of his conservative fellow Germanists in the ID and the MFA was unambiguous on both issues. That position, as expressed by the former, was: "Unification – yes, *Anschluß* – no. Only the socio-economic status of the unified Germany could and should be determined by the Germans. The external, that is, the military-political conditions of unification were to be decided by the Four Powers together with the two German states *before the FRG and the GDR were joined*."[336] Furthermore, in Falin's view, "the Four Plus Two formula reflected the correct priorities. Securing European peace had to come first; once a satisfactory solution was attained on this aspect, solution of the other issue would follow promptly."[337]

In retrospect, the emergence and adoption of the Two Plus Four formula has acquired an almost mythical quality. In the Western context, notably among American officials involved in the management of the international aspects of German unification, it has been portrayed as an example of brilliant statecraft that originated in the State Department.[338] Chernyaev has minimized its importance. In an article co-authored with German expert Alexander Galkin, and in reference to the 26 January *ad hoc* meeting, he states that *he* had been the first to advance this proposal, but that Baker, on many occasions, was to say that the Americans had developed it.[339] In Russian or post-Soviet controversies over the collapse of the Soviet empire and the loss of East Germany, this question has also become a bone of contention, pulled in different directions by supporters and critics of Gorbachev.[340] Falin, for instance, has

---

335 The exact wording of article 23 is that "For the time being, the Basic Law shall apply in the territory of the Länder. ... In other parts of Germany it shall be put into force upon their accession." Article 146 provides: "The Basic Law shall cease to be in force on the day on which a constitution adopted by a free decision of the German people comes into force"; *Grundgesetz der Bundesrepublik Deutschland* (Bonn: Presse- und Informationsamt der Bundesregierung, 1987).

336 Falin, *Politische Erinnerungen*, p. 490 (italics mine).

337 Ibid., p. 491.

338 One does get a strong sense of this, for instance, in Zelikow and Rice, *Germany Unified*, pp. 167-68. The authors credit Secreatry of State Baker's advisers Dennis Ross and Robert Zoellick with having invented the Two Plus Four formula.

339 Galkin and Chernyaev, "Pravdu i tol'ko pravdu," p. 26.

340 This controversy is most apparent in Falin, *Politische Erinnerungen*, pp. 491-92, and Galkin and Chernyaev, "Pravdu i tol'ko pravdu," pp. 26-27.

vehemently attacked both Gorbachev and Shevardnadze for mismanaging the issue, conveying the notion that it had not all been resolved as late as June 1990. Shevardnadze, according to Falin, had returned from the foreign ministers' meeting of the Six in East Berlin, "acting like a *dzhigit* [daring horseman], sitting high on a white horse." He appeared exceedingly confident and caused everyone's hopes to be rekindled. Chernyaev prepared a press release in the president's name, in which the significance of the negotiations as a whole and of the Four Plus Two formula in particular was to be proclaimed. He called Shevardnadze, read the text to him, and the minister approved, except for a "slight 'specification'": the *Two Plus Four* formula was to be preferred. Chernyaev was outraged, not least because Gorbachev had made it absolutely clear that only the Four Plus Two formula was acceptable. The Soviet foreign minister justified this change by saying that "Genscher really pleaded for it, and Genscher is a good person." Nevertheless, despite Chernyaev's purported intervention, the Two Plus Four formula "came into effect" and the Soviet Union, as a result, maneuvered itself into a "dead end."[341] What, then, given the apparent sensitivity of the matter, is its significance?

Chernyaev has reduced apparent complexities to their simple essence: "The important thing was that it should be possible quickly to design a successful mechanism that, on the one hand, would grant the Germans the right to select the path to unification by themselves and, on the other, give the USSR, USA, England, and France a chance to realize their right to advance the interests of the international community and their own in the process of German unification."[342] As for Falin's portrayal of the alleged haphazard and unprofessional reversal of the sequence of the numbers in response to Genscher's pleas, Chernyaev has scathingly dismissed it as a complete fabrication.[343] "[First], no one took any decision on this question. And it would have been strange if someone had. Second, the division of the Six into two groups was of a spontaneous character. Some used the first variant of the 'sum,' others – the second. Each, of course, with a sub-text." Furthermore, he (Chernyaev) "could not have been 'outraged' by the transformation of the Two Plus Four formula because [I] was always indifferent to the sequence of letters, considering that by itself the sequence could have no real influence on the course of events." As for Gorbachev, he too "did not pay any particular attention to the sequence of the numbers. When he mentioned the formula, he would use it either way." As reflected in his talks with Chancellor Kohl in Moscow on 10 February (see below), "this corresponded with his position of principle."[344] Not quite, perhaps. Gorbachev

---

341 Falin, *Politische Erinnerungen*, pp. 491-92.

342 Galkin and Chernyaev, "Pravdu, i tol'lko pravdu," p. 26.

343 Interview with Chernyaev.

344 Galkin and Chernyaev, "Pravdu, i tol'lko pravdu," pp. 26-27.

initially did prefer the Two Plus Four sequence. Thus, in his talks with Baker, according to the American record, Gorbachev had asked: "I say Four Plus Two; you say Two Plus Four. How do you look at this formula?", to which Baker had replied: "Two Plus Four is a better way."[345]

The Soviet consent to German unification occurred most authoritatively and unequivocally during Chancellor Kohl's visit to Moscow on 10-11 February. Eight days earlier, the West German chancellor had finally received a long-awaited letter from the Soviet party leader with the invitation. Upon arrival at Moscow's Vnukovo airport, the chancellor received another letter, this one from Secretary of State Baker, summarizing the content of his talks with the Soviet leaders.[346] When the talks began, therefore, Kohl was well briefed on the new direction of Gorbachev's thinking, but uncertain whether it would be confirmed in *his* talks with the Soviet leader. The initial welcome accorded to Kohl by Gorbachev in the latter's Kremlin office (in the presence of personal assistants Teltschik and Chernyaev and the interpreters) was cool, in the German chancellor's recollection, and Gorbachev appeared deeply pensive. Kohl assured Gorbachev of the German people's empathy with and support for the latter's reform efforts and, in response to a presentation by the general secretary of the problems encountered with perestroika, reiterated that the West German government was prepared, as far as possible, to expand economic relations with the GDR and the USSR. As evident in the delivery of foodstuffs subsidized by the Bonn government in January, it was also willing to extend tangible economic assistance.[347]

Kohl described the deteriorating conditions in the GDR and the accelerated drive in that part of Germany towards the re-establishment of German unity. Presumably

345 Memcon of the talks, as quoted by Zelikow and Rice, *Germany Unified*, p. 182.

346 The letter was handed to him by the West German ambassador in Moscow, Klaus Blech. The subsequent account of the visit by Kohl (accompanied by Teltschik) and Genscher to Moscow is based on Kohl, *Ich wollte Deutschlands Einheit*, pp. 253-82; Teltschik, *329 Tage*, pp. 137-44; and Genscher, *Erinnerungen*, pp. 722-24. The most extensive account is that by Kohl. The account contains some inaccuracies on Soviet internal politics. The two journalists authorized to edit his memoirs (Kai Diekmann and Ralf Georg Reuth) quote Kohl to the effect that, "After the doors had closed behind us [in Gorbachev's office in the Kremlin, in the afternoon on 10 February], I [Kohl] congratulated Mikhail Gorbachev on his assumption of the office of president. In fact, there had been a lively debate about the creation of this office because not everyone supported the [attendant] concentration of power. In the end, however, Gorbachev was elected with a large majority of the votes." This portrayal contains two mistakes. Gorbachev was elected president only with a *small* majority, with only 59 percent of the members of the Congress of Deputies (1,329; only 206 more votes than he needed) voting for him, and the elections did not take place prior to Kohl's Moscow visit but only one month *thereafter*, on 15 March 1990; see *Vneocherednyi tretii s"ezd narodnykh deputatov SSSR, 12-15 marta 1990 g. Stenograficheskii otchet* (Moscow: Izdanie Verkhovnogo Soveta SSSR, 1990).

347 The economic and financial aspects of Gorbachev's acceptance of German unification and his consent to unified Germany's membership in NATO will be discussed in context; see below, pp. 539-58.

conscious of international concern about the West German government's position concerning the finality of Poland's western borders, he clarified that his government had no intention to call in question Poland's current borders, but that he wanted the consent of the German refugees from the areas east of the Oder and Neisse rivers; furthermore, the 1970 Moscow and the 1972 Warsaw treaty had been concluded by the western part of a divided country, not by a united Germany (the implication of that observation being that only the latter could decide on the finality of the border). He also told his host that neutralization of a united Germany would find no acceptance (presumably both domestically and internationally) and that, as developments after 1918 had shown, any special international status for Germany would be a historic mistake. Gorbachev agreed that the issue of Germany's alliance membership was a central problem, and he also endorsed Kohl's interjection that, whereas the Soviet Union wanted to see its security interests safeguarded, Germany wanted to regain full sovereignty.

Discussion then turned to developments in the GDR. Gorbachev wanted to know whether the campaign for the 18 March elections in East Germany was not contributing to a division of society. Kohl rejected that notion and added that a more tranquil development would have been possible if Honecker had decided to introduce reform measures. With an air of resignation, his interlocutor (at variance with the facts) asserted that time and again he had urged Honecker to do just that, but in vain. He then wanted to be informed of Kohl's views on the electoral campaign itself and was told in response that the starting position of the SPD was better than that of the other parties. Thuringia and Saxony had traditionally been strongholds of social democracy and Willy Brandt, Kohl complained, was criss-crossing East Germany like some bishop blessing his flock, a metaphor that was countered by Gorbachev with the remark that he (Kohl), too, wasn't exactly sitting around at home with folded hands and that West Germany (the government, presumably) tried to influence East German affairs through all sorts of channels.

In the course of the conversation, Gorbachev abandoned his detached demeanor, and the atmosphere became more relaxed. Finally, in what was obviously a well prepared statement, Gorbachev formally told Kohl:

> I believe that there is no divergence of opinion between the Soviet Union, the Federal Republic, and the GDR about unity and the right of the people to strive for unity and to decide on the further development. There is agreement between you and me that *the Germans themselves have to make their choice. The Germans in the Federal Republic and in the GDR themselves have to know what road they want to take.*[348]

Gorbachev thus had formally handed to Kohl the key to German unity. "This is the breakthrough! Gorbachev is consenting to German unification," Teltschik confided to

---

348 Kohl, *Ich wollte Deutschlands Einheit*, p. 272 (italics mine).

his diary as having been his reaction to Gorbachev's statement.[349] The West German chancellor, too, was immediately aware of the historic significance of what Gorbachev had said and, wanting to make sure that there was no misunderstanding, repeated the Soviet leader's words. There was no misunderstanding. Teltschik was "jubilant," even though both he and the chancellor refrained from expressing that or any other emotion.

Not only was Gorbachev handing over the key to German unity, but for all practical purposes he was doing so *unconditionally*. He merely elaborated on his formal consent and explained that unification had to occur in the context of realities, including the fact that there had been a war in which the people of the Soviet Union had suffered more than any other. Confrontation and the division now had to be overcome, and he believed that the Germans in East and West had already demonstrated that they had learned from history. What about neutrality as a condition for yielding the key? He knew, Gorbachev said, that German neutrality would be unacceptable for Kohl; that it would be humiliating to the German people; and that it would appear as if all the contributions the Germans had made to peace would be ignored. Nevertheless, he still saw a united Germany outside the military alliances and disagreed with the notion that at least one part of Germany could be in NATO, with the other remaining in the Warsaw Pact.[350] Nowhere in the conversation, however, did Gorbachev pose German neutrality as an inexorable or inalienable end result of unification. "Yet another sensation," Teltschik was to comment in his diary, "Gorbachev does not commit himself to a specific solution; no demand of a price, and certainly no threat. What a meeting!"[351]

What about processes of negotiation and the link between the internal and external aspects of German unification? The two leaders agreed, in accordance with what Gorbachev had told Baker, that representatives of the two German states and the Four Powers should find acceptable solutions. Kohl again rejected an exclusive Four Power framework and Gorbachev assured his guest: "Nothing [will be decided] without you."[352]

The Soviet public was informed of the historic decisions. Earlier, after Modrow's visit, it had been confronted with the fact that the leadership considered German unification inevitable. Now it was being told that the Germans had the right to decide on the speed and direction of the process and that, essentially, Moscow would set no preconditions. In fact, the TASS report on the meeting went even farther than what

---

349 Teltschik, *329 Tage*, p. 140.

350 On this issue, the accounts by Kohl and Teltschik differ somewhat; for details, see the next section.

351 Teltschik, *329 Tage*, p. 141.

352 Ibid., p. 274.

Gorbachev had said (as reported by Kohl and Teltschik in their published accounts) but was closer to what Kohl told an international press conference on the night after the talks. Published on page one of *Pravda*, the report said:

> Gorbachev stated, and the chancellor agreed, that there is at present no divergence concerning the view that the Germans themselves have to solve the question of unity of the German nation and *choose the forms of statehood and at what time, at what speed, and under what conditions* they will realize that unity.[353]

The report also noted correctly Gorbachev's reference to the realities that had to be taken into consideration and that the rapprochement between the two German states should not "damage the positive results that have been achieved in East-West relations and rupture the balance [of power] in Europe."[354] Such qualifications, albeit without any reference to the balance of power in Europe, were publicly reiterated by the West German chancellor at the international press conference. He and Gorbachev had agreed, Kohl stated, that "the German problem can be solved only on the basis of realities, that is, that it must be embedded in the architecture of all of Europe. We must take into account the legitimate interests of our neighbors, friends, and partners in Europe and the world."[355]

In addition to the top private level, the Soviet-West German exchanges occurred in three other venues. First, Shevardnadze and Genscher held separate talks. In what, according to the West German foreign minister, was "obviously coordinated between Gorbachev and Shevardnadze," the external aspects of German unification and the international negotiation process formed the main topic of the conversation. Genscher, apparently not contradicted by Shevardnadze, proposed using the upcoming (12-13 February) Open Skies foreign ministers' conference of the member states of NATO and the Warsaw Pact in Ottawa to agree on the Two Plus Four ("in that order") format.[356] Second, in the evening of 10 February, in the Kremlin's Garnet Room, with the members of the German delegation and some of the major Soviet policy-makers, including Yakovlev and the German experts, assembled around the table, Gorbachev and Shevardnadze explained the results of their talks with Kohl and

---

353 "Vstrecha M.S. Gorbacheva i G. Kolia," *Pravda*, 11 February 1990 (italics mine). On 10 February, late at night, at the Soviet Union's International Press Center, Kohl had said that Gorbachev had "unequivocally agreed that he will respect the decision of the Germans to live in one state and that it is up to the Germans to decide the timing and the road to unification."

354 Ibid.

355 Craig R. Whitney, "Kohl Says Moscow Agrees Unity Issue is Up to Germans," *New York Times*, 11 February 1990.

356 Genscher, *Erinnerungen*, p. 723. Whereas Genscher's account of the talks is exceedingly brief, Shevardnadze's is nonexistent: in his memoirs, he leaves out entirely the 10-11 February Moscow meeting(s), turning directly from a description of his 19 December Brussels speech to his role at the 12-13 February Ottawa conference.

Genscher. Third, conversations took place also during a formal dinner in the St. Catherine's hall of the Kremlin.

The last two venues were instructive of Soviet domestic dissonance. Gorbachev's explanations of the results of his talks with Kohl in the Garnet Room were met with utter disbelief by Falin and Bondarenko; the West German chancellor observed "naked horror on their faces."[357] At the banquet, the two officials as well as Academician Sergei Kovalev failed to share the generally relaxed, almost jocular, spirit: Falin looked "somber," and he and the other two did "not want to loosen up."[358] Evidently with a mixture of pique and irony, Falin told Zagladin that now that the German problem had been solved, they could leave on pension.[359] It is plausible to infer from these reactions that the "professionals" at the MFA and ID had not been informed by Gorbachev about the far-reaching extent of his concessions and that this was also the first major instance of his brushing aside their reservations and hesitations. The MFA, in consequence, could do nothing more than engage in an effort at damage limitation. MFA spokesman Gerasimov thus regretted both the "bias" and "euphoria" in West German journalistic and official comment on the Kohl visit. It was correct, he said, that "we have declared that the Germans themselves have to decide the question of the unification of the German nation, including its speed, dates, conditions, and provisions." But this was not the complete picture. The German problem "does not exist in isolation but in a political, historical, geographic, and even psychological context."[360] Other Soviet officials, similarly, were intent on dispelling the notion that a unified German state could be created under the "NATO roof."[361]

These rear-guard clarifications and qualifications by the foreign ministry were part of a more general assault on Gorbachev's policies, including his policy on the German problem. At the 5-7 February Central Committee plenum, Ligachev, as usual, had taken the lead. "I cannot but mention one other thing," he said at the end of a comprehensive criticism of the way in which important problems in the Soviet Union were (not) being addressed – "the events in Europe."

> We should not overlook the *impending danger of the accelerated reunification of Germany*, or in fact, the engulfment of the German Democratic Republic. It would be unpardonably short-sighted and a folly not to see that on the world horizon looms a *Germany with a formidable economic and military potential.* Real efforts of the world community, of all democratic forces in the world, are needed in order to prevent in

357 Kohl, *Ich wollte Deutschlands Einheit*, p. 275.

358 Ibid., p. 276. "*Auftauen*" is the German original.

359 Teltschik, *329 Tage*, p. 142.

360 Press conference in Moscow, reported by DPA (West German news agency) from Moscow (in German), 12 February 1990.

361 The term was used by Alexander Bondarenko, "A pravda takova," *Trud*, 18 February 1990.

> advance the raising of the issue of the revision of the post-war borders and, to put it directly, not to *allow a new Munich*. I believe the time has come to recognize this new danger of our era and tell the party and the people about it in a clear voice. It is not too late.[362]

But Ligachev's warnings had come too late to have an impact on Gorbachev's position in the talks with Kohl. The conservatives had already lost the battle over the internal aspects of German unification as well as the struggle over the forum of negotiations concerning its external aspects. From Gorbachev's perspective and that of West Germany and its allies, the danger now existed that disaffected, disgruntled, and dissatisfied foreign ministry and party officials would combine forces with high-ranking military officers to influence the *content* of the negotiations among, as they saw it, the Six. Their position was already unambiguous on the central issue of the impending negotiations, that is, united Germany's international status and affiliation with the existing alliances. For them, Germany's membership in NATO, in any shape or form, was completely out of the question.

7. Gorbachev's Consent to United Germany's Membership in NATO

One of the first indications of Gorbachev's realization of the complexities of European security problems that would arise from German unification had occurred in his meeting with Genscher on 5 December. In his blistering attack on Kohl's Ten Points and the West German government's idea of establishing a confederation, he had asked:

> What next? What is meant by confederation? Does confederation envisage a common defense, a common foreign policy? Where would the FRG be – in NATO or in the Warsaw Pact? Or will it perhaps become neutral? But what would NATO be without the FRG? And, in general, what will happen further? Have you thought all of this through?[363]

At that early stage, of course, hardly anyone in the West or in the Soviet Union had thought through the basic problem of whether united Germany should be neutral or allowed to join the Atlantic alliance, or whether its two parts should be members of both NATO and the Warsaw Pact, let alone the myriad of subsidiary questions German unification would pose. Some of the most important related problems that had to be solved can be summarized as follows:

(1) What should be the role of the *United States* in Europe, and what should be the size of its military presence in the center and at the flanks?

(2) What, conversely, should be the role of the *Soviet Union* in European security affairs?

---

362 "Vystupleniia v preniiakh po dokladu. E. K. Ligachev," *Pravda*, 7 February 1990.

363 "Zapis' besedy s Genscherom," p. 34.

(3) Was it legitimate and, for both East and West Europeans, politically acceptable to proceed from the premise of *equivalency,* that is, from the idea that change in one alliance should be replicated by change in the other? If, for instance, the Soviet Union were prepared to heed Eastern European demands and withdraw its forces from Eastern Europe, should the United States pull back its forces from Western Europe, too?

(4) Should *both alliances* be involved in the management of security issues on the European continent? But what about the Warsaw Pact? Should that organization be excluded, since historically it had been the major symbol and instrument of Soviet imperial domination and in 1990 was doomed to oblivion?

(5) If the Warsaw Pact were to disintegrate, what should be the *status of its members other than East Germany*? Should they be allowed to join NATO, too, or would the Soviet political and military leaders consider this to be an unacceptable imposition, if not a provocation?

(6) If, on the other hand, the Warsaw Pact should survive and be involved in the management of European security issues, how much *reform* would be required to make that organization palatable to the new non-communist countries of Eastern Europe and serve their national interests?

(7) Again assuming the continued existence of the Warsaw Pact, even if only for a transitional period, what overall *force levels and military equipment* should the two alliances have in Europe, and what should be the relationship between the Two Plus Four talks and the negotiations on Conventional Forces in Europe (CFE) in Vienna?

(8) What should be the total *strength of united Germany's armed forces*, and should their size be limited in a Two Plus Four or a CFE agreement?

(9) What should be the role of *nuclear weapons* in a new Europe, and what limits (if any) should be placed on their numbers and delivery vehicles, and their modernization? Should they be withdrawn from West Germany?

Daunting as these questions were for any international forum to resolve, they almost paled in comparison with the problems they were likely to cause in the Soviet domestic political context. Ever since its inception, NATO had been portrayed by Soviet political leaders and propagandists as the incarnation of the most aggressive and reactionary tendencies of "American imperialism" and West Germany as the Pentagon's main staging post in Europe. Gorbachev, as late as December 1989, had termed the GDR the Soviet Union's "strategic ally" and a reliable member of the Warsaw Pact to which no harm would come. Now, a few months later, his increasingly unpopular leadership was being called upon not only to impute peaceful intentions to NATO and allocate to it a constructive security role in Europe but also to explain why it would be in the Soviet national interest to hand over the GDR to that alliance!

In the era of the New Thinking, the military had been asked to swallow a series of bitter pills, and it had done so with reasonably good grace. The military in both Czarist Russia and the Soviet Union had traditionally remained aloof from direct political involvement. But to ask it now to cooperate in the dismantling of the Soviet Union's entire strategic glacis and voluntarily agree to a comprehensive realignment of the military balance in Europe could be asking too much. The enormity of the strategic changes contemplated could catapult the armed forces into political action. Acting in conjunction with hard-line factions in the party, the foreign ministry, and the KGB, they could threaten to bring down the whole edifice of the New Thinking as well as its architects. For Gorbachev and the reformers still committed to him and clamoring for a radicalization of the reform effort, the problem was compounded by the likely exorbitant costs of the withdrawal of the approximately 575,000 Soviet troops still deployed in Eastern Europe. The pull-back of forces, furthermore, raised not only the issue of who was going to pay but also how to integrate the decommissioned officers and non-commissioned officers in the disintegrating fabric of the Soviet economy and society.

Understanding Gorbachev's consent to NATO's first eastward expansion and the final act in the dissolution of the Soviet empire in Eastern Europe thus necessitates reconstruction not only of the evolution of his own thinking but also an explanation of why the obvious dangers of a domestic revolt against his policies failed to materialize. The best starting point is a reconsideration of his attitudes to NATO and to the role of the United States in Europe.

Gorbachev and the Atlantic Alliance

In February 1990, Shevardnadze was to acknowledge that until "quite recently our aim was to oust the Americans from Europe at any price."[364] Indeed, on many occasions – both in words and in deeds – his predecessor at the Soviet foreign ministry (Gromyko) had confirmed the existence of this objective. For instance, speaking at the Twenty-third CPSU Congress in 1966, he had recalled Roosevelt's commitment at Yalta to the effect that American troops would be withdrawn from Europe within two years. "Ten times two years have passed," he exclaimed indignantly, "but the American army is still in Europe and by every indication claims

364 E. Shevardnadze, "V mire vse meniaetsia s golovokruzhitel'noi bystrotoi," *Izvestiia*, 19 February 1990. For a detailed analysis of the evolution of Soviet and Russian attitudes, see Hannes Adomeit, "The Atlantic Alliance in Soviet and Russian Perspectives," in Neil Malcolm, ed., *Russia and Europe: An End to Confrontation?* Royal Institute on International Affairs (London: Pinter, 1994), pp. 31-54.

a permanent status here." He also warned the United States that "the peoples of Europe are having their say and will have their say on this score."[365] Kvitsinsky reiterated his chief's complaints a decade and a half later. In an intemperate outburst to his American counterpart in the Geneva negotiations on intermediate-range nuclear forces (INF) he snapped: "You have no business in Europe."[366] What, then, traditionally, were the reasons for Soviet opposition to the American military presence in Europe?

First, the combination of the economic, technological, and military potential of the United States and West Germany, that is, the build-up of US forces in Europe and the addition of the Bundeswehr to NATO's integrated command structure, significantly strengthened the overall military power and effectiveness of the Atlantic alliance. NATO gave its European members confidence to stand up to Soviet military pressures and placed stringent limits on any increase in Soviet political influence in Western Europe.

Second, the stability of East Germany was always in doubt as long as West Berlin was allowed to act as a showcase of the Western system and a "thorn in the flesh" of the GDR. But West Berlin's viability and security depended vitally on the United States and its military presence in the city, in Germany, and in Europe. This had been the clear lesson of Stalin's Berlin blockade of 1948-49 and Khrushchev's protracted pressure on Berlin from 1958 to 1962.

Third, Soviet control in Eastern Europe would have been more effective without the countervailing power of the Atlantic alliance. Just as a strong NATO and a prosperous European Community provided reassurance to its West European members, it gave the Europeans east of the Elbe river reason to believe that Soviet domination and the division of Europe would not last forever. Differentiation and dissent could develop more easily in such conditions. Even today it is difficult to say how much concern there ever was in Moscow about the risks of a direct military clash between NATO and the Warsaw Pact. It probably did exist at the height of the Berlin crisis of 1961. Subsequently, however, the Soviet leaders seemed to be more concerned with the military-political backing NATO could provide for ideological and economic challenges, such as utilization of the economic weaknesses and exploitation of the domestic political instabilities in Eastern Europe.

Finally, while the Atlantic alliance, from Moscow's perspective, perhaps served to discourage West Germany from entering upon a separate German nationalist, militarist, or revanchist road, it was time and again to commit itself to a European

---

365 Gromyko's speech at the Twenty-seventh CPSU Congress, *Pravda*, 3 April 1966.

366 As reported by Strobe Talbott, *Deadly Gambits* (New York: Knopf, 1984), p. 113. Kvitsinsky's outburst would be repeated almost verbatim in 1988 by Institute on Europe deputy director Vladimir Shenaev, who claimed (to the present author) that the United States had "absolutely no business" in Europe; see above, p. 304, n. 378.

settlement that would end the division of Germany and Europe.[367] Although this position, as noted, was not precisely a sincere expression of heart-felt sentiments, it nevertheless did have political consequences and remained a constant irritant to the Soviet leaders for as long as they supported Germany's division.

Since a Europe from the Atlantic to the Urals controlled by the Soviet Union was impossible to achieve, NATO remained vigorous and viable and the American military presence could not be eliminated, the Soviet leaders from Stalin to Chernenko pursued second-best solutions, oscillating between various strategies. These included the "Finlandization" of Europe (aimed at restrictions of autonomy for the Europeans and a high degree of Soviet influence over their internal and external behavior); "pan-European" security (which included American participation but still provided for the curtailment and ultimate eradication of US influence); and variations of de Gaulle's *Europe des patries* (emphasis on European state sovereignty and rejection of the role of "peripheral powers," which in the Soviet interpretation meant that American soldiers and perhaps even businessmen ought to go home, but that the Soviet Union, as a European power, would remain). Gorbachev's Common European Home initially fit the *traditional* approach of attempting to drive wedges between the United States and Western Europe. Between 1986 and 1989, however, specialists at the academic institutes on international affairs and the foreign ministry under Shevardnadze brought about a transformation in attitudes and policy on NATO and the US presence in Europe. The Common House itself was redefined to include the Atlantic dimension.[368] What were the arguments used by this coalition to gain acceptance for such a comprehensive policy change?

First, in contrast to Gorbachev's initial emphasis on a separate continental European identity, the theoreticians of Atlanticism acknowledged that America "is part of Europe, historically, in religion, culturally, and politically."[369] *Second*, they noted that there were close economic bonds between the USA and Western Europe that neither of the two entities could afford to sever.[370] One analyst even asserted that "economically the United States is more a part of Europe than most major European

---

367 The most basic NATO commitment, reiterated time and again, was codified in the report on the "Future Tasks of the Alliance" ("Harmel report"), adopted at the December 1967 NATO ministerial meeting in Brussels. The "German Question" was defined there as the "*first and foremost*" of the "*central political issues in Europe*." The report also asserted that no lasting settlement in Europe would be possible unless the division of Germany and Europe were overcome; see North Atlantic Treaty Organization, *Basic Documents* (Brussels: NATO Information Service, 1981), pp. 103-6 (italics mine).

368 See above, pp. 241-42 and pp. 247-52.

369 Sergei Karaganov, "Amerika v obshcheevropeiskom dome," *Moskovskie novosti*, 13 November 1988 (italics mine).

370 Ibid.

nations."[371] *Third*, the links that had evolved in the security sphere were recognized as being of a fundamental nature. Modern weaponry and armed forces, they contended, had narrowed the Atlantic Ocean "to the size of a Gulf" and made the United States as close to the continent militarily "as England was at the turn of the century."[372] A significant role for the United States in any future system of European security was therefore "logical and necessary."[373] *Fourth*, despite all the talk about shifting its attention to Asia and the Pacific, the United States in reality had no plans to quit Europe and lose influence on the continent. If more attention was now being paid to the Asian-Pacific region in Washington, this was not a substitute but a supplement to its involvement in Europe. *Fifth*, even if it were politically desirable to have the United States leave Europe, from a practical point of view it would be "virtually impossible, even by the concerted efforts of all European nations."[374] To drive wedges between the two geopolitical entities could perhaps produce some temporary tactical advantages. But from a strategic vantage point it would be counterproductive. *Sixth*, they argued, the part played by the United States in the system of European security would serve to preserve, in most cases, the salutary influence of European powers on American policy and military strategy. European countries had helped deter Washington from adventurism in international crises, for instance, in the 1973 Middle East war and in Korea, Vietnam, and the Taiwan Straits, when American policy makers had "contemplated the use of nuclear weapons."[375] *Seventh*, a withdrawal of US forces from Europe could create insecurity among West European countries disadvantageous to Soviet interests. The Europeans, as a result, might be driven to strengthen their own defense efforts. Military integration in Western Europe could be enhanced. And such integration would most likely not be directed against the United States but would run parallel to US defense efforts and

---

371 Yuri Davydov, "The Soviet Vision of a Common European House," Paper Delivered to the International Studies Conference (ISA) in London, 29 March–1 April 1989 (unpublished), p. 10. The author is deputy director of the USA and Canada Institute of the Academy of Sciences.

372 Karaganov, "Amerika v obshcheevropeiskom dome." Davydov similarly wrote: "The nuclear age has drastically shrunk the Atlantic, and now America is as close to Europe in security terms as Great Britain was at the beginning of this century, or even closer"; Davydov, "The Soviet Vision of a Common European House," p. 10.

373 Karaganov, "Amerika v obshcheevropeiskom dome."

374 Davydov, "The Soviet Vision of a Common European House," p. 10; similarly Karaganov, "Amerika v obshcheevropeiskom dome."

375 Karaganov, "Amerika v obshcheevropeiskom dome." The author restated this argument in November 1988 in Brussels, at a conference of the Center for European Policy Studies (CEPS), and in December of the same year in Bonn-Bad Godesberg, at the Bergedorfer Gesprächskreis, a politically and economically independent forum initiated by industrialist Hans Körber; *Süddeutsche Zeitung*, 25 November 1988, and Bergedorfer Gesprächskreis, ed., *Das gemeinsame europäische Haus aus der Sicht der Sowjetunion und der Bundesrepublik Deutschland*, Protocol of the 86th round of talks of the Bergedorfer Gesprächskreis, held in Bonn-Bad Godesberg, 3-4 December 1988 (Hamburg: Körber Stiftung, 1989), p. 78.

enhance NATO's military potential.[376] *Eighth*, an American withdrawal could induce European states, acting individually or multilaterally, to produce and deploy nuclear weapons. De Gaulle, in that view, had "understood before anyone else that the Americans were getting ready to leave Europe and that the French would need nuclear weapons [the *force de frappe*] to balance the colossal economic might of the FRG."[377] *Finally*, in extension of the previous point, the US presence had served as a restraint on West German nuclear ambitions. If the Americans were to leave, Bonn could demand its own nuclear weapons.[378] To summarize, whatever the nuances in the views adopted, the advocates of the New Thinking agreed that the effects of a withdrawal of the United States would be "destabilizing in security terms."[379]

Such perceptions were endorsed by Gorbachev as early as 1986. In talks with West German foreign minister Genscher, he said that he had no wish to undermine NATO: "We are of the opinion that, given the alliances that have taken shape, it is essential to strengthen those threads whose severance is fraught with the danger of a rupture of the world fabric."[380] To Henry Kissinger, in January 1989, he expressed the opinion that the Europeans needed the participation of the USSR and the USA in the "all-European process." Stability in Europe was a "common interest."[381] Similarly, during his visit to Bonn, in June 1989, he told his German hosts that the Joint Soviet-German Declaration

> does not demand that you, or we, should renounce our uniqueness or weaken our allegiance to the alliances. On the contrary, I am confident that maintaining [this allegiance] in our policies will serve to consolidate the contribution of each state to the creation of a peaceful European order as well as to shape a common European outlook.[382]

---

376 Thus Vladimir Baranovsky argued that, in the past, West European military-political integration had proceeded parallel and in tandem with US military efforts in Europe; see his *Zapadnaia Evropa. Voenno-politicheskaia integratsiia* (Moscow: Mezhdunarodnye otnosheniia, 1988), pp. 180-84. Baranovsky was then head of the West European Department at IMEMO.

377 Radomir G. Bogdanov, "Glavnyi protivnik – inertsiia gonki vooruzhenii," *SShA: Ekonomika, politika, ideologiia*, No. 10 (1988), pp. 62-63. Bogdanov was the deputy head of the Institute on the USA and Canada (and known to be a KGB colonel). His concern about the potentially destabilizing effects of an American troop withdrawal was expressed by him also at the MFA's July 1988 Scientific-Practical Conference; see *Vestnik Ministerstva inostrannykh del SSSR*, No. 15 (August 1988), p. 24.

378 Bogdanov in conversation with this author, in Moscow, 4 October 1988.

379 Davydov, "The Soviet Vision of a Common European House," p. 10; and Karaganov, Bergedorfer Gesprächskreis, 86th session, *Das gemeinsame europäische Haus*, p. 78.

380 *Soviet News* (London), No. 23 (July 1986).

381 In talks with former Western political leaders and current members of the Trilateral Commission, including former French president Giscard d'Estaing, Japanese prime minister Nakasone and US secretary of state Henry Kissinger, in January 1989 (in response to a question by Kissinger); *Pravda*, 19 January 1989.

382 "Vizit M. S. Gorbacheva v FRG. Rech' M. S. Gorbacheva," *Pravda*, 13 June 1989.

In Gorbachev's perceptions, the prospect of German unification enhanced rather than detracted from the importance of the two military alliances. "*Now is not the time to break up the established international political and economic institutions*," he told visiting French Foreign Minister Roland Dumas shortly after the opening of the Berlin wall. "Let them be transformed, taking into account internal processes, let them find their place in the new situation and work together."[383] Similarly, in a briefing for the leaders of the Warsaw Pact on the Soviet-American summit meeting on Malta in December 1989, he stated that the two alliances "*will be preserved for the foreseeable future*" because they could make a "contribution to strengthening European security" by becoming a bridge between the two parts of Europe.[384]

It could be argued that the fact that Gorbachev publicly allocated a positive role to the Atlantic alliance in European security affairs – a step unprecedented for a Soviet leader – predetermined Soviet consent to membership of a unified Germany in NATO. There is some validity to this argument. However, the role that he was prepared to grant to both alliances at the end of 1989 and the beginning of 1990 was intimately connected with the "post-war realities" and the existence of not one but *two German states*. The question to be decided in the spring of 1990 was whether NATO should still be regarded as a stabilizing factor in the changed conditions of German unification, the impending disappearance of the GDR, and a crumbling Warsaw Pact. Gorbachev's answer was essentially affirmative, but he continued to cling to the notion of two alliances in Europe and avoided as long as possible to commit himself on the issue of Germany's alliance membership. On the latter issue, he was under severe conflicting pressures. The mainstays of the imperial system and the *germanisty* flatly rejected the idea of an extension of NATO to the eastern part of Germany, as did the East German government until it was replaced in the elections of 18 March. With equally insistence, and increasingly in the spring of 1990, he was being pressured first by the Four and then the Five to allow that extension to occur.

The first major opportunity to set in stone the Soviet position on security matters presented itself in the 26 January *ad hoc* meeting. Gorbachev failed to use this opportunity. Another possible occasion was the visit by East German prime minister Modrow to Moscow on 30 January. Again the matter was left surrounded by vagueness and indecision. The East German prime minister certainly was committed to German neutrality. This was evident in his four-stage plan from confederation to German unity, which, as cited above, posited "military neutrality of the GDR and the FRG on the road to federation."[385] Modrow confirmed his commitment to this goal at

383 Bill Keller, "Gorbachev Urges West to Show Restraint on Turmoil in Eastern Europe," *New York Times*, 15 November 1989 (italics mine).

384 *Pravda* and *Izvestiia*, 5 December 1989 (italics mine).

385 Text as published in Modrow, *Aufbruch und Ende*, appendix 6, pp. 186-88; see *supra*, pp. 482-83.

a press conference in East Berlin shortly after his return from Moscow. German unification, he said, was intimately connected with the idea of building a Common European Home. In constructing that new home, he continued, one

> has to proceed from the idea that already in the stage of confederation, both German states will *step by step detach themselves from their obligations of alliance* toward third countries and attain a state of *military neutrality.*[386]

PDS chief Gysi carried the neutrality ball several yards farther downfield. In accordance with the proceedings at the *ad hoc* meeting, he had been invited to Moscow and on 2 February held talks with Gorbachev, Yakovlev, and Falin. In a subsequent interview, Gysi reported that he and Gorbachev had been of one mind on the point that, at the end of any reunification process, Germany not only had to be neutral but *demilitarized.*[387] The TASS report on the Gysi-Gorbachev meeting, however, did not contain this requirement. It only recorded that Gorbachev had struck a balance between support for the GDR as a sovereign state and recognition of the momentum towards German unity.[388] The Soviet leadership, it would appear, was intent on keeping its options open. In fact, there was ambiguity about what had actually been agreed upon both between Gorbachev and Gysi, and between the Soviet leader and the East German prime minister. Gorbachev, by supporting the Modrow plan, appeared to have bound himself to the goal of neutralization. However, both he – and again the Soviet media – subsequently failed to confirm this. Furthermore, no sooner had Gysi added the disarmament requirement that Modrow backed away from German neutrality altogether. At the World Economic Forum in Davos as well as in interviews with German and foreign journalists he said that he had not meant the neutralization of Germany to be a precondition for unity but simply an "idea for dialogue."[389]

---

386 "Hans Modrow unterbreitet Konzept 'Für Deutschland, einig Vaterland,'" *Neues Deutschland*, 2 February 1990 (italics mine); see above, p. 482. Apparently based on the American memcon of the meeting, Zelikow and Rice (*Germany United*, p. 181) write that Shevardnadze had told Baker on 8 February in Moscow that the requirement that united Germany not only be neutral but also *demilitarized* had not been in the original Modrow plan but had been added in Moscow. Modrow had feared that if he had proposed this additional requirement, it would have spelled the end for him politically. This account is confusing: *neither Modrow's plan nor his explanations of the plan contain the requirement of a disarmed neutral Germany*. It was Gysi who would raise the disarmament issue.

387 Gysi interview with *Washington Post*, 4 February 1990; see also the report in the PDS newspaper, "Nicht nur Neutralität, sondern Demilitarisierung," *Neues Deutschland*, 5 February 1990.

388 "Beseda v TsK KPSS," *Pravda*, 5 February 1990.

389 "Modrow: Vorschläge sind ein Angebot zum Dialog," *Neues Deutschland*, 5 February 1990. Yet he did not completely abandon his idea. Thus, he pointed to international responses which had supported it. He also stated that Oskar Lafontaine, the prime minister of the Saarland and potential SPD candidate for chancellor, had called his proposal worthy of consideration.

The ambiguities persisted in Baker's meetings with Gorbachev and Shevardnadze on 8-9 February. The Soviet foreign minister did not push the idea of neutralization, telling his American counterpart only that Moscow had once supported the idea of a unified Germany, but of a neutral unified country, and that a united Germany could not be adapted to the alliances as they now existed. In the same way as he had previously worried about the possible rise of right-wing and neo-Nazi forces, he was now anxious about the danger of a militarized Germany.[390] In *his* talks with Baker, Gorbachev was less concerned about such dangers than his foreign minister:

> Basically, I share the direction of your thinking [on the favorable possibilities of Soviet-American cooperation to preserve peace]. The process is under way. We have to adjust to this process. We have to adjust to this new reality and not be passive in ensuring that stability in Europe is not upset. Well, for us and for you, regardless of the differences, there is nothing terrifying in the prospect of a unified Germany ... For France and for Britain, the question is who is going to be the major player in Europe. We have it easier. We are big countries and have our own weight.[391]

Nevertheless, he saw advantages to having American troops in Germany (and Europe): "We don't really want to see a replay of Versailles, where the Germans were able to arm themselves. ... The best way to constrain that process is to ensure that Germany is contained within European structures."[392]

Earlier in the conversation, Baker had assured Gorbachev that, if Germany were to remain part of NATO, "*there would be no extension of NATO's jurisdiction for forces of NATO one inch to the east.*"[393] This position was to play an important role several years later in the vehement Russian opposition to any further eastward expansion of NATO.[394] It coincided with the view that Genscher had expressed on 31 January in a speech in Tutzing. Gorbachev may have been conscious of that position, and he certainly knew (as he told Baker) that it had been adopted by Brandt, who had suggested to let West Germany stay in NATO and to work out a special status for the former GDR. Returning to this problem, Baker asked Gorbachev directly whether he would rather see an independent Germany outside of NATO, with no US forces on German soil, or a united Germany tied to NATO but with assurances "that there would be no extension of NATO's current jurisdiction eastward." Gorbachev replied that he was still giving thought to these options. "Soon we are going to have a seminar [a discussion] among our political leadership to talk about all of these

390 Zelikow and Rice, *Germany Unified*, p. 180. In his memoirs, Baker fails to report Shevardnadze's views on the issues of German neutralization and demilitarization; *The Politics of Diplomacy*, pp. 202-5.

391 Ibid., p. 205.

392 Zelikow and Rice, *Germany Unified*, p. 184.

393 Ibid., p. 182 (italics mine).

394 For details of that opposition see *infra*, pp. 533-36.

options." One thing was clear, however: "*Any extension of the zone of NATO is unacceptable*." "*I agree*," Baker replied.[395] Ambiguities in the Western position were conveyed also by Baker's remarks at a press conference after his talks with the Soviet leaders to the effect that the United States favored a unified Germany's "continued membership in, *or association with*, NATO."[396]

At a press conference held immediately prior to the talks between the Soviet leadership and Kohl and Genscher on the following day, Shevardnadze followed the line he had taken with Baker, declining to commit himself on the neutrality issue. "The idea of neutrality is not new," he said.

> This is a good, fine idea. It was proposed right after the war ... [We] were always for a united German nation and one German people but for a neutral, demilitarized Germany. This was our main principle. What is our future position on this issue? Well, today Kohl and Genscher are meeting with Gorbachev. We will try to discuss these issues that are currently very acute both for Europe and the two German states, and I guess for the rest of the world.[397]

Similarly, Gorbachev (as noted above), in his meeting with the German chancellor, stated that he knew that neutrality was not only unacceptable to him (Kohl) but that it was humiliating to the German people. Nevertheless, he saw a unified Germany *outside* the alliances, with national armed forces adequate for national defense. He could not take seriously the idea that one part of Germany should be in NATO and the other in the Warsaw Pact. He also rejected Baker's proposal, according to which a unified Germany should belong to NATO, except for the territory of the former GDR.[398]

To review the state of affairs in mid-February 1990, both the Western and the Soviet position on Germany's future security status was only beginning to take shape. Ambiguity surrounded both positions, although to a lesser degree in the West than in the Soviet Union. The Western preference for a unified Germany's alliance membership was muddied by the discussion of whether the whole of Germany should be a member of the Atlantic alliance politically but remain outside its military organization (that is, have a status similar to that of France); by the question of what an "association" with the Atlantic alliance could look like; and by what was meant by the formula of no extension of the "zone" of NATO or NATO's "jurisdiction." However, the ambiguities in the joint and all-important West German-American

---

395 Ibid., p. 183. Jack Matlock, who was present at the meeting and took his own notes, has confirmed the accuracy of this crucial exchange in conversation with this author on 10 February 1997 in Cambridge, Mass.

396 Thomas L. Friedman, "Gorbachev Accepts Deep Cuts in Europe," *New York Times*, 10 February 1990 (italics mine).

397 Excerpts from the press conference as published in *Pravda*, 11 February 1990 (italics mine).

398 Kohl, *Ich wollte Deutschlands Einheit*, p. 273.

position dissipated very quickly. On 24 February, at a meeting at Camp David, Bush and Kohl agreed that

> a unified Germany should remain a full member of the North Atlantic Treaty Organization, including participation in its military structure. We agreed that US military forces should remain stationed in the united Germany and elsewhere in Europe as a continuing guarantor of stability. The Chancellor and I are also in agreement that in a unified state, the former territory of the GDR should have a special military status [that] would take into account the legitimate security interests of all interested countries, including those of the Soviet Union.[399]

Gorbachev was torn more fundamentally between various positions and refused to commit himself to any of them, essentially until the talks with Kohl in Moscow in July 1990. On the one hand, he recognized the dangers of Versailles (not only because the treaty had been unable to forestall German rearmament, but also because it had encouraged a nationalist backlash in Germany) but on the other, he emphasized the necessity of Four Power cooperation and firm guarantees to be provided within that framework. In accordance with the New Thinking, he allocated important security functions to the Atlantic alliance and American forces in Europe but he opposed the logical extension of this framework to include unified Germany's membership in NATO. The principle of the Freedom of Choice implied letting the Germans and the East Europeans decide the question of what alliance they wanted to belong to, but he sought to place constraints on the application of this principle. For several months, however, it seemed as if the ambiguities had been resolved in Moscow in favor of retrenchment and a hardening of positions on both the internal and external aspects of German unification. The forms, circumstances, and rationales of that apparent reversal need to be explored in some detail.

Soviet Retrenchment

The turn to a more uncompromising stance became evident immediately after the Open Skies foreign ministers' conference in Ottawa. In what can be regarded as having clearly been related to the upcoming Two Plus Four negotiations formally agreed upon at the conference, Gorbachev warned that Moscow would resist Western efforts to dictate the proceedings: "We rule out such a method," he said in an interview with *Pravda* published on 21 February, "whereby three or four [countries] first come to an arrangement between themselves and then set out their already

---

399 Joint Bush-Kohl press conference; excerpts as quoted by Zelikow and Rice, *Germany Unified*, p. 216. Notwithstanding ambiguities in the internal West German government discussion (notably hesitations and modifications by Genscher and the foreign ministry) and vacillation by Britain and France, the joint Bush-Kohl position remained firm. Since the Soviet consent to unified Germany's membership in NATO is at issue here, the differentiations in the Western position will not be pursued.

agreed-upon position before the participants. This is unacceptable."[400] On the form which an agreement should take, he still (or again) thought that there should be a peace treaty. On substance, the treaty should provide for a role of both NATO and the Warsaw Pact, and he called any change in the military-strategic balance between the two alliances "impermissible."[401] New and more intransigent inflections on the German security issue also surfaced in the foreign ministry. Shevardnadze formed a working group, chaired by Deputy Minister Anatoli Adamishin and department head Bondarenko, to deal with the German problem and the Two Plus Four negotiations, and on 24 February assembled the MFA's Collegium, including his deputies and fourteen other officials, ostensibly to drive firm stakes into the international negotiation ground. The Collegium derided the "prescriptions advanced in some Western countries" and specifically the idea that NATO membership of a unified Germany in NATO would be in the Soviet interest. It was unacceptable to the Soviet Union that anyone but she herself should seek to determine what constituted the essence of Soviet security and how best to safeguard it. The USSR had its own notions as to how to do this and "certainly, any variants envisaging the membership of unified Germany in NATO do not correspond to these notions."[402]

As for the hardening of the Soviet position on the internal issues of German unification, Gorbachev ostensibly reconsidered the position he had adopted when he had handed the key to German unity to Kohl and told him that unification was the prerogative of the Germans. In his *Pravda* interview, Gorbachev rejected not only any attempt by three or four of the Six to confront the remaining two countries with an agreed-upon position, but he also objected to a procedure whereby "the Germans agree among themselves and then propose to the others only to endorse the decisions already adopted by them.[403] Similarly, on 6 March, at the second and last of Modrow's visits to Moscow, he again eschewed the terms "German unity" and "unification," asserting instead that it was "by no means a matter of indifference how the rapprochement (*sblizhenie*) of the two German states takes place" and expressed his firm conviction that the "fanning of speculation, the tendency to annex the GDR, and the policy of creating *faits accomplis* do not correspond to a responsible approach to a solution of a problem as sensitive to the fate of Europe and the world as the German question."[404] In other words, article 23 of the Federal Republic's

400 "Otvety M.S. Gorbacheva na voprosy korrespondenta 'Pravdy,'" *Pravda*, 21 February 1990.

401 Ibid.

402 "V MID SSSR. Rassmotren shirokii krug voprosov," *Pravda*, 26 February 1990.

403 Interview in *Pravda*, 21 February 1990.

404 "Vstrecha M.S. Gorbacheva s pravitel'stvennoi delegatsii GDR," *Pravda* and *Izvestiia*, 7 March 1990. Gorbachev's emphasis on *sblizhenie* had been apparent earlier, in his telephone conversation with Modrow on 12 February, "Zapis' osnovnogo soderzhaniia telefonnogo razgovora M.S. Gorbacheva s Predsedatelem Soveta Ministrov GDR Kh. Modrovom, 12

constitution as the point of departure for unification was definitely out of the question.

This apparently firm stance, however, as so many others previously, was severely undercut by the course of events. The parliamentary elections in East Germany on 18 March produced a stunning victory for the conservative parties, which polled 48 percent of the vote. The SPD, which had been regarded as the front-runner, received only 22 percent, and the PDS 16 percent. The most disastrous performance was that of the Alliance 90, the umbrella party for groups like the Neue Forum that had been in the forefront of the democratic revolution of the preceding year; it garnered less than 3 percent of the vote. It was a foregone conclusion that the new government under Prime Minister Lothar de Maizière (CDU) would not support anything but Kohl's preference for unification under article 23.

Concerning the external aspects, Gorbachev now dispelled Western hopes to the effect that his and Shevardnadze's failure to demand a neutral status for unified Germany had presaged Soviet consent to NATO membership. In reference to the talks between Gorbachev and Modrow, TASS reported that

> It was stated with full determination [at the talks] that the inclusion of a future Germany in NATO is inadmissible and will not take place, whatever arguments may be used. One cannot allow the breakdown of the balance [of power] in Europe, the basis of stability and security, and of mutual trust and cooperation.[405]

On the face of it, this settled the question: unified Germany's membership in NATO was unacceptable. Other solutions had to be found.

It is not the purpose of this book to reconstruct in detail the tactical twists and turns adopted by the Soviet negotiators in the Two Plus Four talks at both the foreign ministers' level and that of the ministries' political directors. The protracted talks, extending from a preliminary meeting on 14 March in Berlin and the first ordinary meeting on 5 May in Bonn to the final meeting on 12 September in Moscow, have been described elsewhere.[406] They were characterized on the Soviet side by an erratic but in essence uncompromising treatment of the issue both in and at the sidelines of the Two Plus Four negotiations and the return in rapid succession to several of the positions advanced previously, including ideas such as (1) the settlement of the

---

fevralia 1990 goda," Hoover Institution Archives, box 3, Zelikow-Rice Project on German Unification.

405 "Vstrecha M.S. Gorbacheva s pravitel'stvennoi delegatsii GDR," *Pravda* and *Izvestiia*, 7 March 1990.

406 The best account is that of Zelikow and Rice, *Germany Unified*, pp. 246-63; see also the account by the West German political director in the talks, Frank Elbe, *Die Lösung der äußeren Aspekte der deutschen Frage* (Bonn: Europa Union Verlag, 1993) and, with Richard Kiessler, *Ein runder Tisch mit scharfen Ecken: Der diplomatische Weg zur deutschen Einheit* (Baden-Baden: Nomos, 1993); other sources for the arduous negotiations are the memoirs by Shevardnadze, Baker, and Genscher.

German problem by a peace treaty; (2) synchronization of the unification process with the creation of new security structures in conjunction with the transformation of the military alliances and new machinery to be allocated to the CSCE; (3) retention of the special status of Berlin and the presence of the armed forces of the Four Powers in Germany until after the conclusion of a peace treaty; (4) membership of both unified Germany and the Soviet Union in NATO; and (5) dual membership of Germany in both alliances. Everything on that menu, as Shevardnadze knew well from his talks, was abhorrent to the taste of the two conservative-ruled Germanys and their NATO allies, notably the United States. Nevertheless, the various indigestible dishes of that menu continued to be developed in the proceedings and position papers at closed internal meetings and advertised in public statements, the talks with Western officials and the Two Plus Four negotiations.

Two examples from the internal discussions, both involving the Politburo, may suffice to demonstrate the point. The first concerns the PB's instructions (*direktivy*) for Shevardnadze for his talks with Bush and Baker in Washington on 4-6 April. The directives were issued on 2 April in the form of Politburo approvalfor a draft that had been prepared a few days earlier and sponsored by Shevardnadze, Defense Minister Yazov, KGB chief Kryuchkov, PB foreign policy *kurator* Yakovlev, CC secretary for the military industry Oleg Baklanov, and Deputy Prime Minister Igor Belousov.[407] As for the internal aspects of German unification and their linkage to international security affairs, Shevardnadze was instructed to emphasize to Bush and Baker

> the necessity of ensuring the stage-by-stage unification of the two German states and its synchronization with the all-European process. It is important to prevent the movement toward unity from acquiring uncontrolled forms and speed which would put the Four Powers, Germany's neighbors, and Europe as a whole in a position of [having to] face accomplished facts and seriously hamper the search for mutually acceptable decisions on the external aspects of the building of German unity. The unification process should take place not in the form of an *Anschluß* of the GDR but should be the result of agreements between the two German states as equal subjects of international law. We should emphasize that, naturally, we favor the existence of the GDR as an independent state for as long as possible.

Perhaps needless to repeat, by the time these restrictive directives were issued, the train of article 23 had already departed from the stations in both Bonn and East Berlin.

As for the external aspects, the directives stated:

---

407 "Vypuska iz protokolia No. 184 zasedaniia Politburo TsK KPSS ot 2 aprelia 1990 goda. O direktivakh dlia peregovorov Ministra inostrannykh del SSSR s Presidentom SShA Dzh. Bushem i Gosudarstvennym sekretarem Dzh. Beikerom (Vashington, 4-6 aprelia 1990 goda)." The document is stored in the Russian TsKhSD archives; a copy is available in the archives of the Hoover Institution.

> We should emphasize that the most appropriate form of a German settlement would be a peace treaty that would draw the line under the past war and determine the military-political status of Germany. It should have as its necessary elements the partial demilitarization and the establishment of a reasonable sufficiency (*razumnaia dostatochnost'*) for the armed forces. ... If Baker were to react negatively to the idea of a peace treaty, we should inquire about his vision of the forms for a peace settlement with Germany.

Until the creation of new European security structures, the directives continued, the rights and responsibilities of the Four should be preserved to the full extent. Furthermore, "We should firmly state our negative attitude to the participation of the new Germany in NATO. Germany could become a non-aligned state, preserving [only] its EC membership."[408]

The record does not indicate whether the PB's approval was preceded by much or any discussion.[409] At the beginning of May, however, a "tough" (*zhestkii*) discussion of the German problem at Politburo level did take place.[410] Shevardnadze, assisted by Tarasenko, had prepared a position paper which, following by then well established practice, was redrafted and turned in a more uncompromising direction by Bondarenko's Third Department. The paper was to serve as a point of reference for his upcoming participation in the first round of the Two Plus Four negotiations in Bonn. It was co-sponsored by Shevardnadze, Yakovlev, Yazov, and Kryuchkov but was apparently still not tough enough to satisfy the more conservative PB members, including Ligachev, who severely criticized it. Furthermore, with the exception of Shevardnadze, the sponsors of the new directives remained silent. Gorbachev sided with the conservative majority faction. He burst out heatedly at one point, stating categorically: "*We will not let Germany into NATO, and that is the end of it. I will even risk the collapse of the [CFE] negotiations in Vienna and START but will not allow this.*"[411] The position paper, as a result, essentially was no different from the directives that the PB had endorsed one month earlier.

Chernyaev, who had not been asked for his opinion at the PB meeting, sent a note to Gorbachev on the following day, reflecting both on the decision-making process in the Politburo and the Soviet negotiating position on the German problem. He deplored the fact that, although many PB members lacked any expertise on that problem, they were nevertheless allowed to discuss it. As a result, positions were formed under the influence of Ligachev and his dire warnings about NATO

---

408 Ibid. (italics mine).

409 Chernayev has stated that only one PB session dealt with the German problem, the one at the beginning of May. Tarasenko speaks of two PB meetings, referring perhaps – in addition to the one in May – to the meeting of 2 April; interviews with Chernyaev and Tarasenko.

410 Chernyaev, *Shest' let s Gorbachevym*, p. 347. The record of the meeting has not been made available.

411 Ibid. (italics mine).

approaching the borders of the Soviet Union. Such warnings, he told Gorbachev, were nonsense. They reflected 1945 thinking and pseudo-patriotism of the masses. "Germany will remain in NATOin any case," he predicted, "and we will again try to catch up with a train that has left the station. Instead of putting forward specific and firm terms for our consent, we are heading toward a failure."[412] To Chernyaev, at least, the consequences of the Soviet failure to present terms in accordance with Soviet interests and acceptable to the West were immediately obvious. The telegrams which Shevardnadze sent from Bonn and his report on the Two Plus Four meeting after his return to Moscow indicated that he had been forced to evade the issues by taking recourse to "general phraseology" and that "we lost" another round in the diplomatic game.[413]

How, then, is the hardening of the Soviet position to be explained? One interpretation has been advanced by Tarasenko, Shevardnadze's personal assistant. He has argued that the foreign minister was "from the very beginning [the talks with Kohl and Genscher on 10 February] to the end [the formal Soviet consent in July] committed to the idea of German membership in NATO" and that the crucial task he saw was "how to manage the problem domestically."[414] This interpretation is reflected in Shevardnadze's own account. "Politics is the art of the possible," he has stated.

> We may like it or not, but it is an axiom that has no need of proof. In the real world of politics we could not escape the need for a constant and scrupulous reading of the changing political context. But the *internal situation* of the Soviet Union was the crucial factor. Our position had to coincide with the will of our people.[415]

Although the importance of domestic constraints is undeniable, the interpretation of Shevardnadze as having consistently adhered to the view of unified Germany in NATO as the best bargain for the Soviet Union and of his striving for public endorsement of this solution is not very credible. The most simple and, to a large extent, plausible explanation for the hardening of his position lies in the time-honored diplomatic practice to construct a tough, even maximalist, position at the outset of negotiations. Furthermore, although this cannot be proven beyond doubt, it is questionable whether Shevardnadze, from the very beginning of the negotiation process, did have a firm view not only of what was possible but also of what was desirable. As for Gorbachev and his attitudes on the NATO issue, no claim of constancy and foresight has been advanced either by him or by his supporters. Gorbachev may have been conscious of the disadvantages of a neutral status for a

---

412 Ibid., p. 348.
413 Ibid.
414 Interview with Tarasenko.
415 Shevardnadze, *My vybor*, p. 238 (italics mine).

unified Germany, but (as evident in the PB meeting of early May) he was genuinely and adamantly opposed to Germany's exclusive membership in the Atlantic alliance. He was wedded instead to an idea that would seemingly permit safe passage for the Soviet ship of state between the Scylla of German neutrality (and a possible renationalization of German security policies) and the Charybdis of the GDR's full integration in NATO, namely: *dual membership* of unified Germany in NATO and the Warsaw Pact. As absurd as this idea may appear in retrospect, he tenaciously clung to it for several months, encouraged perhaps by the support it received from experts in the academic institutes on international relations.[416] In a variation on this idea, one of the possibilities he contemplated was that if a unified Germany joined NATO, the Soviet Union should be invited to join NATO as well.[417] Gorbachev's stance, in turn, provides another clue to Shevardnadze's tactical procedure. It undercut the degree of flexibility that the foreign minister may have been prepared to show at the negotiating table. But he was also in all likelihood not prepared openly to challenge Gorbachev on a position that was supported by the pillars of Soviet power and within his own ministry.

A second interpretation of the reasons why the Soviet position hardened in the spring of 1990 is connected with the by now familiar conservative charge of ineptitude and lack of professionalism. Akhromeev and Kornienko, for instance, contend that, prior to the Camp David agreement between Bush and Kohl on 24 February, the Western leaders had not excluded the possibility of a modified or partial membership of a unified Germany in NATO, notably its not entering into the military structure of the alliance, and that "it was only in March, that is, after the NATO train had left the station, that we started to put forward the unacceptability of German inclusion in NATO" and to argue that such a step "would lead to the breakdown of the balance of power in Europe."[418] Only then, on 14 March, did the Soviet foreign ministry issue an official statement that more or less clearly outlined a Soviet concept on German unification. "But it was too late," they charge,

> especially since the elections in East Germany on 18 March had produced a new government headed by [Christian Democrat] de Maizière and the negotiations on German affairs, which were held under the Two Plus Four formula, very quickly turned into a formula of Five Minus One, that is, the USSR became a pariah at these negotiations. Our improvisations to

416 Sergei Karaganov of the Institute on Europe, for instance, asserted that dual membership of Germany in both alliances was not such a strange idea. The United States was not only a member of NATO but also of ANZUS, and previously of SEATO and CENTO; in conversation with this author in Moscow on 5 May 1990.

417 Shevardnadze, too, had advanced this proposal; see Thomas L. Friedman, "Soviets Promise to Pull Back Some Tactical Nuclear Arms," *New York Times*, 6 June 1990.

418 *Pravda*, 7 March 1990, as quoted by Akhromeev and Kornienko, *Glazami marshala i diplomata*, p. 260. Their reference is presumably to the TASS statement on the talks between Gorbachev and Modrow on 6 March; see above, p. 504.

"neutralize Germany" (which was, of course, unrealistic) or by have it enter both alliances, NATO and the Warsaw Pact (which was even more unrealistic, especially under the circumstances where the days of the Warsaw Pact were numbered), of course did not help.

As a result of these ill-advised improvisations, the conservative critics conclude, it was not at all surprising that Gorbachev and Shevardnadze changed course yet again and, "at the time of the July visit of Chancellor Kohl to the USSR, officially removed all Soviet objections to German membership in NATO."[419] Irrespective of whether one agrees with the allegation that the Final Agreement constituted a violation of Soviet (and Russian) security interests, the conservative criticism of Gorbachev and Shevardnadze is well founded at least in one respect. A good case can be made for the argument that, at the time when Gorbachev handed the key to German unification to Kohl and consented to letting the Germans decide on the form and speed of that process, he and Shevardnadze had *not* thought through the practical consequences of that blanket authorization, notably the implications of unification on the basis of article 23 of the West German constitution. Accession of East Germany according to the constitution would mean that West Germany's network of treaties, including the Final Act of 1954 that provided for the Federal Republic's membership in NATO, would automatically be extended to the eastern part of the enlarged Germany and thus would prejudge the outcome of what was ostensibly in the purview of the Two Plus Four negotiations. It would seem that on 6 March Modrow and his government delegation had successfully impressed upon Gorbachev, from their perspective, the negative implications of article 23.

A third interpretation sees the hardening of the Soviet position as a result, at least in part, of a reassertion of the interests of the Soviet armed forces on the German issue. Scrutiny of role of the armed forces in decision-making on Germany's membership in NATO confirms the enervation of their influence on overall Soviet international security affairs. As described in the previous chapter, this assessment may run counter to conventional wisdom. Given the trends toward the dissolution of the Warsaw Pact and the inclusion of unified Germany in NATO, one should have expected a determined effort by the armed forces in conjunction with the party to forestall both. Such an effort, however, was not made. A more thorough analysis of this phenomenon, drawing on the earlier discussion of military and party influence on policy-making in the Gorbachev era, is appropriate .

Military and Party Opposition

Expressions of dissatisfaction with the political leadership's handling of international security matters by military officers in the crucial period between February and July

419 Ibid.

1990 can certainly be found. In that period, the military's position on the central question of the possible inclusion of unified Germany in NATO seemed to be consistent. As expressed by General Staff department head Col. Gen. Nikolai Chervov as late as July 1990, such a measure would "definitely be unacceptable, both politically and psychologically, to the Soviet people. It would seriously upset the military balance of strength that has developed in Europe."[420] Furthermore, as Mikhail Moiseev, the chief of general staff, had warned several months earlier, any Soviet withdrawal from Eastern Europe, including from East Germany, had to be matched by Western, foremost American pull-backs. The Soviet Union, he told French journalists in early February, was ready "to withdraw its forces from the GDR completely *if* those of the United States, Britain, and France were withdrawn from the FRG."[421] His position remained unchanged as late as July 1990. He bluntly told German visitors that Soviet soldiers would remain in Germany "as long as there are American troops in the Federal Republic."[422] Similarly, with impeccable military logic Lt. Gen. Igor Sergeev, deputy chief of the strategic rocket forces, told the weekly *Moskovskie novosti* that a mass pullout from Czechoslovakia, Poland, and Hungary would upset strategic parity with NATO and overturn Soviet military calculations:

> We will lose ground and be that much closer to danger. If someone loses in parity, then someone else naturally gains. Forthcoming changes in the Warsaw Pact of course mean losses for us from the military standpoint. All the theoretical discussions about changing from a military to a political pact are cold comfort. It's playing with words.[423]

Even more strident criticism of the allegedly disastrous drift of Soviet security policies was expressed by military officers at the Congress of People's Deputies and the founding congress of the Russian Communist Party, which took place from 19 to 23 June and the Twenty-eighth Party Congress, held from 2 to 13 July. Its exponents were Albert Makashov, commander of the Volga-Urals Military District; Colonels Viktor Alksnis and Nikolai Petrushenko; Generals Alexei Lizichev, head of the Main Political Administration of the Soviet Army and Navy; Nikolai Boiko, his counterpart in the Air Defense Forces; Ivan Mikulin, chief of the Southern Group of Forces' Political Directorate; and Admiral Gennadi Khvatov, commander of the Pacific Fleet.

Gen. Makashov's diatribes were particularly scathing and insulting to the political leadership. Warning of the dangers inherent in the impending incorporation of a

---

420 Col. Gen. Nikolai Chervov, "United Germany Should Not Be NATO Member," *Svenska Dagbladet* (Stockholm), 1 July 1990, quoted in Foreign Broadcast Information Service, Daily Report, Soviet Union, FBIS-SOV-90-129, pp. 4-5.

421 "UdSSR bereit zu sofortigem Truppenabzug aus der DDR," *Neues Deutschland*, 5 February 1990 (italics mine).

422 *Der Spiegel*, 16 July 1990, p. 27.

423 *Moskovskie novosti*, 21 February 1990.

unified Germany into NATO and the emergence of a powerful Japan in the Far East, he charged sarcastically that "only our learned peacocks are crowing that no one is going to attack us."[424] The strange birds he figuratively referred to were obviously the academic specialists who had been elevated by the political leadership to a preeminent role in international security decision-making. Reinforcing his sarcastic comment, he fumed that the president ought to meet "not only with the intelligentsia and owners of cooperatives but also with the defenders of the state." Presumably contemptuous of Gorbachev for his lack of military experience and expertise, he suggested that military service should be made mandatory for future presidents and that newly elected leaders should undergo three months of training at the General Staff Academy. On foreign policy and the loss of empire in Eastern Europe, and in obvious criticism of Shevardnadze and by implication again of Gorbachev, he deplored that, "because of the so-called victories of our diplomacy, the Soviet army is being driven without a fight out of countries that our fathers liberated from fascism." Furthermore, he pointedly asked why NATO was continuing to strengthen itself despite the erosion of the Warsaw Pact. He even went as far as claiming that "the realities of the world today are such that continuing unilateral disarmament would be an act of stupidity, or a crime." [425]

Some of that criticism, albeit less ominous and vitriolic, was in evidence also at the Twenty-eighth CPSU Congress. At the outset of the congress, the chances of a full-fledged political battle developing over international security issues seemed high. Not only was the military establishment represented by a contingent of 269 delegates, but a high percentage of those officers were drawn from the conservative High Command. Furthermore, evidence gathered at a series of military party conferences that preceded the congress indicated that the military leadership had manipulated the selection of delegates to ensure a predominantly conservative slate.[426] The most disparaging comments were voiced during a stormy meeting of the working group on international affairs on 5 July. At that meeting, Mikulin laid the blame for the ouster of Soviet forces from Eastern Europe to the New Thinking and its architects. He also charged that the idea that the Common European Home would eliminate the

---

424 *Sovetskaia Rossiia*, 21 June 1990. This account of the military's criticism of the political leadership on defense and international security issues follows Stephen Foye, "Military Hard-Liner Condemns 'New Thinking' in Security Policy," *Report on the USSR* (Radio Liberty, Munich), Vol. 2, No. 28, 13 July 1990, pp. 4-6.

425 Ibid.

426 Stephen Foye, "Defense Issues at the Party Congress," *Report on the USSR* (Radio Liberty, Munich), Vol. 2, No. 30 (July 1990), pp. 1-4, and *id.*, "The Soviet Armed Forces: Lead-Up to the Party Congress," *Report on the USSR* (Radio Liberty, Munich), Vol. 2, No. 28 (July 1990), pp. 1-4.

opposing military blocs was simply a "myth."[427] Admiral Khvatov summed up the allegedly dire security position that the New Thinking (rather than pre-Gorbachev policies) had produced: "We have no allies in the West. We have no allies in the East. Consequently, we are back to where we were in 1939."[428]

There is little doubt that such sentiments were widely shared in the military officers' corps. The imminent inclusion of unified Germany in NATO, the withdrawal of forces from Eastern Europe, and large asymmetrical cuts in CFE were, after all, merely some more milestones marking the sharp decline of military factors in Soviet foreign policy and the emasculation of the military's influence in decision-making. To that extent, the important point to consider is not whether the military's criticism at the Russian and Soviet party congresses was the tip of an iceberg of military grumbling and dissatisfaction – a point that can be taken for granted – but whether its exponents were the spearhead of a coordinated effort to intervene in politics or even the organizational core of a military coup. It is doubtful, at least for that stage in the demise of the Soviet empire and the Soviet Union, that such far-reaching conclusions can be drawn. The following reasons warrant doubt.

One is the low rank of some of the most vociferous military critics. Alksnis and Petrushenko were merely colonels – the "black colonels" as they were called derisively by civilian reformers – and they lacked the standing and a wider base in the military establishment that would justify considering them leaders of a political revolt. Neither was Russian (Alksnis was Latvian and Petrushenko was Belorussian). Their support and that of the conservative Soyuz parliamentary group, where they played a prominent role, was drawn mostly from assimilated non-Russians or Russians from outside the RSFSR.[429] Makashov's extreme reactionary diatribes could only serve to undermine, rather than support the formulation of a politically sound and coordinated military position that could be taken seriously and become politically effective. Lizichev, Boiko, and Mikulin were political officers and because of that function presumably more representative of the party than of the professional officers' corps. Only Khvatov was a high-ranking professional military officer but his position and influence in the armed forces, like that of the others critics, was also not

---

427 Foye, "Defense Issues at the Party Congress," p. 2; Paul Quinn-Judge, "Military Assails Concessions to West, Arms Cuts," *Boston Globe*, July 6, 1990. The intended targets of the military criticism did not fail to respond. Shevardnadze, for instance, stated: "I was told that some comrades said at the section's session that the idea of a Common European Home is an illusion or a myth. Thinking like that means failing to notice what is going on around us and closing one's eyes to the facts"; "Otvety na voprosy uchastnikov s"ezda. E.A. Shevardnadze," *Pravda*, 11 July 1990.

428 John-Thor Dahlburg, *Los Angeles Times*, 6 July 1990, as quoted by Foye, "Defense Issues at the Party Congress," p. 2.

429 Miller, *Gorbachev*, p. 164.

comparable to that of, say, the commanders of the five branches of the Soviet armed forces or the chiefs of the Moscow and Leningrad military districts.

Another reason for questioning the validity of the theory that the military critics at the party congresses were the spearhead and organizational core of a coordinated effort to topple the political leadership and change security policy is the failure of the *top* military leaders, at a crucial juncture of Soviet domestic politics, to provide public backing for the critics' frontal attack. Whereas Yazov, in two interviews at the end of June, had indeed associated himself with some of the positions at variance with those of the political leadership and had again rejected the ideas of German NATO membership and asymmetrical cuts in conventional weapons,[430] he gave an essentially bland and non-committal speech at the Twenty-eighth Party Congress. In the circumstances, this could be interpreted as support, albeit lukewarm, for the president. Moiseev's speech was more critical, but at the same time he de facto defended Gorbachev against some of the charges of complacency and failure to meet rising dangers, stating that the Soviet Union possessed "a reliable rocket shield that ensures its full security."[431]

Another reason lies in the attention paid by the congress to a myriad of other issues. In relative perspective, Eastern Europe and unified Germany's membership in NATO were neither treated extensively nor were they the most contentious. Scrutiny of the transcripts indicates that the most controversial issues were personnel and party power and organization; "depolitization" and "departization," that is, dissolution of the party structures, in the armed forces, the internal security ministry, and the KGB; the crisis of ideology; the abysmal state of the economy; the problems of national emancipation in the USSR, such as the Baltic crisis and the conflict between Armenia and Azerbaijan over Nagorno-Karabakh; the extent of republican sovereignty; and the resignation of the Democratic Platform from the CPSU, including its leading members Yeltsin, Gavril Popov, and Anatoli Sobchak (the mayors of Moscow and Leningrad), and the historian Yuri Afanasev.

Yet another reason for doubting the organizational cohesion and political effectiveness of military opposition lay in the fact that the armed forces were internally divided. There was no unanimity even on the issue that could be considered central to the military's concerns: united Germany's membership in NATO. Maj.-Gen. Geli Batenin is an example of the divergence of views. In an article for an East German newspaper published on 4 May, he rejected both the concept of dual membership of a united Germany in the two blocs – a concept, he thought, "favored

---

430 *Rabochaia tribuna*, 26 June 1990, and TASS, 27 June 1990, as quoted by Foye, "Military Hard-Liner Condemns 'New Thinking,'" p. 6.

431 TASS, 5 July 1990, as quoted by Foye, "Defense Issues at the Party Congress," p. 2.

by the Soviet foreign minister" – and German neutrality.[432] He based his case against the *dual membership* idea on the premise that such a solution would be useful only if the Warsaw Pact had some prospects to become a viable organization. After the formation of the new governments in Central and Eastern Europe, however, he saw no chance of that happening: "Czechoslovakia, one of the most important Warsaw Pact countries in military terms," he wrote, "is practically on the verge of leaving the alliance. Similar developments can be observed in Hungary and Romania." Furthermore, he reasoned that dual membership would have a destabilizing effect "on the process of unification of the two Germanys because in this way confrontation between the Warsaw Pact and NATO will continue to be focused on the territory of the united Germany."

Batenin also argued that a *neutral or non-aligned* Germany would not be in line with European security interests. "The military and economic potential of a unified Germany concentrated in the center of Europe," he contended, "would give rise to serious concerns among its neighbors." The chances were slim, he continued, that a united Germany would voluntarily accept military-political impotence, and it was for that reason that demilitarization of Germany should also be ruled out, except within the context of coordinated and comprehensive European disarmament measures. The best solution in Batenin's view, therefore, was

> *to include the whole of Germany into the political organization of NATO.* The military jurisdiction of NATO will remain effective on the territory of the present-day FRG. In other words, concerning its military incorporation in NATO, Germany will retain its current status during the entire transition period [of perhaps five to ten years]. The Bundeswehr, being part of NATO's integrated command structure, will remain within the boundaries of the western part of a united Germany. In the eastern part, the National People's Army will continue to exist but *it will no longer be under the operational control of the Warsaw Pact.*[433]

Even more at variance with conservative military opinion, in an earlier interview with a German defense specialist, he had stated: "To maintain a dividing line between Germany and Germany, or between Germany and Poland, is unacceptable. That would mean to remain stuck in outdated thinking. ... Both alliances [for the duration

---

432 Maj. Gen. Geli Viktorovich Batenin, "Vorgezogene Version: Ganz Deutschland in der NATO," *Berliner Zeitung*, 4 May 1990. At the time when his article was published, Batenin was assigned to the Central Committee's Ideological Department. Importantly for the current context, he was not a political officer without professional experience. According to information which he himself provided in an interview with Hans-Henning Schröder of the Bundesinstitut für ostwissenschaftliche und internationale Studien, he born in Vladivostok, entered officer's school in the 1950s, was commissioned first as an artillery officer and then in the rocket forces (*raketchik*), served in the General Staff specializing in nuclear strategy and, in 1989-90, was involved in drafting the Soviet position in the CFE negotiations. He was also a member of the Soviet delegation during Gorbachev's visit to West Germany in June 1989.

433 Ibid. (italics mine).

of the Warsaw Pact's existence] have to link up with each other in order to overcome this division."[434]

One of the possible options for the military to delay, deflect, or derail Gorbachev's impending decision on Germany's NATO membership in the spring and summer of 1990 was to forge an alliance with conservative party officials. The CPSU, however, was in disarray.[435] The legislatures, state institutions, and the emerging presidential structures were replacing its power and influence; its Marxist-Leninist foundation lay in shambles; and its popularity was being eroded by glasnost. A neo-Stalinist Communist Party of Russia was created to compete against both its communist parent and the decidedly more democratic and liberally inclined Russian Congress of People's Deputies. Another split, one involving the CPSU itself, was imminent, with the members of its Democratic Platform, as mentioned, about to leave the party and perhaps intent on creating a new social-democratic entity. In March 1990, the constitutional article guaranteeing a political monopoly to the CPSU had been abolished; the Central Committee was involved in a bitter dispute with "social" organizations," such as the Komsomol and labor unions; its Secretariat had been emasculated; and rank-and-file members were leaving in droves.

Furthermore, the once mighty Politburo was now a stricken and internally divided group that had seen its decision-making power and authority curtailed progressively since the October 1988 party reorganization and was scheduled to be further emasculated at the Twenty-eighth congress. At that congress, its full and alternate members had to answer for the massive failures of the Soviet economy and other domestic ills: Prime Minister Ryzhkov and his deputy and planning chief Yuri Maslyukov on the economic decline; Vadim Medvedev on the demise of Marxism; Lev Zaikov on the bloated and inefficient military-industrial complex; and Georgi Razumovsky on personnel policy and the drain of the party membership. Ligachev, who had vehemently attacked Gorbachev's policy on the German issue at the February Central Committee plenum and was to do so again at the Twenty-eighth Party Congress, certainly was one of the potential organizers of a revolt against the president. But the PB, in conjunction with the CC, could no longer remove Gorbachev from the office of General Secretary, let alone from the presidency.[436] Furthermore, Ligachev's power was waning and, at the congress, he was ousted.

---

434 Batenin interview with Hans-Henning Schröder, Moscow, 4 April 1990.

435 This analysis of the role of the CPSU and CPR in Soviet decision-making on unified Germany and NATO draws on Fredo Arias-King, "Essence of a Soviet Decision: Allowing a United Germany to Join the North Atlantic Treaty Organization. An Organizational-Bureaucratic Approach," Research Paper, the Kennedy School of Government, Harvard University, January 1996 (unpublished), pp. 1-16.

436 This required a two-thirds vote of the legislature.

Although in no way an action channel for Soviet foreign policy or even domestic politics, the Communist Party of Russia exerted some influence on decision-making but in ways quite contrary to its members' intentions. Given its utterly reactionary and unrepresentative nature, the fierce attacks directed at the founding congress against Gorbachev, Yakovlev, Shevardnadze as well as against moderate or conservative party officials not only served to further delegitimize communism but forced moderate party leaders to side with the reformers. This occurred, for instance, at the Russian Congress of People's Deputies, held at the same time as the CPR's inaugural congress. At the former congress, CPR spokesmen blasted a large part of the CPSU's moderate strata, insulting even the stalwart economist Leonid Abalkin and vowing to cleanse "cancerous tumors," including *Pravda* (!), and to reimpose censorship. What about a possible alliance between the hard-line military opposition, like-minded officials in the CPSU, and the CPR? This, too, would have been counterproductive. Even Ligachev was averse to associating himself with this new party entity and Igor Polozkov, its new leader, and openly criticized him. Similarly, on the day of his election as CPR chairman, the nightly news program Vremya chose not to cover the proceedings, featuring instead a story on Yeltsin and Popov.[437]

To summarize, although the military criticism of the political leadership's policies on the withdrawal of the Soviet armed forces from Eastern Europe and NATO's first eastern enlargement was certainly indicative of wide-spread dissatisfaction in the armed forces, it should not be interpreted as proof of a coordinated attempt to interfere in domestic politics. This was because of the relatively low rank and standing of the most vociferous critics in the military establishment; the disassociation of the top military leadership from both extreme positions and direct involvement in politics; and internal divisions concerning the most appropriate response to a rapidly changing security environment in East Germany and Eastern Europe. As for military and party collusion, by the spring and summer of 1990 Gorbachev had effectively emasculated the party apparatus and curtailed the party's and the military's influence in international security decision-making by transferring many of their previous functions to a combination of reformist foreign ministry personnel, academic specialists, and a small circle of decision-makers. There was no unanimity of views in the military. The party was hopelessly divided, and the creation of the reactionary Russian Communist Party unwittingly served to undercut the construction of a reasonable conservative alternative to Gorbachev's international security policies and drive moderate party leaders into his camp. The Twenty-eighth Party Congress, therefore, contrary to his and his supporter's anxiety, did not turn into

---

437 Arias-King, "Essence of a Soviet Decision," p. 11; Alexander Rahr, "The Russian Triangle: Gorbachev, Yeltsin, Polozkov," *Report on the USSR* (Radio Liberty, Munich), Vol. 2, No. 27 (July 1990), p. 5.

a major impediment to his policies but, perhaps paradoxically, even helped facilitate his consent to unified Germany's membership in NATO.

In the remaining sections, the timing and circumstances of that consent will be described. Three possible explanations will be examined. First, the Soviet Union may have been running out of viable alternative options. Second, the West may have offered sufficiently favorable conditions. Third, Gorbachev came to accept that unified Germany's membership in NATO served Soviet security interests better than any other possible solution.

The Consent to NATO Membership

When Chernyaev was asked, when it was that Gorbachev consented to unified Germany's membership in NATO, he unhesitatingly replied: "At the Soviet-American summit." When the supplementary question was put to him, what had induced the Soviet leader to change his mind, the answer was equally short and precise: "Baker's nine points."[438] From 16 to 19 May, Baker had again visited Moscow and talked to Gorbachev and Shevardnadze, with the German problem as the main focus of the discussions. The secretary of state presented a comprehensive package of incentives designed to persuade Gorbachev to accept the basic foundation of all subsequent and supplementary measures for a German settlement. As Baker has explained in his memoirs, the nine points had been advanced individually, "but by wrapping them up in a package and calling them 'nine assurances,' we greatly enhanced their political effect."[439] The nine points were as follows:

1. Limitation of the size of armed forces in Europe, including in Central Europe, in a CFE agreement, with further reductions to be provided for in CFE follow-on negotiations.
2. The beginning of arms control negotiations on short-range nuclear missiles to be moved up.
3. Reaffirmation by Germany that it would neither possess nor produce nuclear, biological, or chemical weapons.
4. No NATO forces to be stationed on the former territory of the GDR during a specified transition period.
5. An appropriate transition period to be agreed upon for the withdrawal of all Soviet troops from German territory.
6. A comprehensive review of NATO strategy and change of NATO's conventional and nuclear force posture.
7. Settlement of Germany's future borders, that is, essentially confirmation of the Polish-German frontier.

---

438 Interview with Chernyaev.

439 Baker, *The Politics of Diplomacy*, p. 251n.

8. Enhancement of the functions of the CSCE to ensure a significant role for the Soviet Union in Europe and linkage of a summit meeting of that organization with the finalization of a CFE treaty, both to take place at the end of 1990.
9. Development of Germany's economic ties with the Soviet Union, including fulfillment of the GDR's economic obligations to the USSR.[440]

Gorbachev took copious notes of Baker's presentation. But his reaction was contradictory. He approved much of what the secretary of state had said but adhered to the by then standard Soviet position that it was impossible for the Soviet Union to accept a unified Germany in NATO. This would constitute a fundamental shift in the strategic balance of forces and jeopardize his program at home. "It will be the end of perestroika," he warned. Although he knew that Germany would be closer to the United States, it still should not be in the Western alliance. If that was unacceptable to the United States, then perhaps the Soviet Union should be admitted to NATO.[441] His ambiguous and conceptually incoherent position was reflected also in his reply to Baker's question as to whether, by insisting that Germany remain outside NATO, he was talking about a *neutral* Germany. "I don't know if I'd call it that," Gorbachev said. "Maybe I'd call it nonaligned."[442]

The nine points also figured prominently at the Soviet-American summit in Washington, 30 May-3 June.[443] On 31 May, in response to President Bush's review of the assurances, Gorbachev initially reiterated the intransigent Soviet position (letting a united Germany join only NATO would "unbalance" Europe), and he repeated the alternatives he preferred: Germany should either be a member of both alliances or not belong to any alliance. Shevardnadze supported the dual membership idea and Gorbachev added that perhaps *any* country could join either alliance, musing (again) whether the Soviet Union should apply for NATO membership. (Bush, with a smile, wondered how Marshal Akhromeev – sitting across the table – would like serving under an American NATO commander.) The American president then introduced an argument that other US and West German officials had begun to employ at lower

---

440 Ibid, pp. 250-51; and Zelikow and Rice, *Germany Unified*, pp. 263-64. The nine points were prepared by National Security Council staff member Robert Zoellick. Earlier on the same day, Zoellick, National Security Council expert on Soviet affairs Condoleezza Rice and Raymond Seitz of the State Department's European bureau had discussed these points with Kvitsinsky and Bondarenko. Confirmation of this and other points related to the U.S.-Soviet summit as provided by Zoellick in conversation with the author at a conference of the Freie Universität Berlin on 5 July 1994, attended by the Political Directors of the Two Plus Four negotiations.

441 Zelikow and Rice, *Germany Unified*, p. 265.

442 Baker, *The Politics of Diplomacy*, p. 251.

443 On 30 May, Gorbachev had arrived in Washington from Ottawa. In talks with Canadian prime minister Brian Mulroney, the Soviet president had shown no flexibility on the German problem. The account of the proceedings at the Soviet-American summit follows Zelikow and Rice, *Germany Unified*, pp. 276-81. An earlier, less detailed, account of the meeting can be found in Beschloss and Talbott, *At the Highest Levels*, pp. 215-30.

levels. Under the CSCE's principles in the Helsinki Final Act, all nations had the right to choose their own alliances. Should Germany, too, not have the right to decide for itself which alliance it would want to join? Gorbachev nodded and agreed matter-of factly that it did.[444]

From the American viewpoint, it was important to ascertain whether Gorbachev's change of position was merely a *lapsus linguae* and temporary aberration or, if not, to induce him to commit himself publicly to it. Prompted by a note from Robert Blackwill, Bush said: "I am gratified that you and I seem to agree that nations can choose their own alliances." Gorbachev reiterated his change of position: "So we will put it this way. The United States and the Soviet Union are in favor of Germany deciding herself [after a Two Plus Four settlement] in which alliance she would like to participate."[445] As for a public commitment to the change of position, the NSC staff prepared a statement for the president to be delivered on 3 June, at the end of the summit conference. It submitted the draft statement to Soviet ambassador Alexander Bessmertnykh for his review and approval by Gorbachev. There were no objections. The statement read:

> On the matter of Germany's external alliances, I believe, as do Chancellor Kohl and members of the Alliance, that the united Germany should be a full member of NATO. President Gorbachev, frankly, does not hold that view. But we are in full agreement that the matter of alliance membership is, in accordance with the Helsinki Final Act, a matter for the Germans to decide.[446]

The de facto consent to unified Germany's membership in NATO was completely unexpected by any of the participants, American or Soviet. On the Soviet side, there had been no prior consultation or coordination. Gorbachev had acted unilaterally and spontaneously. Even his personal assistant on foreign policy had not been alerted to the impending change of his chief's position.[447] In the White House's Cabinet Room on 31 May, there was consequently a palpable atmosphere among Soviet participants, who almost physically distanced themselves from Gorbachev's remarks. Akhromeev and Falin could be observed uncomfortably shifting in their seats.[448] Gorbachev

---

444 Zelikow and Rice, *Germany Unified*, p. 277. Participants in the meeting on the Soviet side included Shevardnadze, Chernyaev, Akhromeev, Falin, Dobrynin, and Alexander Bessmertnykh, the Soviet ambassador in Washington.

445 There is a discrepancy in the rendering of the conversation between the American account, as reconstructed by Zelikow and Rice, and the Soviet version, as contained in Gorbachev's and Chernyaev's memoirs. According to the latter account, "the Soviet Union" was omitted in Gorbachev's reply (Gorbachev, *Zhizn'*, Vol. 2, p. 175; Chernyaev, *Shest' let s Gorbachevym*, p. 348).

446 Zelikow and Rice, *Germany Unified*, p. 281.

447 Interview with Chernyaev.

448 Zoellick, personal communication to the author (see above, n. 440); Baker, *The Politics of Diplomacy*, p. 253; and Zelikow and Rice, *Germany Unified*, pp. 277-78.

slipped a piece of paper to the latter, asking him to explain the legal, political, and military rationales that made a pro-Atlantic solution unacceptable. Falin replied on that paper that he was ready to do so.[449] While he launched into his presentation, Gorbachev conferred with Shevardnadze. When Gorbachev reentered the discussion, he proposed that Shevardnadze work with Baker on the German issue. Oddly, Shevardnadze at first refused, right in front of the Americans, saying that the matter had to be decided by the heads of government.[450]

It is appropriate to clarify at this stage that Gorbachev's agreement with the Western position that Germany be allowed to choose the alliance membership it wanted was neither unconditional nor irreversible. In *his* mind, at least, there vaguely still existed different options, one of which would somehow make it possible to avoid Germany's full membership in NATO.[451] The ambiguities of his position were reflected in his public stance. On 12 June, in his report on the Soviet-American summit to the Supreme Soviet, Gorbachev said that he had "told the president that I think that the American presence in Europe, since it fulfills a certain role in maintaining stability, is an element of the strategic situation and does not represent a problem for us." He also outlined a solution, according to which "the Bundeswehr would, as before, be subordinate to NATO, and the East German troops would be *subordinate to the new Germany,*" which obviously meant that they would no longer be subordinate to the Warsaw Pact.[452] However, this applied only to a "transition period." What, if anything, would happen thereafter was left open by Gorbachev. The murky security waters were muddied further by the ideas, also mentioned in his report, of "associate membership" of the GDR in the Warsaw Pact and a unified Germany having to "honor all obligations" inherited from the two Germanys, and by his return to the "dual membership" proposal.[453] Only one thing was crystal clear: there was a complete and deliberate lack of clarity in the Soviet stance, except for the fact that the notion of a unified Germany in NATO as being absolutely unacceptable was no longer valid.

This applied also to Shevardnadze's position. His initial recalcitrance at the Soviet-American summit to work with Baker on details of a security arrangement that would – in accordance with Gorbachev's spontaneous consent – proceed from the premise of unified Germany's membership in NATO did not mean that the foreign minister objected to the principle of the revised Soviet stance. In the internal management of the issue, however, it was sensible for him to let *Gorbachev* take responsibility rather

449 Falin, *Politische Erinnerungen*, p. 493.

450 Zelikow and Rice, *Germany Unified*, p. 278.

451 Interview with Chernyaev.

452 "Vystuplenie M.S. Gorbacheva na tret'ei sessii Verkhovnogo Soveta SSSR," *Pravda* and *Izvestiia*, 13 June 1990.

453 Ibid. (italics mine).

than leading or leaving the conservative opposition to believe that yet another fundamental change in international security policy had unilaterally been decided by the foreign minister.

If it is correct that Gorbachev, Shevardnadze, and Yakovlev were tilting towards a formula that would allow unified Germany to join NATO[454] and that could assuage the conservative opposition and be made acceptable to the public, much depended now on whether the political leadership could deliver on two crucial issues: transformation of NATO and transitional arrangements until the consolidation of a new European security system. As for the *transformation of the Atlantic alliance*, for domestic political purposes it was vitally important for the Soviet leadership to be able to present to the public a NATO that would be transformed from a primarily military alliance to one emphasizing its political character – a demand that had figured prominently as soon as German unification had been put on the international agenda. At the 5 July London summit, as will be shown below, the West would make an effort to accommodate this demand. Concerning the issue of *transition*, this meant many things to Soviet and Western political leaders and diplomats. It pertained to several different processes and implied different answers to the questions how long the transition should last and what should be its end result. From the Soviet perspective, these questions had political and psychological as well as practical and technical dimensions. To borrow a phrase from the American discussion on Vietnam, a "decent interval" was needed to save face. Furthermore, the length of time the Soviet armed forces should be allowed to stay in East Germany, as well as their status, had to resolved. Also to be decided was the question of whether – in accordance with the equivalency principle – the Western allied forces, like those of the Soviet Union, should only be permitted to stay for a specified period and then be withdrawn from Germany. Finally and most far-reaching, a decision was needed whether the alliances themselves should only exist for a transitional period and then be dissolved in favor of a new European security system.

---

454 Yakovlev's role at this stage was connected much more with the management of the seemingly intractable Baltic issue and other nationality problems. However, in an attempt to dispel the notion that Gorbachev single-handedly and without consultation with senior members in the leadership decided the issue of Germany's NATO membership, Chernyaev has asserted that Shevardnadze and Yakovlev were aware of all the options and that Gorbachev discussed these options with them separately (interview with the author). Yakovlev, furthermore, was a firm adherent to the principle of the Freedom of Choice, which had prompted Gorbachev's change of position on the NATO issue in Washington. For instance, in the 15 June 1990 meeting of the Central Committee's Commission on International Policy, where Falin expounded the conservative position on the changes in Eastern Europe and the loss of East Germany, Yakovlev had stated: "Since we have declared the principle of the Freedom of Choice, we should firmly stick to it"; "Peremeny v Tsentral'noi i Vostochnoi Evrope. S zasedaniia Komissii TsK KPSS po voprosam mezhdunarodnoi politiki 15 iiunia 1990 g.," *Izvestiia Tsk KPSS*, No. 10 (October 1990), p. 113.

At the 11 June meeting between Shevardnadze and Genscher in Brest, the Soviet foreign minister had explained the basic rationale of the demand for a transitional period. If there was to be no such period, he argued, the Soviet Union would be isolated. The political and military balance in Europe would be changed. The GDR would be part of NATO. And the Soviet Union would have no guarantees for its security.[455]

This exposé of Soviet interests differed significantly from the provisions of a draft treaty prepared by the MFA's Third Department (Bondarenko) and tabled by Shevardnadze at the 22 June Two Plus Four meeting in East Berlin. For at least five years after unification, according to the draft, all the GDR's international agreements would remain in force; the competence of the Warsaw Pact and NATO could not be changed and would not extend to territories that had previously not been within their scope; ceilings on German armed forces would be imposed in quantity (no more than 200,000 to 250,000 troops) and in quality, with implementation of the reductions and structural changes within three years. After five years, the troop contingents of the Four Powers would either be withdrawn or retained at token levels; the Bundeswehr and the East German National People's Army would be confined to their former territories. The settlement of these issues would remain in effect until both NATO and the Warsaw Pact were dissolved or Germany withdrew from both alliances.[456]

The Soviet draft on various transitional security arrangements itself, like so many others before, had a transitional character. It quickly passed into oblivion. In the 22 June meeting, as Shevardnadze was speaking, Baker passed a note to Genscher asking, "What does this mean?" Genscher (accurately) replied: "Window dressing."[457] The West German foreign minister was apparently confident that the presentation of the draft was essentially a holding operation designed to gain time and to prepare the Soviet foreign policy establishment and public opinion to accept the inevitable. That confidence he derived from another meeting with Shevardnadze, on 18 June in Münster, where Frank Elbe, his aide, had been given a "non-paper" by Tarasenko that did not contain any reference to the retention of Four Power rights after the end of a transition period, and where he (Elbe) had been told "not to worry." Everything would "proceed as [outlined] in this paper."[458]

To return to the central issue of the Soviet leadership's consent to unified Germany's membership in NATO, at the beginning of July the stage for the formal consent was set: various alternative options had been presented and rejected by the West; a plethora of private talks and the Two Plus Four meetings at the foreign

---

455 Genscher, *Erinnerungen*, p. 811.

456 Zelikow and Rice, *Germany Unified*, pp. 296-97.

457 Genscher, *Erinnerungen*, pp. 824-25.

458 Ibid., p. 821, and Kiessler and Elbe, *Ein runder Tisch*, p. 159.

ministers' level had clarified the form that could be attached to NATO's first eastward expansion: non-integrated German units could be stationed in the former GDR immediately after Germany regained full sovereignty, and German NATO-integrated forces after the withdrawal of Soviet troops, but no allied forces; Germany would not produce or possess nuclear, bacteriological or chemical weapons; NATO, at its London summit, had ostensibly committed itself to a transformation of its structure and its role in Europe; the G-7, at its meeting in Houston, had held out the prospect of economic assistance; Kohl had committed himself to codifying a complete rearrangement of German-Soviet political and economic relations in a comprehensive bilateral treaty and to accept the Polish-German borders as final; Lithuania had created favorable conditions for a policy change in Moscow by suspending its declaration of independence; and the conservative opposition of Soviet party and foreign ministry officials and military officers had been outmaneuvered or isolated itself and certainly was politically ineffective as both the Russian and Soviet party congresses had demonstrated. The stage was set for the formal consent to unified Germany's membership in NATO during Chancellor Kohl visit to the Soviet Union from 14 to 16 July.[459]

On 11 July, in a letter to Kohl, Gorbachev had confirmed his invitation for the German chancellor to visit the Soviet Union, including the suggestion for a side-trip to Stavropol, the town and krai where he had grown up and begun his career, and the small North Caucasian mountain resort of Arkhyz, about 100 miles south of the city. The suggestion was obviously meant to provide a personal touch to the visit and set the stage for a repetition of the informal conversations which the two leaders had had in June 1989 along the banks of the Rhine, and it augured well for what the German participants could expect from the talks.[460] According to the accounts provided by Chernyaev and Teltschik, the breakthrough on the main issues took place on 15 July in Moscow, in the guest house of the Soviet foreign ministry on Tolstoy street. The private conversations between Kohl and Gorbachev were witnessed only by the two aides and interpreters.[461]

---

459 The significance of the Lithuanian decision and of the results of the London and Houston summits will be discussed below.

460 This was recognized by Teltschik, *329 Tage*, p. 310; for the informal conversations between Kohl and Gorbachev on the banks along the Rhine, see above, p. 396. Gorbachev's commitment to hold talks in the second half of July and to include the Caucasus as their venue had occurred on 14 May, when Teltschik had been on a secret mission to Moscow; see below, p. 543.

461 The subsequent account of the 15 July talks is based on ibid., pp. 319-24 and Chernyaev, *Shest' let s Gorbachevym*, pp. 358-59. Kohl's memoirs essentially confirm these accounts; Kohl, *Ich wollte Deutschlands Einheit*, pp. 421-44. There are some important differences in the portrayal and interpretation of the talks between Teltschik and Chernyaev on the one hand, and Kohl on the other. These will be noted below. A note on decision-making processes in the Soviet Union: immediately prior to the Kohl visit, Falin had become a footnote to history on the German problem. According to his own account, as Kohl was already on his way to Moscow, he called

The German chancellor pointed out that these were historic times and that the opportunities that presented themselves should be used to good effect. Bismarck had once said that one had to seize the coattails of history. Gorbachev replied that he had not been aware of this remark but that he found it quite interesting and agreed with it. Kohl reminded his host that they both belonged to the same generation – too young to fight in the Second World War but old enough consciously to experience these years. Against the background of their common experience, the German chancellor continued, they had an obligation to use the opportunities for change.

Kohl had apparently struck a responsive cord in Gorbachev. He replied that he was ten years old when the war began and that he could remember very well the events that had occurred during the war. He said that he shared Kohl's view that their generation possessed unique experiences and he also agreed that, if unique opportunities for change existed now, it was the task of that generation to use and shape them. He was impressed above all by the fact that there was less talk now as to who had won or lost the war and a greater understanding of one world.

The German chancellor then spoke of the trust that he thought had developed between them in their conversations in Bonn in June 1989, in the park of the chancellor's office, on the banks of the Rhine. On that occasion, they had talked of their common obligation to shape the future of their peoples and to develop relations of friendship, he reminded Gorbachev. He, Kohl, still considered this exchange to have been an event of fundamental importance that had established a relationship of trust between them.

The next portion of the exchange between the two leaders is of crucial importance for appreciating a new frame of reference that apparently had taken hold in Gorbachev's mind. Rather than continuing to see the world through the prism of Marxism-Leninism and the state interests of the Soviet Union, he reverted to national images. He introduced what he himself called thoughts of a basic nature. A situation was now developing, he said, that had to bring *Russia* and Germany together again. If both *peoples* had been separated in the past, they now had to come together again. For him that goal was of equal importance as the normalization of relations with the

---

Gorbachev and asked for ten to fifteen minutes of his time. Shortly before midnight, the Soviet leader obliged and returned the call. Falin wanted to impress three points on Gorbachev for the upcoming negotiations. (1) An *Anschluß* on the basis of article 23 should be ruled out. (2) Unified Germany should not be allowed to become a full member of NATO. At the very least, if he were to agree to it nevertheless, Germany's status should be similar to that of France, but under no circumstances should nuclear weapons be stationed in any part of Germany. (3) No agreement on the political issues should be signed unless all matters concerning Soviet assets in the GDR were settled. Gorbachev asked a few polite questions and concluded the conversation by saying, "I will do what I can. Only I fear that the train has already left." Falin, *Politische Erinnerungen*, pp. 493-94.

United States. If it were possible to find a new quality in the relations between Russia and Germany, both peoples and all of Europe would benefit.

The German chancellor agreed and provided incentives for Gorbachev to consent to German demands. The Federal Republic, he said, was prepared to conclude a comprehensive treaty with the Soviet Union to cover all areas of cooperation. To be included in such a treaty could be principles such as the renunciation of force and non-aggression, along the lines of provisions contained in the declaration adopted at the July NATO summit meting in London. Furthermore, reporting on the results of the summit meetings of the European Council in Dublin, NATO in London, and the G-7 in Houston, he assured Gorbachev that the common theme at all of these meetings had been the conviction that the processes of reform in the Soviet Union had to be supported. Kohl then added another incentive by stating that, in his view, economic and financial cooperation were an integral part of the total package.

He also addressed the dynamic processs of German unification and described the still deteriorating conditions in the GDR. As if still in response to what had been a recurrent Soviet warning since the autumn of 1989, he assured Gorbachev that he was not attempting to accelerate matters artificially. From the very beginning, he had had different ideas as to the time scale of unification. He would have liked to have had more time, he said regretfully, but the economic decline of the GDR had been dramatic. Turning to specific problems to be resolved, Kohl mentioned three areas in which agreement had to be reached if the time-table for the conclusion of the Two Plus Four talks and the CSCE summit conference were to be met: the withdrawal of Soviet Union forces from East Germany; membership of a united Germany in NATO; and the numerical strength of the armed forces of the united country. Restoration of full sovereignty of Germany had to be the final result of the Two Plus Four talks.

The two leaders exchanged papers containing their mutual ideas concerning the provisions to be contained in a treaty on partnership and cooperation between the Soviet Union and Germany. Gorbachev then returned to security issues. Germany, he acknowledged, should regain full sovereignty. On the central issue of NATO, Gorbachev said that membership of unified Germany in that alliance constituted the most important problem. *De jure* the question was unambiguous. *De facto* matters were more complicated. NATO authority could not (immediately) be extended to the former territory of the GDR. A transitional period was necessary. Kohl and Teltschik, like Bush and his advisers six weeks earlier, were stunned, but the German chancellor outwardly reacted calmly and was eager to make sure that there had been no misunderstanding. Pressed by him, Gorbachev clarified that *Germany could remain in NATO,* but NATO had to take into consideration that its authority could not be extended to the territory of the former GDR for a transitional period, that is, for as long as Soviet troops continued to be stationed there. He reinforced this historic concession by a second commitment. The final settlement in the Two Plus Four framework should provide for the *immediate* abolition of Four Power rights. A separate treaty should govern the status of the Soviet armed forces on the territory of the former GDR.

The historical record at this point remains somewhat unclear. Kohl and Teltschik's account differ on both what Gorbachev said subsequently and on the implications of what he had said. Concerning the issue of the status of the Soviet forces and a future treaty on the modalities of their withdrawal, Gorbachev – according to Kohl – had stated that negotiations on that issue could begin after an (unspecified) transitional period.[462] Teltschik, in contrast, does not record Gorbachev mentioning anything about the beginning of such negotiations. He also has Gorbachev saying that the treaty ought to govern the presence of the Soviet forces for a period of three to four years.[463] The inference to be drawn from this is that negotiations could begin immediately, without any transitional period.

The second issue of divergence concerns Gorbachev's distinction between Germany's *de jure* and *de facto* NATO membership. What Gorbachev seemed to have in mind, according to Kohl, was to limit NATO for all practical purposes to the western part of Germany, and that any change of that restriction could be agreed upon only later, after the successful conclusion of the negotiations on the withdrawal of Soviet forces. Contrary to his host's assurances, as Kohl has commented, the Federal Republic would not have regained sovereignty after all. The later negotiations on the withdrawal of forces would have provided Moscow with a lever with which to exert pressure on Bonn to accede to Soviet demands on the alliance problem.[464] Apparently sensing the disappointment of his guest, Kohl continues, Gorbachev said reassuringly: "We have [only] begun our talks here in Moscow and will continue them in the Caucasus mountains. In the mountain air, things will be seen much more clearly."[465]

Teltschik did not share Kohl's skepticism. For Chernyaev, too, the matter was settled. In his view, his chief had no longer suggested any "diluted versions" on Germany's full membership in NATO. In accordance with his position and protocol, Chernyaev should have accompanied his chief to the Caucasus. However, he talked his way out of it. "The issue has already been settled in Moscow," he thought, "and I would only get in the way." As a reflection of the tremendous strain under which he and others in Gorbachev's entourage were working, he had another, and more

462 Kohl, *Ich wollte Deutschlands Einheit*, p. 425.

463 Teltschik, *329 Tage*, p. 324.

464 Kohl, *Ich wollte Deutschlands Einheit*, p. 425.

465 Ibid., p. 426.

important reason why he chose not to go along: "I had taken a dislike to Gorbachev since the events at the two party congresses. I did not want to be near him. In my opinion, he did not even notice my absence on the trip. More and more often I thought of resigning."[466]

It was only on 16 July in Arkhyz, after having "argued back and forth," as Kohl writes, with Gorbachev "yielding step by step to our tenacious urging," that the Soviet president relented and agreed that German troops, as part of NATO's integrated command structure, could be stationed on the territory of the former GDR.[467] The final agreement reached at the talks was announced at the neighboring spa of Zheleznovodsk. It consisted of the following eight points:

1. A unified Germany shall comprise the Federal Republic, the GDR, and Berlin.
2. The rights and responsibilities of the Four Powers will end after the achievement of German unification, and unified Germany will enjoy full and unrestricted sovereignty.
3. The unified Germany, exercising its unrestricted sovereignty and in accordance with the Helsinki Final Act, may decide freely and by itself which alliance it wants to belong to.
4. The unified Germany and the Soviet Union will conclude a bilateral treaty providing for the withdrawal of Soviet troops from the GDR within three to four years. Another treaty will cover the consequences of the introduction of the Deutschmark in the GDR for this transitional period.
5. For as long as Soviet troops remain stationed on the territory of the former GDR, NATO structures will not be extended to this part of Germany. The immediate applicability of articles 5 and 6 of the NATO treaty will remain in effect. Non-integrated units of the Bundeswehr – that is, unites of the Territorial Defense – may be stationed immediately after unification on the territory of the GDR and Berlin.
6. Troops of the three Western powers shall remain in Berlin for the duration of the presence of Soviet troops on former GDR territory. The Federal government will seek to conclude corresponding agreements with the three Western governments.
7. The Federal government is willing to make a binding declaration in the current CFE talks in Vienna to reduce the level of the armed forces of a unified Germany to a personnel strength of 370,000 within a period of three to four years.

---

466 Chernyaev, *Shest' let s Gorbachevym*, p. 359.

467 Kohl, *Ich wollte Deutschlands Einheit*, p. 435. Genscher appears to concur with the interpretation that this issue was settled only in Arkhyz; Genscher, *Erinnerungen*, pp. 839-40.

8. A unified Germany will refrain from producing, storing, or controlling nuclear, biological, and chemical weapons and continue to adhere to the Non-Proliferation Treaty.[468]

It is now appropriate to return to the rationale and reasons why Gorbachev relented and acceded practically without dilution or modification to all the positions on the international security status of a unified Germany as developed by the West, foremost by the United States and West Germany. The domestic dimension of his consent has amply been covered. What remains to be examined in conclusion in more detail are some of the important international dimensions of his agreement and their "price tag."

The Warsaw Pact and NATO

The central point to be made about the international dimension of Gorbachev's consent to unified Germany's membership in NATO is that in the spring of 1990 the Soviet Union was running out of options: the neutralization of Germany failed to attract support in both Eastern and Western Europe and in the United States, and ideas such as "dual membership" of Germany in both alliances and "associate membership" of the eastern part of Germany in the Warsaw Pact were rendered obsolete by the rapid disintegration of the latter alliance. Were Gorbachev, his close advisers, and Shevardnadze conscious of these constraints?

Concerning the issue of neutralization, matters were fairly simple. At the February 1990 Open Skies foreign ministers' meeting of NATO and the Warsaw Pact in Ottawa, it had become apparent that only two foreign ministers were calling for the neutralization of Germany: Shevardnadze and East German Foreign Minister Oskar Fischer. At the mid-March 1990 Warsaw Pact foreign ministers' conference in Prague, the USSR again found itself in a minority on the issue. At the closing news conference, Czechoslovak foreign minister Jiři Dienstbier said that neutrality would be "the worst alternative."[469] And even the Polish foreign minister, Krystof Skubiszewski, stated that a neutral Germany would "not be good for Europe"; it would "foster some tendencies in Germany to be a great power acting on its own."[470] Only the East German foreign minister, a member of the communist old guard, still supported his Soviet colleague. But he was to be replaced a few weeks later as a

468 This enumeration is derived from Kohl's statement at the 16 July press conference in Zheleznovodsk, as carried by the German news agencies and TASS; see "Press-konferentsiia M.S. Gorbacheva i G. Kolia," *Pravda* and *Izvestiia*, 18 July 1990, and "Excerpts from Kohl-Gorbachev News Conference," *New York Times*, 17 July 1990. The announcement was structured in seven points; point five and six, as presented here, were merged in Kohl's statement.

469 Celestine Bohlen, "Warsaw Alliance Split on Germany," *New York Times*, 18 March 1990.

470 Ibid.

result of the free elections in the GDR. This settled the matter of neutralization once and for all.

As for the role of the Warsaw Pact in Europe, as mentioned above, Gorbachev had initiated a retreat from the traditional Soviet dissolution-of-the-blocs campaign during his June 1989 visit to West Germany and confirmed that retreat in talks with French foreign minister Dumas in November, after the fall of the Berlin wall, saying that now was not the time to break up the established international political and economic institutions.[471] That line continued into the spring of 1990. On 12 June, for instance, Gorbachev – reporting to the Supreme Soviet on the results of the Soviet-American summit in Washington – stated that the rival blocs would continue to exist "for longer than might be imagined."[472] Was a new Europe then, with NATO but without the Warsaw Pact, inconceivable to Soviet decision makers? Was there a direct connection between the Soviet consent to membership of united Germany in NATO and the continued existence of the Warsaw Pact? But if so, how could Gorbachev ever have believed that it could be possible to salvage the Pact from the revolutions of 1989 in East Central Europe?

The answer may lie in the willingness of the Soviet political leadership and, *nolens volens*, the military to convert the Warsaw Pact from an instrument of Soviet domination and control to a *political* institution respecting the sovereignty of its member nations. Only in the medium to long term would the alliances be dissolved in favor of a new European security structure. A transformation of the Warsaw Pact, they hoped, would be feasible even after the systemic changes in Eastern Europe because the "state interests" of the member countries of the Pact would remain essentially unchanged. Marshal Akhromeev, in November 1989, had expressed this idea as follows:

> First of all, there's the stability of the territory and state boundaries. Second, there are the economic interests of the states. After all, they've been linked for many decades. That is why the military-political alliance remains. The *state interests of both alliances still remain*, and the contradictions remain. And a certain quantity of arms and armed forces will remain. But what matters is that it be such a quantity which would not permit the country to start a war, even if it wanted to.[473]

In conformity with such rationales and rationalizations, the head of a department of the Soviet General Staff, Col. Gen. Nikolai Chervov, announced at a meeting of military chiefs from thirty-five nations held in Vienna in January 1990 to discuss military doctrine that the Warsaw Pact would be thoroughly restructured. The Pact's

---

471 See above, p. 498.

472 "Vystuplenie M.S. Gorbacheva na tret'ei sessii Verkhovnogo Soveta SSSR," *Pravda* and *Izvestiia*, 13 June 1990.

473 Interview with Bill Keller, "Gorbachev's Hope for Future: 'A Common European Home,'" *New York Times*, 30 November 1989 (italics mine).

future, as a Soviet foreign ministry participant in the meeting explained, would be shaped by political and regional interests rather than by ideological solidarity.[474]

The hope that after injection of a reformist antidote the moribund Warsaw Pact would survive and return to the life of European politics was encouraged by attitudes in Poland in the first half of 1990. For a brief time interval, reflecting anxiety about the reconstitution of a potentially powerful Germany at its western borders, Poland remained committed to cooperation with the Soviet Union in a reformed Pact. The then Polish prime minister, Tadeusz Mazowiecki, made this clear when he said that, in its alliance with its eastern neighbor, Poland had passed from the ideological level to the state level. But this did "not mean that at the state level we do not see the importance of this alliance for the problem of security for our borders." He even argued that Soviet troops should remain in Poland because of "the German problem."[475] Obviously under the impression of such statements, Gen. Batenin still thought in April that Poland would want to retain a Soviet military presence in the country and that the organization would still be viable, at least for a transitional period: "The USSR and Poland – only two fingers are needed to count the members." But other countries would be interested as well. "Czechoslovakia, no matter what, will remain a member of the Warsaw Pact. [Czechoslovak president] Havel is now in an exceptional mood, [caught up in] the euphoria of power." However, this mood would dissipate.[476]

The Soviet concept for reform of the alliance was presented to the Pact members at two meetings in the spring of 1990. One was the 7 June conference of the Political Consultative Committee in Moscow, the other the Military Committee's gathering on 14-15 June in Strausberg near East Berlin. Despite some differences of position, the trend that emerged from the final document adopted by the PCC and statements of participants at both meetings was clear. The member states, according to the declaration adopted at the Warsaw Pact summit meeting, would review the Warsaw Treaty and "initiate efforts to transform it into a treaty of sovereign, equal states that is based on democratic principles."[477] The "character, functions, and activities of the Warsaw Pact" were to be thoroughly reviewed. The organization was to change from a military alliance to a political organization with military consultation; the centralized, Soviet-controlled command structure was to be abandoned, which in practice meant that a Soviet deputy minister of defense would no longer be the Pact's commander in chief and that perhaps the Supreme Joint Command would be

---

474 Alan Riding, "At Conference Soviet General Sees Changes in Warsaw Pact," *New York Times*, 18 January 1990; see also Maj. Gen. Yuri Kirshin, "Why is Military Reform Needed," *New Times* (Moscow), No. 12 (March 1990), pp. 30-31.

475 In a news conference in Warsaw, Associated Press (from Warsaw), 21 February 1990.

476 Batenin interview with Hans-Henning Schröder in Moscow, 4 April 1990.

477 Text of the declaration as published in *Pravda*, 8 June 1990.

dissolved; the member states would gain control of their own national forces in conformity with the principle of full national sovereignty; and for the duration of the existence of multilateral institutions representatives of the member states would fill positions by rotation. Nothing, however, was said of a possible dissolution of the Pact.

To use the convenient metaphor of departing trains again, this time the Soviet political leadership was on the Warsaw Pact reform train. In fact, it was in the driver's seat. However, as it recognized to its dismay, most of the member countries of that organization, while negotiating reform, at the same time were preparing to leave that train.[478] Above all, the new governments in two of the four countries where Soviet troops were stationed, Czechoslovakia and Hungary, made it clear early on that they wanted the Soviet forces out as quickly as possible.[479] Gorbachev acceded to these demands. In both cases the withdrawal negotiations dealt almost exclusively with the logistics of the pullout of Soviet forces, not with the principle of their withdrawal. Although Soviet negotiators insinuated that unilateral withdrawals would adversely affect the Warsaw Pact's negotiation position at the CFE talks in Vienna, they made no serious effort to try to retain a residual force. During President Vaclav Havel's visit to Moscow in late February, the Czechoslovak and Soviet foreign ministers signed an agreement calling for the bulk of the Central Group of Forces to be out of Czechoslovakia by the end of May 1990 and for all of the troops and equipment to be withdrawn no later than the end of June 1991. On 9 March, Hungarian and Soviet negotiators concluded an agreement that stipulated the same final withdrawal date for the Southern Group of Forces, that is, June 1991. As these negotiations and the Two Plus Four talks progressed, the Polish government revised its position on the German danger and also began calling for the withdrawal of Soviet forces.

These developments put the Soviet Union in an awkward position. In the preceding era, its armed forces had fulfilled important political and strategic functions, foremost, to maintain its vassals in power and safeguard the empire against external threats. In the form of status of forces agreements, their presence had some legal justification. But after the revolutions of 1989, these rationales no longer existed: the socio-economic systems changed fundamentally; NATO was no longer regarded as a threat; and the legal basis of the presence of Soviet troops was put in

478 Interview with Shakhnazarov.

479 This account, in the next two paragraphs in part *verbatim*, follows Douglas L. Clarke, "Soviet Troop Withdrawals from Eastern Europe," *Report on Eastern Europe* (Munich, Radio Liberty / Radio Free Europe), 30 March 1990, pp. 43-44. A more detailed and well documented analysis is Daniel N. Nelson, "Watching the Pact Unravel: The Transformation of East European Political-Military Policies," Bundesinstitut für ostwissenschaftliche und internationale Studien (Cologne), Research Report, No. 32 (1990).

doubt. The repercussions of these developments on the Soviet forces in Germany were considerable. If the Northern, Central, and Southern Groups of Forces were to be withdrawn, the Western Group of Forces in Germany would find itself in a militarily untenable position: its supply lines would be cut. Furthermore, after the 18 March elections, these forces would find themselves in a political environment that would make them an unwanted anachronism. Moscow would also be pushed into another race against time. Agreement between the United States and the Soviet Union on the level of their forces in Europe could enshrine the legitimacy of the Soviet military presence, perhaps even an equal number of forces of the two superpowers, and the continued existence of the Warsaw Pact. But the pressures from the Central and Eastern European countries for a speedy *unilateral* withdrawal of the Soviet forces and the dissolution of the Warsaw Pact, regardless of developments in NATO, threatened to render obsolete any such agreement. This race against time can be demonstrated in reference to the negotiations on the level of Soviet and American forces in Europe.

At the beginning of February, in his State of the Union address, Bush had proposed limits of 195,000 American and Soviet troops in Central Europe, which he defined as embracing West Germany, the Benelux countries, Denmark, and all of Eastern Europe except Romania and Bulgaria. The proposal also envisaged retention of 30,000 American troops at the "flanks," that is, in countries like Britain and Turkey. Gorbachev's counterproposal reflected completely unrealistic notions about the future level of Soviet forces in Europe. It rejected any asymmetry in the level of Soviet and American forces and stipulated that both the USSR and the USA reduce their troops in Europe to either 195,000 or 225,000 each.[480] Where, it is appropriate to ask, did the Soviet political and military leaders expect this enormous number of forces to be stationed? Which governments did they think would be prepared to agree even to a token presence of Soviet troops? In 1990, except for allusions to on-going negotiations with NATO and within the Warsaw Pact, no answer was given in Moscow to these pertinent questions. This was confirmed in mid-May, when Moscow halted the withdrawal of forces from East Germany (by that time two Soviet tank divisions and other military units had been pulled back). A Soviet foreign ministry spokesman merely explained that "a further decision on questions connected with the withdrawal of Soviet troops from the GDR will depend on the results of the Vienna talks on the reduction of conventional armaments in Europe and a political solution to the German question."[481]

480 Thomas L. Friedman, "Gorbachev Accepts Deep Cuts in Europe if Forces Are Equal," and Michael R. Gordon, "A Troop-Cut Assent: Gorbachev Accepts Vital Part of Plan by Bush to Reduce Forces in Europe," *New York Times*, 10 February 1990.

481 The explanation was provided by foreign ministry spokesman Gennadi Gerasimov, TASS International Service, in Russian, 17 May 1990.

The results obtained after difficult negotiations in Vienna, codified in the Paris CFE agreement on 19 November 1990, skillfully sidestepped the issue of whether the Warsaw Pact would continue to exist. Although the agreement *de facto* embodied the bloc-to-bloc structure of the Cold War and the military alliances were called upon to decide among themselves how to apportion cuts in the treaty-limited equipment, it was multilateral in nature and divided the signatories into *Groups*, thereby avoiding the term alliance. The agreement, therefore, was not prejudicial to the continued existence of the alliances. Simply put, the CFE agreement was designed to survive any dissolution of the Warsaw Pact. Furthermore, the zones of reduction that were devised and the ceilings for Soviet and American forces that were set would make a complete withdrawal of Soviet forces from Eastern Europe possible while allowing the continued presence of American forces in Western Europe.[482]

If the Warsaw Pact could perhaps be reformed and at least temporarily be preserved as a political organization, changes in the *Western* military alliance were indispensable from Gorbachev's perspective. If not the reality, at least the semblance of change was necessary to facilitate his task of justifying Soviet consent to Germany's NATO membership. Specifically, an appropriate response was required to the Warsaw Pact summit meeting's call for "constructive cooperation" between the two blocs and a Europe "without artificial barriers and ideological hostility."[483] The reply was duly provided in the declaration adopted by NATO's summit conference in London on 6 July. The Atlantic alliance, according to the declaration, extended the "hand of friendship" to the countries of the East. NATO was ready "to enhance the political component of our Alliance"; to intensify military contacts with "Moscow and other Central and East European capitals"; to field, after the conclusion of the CFE negotiations, "smaller and restructured active forces"; to move "away from 'forward defense;'" and to reduce its "reliance on nuclear weapons."[484]

To conclude the discussion of the security dimensions of German unification, it is appropriate to pose two sensitive questions that form part of current controversies in Russia about her national interests and NATO's enlargement to the east. (1) Did the West in the 1990 negotiations commit itself not to expand eastward beyond the former territory of East Germany? (2) Did the agreement, as outlined in basic form in Moscow and Arkhyz, refined in the Two Plus Four negotiations and codified on

---

482 Richard A. Falkenrath, *Shaping Europe's Military Order: The Origins and Consequences of the CFE Treaty*, Center for Science and International Affairs (CSIA), John F. Kennedy School of Government, Harvard University (Cambridge, Mass.: The MIT Press, 1995), pp. 54-61, 76-77; Jonathan Dean and Randall Watson Forsberg, "CFE and Beyond: The Future of Conventional Arms Control," *International Security*, Vol. 17, No. 1 (Summer 1992), pp. 76-121; Jeffrey D. McCausland, "Conventional Arms Control and European Security," Adelphi Paper 301 (London: IISS, 1996), p. 14.

483 Communiqué of the PCC's Moscow meeting, *Pravda*, 8 June 1990.

484 Text of the London declaration of NATO, *New York Times*, 7 July 1990.

12 September in the Final Settlement, constitute the best possible deal from the Soviet perspective, or did it violate basic Soviet security interests? Concerning the first question, former Soviet and current Russian officials, including Chernyaev and First Deputy Defense Minister Andrei Kokoshin, have repeatedly and vehemently asserted that the West had given assurances to the effect that there would be no further NATO eastward expansion.[485] Ambassador Matlock has supported their contentions: "We gave categorical assurances to Gorbachev back when the Soviet Union existed that if a united Germany was able to stay in NATO, NATO would not be moved eastward."[486] Western scholars have accepted this version and asserted that at the Ottawa "Open Skies" meeting the Western foreign ministers had "agreed not to extend NATO to the east and to let the Soviets know that the Western alliance would not accept the former Warsaw Pact states as members in NATO.[487]

The facts of the matter are that on 9 February Baker, as cited above, had indeed assured Gorbachev that if Germany were to remain part of NATO, "there would be no extension of NATO's jurisdiction for forces of NATO one inch to the east." But even then, it is clear from the context that "east" meant East Germany. Furthermore, the ambiguities about NATO "jurisdiction" and any special political status for the former GDR were unequivocally resolved on 24 February in the Bush-Kohl meeting at Camp David: although there would be a special military status for the former East Germany, NATO *would* move eastward and unified Germany would be a full member of NATO. The new stance, as amply reconstructed here, was immediately made public; presented directly to Gorbachev by Baker in Moscow on 18 May, to Bush on 31 May in Washington, and to Kohl on 15-16 July in Moscow and Arkhyz; discussed at length and in detail in the Two Plus Four negotiations; and codified in the Final Settlement. There is no evidence that further NATO enlargement eastward

485 Chernyaev, for instance, made this point at annual meeting of the Göttinger Arbeitskreis, in Mainz, 4-6 May 1995, where he promised proof of the Russian contentions in the form of an 800-page documentary collection; Kokoshin argued the case at the 3-4 February 1996 Wehrkundetagung in Munich; for details see Fred Oldenburg, "Deutsche Einheit und Öffnung der NATO," Berichte des Bundesinstituts für ostwissenschaftliche und internationale Studien, No. 52 (1996), pp. 5-6. Gennadi Seleznev, chairman of the State Duma, reiterated this point on a visit to Norway; ITAR-TASS (in Russian), 29 May 1979. The thus far most ambitious attempt to prove the case was made by Alexei Pushkov, ORT's (Russian television) director for international relations. The evidence he presents in support of the argument, however, is exceedingly thin; see his article "Lidery Zapada ne zderzhali obeshchanii," *Nezavisimaia gazeta*, 19 March 1997.

486 As quoted by Philip Zelikow, "NATO Expansion Wasn't Ruled Out," *International Herald Tribune*, 10 August 1995. Matlock has maintained his position on this issue; conversation with the author, Cambridge, Mass., 10 February 1997.

487 Szabo, *The Diplomacy of German Unification*, p. 64, based on an article in *Der Spiegel*, No. 9, 26 February 1990, p. 21. Uncritically, another analyst accepts this contention as fact; Michael Mandelbaum, *The Dawn of Peace in Europe* (New York: The Twentieth Century Fund Press, 1996), p. 63.

was dealt with at any time in any of the negotiation fora. The issue could and, perhaps from the Soviet perspective, should have been raised by Gorbachev. But there is no evidence that he did. Nor, as far as this writer is aware, did any of his later conservative critics and *germanisty*, including Kvitsinsky, Falin, and Bondarenko, or anyone else in a responsible position in the Soviet Union in 1990. There was a good reason why the issue was never put on the negotiating table. The negotiations and Soviet internal controversies in the spring and summer of 1990 were focused on *Germany*. Like unified Germany's NATO membership initially, it seemed inconceivable that any of the non-Soviet members of the Warsaw Pact in addition to East Germany would one day want to join the Western alliance. But there had been some harbingers that this could happen. For instance, in a discussion in Budapest on European security matters at the end of February 1990, Hungarian Foreign Minister Gyula Horn had said that "a new approach is possible in the framework of which one could not even exclude membership of Hungary in NATO."[488] The notion that NATO enlargement would stop at the eastern borders of the new Germany was certainly a prevalent Soviet (and Western) assumption and a strong Soviet expectation. Harbingers to the contrary, such as Horn's vision of the future, therefore, either went unnoticed or were considered politically too painful and embarrassing in Moscow to be raised officially in the negotiations or private talks with Western leaders.

If there is nothing, as far as one is able to ascertain, in the letter of the Two Plus Four and other agreements in 1990 that would rule out a second NATO eastern enlargement, what about such a move violating their logic or spirit? A better case can be made for such an interpretation. This argument could proceed from the fact that a strong consensus existed in Moscow on three major security issues. (1) If a unified Germany *were* to be allowed to be a full member of NATO, there should at least be no stationing or deployment of foreign military forces in the eastern part of the country and, *ceteris paribus*, on the territory of any other member of the Warsaw Pact. (2) Not only should there be a fundamental transformation in the character of NATO – particularly if the Warsaw Pact were to be dissolved – but the military balance should not be substantially changed to the disadvantage of the Soviet Union. From the Soviet perspective, a common understanding existed to that effect and was reflected, for instance, in bilateral talks and the multilateral CFE agreement that the total number of German forces and the total military inventory of the German armed forces would not exceed the level that West Germany would have had under the CFE regime before unification. Such an interpretation could be based also on the CFE signatories implicitly ceding the East German equipment entitlements to the other six

488 This view was reported verbatim by *Vremia* (Central Soviet television, evening news), 23 February 1990.

states in the eastern Group.[489] (3) In conjunction with the transformation of both alliances or the disappearance of the Pact, a security system should be constructed on the continent in which all-European institutions, such as the CSCE, rather than any single alliance would be dominant. Shortly prior to the Soviet-American summit, Gorbachev had expressed this Soviet consensus in the form of a strong warning. For the Soviet people, he said in an interview with *Time* magazine,

> NATO is associated with the cold war [and regarded as] as an organization designed from the start to be hostile to the Soviet Union, as a force that whipped up the arms race and the danger of war. Regardless of what is being said about NATO now, for us it is a symbol of the past, a dangerous and confrontational past. And we will *never agree to assign it the leading role in building a new Europe*. I want us to be understood correctly on this.[490]

NATO enlargement to the east, to extend this argument, could be considered to allocate such a role to the Western alliance.

As for the question of whether the Final Settlement served or violated Soviet security interests, the proper yardstick of assessment is again the decisive issue. In particular, the answer depends on whether one uses as a measuring device the principles of the New Thinking and Euro-Atlantic cooperation or the traditional ideological and imperial paradigm, Eurasianist concepts and Russian Great Power images. Using the former yardstick of evaluation, what is it that the Soviet Union gained? (1) The Soviet Union, and thereby Russia, was finally able to rid itself of an empire that was politically non-viable and economically inefficient and that could only be preserved by means of recurrent military intervention. (2) Moscow was no longer saddled with the task of having to maintain the division of Germany through the threat or the use of force but was free to construct an entirely new, cooperative relationship with the new Germany. (3) The policies of unified Germany would be more predictable since it would remain firmly anchored in Western institutions and in a Western military alliance. (4) NATO had committed itself to structural reforms and to abandoning its previous anti-Soviet political and military orientation, permitting the Soviet Union to scale down its armament efforts and concentrate on internal reform. (5) To the extent that NATO could still be considered a military competitor in Europe, the problem was mitigated by the fact that foreign armed forces and nuclear weapons or their carriers would not be stationed in the former East Germany. (6) The risk of a new security threat in Europe was obviated or at least significantly lessened by unified Germany's NATO membership; the presence of American forces in that country and in Europe; limitation of its armed forces to 370,000 servicemen; and its

489 Falkenrath, *Shaping Europe's Military Order*, p. 73.

490 *Time*, 4 June 1990 (italics mine). Although the interview appeared after the conclusion of the Soviet-American summit, it was granted prior to Gorbachev's departure for Washington.

reaffirmation that it would not produce or possess nuclear, biological, and chemical weapons.

An assessment of the settlement on the basis of the traditional Soviet and current Russian Great Power paradigm yields different results. (1) The Soviet Union and, *mutatis mutandis*, Russia suffered a disastrous defeat in the competition with the United States and Germany, losing its traditional sphere of influence in Europe and exposing itself yet again to the risk of the emergence of a powerful Germany in Europe. (2) In negotiations conducted unprofessionally and in complete ignorance of military affairs, the officials responsible needlessly consented to a fundamental shift in the balance of power, committing the Soviet Union to large-scale asymmetrical reductions and the unilateral dismantling of its force posture in Europe. (3) These negotiators missed the opportunity to provide for a neutralized and demilitarized Germany and thereby squandered the chances of constructing a new European security system without military blocs. (4) They agreed instead to a significant strengthening of NATO by abandoning the GDR and handing that country over to the adversary; endorsed the continued stationing of foreign troops and nuclear weapons on West German soil; consented to an excessively high number of German conventional forces as part of NATO's integrated command structure; accepted at face value unilateral NATO commitments that could be rescinded at any time at that organization's convenience; and failed to provide safeguards against a further NATO expansion eastward.

To provide the flavor of the conservative criticism of the Final Settlement, it is useful to refer again to Akhromeev and Kornienko. They write that Gorbachev, his associates and advisors, and Shevardnadze essentially used three arguments in their attempt at justifying their consent to what they only yesterday had called unthinkable and a violation of the global balance of power. First, at its London summit, NATO had adopted a declaration to the effect that the alliance would transform itself into an organization emphasizing its political character and reexamine its military doctrine. Second, the West German chancellor had pledged that a unified Germany would not deploy foreign troops on the soil of the former GDR and would not to allow the stationing of nuclear weapons there. Third, he had also committed Germany to a ceiling of 370 000 officers and men for Germany's armed forces, meaning that the total number of troops would be only half the size of the combined forces of the FRG and the GDR before unification.[491]

In their rebuttal of the first argument, Akhromeev and Kornienko state that "time keeps moving and the promises of a reevaluation of the organization of NATO still remain nothing more than projects, while at the same time the Warsaw Pact has ceased to exist altogether and Soviet military doctrine was redesigned three years

491 Akhromeev and Kornienko, *Glazami marshala i diplomata*, pp. 260-61.

before the London NATO summit meeting. Consequently, the restructuring of the Soviet military forces has commenced and is proceeding right now." They then quote Gorbachev telling Genscher on 18 March 1991 that "we do not see much of a transformation of NATO from the perspective of the formulation of an all-European security system. What is being discussed is rather a strengthening of the security structures for those who belong to the [Western military] organization."[492]

In refutation of the second argument, they acknowledge that not deploying foreign troops and nuclear weapons on the territory of East Germany was, of course, advantageous for the USSR. But in the context of the self-dissolution of the Warsaw Pact and the withdrawal of Soviet forces not only from East Germany but also from Hungary, Czechoslovakia, and Poland, one could not fail to raise the following question: why, under these conditions must foreign forces and nuclear weapons remain on the territory of *West* Germany? This question had been asked not only in the Soviet Union. Egon Bahr, for instance, had put it the following way: "Honestly speaking, I am amazed at Gorbachev's consent to the inclusion of a united Germany in NATO. I was [also] surprised that the fate of nuclear weapons was not touched upon. You can say that NATO has achieved a tremendous victory."[493]

In their criticism of the third alleged advantage derived from the Soviet Union from the Final Settlement, they assert that it was logically unsustainable to maintain that the limitation of the size of the German forces to 370 000 officers and men was fair to the Soviet Union because the limitation constituted a reduction to half the combined armed strength of the East and West German armed forces before German unification. Previously, these two armies existed on opposite sides of the barricade. It had been inappropriate, therefore, to combine them for the purpose of calculating respective gains and losses. Logic would have demanded that the number of forces of the East German forces (173,000) be subtracted from the number of forces of the Bundeswehr (previously 495,000). This would have meant to settle on no more than 322,000 officers and men for the armed forces of the new Germany rather than the 370,000 agreed upon.[494]

The central focus of the conservative criticism is not on the details of the Final Settlement but the principle of unified Germany's membership in NATO. Akhromeev, Kornienko, Kvitsinsky, Falin, Bondarenko, and many other Soviet and

---

492 *Pravda*, 19 March 1991, as quoted by Akhromeev and Kornienko, *Glazami marshala i diplomata*, p. 261.

493 *Pravda*, 19 July 1990, as quoted by Akhromeev and Kornienko, *Glazami marshala i diplomata*, p. 261.

494 Ibid., p. 262. Akhromeev and Kornienko were in all likelihood conscious of what Shevardnadze had said. On 3 July 1990, evidently in anticipation of the Moscow and Arkhyz accords, he had asked the delegates to the Twenty-eighth CPSU Congress: "What is better for us? To deal with a half-million strong Bundeswehr of the FRG, or, say, an army half that size of a united Germany?"

current Russian government officials and members of the military establishment thought – and those still alive today continue to believe – that a neutral Germany would have served Soviet and Russian security interests better than a Germany in NATO. This belief is certainly debatable. On balance, however, it would seem that the latter solution was far more advantageous for Russia, and for Germany and her European neighbors as well. Gorbachev ultimately came to see it that way. When the question was put to Chernyaev as to what convinced his chief to opt for this solution, his reply concerning the modalities of German NATO membership (as noted) were Baker's nine points or incentives. On the principle, he mentioned two considerations. (1) Gorbachev was impressed by the reasoning that a neutral Germany could, and one day might, seek access to nuclear weapons. (2) "The West had the better arguments."[495]

This reconstruction of the Soviet consent to unified Germany's membership in NATO as well as of its presumed and actual advantages and disadvantages from the Soviet perspective has focused exclusively on its political and international security dimensions. What is missing is a discussion of economic factors in that decision.

8. The "Price Tag" of the Consent

Several questions need to be posed in a discussion of economic factors in the Soviet decision to consent to unified Germany's membership in NATO. Are the conservative Russian critics correct in contending that Gorbachev traded vital long-term Soviet security interests for short-term economic gain? How well did Soviet negotiators succeed in integrating security and financial issues in one comprehensive negotiating package? Did they, from their own perspective, strike a good bargain? How significant were the sums of money received? These questions can meaningfully be addressed only in the larger context of the economic dimension in the Soviet imperial decline and collapse and what many observers consider to be the most fundamental of all questions: did the economic crisis lie at the root not only of the disintegration of the Soviet empire in Eastern Europe but did it determine Gorbachev's consent to German unification and unified Germany's membership in NATO?

The record of Soviet economic performance between 1985 and 1987 may be debatable. It seems that there may even have been some stabilization due to the traditional Soviet approach of administrative streamlining, anti-corruption measures, and pressures exerted on the middle levels of the economic bureaucracy from the top.[496] From 1988 to 1990, however, some of the measures adopted previously and

495 Interview with Chernyaev.

496 The argument made in this and the next paragraph closely follows Michael Ellman and Vladimir Kontorovich, "Overview," in Michael Ellman and Vladimir Kontorovich., eds., *The Disintegration of the Soviet Economic System* (London: Routledge, 1992), pp. 1-39, and

new decisions by the political leadership pulled the economy into a severe downturn, with fateful consequences. The essence of the problem lay in a sharp divergence of the pace of political and economic reform; the conscious curtailment of the party's power in economic decision-making; erosion of the ideological basis on which the party's authority in economic management had rested; the deliberate dismantling of the command bureaucratic system; a disastrous reorganization of the agro-industrial complex; and the replacement of the centrally organized supply system by market relations between enterprises. Laudable as the intentions of the political leadership and its economic advisers may have been, the consequences of the reform measures were enormous. They included a decline in output; the disruption of the supply system; severe shortages in consumer goods and agricultural products; significant differentials in state and market prices; budget and foreign trade deficits; the destabilization of fiscal and monetary relations; the reemergence of barter trade; and widening queues and strikes in the mining and transportation industries. Attempts were made to counter perceived negative developments in a nascent private economic sector by the widespread introduction of rationing and sweeping powers given to the KGB and the police to combat purported profiteering and an increasingly powerful mafia. These and other measures, however, were to no avail. As Michael Ellman and Vladimir Kontorovich have concluded, the collapse of the Soviet economic system was the "unintended result of a small number of disastrous decisions by a few individuals" who based their actions on "a mistaken belief in the boundless reformability of the traditional system" but who, in economic affairs, displayed "monumental incompetence."[497]

What about the subjective dimension of the problem? Was Gorbachev aware of the serious economic problems? And, if so, how did he propose to address them? On 29 January 1990, in what Chernyaev has described as a "stormy" meeting of the Politburo, one of the main items on the agenda was the economic and fiscal state of affairs of the Soviet Union. Prime Minister Ryzhkov introduced the discussion by saying: "The situation is difficult, if not critical, and continues to worsen. The apex of the crisis of 1989 has not been overcome."[498] Planning chief Slyunkov reinforced this gloomy appraisal: "One can no longer call the state of affairs difficult. The people no longer see any way out. And, in fact, there will be [no way out] if the government is incapable of balancing expenditure and revenue." As a reflection of the continuing stalemate in the top leadership on the central issue of economic reform, Slyunkov advocated an immediate price liberalization and drastic reform measures, many of

---

Vladimir Kontorovich, "The Economic Fallacy," *The National Interest*, Vol. 31 (Spring 1993), pp. 35-44.

497 Ellman and Kontorovich, "Overview," p. 32; Kontorovich, "The Economic Fallacy," p. 44.

498 Chernyaev, *Shest' let s Gorbachevym*, p. 332.

which later formed part of Grigori Yavlinsky's 500 Days Plan for a rapid transition to a market economy. He was supported by Yakovlev and Medvedev and, in vivid testimony to the depth of the crisis, also by Ligachev. Kryuchkov, however, thought: "Perhaps we ought to rescind some of the measures (of perestroika)." Gorbachev summarized the discussion by saying that the economic turn promised for 1989 had not been achieved. People would lose confidence. "We can't go on this way. That concerns everyone in this room. If we go on working like this, our days are numbered. The people will depose us."[499]

The impact of such perceptions on Soviet foreign policy was twofold: (1) the leadership's willingness to prop up an economically inefficient empire was even more rapidly being eroded in 1988-90 than in 1985-87; and (2) not only had any disruptive shocks potentially emanating from the world economy to be avoided, but Western economic and financial assistance became part of the political leaders' hopes for their own survival and that of perestroika. Requests for such assistance, however, posed painful dilemmas for Gorbachev. In the interest of an effective negotiation stance on the German problem, it was advantageous not to convey the impression that the Soviet Union's bargaining position was weak. But failure to raise significant sums of hard currency would surely accelerate the economic crisis, with potentially disastrous political consequences.

The first initiative to alleviate economic and financial stringencies by relying on West German assistance was an urgent request for food deliveries. On 15 January 1990, Ambassador Kvitsinsky asked for a meeting with Teltschik and gave him a list of supplies that were immediately required. The request, one may comment, perhaps more clearly than anything else, revealed how far the once mighty country had fallen. Significantly for the nexus between economic and political issues, an agreement between West Germany and the Soviet Union on the deliveries requested was signed on 9 February, one day before Kohl's departure to Moscow. The Federal Republic would supply 52,000 tons of canned beef, 50,000 tons of pork, 20,000 tons of butter, 15,000 tons of milk powder and 5,000 tons of cheese as well as clothing and other consumer goods. The deliveries were to be subsidized by the federal government with DM 220 million (about $100 million).[500] On 10 February, Gorbachev thanked Kohl for the assistance provided by West Germany, adding – presumably for the reasons mentioned above – that some time ago (when Kvitsinsky had made the request?) matters looked as if everything was up in the air. But that had completely changed in the meantime.[501]

---

499 Ibid.

500 Teltschik, *329 Tage*, pp. 108, 114; Kohl, *Ich wollte Deutschlands Einheit*, pp. 280-81.

501 Ibid., p. 270.

Although the deliveries agreed upon were designed to deal with short-term supply bottlenecks and involved only small sums of federal money, the connection between economic issues and German unification involved much more substantial and long-term issues. In the era of the Cold War, whenever West German political leaders and pundits had discussed the question as to how Moscow could ever be persuaded to yield the key to German unification, substantial economic concessions had been considered an indispensable part of a more comprehensive package. Consequently, when Gorbachev visited West Germany in June 1989, Kohl had outlined his vision of a complete rearrangement of Russian-German relations and the conclusion of a Grand Treaty that would integrate political, security, and economic dimensions.[502] Kohl returned to this theme during his visit to Moscow in February 1990. He also noted that East Germany, as a principal supplier of manufactured goods to the Soviet Union, was defaulting on its delivery contracts. A unified Germany could do better. It could furnish supplies of a higher quality, more cheaply, and more reliably, and it could provide the Soviet Union with access to the European Community market.[503] The German chancellor thereby *de facto* reinforced the advice Gorbachev was receiving from his market-oriented economists, such as Stanislav Shatalin, Nikolai Petrakov, Nikolai Shmelev, and Boris Fyodorov, to the effect that large-scale Western involvement was crucial for a revitalization of perestroika. In the summer of 1990, their advice was to take concrete shape in Yavlinsky's 500 Days Plan and the later Shatalin Plan as well as the Yavlinsky-Allison Grand Bargain.

Four months later the Soviet Union again turned to West Germany for assistance.[504] On 4 May, using the occasion of the Two Plus Four meeting in Bonn and acting in accordance with instructions by Gorbachev and Prime Minister Ryzhkov, Shevardnadze explored the possibilities of a government-guaranteed credit. On the following day, Kvitsinsky conveyed the details of the Soviet request: a credit in the amount of DM 20 billion ($12 billion) with a duration of five to seven years. His reaction to the aid request he had been obliged to transmit is instructive of both the political sensitivity and internal opposition to any tradeoff between Western economic assistance and Soviet concessions on unified Germany's membership in NATO. Kvitsinsky deplored the fact that his chief had lent himself to raising the aid issue although "Shevardnadze had no direct responsibility for economic management in the country." He also objected to the very principle of the request and criticized those who had told Shevardnadze to submit it. It was clear to him that the credit, if it

---

502 Ibid., pp. 42-44.

503 Zelikow and Rice, *Germany Unified*, p. 188. The account of the economic details is based on what Teltschik told American officials after the Moscow talks. They are not contained in Teltschik's and Kohl's memoirs.

504 The account that follows is drawn from Teltschik, *329 Tage*, pp. 221, 226-28, 230-35, and Kwizinskij, *Vor dem Sturm*, pp. 25-31.

were to granted, would be "eaten up" within a few months. It would provide no impulse to an acceleration of reforms in the Soviet Union because the government simply had no concept as to how to increase exports or gain hard currency, let alone how to lead the country out of the crisis. In Kvitsinsky's view, the conclusion to be drawn was obvious:

> The request for a financial credit could only be the beginning of a long chain of similar pleas, which would lead to ever more humiliations and induce the West to pose ever more disagreeable political demands. ... To have sent off [Shevardnadze] to beg for money meant that we ourselves, whether we intended it or not, were hinting at a connection between the solution of the German problem and the extension of credit.[505]

The West German government, of course, saw such a connection. It was prepared to act upon the request in full consciousness of its political implications, that is, that foreign assistance could help keep Gorbachev in power and could serve to persuade Gorbachev to accept unified Germany's membership in NATO.[506] Given the sensitivity of the issue, it decided to proceed in secrecy. On 13 May, accompanied by Hilmar Kopper of Deutsche Bank and Wolfgang Röller of Dresdner Bank, Teltschik flew to Moscow on a West German military aircraft. In the morning of the following day, the three held talks in the Kremlin with Ryzhkov, Shevardnadze, Deputy Prime Minister Sitaryan, Yuri Moskovsky (the chairman of the Bank for Foreign Trade) and Kvitsinsky in his new role as deputy foreign minister with responsibility for European affairs.[507] In the afternoon, they met separately with Gorbachev in his Kremlin office, with only Ryzhkov and Kvitsinsky present.

Characterizing the first round of meetings, Kvitsinsky observed a difference in the approach of the two sets of participants: whereas the German envoys tried to link financial issues and the German problem, the Soviet participants attempted to *separate* the two issues. Thus, at the outset of what was to be an extensive survey of Soviet economic difficulties, Ryzhkov stated that the Soviet leadership was, of course, paying attention to German unification, but it also imparted great importance to the proper management of economic affairs in the triangular relationship USSR-GDR-FRG. For the purpose of such management, he said, six commissions would be

---

505 Kwizinskij, *Vor dem Sturm* p. 25.

506 In his talks with Bush in Washington and Camp David, Kohl had reportedly said: "The Soviets are negotiating. But this may end up as a matter of cash. They need the money. ... There will be security concerns for the Soviets if Germany remains in NATO. And they will want to get something in return"; Baker, *The Politics of Diplomacy*, p. 213.

507 Kvitsinsky was charged with the responsibility of ensuring that the West German mission to Moscow would indeed be kept secret. Corresponding measures, to be agreed upon with Teltschik, pertained to the route the plane would be taking to Moscow, non-disclosure of the identity of the members of the German delegation, and confidentiality of their reception at the airport. Not even the West German embassy in Moscow was to be informed of the trip; Teltschik, *329 Tage*, p. 230; Kwizinskij, *Vor dem Sturm*, p. 25.

established at the Council of Ministers. Shevardnadze later endeavored to delink the two dimensions by postulating the preferred Soviet sequence. In an interjection to Teltschik's remark that "if we are able to come to an agreement today [on economic and financial matters], this will contribute to calming the controversy in the area in which Shevardnadze is conducting negotiations," he quipped: "Or vice versa."[508]

Ryzhkov justified the Soviet aid request as follows: between 1985 and 1987, economic reforms had been prepared, and in the following two years their implementation had begun. The rigid system of central planning was gradually being abandoned, but neither the infrastructure nor models for a new economic system had as yet been developed. Many problems had arisen, including a disproportion between the volume of money in circulation and the availability of goods. Concerning foreign trade, he deplored that in 1990 the Soviet Union year would have to import 42 million tons grain at the cost of 4.5 billion rubles ($2.7 billion), which constituted 25 percent of the country's hard currency earnings. The chances for an improvement were limited because of the "unauthorized" export of raw materials and metals and decreasing prices for oil on the world market. Overall, the country had to overcome a very complicated stage in its development and needed foreign aid. The transition problems could be solved without such assistance, but this would mean that the standard of living of the population would have to be lowered, which would imperil not only perestroika but also the future of the Soviet Union and of the whole world. Specifically, he asked West Germany for an unconditional credit in the amount of 1.5 to 2 billion rubles ($900 million to $1.2 billion) to meet current payment requirements. This sum would be part of an overall package of 10 to 15 billion rubles ($6 to $9 billion), to be repaid over ten to fifteen years, with no payment due for five years.[509]

Gorbachev, in essence, reiterated Ryzhkov's plea for assistance as well as the main line of reasoning that made such assistance necessary.[510] He, too, spoke of a very complicated transitional stage which the country was experiencing but thought that this phase could be overcome within two to three years. An overall improvement of the economy could be achieved within five to seven years. He considered foreign assistance for the Soviet Union to be a fundamental and strategically important issue. Europe had arrived at a turning point, and it would be parochial pragmatism if attempts were made now to exploit instabilities for egoistic reasons. In obvious allusion to differences in approach between West Germany and the United States on the issue of credit to the Soviet Union, he regretted that Washington was still

508 Ibid., p. 26

509 Ibid., pp. 27-28; Teltschik, *329 Tage*, pp. 23-32.

510 Since Gorbachev's approach was almost identical to that adopted by Ryzhkov, there is no need to repeat it here in detail. Only some important additions will be noted.

hesitating and was not conducting a far-sighted policy. As for the total Soviet credit requirement, he thought that what was needed were between 15 and 20 billion rubles ($9 to $12 billion), with a grace period for repayment of about seven or eight years.[511] Gorbachev, too, eschewed the idea of linkage. Nevertheless, he agreed with Teltschik that it was appropriate to link all issues in a comprehensive treaty to be concluded after the achievement of German unification, with preparatory work to begin immediately. Furthermore, it was at this meeting where Gorbachev not only proposed another Soviet-West German summit – to be held, as he mentioned, *after* the Twenty-eighth CPSU Congress – but also responded positively to the German suggestion for the two leaders to meet in the Caucasus.[512]

What, then, was the fate of Gorbachev's request for West German financial assistance? The Bonn government agreed to provide guarantees for an unconditional bank credit in the amount of up to DM 5 billion ($3 billion). The lack of conditionality, however, applied only to the financial technicalities. Unmistakably, there were political strings attached. As Kohl explained to Gorbachev in a letter on 22 May, the extension of credit required a considerable political effort. He expected, therefore, that the Soviet government would, in a spirit of cooperation, do everything in its power to help settle as yet unresolved issues in the Two Plus Four negotiations. As for additional and more long-term loans, he said that common action of all the Western industrialized countries was necessary and promised to pursue the matter in talks with his partners in the European Community, the G-7 and the Group of 24.[513]

Despite the urgency of the loan from Moscow's perspective and its perceived political importance in Bonn, it took until early July for the package to be assembled and approved by the government. In vivid testimony to the liquidity crisis facing the Soviet Union, the full amount was called up within a week after approval.[514] However, as Kvitsinsky correctly comments, the credit was quite insufficient to meet the Soviet leadership's objectives of putting the Soviet Union into a position to fulfill its payment obligations and to eradicate concern on the international financial markets about the country's credit standing.[515] For a larger loan approximating the amounts that Gorbachev had suggested to the German delegation on 14 May, and as Kohl had said in his letter, a more comprehensive international effort of both banks and governments was needed, and this would certainly have to include the United States and Japan. In fact, only four days after the Teltschik mission, the Soviet

511 Kwizinskij, *Vor dem Sturm*, pp. 29-30.

512 Teltschik, *329 Tage*, pp. 233-34; Kwizinskij, *Vor dem Sturm*, p. 31.

513 Teltschik, *329 Tage*, pp. 243-44.

514 Theo Waigel, the West German finance minister, communicated this fact to the chancellor on 13 July; Teltschik, *329 Tage*, p. 316. In the memoir literature (Kohl, Genscher, Teltschik, and Kvitsinsky), there is no explanation why it took so long for the credit to be made available.

515 Kvitsinsky, *Vor dem Sturm*, p. 28.

president and party chief repeated his plea for international financial assistance to Baker in Moscow, although now with a focus on the United States and an increase in the total amount of credit required. The next few years would be critical because the Soviet Union was going to move to a market-based economy, he told Baker. To cushion the impact and expedite the transition, it had to buy consumer goods and invest in the conversion of defense industry to civilian production. To cover the costs of imports and structural change, it needed hard-currency credits in the amount of $20 billion.[516]

West Germany, mainly for incontrovertible political reasons, was prepared to participate in an international assistance effort and, more specifically, be instrumental in the establishment of an international banking consortium to finance Soviet requirements. However, the political impediments to such an approach were daunting. Neither the Japanese government nor the Japanese banks would subscribe to it for as long as Moscow failed to make concessions on the Kurile islands or Northern Territories issue (more of this later). As for the United States, as Bush told Kohl on 17 May in Washington, his hands were tied because of the Baltic problem. Given the pressure tactics Gorbachev had adopted toward Lithuania, including an economic blockade, and opposition in Congress, neither most-favored-nation status (MFN) nor large American loans could be granted. Bush also maintained that the Soviet Union would be unable to repay substantial loans.[517]

The American president adhered to that position at the Soviet-American summit. He wanted to help, Bush told Gorbachev, but American credits at this stage would not be forthcoming. The right conditions had to be created first. What was needed were more far-reaching economic reforms, movement on Lithuania, a reduction of subsidies to Cuba, and progress on the German problem. The only concession he was willing to make was the promise that the G-7 summit meeting, scheduled to take place in Houston from 9 to 11 July, would consider the possibilities of a multilateral assistance program.[518] As for American trade benefits, including MFN, as Gorbachev observed in retrospect, "of all the agreements concerning the further development of our relations, none was more bitterly fought over than the planned trade treaty."[519] The major obstacle here, in addition to those previously mentioned, were the continuing restrictions on the emigration of Soviet Jews and the failure of the Supreme Soviet to adopt a liberal emigration law. Emigration had been the issue that had led to the collapse of the 1972 Foreign Trade Act in the fall of 1974 and contributed to the demise of detente. In 1990, the linkage between the two issues

---

516 Baker, *The Politics of Diplomacy*, p. 249.
517 Teltschik, *329 Tage*, pp. 237-38.
518 Zelikow and Rice, *Germany Unified*, p. 282.
519 Gorbachev, *Zhizn'*, Vol. 2, p. 183.

remained as close as ever. Both Gorbachev and Shevardnadze were emotional on the conclusion of a trade treaty, the latter exclaiming at one point to Baker: "I've rarely spoken like this with you, but it's *extremely important* that this be done."[520] Bush finally relented and consented to signing the treaty but not without having clarified first that the ultimate fate of the act would depend on Moscow adopting the emigration law and lifting the economic blockade on Lithuania.[521]

To return to the issue of a multilateral aid package, on 11 June, in another letter to Kohl, Gorbachev formalized his request for such a package to be assembled and asked the chancellor to use his good offices for that purpose.[522] At the 25-26 June EC summit in Dublin, Kohl obliged and was supported by Mitterrand. Thatcher, however objected. She did not want Western money to become "an oxygen tent for the survival of much of the old system" and found the lack of serious economic analysis at the summit appalling, arguing that "no board of directors of a company would ever behave in such an unbusinesslike way."[523] The criticism was, in essence, well founded: neither had a serious study been made nor had a plan been developed in West Germany (or as yet in the Soviet Union) to ascertain how the $15-20 billion Gorbachev had suggested would be used so that they would effectively contribute to the restructuring of the Soviet economy; the *political* rationale for an international loan package was seen as more important in Bonn. The split in the Western position did not augur well for the Houston summit of the G-7. In fact, the divisions were replicated there. Whereas the European members, except Britain, argued for a speedy multilateral effort, the United States, Canada, and Japan were reluctant. As a result, and as so often in such cases of disagreement, the resolution of the problem was postponed and transferred to the IMF, the World Bank, and the European Bank for Reconstruction and Development for further study.[524]

To review the state of affairs prior to the Soviet-German negotiations in Moscow and Arkhyz in mid-July, the Soviet Union had, on balance, been unsuccessful in its attempt to involve the Western industrialized countries in a comprehensive program to underpin perestroika. An international banking consortium for that purpose had

---

520 Beschloss and Talbott, *At the Highest Levels*, p. 218 (emphasis in original); on the trade and emigration issues see also ibid., pp. 222-23.

521 Ibid., p. 223; Zelikow and Rice, *Unified Germany*, p. 281. Gorbachev has correctly said in retrospect that "the first demand, [passage of] the emigration law, presented no big problem. ... But Lithuania was a different problem"; Gorbachev, *Zhizn'*, Vol. 2, p. 183.

522 Kohl, *Ich wollte Deutschlands Einheit*, p. 397; Teltschik, *329 Tage*, p. 265. On 4 July, Gorbachev also sent a similar letter to Bush in his capacity as chairman of the G-7 summit meeting in Houston, reiterating his plea for international financial and economic assistance for the Soviet Union; ibid., p. 304.

523 Thatcher, *The Downing Street Years*, pp. 762-63.

524 Kohl, *Ich wollte Deutschlands Einheit*, pp. 416-18; Teltschik, *329 Tage*, pp. 306-10; Genscher, *Erinnerungen*, pp. 829-30.

failed to materialize. To the extent that aid or aid commitments existed, they were bilateral and scarce, and extended by countries like France and Italy, whose financial assistance potential was limited. Japanese assistance was blocked by the Kurile islands issue. The only country with major resources that was both able and willing to help was West Germany. But what were its commitments thus far? In January, the government in Bonn had subsidized the export of foodstuffs and clothing with DM 220 million; in early July, it had approved federal guarantees for a bank credit in the amount of 5 billion German marks; in the same month, it had expressed its willingness to honor the economic obligations the GDR had assumed vis-à-vis the Soviet Union, at an uncertain cost; and it had agreed to meet the East German financial obligations for the stationing of Soviet forces for the year 1990, at an estimated cost of 1.4 billion marks.[525] By any measure of comparison and, in particular, relative to West Germany's large hard-currency reserves, the sums involved were modest. If Gorbachev intended to establish a firm *quid pro quo* between Soviet consent to unified Germany's membership in NATO and large-scale West German economic and financial aid, and drive a hard bargain, the opportunity to do so presented itself at the Soviet-West German summit. The opportunity, however, essentially was not used.

In fact, it is astounding how little was said about economic and financial matters at the summit. There was hardly any discussion of specific figures. This applies not only to the exchanges among the top political leaders but also to the talks at the ministerial level. Kohl assured Gorbachev that the common theme at the European Council in Dublin, NATO in London, and the G-7 in Houston had been the idea that the processes of reform in the Soviet Union had to be supported.[526] He reiterated the theme that to him economic and financial cooperation was an integral part of the total package. Gorbachev spoke about the great economic opportunities that existed for the *Federal Republic* in the Soviet Union and said that the USSR was not concerned about (economic) dependency on Germany. He also expressed his gratitude for the DM 5 billion loan that West Germany had extended to the Soviet Union. Ryzhkov raised three specific issues. (1) He said that some solution had to be found for the 370 economic framework agreements concluded between the GDR and the USSR – a point readily conceded by the German participants who said that the unified Germany would honor East Germany's economic obligations. (2) He also introduced the point, to which Gorbachev later returned, that Germany should contribute beyond 1990 to the financing of Soviet troops transitionally stationed in the eastern part of

---

525 Teltschik, *329 Tage*, p. 279.

526 This account is based on Teltschik, *329 Tage*, pp. 319-42; Kohl, *Ich wollte Deutschlands Einheit*, pp. 421-44; Theo Waigel and Manfred Schell, *Tage, die Deutschland und die Welt veränderten: Vom Mauerfall zum Kaukasus. Die deutsche Währungsunion* (Munich: Bruckmann, 1994), pp. 26-56: and interviews of this author with Teltschik.

Germany.[527] (3) Finally, Ryzhkov advanced claims for compensation for Soviet assets in the GDR, mentioning a figure of DM 20 billion – a figure that was immediately rejected by the German finance minister as unacceptable. Kohl only promised that the issue could be raised in later negotiations.[528] Sitaryan, in separate discussions with Waigel in Moscow, explored the possibilities of further unconditional financial credits and was brushed off by the latter with the explanation that German credits could not be increased infinitely; that an international aid effort was needed; and that all short-term payment problems should be referred to the IMF.[529] In Arkhyz, in the early morning hours, the Soviet deputy prime minister made another attempt to discuss with the German finance minister specific sums for German financial commitments across various dimensions; this attempt, too, was unsuccessful.[530]

To summarize the various fragments of discussion in Moscow and Arkhyz, there was agreement on several principles: the Federal Republic should play a major role in the reconstruction of the Soviet economy; honor the GDR's economic agreements with the USSR; embark upon negotiations on compensation for Soviet assets in the GDR; contribute to the financing of Soviet troops stationed in East Germany for the transition period until their complete withdrawal; and help pay for the resettlement of the Soviet military officers in their homeland. As for the mechanics and machinery of addressing these problems, two agreements were to be negotiated, one on the transitional presence of the Soviet armed forces, the other on the modalities of their withdrawal. The two treaties would contain specific figures for the financing of the Soviet forces' transitional presence, withdrawal, and reintegration.[531]

Apart from the rather unspecific and indeterminate treatment of the economic and financial issues in Moscow and Arkhyz, another anomaly was the delay that occurred at the beginning of serious negotiations. It was not until 23-24 August that Sitaryan and Waigel met in Moscow for a first round, with the second round taking place on

---

527 Ryzhkov also gave some indication as to the likely costs that might arise, saying that the Soviet Union had previously paid for the stationing costs with the equivalent of 6 million tons of oil. After the establishment of the economic and financial union between the two Germanys on 1 July 1990 and the necessity for Moscow to pay in hard currency, the equivalent volume had risen to an estimated 11 million tons; Waigel and Schell, *Tage*, pp. 37, 45.

528 Waigel and Schell, *Tage*, p. 46; Teltschik, *329 Tage*, p. 337.

529 Waigel and Schell, *Tage*, p. 31.

530 Ibid., p. 49.

531 The two agreements were concluded on 9 October 1990; see "Abkommen zwischen der Regierung der Bundesrepublik Deutschland und der Regierung der Union der Sozialistischen Sowjetrepubliken über einige überleitende Maßnahmen," and "Vertrag ... über die Bedingungen des befristeten Aufenthalts und die Modalitäten des planmäßigen Abzugs der sowjetischen Truppen aus dem Gebiet der Bundesrepublik Deutschland," Press- und Information Office of the Federal Government, *Bulletin*, No. 123, 17 October 1990, pp. 1281-1300.

3-4 September in Bonn.[532] The negotiations were rife with controversy, with the final figures left unresolved until high-level intervention. One issue discussed was the significant deficit in Soviet-East German trade, expressed in so-called "transferable rubles," an artificial unit of account and the very antithesis of transferable currency. Sitaryan argued that the imbalance had been caused by the preferential conditions accorded to the GDR in its trade with the Soviet Union, foremost the low prices for oil. Waigel countered this explanation by saying that East German commodities had been undervalued in the bilateral trade. The total debt figure was as yet unknown but likely to rise in the remaining months of 1990. There had been a substantial decrease in Soviet-East German trade as a result of the Soviet economic crisis; the rise in export prices charged by East German firms and now to be paid by Soviet importers in hard currency; and a slackening of demand in the eastern part of Germany for Soviet commodities. The two sides agreed to establish the precise figure of the Soviet trade debt at the end of the year and, by 30 June 1991, to express it in a hard currency equivalent.[533]

A second issue were the costs for the transitional stationing of the Soviet forces. Waigel's proposal to agree upon a total sum for 1991 to 1994 was rejected. Sitaryan demanded instead DM 2.5 billion for 1991 alone – a sum that was allegedly based on the number of forces that would still be on German soil after partial troop withdrawals in that year. The sum was rejected as too high by the German finance minister, who also argued that lower costs in that category would free financial resources for other types of payment. Resolution of this matter, too, was postponed.[534]

A third issue were the costs for the withdrawal of the Soviet armed forces. The Soviet side envisaged sums in amount of DM 2 to 3 billion, based on Comecon prices, for the transportation of the troops to the Soviet border. The German negotiators rejected covering transportation costs in principle and were prepared only to provide and pay for "technical assistance," such as supplying container vessels and services of the German railways.[535]

---

532 The account of the negotiations draws on Waigel and Schell, *Tage*, pp. 53-55. For a discussion of the difficulties in reaching agreement on the various economic and financial issues, see "Bonn und Moskau uneins über finanzielle Hilfe beim Truppenabzug," *Frankfurter Allgemeine Zeitung*, 7 September 1990.

533 Later in the year, the trade debts of the USSR with the GDR at the end of 1990 were estimated by the German government to amount to 5 billion transfer rubles, or DM 11.70 (at an exchange rate of 1 TF = DM 2.34); "Der Osthandel der ehemaligen DDR bricht zusammen," *Frankfurter Allgemeine Zeitung*, 1 November 1990. In negotiations conducted between Moscow and Bonn in 1991, it turned out that the Soviet Union wanted to pay as little as possible of its trade debt, preferably nothing at all; see "Bonn pocht auf Guthaben in Transferrubel," ibid, 10 July 1991.

534 Waigel and Schell, *Tage*, p. 54.

535 Ibid.

A final issue was the resettlement of the WGF officers in their homeland. The Soviet negotiators wanted the German contribution to a concomitant program to be based on the volume of housing necessary for 72,000 officers, with Bonn covering the requirements of half of that total number. They suggested comprehensive investments in the infrastructure of housing compounds, with projects in almost twenty Soviet cities, including Minsk, Kiev, Rostov, and Odessa. From the German perspective, the area slated for both infrastructure and housing construction was enormous. Waigel therefore suggested a financial ceiling to be put on the total cost. No agreement was reached on such a ceiling.[536]

On 5 September, presumably in response to the obvious disagreements and deadlock on issues of principle and specific costs, the new ambassador in West Germany, Vladislav Terekhov, presented a huge bill to the West German government. The bill included (1) contributions to the cost of the stationing of the Western Group of Forces in the period from 1991 through 1994 in the amount of DM 3.5 billion; (2) payment of transportation costs for the withdrawal of Soviet forces amounting to DM 3 billion; (3) a share in the construction of 72,000 apartments, including a supporting infrastructure consisting of kindergartens, shops, and pharmacies, at a sum total of DM 11.5 billion; (4) the financing of retraining schemes for returning officers and non-commissioned officers and their integration in the Soviet economy at DM 500 million; and (5) compensation for Soviet assets in the GDR in the sum of DM 17 billion to DM 17.5 billion. The grand total of this bill as an integral part of the German settlement amounted to about DM 36 billion. But all of this money was directly related to the stationing and withdrawal of the Soviet forces only. It did not include any other type of German government assistance. The sum stood also in stark contrast to what Germany was willing to pay, namely DM 6 billion, which was to be used primarily for the construction of housing.[537] Nothing was mentioned about Soviet assets, with another huge bill presumably still to be presented unless the USSR chose to follow the precedents established in its negotiations with Hungary and Poland, which provided that the costs of environmental clean-up would be set off against the presumed value of the military installations.

The large gap between the Soviet and the German figures was both a mutual embarrassment and a practical problem that urgently needed to be dealt with. The gap was bridged in what must probably be ranked as two of the most expensive telephone conversations in recent Russian-German history. In a first telephone conversation with Gorbachev on September 7, the German chancellor suggested a total of DM 8 billion. Gorbachev reacted harshly and said that DM 11 billion would be

---

536 Ibid.

537 Teltschik, *329 Tage*, pp. 357-58.

required for housing construction alone. He also now linked directly possible Soviet concessions and final agreement in the Two Plus Four negotiations with sums to be obtained from Germany. He was unsure what instructions he should give to Shevardnadze in these negotiations. "For me," he continued, "the situation is alarming. *I have the impression that I have fallen into a trap.*"[538] If this was an expression of genuine belief, it was obviously based on misperception. To be blamed for the existence of the wide discrepancy between what he now demanded and what Kohl was willing to pay was not, it would seem, bad faith shown by the West German government but, in this case at least, inept Soviet negotiating tactics (more on how to interpret Soviet behavior below). The telephone conversation ended without a resolution of the problem and with the German chancellor merely suggesting to talk again three days later. In the telephone conversation on 10 September, Gorbachev was more conciliatory, saying that he did not want to haggle about figures, but he still considered Kohl's counteroffer of DM 11 to DM 12 billion inadequate. He added that, after all, German unification was at stake. Gorbachev finally accepted another offer by Kohl of DM 12 billion plus an interest free credit of DM 3 billion.[539]

In conclusion, it is appropriate to ask two questions pertaining to the discussion of the economic and financial aspects of the Soviet consent to German unification and Germany's NATO membership: (1) How should the DM 15 billion agreed upon for the direct costs of the stationing, withdrawal and resettlement of Soviet forces and other German assistance be considered? Should the sums of money that were provided be regarded as adequate and reasonable or as too low? (2) Why did Gorbachev, until his telephone conversations with Kohl in September, refuse to drive a hard bargain on the economic and financial issues, and why from Kohl's perspective did he put unacceptably high figures on the table only *after* the resolution of the international security provisions of German unification? As for the first question, on 12 September Gorbachev was asked on national television to comment on the impending finalization of the Two Plus Four negotiations and, more specifically, on his two telephone conversations with Chancellor Kohl. He put his explanations in the context of the conclusion of a new comprehensive treaty with a unified Germany and other documents that were being prepared, including a treaty on economic cooperation, and he linked these talks with the troop issue. A direct question was then put to him:

[Interviewer:] And what have we acquired?

538 Kohl, *Ich wollte Deutschlands Einheit*, pp. 467-68 (italics mine).

539 Ibid., p. 468; Teltschik, *329 Tage*, p. 358.

> [Gorbachev:] Yes, and what we have acquired? You are right. The Germans understand the fact that they should participate in the settlement of our returning servicemen.
>
> [Interviewer:] That will be fair.
>
> [Gorbachev:] That will be fair, and they are responding and are ready to do so within the framework of certain amounts – *in my view the amount being obtained is quite good.* I think it is a total of about 15 billion [currency not stated]. Twelve billion will be expenditures on the maintenance and settlement [of the armed forces], and there will be three billion by way of financial aid at the present time. So I would say that everything is being decided on the basis of concord and cooperation – well not immediately and not from the very outset.[540]

Thus, perhaps predictably in view of the necessity to justify the far-reaching strategic withdrawal from Central Europe, Gorbachev expressed satisfaction with the German contribution to its cost. But everything is relative. The sum of DM 15 billion, much of it to be paid over several years, for a country as huge as the Soviet Union, pales in comparison with the net transfer of about *DM 150 billion* in public money allocated *per annum* every year since the achievement of German unity to the reconstruction of the new Länder. But are the DM 15 billion really to be considered the total payment to the Soviet Union for its consent to German unification? The price tag is indeed larger than the figure agreed upon between Gorbachev and Kohl. As shown in Table 6, by mid-1991 the sum of German government and (some) private assistance provided to the Soviet Union amounted to DM 60.1 billion.

Even if one uses the revised figures, it would appear that German unity and unified Germany's membership in NATO were obtained relatively cheaply. The German finance minister certainly is of that opinion. In his memoirs, he quotes from notes by Franz-Josef Strauß written in 1966. He (Strauß) had thought that the Soviet Union might perhaps be tempted by an offer of DM 100 to 120 billion of investment aid to consent to a package consisting of a status for East Germany like that of Austria, exit of West Germany from NATO and the EC, and a German commitment not to pose the question of unification until the end of the century. Waigel calculates that the figure, adjusted for inflation, would have amounted to approximately DM 450 billion in 1990 and concludes that "all of those who consider the price for German unity to have been too high should think about this."[541]

540 "Vremia" news broadcast, 12 September 1990, 5 p.m. GMT; television records, the Harriman Institute, Columbia University (italics mine).

541 Waigel and Schell, *Tage*, p. 56.

Table 6 – The "Price Tag" of German Unification (in billions of DM)[a]

A. Grants and Commodities Free of Charge	
1. Contributions to the Transitional Presence and the Withdrawal of the Soviet Armed Forces Pursuant to the *Überleitungsabkommen*	
– Housing Construction for Returning Officers	7.8
– Stationing Costs	3.0
– Transportation Costs	1.0
– Retraining	0.2
– Interest for the DM 3 Billion Credit	1.5
2. Stationing Costs for 1990	0.7
3. Deliveries from Berlin and Bundeswehr Stocks	0.7
4. Donations by the German People	0.2
5. Grants for Consulting and Training Programs	0.03
6. Germany's Share in EC Grants	0.4
B. Credits and Credit Guarantees	
1. Government Guarantees for Unconditional Financial Credits	
– Balance of Payments Credit of July 1990	5.0
– Credit Pursuant to the *Überleitungsabkommen*	3.0
2. Export Guarantees (Hermes)	19.5
3. Germany's Share in EC Credit Guarantees for Food Exports	0.3
C. Soviet-GDR Trade Imbalance	
1. Transferable Ruble Debt Account	15.0
2. Interest on that Account, 1990-91	1.9
TOTAL	60.1

a Adapted from Christian Meier, "Economic Relations Between the Federal Republic of Germany and the Soviet Union in the Context of Support for Soviet Perestroika," in Armand Clesse and Rudolf Tökés, eds., *Preventing a New East-West Divide: The Economic and Social Imperatives of the Future Europe* (Baden-Baden: Nomos, 1992), pp. 460-67.

As for the second problem, that of why Gorbachev or his negotiators failed to state a high price in the spring or summer of 1990 and why he demanded specific sums only in September, after the resolution of the international security provisions of German unification, five interpretations are possible. The first is that of *inept negotiating tactics*. This view could rest on the idea that Gorbachev and the government either did not recognize the opportunities that existed or were too distracted or overwhelmed by the myriad of domestic problems, including the preparations for the Twenty-eighth CPSU Congress, to deal effectively with the issue. The second interpretation is the opposite of the first, that is, *skillful, if not devious, negotiating tactics*. Soviet negotiators would pretend to agree to all major security aspects of German unification and only later, in the midst of euphoria in Bonn, would present their bill in the full knowledge that West Germany would have to pay whether it liked to or not. The third is that of *good will and faith*. This interpretation could be based on the notion that Gorbachev was quite confident or even certain of Kohl's gratitude and saw no problem, once agreement on the central security issues was reached, to "cash in" later. The fourth is that of a more *comprehensive view of future Soviet-German political and economic relations*, which Kohl had suggested to Gorbachev as early as June 1989 in Bonn. This interpretation implies that Gorbachev assumed that a fundamental change of Soviet-German relations towards cooperation would lead to a substantial expansion of economic exchanges, including both government-guaranteed credits and private investments, and that specific sums to be agreed upon for a transitional phase were less important than the long-term benefits. The final interpretation is that of *domestic considerations and constraints*. Gorbachev, it could be argued, sought to avoid the potentially damaging impression that major concessions on central security problems affecting the position of the Soviet Union for decades to come had been made in exchange for short-term and perhaps short-sighted economic benefit.

Although analytically distinct, the interpretations – except the second, that of devious negotiating tactics – are mutually reinforcing and in all likelihood played some role in the composite set of considerations on the German problem. Certainly, expectations as to the substantial long-term economic benefits of a complete rearrangement of Soviet-German political relations were widely shared in the Soviet Union. For instance, one day after the finalization of the Two Plus Four agreement, *Izvestiia* commentator Alexander Bovin told his readers that German unification would change the European political landscape. He reminded them that West Germany's GNP was the third largest (after the USA and Japan); its share in world trade amounted to a quarter of the total; and its industrial might was as big as its financial clout. In 1989, he explained, it was the world's second largest creditor (behind Japan), and its net financial assets amounted to $427 billion. This economic giant was no longer a political dwarf. "Must we fear [this giant]?," he asked. His reply:

> I am convinced we must not. ... In the FRG a stable democratic society has been formed, and a return to the past is practically excluded. One can assume that trust will be established because of the traditions and experience in economic and political cooperation between the USSR and the GDR, and between the USSR and the FRG. It is not hard to imagine that *a unified Germany will be extremely interested in having a permanent partner with a huge market and constant demand for investment from abroad.*[542]

Another centrally important clue to solving the mystery of the missing price tag in July 1990 and the relatively modest sums ultimately obtained by Moscow lies in Chernyaev's answer to the question of why Gorbachev had not attached stringent

542 Alexander Bovin, "Novaia Germaniia," *Izvestiia*, 14 September 1990 (italics mine).

economic conditions to unified Germany's NATO membership. He replied that the Soviet leader would have considered this to be "undignified."[543] Indeed, as several of the German participants in the Arkhyz talks have implied, appearances played a significant part in Gorbachev's stance. To Kohl, for instance, this was confirmed in the context of a discussion on how to present the security provisions of the Arkhyz agreement. Gorbachev, according to the German chancellor, had thought that "the first question to the federal chancellor would be: 'Did Gorbachev consent to entry of unified Germany into NATO?' It would then be said: 'The Soviet General Secretary has allowed unified Germany's membership in NATO to be bought.'" The procedure he then suggested was for Kohl simply to state that Germany would receive full sovereignty and would decide on her alliance membership (in essence, therefore, he suggested not to address the economic and financial issues).[544] Waigel, similarly, quotes the Soviet leader as having posed the question:

> What will be said when [we announce] that Gorbachev has consented to Germany's entry into NATO? What will be the repercussions on the atmosphere in the Soviet Union? [Our consent] will be interpreted as a trade for credits, as reprehensible. We are conducting Realpolitik. We must find appropriate language in order to gain acceptance.[545]

Negotiations on German Economic Assistance and the Kurile Islands

In conclusion, it may be useful to compare Gorbachev's failure to link security and financial issues on the German problem in a coherent, competent, and timely fashion with Soviet negotiating tactics vis-à-vis Japan and the Kurile islands. This procedure is appropriate given (1) the strong economic and financial position of both Germany and Japan in the world economy and their potential importance for the modernization of the Soviet economy; (2) the opportunity in both cases to link Soviet concessions on territorial and security issues with economic and financial assistance; and (3) the fact that an attempt was made to apply lessons from the negotiations with Germany to those with Japan. Put simply, in the Japanese case, the central question concerned a "cash for the islands" deal. Such a deal had painstakingly been prepared in back-channel negotiations between Arkadi Volsky, chairman of the Union of Industrialists and Entrepreneurs, and Ichiro Ozawa, chairman of the Liberal-Democratic Party. It was meant to form the basis of an agreement to be reached at the April 1991 summit between Gorbachev and Japanese prime minister Toshiki Kaifu.[546]

---

543 Interview with Chernyaev.

544 Kohl, *Ich wollte Deutschlands Einheit*, p. 437.

545 Waigel and Schell, *Tage*, p. 46.

546 The account of the back-channel negotiations on a "cash for the islands" package follows Lisbeth T. Bernstein, "On the Rocks: Gorbachev and the Kurile Islands," unpublished Ph.D. dissertation, The Fletcher School of Law and Diplomacy, May 1997. Her account is based on interviews with

At the end of January 1991, Gorbachev commissioned Vice President Yanaev to hold a meeting of the Preparatory Committee for the Presidential Visit to Japan. The meeting was attended by Volsky, Sitaryan, Vitali Ignatenko (Gorbachev's press secretary), Alexander Panov (head of the MFA's department for the Pacific and Southeast Asian countries), Falin and Andrei Grachev (head and deputy head of the Central Committee's ID respectively), Vassili Saplin (desk officer in charge of Japan at the CC ID), Konstantin Sarkisov (head of the Japan section of the Oriental Institute), Vladylen Martynov (director of IMEMO), Anatoli Milyukov (head of the Economic and Social Forecasting Department at Gorbachev's office), and Vladislav Malkevich (chairman of the Soviet Chamber of Industry and Commerce). Faced with reservations, hesitation, and wavering on the proposed package deal, Volsky burst out in anger:

> This is our last chance. Just think about the food and all sorts of other aid. This [discussion] is all bad. You are all politicians here. To hell with all of you. You understand nothing. Economics is more important, and [returning the islands] is the only way [the Japanese] will give us some money. ... We must go [to Japan] and not just for nothing. We must go for credits. Let's analyze again the Ozawa proposal. The Ozawa plan offers $22 billion. The plan offers short-term credits and gradual credits. What they give us immediately, and we should grab it, is $1.5 billion to buy medicines; $1.5 billion to buy food; 1 billion for consumer goods. For medium-term credits, they give us $8 billion. And for long-term credits, they give us $10 billion.
>
> I spoke to Ozawa, I am in touch with him, as you know. Ozawa said [sarcastically]: "You don't need it [this money]? If you don't need it, then what do you need?" Ozawa then said" "Give me a formula. Let's postpone the actual sovereignty over all the islands for fifteen years, but give a promise to us now that we will have them in fifteen years."
>
> It's a symbolic question, but I support this solution of the so-called "postponed sovereignty" in the following way: we give them two islands immediately, and assure them that they will get [the] two more [remaining islands] within fifteen years. We ourselves are making a mistake. ... If we don't need it [the package deal] then give me a hint and I will stop it. But what shall we do without money? We already owe them $450 million that we cannot pay back.

Volsky then turned to Sitaryan as the official formally responsible for negotiating a deal and told him: "You should do it. My [opinion] is that it should either be the Ozawa line or we should not go to Tokyo."

Earlier in the tense meeting, Sitaryan had indicated his guarded agreement in principle. He cryptically put it in the context of the failure (in essence, his own)

---

several of the participants in the negotiations, including the January meeting, and on personal notes taken by Sergei Grigoriev, assistant to Vitali Ignatenko and executive secretary of the meeting.

effectively to link economic and security issues on the German problem, saying that considering "*our careless activities in the West, we should now learn how to tie things up. So the biggest question is, if we give them the islands, what do we get back*?"[547]

For reasons which go beyond the scope of this book, Gorbachev failed to endorse the proposed package deal. The important point to note, however, is the fact that at least the official chiefly responsible for foreign economic and financial affairs was conscious of deficiencies in the previous negotiations with West Germany and that much larger sums than those agreed upon by Kohl were contemplated as part of a comprehensive settlement with Japan.

---

547 Ibid. (italics mine).

CONCLUSIONS

As explained in the Introduction, the purpose of this book was to examine the reasons why Germany was divided after the Second World War; why the division was maintained for such a long time; why the Soviet Union accepted German unification; and why it consented to unified Germany as a full member in the Atlantic alliance. The inquiry was set into the theoretical framework of the rise, decline, and fall of empires and the specific context of the evolution and collapse of the Soviet empire in Eastern Europe. The examination has produced the following results:

The division of Germany did not occur as a consequence of Stalin's foresight and on the basis of "scientific" analysis derived from Marxism-Leninism. It was also not part of a deliberate, well thought-out Soviet policy of establishing an empire in Eastern Europe with the inclusion of East Germany. Instead, it constituted the outcome of unplanned processes, uncoordinated actions, and a perceived lack of better alternatives. The division thus occurred by default rather than by design. The default, however, was not spurious or accidental. It conformed to a particular logic, which rested in what has been called here the Ideological and Imperial paradigm. Stalin was the unchallenged leader in the Soviet Union after the Second World War. He gave his imprint to the Soviet system. His political philosophy and world view were a decisive factor in the evolution of events. Both centered on the acquisition, maintenance, and expansion of power, no matter whether in the Soviet Union itself or abroad. His was an imperial mind-set. In his approach to international affairs, furthermore, raw indicators of power took center stage, including population size, geographical expanse, natural resources, volume of industrial output, control over human and material resources, and the number and quality of divisions, tanks, aircraft, artillery, and nuclear weapons available to the Soviet Union.

Stalin's drive for personal power and the expansionist tendencies inherent in imperial systems were reinforced by the universalist features of Marxist-Leninist ideology. By ideological definition, the existing world system was considered to be unjust. The *status quo* had to be changed in favor of "world socialism," that is, in favor of the Soviet Union. Since Stalin lacked confidence in autonomous political processes and distrusted unplanned activities "from below," history had to be given a push by bayonets. There was, of course, nothing in Soviet ideology that would have supported the *de facto* preeminence of military and geopolitical factors in Soviet policy over economic considerations. On the contrary, historical materialism posited a world development in which autonomous socio-economic processes determined politics. It was Stalin, if not Lenin, who gave Marxist-Leninism a peculiar bent towards the preeminence of political and military power. At the end of the Second World War, the internal empire constructed on that basis was already firmly in place.

Not much was required for its expansion when the opportunity arose in Eastern Europe. An "informal" empire was added to the existing formal empire. The fate of the part of Germany occupied by the Soviet Union in World War II, that is, the division of Germany, was predetermined by this dual structure and more specifically the confluence of Stalin's personality, Soviet imperial structures, and Marxist-Leninist ideology. A revolutionary transformation of the whole of Germany, as Stalin came to realize, was not a viable option. German nationalism, as he knew, militated against a division of Germany. But the prescriptive or even compelling nature of the paradigm was such that the temptation of holding on to an area under Soviet control was irresistible. At least he considered the risks of doing anything else to be greater than holding onto what he had.

Why, then, did the division of Germany last for such a long time? Part of the answer lies in the compelling nature of the paradigm, another in the *normative Kraft des Faktischen*, or the tendency of facts to establish new norms. The "building of socialism" in the Soviet zone of occupation and the German Democratic Republic within the context of the Soviet imperial system in Eastern Europe, including the Warsaw Pact and CMEA, created powerful vested interests among both Soviet and East German institutions. Bureaucratic inertia is always an important characteristic of imperial systems and was no less so in the Soviet Union under Stalin and his successors. This reinforced pressures not to tamper with imperial possessions. Yet the currency reform in the Western zones and the momentum towards the creation of a separate West Germany allied with the United States posed in a most tangible form the disadvantages of a continued division of Germany. Stalin reacted by imposing the Berlin blockade in 1948. That ill-advised measure underlined the complete lack of conceptual clarity on the German issue. The Soviet leader was unable to convey a clear message as to what it was he wanted: the incorporation of all of Berlin to round off the Soviet empire in Eastern Europe (Berlin as a prize) or the prevention of the formation of a separate West German state (Berlin as a lever). If the former was his goal, he was unprepared to accept the risk of a military confrontation with the United States which it implied. If the latter, he was unwilling to relinquish Soviet control in the Soviet zone of occupation and make a reasonable offer of German reunification. In 1952, he made such an offer. On paper it looked reasonable. But it was not credible. As the archival evidence underlines, the objectives to be achieved to one degree or another were to gain greater influence over West German public opinion; to counteract then current Western initiatives on "free elections" to be held in both parts of Germany under United Nations supervision; to delay or prevent West German defense integration in the framework of the European Defense Community; and to obtain a gradual pullout of Western allied troops from West Germany.

Imperial dilemmas again became dramatically evident in 1952-53. In reference primarily to the mass exodus of East Germans to West Germany, Prime Minister Malenkov had to acknowledge at a meeting of the government in May 1953 that the Soviet leadership faced an internal catastrophe in East Germany and that it was obliged to face the truth and to admit that without the presence of Soviet troops the existing regime in the GDR was not stable. A devastating admission. The available evidence is fairly strong that Beria was prepared to draw appropriate conclusions and do something about the problem but not strong enough to set a price acceptable to the West, let alone to abandon the GDR unconditionally. No one knows in what, if anything, negotiations conducted under Beria's leadership would have resulted. In any case, he was not given a chance to try, and his executors – some of them at least – used both the East German popular uprising of June 1953 and the argument that Beria had embarked upon a criminal scheme towards the GDR as justification, if justification indeed was needed, to stay the course. This meant that the imperial dilemmas would return, as indeed they did in 1958-61. As early as August 1958, Central Committee department head Andropov warned of another critical phase in East Germany caused by another mass exodus of skilled workers and the intelligentsia. Khrushchev's solution after long hesitation and severe pressure exerted on him by Ulbricht was to give his consent to the building of the wall.

After some time, it appeared as if East Germany was becoming a viable political entity after all. The wall induced conformity and cooperation in the GDR, a *Staatsbewußtsein* of sorts. It also produced economic progress and advances in technology. But not enough of it. Imperial dilemmas returned in the form of increasing "costs of empire" and perceptions of East German financial and economic dependency on West Germany with supposedly dangerous political implications. The Soviet leadership had not known that the GDR was so vulnerable to West German pressures, an exasperated Khrushchev had told Ulbricht in November 1960. Rather than making the mistake of thinking that Germany was still one nation, permitting itself to be drawn into dangerous dependencies, and asking the Soviet Union to bail it out, he complained, it should have learned how to walk on its own feet. This problem the wall did *not* solve. In fact, all the Soviet leaders following after Khrushchev – Brezhnev, Andropov, Chernenko, and Gorbachev – warned of the great danger of East Germany's indebtedness to the West. At a meeting in East Berlin in October 1979, for instance, Brezhnev pounded his fist on the table and in front of the assembled SED Politburo accused Honecker of leading the GDR into bankruptcy. To take another example, in August 1984, after the GDR had accepted another major credit from West Germany and after yet again having failed to inform Moscow in advance of plans to that effect, Chernenko severely criticized Honecker. He reminded him that the GDR had expressed agreement in principle with the Soviet Union on all international questions. But in practice it was acting very differently. By accepting new credits it was becoming even more dependent on West Germany. The measures it had adopted in exchange for the credit, that is, the provisions it had made for facilitating contacts and visits of citizens and children from West Germany were unwarranted unilateral concessions to Bonn and dubious from the point of view of internal GDR security. Gorbachev continued to adhere to such views after he had become party leader.

Looked at through the conceptual lenses of the paradigm in force from 1945 until 1985, the GDR was indispensable. It was regarded in Moscow as an integral part of the Soviet empire in Eastern Europe, a bulwark of ideological orthodoxy, a strategic glacis, a staging area for the Soviet armed forces, and a supplier of machinery, chemical products, and uranium. Gorbachev initially did not abandon this frame of reference when he assumed power in March 1985. In fact, in the period of perestroika without democratization, that is, in the modernization, perfection, and acceleration interval of his tenure in office, he exerted pressure on the GDR to help in this endeavor and even to participate in an attempt to counter SDI. However, he abandoned this approach in 1986 and 1987. Three interacting and mutually reinforcing factors produced this effect: (1) the improvement of Soviet-American relations; (2) the growing realization that East Germany's standing as a politically stable, technologically advanced, and economically efficient ally had been overrated; (3) Gorbachev's move away from the paradigm of ideological competition and imperial control to a new framework – the New Thinking – emphasizing political, economic, and social development in domestic affairs and cooperation with the Western industrialized countries in the international arena. Since emphasis in this book was placed on the Gorbachev era, the main conclusions are best presented under separate headings.

Gorbachev and the German Problem. When Gorbachev took office he did, of course, have some notions about Germany and the Germans. However, these essentially appear to have been stereotypes, consisting of a mixture of standard Soviet interpretations and traditional Russian views. His attitudes were also governed more by common sense than by intellectual sophistication or in-depth knowledge. Importantly, however, he proved capable of learning and willing to adjust to ever changing circumstances. One of his beliefs, shared widely in Europe, was the notion that in an era of nationalism and the nation state the division of Germany was unnatural and artificial and could not last. But contrary to that, he also subscribed to the idea that East Germany was basically politically stable, socially integrated, economically viable, and operating in a favorable environment of increasing international acceptance of the division of Germany. Both of these two, in principle, contradictory and irreconcilable notions – "the division of Germany is artificial and cannot endure" and "the division of Germany will last because the GDR is stable and no one really wants reunification" – coexisted in Gorbachev's mind until the summer and fall of 1989.

The Politics of Non-Interference and Deference. One of the ways in which these contradictions were "solved" was typically Gorbachevian and perhaps inspired by Marxist dialectics: history would decide. He, Gorbachev, was *not* to take up the question of the continued division or reunification of Germany but to wait for things to get more mature. For shaping his own political agenda, the "realities" of the division were the decisive frame of reference; and thus there was no point, as he admitted to President Richard von Weizsäcker in July 1987, in worrying about what would be "in a hundred years." His aversion to volunteer for the role of midwife of history in East Germany and Eastern Europe was complemented by his refusal to interfere in order to stop change. The extension of glasnost and the introduction of *demokratizatsiia* as a new priority in domestic politics in January 1987 objectively had the effect of undermining the legitimacy of orthodox, bureaucratic, and neo-Stalinist regimes, including that of Honecker in East Germany. Subjectively, Gorbachev saw no reason to interfere in the course of events, let alone to embark on a coordinated policy initiative within the bloc. In fact, in what may be considered as one of the most astounding features of his tense relationship with Honecker, in the many private conversations with the East German leader he not only abstained from criticism but was complimentary about the GDR's economic and technological achievements, praised its social policies, and even lauded its internal *political* development, comparing it favorably with events in Hungary and Poland. To his close associates in Moscow he complained about Honecker being recalcitrant and arrogant and portraying the GDR as a model of socialist development in the bloc, but in conversation with the East German leader he *de facto* admitted the model character of the GDR's development. He repeatedly complimented Honecker and the GDR for having drawn the appropriate lessons from the scientific-technological revolution and averred that perestroika was essentially the same kind of response to that revolution which East Germany had adopted fifteen years earlier. Whereas his explanations of his program of change in the Soviet Union were defensive, his attitude and tone concerning developments in the GDR were deferential. At no time did he clearly and openly impress upon Honecker the need for democratic change and liberalization in the GDR. His warning in October 1989 in East Berlin that those who are late would be punished by history is characteristic of his indirect and enigmatic – and ineffective – approach and came rather late in the historical demise of the GDR

Gorbachev adopted the same approach to deal with the wide-spread notion, which he shared, that West Germany was deliberately and effectively using large-scale credits, trade preferences, and transfer payments to undermine the "socialist foundations" of the GDR. In contrast to his predecessors, Gorbachev was too polite, too timid, or perhaps only too ill-informed to raise the matter head-on with Honecker. In his many private conversations with the East German leader, he only meekly or weakly alluded to the problem. Only in November 1989, after Honecker's successor Krenz had described in detail the disastrous economic and financial state of the GDR, was Gorbachev to acknowledge that he had not imagined the economic situation to be that precarious and East German dependence on West Germany to be so far-reaching.

Reform Socialism in the GDR. As these observations demonstrate, until the very end of the GDR's existence Gorbachev's approach to that country remained rife with unresolved contradictions. The reason for this in all likelihood was that he hoped for the creation of a reform socialist East Germany that would remain an integral part of the Soviet sphere of influence in Eastern Europe and continue to be an active member of a reformed Warsaw Pact and CMEA. The replacement of Honecker first by Krenz and then by Gysi as party chief and by Modrow as prime minister reinforced rather than detracted from this idea. Although Gorbachev appreciated the fact that it was too early to present a detailed plan of change, as he told Krenz on 1 November 1989, he was nevertheless heartened by the outlines of the main directions of an action program which Honecker's successor had allegedly developed and which Gorbachev considered to be characterized by more socialism, renewal, and democratization. The novelty for the East Germans of being able to exercise new rights and the attractions of the West would wear off, he told a group of parliamentary leaders from West Germany and France shortly after the opening of the Berlin wall. The East Germans would build a reform socialist country. Such ideas persisted until the 18 March parliamentary elections finally destroyed his illusions. They foundered on four realities: (1) socialism with a human face and the harmonious combination of the plan and the market, capable of adapting rapidly to innovation, has never existed and probably can never be realized; (2) ruling communist parties have invariably been opposed to a dilution of their power, and this was just as true for the CPSU as for the SED and its successor, the PDS; (3) whereas a reform socialist metamorphosis was perhaps possible among non-ruling communist parties in a democratic environment, such as in Western Europe, it was hardly likely in Eastern societies, where civil society had to be rebuilt; and (4) a reform socialist GDR as the smaller part of a divided nation could never hope to compete successfully with West Germany and its *soziale Marktwirtschaft.* Objective conditions and Gorbachev's preferences, therefore, diverged considerably. This applied also to his attitudes and policies toward German unification.

Acceptance of German Unification. In retrospect, Gorbachev and his supporters have argued that their primary concern in the period from the opening of the wall on

9-10 November until the end of January 1990 was not the prevention of unification but the management of a process that could have gotten out of control and led to unpredictable consequences. Support for this view could be found in the fact that Gorbachev refrained from adopting the kind of forceful measures at the military level, but also at the political and diplomatic level, that would have been necessary in order to arrest the inexorable movement towards German unity, despite the fact that the means to do so were still available to him in the form of the continued presence of substantial Soviet military forces in Europe. But this interpretation is credible only up to a point. Gorbachev's preferences, as noted, were clear: East Germany was to be transformed from a moribund, orthodox system to a viable, reform socialist country. To that extent he was against unification. It is, therefore, not convincing to argue that his negative attitude towards German unification was essentially tactical and temporary, embarked upon under the assumption that the GDR and with it Soviet empire in Eastern Europe were irretrievably lost. Until the end of 1989 it was still unclear, certainly to Gorbachev, whether the reform experiment in the GDR might not succeed after all. No test was ever run to decide the question of how long this purportedly provisional support for a reformist GDR would have lasted and what its impact would have been on the distribution of power and influence in Central Europe. Paradoxically, therefore, German unification – like the division of Germany – did not occur in accordance with Soviet preferences. It also did not take place on the basis of Soviet policy initiatives. It was not even formally discussed and decided upon as a policy option (more of this below) but *accepted* or ratified at the end of January 1990 as an accomplished fact. This also applied, with some modification, to the Soviet consent to unified Germany's membership in NATO.

Consent to German NATO Membership. Gorbachev was torn fundamentally between various positions and refused to commit himself to any of them, essentially until the talks with Kohl in Moscow in July 1990. On the one hand, he recognized the dangers of Versailles but, on the other, he emphasized the necessity of Four Power cooperation and firm guarantees to be provided within that framework. In accordance with the New Thinking, he allocated important security functions to the Atlantic alliance and American forces in Europe, but he opposed the logical extension of this framework to include unified Germany's membership in NATO. The principle of Freedom of Choice implied letting the Germans and the East Europeans decide the question of what alliance they wanted to belong to, but Gorbachev sought to place constraints on the application of this principle. For several months, in the spring of 1990, it seemed as if the ambiguities had been resolved in favor of retrenchment and a hardening of positions on both the internal and external aspects of German unification. The reversal of that position occurred as a result of several domestic and international factors. (1) There was no viable alternative option to unified Germany's membership in NATO. The Soviet Union was isolated on both the issue of German neutrality and Gorbachev's idea of unified Germany's dual membership in both NATO and the Warsaw Pact. There was no support for it in Western and Eastern Europe, let alone from across the Atlantic. (2) At the end of January 1990, Gorbachev in essence had consented to East Germany's accession to the West German constitution on the basis of article 23. This meant that West Germany's network of treaties, including the Final Act of 1954 that provided for the Federal Republic's membership in NATO, would automatically be extended to the eastern part of the enlarged Germany unless other solutions could be agreed upon with the Western powers. Such an agreement, as described in the previous point, was ruled out. (3) In the spring of 1990, Gorbachev and his military advisor, Marshal Akhromeev, still thought that the Warsaw Pact could be salvaged and would continue, albeit in a thoroughly reformed shape, to provide a counterbalance to NATO. (4) They and other members of the top Soviet leadership came to accept the Western argument that the policies of unified Germany would be more predictable if it were to remain firmly anchored in Western institutions and in a Western military alliance. (5) NATO had committed itself to structural reforms and to abandoning its previous anti-Soviet political and military orientation. To the extent that NATO could still be considered a military competitor in Europe, the problem was mitigated by the fact that foreign armed forces and nuclear weapons or their carriers would not be stationed in the former East Germany. (6) The risk of unified Germany presenting a new security threat in Europe was obviated or at least significantly lessened by the presence of American forces in that country and in Europe; limitation of its armed forces to 370,000 servicemen; and its reaffirmation that it would not produce or possess nuclear, biological, and chemical weapons. (7) Domestically, at the end of January 1990 the idea of unified Germany's membership in NATO had appeared as an unacceptable proposition. Several decades of propaganda had hardened the image in the Soviet foreign policy establishment and in public opinion of NATO as the incarnation of aggressive Western intentions. To reverse that image, at least partially, needed time.

The "Price Tag" of the Consent. The tremendous security implications of unified Germany's membership in NATO for the Soviet Union affected Gorbachev's bargaining position on the price to be exacted for his consent. On that issue, he faced a dilemma. The Soviet economic and financial state of affairs in the spring and summer of 1990 was critical and perceived to be so both in Moscow and internationally. Gorbachev and his political and economic advisors considered involvement of the Western industrialized countries, including West Germany, a matter of top political priority both for the short term (to alleviate severe bottlenecks in the supply of the population with foodstuffs and other consumer goods) and the medium- and long term (to assist the Soviet leadership in its reform effort). However, direct linkage between the security and economic dimensions of the German settlement had to be avoided. The impression had to be dispelled that the leadership of the Soviet Union was making far-reaching concessions on security issues for possibly short-term and short-sighted economic and financial benefit. This at least in part explains the reluctance of Gorbachev and his top economics and trade officials to adopt a tough negotiating stance and demand a high price. It was only after the security issues had been settled in principle that a concomitant attempt to do so was made with results that permit different interpretations. Measured against the vast sums expended by West Germany for the reconstruction of the new *Länder*, the sums obtained by Gorbachev after some tough bargaining at a late stage, in September 1990, can be considered rather modest. Nevertheless, the comprehensive rearrangement of the political relationship between the Soviet Union and Germany created significant economic opportunities which the former country, however, was unable to realize due to its failure to create a viable framework of reform.

Domestic Politics: The Institutional Constraints. (1) None of the established institutions played a significant role in breaking new ground. This applies to the CPSU and its subordinate branches, including the CC's International Department, the middle levels of the foreign ministry, the KGB, and the armed forces. Generating, adapting to, and reconceptualizing the changes unleashed in Eastern Europe, including in East Germany, fell almost entirely to a narrow circle of top leaders and their closest advisors: Gorbachev, Shevardnadze, Yakovlev, Chernyaev, and Shakhnazarov. (2) As the CPSU and its central apparatus were lagging behind in the reform process and losing their mobilizing function in Soviet society, attempts were made by Gorbachev to alter this state of affairs. The October 1988 reorganization of the CC departments dealing with international affairs and their merger in one single, streamlined ID, with Falin as its head, was to serve this purpose. However, Falin's role on the German problem was symptomatic of that of all major leading *germanisty*: He was one of the chief architects of the August 1970 Moscow Treaty and the September 1971 Quadripartite Treaty on Berlin and viewed these agreements as strong pillars of European security. The new ID chief also felt that he had a vested interest in the continuation of the conceptual and practical approaches he had developed. Although times had changed, he was unable or unwilling to change with them. As a result, Falin's attitudes toward German unification and unified Germany's membership in NATO were more conservative than those of Yakovlev, Shevardnadze, and even Gorbachev. (3) Another leading *germanist* was Alexander Bondarenko. From 1971 to 1991, as chief of the MFA's Third European Department, he was responsible, among other countries, for the relations with both Germanys and Berlin and then, after an ill-advised reorganization in 1986, for the western areas of

Central Europe (minus West Berlin). In that function, he played a similar role as Falin – not as valiant head of the advance party on German unification and unified Germany's membership in NATO but as one of the rear-echelon commanders, initially to stop any advance and then, after this proved impossible, to delay or deflect it. Bondarenko was supported in this role by Yuli Kvitsinsky, like Falin another former ambassador to West Germany and, starting from May 1990, deputy foreign minister with responsibility for European affairs. (4) The attitudes of the chiefs of the ID and of the Third European Department and the new deputy foreign minister for European affairs in the MFA, in turn, are representative for the role of these and other institutions. Despite several attempts at structural reorganization, the unwillingness or inability of the main institutions to mend their ways remained an obstacle that constantly had to be overcome by pressure and persuasion from the very top. In the central party apparatus this task was fulfilled by Yakovlev as the *kurator* of the new ID in the Politburo and by Shevardnadze in the foreign ministry. In these institutions, as well as in the KGB and the armed forces, there was wide-spread dissatisfaction and frustration. No attempt was made, however, to assemble oppositional leaders and factions in these institutions in a coordinated endeavor to reverse the top political leadership's course on the German problem or, indeed, stop the accelerating drift towards the dissolution of the Soviet empire and the Soviet Union until it was too late.

Domestic Politics: Decision Making. Theoretically, one of the central analytical tasks could be the attempt to pinpoint the precise date when the Soviet leadership consented to German unification and decided on the basic outlines of united Germany's international status. Ideally, one would be able to identify one or more Politburo meetings where the internal and external aspects of German unification were put on the agenda, discussed, and then resolved. In practice, however, both the internal and external aspects were never formally discussed and decided simultaneously. A formal meeting of the Politburo to consent to German unification or to decide the Soviet position on Germany's international status was never held. A meeting that was held at the end of January 1990 and that involved a select circle of decision-makers, including several Politburo members, simply took German unification for granted. Its participants decided a few procedural questions for negotiations with West and East German leaders but failed to address, let alone resolve, the principles of the Soviet negotiating position on the external aspects of German unification. A formal Politburo meeting on the German problem took place at the beginning of May 1990, but it continued to treat the internal and international problems of the German problem as separate, and the majority of its participants, including Gorbachev, were adamantly opposed to united Germany's membership in NATO. This apparently firm position was reversed less than four weeks later by

Gorbachev, single-handedly, at the Soviet-American summit in Washington – to the surprise of the American and the consternation of the Soviet participants, without prior consultation of other Politburo members and top decision-makers, and contrary to the advice of all the senior experts on Germany. The explanation for this extraordinary state of affairs lies in the deliberate enervation of the power of the traditional decision-making institutions and machinery and their relegation to a secondary role; the disorganization and disruption produced by an incomplete and ineffective shift from a centralized, one-party state to a presidential system with some forms of parliamentary control; the shift in decision-making authority to a small circle of top leaders and their advisers and personal assistants; the exacerbation of conflict between the broad base of conservative bureaucracies and the thin layer of advocates of the New Thinking at the top; and an increase in pressure for more radical reform exerted by the newly created legislative bodies and the politically aware segments of public opinion.

The final problem to be addressed is the role of the German problem in the rise and fall of the Soviet empire and the utility of theories of imperialism as described in the first chapter. An integrative approach is appropriate here, that is, one that uses conceptual lenses provided by various theories. To look at the problem of Soviet empire-building and the attempted inclusion of East Germany in that effort with the help of *metrocentric* theories, the explanations provided by Schumpeter and Nederveen Pieterse, with their emphasis on political and military power and the political will of elite groups, rather than Marxist, neo-Marxist, or radical-liberal economic concepts, probably yield the sharpest and most accurate images. Soviet imperialism, to use their approaches, was not an expression of economic dynamics but primarily a political phenomenon. The quest for power, expressed in the perennial question of *kto-kogo*, or who will beat whom, was a central concern for Lenin, Stalin, Trotsky, Bukharin, Dzerzhinsky, and other leading figures of the Bolshevik revolution. Their drive to gain the upper hand in Russia was so determined that they turned Marxism on its head. They, or rather those of them who remained on top in the domestic power struggle, refused to contemplate Gorbachev-style attitudes and policies of waiting for matters to get more mature, that is, in 1917 for backward Russia to develop capitalism and a strong working class. The Bolshevik leaders rather than "history" established a *political* superstructure with which they constructed *ex post facto* the appropriate socio-economic base for a socialist system. Also, contrary to Marxist ideas about the "withering away of the state," they built strong institutions, including a centralized party, armed forces, and a large security apparatus. These instruments of power served these leaders well in the recreation of the Czarist empire, with the reincorporation of Ukraine, Belorussia, Armenia, Azerbaijan, Georgia, and Central Asia after the First World War and during the civil war, the addition of the Baltic states in the Second World War, and the extension of the empire in modified form to Eastern Europe after the war.

Power and political will were also the determining factors in the reformulation and adaptation of Marxist-Leninist ideology to serve imperial needs. This was evident, among other things, in the Stalinist definition of true internationalism as defense of the Soviet Union "without reservation, without wavering, and unconditionally."

The problem with the primacy of politics over economics in the construction of the Soviet empire, however, was the gap that opened between economic potential and military capabilities and between foreign-policy ambitions and the means for their realization. This problem existed in the Stalin and the Khrushchev era but became acute under Brezhnev in the late 1970s and early 1980s. The Soviet economy became overburdened with a vast and growing bureaucracy, including a large "army" of government officials, economic administrators, police, the KGB, and the armed forces. As described by Paul Kennedy in both general terms and specifically in relation to the Soviet Union, an extraordinarily large portion of the country's resources was allocated to "guns" rather than "butter." This accelerated the country's economic decline, impaired its long-term ability effectively to compete with economically more efficient and innovative adversaries, and eroded its ability to maintain its internal and external empire. To that extent, the problem of overextension started in the metropole, in the form of imperial stagnation and decay.

This obviously had implications for the global position of the Soviet Union and necessitates adoption of an the *international systemic* focus of analysis. Imperial overexpansion was a relative phenomenon, as indeed were the economic problems of the Soviet imperial system. The collapse of both the Soviet external and internal empire, as Kontorovich has convincingly argued, was not the result of an acute economic crisis but of a crisis of ideology and the disintegration of the political system in the Soviet Union. The impetus for fundamental change, including the turn away from empire, was rooted in Gorbachev's realization and that of the advocates of the New Thinking that in comparative perspective the Soviet Union and its East European dependencies were falling behind in the economic and technological competition with the United States, Western Europe, Japan, and some of the newly industrializing countries. Indeed, one is left to wonder how much change there would have occurred even under Gorbachev if the Western system had *not* performed as well as it did. Given the competitive pressures from abroad, however, the costs of empire had to be considered in a completely different light. For the Soviet Union successfully to compete it made a substantial difference whether its European possessions were an asset or a liability. The worsening of the international power position of the Soviet Union necessitated the adoption of conciliatory policies and a reduction rather than an expansion of imperial commitments. Contrary to Snyder's theoretical constructs dressed as empirical observations, a fairly broad coalition of domestic actors, including Gorbachev himself, recognized this objective necessity and acted accordingly. To the extent that there was resistance among the institutions with a vested interest in the maintenance of empire, they had no valid counterarguments.

As for the *pericentric* analytical lens, nothing could cloud more a proper understanding of the relationship between the metropole and the Soviet dependencies in Eastern Europe than the consideration of these relations as "involuntary imperialism" or conforming to a pattern of "autocolonization." The foundation of Soviet empire, to reiterate the point, was predicated upon the center's political will. The fact that the modern-day Soviet equivalents of provincial governors, satraps, or paladins, once they had been put in power by the imperial center, perennially needed and asked for Moscow's support, including intermittently in the form of military intervention, was not an expression of the center's aversion to empire but a function of the non-viability of imperial structures in Eastern Europe. The lack of viability had many reasons. For instance, in contrast to many previous examples of empire-building, including the Russian colonization in Central Asia, where the low level of socio-economic development facilitated the establishment of imperial control, the Soviet system in Eastern Europe had been imposed on economies and societies that were in many ways more advanced than Soviet society. This provided the seeds, to use a favorite Marxist-Leninist term, of contradictions between East European society and the communist regimes and formed the basis for anti-Soviet and anti-Russian national emancipation. Kennan, as he admitted twenty years after the publication of his July 1947 article in *Foreign Affairs*, could have made a much better case for the tenuous nature of Soviet rule if he had added to his analysis the "embarrassments" of imperialism which the Soviet leaders had taken upon themselves with their conquest of Eastern Europe.

In the Stalin era the imperial possessions had still fulfilled their traditional purpose of adding to the power and wealth of the metropole. This was achieved by a blatantly exploitative policy. Khrushchev ended that policy and after 1958 even promoted concepts of voluntary cooperation, supranationality, and the "socialist division of labor." But neither his reformist attempts nor Brezhnev's re-emphasis on bloc discipline could transform the center-periphery relations to a condition of viability and efficiency. Perennial subsidization and recurrent military intervention constituted "costs of empire" which, under Gorbachev, powerfully eroded the metropole's will to empire. As for Gorbachev's attitudes specifically to East Germany, the perceived dependency of the GDR on West Germany as well as Honecker's recalcitrance and arrogance played a large part in the erosion of imperial will.

Because of the widely assumed East German economic and technological progress and political stability, imperial overstretch in that exposed part of the periphery was not the most visible. But it was the most fundamental. There were two reasons for this. First, liberalization meant opening of the borders. For many practical reasons, including the would-be emigrants' unfamiliarity with the language of Western industrialized countries and the difficulty to receive work permits, this was not an unmanageable problem for reform communist regimes as in Hungary and Poland. Liberalization could be used there to enhance domestic stability. In the East German case, there was neither a problem with the language for would-be emigrants to West Germany nor with work permits or citizenship. Liberalization of travel, therefore, tendentially had the opposite effect than elsewhere in Eastern Europe. It led to a population drain and hence to an erosion of stability of the country. Second, the national problem also differentiated the GDR from all other East European countries. The communist regimes in Poland and Hungary, and in Romania as well, could play the national card in order to enhance their legitimacy. This was and turned out to be impossible for the SED. Playing the national card meant raising the issue of German unification and hence tendentially threatened the existence of the GDR as part of the Soviet empire. The unresolved German problem, among many other factors, also made it impossible for Gorbachev to transform the East European empire to a "simple" Soviet sphere of influence and change Soviet-East European relations from imperial domination to hegemony.

This inability, to turn to the *transnational* focus, was compounded by the exposure of the East European societies and economies to Western influence. Western technology, trade and credits, and businessmen and bankers were some of the transnational "forces" that had an important impact on the Soviet empire. Other, equally important agents of change were the Western European social democratic parties; the Eurocommunist parties, notably those of Italy, France, and Spain; the trade unions; cultural and church groups; and the "peace movement." In the East, they existed in the form of reform communist parties or reformist factions in orthodox parties. Such entities and Western Europe's demonstrated success in economic integration exerted a substantial corrosive influence on the Soviet empire. The effectiveness of transnational factors was enhanced by the underpinning they received through such concepts as detente, "bridge building," "constructive engagement," Ostpolitik and *Wandel durch Annäherung*, or change through rapprochement. The Conference on Security and Cooperation in Europe (CSCE) provided a particularly useful umbrella under which they could deploy and operate. East European society, therefore, was thoroughly penetrated. This vastly complicated Soviet control and produced "costs of empire" that were perhaps less tangible than the direct economic and financial costs but no less important because of their political repercussions.

East German society, as the Soviet leaders from Stalin to Gorbachev realized, was the most penetrated of all. This was the result of a flood of radio and television broadcasts from West Germany and West Berlin unhampered by a language barrier, millions of visits in both directions, and East German economic and financial dependencies. The SED, as Honecker repeatedly complained in private conversation with Gorbachev, was put in the awkward (in reality hopeless) position to fight a two-front war: against ideological penetration from West Germany and West Berlin and the effects of glasnost and democratization in the Soviet Union. These effects – irony of history! – reached East Germany primarily from West Germany and West Berlin. Given these problems, one may want to ask, what came first and what was more important in the Soviet aversion to continue to shoulder the imperial burden in the GDR: imperial overexpansion or loss of will? The former rather than the latter, it would seem. This is indicated by Gorbachev's private conversation with Krenz on 1 November 1989. There is little doubt that Gorbachev would have liked to do more than to wish Krenz luck in his endeavor to establish a reform socialist system in East Germany. But given both the dismal state of the Soviet economy and the precarious East German economic conditions, there was not much the Soviet Union could do.

A final problem to be addressed concerns the *relative importance of individual leaders, ideas, and objective forces in history*. In the evolution of events leading to both the division of Germany and to German unification the party leaders – Stalin and Gorbachev – played a central role. It is more than a play on words and stating the obvious that Stalinism would have been impossible without Stalin. The *vozhd* was not merely a party leader but also an institution. He gave Marxist-Leninist ideology a particular bent. His ideas, limited and parochial as they may have been, shaped history. This had the effect that his successors, including Khrushchev in his reform effort, were severely constrained in their freedom of action by the ideological and institutional framework which he had created. Hence, in the more than three decades after Stalin's death objective forces rather than political will proved dominant. It took a severe crisis in all dimensions of policy and another leader with new ideas to change this state of affairs.

For heuristic purposes, Gorbachev's role can be said to lie on a continuum, ranging from control to loss of control, or from planning to subjectivism and spontaneity. On this continuum, two schools of thought can be distinguished. The first interprets Gorbachev's role and the dissolution of empire as a complex and difficult but essentially managed process. The second argues that the Soviet party leader initiated processes over which he lost control. The two schools, in turn, are found in two variants. One variant of the first interpretation sees Gorbachev as a midwife of history, helping to give birth to something new and desirable, with pain obviously to be expected in the process. The other variant, ardently promulgated by orthodox communists, sees him as a more sinister character, full of criminal energy, at the head of a conspiracy to destroy both the Soviet empire and the Soviet Union. The first variant of the second school could be called that of the sorcerer's apprentice. It consists of the idea that the Soviet leader did have some idea as to what certain magic spells, such as perestroika, glasnost, Freedom of Choice, and the Common European Home, might mean, that he – like the sorcerer's apprentice in Goethe's ballad – got the abracadabra to work wonders, but that things then spun out of control. The second variant takes this case to the extreme and accuses Gorbachev of lack of foreign-policy professionalism and foresight, incompetence and ignorance, and as simply reacting to and endorsing events as they unfolded.

The solution to the riddle of Gorbachev's role in history probably lies in a combination of elements of the various interpretations and in a proper assessment of the changing context of his policies. In the first four years of his tenure in office, Gorbachev acted primarily as "midwife of history." Major processes of change were set in motion by his endorsement of the New Thinking and the Common House of Europe in 1985-86, the broadening of glasnost and the introduction of democratization in 1987, and of the Freedom of Choice in 1988. The role of the individual in history and that of ideas was preeminent. In 1989, however, both in domestic politics and in international affairs, Gorbachev essentially lost control. He was no longer guiding the course of events but merely reacting to them. Abroad, the drift became evident first and foremost in Eastern Europe, in Hungary and Poland, and then in East Germany. The uncontrollable dynamics culminated in the torrents that led to the collapse of the Warsaw Pact and CMEA and then of the Soviet Union itself. This also makes Gorbachev a "sorcerer's apprentice" – a prisoner of the new paradigm he had constructed. A prominent place for him in European and world history is well deserved, however, not because of his keen analytical sense and political foresight but because of his willingness to adapt to ever changing realities and his unwillingness to use force in order to arrest or deflect fundamental change.

APPENDIX

Notes on Archival Research

One of the most important sources used here are the archives of the East German communist party, the *Sozialistische Einheitspartei Deutschlands* (SED). They are to be found in the *Institut für Geschichte der Arbeiterbewegung, Zentrales Parteiarchiv* (Institute for the History of the Workers' Movement, Central Party Archives), referred to in the footnotes as SED, Central Party Archives. The archives are now under the administration of the German federal government and called *Bundesarchiv für Partei- und Massenorganisationen der ehemaligen DDR* (Federal Archives of the Party and Mass Organizations of the Former GDR).

The archives are important for a number of reasons. The first is their broad scope, covering the period from 1949 to 1989 and including the *Arbeitsprotokolle,* or official records of the Politburo sessions; personal files of the party chief and Politburo members (Büro Honecker, Krenz, Hager, and Axen, for instance); and the files of the CC secretariats and departments. Apparently not in their worst nightmares did the East German leaders imagine that the records of their private conversations and crimes would see the light of day. This pertains even to the records of private conversations in cars to and from airports and to what the top party leaders told each other in closed session at Warsaw Pact summit conferences. A second reason is their accessibility. The "red Prussians" certainly lived up to their reputation for order and thorough work (*deutsche Ordnung und Gründlichkeit*). Everything is neatly ordered and easy to find. Third, they are highly reliable. Given the importance of the Soviet connection for the survival of the regime, the Politburo wanted to have a complete and accurate record of every nuance and shading of what the "Soviet comrades" said, thought, and did. Because of this, it is difficult to imagine GDR scribes putting a negative or positive slant on the Soviet position as reflected in secret, confidential, or open meetings. Through interviews with the participants he author, furthermore, had the opportunity to gain important insights into the context of conversations, negotiations, and decisions.

Given the importance of the East German communist party archives, it is not surprising that Gorbachev attempted to prevent their publication. A letter dated 13 March 1991 and addressed to Ivan Ivashko, the deputy chief of the CPSU, revealed that Gorbachev had sent a confidential letter to Chancellor Kohl, appealing to him to try to stop the opening of the SED archives. The letter noted that a first request had not borne fruit. But perhaps, it continued, one should renew the request in a coming meeting with Foreign Minister Genscher or by phone with the chancellor. The letter is part of the so-called Special File, a highly secret repository used by the communist party leaders from Lenin to Gorbachev. They were declassified but not published despite or because of the on-going preparations for a constitutional court hearing on the fate of the then banned CPSU.[1]

The reasons for Gorbachev's intervention may have been both personal and political. When he was taking the initiative for the suppression of the documents he was nominally still head of the CPSU. The transcripts in the archives would show him numerous times in confidential conversations and meetings with East German friends and comrades assuring them of the unwavering support they would receive from the Soviet party and its general secretary. But in his capacity as executive president of the Soviet Union he would eventually abandon East Germany and agree to German unification and unified Germany's membership in NATO. In the internal struggles in the party and with the nationalist opposition this would be further proof of Gorbachev's treacherous double-dealing.

But another reason was probably more important. The East German archives, he told Ivashko, contained "documents connected with the activities of illegal communist parties, which the SED has assisted in coordination with us" and of secret assistance provided to West German organizations. This is also the reason why Gregor Gysi, the last party chief of the SED and also the head of its successor organization, the PDS, had warned Falin in a confidential conversation the day before Gorbachev's letter that publication of the archives would be "a real catastrophe."[2]

Some of the transcripts are in direct speech, others in indirect speech. To preserve consistency and readability, direct speech has been used throughout in this book,. When indirect speech was used in the original, this has been indicated accordingly in the footnote.

---

1 The documents were shown to Paul Quinn-Judge, Moscow correspondent of the *Boston Globe*; a report on the circumstances and the content of the letter was published by the paper on 29 May 1992.

2 Ibid.

Biographical Notes

The biographical data are not meant to be exhaustive. For the most part, information has been provided about the offices held by Soviet and German officials only where this appeared relevant to an understanding of their decision-making role on the German problem.

Arbatov, Georgi A., 1968-96, Director of the Institute for the Study of the USA and Canada under the Soviet (later the Russian) Academy of Sciences, member of the Academy of Sciences, the Central Committee of the CPSU, and the Supreme Soviet of the USSR; advisor to all six Soviet and Russian leaders, from Khrushchev to Yeltsin.

Axen, Hermann, 1970-89, Politburo member and secretary of the SED CC for foreign relations.

Boldin, Valeri, 1981 joined Gorbachev's staff as an adviser on agricultural questions and advanced in conjunction with his chief's career; 1986 candidate member and 1988 full member of the Central Committee; 1987-90, head of the CC's General Department; 1990-91, Gorbachev's chief of staff and in that capacity helped execute the August 1991 coup attempt against the president.

Bykov, Vladimir L., 1986-91, section head in the Fourth European Department of the Soviet foreign ministry dealing with the socialist countries of Europe, including the GDR.

Chernyaev, Anatoli S., 1970-86, deputy head of the CPSU CC International Department; starting from February 1986, chief foreign policy advisor to Gorbachev.

Dashichev, Viacheslav I., sector head, professor and German expert at the Institute for the Study of the Economy of World Socialism at the USSR Academy of Sciences in Moscow.

Falin, Valentin M., 1971-78, Soviet ambassador to West Germany; 1978-83, deputy head of the CPSU CC's International Information Department; 1983-86, political commentator for *Izvestiia*; 1986-88, chief of Novosti press agency; 1988-91, head of the reorganized ID.

Gerasimov, Gennadi I., 1986-90, Soviet foreign ministry spokesman under Shevardnadze; 1991, Soviet ambassador to Portugal.

Gorinovich, Gorald N., 1971-84, *chargé d'affaires* at the Soviet embassy in East Berlin; 1984-86, deputy head of the Third European department at the Soviet foreign ministry; 1986-90, chief of the MFA's department for European socialist countries.

Grigoriev, Sergei A., 1984-90, official in the American section of the ID; from October 1990 until July 1991 deputy press spokesman for Gorbachev.

Honecker, Erich, 1971-89, General Secretary of the SED; 1973-89, chairman of the State Council of the GDR.

Kornienko, Georgi M., 1977-86, first deputy foreign minister of the Soviet Union; 1986-91, deputy chief of the ID.

Krenz, Egon, 1976-89, candidate member and – after 1983 – full member of SED Politburo; 1983-89, CC secretary responsible for security; replaced Erich Honecker as party chief on 18 October 1989.

Kvitsinsky, Yuli A., 1959-65, Soviet embassy official in East Berlin; 1978- 81, Soviet embassy official in Bonn; 1981-83, head of the Soviet delegation at the Geneva INF talks; 1986-90, ambassador in Bonn; May 1990 until September 1991, deputy and first deputy foreign minister.

Maksimychev, Igor F., one of the few progressive *germanisty* in the Soviet foreign ministry under Shevardnadze; 1956-58, official at the Soviet consulate in Leipzig; 1958-60 and 1976-84, posted to the Soviet embassy in Bonn; 1987-92, deputy chief of mission at the Soviet embassy in East Berlin.

Medvedev, Vadim A., 1986-90, Secretary, CC CPSU; 1988-90, full member of the Politburo; 1986-88, head of the Department for Liaison with Communist and Workers' Parties of Socialist Countries; 1988-90, CC secretary responsible for ideological questions, chairman of the CC's Ideological Commission, and member of the Politburo's Commission for Further Study of Materials and Documents Related to the Repressions of the Stalin Years.

Mittag, Günter, 1986-89, SED Politburo member and CC secretary responsible for economic affairs.

Rykin, Viktor S., 1970-90, official in the CPSU Central Committee's international department, responsible for relations with Western political parties and movements, notably the social-democratic parties of Western Europe; 1988-90, ID deputy head; interpreter for Gorbachev on numerous occasions, including Gorbachev's first visit to West Germany in 1975.

Schabowski, Günter, 1985-89, Politburo member and first secretary of the SED's Berlin district.

Shakhnazarov, Georgi K., 1969 deputy head, 1986 - October 1988, first deputy head of the Department for Liaison with Socialist Countries; October 1988, appointed special assistant to Gorbachev for relations with the socialist countries; in addition, from autumn 1989, special assistant to Gorbachev on Soviet legal issues; 1989-91, member of Supreme Soviet and Congress of People's Deputies.

Steinbach, Thilo, March 1990 - October 1990, foreign policy aide to East German Prime Minister Lothar de Maizière.

Tarasenko, Sergei P., 1986-90, personal aide to foreign minister Shevardnadze.

Teltschik, Horst, 1982-91, department head in the West German chancellery's office and chief advisor to Chancellor Kohl on foreign policy.

Tsipko, Alexandr S., December 1986 - November 1989, Central Committee consultant in the Department for Liaison with the Communist and Workers' Parties of Socialist Countries (later renamed Department for Relations with Communist and Workers' Parties of Eastern Europe), with GDR and Poland as a special sphere of responsibility.

Wolf, Markus, 1951-87, GDR Ministry of Security; his last position was chief of the main intelligence directorate and deputy minister.

Yakovlev, Alexander N., June 1987 - July 1991, member of CPSU Politburo, secretary of the CPSU Central Committee; 1988-90, CC secretary in the Politburo responsible for the ID (that is, ID *kurator*); January 1990 - July 1991, head of the CC Foreign Policy Commission; one of Gorbachev's closest and most influential advisers.

Zagladin, Vadim V., 1967-88, first deputy head of Central Committe's International Department.

List of Interviews

The author conducted interviews with the following Western, Soviet, and East German party or government officials:

Blech, Klaus, ambassador, May 1991, March 1992, and June 1993, in Moscow.

Braithwaite, Sir Roderic, ambassador, 30 April 1994, in St. Petersburg.

Bykov, Vladimir L., 29 June 1993, in Bonn.

Chernyaev, Anatoli S. , 25 June 1993 and 29 April 1994, in Moscow.

Dashichev, Viacheslav I., 29 June 1993, in Bonn.

Gerasimov, Gennadi I., 25 June 1993, in Moscow.

Grigoriev, Sergei A., 23 and 27 March 1994, in Boston.

Krenz, Egon, 23 and 26 July 1993, in Berlin.

Kvitsinsky, Yuli A., 5 June 1994, in Berlin.

Maksimychev, Igor F., 2 June 1993, in Moscow.

Palazchenko, Pavel R., 10 February 1995, in Boston.

Pavlov, Nikolai, 9 June 1993, in Moscow.

Rykin, Viktor S., 11 June 1993, in Moscow.

Shakhnazarov, Georgi K., 3 December 1994, in Providence, Rhode Island.

Steinbach, Thilo, 15 May 1990, in East Berlin and in 1992-93 at the Fletcher School of Law and Diplomacy, Medford, Mass.

Tarasenko, Sergei P., 29 April 1994, in Moscow.

Teltschik, Horst, 26 July 1994, in Munich.

Tsipko, Alexandr S., 28 July 1995, in Moscow (conducted on the author's behalf by Alexander Kokeev).

Zagladin, Vadim V., 10 June 1993, in Moscow.

Bibliography

Abel, Elie, *The Shattered Bloc* (Boston: Houghton Mifflin, 1990).

Adomeit, Hannes, "Russia as a 'Great Power' in World Affairs: Images and Reality," *International Affairs* (London), Vol. 71, No. 1 (January 1995), pp. 35-68.

--- "Gorbachev, German Unification, and the Collapse of Empire," *Post-Soviet Affairs* (Berkeley, Calif.), Vol. 10, No. 3 (July–September 1994), pp. 197-230.

--- "The Atlantic Alliance in Soviet and Russian Perspectives," in Neil Malcolm, ed., *Russia and Europe: An End to Confrontation?*, published under the auspices of the Royal Institute on International Affairs, London (London: Pinter, 1994), pp. 31-54.

--- "Rußland, Deutschland und die 'neue' Weltordnung," in Gustav Schmidt, ed., *Ost-West-Beziehungen: Konfrontation und Détente, 1945-1989* (Bochum: Universitätsverlag, 1993), pp. 18-36.

--- "Gorbachev and German Unification: Revision of Thinking, Realignment of Power," *Problems of Communism*, Vol. 39, No. 4 (July-August 1990), pp. 1-23.

--- "Soviet Perspectives on Tomorrow's Germany," in Gary L. Geipel, ed., *The Future of Germany* (Indianapolis, Ind.: The Hudson Institute, 1990), pp. 164-183.

--- Hans-Hermann Höhmann and Günther Wagenlehner, eds., *Die Sowjetunion unter Gorbatschow* (Stuttgart: Kohlhammer, 1990).

--- "The Impact of Perestroika on Soviet European Policy," in Tsuyoshi Hasegawa and Alex Pravda, eds., *Perestroika: Soviet Domestic and Foreign Policies*, published under the auspices of the Royal Institute of International Affairs (London: Sage Publications, 1990), pp. 242-266.

--- "Soviet Security Perspectives on Germany," in Robbin F. Laird and Susan L. Clark, eds., *The USSR and the Western Alliance* (Boston, Mass.: Unwin & Hyman, 1990), pp. 181-215.

--- "Auswirkungen von Reformpolitik und Systemwandel in der Sowjetunion auf die Ost-West-Beziehungen in Europa," Stiftung Wissenschaft und Politik (Ebenhausen), Research Report, SWP–AP 2636 (February 1990).

--- "Soviet Policy Toward the United States and Western Europe: 'Atlanticism' Versus the 'Common House,'" in Lawrence W. Lerner and Donald W. Treadgold, eds., *Gorbachev and the Soviet Future* (Boulder, Colo.: Westview, 1988), pp. 188-206.

--- "Gorbatschows Westpolitik: Vorrang für die Beziehungen zu den Vereinigten Staaten," *Osteuropa*, Vol. 38, No. 12 (December 1988), pp. 1091-1105.

--- "Gorbatschows Westpolitik: Die Beziehungen im 'gemeinsamen Haus'," *Osteuropa*, Vol. 38, No. 9 (September 1988), pp. 816-834.

Adomeit, Hannes, "Gorbatschows Westpolitik: 'Gemeinsames europäisches Haus' oder atlantische Orientierung?," *Osteuropa*, Vol. 38, No. 6 (June 1988), pp. 419-34.

--- Hans-Hermann Höhmann and Günther Wagenlehner, eds., *Die Sowjetunion als Militärmacht* (Stuttgart: Kohlhammer, 1987).

--- "Widersprüche im Sozialismus: Sowjetpolitik in Osteuropa im Kontext der Ost-West-Beziehungen, Stiftung Wissenschaft und Politik (Ebenhausen), Research Report, SWP–AZ 2412 (February 1985).

--- "The German Factor in Soviet Westpolitik," *The Annals of the American Academy of Political and Social Science* (September 1985), pp. 15-28.

--- "Soviet Policy Toward the West: Costs and Benefits of Using 'Imperialist Contradictions'," in Uwe Nerlich and James A. Thomson, eds., *The Soviet Problem in American-German Relations* (New York: Crane, Russak, 1985), pp. 187-234.

--- "Relations Between Eastern and Western Europe: Prospects for Change," in *The Conduct of East-West Relations in the 1980s*, Adelphi Paper (London: International Institute for Strategic Studies, 1984), pp. 1-11.

--- "Capitalist Contradictions and Soviet Policy," *Problems of Communism*, Vol. 33, No. 3 (May-June 1984), pp. 1-18.

--- "Sowjetische Westpolitik: Möglichkeiten und Grenzen der Nutzung von 'Widersprüchen im Imperialismus'," in Uwe Nerlich and James A. Thomson, eds., *Das Verhältnis zur Sowjetunion: Zur politischen Strategie der Vereinigten Staaten und der Bundesrepublik Deutschland* (Baden-Baden: Nomos Verlagsgesellschaft, 1984), pp. 193-243.

--- with an introduction by Richard Löwenthal, *Die Sowjetmacht in internationalen Krisen und Konflikten: Verhaltensmuster, Handlungsprinzipien, Bestimmungsfaktoren* (Baden-Baden: Nomos, 1983).

--- "The Political Rationale of Soviet Military Capabilities and Doctrine," in *Strengthening Conventional Deterrence in Europe: Proposals for the 1980s*, Report of the European Security Study (ESECS) (London: Macmillan, 1983), pp. 67-104.

--- "Nach Breshnew – Tendenzen, Perspektiven," *Osteuropa*, Vol. 33, No. 6 (June 1983), pp. 437-448.

--- *Soviet Risk Taking and Crisis Behavior* (London: Allen & Unwin, 1982).

--- "Außen- und Sicherheitspolitik unter Andropov: Tendenzen, Perspektiven," Stiftung Wissenschaft und Politik (Ebenhausen), Research Report, SWP – AP 2358 (April 1983).

--- "Ideology in the Soviet View of International Affairs," in Christoph Bertram, ed., *Prospects of Soviet Military Power in the 1980s* (London: Macmillan, 1980), pp. 103-110.

Adomeit, Hannes, "Ideology in the Soviet View of International Affairs," in Christoph Bertram, ed., *Prospects of Soviet Power in the 1980s* (London: Macmillan, 1980), pp. 103-110.

--- "Soviet Perceptions of Western European Integration," *Journal of International Studies* (London), Vol. 8, No. 1 (Spring 1979), pp. 1-24.

Akhromeev, [Marshal] Sergei F., and Georgi Kornienko, *Glazami marshala i diplomata* (Moscow: Mezhdunarodnye otnosheniia, 1992).

Albats, Yevgenia, *The State Within a State: The KGB and Its Hold on Russia – Past, Present, and Future*, transl. Catherine A. Fitzpatrick (New York: Farrar, Straus, Giroux, 1994).

Aleksandrov-Agentov, Andrei, *Ot Kollontai to Gorbacheva* (Moscow: Mezhdunarodnye otnosheniia, 1992).

Alexiev, Alex R., "The Soviet Campaign Against INF: Strategy, Tactics, and Means," *Orbis*, Vol. 29, No. 2 (Summer 1985), pp. 319-350.

Andert, Reinhold, and Wolfgang Herzberg, *Der Sturz: Erich Honecker im Kreuzverhör* (Berlin: Aufbau Verlag, 1990).

Andropov, Yurii N., "Uchenie Karla Marxa i nekotorye voprosy sotsialisticheskogo stroitel'stva v SSSR," *Kommunist*, No. 3 (February 1983).

Andrew, Christopher, and Oleg Gordievsky, *KGB: The Inside Story of Its Foreign Operations from Lenin to Gorbachev* (London: Hodder and Stoughton, 1990).

Arbatov, Aleksei G., "Skol'ko oboronoy dostatochno'?," *Mezhdunarodnaia zhizn'*, No. 3 (March 1989), pp. 33-47.

--- *Bezopasnost' v iadernyi vek* (Moscow: Politizdat, 1980).

Arbatov, Georgii, with an introduction by Strobe Talbott, *The Soviet System: An Insider's Life in Soviet Politics* (New York: Random House, 1992).

Arias-King, Fredo, "Essence of a Soviet Decision: Allowing a United Germany to Join the North Atlantic Treaty Organization. An Organizational-Bureaucratic Approach," Research Paper, the Kennedy School of Government, Harvard University, January 1996 (unpublished).

Arnold, Heinz, *Die ersten hundert Tage des Hans Modrow* (Berlin: Dietz Verlag, 1990).

Ash, Timothy Garton, *In Europe's Name: Germany and the Divided Continent* (New York: Random House, 1993).

--- *The Uses of Adversity* (New York: Random House, 1989).

--- "Mitteleuropa?," *Daedalus*, Special issue, (Winter 1989), pp. 1-21.

--- "The Decline of the Soviet Empire," *New York Review of Books*, Nos. 14, 15, 16 (1988).

Åslund, Anders, *Gorbachev's Struggle for Economic Reform* (Ithaca, N.Y.: Cornell University Press, 1989).

Asmus, Ronald D., *German Unification and Its Ramifications*, Rand Research Report, Santa Monica, Cal., The Rand Corporation, R-4021-A, 1991.

--- "A United Germany," *Foreign Affairs*, Vol. 69, No. 2 (Spring 1990), pp. 63-76.

--- "Evolution of Soviet-East European Relations under Mikhail Gorbachev," Radio Free Europe Research, *Background Report*, No. 153 (Eastern Europe), 22 August 1989.

--- "The Dialectics of Detente and Discord: The Moscow – East Berlin – Bonn Triangle," *Orbis*, Vol. 28, No. 4 (Winter 1985), pp. 748-774.

Azrael, Jeremy R., *The Soviet Civilian Leadership and the Military High Command*, Rand Research Report, Santa Monica, Cal., The Rand Corporation, R-3521-AF, June 1987.

Baker, James A., with Thomas M. Defrank, *The Politics of Diplomacy: Revolution, War and Peace, 1989-1992* (New York: G. P. Putnam's Sons, 1995).

Baranovsky, Vladimir G., *Zapadnaia Evropa: Voenno-politicheskaia integratsiia* (Moscow: Mezhdunarodnye otnosheniia, 1988).

Baranovsky, Vladimir, and Hans-Joachim Spanger, *In from the Cold: Germany, Russia, and the Future of Europe* (Boulder, Colo.: Westview, 1992).

Baras, Victor, "Beria's Fall and Ulbricht's Survival," *Soviet Studies*, Vol. 27, No. 3 (July 1975), pp. 381-395.

Barron, John, *KGB: The Secret Work of Soviet Secret Agents*, A Corgi Book (London: Transworld, 1974).

Becker, Abraham S., *Sitting on Bayonets: The Soviet Defense Burden and the Slowdown of Soviet Defense Spending*, Rand/UCLA Center for the Study of Soviet International Behavior, JRS-01, December 1985.

--- *Economic Leverage on the Soviet Union in the 1980s*, The Rand Corporation, Santa Monica, Cal., R-3127-USDP, July 1984.

Bergedorfer Gesprächskreis, *Das gemeinsame europäische Haus aus der Sicht der Sowjetunion und der Bundesrepublik Deutschland*, Protocol of the 86th round of talks of the Bergedorfer Gesprächskreis, a politically and economically independent forum, held in Bonn-Bad Godesberg, 3-4 December 1988 (Hamburg: Körber Stiftung, 1989).

--- *Systemöffnende Kooperation? Perspektiven zwischen Ost und West*, Protocol of the 84th round of talks of the Bergedorfer Gesprächskreis, a politically and economically independent forum, held in Berlin 25 March 1988 (Hamburg: Körber Stiftung, 1988).

Bernstein, Lisbeth T., "On the Rocks: Gorbachev and the Kurile Islands," unpublished Ph.D. dissertation, The Fletcher School of Law and Diplomacy, May 1997.

Bertram, Christoph, "The German Question," *Foreign Affairs* (Spring 1990), pp. 45-62.

Beschloss, Michael R., and Strobe Talbott, *At the Highest Levels: The Inside Story of the End of the Cold War* (Boston: Little, Brown & Company, 1993).

Beyme, Klaus von, *The Soviet Union in World Politics* (Aldershot, Hants.: Gower, 1985).

Birnbaum, Karl E., *East and West Germany: A Modus Vivendi* (Westmead, England: Saxon House, D.C. Heath, 1973).

Blagovolin, S. E., "K voprosu o globalizatsii deiatel'nosti voenno-promyshlennykh kompleksov," in *Puti k bezopasnosti* (Moscow: Scientific Council for the Study of Peace and Disarmament, 1988).

Bluth, Christoph, *New Thinking in Soviet Military Policy*, Chatham House Papers, published under the auspices of the Royal Institute of International Affairs (London: Pinter, 1990).

Bogdanov, Radomir G., "Glavnyi protivnik – inertsiia gonki vooruzhenii," *SShA: Ekonomika, politika, ideologiia*, No. 10 (1988), pp. 61-65.

Bogomolow, Oleg, and Heinrich Vogel, eds., *Rußland und Deutschland: Nachbarn in Europa*, under the auspices of the Bundesinstitut für ostwissenschaftliche und internationale Studien, Cologne (Baden-Baden: Nomos, 1992).

Boggs, Carl, *The Impasse of European Communism* (Boulder, Colo.: Westview, 1982).

Boldin, Valery, *Ten Years that Shook the World: The Gorbachev Era As Witnessed by His Chief of Staff* (New York: Basic Books, 1994).

--- *Kruzhenie piedestala. Shrikhy k portretu M. S. Gorbacheva* (Moscow: Respublika, 1995).

Bortfeldt, Heinrich, *Washington – Bonn – Berlin: Die USA und die deutsche Einheit* (Bonn: Bouvier, 1993).

Bölling, Klaus, *Die fernen Nachbarn: Erfahrungen in der DDR* (Hamburg: Gruner and Jahr, 1983).

Bond, Daniel, *Trade or Aid? Official Export Credit Agencies and the Economic Development of Eastern Europe and the Soviet Union* (New York: Institute for East-West Security Studies, 1991).

Brandenburg, Ulrich, "The 'Friends' Are Leaving: Soviet and Post-Soviet Troops in Germany after Unification," Bundesinstitut für ostwissenschaftliche und internationale Studien (Cologne), Research Report, No. 33 (1992).

Brown, Archie, *The Gorbachev Factor* (Oxford: Oxford University Press, 1996).

Brown, J. F., *Eastern Europe and Communist Rule* (Durham and London: Duke University Press, 1988).

Brzezinski, Zbigniew, *Alternative to Partition* (New York: McGraw Hill, 1965).

Buchan, David, *Western Security and Economic Strategy towards the East*, Adelphi Paper No. 192 (London: IISS, 1984).

[Cecchini Report] Paolo Cecchini, *Europa '92: Der Vorteil des Binnenmarkts*, published under the auspices of the Steering Committee for the Research Program on "The Costs of Non-Europe", Chairman: Paolo Cecchini, Coordinator: Michael Loy (Baden-Baden: Nomos, 1988).

Central Intelligence Agency (CIA) and Defense Intelligence Agency (DIA), *The Soviet Economy under a New Leader*, A Paper Prepared Jointly by the Central Intelligence Agency (CIA) and the Defense Intelligence Agency (DIA) for Submission to the Subcommittee on Economic Resources, Competitiveness, and Security Economics of the Joint Economic Committee, Congress of the United States, 19 March 1986, Washington 1986.

--- *USSR: Measures of Economic Growth and Development, 1950-1980*, Study Prepared for the Use of the Joint Economic Committee, U.S. Congress, Washington, D.C., December 1982.

Chazov, Yevgenii, *Zdorove i vlast'* (Moscow: Novosti, 1992).

Chernyaev, Anatolii S., *Shest' let s Gorbachevym: Po dnevnikovym zapisiam* (Moscow: Izdatel'skaia gruppa "Progress," "Kultura," 1993).

"'Chinesische Lösung': Wollten Stasi-Leute ein Blutbad unter Demonstranten provozieren?," *Der Spiegel* (Hamburg), 18 December 1989.

Christians, F. Wilhelm, *Paths to Russia: From War to Peace* (New York: Macmillan, 1990).

Clark, Michael T., and Simon Serfaty, eds., *New Thinking and Old Realities: America, Europe and Russia*, published in association with the Johns Hopkins Foreign Policy Institute (Washington, D.C.: Seven Locks Press, 1991).

Clarke, Douglas L., "Soviet Troop Withdrawals from Eastern Europe," *Report on Eastern Europe* (Munich, Radio Liberty/Radio Free Europe), 30 March 1990, pp. 41-49.

Cohen, Ariel, *Russian Imperialism: Development and Crisis* (Westport, Conn.: Praeger, 1996).

--- "The End of Empire: Russian Imperial Development and Decline," Ph.D. thesis, The Fletcher School of Law and Diplomacy, Tufts University, December 1993.

Cohen, Benjamin J., *The Question of Imperialism* (New York: Basic Books, 1973).

Coker, Christopher, ed., *Drifting Apart? The Superpowers and their European Allies* (London: Brassey's Defence Publishers, 1988).

"The Cold War in Asia," Woodrow Wilson International Center for Scholars, Washington, D.C., *Cold War International History Project Bulletin,* Nos. 6-7 (Winter 1995/96).

CPSU, CC. Top Secret, Plenum TsK KPSS, Jiul' 1953 goda. Stenograficheskii otchet, "O prestupnykh antipartiinykh i antigosudarstvennykh deistviiakh Beriia," 2-7 July 1953, *Izvestiia TsK KPSS*, No. 1 (1991), pp. 140-214 and No. 2 (1991), pp. 141-208.

--- CC. "Informatsionnoe soobshchenie o Plenume Tsentral'nogo Komiteta Kommunisticheskoi Partii Sovetskogo Soiuza," *Pravda*, 7 February 1990.

--- CC. "Tezisy Tsentral'nogo Komiteta KPSS k XIX Vsesoiuznoi partiinoi konferentsii," *Pravda*, 27 May 1988.

CPSU, Conferences. "XIX Vsesoiuznaia konferentsiia KPSS. Vneshniaia politika i diplomatiia. Doklad chlena Politburo TsK KPSS, ministra inostrannykh del SSSR E.A. Shevardnadze na nauchno-prakticheskoi konferentsii MID SSSR, 25 iiulia 1988 goda," *Mezhdunarodnaia zhizn',* No. 9 (September 1988), pp. 3-35.

--- Conferences. "XIX Vsesoiuznaia konferentsiia KPSS: vneshniaia politika i diplomatiia. Doklady rukovoditelei sektsii ob itogakh raboty," *Mezhdunarodnaia zhizn',* No. 9 (September 1988), pp. 36-53.

Cracraft, James, ed., *Major Problems in the History of Imperial Russia* (Lexington, Mass.: D.C. Heath, 1994).

CSCE. "Itogovyi dokument Venskoi vstrechi predstavitelei gosudarstv-uchastnikov Soveshchaniia po bezopasnosti i sotrudnichestvo v Evrope," *Mezhdunarodnaia zhizn',* No. 3 (March 1989), pp. 130-61.

Cuthbertson, Ian M., and David Robertson, eds., *Enhancing European Security: Living in a Less Nuclear World,* in association with the Institute for East-West Security Studies (New York: St. Martin's Press, 1990).

Dallin, Alexander, "Linkage Patterns: From Brest to Brezhnev," in Seweryn Bialer, ed., *The Domestic Context of Soviet Foreign Policy* (Boulder, Colo: Westview, 1981), pp. 344-347.

--- "Soviet Foreign Policy and Domestic Politics: A Framework of Analysis," *Journal of International Affairs*, No. 2 (1969), pp. 250-265; reprinted in Hoffmann and Fleron *The Conduct of Soviet Foreign Policy* (London: Butterworths, 1972), pp. 36-60.

Davison, Walter Philips, *The Berlin Blockade: A Study in Cold War Politics* (Princeton, N.J.: 1958).

Davydov, Yuri, "The Soviet Vision of a Common European House," Paper delivered to the International Studies Conference (ISA) in London, 29 March – 1 April 1989 (unpublished).

Dawisha, Karen, *Eastern Europe, Gorbachev, and Reform: The Great Challenge*, 2nd ed. (Cambridge: Cambridge University Press, 1990).

--- and Bruce Parrott, eds., *The End of Empire? The Transformation of the USSR in Comparative* Perspective, Series The International Politics of Eurasia, Vol. 9 (Armonk, NY: M.E. Sharpe, 1997).

Dean, Jonathan, "Conventional Arms Talks: A First Good Round," *The Bulletin of the Atomic Scientists* (October 1989), pp. 26-31.

De Nevers, Renée, *The Soviet Union and Eastern Europe: The End of an Era*, Adelphi Paper No. 249, International Institute for Strategic Studies (London), March 1990.

Djilas, Milovan, *Conversations with Stalin*, transl. Michael B. Petrovich (New York: Harcourt Brace & World, 1962).

Dobrynin, Anatoly, *In Confidence: Moscow's Ambassador to America's Six Cold War Presidents (1962-1986)* (New York: Random House, 1995).

Donnelly, Christopher, *Gorbachev's Revolution: Economic Pressures and Defense Realities* (Alexandria, Va.: Jane's Information Group, 1989).

Doyle, Michael W., *Empires* (Ithaca, N.Y.: Cornell University Press, 1986).

Duisberg, Claus J., "Der Abzug der russischen Truppen aus Deutschland: Eine politische Erfolgsbilanz," *Europa-Archiv*, No. 16 (1994), pp. 461-469.

Eisfeld, Alfred, ed., *Die Rußlanddeutschen* (Munich: Langen Müller, 1992).

Elbe, Frank, *Die Lösung der äußeren Aspekte der deutschen Frage* (Bonn: Europa Union Verlag, 1993).

--- and Richard Kiessler, *Ein runder Tisch mit scharfen Ecken: Der diplomatische Weg zur deutschen Einheit* (Baden-Baden: Nomos, 1993).

--- and Richard Kiessler, *A Round Table with Sharp Corners* (Baden-Baden: Nomos, 1993).

Ellison, Herbert J., ed., *Soviet Policy toward Western Europe: Implications for the Western Alliance* (Seattle: University of Washington Press, 1983).

Ellman Michael, and Vladimir Kontorovich, eds., *The Disintegration of the Soviet Economic System* (London: Routledge, 1992).

Emerson Vermaat, J. A., "Moscow Fronts and the European Peace Movement," *Problems of Communism*, Vol. 31, No. 6 (November-December 1982), pp. 43-56.

Enders, Thomas, "Die SPD und die äußere Sicherheit. Zum Wandel der sicherheitspolitischen Konzeption der Partei in der Zeit der Regierungsverantwortung, 1966-1982," Research Report No. 64, Konrad-Adenauer-Stiftung (Melle, West Germany: Knoth, 1987).

ESECS Report, *Strengthening Conventional Deterrence in Europe: Proposals for the 1980s*, Report of the European Security Study (ESECS) (London: Macmillan, 1983).

ESG Report, *The Gorbachev Challenge and European Security*, Report by the European Strategy Group (ESG), (Baden-Baden: Nomos, 1988).

Falin, Valentin, *Politische Erinnerungen* (Munich: Droemer Knaur, 1993).

Faramazian, F. A., ed., *Gonka vooruzenii v stranach NATO*, published under the auspices of the Scientific Council for Research on Problems of Peace and Security at the Institute for World Economy and International Relations (Moscow: Mezhdunarodnye otnosheniia, 1988).

Federal Institute for East European and International Studies, ed., *The Soviet Union 1988-1989* (Boulder, Colo.: Westview, 1990).

--- *The Soviet Union 1986-1987* (Boulder, Colo.: Westview, 1989).

--- *The Soviet Union 1984-1985* (Boulder, Colo.: Westview, 1986).

Fehe'r, Ferenc, and Agnes Heller, *Osteuropa unter dem Schatten eines neuen Rapallo*, Research Project on Crises in Soviet-type Systems, directed by Zdenek Mlynar, Research Report No. 6 (Cologne: Index, 1985).

Feis, Herbert, *From Trust to Terror: The Onset of the Cold War, 1945-1950* (London: Bond, 1971).

Filitov, Aleksei M., *Germanskii vopros. Ot raskola k ob"edineniiu* (Moscow: Mezhdunarodnye otnosheniia, 1993).

Foye, Stephen, "Defense Issues at the Party Congress," *Report on the USSR* (Radio Liberty, Munich), Vol. 2, No. 30 (July 1990), pp. 1-4.

--- "The Soviet Armed Forces: Lead-Up to the Party Congress," *Report on the USSR* (Radio Liberty, Munich), Vol. 2, No. 28 (July 1990), pp. 1-4.

--- "Military Hard-Liner Condemns 'New Thinking' in Security Policy," *Report on the USSR* (Radio Liberty, Munich), Vol. 2, No. 28 (July 1990), pp. 4-6.

Frantseva, Inessa S., *Otnosheniia SEV-ES. Istoriia, sovremennost', perspektivy*, published under the auspices of the Institut for Scientific Information in the Social Sciences (INION) at the USSR Academy of Sciences of the USSR (Moscow: INION, 1988).

Fricke, Karl-Wilhelm, "Okkupanten oder Waffenbrüder? Die Gruppe der Sowjetischen Streitkräfte in Deutschland," *Deutschland-Archiv*, Vol. 15, No. 3 (March 1982), pp. 269-276.

Gaddis, John Lewis, "International Relations Theory and the End of the Cold War," *International Security*, Vol. 17, No. 3 (Winter 1992/93), pp. 5-58.

--- "The Rise, Fall, and Future of Detente," *Foreign Affairs*, Winter 1983/84.

Galkin, Alexander, and Anatoli Chernyaev, "Pravdu i tol'ko pravdu. Razmyshleniia po povodu vospominanii," *Svobodnaia mysl'*, No. 3 (1994), pp. 19-29.

Garthoff, Raymond L., *The Great Transition: American-Soviet Relations and the End of the Cold War* (Washington, D.C.: Brookings, 1994).

--- *Detente and Confrontation: American-Soviet Relations from Nixon to Reagan* (Washington, D.C.: Brookings, 1985).

Gati, Charles, *The Bloc that Failed: Soviet-East European Relations in Transition* (Bloomington, Ind.: Indiana University Press, 1990).

--- "The Stalinist Legacy in Soviet Foreign Policy," in Robbin P. Laird and Erik P. Hoffmann, eds., *Soviet Foreign Policy in a Changing World* (New York: Aldine, 1986), pp. 16-28.

Gedmin, Jeffrey, *The Hidden Hand: Gorbachev and the Collapse of East Germany*, published under the auspices of the American Enterprise Institute (Washington, D.C.: The AEI Press, 1992).

Geipel, Gary L., ed., *The Future of Germany* (Indianapolis, Ind.: The Hudson Institute, 1990).

Gelman, Harry, *The Rise and Fall of National Security Decision Making in the Former USSR: Implications for Russia and the Commonwealth*, The Rand Corporation, Santa Monica, Cal., R-4200-A, 1992.

--- *Gorbachev's Policies toward Western Europe: A Balance Sheet*, The Rand Corporation, Santa Monica, Cal., R-3588-AF, October 1987.

--- ed., *The Future of Soviet Policy toward Western Europe*, The Rand Corporation, Santa Monica, Cal., R-3254-FF/NATO, September 1985.

--- *The Brezhnev Politburo and the Decline of Detente* (Ithaca: Cornell University Press, 1984).

"Gemeinsame Mitteilung über die Gespräche des Bundeskanzlers mit dem Ministerpräsidenten der DDR in Dresden," Press and Information Office of the Federal Government, *Bulletin*, No. 148, 20 December 1989, pp. 1249-1252.

Genscher, Hans-Dietrich, *Erinnerungen* (Berlin: Siedler Verlag, 1995).

Ginsburgs, George, and Alvin Z. Rubinstein, eds., *Soviet Foreign Policy toward Western Europe* (New York: Praeger, 1978).

Glynn, Patryck, "Peredyshka, Appeasement, Isolationism: NATO's Uncertain Future," Paper presented to the Conference on Planning for Defense and Arms Control: The Quest for Integration, organized by the Washington Strategy Seminar and the Atlantic Strategy Forum, King's College, London, 2-4 April 1989 (unpublished).

Goeckel, Robert F., *The Lutheran Church and the East German State: Political Conflict and Change under Ulbricht and Honecker* (Ithaca, N.Y.: Cornell University Press, 1990).

Goettemoeller, Rose E., and Paul F. Langer, *Foreign Area Studies in the USSR: Training and Employment of Specialists*, The Rand Corporation, Santa Monica, Cal., R-2967-RC, January 1983.

Gorbachev, Mikhail S., *Zhizn' i reformy*, 2 vols. (Moscow: Novosti, 1995).

--- Michail Gorbatschow, *Erinnerungen* (Berlin: Siedler, 1995).

--- "Gorbatschow und die deutsche Einheit," interview with Brigitte Seebacher-Brandt, *Frankfurter Allgemeine Magazin*, No. 746, 17 June 1994, pp. 23-29.

--- *Gody trudnykh reshenii. Izbrannoe, 1985-1992*, ed. under the auspices of the Gorbachev Foundation by Aleksandr Gal'kin and Anatolii Chernyaev (Riazan': "Sapienti sat' Regional Publishing House, 1993).

--- "Mir na perelome," *Svobodnaia mysl'* (Moscow), No. 17 (November 1992), p. 10.

--- "Iz Arkhiva Gorbacheva: M. S. Gorbachev – W. Brandt," Transcript of a meeting between Gorbachev and Brandt, held in Moscow on 17 October 1989, *Svobodnaia mysl'*, No. 17 (November 1992), pp. 22-29.

--- Interview with *Time* Magazine, 4 June 1990.

--- Michail Gorbatschow, *Das gemeinsame Haus Europa und die Zukunft der Deutschen* (Düsseldorf: Econ, 1990).

--- "Sotsialisticheskaia ideia i revolutsionnaia perestroika," *Pravda*, 28 November 1989.

--- "Prazdnik sotsializma na nemetskoi zemle. Rech' M.S. Gorbacheva," Speech at the 40th anniversary of the founding of the GDR in East Berlin on 6 October 1989, *Pravda*, 7 October 1989.

--- "Vystuplenie M.S. Gorbacheva pered uchastnikami Leningradskogo obkoma KPSS," *Izvestiia*, 14 July 1989.

--- "Obshcheevropeiskii protsess idet vpered. Rech' M. S. Gorbacheva," Speech to the Parliamentary Assembly of the European Union, *Pravda*, 7 July 1989.

--- "Press-konferentsiia v Parizhe," Joint press conference with François Mitterrand, *Pravda*, 7 July 1989.

--- "Gorbachev v FRG. Sovmestnoe zaiavlenie," *Izvestiia*, 15 June 1989.

--- "Vstrecha s kitaiskoi obshchestvennost'iu. Vystuplenie M. S. Gorbacheva," *Pravda*, 18 May 1989.

--- "Interv'iu M.S. Gorbacheva kitaiskomy televideniiu," *Pravda*, 18 May 1989.

--- *Perestroika i novoe myshlenie dlia nashei strany i dlia vsego mira* (Moscow: Politizdat, 1988).

Gordon, Lincoln, ed., *Eroding Empire: Western Relations with Eastern Europe* (Washington, D.C.: Brookings Institution, 1987).

Goskomstat, "Sotsial'no ekonomicheskie razvitie SSSR za deviat' mesiatsev 1989 goda. Soobshchenie Goskomstata," *Pravda*, 28 October 1989.

Götz-Coenenberg, Roland and Hans-Henning Schröder, Schwerter zu Pflugscharen, Atomsprengköpfe zu Molkereimaschinen, *Aktuelle Analysen*, Bundesinstitut für ostwissenschaftliche und internationale Studien, Cologne, 30 November 1988.

Grachev, Andrei S., *Kremliovskaia khronika* (Moscow: EKSMO, 1994).

Graml, Hermann, "Die Legende von der verpaßten Gelegenheit: Zur sowjetischen Notenkampagne des Jahres 1952," *Vierteljahrshefte für Zeitgeschichte*, Vol. 29, No. 3 (1981), pp. 307-341.

Gratchev [Grachev], Andrei S., *L'histoire vraie de la fin de l'URSS: Le naufrage de Gorbatchev* (Monaco: Editions du Rocher, 1992).

Griffith, William E., "The Soviets and Western Europe," in Herbert J. Ellison, ed., *Soviet Policy toward Western Europe: Implications for the Western Alliance* (Seattle: University of Washington Press, 1983).

Grigoriev, Sergei, "The International Department of the Central Committee of the Communist Party of the Soviet Union and Gorbachev's Attempts to Reform the Party Apparat: A Case Study of Disintegration of Authority," unpublished Ph.D. dissertation, Tufts University, May 1996.

--- "The International Department of the CPSU Central Committee: Its Functions and Role in Soviet Foreign Policy-Making and its Rise and Fall Following the Major Reorganization of the Central Party Apparatus under Gorbachev," Strengthening Democratic Institutions Project, Harvard University, John F. Kennedy School of Government, December 1995.

Gromyko, Anatolii, and Vladimir Lomeiko, *Novoe myshlenie v iadernyi vek* (Moscow: Mezhdunarodnye otnosheniia, 1984).

Gromyko, Andrei, *Memoirs*, Foreword by Henry A. Kissinger, transl. Harold Shukman (New York: Doubleday, 1989).

Grosser, Dieter, Stephan Bierling and Friedrich Kurz, *Die sieben Mythen der Wiedervereinigung: Fakten und Analysen zu einem Prozess ohne Alternative* (München: Ehrenwirt, 1991).

Griffith, William E., ed., *Central and Eastern Europe: The Opening Curtain?* (Boulder, Colo.: Westview, 1989).

Grube, Frank, and Gerhard Richter, *Flucht und Vertreibung: Deutschland zwischen 1944 und 1947* (Hamburg: Hoffmann und Campe, 1980).

Hacker, Jens, *Deutsche Irrtümer: Schönfärber und Helfershelfer der SED-Diktatur* im Westen (Berlin: Ullstein, 1992).

Haigh, R. H., D. S. Morris and A. R. Peters, *German-Soviet Relations in the Weimar Era: Friendship from Necessity* (Aldershot, Hants.: Gower, 1985).

Halecki, Oscar, *The Limits and Divisions of European History* (Notre Dame, Ind.: University of Notre Dame Press, 1962).

Hamilton, Daniel, *After the Revolution: The New Political Landscape in East Germany*, German Issue Series, No. 7 (Washington, D.C.: American Institute for Contemporary German Studies, 1990).

Hanrieder, Wolfgang, *Germany, America, Europe: 40 Years of German Foreign Policy* (New Haven, Conn.: Yale University Press, 1987).

Hanson, Philip, "Is there a 'Third Way' between Capitalism and Socialism?," *Report on the USSR*, August 30, 1991.

Harkavy, Robert E., *Bases Abroad: The Global Military Presence* (Oxford: Oxford University Press, 1989).

Harrison, Hope, "Ulbricht and the Concrete 'Rose': New Archival Evidence on the Dynamics of Soviet-East German Relations and the Berlin Crisis, 1958-61," Cold War International History Project, Woodrow Wilson International Center for Scholars, Working Paper, No. 5, May 1993.

Haslam, Jonathan, *The Soviet Union and the Politics of Nuclear Weapons: The Problem of the SS-20* (Houndmills and London: Macmillan, 1989).

Hassner, Pierre, "Moscow and the Western Alliance," *Problems of Communism*, Vol. 30, No. 3 (May-June 1981), pp. 37-54.

Herrnstadt, Rudolf, *Das Herrnstadt-Dokument. Das Politbüro der SED und die Geschichte des 17. Juni 1953*, ed. by Nadja Stulz-Herrnstadt (Reinbek: Rowohlt, 1990).

Herspring, Dale, "On Perestroika: Gorbachev, Yazov, and the Military," *Problems of Communism*, Vol. 35, No. 4 (July-August 1987), pp. 99-107.

Hertle, Hans-Hermann, "Der ökonomische Untergang des SED-Staates," *Deutschland-Archiv*, Vol. 25 (October 1992), pp. 1019-1030.

--- "Gespräch mit Gerhard Schürer," *Deutschland-Archiv*, Vol. 25 (October 1992), pp. 1031-1039.

--- and Igor Maksimychev, "Die Maueröffnung: Eine russisch-deutsche Trilogie," *Deutschland-Archiv*, Vol. 27 (November 1994), pp. 1137-1158.

Hoffmann, Stanley, "The Western Alliance: Drift or Harmony?," *International Security*, Vol. 6, No. 2 (Fall 1981), pp. 105-125.

Holloway, David, *Stalin and the Bomb: The Soviet Union and Atomic Energy, 1939-1956* (New Haven: Yale University Press, 1994).

Holzman, Franklyn, *International Trade under Communism* (New York: Basic Books, 1976).

Horelick, Arnold, and Myron Rush, *Strategic Power and Soviet Foreign Policy* (Chicago: University of Chicago Press, 1966).

Horn, Gyula, *Freiheit, die ich meine: Erinnerungen des ungarischen Außenministers, der den Eisernen Vorhang öffnete*, transl. Angelika and Péter Máté (Hamburg: Hoffman and Campe, 1991).

Hough, Jerry F., *Opening Up the Soviet Economy* (Washington, D.C.: Brookings, 1988).

--- *Russia and the West: Gorbachev and the Politics of Reform* (New York: Simon and Schuster, 1988).

Hyde-Price, Adrian, *European Security beyond the Cold War: Four Scenarios for the Year 2010*, for the Royal Institute of International Affairs (London: Sage Publ., 1991).

Ivanov, V., "Bez'iadernyi mir i obshchestvennoe soznanie," *Kommunist*, No. 5 (March 1987), pp. 117-119.

Jackson, John H., *Restructuring the GATT System*, Chatham House Papers, published under the auspices of the Royal Institute of International Affairs (London: Pinter Publishers, 1990).

Jahn, Egbert, "Wo befindet sich Osteuropa?," *Osteuropa*, Vol. 40, No. 5 (May 1990), pp. 418-440.

Joffe, Josef, "The 'Revisionists:' Germany and Russia in a Post-Bipolar World," in Michael T. Clark and Simon Serfaty, eds., *New Thinking and Old Realities: America, Europe, and Russia*, Published in association with the Johns Hopkins Foreign Policy Institute (Washington, D.C.: Seven Locks Press, 1991).

Judt, Tony, "The Rediscovery of Central Europe," *Daedalus*, (Winter 1989), pp. 23-54.

Kaiser, Karl, *Deutschlands Vereinigung: Die internationalen Aspekte*, published under the auspices of the Deutsche Gesellschaft für Auswärtige Politik (Bergisch-Gladbach: Bastei Lübbe, 1991).

Kaiser, Robert G., *Why Gorbachev Happened: His Triumphs and His Failure* (New York: Simon & Schuster, 1991).

Karaganov, Sergei, "Implications of German Unification for the Former Soviet Union," in Paul B. Stares, ed., *The New Germany in the New Europe* (Washington, D.C.: Brookings Institution, 1992), pp. 331-364.

--- "Chto vmesto modernizatsii?" *Moskovskie novosti*, 9 April 1989.

--- "Amerika v obshcheevropeiskom dome," *Moskovskie novosti*, 13 November 1988.

Keohane, Robert O., Joseph S. Nye, and Stanley Hoffman (Cambridge, Mass.: Harvard University Press, 1993).

Kennan, George F., *Memoirs: 1925-1950* (Boston: Little, Brown & Co., 1967).

Khrushchev, Sergei, "Pensioner soiuznogo znavheniia," *Ogonek*, Nos. 40-43 (October 1988).

Kitrinos, Robert W., "The International Department of the CPSU," *Problems of Communism*, Vol. 33 (September-October 1984), pp. 47-76.

Klein, Hans, *Es begann im Kaukasus. Der entscheidende Schritt in die Einheit Deutschlands* (Berlin and Frankfurt/M: Ullstein, 1991).

Kohl, Helmut, "*Ich wollte Deutschlands Einheit*," as portrayed by Kai Diekmann and Ralf Georg Reuth (Berlin: Propyläen, 1996).

Kokoshin, Andrei A., "The New Soviet Military Doctrine and Unilateral Cuts of the USSR Armed Forces," Statement before the Armed Services Committee, U.S. House of Representatives, 10 March 1989 (unpublished mimeograph).

--- and V. Larionov, "Protivostoianie sil obshchego naznacheniia v kontekste obespecheniia strategicheskoi stabil'nosti," *MEIMO*, No. 6 (June 1988), pp. 23-31.

--- and V. Larionov, "Kurskaia bitva v svete sovremennoi oboronitel'noi doktriny," *MEIMO*, No. 8 (August 1987), pp. 32-40.

Kontorovich, Vladimir, "The Economic Fallacy," *The National Interest*, Vol. 31 (Spring 1993), pp. 35-44.

Kornienko, Georgi, *Kholodnaia voina. Svidetel'stvo ee uchastnika* (Moscow: Mezhdunarodnye otnosheniia, 1994).

Kotschemassow, Wjatscheslaw [Kochemasov, Viacheslav], *Meine letzte Mission: Fakten, Erinnerungen, Überlegungen* (Berlin: Dietz, 1994).

Kramer, Mark, "The CPSU International Department: Comments and Observations," in Sergei Griogirev, ed., The International Department of the CPSU Central Committee: Its Functions and Role in Soviet Foreign Policy-Making and its Rise and Fall Following the Major Reorganization of the Central Party Apparatus under Gorbachev, Strengthening Democratic Institutions Project, Harvard University, John F. Kennedy School of Government, December 1995.

--- "The Role of the CPSU International Department in Soviet Foreign Relations and National Security Policy," *Soviet Studies*. Vol. 42, No. 3 (July 1990), pp. 429-448.

--- "Beyond the Brezhnev Doctrine: A New Era in Soviet-East European Relations?," *International Security*, Vol. 14, No. 3 (Winter 1989/90), pp. 25-67.

Kraus, Michael and Ronald D. Liebowitz, *Perestroika and East-West Economic Relations: Prospects for the 1990s* (New York: New York University Press, 1990).

Krenz, Egon, "Honecker und Gorbatschow," *Neues Deutschland*, 25 January 1993.

--- "Anmerkungen zur Öffnung der Berliner Mauer im Herbst 1989," *Osteuropa*, No. 4 (1992), pp. 365-369.

--- with Hartmut König and Gunter Rettner, *Wenn Mauern fallen. Die friedliche Revolution: Vorgeschichte, Ablauf, Auswirkungen* (Vienna: Paul Neff, 1990).

Kuhn, Ekkehard, *Gorbatschow und die deutsche Einheit: Aussagen der wichtigsten russischen und deutschen Beteiligten* (Bonn: Bouvier, 1993).

Kupchan, Charles A., *The Vulnerability of Empire* (Ithaca, N.Y.: Cornell University Press, 1994).

Kwizinskij, Julij A., *Vor dem Sturm: Erinnerungen eines Diplomaten* (Berlin: Siedler, 1993).

Kvitsinsky, Yuli A., "Posol'stvo na Reine," *Mezhdunarodnaia zhizn',* No. 4 (April 1989), pp. 38-48.

Laird, Robbin F., *The Soviets, Germany, and the New Europe* (Boulder, Colo.: Westview, 1991).

--- and Susan L. Clark, eds., *The USSR and the Western Alliance* (Boston: Unwin & Hyman, 1990).

--- and Erik P.Hoffmann, eds., *Soviet Foreign Policy in a Changing World* (New York: Aldine, 1986).

Laqueur, Walter, *Russia and Germany: A Century of Conflict* (New Brunswick, N.J.: Transaction Publishers, 1990).

Larrabee, Stephen F., ed., *The Two German States and European Security,* in association with the Institute of East-West Security Studies (Houndmills and London: Macmillan, 1989).

Lenin, V.I., *Imperialism: The Highest Stage of Capitalism* (New York: International Publishers, 1939, new. ed.: 1969).

Leonhard, Wolfgang, *Child of the Revolution* (Chicago: H. Regnery, 1958).

Lewin, Moshe, *The Gorbachev Phenomenon: A Historical Interpretation*, expanded edition (Berkeley, Cal.: University of California Press, 1991).

Ligachev, Yegor, *Zagadka Gorbacheva* (Novosibirsk: SP Interbook, 1992).

MacGregor, *The Soviet-East German Military Alliance* (Cambridge: Cambridge University Press, 1989).

Malashenko, Igor, "Warum bauen wir mehr Raketen ab?," *Neue Zeit* (Moscow), No. 7 (1988), p. 21.

Mastny, Vojtech, *The Cold War and Soviet Insecurity: The Stalin Years* (Oxford: Oxford University Press, 1996).

--- "Soviet Troop Withdrawals from Eastern Europe as a Political Problem: Past, Present and Future," Research Report, Bundesinstitut für ostwissenschaftliche und internationale Studien (Cologne), No. 1, January 1989.

Matlock, Jack F., Jr., *Autopsy of an Empire: The American Ambassador's Account of the Collapse of the Soviet Union* (New York: Random House, 1995).

Maull, Hanns W., "Germany and Japan: The New Civilian Powers," *Foreign Affairs*, Vol. 69, No. 5 (Winter 1990/91), pp. 91-106.

McAdams, A. James, *Germany Divided: From the Wall to Reunification* (Princeton: Princeton University Press: 1993).

--- "The New Logic in Soviet-GDR Relations," *Problems of Communism*, Vol. 37, No. 5 (September-October 1988), pp. 47-60.

Maksimychev, Igor, "Berlinskaia stena. Ee padenie glazami ochevidtsa," *Nezavisimaia gazeta*, 10 and 12 November 1993.

--- "Krushenie. Rekviem po GDR," in Igor Maximychev and Hans Modrow, *Poslednii god GDR* (Moscow: Mezhdunarodnye otnosheniia, 1993), pp. 9-156.

--- "Possible 'Impossibilities'," *International Affairs* (Moscow), No. 6 (June 1993), pp. 108-17.

Medvedev, Vadim, *V komande Gorbacheva. Vzgliad iznutri* (Moscow: Bylina, 1994).

--- *Raspad. Kak on nazreval v "mirovoi sisteme sotsializma"* (Moscow: Mezhdunarodnye otnosheniia, 1994).

--- *East Germany and Détente: Building Authority after the Wall* (Cambridge: Cambridge University Press, 1985).

Medvedev, Zhores, *Gorbachev* (Oxford: Basil Blackwell, 1986).

Meissner, Boris, "The GDR's Position in the Soviet Alliance," *Aussenpolitik*, Engl. ed., No. 4 (1984), pp. 369-389.

Mel'vil', A. Iu, "'Obraz vraga' i novoe politiceskoe myshlenie," *SShA*, No. 1 (January 1988), pp. 29-39.

Miller, John, *Mikhail Gorbachev and the End of Soviet Power* (New York: St. Martin's Press, 1993).

Mittag, Günter, *Um jeden Preis: Im Spannungsfeld zweier Systeme* (Berlin: Aufbau Verlag, 1991).

Modrow, Hans, *Aufbruch und Ende* (Hamburg: Konkret Literatur Verlag, 1991).

--- "Abschied von der zweiten Heimat," *Die Zeit*, 27 April 1990.

[Molotov, Viacheslav M.], *Sto sorok besed s Molotovym. Iz dnevnika F. Chueva* (Moscow: Terra, 1991).

Moreton, Edwina, ed., *Germany Between East and West*, Published in association with the Royal Institute on International Affairs (Cambridge: Cambridge University Press, 1987).

--- and Gerald Segal, *Soviet Strategy toward Western Europe* (London: George Allen & Unwin, 1984).

--- *East Germany and the Warsaw Alliance: The Politics of Detente* (Boulder, Colo.: Westview, 1978.

Naimark, Norman M., *The Russians in Germany: A History of the Soviet Zone of Occupation, 1945-1949* (Cambridge, Mass.: The Belknap Press of Harvard University Press, 1995).

[NATO], A Comprehensive Concept of Arms Control and Disarmament, NATO Press Communiqué, M-1 (89) 20, released 30 May 1989.

--- Declaration of the Heads of State and Government Participating in the Meeting of the North Atlantic Council in Brussels, 29-30 May 1989, NATO Press Communiqué, M-1 (89) 21, released 30 May 1989.

--- Report of the Council. Annex to the Final Communique of the Ministerial Meeting, December 1967, "The Future Tasks of the Alliance," in *NATO Final Communiqués 1949-1974* (Brussels: NATO Information Service, 1975), pp. 195-202.

Nederveen Pieterse, Jan P., *Empire and Emancipation* (New York: Praeger, 1989).

Nelson, Daniel N., "Watching the Pact Unravel: The Transformation of East European Political-Military Policies," Bundesinstitut für ostwissenschaftliche und internationale Studien (Cologne), Research Report, No. 32 (1990).

--- *Alliance Behavior in the Warsaw Pact*, Westview Special Studies on the Soviet Union and Eastern Europe (Boulder, Colo.: Westview, 1986).

Nerlich, Uwe, and James A. Thomson, eds., *The Soviet Problem in American-German Relations* (New York: Crane, Russak, 1985).

--- ed., *The Soviet Asset: Military Power in the Competition over Europe* (Cambridge, Mass.: Ballinger, 1983).

Nye, Joseph S., Jr., and Robert O. Keohane, "Transnational Relations and World Politics," *International Organization*, Vol. 25 (Summer 1971), pp. 325-349.

Novikov, Nikolai V., *Vospominaniia diplomata. Zapiski 1938-1947* (Moscow: Politizdat, 1989).

Oldenburg, Fred, "Deutsche Einheit und Öffnung der NATO," Research Report, Bundesinstitut für ostwissenschaftliche und internationale Studien (Cologne), No. 52, October 1996.

--- "Das Dreieck Moskau-Ost-Berlin-Bonn, 1975-1989," Research Report, Bundesinstitut für ostwissenschaftliche und internationale Studien (Cologne), No. 54, September 1994.

--- "Der Zusammenbruch des SED-Regimes," in *Die revolutionäre Umwälzung in Mittel- und Osteuropa*, Series Göttinger Arbeitskreis, Vol. 10 (Berlin: Duncker & Humblot, 1993), pp. 103-161.

Oldenburg, Fred, "Sowjetische Osteuropapolitik und die Lösung der deutschen Frage," *Osteuropa*, No. 8 (August 1991), pp. 751-773.

Oschlies, Wolf, "'Russischkenntnisse? In der DDR eine Seltenheit'! Ausmass und Ursachen einer Fremdsprachenmisere," Research Report, Bundesinstitut für ostwissenschaftliche und internationale Studien (Cologne), No. 49, October 1989.

Parker, Geoffrey, *The Geopolitics of Domination* (London and New York: Routledge, 1988).

"Peremeny v Tsentral'noi i Vostochnoi Evorope. S zasedaniia Komissii TsK KPSS po voporsam mezhdunarodnoi politiki 15 iiunia 1990 g.," *Izvestiia Tsk KPSS*, No. 10 (October 1990), pp.102-113.

Pinder, John, *The European Community and Eastern Europe*, Chatham House Papers, published under the auspices of the Royal Institute of International Affairs (London: Pinter Publishers, 1991).

Pipes, Richard, *Russia under the Bolshevik Regime* (New York: Random House, 1995).

--- ed., *Soviet Strategy in Europe* (New York: Crane, Russak, 1976).

Pittman, Avril, *From Ostpolitik to Reunification: West German-Soviet Political Relations Since 1974*, Soviet and Eastern European Studies Series, No. 85 (Cambridge: Cambridge University Press, 1992).

Ploss, Sidney I., *Moscow and the Polish Crisis: An Interpretation of Soviet Policies and Intentions*, Westview Special Studies on the Soviet Union and Eastern Europe (Boulder, Colo.: Westview, 1986).

Pond, Elizabeth, *Beyond the Wall: Germany's Road to Unification*, A Twentieth Century Fund Book (Washington, DC: The Brookings Institution, 1993).

--- *Germany after the Wall: Assessing the "Tectonic Change" that Still Rumbles Through Europe* (Washington, D.C.: The Brookings Institution, 1993).

--- "A Wall Destroyed: The Dynamics of German Unification in the GDR," *International Security*, Vol. 15, No. 2 (Fall 1990), pp. 35-66.

Pridham, Kenneth, "The Soviet View of Current Disagreements between the United States and Western Europe," *International Affairs* (London), Vol. 49, No. 1 (Winter 1982/83), pp. 17-31.

Primakov, Yevgeni, "USSR Policy on Regional Conflicts," *International Affairs* (Moscow), No. 6 (June 1988).

Proektor, Danil, "Wenn die letzten Limits fallen," *Neue Zeit* (Moscow), No. 19 (May 1984), pp. 18-21.

Przybylski, Peter, *Tatort Politbüro: Honecker, Mittag und Schalck-Golodkowski*, Vol. 2 (Berlin: Rowohlt, 1992).

Przybylski, Peter, *Tatort Politbüro: Die Akte Honecker* (Berlin: Rowohlt, 1991).

Rachwald, Arthur R., *Poland between the Superpowers: Security vs. Economic Recovery*, A Westview Replica Edition (Boulder, Colo.: Westview, 1983).

Recktenwald, Marion, "Perestrojka in den sowjetischen Streitkräften," Research Report of the Bundesinstitut für ostwissenschaftliche und internationale Studien, Cologne, No. 10 (1987).

Remnick, David, *Lenin's Tomb: The Last Days of the Soviet Empire* (New York: Random House, 1993).

Reuth, Ralf Georg, and Andreas Bönte, *Das Komplott: Wie es wirklich zur deutschen Einheit kam* (Munich: Piper, 1993).

Riese, Hans-Peter, "Die Geschichte hat sich ans Werk gemacht: Der Wandel der sowjetischen Position zur Deutschen Frage," *Europa-Archiv*, No. 4 (1990), pp. 117-126.

Rollo, J. M. C. et al., *The New Europe: Western Responses*, Chatham House Papers, published under the auspices of the Royal Institute of International Affairs (London: Pinter Publishers, 1990).

Royen, Christoph, *Die sowjetische Koexistenzpolitik im Wandel: Voraussetzungen, Ziele, Dilemmata*, Series Internationale Politik und Sicherheit, Vol. 2 (Baden-Baden: Nomos, 1987).

Rubinstein, Alvin Z., *Soviet Foreign PolicysSince World War II* (Boston: Little, Brown, and Co., 1985).

Ruehl, Lothar, *MBFR: Lessons and Problems*, Adelphi Paper No. 176, (London: IISS, 1982).

Ruge, Gerd, *Gorbachev: A Biography* (London: Chatto & Windus, 1991).

Rumer, Eugene B., "The German Question in Moscow's 'Common European Home:' A Background to the Revolutions of 1989," Rand Note, The Rand Corporation, Santa Monica, Cal., N-3220-USDP, 1991.

Rykin, V. S., ed., *Lidery sovremmenoi sotsial-demokratii* (Moscow: Mezhdunarodnye otnosheniia, 1991).

Schabowski, Günter, *Das Politbüro: Ende eines Mythos. Eine Befragung*, ed. by Frank Sieren and Ludwig Koehne, Series rororo aktuell (Reinbek: Rowohlt, 1991).

--- *Der Absturz* (Berlin: Rowohlt, 1991).

Schäuble, Wolfgang, *Der Vertrag: Wie ich über die deutsche Einheit verhandelte*, with an introduction by Dirk Koch and Klaus Wirtgen (Stuttgart: Deutsche Verlags-Anstalt, 1991).

Schneider, Peter, "Is Anyone German Here? A Journey into Silesia," *The New York Times Magazine*, April 15, 1990.

Schröder, Hans-Henning, "Gorbatschow und die Generäle: Militärdoktrin, Rüstungspolitik und öffentliche Meinung in der 'Perestrojka,'" Research Report, Bundesinstitut für ostwissenschaftliche und internationale Studien, Cologne, No. 45 (1987).

Schulz, Eberhard, and Peter Danylow, "Bewegung in der deutschen Frage? Die ausländischen Besorgnisse über die Entwicklung in den beiden deutschen Staaten," 2nd ed., Research Paper No. 33, Research Institute of the Deutsche Gesellschaft für Auswärtige Politik, Bonn, April 1985.

Schumpeter, Joseph A., *Imperialism and Social Classes*, transl. Heinz Norden, ed. and with an introduction by Paul M. Sweezy (New York: Augustus M. Kelley, 1951).

SED Politburo, *Arbeitsprotokolle. Sozialistische Einheitspartei Deutschlands, Zentralkomitee, Politbüro* [Transcripts of the SED Politburo meetings, 1949-1989, documentary collection], IfGA, ZPA, Institut für Geschichte der Arbeiterbewegung, Zentrales Parteiarchiv (Institute for the History of the Workers' Movement, Central Party Archives).

Seiffert, Wolfgang, *Die Deutschen und Gorbatschow: Chancen für einen Interessenausgleich* (Erlangen: Straube, 1989).

Semjonow, Wladimir S. [Semenov, Vladimir S.], *Von Stalin bis Gorbatschow: Ein halbes Jahrhundert in diplomatischer Mission, 1939-1991* (Berlin: Nicolai, 1995).

Shakhnazarov, Georgi K., *Tsena svobody. Reformatsiia Gorbacheva glazami ego pomoshchnika* (Moscow: Rossika, Zevs, 1993).

Shebarshin, Leonid V., *Iz zhizni nachal'nika razvedki* (Moscow: Mezhdunarodnye otnosheniia, 1994.

Shevardnadze, Eduard Ambrosievich, *Moi vybor. V zashchitu demokratii i svobody*, 2nd ed. (Moscow: Novosti, 1991).

Shulman, Marshall D., "Soviet Proposals for a European Security Conference," *Studies for a New Central Europe*, No. 3/4 (1968-69), pp. 67-80.

--- "'Europe' versus 'Detente,'" *Foreign Affairs* (April 1967), pp. 389-402.

--- *Stalin's Foreign Policy Reappraised* (New York: Atheneum, 1965).

Shumaker, David H., *Gorbachev and the German Question: Soviet-West German Relations, 1985-1990* (Westport, Conn.: 1995).

Sheehy, Gail, *The Man Who Changed the World* (New York: Harper Collins, 1990).

Simes, Dmitri "The Death of Detente," *International Security* (Summer 1980), pp. 3-25.

Snyder, Jack, *Myths of Empire: Domestic Politics and International Ambition* (Ithaca, N.Y.: Cornell University Press, 1991).

Snyder, Jack, "Averting Anarchy in the New Europe," *International Security*, Vol. 14, No. 4 (Spring 1990).

Sodaro, Michael J., *Moscow, Germany, and the West from Khrushchev to Gorbachev* (Ithaca, N.Y.: Cornell University Press, 1991).

Stalin, J. V., *Sochineniia*, Vol. 6 (Moscow: Politizdat, 1947).

--- *Sochineniia*, Vol. 10 (Moscow: Politizdat, 1948).

Steininger, Rolf, *Eine vertane Chance: Die Stalin-Note vom 10. März 1952 und die Wiedervereinigung. Eine Studie auf der Grundlage unveröffentlichter britischer und amerikanischer Akten* (Berlin: Dietz Verlag, 1990).

Stent, Angela, ed., *Economic Relations with the Soviet Union: American and West German Perspectives* (Boulder: Westview, 1985).

--- "Soviet Policy toward the German Democratic Republic," in Sarah Meiklejohn Terry, ed., *Soviet Policy in Eastern Europe*, Council of Foreign Relations (New Haven: Yale University Press, 1984), pp. 33-60.

--- *From Embargo to Ostpolitik: The Political Economy of West German-Soviet Relations, 1955-1980* (New York: Cambridge University Press, 1982).

--- "The USSR and Germany," *Problems of Communism*, Vol. 30, No. 5 (September-October 1981), pp. 1-24.

Strany SEV: Perestroika ekonomicheskogo sotrudnichesta (Moscow: Mezhdunarodnye otnosheniia, 1989).

Starchey, John, *The End of Empire* (London: Victor Gollanz, 1959).

Strauß, Franz Josef, *Die Erinnerungen* (Berlin: Siedler Verlag, 1989).

Sudoplatov, Pavel, *Razvedka i Kreml'. Zapiski nezhelatel'nogo svidetelia* (Moscow: TOO "Geia," 1996).

Teltschik, Horst, *329 Tage: Innenansichten der Einigung* (Berlin: Siedler Verlag, 1991).

Timmermann, Heinz, "Die sowjetische Aussenpolitik im Zeichen von 'neuem Denken' und Handeln," Research Report, Bundesinstitut für ostwissenschaftliche und internationale Studien (Cologne), No. 48, September 1989.

Tolz, Vera, "The Soviet Union Retreats from Marxism-Leninism," *Report on the USSR* (Munich, Radio Liberty / Radio Free Europe), October 20, 1989, pp. 9-14.

Tsipko, Aleksandr, "O Gorbacheve, 'predateliakh' i russkoi dushe," *Nezavisimaia gazeta*, 6 April 1995.

Turner, Henry Ashby, Jr., *The Two Germanies Since 1945* (New Haven, CT: Yale University Press, 1987).

Ulam, Adam B., "Europe in Soviet Eyes," *Problems of Communism* (May-June 1983), pp. 22-30.

Ulam, Adam B., *Expansion and Coexistence: The History of Soviet Foreign Policy* (New York: Praeger, 1968).

U.S. Department of State, Central Confidential Files, *The Soviet Union: Internal Affairs, 1945-1949*, on microfilm (Frederick, MD: University Publications of America, n.d. [1989]).

--- *The Soviet Union: Foreign Affairs, 1945-1949*, on microfilm (Frederick, Md.: University Publications of America, n.d. [1989]).

--- *The Soviet Union: Internal Affairs, 1950-1954*, on microfilm (Frederick, Md.: University Publications of America, n.d. [1989]).

--- *The Soviet Union: Foreign Affairs, 1950-1954*, on microfilm (Frederick, Md.: University Publications of America, n.d. [1989]).

Van Brabant, Jozef M., *A Central European Payments Union: Technical Aspects* (New York: Institute for East-West Security Studies, 1991).

Van Dijk, Ruud, "The 1952 Stalin Note Debate: Myth or Missed Opportunity?", Cold War International History Project, Woodrow Wilson International Center for Scholars, Working Paper, No. 14, May 1996.

Van Oudenaren, John, *Détente in Europe: The Soviet Union and the West since 1953* (Durham, N.C.: Duke University Press, 1991).

--- *The Role of Shevardnadze and the Ministry of Foreign Affairs in the Making of Soviet Defense and Arms Control Policy*, The Rand Corporation, Santa Monica, Cal., R-3898-USDP, July 1990.

--- *Soviet Policy toward Western Europe: Objectives, Instruments, Results*, The Rand Corporation, Santa Monica, Cal., Research Report, R-3310-AF, February 1987.

Vincent, R. J., *Military Power and Political Influence: The Soviet Union and Western Europe*, Adelphi Paper No. 119 (London: IISS, 1975).

Vine, Richard D., ed., *Soviet-East European Relations As a Problem for the West*, A Research Volume for the Atlantic Institute for International Affairs (London: Croom Helm, 1987).

Von Borcke, Astrid, "The KGB and Perestroika," in Federal Institute on Soviet and International Studies, ed., *The Soviet Union 1988-1989* (Boulder, Colo.: Westview, 1990), p. 61-66.

--- "KGB International: The Role of the Secret Service in Soviet Foreign and Security Policy," in Federal Institute on Soviet and International Studies, ed., *The Soviet Union 1986-1987* (Boulder, Colo.: Westview, 1989), pp. 306-316.

--- *KGB: Die Macht im Untergrund* (Stuttgart: Hänssler, 1987).

Von Flocken, Jan, and Michael Klonovsky, *Stalins Lager in Deutschland 1945-1950. Dokumentation. Zeugenberichte* (Berlin and Frankfurt a.M.: Ullstein, 1992).

Vorotnikov, Vitalii, *A bylo tak. Iz dnevnika chlena Politburo TsK KPSS* (Moscow: SI-MAR, 1995).

Waigel, Theo, and Manfred Schell, *Tage, die Deutschland und die Welt veränderten: Vom Mauerfall zum Kaukasus. Die deutsche Währungsunion* (Munich: Bruckmann, 1994).

Walters, Vernon, "Die ersten Raketen werden auf uns und nicht auf Europa fallen," interview, *Süddeutsche Zeitung*, 6-7 May 1989.

[Warsaw Pact], "Kommiunike zasedaniia Komiteta ministra inostrannykh del gosudarstv-uchastnikov Varshavskaia Dogovora," *Pravda*, 13 April 1989.

--- "Zaiavlenie gosudarstv-uchastnikov Varshavskaia Dogovora po takticheskomu iadernomu oruzhiiu v Evrope," *Pravda*, 13 April 1989.

Weathersby, Kathryn, "Soviet Aims in Korea and the Origins of the Korean War, 1945-1950," Cold War International History Project, Woodrow Wilson International Center for Scholars, Working Paper No. 8, November 1993.

"Wer sind die Deutschen? Geheimprotokoll eines von Premierministerin Thatcher einberufenen Deutschland-Seminars," *Der Spiegel* (Hamburg), No. 29 (1990), pp. 108-112.

Wertheim, W.F., *Evolution and Revolution: The Rising Waves of Emancipation* (Harmondsworth: Penguin, 1974).

Wessell, Nils H., "The New Europe: Revolution in East-West Relations," Academy of Political Science, *Proceedings*, Vol. 38, No. 1 (1991).

Wettig, Gerhard, "Die sowjetische Rolle beim Umsturz in der DDR und bei der Einleitung des deutschen Einigungsprozesses," in Jürgen Elvert, ed., *Der Umbruch in Osteuropa* (Stuttgart: Franz Steiner Verlag, 1993), pp. 39-63.

--- "Die Deutschland-Note vom 10. März 1952 auf der Basis diplomatischer Akten des russischen Außenministeriums," *Deutschland-Archiv*, No. 7 (June 1993), pp. 786-805.

Whetten, Lawrence L., ed., *New International Communism: The Foreign and Defense Policies of the Latin European Communist Parties* (Lexington, Mass.: Lexington Books, 1982).

Windsor, Philip, *Germany and the Western Alliance: Lessons from the 1980 Crises*, Adelphi Paper No. 170 (London: IISS, 1981).

Wagenlehner, Günther, ed., *Die deutsche Frage und die internationale Sicherheit* (Koblenz: Bernard & Graefe Verlag, 1988).

Wolf, Markus, *In eigenem Auftrag: Bekenntnisse und Einsichten* (Munich: Schneekluth, 1991).

Wolfe, Thomas W., *Soviet Power and Europe: 1945-1970* (Baltimore and London: Johns Hopkins University Press, 1970).

Woodby, Sylvia, *Gorbachev and the Decline of Ideology in Soviet Foreign Policy*, Westview Special Studies on the Soviet Union and Eastern Europe (Boulder, Colo.: Westview, 1989).

Yakovlev, Aleksandr N., *Gor'kaia chasha: Bol'shevism i reformatsiia v Rossii* (Yaroslavl: Verkhnye-volzhskoe knizhnoe izdatel'stvo, 1994).

--- *Predislovie, obval, posleslovie* (Moscow: Novosti, 1992).

--- *Muki prochteniia bytiia: Perestroika – nadezhdy i real'nosti* (Moscow: Novosti, 1991).

Yazov, Dmitri T., "Voennaia doktrina Varshavskogo dogovora – doktrina zashchity mira i sotsializma," *Pravda*, 27 July 1987.

Yergin, Daniel, *Shattered Peace: The Origins of the Cold War and the National Security State* (Boston: Houghton Mifflin, 1978).

"Zapis' osnovnogo soderzhaniia telefonnogo razgovora M.S. Gorbacheva s Predsedatelem Soveta Ministrov GDR Kh. Modorovom, 12 fevralia 1990 goda," Hoover Institution Archives, Box 3, Zelikow-Rice Project on German Unification.

"Zapis' besedy M.S. Gorbacheva s ministrom inostrannykh del FRG F.-D. Genscherom, 5 dekabria 1989 goda," Hoover Institution Archives, Box 3, Zelikow-Rice Project on German Unification.

Zhurkin, V., S. Karaganov and A. Kortunov, "Vyzovy bezopasnosti – starye i novye," *Kommunist*, No. 1 (January 1988), pp. 42-50.

--- S. Karaganov and A. Kortunov, "O razumnoi dostatochnosti," *SShA*, No. 12 (December 1987), pp. 11-21.

Zelikow, Philip, and Condoleezza Rice, *Germany Unified and Europe Transformed: A Study in Statecraft* (Cambridge, Mass.: Harvard University Press, 1995).

Zimmerman, William, *Soviet Perspectives on International Relations: 1956-1967* (New York: Columbia University Press, 1970).

Zubok, Vladislav, and Constantine Pleshakov, *Inside the Kremlin's Cold War: From Stalin to Khrushchev* (Cambridge, Mass.: Harvard University Press, 1996).

Zubok, Vladislav, "Khrushchev and the Berlin Crisis, 1958-1962," Cold War International History Project, Woodrow Wilson International Center for Scholars, Working Paper, No. 6, May 1993.

Glossary and Abbreviations

ANZUS	Australia, New Zealand, and United States Treaty Organization
APN	Agentstvo pechati novosti, the Soviet news agency
BBC	British Broadcasting Corporation
Bundestag	Lower house of parliament of the Federal Republic of Germany
CC	Central Committee
CDU	Christlich-Demokratische Union (Christian Democratic Union)
CGF	Central Group of Forces
Cheka	Vserossiiskaia chrezvychainaia komissiia (All-Russian Extraordinary Commission), the name of the secret police in the first years after the Bolshevik revolution
CIP	Commission on International Policy
CMEA	Council for Mutual Economic Assistance, also referred to as Comecon, the Soviet bloc's trade organization
CPI	Communist Party of Italy
CPSU	Communist Party of the Soviet Union
CSCE	Conference on Security and Cooperation in Europe
DGAP	Deutsche Gesellschaft für Auswärtige Politik
DKP	Deutsche Kommunistische Partei (German Communist Party)
EDC	European Defense Community
ESG	European Strategy Group
FBI	Federal Bureau of Investigations
FBIS	Foreign Broadcast Information Service
FCD	First Chief Directorate
FDJ	Freie Deutsche Jugend (Union of Free German Youth)
FRG	Federal Republic of Germany
GATT	General Agreement on Tariffs and Trade
GDR	German Democratic Republic
GRU	Glavnoie razvedyvatelskoe upravlenie (Chief Intelligence Department), the military intelligence organization in the Soviet era
GSFG	Group of Soviet Forces in Germany, the term used for the Soviet armed forces in East Germany, renamed Western Group of Forces in June 1989
ID	International Department
IEMSS	Institut ekonomiki mirovoi sotsialisticheskoi sistemy (Institute for the Economy of the World Socialist System)

IMEMO	Institut mirovoi ekonomiki i mezhdunarodnykh otnoshenii (Institute of World Economy and International Relations) of the Soviet – now the Russian – Academy of Sciences
IMF	International Monetary Fund
INF	Intermediate-range nuclear forces
IPE	International Political Economy
ISKAN	Institut SShA i Kanady (Institute for the Study of the USA and Canada) of the Soviet – now as ISKRAN of the Russian – Academy of Sciences
KGB	Komitet gosudarstvennoi bezopasnosti (Committee for State Security)
KPSS	Kommunisticheskaia partiia Sovietskogo Soyuza (Communist Party of the Soviet Union)
Land	State; constitutional entity, comparable to the states of the United States or the provinces of Canada, forming part of the federal structure of the Federal Republic of Germany; Länder is the plural form
MBFR	Mutual Balanced Forces Reduction
Memcon	Memorandum of conversation
MEMO	Mirovaia ekonomika i mezhdunarodnye otnosheniia (World Economy and International Relations), journal of the IMEMO
MFA	Ministry of Foreign Affairs
MfS	Ministerium für Staatssicherheit (Ministry for State Security)
MGIMO	Moskovskii gosudarstvennyi institut mezhdunarodnykh otnoshenii (Moscow State Institute for International Relations)
MIC	Military-Industrial Complex
MOD	Ministry of Defense
MPA	Main Political Administration, one of the CPSU's instruments of political control in the Soviet armed forces
NGF	Northern Group of Forces
NHP	Nuclear History Program
NPD	Nationaldemokratische Partei Deutschlands (National Democratic Party of Germany)
NSC	National Security Council
NVA	Nationale Volksarmee (National People's Army)
PB	Politburo
PCC	Political Consultative Committee, the highest organ of the Warsaw Pact and the official term for the summit meetings of the Pact's party leaders
PDS	Partei des Demokratischen Sozialismus (Party of Democratic Socialism)
RSFSR	Russian Soviet Federative Socialist Republic
SALT	Strategic Arms Limitation Talks

SEATO	Southeast Asia Treaty Organization
SED	Sozialistische Einheitspartei Deutschlands (German Socialist Unity Party)
SEW	Sozialistische Einheitsparty West-Berlins (West-Berlin Socialist Unity Party)
SGF	Southern Group of Forces
SMA	Soviet Military Administration
SPD	Sozialdemokratische Partei Deutschlands (Social Democratic Party of Germany)
Stasi	Staatssicherheitsministerium ([East German] Ministry for State Security)
SWB	Summary of World Broadcasts
TsKhSD	Tsentr khraneniia sovremennoi dokumentatsii (Center for the Storage of Contemporary Documents)
UN	United Nations
VPK	Voenno-promyshlennaia kommissiia (Military-Industrial Commission)
VTsIOM	Vserossiiskii tsentr issledovaniia obshchestvennogo mneniia (All-Union Center for the Study of Public Opinion)
WGF	Western Group of Forces, after June 1989 the term for the Soviet armed forces stationed in East Germany